The Family Dynamic: A CANADIAN PERSPECTIVE

FOURTH EDITION

The Family Dynamic: A CANADIAN PERSPECTIVE

FOURTH EDITION

MARGARET WARD

THOMSON

NELSON

Australia   Canada   Mexico   Singapore   Spain   United Kingdom   United States

THOMSON

NELSON

The Family Dynamic: A Canadian Perspective,
Fourth Edition

by Margaret Ward

Associate Vice President, Editorial Director:
Evelyn Veitch

Publisher:
Joanna Cotton

Senior Acquisitions Editor:
Cara Yarzab

Marketing Manager:
Laura Armstrong

Developmental Editor:
Sandra de Ruiter

Photo Researcher:
Kristiina Bowering

Senior Production Editor:
Natalia Denesiuk

Copy Editor:
Lisa Berland

Proofreader:
Kate Revington

Indexer:
Edwin Durbin

Senior Production Coordinator:
Hedy Sellers

Design Director:
Ken Phipps

Interior Design Modifications:
Liz Harasymczuk

Cover Design:
Peter Papayanakis

Cover Image:
Banana Stock/PictureQuest

Compositor:
Carol Magee

Printer:
Webcom

Library and Archives Canada Cataloguing in Publication Data

Ward, Margaret, 1935–

  The family dynamic : a Canadian perspective / Margaret Ward. — 4th ed.

Includes bibliographical references and index.

ISBN 0-17-640609-3

  1. Family. 2. Family—Canada. I. Title.

HQ560.W37 2005   306.85
C2005-905303-8

BRIEF TABLE OF CONTENTS

DETAILED TABLE OF CONTENTS

PART 4: MIDLIFE AND BEYOND

PREFACE

The Family Dynamic serves as a basic introduction to family studies, particularly for people who are interested in finding employment in a human services field. As such, it provides a firm theoretical grounding. Because postsecondary students, like all of us, learn best if they can relate concepts to their own experience or that of others, I have provided many examples throughout the text, as well as in boxes and in questions at the end of each chapter.

The Family Dynamic is set up to help students approach the subject matter. Each chapter begins with learning objectives and ends with a summary, definition of key terms, and questions for assignment or discussion. Within the chapters, boxes are included to amplify points made within the text or to present issues (some of them diverting) for class discussion. An appendix at the end of the book summarizes principal sociological theories for students who do not already have this background. This is followed by a glossary that allows quick reference to key terms.

As with previous editions, I have not attempted to write an exhaustive study of Canadian families, but rather to open up the subject and present the variety in our family experiences. I have also introduced challenges and issues to stimulate thought and discussion about the current state and the future direction of families. When exploring these issues, I have tried not to take sides, although I do have beliefs and opinions; rather, I have attempted to lay out arguments for competing positions to encourage students to form their own beliefs. The orientation of the book is practical and tries to show how the theory relates to the students' lives and their future work situations.

Early in the writing process, one reviewer referred to this work as a "smorgasbook," a term I consider a compliment. In this edition, as in earlier ones, I have tried to spread out a sampling of the rich fare of information available on Canadian families in the hope that readers will be tempted to feast where they have tasted.

NEW TO THE FOURTH EDITION

An advantage of a new edition is the chance to benefit from the feedback of those who have used the text. In addition to updating the statistics and references, the following improvements have been made:

- Current material is included in a number of boxes. In some cases existing examples, such as the account of the Bountiful commune in British Columbia (Chapter 4), have been updated to reflect recent events. In others, new developments are outlined, such as the new law regulating the use of reproductive and genetic technologies (Chapter 5).
- I have added a discussion of the court cases and legislation leading up to the legalization of same-sex marriages (Chapter 4).
- In many parts, the discussion of same-sex families has been "normalized." That is, I have included them in the sections on all couples and families, noting similarities and differences, rather than singling them out for special attention.

- In Chapter 2, I have arranged the topics in a more logical order. I start with describing the many differences in families, then go on to consider social attitudes toward differences. I have also expanded the information on immigration to Canada and the experiences of newcomers, both in this chapter and elsewhere in the book.
- Chapters 3 and 4 have been more clearly separated. The former looks at beginning relationships. The latter considers longer-term pairings, through both marriage and cohabitation.
- The new ancillary support package includes a printed Instructor Manual/Test Bank, an Instructor Resource CD-ROM containing a Computerized Test Bank and PowerPoint© Presentation, and a text-specific website loaded with additional information and resources for both instructors and students.
- To help students explore various topics further, I have used a feature called "Webmarks." In the margins near key passages throughout the text, the reader will find icons that direct the student to the website associated with this book, where he or she can find Internet resources providing further insight and information on the topic at hand. In addition to weblinks organized by chapter, students will find quiz questions, information on degrees and careers in sociology, and other resources to assist them in their studies. The website associated with *The Family Dynamic*, Fourth Edition, is at www.TheFamilyDynamic4e.nelson.com.

ACKNOWLEDGMENTS

It is a joy to be able to thank people publicly for their many private kindnesses. I offer my gratitude

- foremost, to my students over the years, who both infuriated and challenged me in ways impossible to catalogue through their questions, arguments, comments, and stories;
- to my former colleagues at Cambrian College for their support over the years;
- to all the librarians who helped me, for their good nature and invaluable assistance in tracking down resources and information;
- to the editors and marketing manager at Thomson Nelson—Cara Yarzab, Sandra de Ruiter, Natalia Denesiuk, and Laura Armstrong—for their expertise, patience, helpfulness, and generosity;
- to my colleagues who reviewed the third edition of this text: Karen Kobayashi at the University of Victoria; Linda McKinlay at Okanagan University College; Solly Sader at Saskatchewan Institute of Science and Technology; Mary Ann Smith at Fanshawe College; and Sheila Task at College of the North Atlantic for their thoughtful responses;
- to Mary Ward and Barbara and Brian Clark for their continuing practical help and interest, to Ruth Ward for suggesting resources and discussing issues, to Megan McHugh for her generosity in sharing her experiences, to Jonathan Ward for allowing me to write, and to Kay and Bill Bigglestone for their morale-boosting;
- to my children and siblings for demonstrating so many variations on family living;
- and finally to my friend Jim Douthit, for his generous practical help and unfailing interest and encouragement. I dedicate this book to him.

ABOUT THE AUTHOR

Margaret Ward holds a B.A. in English from the University of Toronto, a Masters in Child and Development Studies from Laurentian University, and a Ph.D. in Human Development and Family Systems from the Union Institute in Cincinnati, Ohio. She has written extensively on issues that impact the family—several of her published articles are listed in the references section at the back of this text.

Outside of her academic pursuits, Professor Ward served as a member and secretary of the Board of Directors for the Sudbury Juvenile Services from 1981 to 1983. She also served on the Board of Directors of the Children's Aid Society for the Districts of Sudbury and Manitoulin from 1974 to 1982. The mother of eleven children, eight of whom are adopted, she has received two Adoption Activist Awards for her writings on adoption.

Prior to her retirement, Professor Ward was a member of the Cambrian College faculty where she had taught since 1985. During her tenure, she presented several courses, including Developmental Psychology, Marriage and the Family, and Introductory Behavioural Science. Before joining Cambrian, she had taught at a number of high schools in the Sudbury area.

Margaret now divides her time between Ontario and Arizona.

Part One

© Chris Arend/Getty Images

Chapter 1

What Is a Family?

OBJECTIVES

- To introduce the concept of family and to review a variety of definitions
- To consider theoretical views of the family, along with their strengths and weaknesses
- To review ways researchers study families

Dear Ann Landers: I am writing to you with a simple yet confusing question. Please bear with me.

My parents were divorced years ago. The divorce was final May 30, and my father was remarried June 5 of the same year. It was some time before I accepted his new wife, Donna. After they had been married for about two years, I was asked if I would mind sharing my birthday dinner with Donna's brother, Ron. I said it would be just fine. We had a joint birthday dinner on Dec. 13 and had a super time. Ron and I went together to my father's New Year's Eve party. By March we were madly in love, and we were married July 23. Ron is 10 years older than I, and Donna is about 10 years younger than my father.

Two years later Ron and I decided to have a baby. Now comes the tricky part. What is the relation between our new baby girl and Donna? Is she her grandma or her aunt? Donna prefers to be her aunt. What relation is my father to our child? Is he her grandpa or her uncle? Is my father still my father or is he my brother-in-law? Is Donna still Ron's sister or is she his mother-in-law? My father and I have the same in-laws. The only thing that seems quite clear is that my in-laws are the baby's grandparents any way you look at it. However, since they are also my father's wife's parents, doesn't that make them the baby's great-grandparents?

When I tell this story I get confused looks. There is no incest involved yet people think we are quite strange. Please help me sort this out before our baby can talk so we can explain to her who's who and what's what. Thanks for your help.

—DaughterSister-in-law, Columbus, Ohio

Dear Columbus: I don't know whether this requires an effort of the left brain or the right brain but you lost me right after your daughter was born.

Source: Ann Landers, *Sudbury Star,* September 17, 1991, p. B3.

What is a family? Almost all of us have been members of at least one family. We see families all around us, both in real life and in the media. We all know what families are, yet when we actually try to define "family," as the Ann Landers column shows, the task is not so simple after all. Do we include only the people who live in our household? Should we count all of our relatives? One of the difficulties in defining "family" is that we use the word for many different things—our ancestors, our parents, brothers, and sisters, all of our relatives, and our spouses and children. One commonly used definition in North America is of the "traditional" family; this includes father, mother, and their children.

WHAT IS A FAMILY?

Definitions of the family have changed according to time and place. For example, in England during the Middle Ages, the town-dwelling family was not a private unit of parents and children. Husband, wife, and children shared their living space and daily activities such as work, meals, and prayers with servants, apprentices, journeymen, and unmarried or widowed relatives (Coontz, 2000). Nowadays we would tend to think of such a grouping as a "household" rather than a family. According to Statistics Canada (2004a), a **household** refers to people who occupy the same dwelling, and can consist of one or more families, a single person, or a group of related or unrelated people, for example, brothers and sisters, a live-in nanny, or apartment mates.

In other social groups, the family has been based on one person married to several others of the opposite sex. The general term for this practice is **polygamy.** Polygamy is currently the practice in many Muslim countries and was encouraged among the early Mormons in the United States. It is still reported occasionally in the popular press (e.g., "Hunting Bountiful," 2004). While these practices may seem far removed from those raised in a society that upholds **monogamy** (marriage to only one person at a time) in its customs, religious beliefs, and laws, they do have some practical implications. For example, if a family consisting of one husband and several wives applies for immigration status in Canada, should they all be accorded marital status? If so, are these marriages considered legal in the new country as they were in the country of origin? If not, who is considered the sole wife, and what becomes of the "extras"? Is it fair to exclude polygamous individuals as potential immigrants?

Communal living, which exists in Canada among some groups, provides still another image of family. Acting on the basis of their religious beliefs, the Hutterites traditionally share financial resources, work assignments, and even meals on a community basis. Accommodation, furniture, and clothing are provided according to need. From about the age of three, children spend most of their days in school. They eat their meals in the communal dining hall, seated separately from their parents, according to their age and sex. The community takes precedence over the family unit. The Hutterites have met with prejudice in some areas where they have settled, partly because their communal farming methods were seen as unfair competition, and partly because their lifestyle was so different from that of their neighbours (Peter, 1987; Smith & Ingoldsby, 2003).

The Legal Family

In Canada, the term "family" differs according to who is defining it. A variety of legal definitions exist. The census, which is taken every five years, counts what it calls the census family (see Box 1.1) (Statistics Canada, 2004a). Family members are also defined in a host of laws and regulations. For example, people cannot marry certain categories of relatives, such as parents or brothers and sisters, because they are too closely related. Child welfare laws define parents and specify which relatives are close enough to be allowed to adopt a child without agency approval (e.g., Ministry of Children and Youth Services, Ontario, 2003). Immigration law considers certain relatives to be close family members, and thus to be given preference in entering the country. Government regulations determine family for such services as medical and family benefits and special visiting programs in penitentiaries (Correctional Service of Canada, 2004). In fact, everyone who works in a human services field must learn specific legal definitions of the family in the course of their work.

Legal definitions are not fixed, however; they have changed as a result of court cases and legislation. For example, common-law spouses have been given many of the rights and responsibilities of married couples as to support, employment benefits, and custody and support of children. In 2003, same-sex couples were given the right to marry in British

SOME DEFINITIONS OF THE FAMILY

STATISTICS CANADA
Census family: Refers to a now-married couple (with or without children of either or both spouses), a couple living common-law (with or without children of either or both partners), or a lone parent of any marital status, with at least one child living in the same dwelling. A couple living common-law may be of opposite or same sex. "Children" in a census family include grandchildren living with their grandparent(s) but with no parents present.

Source: Adapted from Statistics Canada, "2001 Census Dictionary," Catalogue 92-378, p. 146.

UNITED CHURCH OF CANADA
By family we mean persons who are joined together by reasons of mutual consent (marriage, social contract, or covenant) or by birth or adoption or placement.

Source: Reprinted by permission of The United Church of Canada, Sexuality, Marriage, and the Family Working Unit, 1987.

CORRECTIONAL SERVICE OF CANADA
The following family members are eligible to participate in the [Private Family Visiting] program: spouse, common-law partner, children, parents, foster-parents, siblings, grandparents and persons with whom, in the opinion of the institutional head, the inmate has a close familial bond, provided they are not inmates.

Source: Reproduced with the permission of the Minister of Public Works and Government Services Canada, 2005.

Columbia, Ontario, and Quebec (Lahey & Alderson, 2004). Other provinces and territories have followed suit. In 2005, the federal government introduced a law making same-sex marriages legal.

Social Definitions of the Family

Various groups and social institutions also define the family. A number of churches have studied the family and, in the process, have had to state what they consider a family (e.g., Canadian Conference of Catholic Bishops, 1980; United Church of Canada, 1987). Hospital intensive-care units usually permit visits by immediate family members only. Schools accept permission and absence notes from parents only, unless they are informed otherwise.

Various ethnic groups may also regard family membership in different ways. For example, Aboriginal peoples in Canada tend to have a very broad definition of family membership, and children are often cared for by relatives as a matter of course. If a child welfare worker defines a family as consisting of parents and children only, then he or she may feel that some Aboriginal parents are neglecting or even abandoning their children, when these parents feel their offspring are safe within their caring family circle. Such misunderstandings have led to unnecessary removal of children from their families (Waterfall, 2003).

Underlying many of the differences in the way people regard families are two basic concepts: the **nuclear family** and the **extended family.** The nuclear family is usually regarded as married parents and their children. This is sometimes called the "standard North American family" or SNAF (Smith, 1993) and forms the basis for what advocates call "traditional family values" (Erera, 2002). Nuclear families come in two forms, depending on our perspective: families of origin or orientation are those we are born into and raised in; families of procreation are those we form through marriage or cohabitation, and in which we raise our children. We can imagine society made up of interlocking sets of nuclear families with many individuals being members of two or more. But this pattern works neatly only if all couples get married, have biological children, and never divorce. As it is, many families do not fit this description. Children may have more than one family of orientation. When parents divorce, their children may have two families to which they are connected, with one parent in each. Adopted children start out in one family, which they may or may not remember, and are raised in another. With the current trend toward making contact with birth parents, adoptees may resume membership in their birth families. Some adults have more than one procreated family. This occurs most often with single mothers who later marry and with individuals who remarry. Occasionally two families result when an individual enters an illegal, bigamous relationship or lives common-law while still married to someone else.

The second concept is the extended family, which encompasses the nuclear family and all other relatives. Once again, there is variation in what constitutes membership. Some people include more distantly related cousins, for example, than others. In the past, most families that lived in small rural communities in Canada were related through marriage or descent. For these individuals, the entire community could be considered their extended family. In both nuclear and extended families, genetic or "blood" relationship is important, although other types of relationships, such as marriage or adoption, are recognized by most people.

Personal Definitions of the Family

Some definitions of the family are quite personal. In many families, a close friend is counted as a member. In other cases, such as those where there has been a high level of conflict and where there is continuing bad feeling, a family may not consider one member as belonging, even though he or she is a legal member. This is especially true when parents have disowned a child or when a marital partner has disappeared but no divorce has occurred. Different family members may have separate ideas of who belongs. For example, a child may include her divorced father, while her mother does not.

THINKING ABOUT FAMILIES

Just as there are many definitions of the family, so there are many theories about what makes families work and how they relate to society as a whole. A **theory** provides a general framework of ideas that can be used to answer questions about the world (Ingoldsby, Smith, & Miller, 2004). Sociologists have used a number of approaches, either singly or in combination, to look for some order and meaning to these questions. To study the theories that have resulted is important because they help shape government policy, agency regulations, methods of therapy, and other ways society relates to families. Each approach tells us something of interest about families; each, however, also has limitations on how much it can explain. They also tend to ignore some realities of family life such as time pressures (scheduling activities) or spatial matters (length of commute or play space for children); (Daly, 2003). As we discuss theories, we should keep in mind the following questions:

1. How does the theory account for both change and continuity in family patterns?
2. Does the theory show the way society and the family influence each other?
3. What does the theory say about relationships within the family?
4. How has the theory affected the policies and practices of government, social agencies, and others who deal with families?

HOW DOES SOCIETY INFLUENCE FAMILIES?

Families do not exist in isolation—they are part of a vast network. Family members are part of the larger society in which they live through their membership and participation in their neighbourhoods, schools, work, religious organizations, and social and recreational groups. The influence of society operates through social institutions, such as schools and religious groups; laws; political and economic factors; pressure from activist groups; and the mass media. Society provides expectations for behaviour. For example, family members are supposed to look after one another physically and emotionally, and are not supposed to harm one another. They are expected to socialize children to meet certain standards of behaviour. Society also limits family behaviour by means of laws such as those against violence, by the level of benefits provided through social assistance, and through stigma and labelling of those who do not conform to societal expectations.

The ecological theory looks at the relationship of family and society. According to James Garbarino (1992), families are a part of interlocking systems that influence each other at four levels. (See Figure 1.1.)

Level 1—The Microsystem

The **microsystem** consists of the small groups in which people interact face-to-face. For adults this might involve family, workplace, and organizations of which they are members. The microsystem most directly affects the quality of life through relationships with individuals; therefore, its nature and quality are important. Each family member has a different microsystem; for example, those of young children include whoever cares for them during the day, such as a babysitter or daycare centre (Palacio-Quintin, 2000).

Level 2—The Mesosystem

The **mesosystem** is made up of the relationships between two or more groups of which the individual is a member. A child's mesosystem would consist of the relationship between parents and the daycare centre, or between parents and the school, or between parents and the neighbourhood. The quality of the connections is important—whether they are weak or

Figure 1.1

THE ECOLOGY OF HUMAN DEVELOPMENT

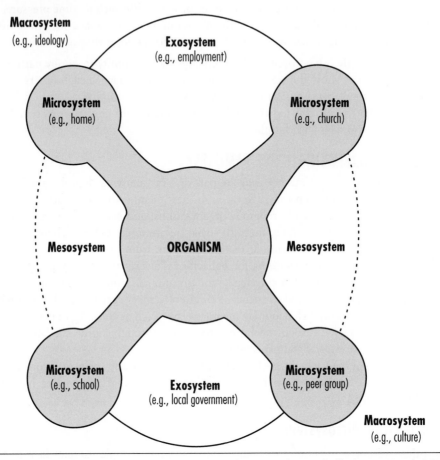

Source: Reprinted with permission from James Garbarino, *Children and Families in the Social Environment*, 2/e. (New York: Aldine de Gruyter). Copyright © 1992 Walter de Gruyter, Inc., New York.

strong, negative or positive. For parents, the mesosystem might consist of the relationship between the family and the workplace.

Level 3—The Exosystem

The **exosystem** is a setting in which individuals do not take an active part, but which has an effect on them through the mesosystem or microsystem (Garbarino, 1992). For children, this could consist of expectations in the parent's workplace or decisions made by the school board. For parents, it might also involve the school board, which can affect family life by closing the school on a workday to allow for staff development, thus forcing parents to make special arrangements for the care of their children.

Many of the important decisions made by exosystems that affect the family are not even thought of as family-related (Garbarino, 1992). Some obviously are, such as funding provided to daycare centres to permit subsidies for low-income families. In the workplace, fringe benefits are clearly family oriented; even these are affected, however, by which definitions of the family are used. Other policies, in both the government and the private sector, although not seen as "family" issues, also affect families. Governmental decisions such as the location of major highways can affect children's routes to school or travel time to the daycare centre or place of employment. Policies and assumptions in the workplace can also have an impact on family life. One assumption, for instance, is that if you are on the executive track, you will work long hours and "move to move up." The time demanded can interfere with family life, and relocating, which is often required for moving up, can disrupt natural support networks, such as the extended family.

Although the exosystem may seem to be made up of immovable institutions, individuals and groups have often been successful in changing it. For example, unions have affected working conditions; parent groups have prevented the closing of local schools; and many pressure groups working together have forced government to increase funding for daycare.

Level 4—The Macrosystem

The **macrosystem** consists of a society's ideology and culture. These shared beliefs and ways of doing things are, taken together, the basis on which policy decisions are usually made (Garbarino, 1992). Most social policies are based on assumptions concerning the pattern of relationships between the sexes, such as the division of labour between males and females both inside and outside the family. Such policies tend to be adjusted in response to problems that arise out of changing economic or political situations; however, these kinds of adjustments are often slow in coming.

Evaluation of the Ecological View

Ecological theory better explains change that occurs in families than it does change that occurs in society as a whole. In addition, it deals more with growth than with decline, as in old age (White & Klein, 2002). Although this theory does address family relationships in the microsystem, its real strength is in its explanation of how society and family interact. The ecological view, for example, can help service providers understand how ethnic and minority families differ from mainstream ones in their relationships with their extended families and with organizations like schools, police systems, and social service agencies (Phenice & Griffore, 1996). In addition, the awareness that a policy in one area may have quite unintentional effects on the family can be important if service is provided by more than one social agency.

MACRO OR MICRO?

We can use Garbarino's diagram (in Figure 1.1) to help classify other theories, most of which concentrate on either the macrosystem or the microsystem. Macro theories principally study the values of a society and the way those values affect the family. These viewpoints include the structural-functional and conflict theories. Micro theories emphasize relationships within individual families. Among these are the symbolic-interaction and exchange theories. Family systems theory has both macro and micro branches. We will consider first the macro and then the micro theories of the family.

THE FAMILY AS AN INSTITUTION

The structural-functional theory views the family as an institution among other social institutions, such as the legal and educational systems. As such, it has a structure and function that both connect it with society as a whole and separate it from other institutions.

According to this view, the family has a number of important functions in society. First, it provides for the physical protection of its members. Usually this means that one or more family members must have a job or some source of income to support the family. Second, the family provides for the emotional well-being of its members. Third, it produces and shapes new individuals who will, as adults, be prepared to take their place in society. This shaping process is called **socialization** (Parsons & Bales, 1955).

A major contribution of the structural-functional theory is its development of the concepts of values and norms, and how they are passed on from one generation to the next. **Values** are social principles accepted by a society as a whole or by groups within that society. One example is the principle of one marriage for life. Many people do not have such a marriage, but may still hold it as their ideal; that is, they value it. Values often vary among different groups in society. Some groups give drug dealers high status because they can make large amounts of money; others consider them to be dangerous parasites.

Ways of behaving that are typical of a certain group are called **norms.** Often social groups feel that norms are also values—that is, that people ought to behave like most others if they are to be considered worthwhile members of society. In some groups nowadays, it is the norm for a young man to have had sexual experience with young women before he graduates from high school. If he does not have such experience, some of his peers may wonder if he is abnormal. In their eyes, if he does not behave like the others (by following the norm) something is wrong with him. To such people no sexual experience whatsoever and homosexuality are both unacceptable. In groups that value individual freedom of choice, however, any of these forms of behaviour are seen as acceptable options.

More generally, knowledge of the "proper" way of doing things in society—mainly, how to survive and how to take part in social life—is passed on to each generation through the process of socialization. Socialization can occur directly through teaching—for example, in learning manners—or indirectly, through examples and unstated expectations of the people around us. Most of us have formed ideas of how newlyweds, parents, or teachers "ought" to act. The cultural rules that tell us what, where, when, how, and why we should do something are referred to as **social scripts.** If people don't behave in the expected way, they leave themselves open to criticism or subtle pressure to conform (Atwood, 1996).

According to structural-functionalists, the family is organized around three statuses: husband/father, wife/mother, and child. A **status** is a social position that carries a set of expectations concerning suitable behaviour, regardless of who fills the position. This behaviour is termed a **role.** Structural-functionalists believe that role specialization increases the efficiency with which families function. In particular, they state the husband/father is an instrumental (active or doing) specialist and the wife/mother is an expressive (emotional) specialist. Thus the man is responsible for economic support of the family members and the woman for their physical and emotional nurture (Parsons & Bales, 1955).

Evaluation of the Structural-Functional View

The most important strength of the structural-functional theory is its explanations of how the family is related to other institutions and how it contributes to society as a whole. It also emphasizes family strengths, such as cooperation between members, rather than weaknesses. However, there are a number of difficulties with the structural-functional approach. Although this theory usually provides good explanations of why society maintains values across generations, it is not as clear in explaining why families and society change. The structural-functional theory often ignores topics such as family violence and sexual abuse, and sees delinquency and crime as social rather than as family problems (Porter, 1987).

Another difficulty is that this view is not very tolerant of differences from the SNAF ("standard North American family"). Anything that departs from the breadwinner-father and homemaker-mother raising their children—in other words, the majority of Canadian families—is regarded as abnormal or defective in some way (Smith, 1993).

Nevertheless, because it has long been the basis for providing social services to families, understanding structural-functional theory is important for anyone involved in human services delivery. If a man, woman, and children are living together, they are assumed to be a family. The father/husband has been seen as responsible for supporting the family and the mother/wife has been seen as responsible for the personal care of family members, especially childcare. It was therefore often easier for a man to receive homemaking and other household help when there was no woman present in the home, and for a woman to receive financial support when there was no man present, than vice versa. This idea of the family has been responsible for "man in the house" rules, according to which a woman could lose her social assistance benefits if a man were living with her. In all provinces, welfare benefits used to be restricted to single mothers and their children. Single fathers were not eligible until the regulations were successfully challenged in the courts as being unconstitutional (Baker, 1995). In addition, the structural-functional view tends to assume that society has one set of norms and values. This is not true of a multicultural society such as Canada. Different groups have their own norms for choosing marriage partners, for deciding whether the new couple should live with relatives or by themselves, for the division of labour between husband and wife, and for many other aspects of family life.

A father's work is never done.

Source: Reprinted by kind permission of Barrie Maguire.

THE FAMILY AS CENTRE FOR CONFLICT

As with structural-functionalism, conflict theories tend to view the family from the perspective of society. Instead of emphasizing the positive aspects of the relationship, however, they stress negative influences. Conflict theories are particularly concerned with power relationships. Marxism, for example, views the family as part of a system in which a few people exploit the majority and reap the benefits of their labour. Currently, the most influential conflict-based theory is feminism. Although feminist thinkers differ in their views on other issues, they generally agree that family relations, and society as a whole, are based on the power and authority of men. As a result, women are limited in their choices and are denied opportunities to develop themselves (Fox & Murry, 2000).

Feminist thinkers criticize structural-functionalism for supporting the patriarchal view of the family. They state that the political and social control men hold over women is tied to the belief that a man is naturally head of the family. Within the family, as in the wider society, men tend to have more power and control than women and tend to receive more benefits (Fox & Murry, 2000). This is reflected, for example, in the imbalance in responsibility for household work that occurs when both spouses are employed (Robinson & Godbey, 1997). Focusing power in the hands of one family member can also lead to abuse of that power, including the use of violence.

The values that support men in a power role are widespread in our society. The inequality between men and women begins in the socialization of earliest childhood. Boys are expected to be active and aggressive, and girls to be nurturing and sensitive to others. Often the differences that result from socialization are pointed to as "natural" differences between men and women; these then form the basis for further socialization (Fox & Murry, 2000). In adulthood, it may be difficult for a woman to choose not to marry and have children. The idea that a woman can be fulfilled only as a wife and mother still has widespread acceptance (Douglas & Michaels, 2004).

Feminists also point to higher levels of pay in traditionally male-dominated occupations such as mining, construction, law, and medicine. Traditional "female" occupations such as providing childcare, preparing and serving food, and cleaning tend to be lower paid. Part of the original basis for lower pay was the notion that women's work merely provided luxuries for the family; it was the man's work that supported the family. Furthermore, women, rather than men, are expected to take time off from work for childcare (Fox & Murry, 2000). This, in turn, reduces their ability to advance their careers and makes them more dependent on men.

Evaluation of Conflict Theories

Conflict theories, including feminism, explain why families and societies change—a result of shifts in the balance of power. They point to the way that values in society are passed from generation to generation, and how they affect family life. Conflict theories are not strong, however, in demonstrating how families contribute to society as a whole. Neither are they good at explaining why society's norms and values for families tend to change slowly (Klein & White, 2002).

Feminist thought, in particular, has a continuing and growing impact. It is the driving force for much current research on the family, by both men and women. One example already mentioned is the study of the difference in the amount of housework done by men and women. Feminists have also supported equity in the workplace, including pay and promotion opportunities.

THE FAMILY SYSTEM

The systems approach to the family has both macro and micro aspects. That is, it looks both at how the family is connected with society and at how individual members interact. The family systems concept comes partly from structural-functional thought, which regards the family as an important part of the social system. It has also grown out of general systems theory, which originated in the field of engineering, but soon expanded into many other areas (Cheal, 1991).

A **system** contains a set of interrelated and interacting parts. Like all systems, anything that affects one part of the family will affect all parts (Montgomery & Fewer, 1988). For example, if one parent loses his or her job, all family members have to make do with less money.

In the family system, there is a complementarity of roles. This means that if there is one social role such as parent, there must be the corresponding role of child. Similarly, it is impossible to be a spouse without having a husband or wife, or a sister or brother without having a sibling. Society expects certain patterns of behaviour from a person who fills a particular role. A parent is expected to be nurturing and self-sacrificing, while a child is expected to be loving and reasonably obedient. Difficulties may arise if the individual, for example a stepmother, does not fit the role, or if a person has no recognized role.

Families also contain **subsystems** (Montgomery & Fewer, 1988), or smaller groupings of members within the family. The most common are the spouse (or marital), parent, and sibling subsystems. In large families, the sibling subsystem is often further subdivided into smaller groupings based on age, sex, and interest (Bossard, 1975). In families where the separation of sex roles is marked, there may be clear male and female subsystems. In such cases, chores may be divided along sex lines, with the men and boys doing outside and maintenance work, and the women and girls responsible for housekeeping and childcare. Some families do not have all of the groupings; some, for example, have no marital subsystem because the parent is unmarried or has been separated or divorced. In many such families, however, both parents are still highly involved with their children and form the parental subsystem even though they do not live in the same household. Childless families have no parental subsystem, and one-child families have no sibling subsystem.

Systems and subsystems have **boundaries** (Montgomery & Fewer, 1988), which mark who is a member and who is not. In our society, boundaries have to be open enough to allow interaction with the outside world. For example, most of us would have difficulty surviving physically without income from a job or some other source. Other input sources include school, religious organizations, friends, and social organizations (Broderick, 1993). The same holds true for subsystems within the family. Children need to be able to interact with adults to receive adequate nurture and have appropriate adult behaviour modelled for them.

Most families operate in much the same way from day to day; that is, they have a steady state made up of familiar routines, rituals, and patterns of interaction (Ward, 1995). Every family gradually develops its own rules for regulating how members interact. This fact helps explain why families behave in completely different ways in the same situation, for example, the loss of a job, or a parent-adolescent argument. Some rules are explicit—in other words, they are stated. Rules of this sort might cover curfews, who drives the family cars, and who shovels the driveway. Although other rules are implicit, or unstated, members are still expected to follow them. Such rules might govern how fights are settled or control other forms of family interaction (Broderick, 1993).

When new circumstances or problems arise in families, members often use tried-and-true methods to bring the situation back to the normal, steady state. Even if a family member wishes for change, others may use approval or punishment to maintain familiar ways of interacting (Montgomery & Fewer, 1988). At times a family system is pushed further and further from its steady state by changes in the family, such as maturing children or chronic illness, or changes in the environment, such as job loss. Family members suddenly find that their usual ways no longer work. At this point, some families fall into confusion and others change rapidly. Such changes can occur through positive feedback, in which the behaviour of one family member sparks a response from others that increases the original behaviour, which in turn intensifies the response. For example, couples' arguments can escalate until they are caught in a vicious cycle of anger and blame. On the positive side, parents may use praise when they want a child to repeat a desired behaviour, like picking up toys. By analogy to the biological formation of organs, this process of change is called **morphogenesis** (Broderick, 1993; Ward, 1995).

Evaluation of Family Systems Theory

The main strength of family systems theory is its ability to account for the impact of the behaviour of one individual on all members of the family. It also explains why behaviour continues in destructive patterns, even through generations. For these reasons, many therapists have used it as a basis for their work with families.

There have been criticisms of this theory, however. First, the theory takes for granted that all members want the family to stay together, and this is not always true. Second, the concentration on the family system as a whole overlooks the experience of individuals, especially women. This is particularly true in cases of wife assault. Systems theory assumes that destructive behaviour is the result of a vicious cycle. This explanation comes suspiciously close to blaming the victim for her own misfortune. Third, theorists often make little or no reference to important social factors, such as unemployment, that affect family life, even though systems theory is quite capable of including such influences (Cheal, 1991).

THE FAMILY AS INTERACTING MEMBERS

In contrast to structural-functional and conflict theories, symbolic-interaction theorists use a micro approach to family relationships. They feel that the best way of understanding relations between family members is to examine the meanings each sees in other members' words and actions. Such meanings affect behaviour directly (Burgess & Locke, 1960). For example, one spouse may say to the other, "Why are you reading that book?" The partner might interpret the question to mean "Why are you wasting your time?" or "Why did you choose that book and not another?" or something else again. The response will differ according to the meaning read into the question. Interpretations develop in this way out of the history of interactions between family members. Behaviour and objects gain meaning, that is, become symbols, through the process of interaction (Ingoldsby, Smith, & Miller, 2004).

A major contribution of the symbolic-interaction theory is an expansion of concepts about roles. In contrast to structural-functionalists, who study roles from the viewpoint of society, symbolic interactionists study roles from the viewpoint of the individual. The latter concepts are often referred to as "role theory." According to this theory, individuals develop a sense of self through the attitudes of others and through relationships with parents, peers, and other individuals significant to them. They also develop a sense of the roles they are expected to fulfill. As they interact with others, individuals can anticipate the behaviour of others, and can tailor their own to match. This putting oneself in another's place is called role-taking. Role expectations come from past experiences. For example, husbands and wives may have different notions of how they should behave in marriage based on their experiences in their families of origin. As a result they may have problems because their role expectations clash. Role strain is a sense of discomfort or tension felt by one who has difficulty meeting role expectations. An example of the latter is the stepmother. The only roles available for her are either the biological mother or the stereotypical wicked stepmother, neither of which fits the reality of most families (Church, 2004). When a situation like this occurs, people are described as experiencing role strain.

Evaluation of the Symbolic-Interaction Position

One of the values of symbolic interaction is the emphasis it places on the individual's responsibility in shaping his or her view of the world. Since it explains individual sameness and change, it has been used as a basis for family therapy. If a therapist can help family members change their interpretations of behaviour, the quality of their interaction can be improved. However, symbolic interaction has been criticized for the micro view that is its main strength; it pays little attention to the impact of the wider society on family relationships. Thus it ignores factors such as laws, economics, social class, or values, and does not explain society-wide changes in families.

FAIR TRADE

According to exchange theory, much of family life can be viewed in terms of costs and benefits. Most of us have an idea of how much we are worth in terms of our abilities, personality, appearance, and even possessions. We expect to get the best return for what we provide in relationships at the least cost to ourselves. For example, if we feel we are reasonably attractive, we usually choose as a mate someone who is also good-looking, or we look for some other benefit, such as an exceptionally pleasant personality. We also go by the rule that when we receive favours, they must be repaid. Similarly, we expect favours we have given to be returned (Brinkerhoff & Lupri, 1989).

Critique of Exchange Theory

Exchange theorists have helped us understand decision-making in families. For the most part, exchange theorists have focused on husband–wife relationships. For instance, they have studied marital interaction as a bargaining process that occurs when one member wishes to change family rules. Power in families is not shared equally by the spouses; in many families, the husband has the advantage in education, income, prestige, social status, and even size. As a result, he has more resources with which he can bargain. In such situations, the exchange is not equal; rather, one spouse exerts power over the other (Brinkerhoff & Lupri, 1989). Exchange theory is limited, however, in its ability to explain family dynamics because it is based on individual rather than on family needs. It also assumes that people behave with self-interest. This is not always true. A small study, for example, found that wives earning much more than their husbands still did well over half the household chores (Tichenor, 1999). In addition, people keep having children even though children are a financial drain on the family (Klein & White, 2002).

THE FAMILY THROUGH TIME

Looking at the family using one of the frameworks we have discussed is rather like looking at a snapshot that has frozen a moment in time. As we leaf through a photo album, we develop a different perspective on our families. Over the years, old faces change or disappear and new ones are added. Often the pictures mark special events—birthdays, weddings, graduations, visits, and trips. Some theorists take the "album" approach to studying the family rather than that of a single snapshot.

Developmentalists look at the entire life cycle of the family from its formation to its end. They divide the cycle into stages, the number varying according to the theorist. Two developmental theories are described in Box 1.2. Stages in Duvall and Miller's (1985) framework are based on the age of the oldest child. Later theorists such as Carter and McGoldrick (1999b) do not link the stages as closely to child development. At each stage the family changes in predictable ways. Having a baby, for instance, calls on parents to accomplish

BOX 1.2

TWO DEVELOPMENTAL THEORIES

DUVALL AND MILLER'S EIGHT-STAGE FAMILY LIFE CYCLE

STAGE

1. Married couples (without children)
2. Childbearing families (oldest child's birth–30 months)
3. Families with preschool children (oldest child 2½–6 years)
4. Families with schoolchildren (oldest child 6–13 years)
5. Families with teenagers (oldest child 13–20 years)
6. Families launching young adults (first child gone to last child's leaving home)
7. Middle-aged parents (empty nest to retirement)
8. Aging family members (retirement to death of both spouses)

CARTER AND McGOLDRICK'S SIX-STAGE FAMILY LIFE CYCLE

STAGE

1. Leaving home: single young adults
2. The joining of families through marriage: the new couple
3. Families with young children
4. Families with adolescents
5. Launching children and moving on
6. Families in later life

Sources: Adapted from Duvall, Evelyn Mills, & Miller, Brent C., *Marriages and Family Development*, 6/e. Copyright © 1985 by Pearson Education; and from Carter, B., & McGoldrick, M., *The Expanded Family Life Cycle*, 3/e. Copyright © 1999 by Pearson Education. Both published by Allyn and Bacon and reprinted by permission of the publisher.

certain **developmental tasks.** The idea of tasks was borrowed from child development theory. According to Robert Havighurst (1952), who helped popularize the concept during the 1950s, a developmental task is a task that an individual is expected by society to achieve at a particular stage in his or her development. Success in this task leads to happiness and success in later tasks; failure brings unhappiness, social disapproval, and difficulty completing later tasks. New parents, for instance, must adjust their family arrangements to meet the physical and emotional needs of the baby as well as their own. If they do not do so, say developmentalists, the family will often experience difficulties at later stages.

The stages and tasks are related to the **social time clock,** that is, to a socially approved timetable for certain life events. If individuals are significantly off-schedule, they may experience difficulties. For example, our society is not geared to provide for adolescent mothers. They have not finished school and have difficulty supporting themselves financially. If they wish to continue their education, the system is usually not very supportive and flexible regarding childcare and school attendance. Officialdom often assumes that adolescent mothers are not competent to care for their children; this is reflected in such expressions as "children raising children" (Luker, 1996).

Evaluation of Developmental Theories

A number of criticisms of developmental theories have been made. First, they have been described as providing a form of lockstep that real families do not fit. For example, if stages are determined by the age of the eldest child, as with Duvall and Miller (1985), families with "caboose" babies or other large variations in age between oldest and youngest child do not really fit the category (Ingoldsby, Smith, & Miller, 2004).

A second criticism is that such theories depend on the concept of the nuclear family. Early developmental theorists assumed that the family consisted of the husband/father, wife/mother, and children who were born at a suitable interval following their parents' marriage. In the 1940s, when the theory was developed, most families did follow this pattern (Aldous, 1996). Other types of families were considered defective in some way; for instance, a single-parent family was considered to be missing either the husband/father or wife/mother. Of course, many present-day families do not fit the two-parents-plus-children pattern. Originally, developmental theorists also treated men's and women's family experiences as being similar, although women's life experiences are actually more variable than men's (Cheal, 1991).

Developmental theorists are responding to changing family forms. Carter and McGoldrick (1999a), for example, have added four developmental stages for divorce, two for the post-divorce family (one each for the custodial and noncustodial parent), and three for remarriage. McGoldrick (1999b) also describes family life cycles of women, distinct from those of men. Life patterns among women have also been compared, ranging from those undertaking professional education to those having their first child in adolescence, prior to marriage (Luker, 1996). There has also been some discussion of family life cycles of lesbians and gay men (Johnson & Colucci, 1999). A somewhat different approach has been taken by

Aldous (1996), who describes family careers or paths. These include marital career, parental career, and sibling career. Not all families include all these paths or follow them in the same order. For some families, parenthood may come before marriage; for others, it may never arrive. Within each path, however, certain things can be expected, for example, the increased demands on a parent's time in looking after a new baby. The family career approach answers the "lockstep" criticism of family development theories.

A third criticism is that developmental theories focus on a single generation, and thus overlooks intergenerational relationships. For example, if we concentrate on midlife, we may ignore young adults or the grandparent generation. This problem can be overcome through using a combination of systems and developmental views (Laszloffy, 2002).

In spite of its drawbacks, the developmental view does have advantages. It allows researchers to compare family life in different cultures, even those as similar as the United States and Canada. In both countries, for example, fertility rates fell sharply from the mid-1960s until the mid-1970s, when the birth rate for the United States began to rise again while the Canadian rate continued to drop. During this period, Canadian women went from having children earlier than Americans to having them later (Bélanger & Ouellet, 2002). Thus the timing of transitions among developmental stages will differ. Also, the developmental perspective is fairly easy to relate to the stages in both child and adult development, such as those described by Erik Erikson (1982).

RESEARCHING THE FAMILY

Where do we get all of the information we have about families? Sociology, including family studies, uses many of the same methods of research as other social sciences. Investigators use two main approaches in studying the family. **Quantitative research** is widely used in the scientific community. Information is presented in the form of numbers which are analyzed using statistical techniques (Greenstein, 2001). Typical quantitative methods are surveys and experiments. Yet, "the things we can easily count are not always the things that count most for families" (Coontz, 2000, p. 292). **Qualitative research** is concerned more with verbal descriptions of behaviour based on reports from people being studied, on observation, and on the analysis of patterns (Greenstein, 2001). Qualitative methods include in-depth interviews, direct observation, and document analysis. This type of research often helps identify questions which are then studied quantitatively.

A common quantitative method is the **survey,** which involves approaching people for information face-to-face, over the telephone, by mail, or over the Internet. The survey method has the advantage of getting answers from a large number of people; on the other hand, it is difficult to investigate a topic in any depth using this method (Greenstein, 2001). One of the most important survey researchers is Statistics Canada. As well as conducting a census every five years, Statistics Canada investigates many areas of Canadian life on a continuing basis. (See Table 1.1.) For example, it provides annual estimates of poverty in families. Many sociologists are also involved in survey research. In addition, magazines often publish the results of questionnaires completed by their readers. However, we must be careful

TABLE 1.1

STRUCTURE OF FAMILIES IN CANADA, 2001 CENSUS

	Number	Percentage
Total families	8 371 020	100.0
Married families	5 901 420	70.5
Common-law families	1 158 410	13.8
Lone-parent families	1 311 190	15.7

Source: Adapted from Statistics Canada, "Profile of Canadian families and households: Diversification continues, 2001 Census," Catalogue 96F0030, October 22, 2002, p. 24.

Note: In 2001, there were 34 200 same-sex common-law couples, 0.5% of all couples. Slightly more than half of these were male.

about accepting the opinions they report as typical of Canadians, because many of the publications originate in the United States, and the opinions and experiences of Americans may be different from our own. Also, there is no way of knowing how well readers who fill out magazine questionnaires represent all ages and classes of people. Another problem is that with any kind of research that involves self-reporting, participants may knowingly or unknowingly distort the facts. On one questionnaire, teenagers mischievously said they were adopted when they were not and stated they had many serious problems (Fan et al., 2002).

Experiments involve changing conditions deliberately, and observing any changes in behaviour that result. In some cases, researchers perform experiments to test relationships, for example, the physiological arousal of couples during arguments as measured by instruments similar to lie detectors (Gottman, 1991). In spite of the ability to control factors, experiments do have drawbacks. Since the research laboratory is not a natural family setting, the behaviour there may not be typical of the individual family members. It is also unethical to conduct experiments that may damage a person physically or emotionally. For example, it would be unethical to isolate a baby from its mother to learn the effects of maternal deprivation.

Probably the most common form of qualitative research is the in-depth **interview.** This involves more detailed and lengthier face-to-face questioning than the survey method. Interviews are often too time-consuming and costly to involve huge numbers of subjects (Patton, 1990). The interview method is often used when the researcher is looking for information that cannot easily be transformed into numbers. One such study concerned how children felt about the support and punishment by parents in one-parent, stepparent, and two-parent families (Amato, 1987). At times, interview research is used as a basis for questionnaires that can be given to a larger number of individuals.

Direct observations by researchers avoid the problems found in self-reporting. In one form, naturalistic observation, the researcher is detached from the people studied, and will try to watch and record normal activities as unobtrusively as possible. Sometimes, audio or video recording equipment is used and tapes are later analyzed in the office or laboratory. For example, in one study of marital relationships, researchers videotaped couples discussing a problem topic and coded their facial expressions. They found that couples who later separated were more likely to have miserable smiles and to show disgust (Gottman, 1991). In another form of observation, the investigator actually takes part in the activities of the subjects and reports on his or her experiences. This method is often used when researchers, more often anthropologists than sociologists, study different cultures. By living in the society, it is possible to observe small details that the outside observer might miss, and to understand the meanings of certain activities.

Researchers also look at the forms of communication used during the period they are studying (Patton, 1996); for example, historical material on the family often depends on both popular and scholarly reports. Sheila Kieran (1986), in her book on family law in Ontario, quotes letters and diaries, particularly ones from the first half of the 19th century; these types of sources help bring to life official documents that can be dry. Researchers have even examined changes in how fathers have been portrayed in comic strips over the past 60 years (LaRossa, Jaret, Gadgil, & Wynn, 2000).

Once the researchers have gathered data, they often perform statistical analyses. This is, of course, a characteristic of quantitative research, but it may also be used by qualitative researchers following many interviews or observations. One of the simplest and most common forms is **correlation,** which attempts to find a strong relationship between two or more factors or variables (Greenstein, 2001). (Correlations cannot, however, prove that one factor or event caused another.) For example, in a study of marital satisfaction, researchers found a correlation between life events such as the birth of a child or children leaving home and the level of satisfaction (Lupri & Frideres, 1981).

In comparing life stages or historical periods, it is important to keep in mind two different approaches to research. **Cross-sectional research** studies individuals of different ages and compares them in relation to the factor under investigation. A major problem with comparing attitudes (toward sexuality, for example) among people of different age groups is that these are affected by different historical events and values, and the differences in attitude may not be the result of age but of changing times. This is referred to as a **cohort effect.** The findings of Lupri and Frideres (1981) concerning marital satisfaction may be showing cohort influences rather than the effect of the life stage. Cohort influences can be overcome by **longitudinal research**—that is, by following the same people over a long period of time. Human Resources Canada and Statistics Canada, for example, are jointly studying the way children grow and develop from birth to adulthood. The first group, aged zero to eleven in 1994, numbers about 15,000, with younger children being added to the study (Brink & McKellar, 2000). One difficulty with longitudinal studies is the many years needed before results are available. In the interval, subjects may lose interest or disappear. Sometimes, to get information faster and yet reduce cohort effects, a combination of cross-sectional and longitudinal studies is used (Baltes, Reese, & Nesselroade, 1977).

Whatever method of investigation is used, the results are affected by the theoretical approach to the family because it determines which questions are asked. If a structural-functionalist wished to study decision-making in the family, the question may be, "How is decision-making related to traditional roles?" A feminist, however, would ask, "How is decision-making related to power in the family?" A family systems theorist might want to know the impact of decision-making on subsystems in the family, and a developmentalist how decision-making differs at the various stages.

THE APPROACH OF THIS BOOK

Much of this book will follow the developmental view of the family, using the family career approach. It will look at how couples get together and consider their relationships in several variations—unmarried cohabitation, marriage, and same-sex unions, among others. Then, after examining the decision to become parents and the process of raising children, the book moves on to discuss the middle and later years. Next, it explores recent changes in trends to do with families, such as divorce and remarriage, and the family's relationship to the workplace. Despite its drawbacks, the developmental view offers some benefits: it enables us to tie the events in family life to studies in human development, and it allows comparisons of present-day families with those of other times and places. We can also add insights from other theories where they will help our understanding.

In order to overcome some of the developmental view's drawbacks, we will need to pay attention to the variations that are common in our society, such as single-parent families and stepfamilies. Some issues, such as family violence and poverty, affect all age groups, and these will be discussed separately. Finally, we will need to consider how governments and social institutions affect family life.

DEFINING THE FAMILY. Families have been defined in different ways according to time and place. In Canada today, there are several legal definitions of family, as well as social and personal definitions. Two ideas of family common in North America are the nuclear family, consisting of parents and children, and the extended family, which includes other relatives.

THEORIES OF THE FAMILY. Sociologists have suggested a number of theories to explain what happens in families.

1. The ecological view regards families as part of interlocking systems that influence each other at four levels: the microsystem, made up of small groups with face-to-face interaction; the mesosystem, made up of relationships between two or more small groups; the exosystem, which affects families through the mesosystem or microsystem; and the macrosystem, or a society's culture and ideology.
2. The structural-functional theory views the family as an institution among other social institutions. Families fulfill important functions in society: caring for the physical and emotional well-being of its members, and producing and shaping new members for society. According to this view, much of behaviour is governed by the values and norms within a society; these are transmitted to new generations through the process called socialization. Families are organized around the statuses of husband/father, wife/mother, and child, who each have roles assigned by society.
3. Conflict theories are concerned with power relationships. One such theory is feminism, which points to the political and social control enjoyed by men. This control is supported by the view that men head the household, by the assumption that caring for a family is a woman's responsibility, and by the higher levels of men's earnings, compared with those of women.
4. Systems theory regards a family as a set of interrelated parts in which anything that affects one part affects all of them. Families also contain subsystems, which are smaller groupings. Boundaries set out who belongs to a family or its subsystems. Families operate according to rules. These are related to feedback and, in a new situation, may produce a vicious cycle, confusion, or formation of new rules.
5. Symbolic-interaction theories look at the meanings individuals see in the words and actions of others. These meanings develop from the history of family members' interactions. Symbolic interactionists have contributed the concepts of role-taking, role expectations, and role strain.
6. Exchange theorists look at the costs and benefits of family life to its members. They have been especially concerned with how husbands and wives make decisions.
7. The developmental view considers families from their formation to their end. At each stage of the family life cycle, members must accomplish developmental tasks. These are related to the needs of members and to social expectations. More recently, developmental

theories have expanded to include couple and parent "careers." Although this perspective has drawbacks, it forms much of the basis of this book.

STUDYING THE FAMILY. Researchers use two approaches to studying families—quantitative and qualitative. Typical quantitative methods are surveys and experiments, which are followed by statistical analysis. Qualitative research uses in-depth interviews, direct observation, and document analysis. Cross-sectional research compares people of different ages at the same moment in time. Longitudinal studies follow the same individuals for a period of time.

KEY TERMS

boundary: an imaginary line marking who belongs to a system (p. 14)

cohort effect: characteristics or attitudes that result from the period of history in which people have lived (p. 21)

communal living: a group of people, who may or may not be related by birth or marriage, sharing financial resources and living arrangements (p. 4)

correlation: a mathematical method for showing whether a relationship exists between factors (p. 21)

cross-sectional research: a method of research that studies individuals of different ages and compares them in relation to the factor under investigation (p. 21)

developmental task: a task that an individual is expected to achieve at a particular stage in development (p. 18)

direct observation: a research method in which the researcher watches and records behaviour (p. 20)

exosystem: institutions and organizations in society in which individuals do not take an active part, but that affect them through the mesosystem or microsystem (p. 8)

experiment: a research method that involves changing conditions deliberately and observing any changes in behaviour that result (p. 20)

extended family: the nuclear family and all other relatives (p. 6)

household: a person or group of persons who occupy the same dwelling (p. 3)

interview: a research method in which the researcher asks questions face-to-face (p. 20)

longitudinal research: a research method in which the same individuals are studied for a period of time (p. 21)

macrosystem: society's culture and ideology (p. 9)

mesosystem: the relationships between two or more microsystems (p. 7)

microsystem: small groups in which people interact face-to-face (p. 7)

monogamy: marriage to one person at a time (p. 4)

morphogenesis: development of new forms of behaviour (p. 14)

norms: ways of behaving that are typical of a certain group (p. 10)

nuclear family: a family consisting of a husband, a wife, and their children (p. 6)

polygamy: marriage of one person to more than one person of the opposite sex (p. 4)

qualitative research: research methods that provide verbal descriptions of behaviour (p. 19)

quantitative research: research methods widely used in the scientific community that present information in the form of numbers (p. 19)

role: a function expected of a person who has a particular status (p. 11)

socialization: the passing on of the basic knowledge of a culture's ways of thinking and acting, including how to survive and how to take part in social life (p. 10)

social scripts: cultural rules that tell us what, where, when, how, and why we should do something (p. 11)

social time clock: socially approved timetable for certain life events (p. 18)

status: a social position that carries a set of expectations concerning suitable behaviour (p. 11)

subsystem: smaller groupings within a system (p. 14)

survey: a method of research that involves getting information from many individuals (p. 19)

system: a set of interrelated and interacting parts (p. 13)

theory: general framework of ideas that can be used to answer questions about the world (p. 6)

values: social principles that are accepted by society as a whole or by a group within that society (p. 10)

CLASS ASSIGNMENTS

Complete one or both of the following assignments, as directed by your instructor:

1. Select an occupation you are interested in. Do some library research or interview someone who is familiar with that occupation. Try to learn how knowledge of the family is important in the occupation. You might consider definition, family history, and influences of the family on the individual.

2. Often, cultural differences can be observed in customs of religious festivals. Interview a friend, neighbour, acquaintance, or classmate about the religious event most important to his or her family. Find out what practices are followed, such as worship, family events, special foods, and other possible activities. Learn how these have affected the person's relationship with others of the same faith and with people of other faiths. Discover the values the individual sees in this event.

PERSONAL ASSIGNMENTS

The following assignments are designed to help you gain insight into your own family experiences:

1. Think about your own family. What are some of the events that have occurred that might affect your ability, either positively or negatively, to provide service to others? Are there any individuals you might have difficulty helping? Why?

2. Make a list of the many roles that you fill (e.g., student, friend, son/daughter, employee, parent). What is expected of you in each role? Where do you foresee conflicts related to family life? Which roles hold priority for you? Why?

Chapter 2

Being Different

© Laureen March/Corbis

OBJECTIVES

 To examine the differences in family experiences of males and females in our society

 To introduce some issues in which differences among families challenge the majority

 To consider social and ethnic differences among English Canadians, French Canadians, Aboriginal peoples, and recent immigrants, and to look briefly at the history behind such differences

 To examine discrimination against minority groups and minority group responses

I have Usher Syndrome, type 2. This is a combination of nerve deafness and retinitis pigmentosa (RP), a form of blindness. I was born with hearing loss and this gradually deteriorated. I was profoundly deaf by the time I was in my mid- to late teens. I had normal vision when I was younger but now have only a very small tunnel of vision. I also have huge problems with glare from bright lights, and have very little night vision.

My hearing loss meant that I was always pretty much left out at family get-togethers because I couldn't follow conversations and really did not feel like I belonged anywhere. Sometimes my parents and brother would get very frustrated or impatient with me when I couldn't understand what they were telling me. Schoolmates didn't bother including me because they didn't want to repeat what was going on. Many times I would look stupid because I would misunderstand and then say something that had nothing to do with what was being discussed. Because of this, I immersed myself into sports, at which I was pretty good, so I got a certain level of respect from my peers.

My parents really did not want to accept that I was losing my vision. It is fairly common that family members, especially parents, do not want to acknowledge the "horrible possibility" that their child is going blind, so they prefer to deny and ignore it as long as they can. There can also be resentment or frustration if the person with the disability needs extra help. For example, since I am no longer able to drive, my parents, especially my dad, have to give me rides to a lot of places. It can also make me feel like a burden at times. Another way an acquired disability like RP affects the family is that the person who is losing their vision can go through periods of depression, grief, denial, and frustration. This creates a strain on the family as well.

People frequently act as if I am stupid and will address questions to someone I am with instead of asking me directly. They also make assumptions about what I can and cannot do, based on their own prejudices and preconceived notions. People also sometimes act as if I am extremely fragile and am about to get hurt any moment.

Source: Used with permission from Megan McHugh.

As we study the family life cycle, we must remain aware of the many differences that exist in families. Frequently, people discussing the family assume that it involves being married, becoming parents, and living together. The one-size-fits-all approach, however, ignores important family variations (White & Klein, 2002). Some people never marry but live in family-like groupings such as those in religious orders. Others who choose not to marry or never find a marriage partner keep close ties with relatives or friends. Same-sex couples often find family-like support and acceptance among friends. Many gay men and lesbians are parents, sometimes because they married before "coming out," sometimes through artificial insemination or adoption. Other couples choose not to have children. Some two-career families are built around commuter couples who live in different cities. In addition, many immigrants bring a different image of family to Canada.

Thus, differences may occur among family members, for example, differences between males and females, in abilities, and in sexual orientation. They can also arise between families, as in different family arrangements, including single-parent and stepfamilies. There are also differences in the family experiences of various racial and ethnic groups, including recent immigrants and interracial marriage. In this chapter, we will consider some of these differences and discuss the reactions of others to them. We will conclude by looking at the importance of differences and of social attitudes for all of us.

WOMEN AND MEN

Sex and Gender Differences

Among the most important differences in family experiences is that between males and females. These differences have three sources: (1) the physical and genetic differences between the sexes, (2) the routine ways of behaving we develop over the years, and (3) our individual ideas and values (Dannefer & Perlmutter, 1990). Thus they arise from both nature and nurture.

The word *sex,* used alone, refers to the appearance of the genitals (LeVay, 1993). In addition to differences in physical appearance, men and women differ bodily in other ways. Male and female sex hormones are, of course, responsible for differences in the reproductive systems. Only women can become pregnant, give birth to babies, and nurse them. They can produce only a limited number of children in their lifetimes. For a woman to have as many as 20 babies is rare but possible, especially when there are multiple births. Men, on the other hand, can father many children, especially if they have many partners (Rowe, 1994). Until DNA testing became available, proving that a man had fathered a child was often difficult; for women, parenthood was obvious.

There are other physical differences. Men, on average, are taller and more muscular than women (LeVay, 1993; Rowe, 1994). Women, however, tend to live longer than men and, generally, to be healthier except in countries where there are many childbirth deaths (Bélanger & Martel, 2003). Sex hormones also appear to affect brain development. Males tend to be more sensitive to sight and females to sound, touch, and odour. Males tend to be better at tracking direction and in mentally manipulating objects. They also have higher levels of activity and aggression. Females, on the other hand, tend to be more fluent in language. They are also more sensitive to nonverbal cues, a skill that makes them more sensitive to babies' signals (LeVay, 1993; Rossi, 1984).

We cannot, however, separate the physical from the environment; physical differences can only be expressed in the family and society in which we live (Moore, 2001). Socially, the sex of an individual is important. On television, as in real life, the first exclamation when a baby is born is usually "It's a girl!" or "It's a boy!" That is, the sex of the child is publicly announced. This knowledge is being pushed even earlier with the routine use of ultrasound and other kinds of testing before birth. Knowing the sex of an individual helps shape how we behave toward that person, even from the first moments of life. Physical differences in reproduction, for instance, can lead to a double standard in sexuality, where men are allowed much more freedom than women. Some societies, for example in India and in Arab countries, almost completely separate male and female roles. Others, like ours in Canada, favour greater equality, but even here boys and girls are often expected to behave in different ways, with boys expected to be more aggressive than girls.

We learn habitual ways of interacting with each other through the process of socialization. Thus **gender roles** (the socially approved ways of behaving as males and females in our society) become second nature to us (Dannefer & Perlmutter, 1990). Gender socialization prepares children and adolescents for the kinds of tasks they are expected to perform as boys and girls and will be expected to perform as men and women. As we saw in the last chapter, people learn the values, attitudes, and patterns of behaviour that their society considers desirable through socialization. These forms of behaviour often become so ingrained that they are considered inevitable. For example, women are considered to "naturally" be nurturers and men to "naturally" be go-getters (Haddock, Zimmerman, & Lyness, 2003). Such patterns of behaviour are sustained through day-to-day interaction with those around us.

If parents' values differ from those of society at large, they can influence their children, but this influence may be limited. When young people are in a situation where they do not quite know how to behave, they usually follow the tried-and-true method of doing what others do. This copycat behaviour also occurs in learning what behaviour is considered appropriate for males and females. As children become older, they are influenced not only by parents, but also by other adults such as teachers, by peers, and by the media. In turn they influence those around them (Shanahan & Sobolewski, 2003). This process of socialization is discussed in more detail in Chapter 6.

As we can see in differences among societies and in changes in our own culture, gender roles do not always stay the same. For example, the tough frontiersman of the pioneer days and the swooning female of Victorian novels are no longer accepted as norms. Following World War II, child psychologists helped change the standard for mothering. Now mothers became responsible not only for the physical and moral upbringing of children, but also for their emotional well-being (Gleason, 1999).

Our values, beliefs, and practices do not depend only on physical differences or how we have been socialized. We also make our own decisions as to how we should behave. This explains why, for example, traditional parents may have children who believe in equally sharing both family support and household responsibilities.

Gender Differences and Family Relationships

Gender differences affect both the nature of relationships and all aspects of family life. In the 19th century, traditional differences between male and female roles were supported by all aspects of society. Both the Roman Catholic Church and many Protestant denominations, for example, regarded men as practical, active, and rational. Women, in contrast, were thought of as moral, spiritual, and emotional. In marriage the two aspects were combined to make a holy union (Westfall, 1989). A birth announcement a few years ago puts it in capsule form: "We have the Cheerleaders and now we have the Quarterback" ("Births," 2000). So-called family values advocates currently support such views (Erera, 2002). In more practical terms, these ideas meant that men were expected to go out into the world to make a living and to protect the family from danger. Women's task was to make the home into a place where family members were nurtured. This division still continues in the idea that women are responsible for making an intimate relationship work and for keeping family peace. If problems arise, they may feel guilty for failing in their responsibility.

In our society, men and women, boys and girls, are still brought up to relate to one another in different ways. Females, according to sociologists, tend to focus on relationships and connections between people. Males, on the other hand, are taught to value independence and self-direction (Haddock, Zimmerman, & Lyness, 2003). For example, when children are injured, adults tend to be less sensitive to boys' pain than to girls'. That is, girls are more likely to be comforted, while boys are dusted off and told not to cry (Mathews, 2002). Adolescent girls are less likely to use physical aggression than boys. Rather, they rely on social aggression, such as shunning or spreading rumours (Underwood, 2003). Girls are also less likely to commit violent crimes than boys (Fitzgerald, 2003).

Another area where differences have been observed is in communication. When men talk, they tend to be concerned with reasoned arguments and with their own or others' power and authority. Women, on the other hand, usually talk to form connections with others. As a result, men's and women's body language is different, and men tend to interrupt more than women do (Wood, 1996b). Women are usually better at reading and sending nonverbal messages than men, especially those regarding emotions. Like others who are less powerful, women often use intelligence, interpersonal skill, sexuality, deception, and avoidance to get what they want (Lipman-Blumen, 1984). For instance, Hutterite women will refuse to be "nice" sexually to their husbands as a form of manipulation (Peter, 1987). Men are not as dependent on the immediate situation in their thinking (Wood, 1996b). These differences in communication that affect how individuals both start and maintain a relationship will be explored in the next two chapters.

There are other differences. It is commonly accepted that males, in general, are more likely to take part in sexual acts without being in a love relationship, while women much more often become romantically attached first. Men also tend to initiate sexual relations more often than women do. Because, unlike women, men are socialized to be independent and unemotional, it may be harder for them to become committed to a relationship, while women tend to try to maintain the relationship. Sexual fidelity after marriage is expected of both spouses, but affairs by men are often regarded more leniently than women's affairs (Regan, 2003).

When it comes to family responsibilities, the man is more often the principal earner because traditionally male occupations, like lawyer or heavy equipment operator, are usually better paid than traditionally female ones, like daycare worker or nurse. Women are more often considered responsible for child-rearing. Usually women, rather than men, take parental leave when a child is born, so that there are breaks in their employment and thus in their opportunities for promotion. When it comes to a choice between family and career, males see less conflict than females. Indeed, many men feel they meet family responsibilities if they work. Women, on the other hand, must explain why they are not bad mothers if they have jobs. Women usually take more responsibility for housework than men do, even when both are employed (Haddock, Zimmerman, & Lyness, 2003).

"Okay, I believe you now."

Source: Reprinted by kind permission of Barrie Maguire.

As we shall discuss in more detail in later chapters, women's family experiences are often quite different from men's. Social norms encourage fathers to be more involved in raising sons than daughters (Maccoby, 2003). In addition, marital satisfaction tends to be lower after the birth of a daughter, especially if unplanned (Cox, Paley, Burchinal, & Payne, 1999). Women are more likely than men to be single parents, to live in poverty, to live alone, and to be widowed. On the other hand, men are more likely to be living with a partner, and are more likely to remarry if they are widowed or divorced. Women and girls experience more physical and sexual abuse than do men (Brzozowski, 2004). To underline differences between men's and women's experiences, sociologists talk of "his and her marriage" (Haddock, Zimmerman, & Lyness, 2003) or "his and her" experiences of parenthood (Cowan et al., 1985). Feminists point out gender inequality in families, with the bulk of power held by men (White & Klein, 2002).

CHANGING FAMILY FORMS

The "traditional" family model of breadwinner father, homemaker mother, and their two or three biological children persists as an ideal in much thinking about the family. For example, high divorce rates, teen pregnancy, and lone parenthood have been blamed for many social ills such as delinquency, child neglect and abuse, and poverty (Erera, 2002). The remedy, some feel, is to encourage marriage, make divorce more difficult, and otherwise return to "family values." Government policy usually assumes that the household and family are the same—that the man and woman living together are husband and wife, and that they are parents of children living with them. Thus people are responsible for supporting children in the household, whether or not they are the parents. Similarly, after the lapse of some specified time that varies from province to province, the individuals are assumed to be married according to common law and are responsible for each other (Bala, 2004). It has been an uphill battle, however, for some partners (same-sex couples, for instance) to be recognized as families (Lahey & Alderson, 2004).

The 2001 census shows that only a minority of families fit the "traditional" model. Couples with children living at home, including common-law couples, made up less than half (44 percent) of all families. The percentage of stepfamilies has increased. A growing number of children lived with parents in common-law unions. About one-fifth (19 percent) of children lived with one parent, usually their mother, or occasionally with others, most often a relative. There is an increase of couples without children at home, the result of a falling birth rate, postponement of childbearing, and longer life after children are grown (Statistics Canada, 2002d). In addition, medical advances and social changes have dramatically altered the options of those wishing to become parents—in vitro fertilization and other treatments for infertility, and older-child and international adoptions. Family types vary in different regions of the country. Alberta has the highest proportion of married parents (74.0 percent), compared with Quebec (52.1 percent) and Nunavut (46.8 percent). Both Quebec and the territories have a higher percentage of common-law unions than other provinces. Nunavut also has the highest proportion of children living with a single parent (Statistics Canada, 2002d). In addition, the number of homemaker wives has declined. In 2003, 72 percent of all women with children under 16 had paid jobs, compared with 39 percent in 1976 (Statistics Canada, 2004k).

Changes in family patterns challenge accepted practices in many ways. The following are a few examples:

1. The increasing number of families with two working parents poses one such challenge. For example, suspending a young child from school ignores the fact that often no parent is home during the day. Similarly, appeals for parents to chaperone daytime school outings may receive little response. Young offenders are expected to appear in court with a parent; this means someone will have to take time off work, with a loss in pay they may not be able to afford.

2. Many children have a variety of parent figures. These include adoptive parents, foster parents, stepparents, babysitters, and daycare staff. The expectation that children live only with biological parents overlooks reality and tends to cloud the emotional effect some of the family differences may have on children. Not all parents fill traditional roles. For example, it was easier in the past for mothers to get child support and fathers to get childcare help than vice versa. Now, however, most provinces will grant family support payments to a single father staying home with young children (Eichler, 1987).

   Despite the best of intentions, some school practices discriminate against children from nontraditional families. Family trees, for instance, single out children from lone-parent, stepparent, adoptive, or foster families. Who should be counted as parents? The issue becomes particularly troubling if family change has been recent, or if the child is attached to a substitute parent and wants that person included in the tree (Shreck, 2001). Mother's Day and Father's Day cards may also highlight differences.

3. Advances in artificial reproductive techniques and greater openness about using them are reflected in media stories. People today are less likely to pretend that they are a conventional family than in the past. There is still some resistance, however, to granting nontraditional methods the same status as biological reproduction. For example, one mother of both biological and adopted children has been asked often, "Which ones are your own?" (meaning biological). Social workers are beginning to question the secrecy surrounding artificial insemination (individuals conceived by this method are usually denied knowledge of their genetic background). Adoptees have insisted that such knowledge is important to a healthy sense of identity (Freundlich, 2001). Questions have centred especially on using such technology to aid unmarried women, and most particularly lesbians, to become parents.

4. Mentally and physically challenged members of the community, like Megan (in the introduction), are demanding the same rights as others. Within the school system, this has emerged as **mainstreaming**—that is, integrating children with exceptional needs into regular classrooms. Children with mental and physical challenges now live at home or in substitute homes within the community rather than in large institutions. As adults, they want jobs and normal family life, including marriage and children. Society has had to respond to the necessity of sex education for those with disabilities; no longer can it be assumed that those with mental and physical challenges are sexless beings (Royal Adelaide Hospital, 1999). Society also needs to plan for the supports and services such individuals need to become the best possible parents.

5. Same-sex couples have received recognition, first as common-law partners, and more recently as eligible to marry. A number of lesbians and gay men are parents through earlier heterosexual marriages. Others are part of what has been called the "lesbian baby boom," often as the result of artificial insemination. Some children live in gay or lesbian stepfamilies. Children in same-sex families may face the decision over coming out of the closet at school and in the neighbourhood, and the need to explain having two mothers or two fathers. There may also be questions around the legal status of the non-biological parent. Some critics have questioned the fitness of homosexual individuals to be parents at all (Erera, 2002; Lahey & Alderson, 2004; Snow, 2004).

RACIAL AND ETHNIC DIFFERENCES

In addition to the variety in family types, there has also been an increase in the racial and ethnic diversity of Canadians. In the 2001 census, fewer than half the non-Aboriginal population (46 percent) reported that their ancestors were British, French, Canadian, or a mixture of these. Another fifth (19 percent) came from other European countries. Those of non-European ancestry (most often Chinese and East Indian) made up 13 percent of Canadians. The remainder had mixed heritage or didn't know what it was (Statistics Canada, 2003c). About one in six (18 percent) stated their mother tongue, that is, the first language they learned at home and still understood, was neither English nor French. Although the

BOX 2.1

IS SHE ENTITLED TO SUPPORT?

It is all too common. A couple in a long-term relationship, but not legally married, split up. They met nearly every standard for a common-law marriage. They lived together in a sexual relationship and shared household responsibilities. They went to social affairs together and were seen by their friends and acquaintances as a couple.

After the split, one partner—let's call her M—applied for support from the other, as any common-law partner in Ontario is entitled. But instead of receiving a routine hearing, the application went all the way to the Supreme Court of Canada. You see, M and her former partner H are lesbians. No one knew if M was entitled to apply for alimony, let alone receive it. The Ontario Family Law Act only permitted partners of the opposite sex to make a claim for spousal support. The Ontario Court (General Division) and the Ontario Court of Appeal both ruled that the Family Law Act violated the Charter of Rights. On May 20, 1999, the Supreme Court of Canada agreed. As a result, Ontario revised its laws, but used the term "partners" rather than "spouses" to refer to same-sex couples. In the meantime, M and H had settled the matter privately. This case set an important precedent leading up to the legalization of same-sex marriage.

Sources: EGALE, 1999a; EGALE, 1999b; EGALE, n.d.; Lahey & Alderson, 2004.

---

total number of anglophones and francophones increased, their proportion of the population declined. The fastest-growing mother tongues were Chinese, Punjabi, Arabic, Urdu, and Tagalog. These language changes, of course, related to trends in immigration. Among Aboriginal peoples, Cree was the most common language, followed by Inuktitut and Ojibway (Statistics Canada, 2002f).

English Canadians and French Canadians

The character of English-Canadian society had roots in Britain. Canada became part of the British Empire as a result of conquest and colonization. In order to further expansionist goals, the traditional "masculine" characteristics were encouraged—enterprise, aggression, and responsibility for the weaker or less civilized (Mann, 2001). Many immigrants from the British Isles were troublemakers "sent to the colonies" or younger sons whose families could not support them. Thus they had incentives to seek their individual fortunes. Second, many were members of Protestant denominations and sects, some of them at loggerheads. This religious diversity did not encourage community-wide cooperation, as did the Roman Catholic Church in Quebec or Aboriginal cultural and religious practices. English Canadians have always seen the family as responsible for its members. Their definition of family and its responsibilities has, however, been rather narrow. The chief responsibility was to nuclear family members and entailed providing opportunities to advance themselves.

Aboriginal families and, to a lesser degree, French-Canadian families usually value ties with extended family members more than English Canadians.

In Quebec, the French government encouraged a society that mirrored the homeland and discouraged dissidents. The traditionally accepted view of Quebec society, which continued until about 1960, emphasized four elements to preserving French-Canadian society. First, the Catholic Church defined both family roles and educational goals. Second, rural lifestyle was central. Third, large families were idealized. Men were patriarchs and women found their chief glory in motherhood. The fourth underpinning was the French language (Valois, 1993). If English Canadians valued "masculine" qualities, French Canadians were perceived as "feminine"—religious, elegant, and civilized (Mann, 2001).

After years of gradual change, a new definition of Quebec identity blossomed during the 1960s. Gone was the authority of the Roman Catholic Church. Education replaced religion as the chief socializer. Modern industrial economy replaced the rural lifestyle as a central value. The large family lost its prestige under the influences of the sexual revolution and the contraceptive pill. Only the importance of the French language remained unchanged, but it was made central only to Quebec society, rather than to French-Canadian culture as a whole (Valois, 1993). The provincial government has taken over social services and Quebec's family support programs have become the strongest in Canada (Vastel, 1994). There are other differences between Quebec and the rest of Canada; for example, more couples in Quebec choose to live together instead of marry than in the other provinces (Statistics Canada, 2002a). Even though they speak the same language, francophones living outside Quebec differ from Quebeckers because they do not have the same official supports for language and culture.

Aboriginal Peoples

Historically, Aboriginal families in North America did not have just one pattern of family relationships. They displayed two basic types of societies, based either on clans or on small migratory hunting groups. Clan lineages, such as Iroquoian and Pacific-slope societies, held rights to specific tracts of land for farming, hunting, or offshore fishing, and controlled specific trading routes. In the Iroquoian confederacy, conflicts and other issues were settled by consensus rather than force. Pacific-slope societies used feasts or potlatches as a way of handling conflicts and settling such issues as inheritance rights (Ray, 1996).

Small migratory hunting groups developed in the Subarctic or the Arctic and included the Inuit, northern Ojibway, and Swampy Cree. These groups consisted of a few closely related hunters and their wives, children, parents, and grandparents. Leadership varied as the task at hand varied. In the summer villages, groups came together. This was a time for matchmaking because people married outside their winter group. These societies were based on social bonds rather than rigid territorial boundaries (Ray, 1996).

Plains buffalo-hunting societies resembled both the clan and migratory groups, because camp sizes varied greatly with the seasons. Most of the year, their organization was similar to that of the summer villages of the nations of the northern forests. During late summer, the buffalo-hunting and sun-dance camps were as large as the winter villages of the Iroquoian and Pacific-slope nations. In these societies, status was earned not through gift-giving or holding territorial rights, but through men's prowess in fighting and hunting (Ray, 1996).

Missionaries and government officials considered divergence from European-based society, especially regarding family relations and business practices, as backward, and they tried to change Aboriginal practices to match their own. One way was by taking children from their homes and educating them in boarding schools. Here, they were isolated from their families and culture. They were subjected to a harsh military-like regime in the schools and suffered both physical and sexual abuse. The schools cut them off from models of healthy family interaction, so institutional graduates had few skills and little knowledge when they came to raise their own families. They were taught farming and relevant crafts, such as wagon building, but none of the traditional Aboriginal forms of livelihood. In any case, these forms were eroded by the spread of migrants from eastern Canada and Europe and by the development of the reserve system. Many families lived in dire poverty. As a result of both poverty and family breakdown, many children were removed by child welfare authorities. Most were placed in non-Aboriginal homes (Milloy, 1999; Waterfall, 2003).

In recent years, the First Nations (registered Indian) population has been growing nearly three times faster than the Canadian population as a whole. There are three reasons for this trend. First, Aboriginal people as a group are younger; therefore more are of child-bearing age. Second, women who lost their Indian status by marrying a man who was not a registered Indian are now able to have their membership reinstated. Third, more individuals count themselves as Aboriginal. Although the largest number of Aboriginal people live in British Columbia and Ontario, the proportion of the population is higher in the prairie provinces and the territories. About half live in cities. As a whole, the opportunities of Aboriginal people are more limited than those of the general Canadian population, but the gap is decreasing. Aboriginal communities are becoming more diverse so that there is much variety in levels of education, income, and health (Castellano, 2002).

Extended family networks living on reserves traditionally took on responsibility for the care and nurture of their members. These networks still provide a stable base for young people who leave reserves for education or employment. Nuclear two-generation families are becoming more common. Especially in cities, "families of the heart," that is, voluntary groups that aim to preserve traditional ways, are assuming some of the functions of extended family members. Community services on reserves are also filling part of the role of the extended family, for example, by providing home care for the elderly. Aboriginal child and family services provide prevention, protection, and foster care services, and are more successful than provincial agencies in finding Aboriginal foster homes. However, legal jurisdiction for child welfare often does not rest with these agencies (Castellano, 2002).

Aboriginal cultural practices are showing new life. In nonreserve areas, about one-third of Aboriginal children are involved in traditional cultural activities, such as learning from elders and taking part in drum and dance groups. There is also evidence that some individuals are learning an Aboriginal tongue later in life as a second language (O'Donnell & Tait, 2003; Turcotte & Zhao, 2004).

PATTERNS OF IMMIGRATION TO CANADA

It is impossible to talk about immigrants as a single group. Many factors affected who was allowed to immigrate, including both the countries they came from and how many arrived in a particular period. These include the desire to maintain the "British" character of Canada, the need for labour to develop the country, and humanitarian motives.

The Desire to Retain Canada's "British" Character

Before 1900, many newcomers came from the British Isles and the United States, including many who were loyal to the British at the time of the American Revolution. A large Aboriginal population, located mainly in the North, and defined pockets of other minorities, mainly Asians and Blacks, made up Canada's **visible minority** presence. Blacks originally came to Canada as slaves; slavery existed in Eastern Canada until the early 1800s. Some came as Black Loyalists. Although they were promised land and adequate food and shelter, many did not receive them. In 2001, over 80 percent of Blacks living in Halifax were at least third-generation Canadians (Milan & Tran, 2004). Although Canada encouraged immigration from France, this was resisted by the French government. Instead, French Canadians who had found work in the United States were encouraged to return (Knowles, 2000).

For many years both federal and provincial governments placed many barriers to the immigration of non-whites, of certain religious groups, and of others regarded at various times as being hard to assimilate into British-based culture. For example, Chinese who originally came to Canada because of labour shortages in British Columbia in mining, railway construction, and domestic services faced growing prejudice. The result was passage of numerous bills in British Columbia to restrict the civil rights of the Chinese, such as the right to vote, to enter certain professions, or to reside in the provincial home for the aged and infirm. In 1923, the federal government passed the Chinese Immigration Act, which made it nearly impossible for Chinese to enter Canada and thus prevented family reunification until it was repealed in 1947. The result was a society of "married bachelors." Concerned that many Asians were coming to Canada by way of Hawaii, the federal government ruled that immigrants had to come from their lands of origin in a continuous journey. Because there were no ships coming directly from India, potential immigrants were automatically disqualified. One dramatic episode involved the ship the *Komagata Maru* (see Box 2.2). At various times, Ukrainians, Mennonites, Jews, Hutterites, and Doukhobors were discouraged or completely banned from immigration (Knowles, 2000; Li, 1998).

There are many other examples of prejudice and racism. Between the two world wars, the Ku Klux Klan recruited members in Canada. In addition to visible minorities, they were against Jews, Catholics, and French Canadians (Appleblatt, 1976). Just prior to World War II, some groups in Toronto flaunted the swastika at a sports event involving Jewish teams; the result was a riot (Levitt & Shaffer, 1987). In the 1930s, Jews fleeing Nazi Germany were turned away by Canada. During World War II, Japanese were interned inland from the west coast, losing their businesses, houses, and other property in the process. They were not released until after the war. Even then, many were encouraged to return to Japan, even

BOX 2.2

THE *KOMAGATA MARU* INCIDENT

The most dramatic challenge [to the continuous-journey regulation] occurred on 23 May 1914, when 376 East Indians (22 were returning Canadian residents) arrived in Vancouver harbour on board the *Komagata Maru*, a Japanese tramp steamer hired by a wealthy Sikh merchant and former labour contractor from Hong Kong, Gurdit Singh Sarhali. The steamer met with an unmitigatedly hostile reception. In fact, for weeks the vessel lay in harbour, its human cargo deprived of food and water by Canadian authorities who sought to weaken their resolve.

Finally, on 20 June, in the face of impending starvation, a passengers' committee agreed to the Canadian government's demand that a test case go before an Immigration Board of Enquiry. A week later the case of Munshi Singh, a young Sikh farmer, was heard and he was ruled inadmissible on the grounds that he had violated three Orders in Council, in particular the continuous-journey regulation.... The way was paved for Munshi Singh and all the remaining passengers to be deported. This happened exactly two months after the arrival of the doomed ship in Vancouver harbour. With the local citizenry cheering from the docks, Canada's *HMCS Rainbow* escorted the *Komagata Maru* to international waters. The steamer then sailed to India, having left behind just a handful of passengers, previous residents of British Columbia, who had been allowed to land by the federal government.

Source: From "Forging Our Legacy: Canadian Citizenship and Immigration, 1900–1977," by Valerie Knowles. Catalogue C151-93/2000E. Adapted with the permission of the Minister of Public Works and Government Services Canada, 2005.

though they were born in Canada and were citizens (Knowles, 2000). The children of a breakaway Doukhobor sect, the Sons of Freedom, were placed in a boarding school, described by one child as being caged in a zoo, because their parents would not send their children to school or were in prison. This sect—whose members would rid of themselves of as many worldly goods as possible, including houses and clothing—became the **stereotype** for all Doukhobors, although most were industrious and law-abiding (Institute of Canadian Studies, 2002; Ombudsman of British Columbia, 1999). More recently, following the assaults on New York and Washington on September 11, 2001, Muslims and those perceived as Muslims have suffered attacks (Badr, 2003; Bell & Prokaska, 2001; Kallen, 2003).

The Need for Labour

Often, the desire to keep Canada "British" conflicted with the need for labour, for example in mining, lumbering, and railway construction, and the desire to develop agriculture across the prairies. Chinese, Sikhs, and Japanese were brought in because they would accept low wages and primitive conditions in work camps, which British immigrants would not. From about 1890 to 1914, Ukrainian farmers were encouraged to settle in clusters across the prairies. In part, this strategy was designed to attract still more immigrants. Eventually their communities stretched from Manitoba to the Edmonton area. Later, Ukrainians became a source of cheap labour in other types of work. Italians also worked in mining and manufacturing. After World War II, some companies were allowed to bring in groups of workers into Canada in a "bulk-labour" program (Knowles, 2000).

In boom times, such as the early 1900s or after World War II, both employers and the federal government fostered the influx of workers. During recessions and the Great Depression, such immigration was discouraged. Unions opposed bringing in cheap labour because of its impact on wages. During the recession immediately following World War I, there was pressure on companies to release foreign labourers so as to provide jobs for returning veterans. One company that complied was International Nickel in Sudbury, Ontario; it fired 2200 of 3200 employees, most of them foreign-born (Knowles, 2000). Thus, preferential treatment for certain groups in the population had dire results for immigrant families.

Humanitarian Motives

Many groups were admitted to Canada for humanitarian reasons. For example, fugitive slaves who had escaped from the United States came to Canada once new slavery was banned here in 1793 and abolished in 1834. The principal end of the Underground Railway, as the escape network came to be called, was in southwestern Ontario (Prince, 2004). The list of humanitarian immigrants is long. Doukhobors, persecuted by the Russians for refusing military service and for their communal ways, migrated to Saskatchewan and then British Columbia. Others included Jewish war orphans and Jews expelled from Romania during the inter-war period; Estonian boat people after World War II and Vietnamese ones following the conflict in Southeast Asia; Hungarians in 1956–1957 fleeing after an unsuccessful uprising against their Communist government; American draft dodgers and deserters during the conflict in Vietnam; and Asians expelled from Uganda in 1972. Between 1947 and 1962, nearly 250 000 refugees and people displaced by World War II, mainly European, were admitted to Canada, more than to all other overseas countries combined. Sometimes strings were attached. Polish war veterans were required to work on a farm for a year. There were also "accidental immigrants," for example anti-Nazi German male civilians sent from Britain to Canada and then interned. After the war, many accepted the invitation to become Canadian citizens. Some refugees were well educated. The Hungarians, for instance, included a large part of the faculties of Forestry and of Mining Engineering at the University of Sopron; they were integrated into the University of British Columbia and the University of Toronto (Knowles, 2000).

Changes to Citizenship and Immigration since World War II

Before 1947, Canadians were officially regarded as British subjects. In addition, married women automatically assumed the nationality of their husbands, an easy way to bypass standard requirements but also a way to lose citizenship. The *Canadian Citizenship Act* of 1947 changed that. It created the category of Canadian citizen, and permitted married women to be citizens in their own right. In the early 1960s, limitations were placed on which relatives could be sponsored for immigration. New regulations also nearly eliminated racial discrimination among unsponsored immigrants, as long as they had a job waiting for them or could support themselves while they found one, were not criminals or terrorists, and did not have a disease that was a danger to public health. Immigration appeals, allowed on many grounds, created a logjam in the system. In 1973, appeal rules were made tighter. To reduce the backlog, in what amounted to an amnesty, about 39 000 legal and illegal immigrants were granted landed immigrant status. The *Immigration Act*, which came into force in 1978, established four categories of immigrants: the family class, whereby nuclear family members and aging parents and grandparents can be sponsored; the humanitarian class, which includes refugees and persecuted and displaced persons; the independent class, which is admitted on a points system recognizing such factors as age, education, and occupational field; and assisted relatives, who are sponsored by relatives in Canada but must meet some of the criteria of the independent class (Knowles, 2000).

The pattern of immigration to Canada has shifted dramatically over the past several years. Before 1967, immigration rules favoured those from Europe or countries of European heritage, such as the United States. Now nearly three-quarters of immigrants come from Africa, Asia, the Caribbean, and Latin America, and only one-quarter from Europe. Currently, the largest group of recent immigrants is the Chinese, especially those from Hong Kong and the People's Republic of China (Bélanger & Martel, 2003). Indeed, immigrants from Asia between 1996 and 2001 nearly equalled the total number who have come from the British Isles since 1961 (Statistics Canada, n.d.). By 2017, about one Canadian in five (between 19 percent and 23 percent) will be a member of a visible minority group. Roughly half of these will be South Asian or Chinese (Bélanger & Malenfant, 2005).

Most newcomers settle in Ontario, British Columbia, and Quebec, especially in Toronto, Vancouver, and Montreal. Chinese comprised the largest group coming to these

TABLE 2.1

NUMBER OF IMMIGRANTS BY TEN MAIN COUNTRIES OF BIRTH, 2001

Country of Birth	Number
China and Hong Kong	43 770
India	30 793
Pakistan	16 027
Philippines	13 627
South Korea	9 544
Iran	6 164
Sri Lanka	5 844
Romania	5 714
United States	5 271
Russia	5 193

Source: Adapted from Statistics Canada, "Report on the demographic situation in Canada, 2001–2002." Catalogue 91–209, December 22, 2003, p. 64

provinces. Those settling in Quebec were more likely to come from French-speaking countries (Bélanger & Martel, 2003). Many newcomers move into visible minority neighbourhoods in large cities. Most of such neighbourhoods are Chinese, followed by South Asian. Some of the minority neighbourhoods have replaced earlier enclaves like "Little Italy" or "Little Greece" (Hou & Picot, 2004).

The Experience of Immigrants in Canada

Many immigrants have seen Canada as the "promised land" with many opportunities for bettering themselves. For some, the promise takes a long time to be fulfilled. Men who came to Canada in the 1990s earned less than those coming in the 1980s. This was partly the result of the general shift from new full-time paid jobs to self-employment, a change that was especially difficult for those without local connections and experience (Chui & Zietsma, 2003). In cities, recent immigrants are nearly twice as likely to have low incomes, especially in Toronto and Vancouver (Heisz & McLeod, 2004). Later in this book, we will discuss the many ways poverty affects family life. About two-thirds of immigrants between October 2000 and September 2001 were in the economic class; that is, they were selected on the basis of their ability to fit into the Canadian economic system. Eighty-five percent of all immigrants planned to work. After six months, 44 percent had actually found a job. Visible minority immigrants had the poorest employment rate, especially those coming from Africa. Over half the newcomers did not work in the same field as in their former country. Reasons included the lack of Canadian experience, problems in having their qualifications recognized, and lack of fluency in English or French (Statistics Canada, 2003c; Tran, 2004).

Young adult and elderly immigrants are more likely to live with relatives (Ghalam, 1996), partly because of cultural practices, partly through economic necessity. Many live in ethnic enclaves, which support their cultural traditions. Yet there can be a misfit between accustomed family roles and Canadian realities. One such area is in gender roles. When men cannot find work that will support their families, their wives will also find jobs. Thus, women become co-providers, with a resulting growth in their power in making family decisions. Their husbands do not always welcome this change. In addition, women may still be expected to fulfill their traditional homemaker role, with the danger of overload and exhaustion (Hune, 2000). Many Asian elders are upset by their children's and grandchildren's loss of respect for them. In some cases, the male head of the family cannot find work and instead cares for his grandchildren. In other cases, the younger generation takes the lead and women may become heads of households. This kind of dislocation entails a loss of the elder's basic identity (Parker, 2004).

Children of immigrants may have difficulty growing up in two cultures. At school, they are encouraged to be independent, spontaneous, outspoken, and aggressive. Television also encourages these values. At home, many are expected to be modest, respectful, and concerned with the family as a whole. Thus there can also be a clash of values. Parents may emphasize thrift and saving so that the family may get ahead economically, while children hope for luxuries like designer clothing their classmates wear. Some also feel pressure from their parents to excel in school and extracurricular activities. As they settle into Canadian ways, some children become less willing to speak the language they share with their parents. Some also have to become interpreters when their parents do not understand English or French. As a result, there may be problems in communication within the family and with maintaining the parents' authority (Balcazar & Qian, 2000; Umaña-Taylor, 2003; Zhou, 2000).

Immigration may mean separation from family members. Female domestic workers may leave children and extended family members behind when they come to Canada on temporary visas. Some form family-like relationships with others in their situation. The immigrant woman who comes to Canada with her husband's family and leaves her own relatives behind in the old country may be especially isolated and have few sources of support if she has conflicts with his parents or brothers. It is even more difficult for her if she does not know English or French because she cannot access services outside her ethnic community. The matter is made worse because there are few government services, such as English classes, available for dependent spouses (Das Gupta, 2000).

Many immigrants, especially the more recent newcomers, have a strong sense of belonging to their ethnic or cultural group. A person's identity as "Canadian" increases with the number of generations since immigration. About 20 percent of visible minority individuals, Blacks more than others, report that they have experienced discrimination (Statistics Canada, 2003c). Many families keep their ethnic identity in large or small ways; food preference is a common example. Other practices are tied to religion, such as dress codes, for instance the hijab (head covering) of Muslim women or the turbans of Sikh men. Cultural practices are often modified in North America. A newspaper story describes a Muslim graduation prom, which included dinner, entertainment, and prayers, with males and females in separate rooms (Prete, 2003). Arranged marriages may be combined with individual choice, with parents suggesting several suitable candidates and the individual making the final selection (Saleem, 2003). Two practices that have received considerable publicity in recent years are female genital mutilation and "honour" killings, whereby men kill female relatives who have "shamed" them. These practices are often linked with Islam. Yet, they are culturally based in parts of Africa and the Middle East and cross religious boundaries (Muslim Women's League, 1999a, 1999b). There is no record how often such events occur in Canada.

Differences within ethnic groups may arise from the individual's social class, religion, level of education, and part of the country they came from (Hernandez & McGoldrick, 1999). In addition, some people closely follow traditional ways while others keep some customs from their homelands but otherwise blend in with mainstream society (Balcazar & Qian, 2000). Immigrants who left their former countries by choice differ from refugees, who were forced to leave their home countries. The former, for example, can keep up family connections in their homeland. Not all refugees are from visible minorities—for example, those from the former Yugoslavia and Serbia, who, like most other refugees, experienced a great deal of terror and violence that can continue to affect their family relationships in Canada (Beiser, Dion, Gotowiec, Hyman, & Vu, 1995).

PROVIDING SERVICES TO RACIAL AND ETHNIC MINORITIES

Demand for service agencies to develop policies that are sensitive to the cultural traditions of their clients has been growing. The need will probably increase, for a variety of reasons. The Aboriginal population continues to be young, partly because its birth rate is higher than for the general population and partly because life expectancy is shorter. In addition, fewer Aboriginal people are choosing to pass as white (Castellano, 2002). Since most immigrants are young adults with children, they are concerned with government and agency policies regarding childcare and education (D'Costa, 1987). Many go to small, ethnic organizations for help rather than to mainstream agencies like Children's Aid Societies or child welfare departments that they fear do not respect the values of their group (Doyle & Visano, 1987). When provincial agencies become involved, they may be unwilling or unable to provide culturally sensitive services. For example, Muslims criticized an Ontario agency for placing Muslim children with Christian parents who did not support their religious and dietary practices (Van Harten, 2004). Agreements between Aboriginal bands and provincial and federal governments have permitted formation of child welfare and family service agencies that are culturally sensitive. However, such services are not available nationwide (Castellano, 2002). Immigrant groups do not have even this level of legal protection. They could, however, be better served by developing closer ties between mainstream agencies and existing or new ethnic organizations.

IS BEING DIFFERENT ACCEPTABLE?

In theory, we Canadians accept and even encourage differences. We point with pride to our federal Charter of Rights and Freedoms, provincial legislation recognizing the fundamental rights of all people, and our multicultural society, yet there are limits to what we view as socially acceptable.

According to Evelyn Kallen (1989), a minority is created by society. The **majority** is the group in a society that is the largest in number or that holds the most power. The stability of any society and its continued existence depend on the majority. According to structural-functional thinkers, when large numbers in society share the same values and beliefs, change will evolve slowly. New generations absorb the dominant social scripts from many sources in society and mould their lives on them. Feminist theorists point out, however, that social stability comes about because those with power resist change (White & Klein, 2002). People who do not fit the accepted social script, do not hold the same values as the majority, or do not have power can encounter serious difficulties.

A **minority** is any social category that is seen by the majority in society as being incompetent and inferior, or abnormal and dangerous; that is, it offends against the norms of society. The members of a minority group experience negative actions, or **discrimination,** by the majority, and thus are denied political, economic, and social rights. As a result, members of this group become disadvantaged and stigmatized. A minority is not necessarily smaller than the majority; Kallen (1989) points out that, under apartheid, Blacks in South Africa fit the definition of a minority even though they far outnumbered whites. So, too, have women been discriminated against throughout much of history, as when they have not been allowed to own property or to vote. In fact, many argue that women are still disadvantaged with respect to pay and opportunities for promotion. In much of Canada, social acceptability is based on white, middle-class, and male society and norms, and relies on values that have come from our British rather than our French heritage (Kallen, 2003; White & Klein, 2002).

We need to look at several aspects of majority–minority relationships if we are to understand their impact on families: for example, discrimination based on majority values can profoundly affect the family life of minority-group members. Child welfare workers who are members of the majority group may regard the traditional child-rearing methods of some minority groups as poor parenting. Churches and educational and social service organizations have provided programs, often with the best of intentions, that worked to destroy family life and family ties among Aboriginal people. For example, gift-giving that accompanied traditional Kwakiutl marriage practices was interpreted by missionaries as bride selling; therefore, they tried to stamp out the custom (Ray, 1996). One aspect of family that differs across cultures is the extent to which extended family members are considered part of the immediate family. Many misunderstandings about the caring and competence of parents have centred on just this difference. In the case of Aboriginal families, many social workers felt that the custom of allowing grandparents or other relatives to care for children showed indifference and neglect on the part of the parents. As a result, they placed the children with families who followed the majority cultural practices. The parents, however, felt that they were behaving responsibly since their children were being looked after by caring family members (Das Gupta, 2000).

Stigma

Members of minorities are often stigmatized by the majority. A **stigma** is any quality that is seen as offensive by the majority—anything that is considered wrong, crazy, disgusting, strange, or immoral, especially if it is labelled "unnatural." During World War II, for instance, Japanese Canadians were interned far from the west coast because they were seen as dangerous aliens (Knowles, 2000). Gay men and lesbians are also stigmatized (Erera, 2002).

Unfortunately, stigma has a way of spreading to other aspects of the individual; if one part is considered wrong, the whole person is considered faulty. For example, blind individuals may be spoken to loudly as if their hearing is also impaired. In the chapter introduction, Megan describes similar attitudes to the hearing impaired. The caricature formed through this process is then used as a basis for justifying discrimination against a whole group of people. Physically challenged people, for example, have been considered unsuitable adopters since they are seen as being "impaired" in their ability to parent as well. The few who have successfully overcome this prejudice have proven themselves as competent as those parents with no obvious physical challenges.

Stigma can spread to others outside the minority group. If one associates too much with members of a minority group, one is regarded as being just like them. This is reflected in proverbs like "A man is known by the company he keeps." If a person works with an AIDS-awareness group, one suspects that he or she is homosexual.

Inferior or Dangerous Too?

Minority groups tend to be regarded either as inferior only, or as both inferior and dangerous (Kallen, 1989, 2003). For example, much of the discussion of whether mentally challenged people should have children centres on the notion that their level of functioning makes them unsuitable parents (inferior). Some argue, however, that allowing them to become parents will lower the intellectual level of the population as a whole, or will produce children who don't know how to behave properly in society (dangerous). The first attitude leads to attempts to deny parenthood to individuals "for their own good." The second tries to control their fertility, to permit sterilization without the consent of the individual, "for the good of society" (Gosden, 1999). Minorities regarded as dangerous may also be considered not quite human (Day, 2000). For example, Aboriginal peoples were regarded as "savages" in need of civilizing (Milloy, 1999).

If a particular characteristic is regarded as unnatural, it is considered particularly dangerous. One notable example is continuing prejudice against gay and lesbian individuals. **Prejudice** is a negative attitude toward a minority group that is not based on fact. Over the years, homosexual people have been continually harassed by both private citizens and members of the social work and legal professions. Homosexual parents, for example, have experienced many problems in gaining custody of their children; when they have managed to do so, generally it has been because they have shown themselves to be the far superior parent. Although research has shown that adult children of homosexuals generally have relationships with members of the opposite sex (Erera, 2002), the fear that the morals of these children will be corrupted and that they will follow their parent's "unnatural" lifestyle continues; this feeling is especially prevalent when the parent has a live-in lover.

Voluntary or Involuntary?

Minority groups are judged also on whether differences in behaviour or characteristics are voluntary or involuntary (Kallen, 1989). If the differences are judged to be voluntary, the individual is presumed to be able to change the behaviour or quality. If change does not occur, the individual is presumed to have chosen minority status. The entire justice system works on a similar principle—that is, with the inherent assumption that people have chosen to be criminals and therefore must suffer a penalty. Age is a factor in determining whether a behaviour or characteristic is voluntary. Children under a certain age—and this has changed over the centuries—are considered to have insufficient understanding to control their behaviour. Age of responsibility varies, of course, with activity; having dry pants or obeying a parent is expected at a much younger age than is the ability to care for a child.

The degree of stigma attached to a particular behaviour or status sometimes changes with time. For example, in the past, divorce was regarded as shameful, especially for women who chose to leave their husbands. Financial support was available for women who were abandoned but not for those who abandoned their husbands, regardless of the cruel or degrading circumstances of their marriage. Custody of children was generally granted to the father if his wife had left the family, unless the child was a baby, dependent on mother's milk (Kieran, 1986; McKie, Prentice, & Reed, 1983). Now, no distinctions are made between men and women in assessing grounds for divorce, and financial support is determined by need rather than by fault. Although, as we shall see in a later chapter, social stigma against lone parenthood continues, it is not embodied in social policies to the same degree as in the past.

The Majority's Sense of Superiority

Central to the discussion of minorities is the majority's sense of superiority—the notion that its way is the right way, and that any other is somehow wrong, or at best inferior. In part this is a power issue—changes in norms may threaten the majority's control over much of social life (Kallen, 2003). Since many regard the family as the heart of society, they see any differences or changes in family patterns as a threat to society itself. In the past, freer divorce laws were feared because it was felt that the family would be destroyed. We can see a similar fear expressed in statements on television or in newspapers that AIDS is God's judgment on homosexuality. The implication is that if we have sexual relations with the opposite sex within marriage (the traditional family), we are safe. This sense of superiority and the fear that what we value most will be destroyed provokes the most violent forms of prejudice.

Responses to Stigma and Discrimination

There are three main responses to minority status: separation, assimilation, and accommodation. Different ethnic and social groups fall along a continuum, with nearly complete separation from the dominant society at one extreme and **assimilation** (i.e., taking on the values and practices of the majority group) at the other.

Separation can occur by choice or can be forced on a particular group (Cook, 2003). For example, the Hutterites, whom I discussed in Chapter 1, have chosen to keep apart from mainstream society. This may also hold true for new immigrants living in enclaves. On the other hand, Chinese who came to Canada during construction of the Canadian Pacific Railway faced such discrimination that they were forced to live in ghettos. Forced separation also includes segregation and, at the extreme, genocide (Cook, 2003).

Like separation, assimilation can be voluntary or forced on a minority. Immigrants may choose to take on the customs and values of the majority culture in Canada. For example, immigrants from India may opt to choose their own marriage partners instead of agreeing to arranged marriages. In general, minority members choosing to assimilate regard this as a road to opportunity (Cook, 2003). On the other hand, the original purpose of residential schools was to force Aboriginal children to change from so-called "savages" to "civilized" beings, that is, to assimilate them into non-Aboriginal society (Milloy, 1999).

Due to discrimination, members of minority groups sometimes attempt to **pass** as a member of the majority group. Usually this involves accepting the stigma society places on the individual and trying to hide it in some way. Cultural assimilation is one form of passing.

In the 1950s, as another example, one of the advantages claimed by adoption agencies over private adoptions was that they could give prospective parents a child that would resemble as closely as possible one they would have produced themselves. Matching of child to parents encourages what sociologist David Kirk (1984) calls "rejection of difference"; in other words, it encourages parents to pass the child off as their biological child and to pass themselves off as fertile adults. In this way they avoid the stigma of illegitimacy or abandonment for their child and the stigma of infertility for themselves. Not telling a child he or she is adopted is a similar kind of denial.

One problem with trying to pass is that it forces the individual to live a double life. This, by itself, causes a strain. Often, there will be uneasy moments as children or other relatives ask questions. Family members sense that this is a taboo subject. Such secrets can have long-lasting and quite unintentional effects on family relationships since they interfere with openness in family communication (Imber-Black, 1993; Kirk, 1984). In addition, one is made tense by the fear that the secret will be discovered. Thus there is a great deal of anxiety and role strain in the attempt to pass.

A third approach to difference is **accommodation**, that is, recognition and respect of both similarities and differences between majority and minority (Cook, 2003). One example is the hyphenated Canadian (e.g., Polish-Canadian, Chinese-Canadian). Another is the growth of multiculturalism. When accommodation is not available, minority groups may challenge the majority to gain greater inclusion. In the past, women campaigned for the vote and for equal rights within families. Adoptees and birth parents have advocated the opening of adoption and birth records. Gay rights activists want same-sex couples granted the same rights as heterosexual couples, including the rights to marry and to divorce.

In the future, we can expect to see continuing pressure for the differences and rights of minority groups to be recognized under human rights legislation. In response, however, the majority may feel endangered. If this occurs, we can expect a backlash against minorities and against rights movements to protect against what majority members feel is a threat to society. Indeed, there is evidence of this reaction in the formation of political parties and other organizations that emphasize the primacy of one race or ethnic group, or one model of the family. Unfortunately, the risk of violent confrontation exists on either side.

DIFFERENCES AND THE STUDY OF THE FAMILY

Why is it important for us to be aware of differences between families? First, since all of us are likely to be part of a minority at some point in our lives, we need to understand that different does not equal inferior. Rather, we must realize that we have all been shaped by our past experiences. They help us develop our individual knowledge, strengths, vulnerabilities, and expectations as we go through life. Our experiences have also shaped how we perceive others. For example, if we have been subjected to prejudice by a particular group, we may be suspicious of its members in the future. On the other hand, we may see others like us as allies.

Second, we will all be affected by changes resulting from pressure for equal rights. New regulations may affect our eligibility to receive services. An expansion of services may mean a heavier tax burden. For those of us who work with people, new rules and policies may affect our working conditions. For example, the current pressure on police over alleged racial discrimination will probably result in changes in regulations concerning the use of force and in new hiring practices. We also need accurate knowledge about the customs and values of minority groups if we are to understand them and provide the kinds of services they need (Sherif-Trask, 2004).

In much of the remainder of this book, we will be looking at the stages of the family life cycle. It is important for us to remember that many individuals and families do not go through the stages in a neat, orderly manner. Some take detours. Others vary the order in which they move through stages, while still others may miss some completely. These variations contribute to the richness of human experience.

SUMMARY

MALE/FEMALE DIFFERENCES. Differences between males and females in our society arise partly because of physical differences and largely because of gender-role socialization. Females are encouraged to focus on relationships, and males on independence and self-direction. Family experiences of the two sexes also differ, with women and girls more likely to have responsibility for family care and to live in poor single-parent families.

FAMILY VARIATION. There are many types of families that differ from the "traditional" one consisting of breadwinner husband and homemaker mother and their children. These include lone-parent families, families with mothers in the workforce, divorced and remarried families, those with same-sex partners, and those with members who have exceptional needs.

RACIAL AND ETHNIC DIFFERENCES. Canadians differ as to culture, ethnicity, and racial group. Their experiences differ according to when they arrived and the power they have held. Until quite recently, the English-Canadian majority has tried to keep the "British" character of the country, although visible minorities or non-British groups have been admitted when needed for labour or on humanitarian grounds. Many visible-minority individuals have experienced discrimination.

MAJORITY/MINORITY RELATIONS. A minority is created by society. It is often seen as incompetent and inferior, or as abnormal and dangerous; thus minority group members may be pitied or blamed. Often minority groups are stigmatized by the majority. The negative attitude may spread to other characteristics of the individuals or to those who associate with them. If they are considered to have voluntarily broken the norms of society, they suffer greater blame than if they are seen as unwilling victims. Often the minority-group members are considered in need of protection.

RESPONSES OF MINORITY GROUPS. There are three general responses to minority status: separation, assimilation, or accommodation. Separation and assimilation can be either voluntary or involuntary. When individuals try to pass, that is, try to hide the conditions that cause stigma, they may experience strains. Minority groups may also challenge the majority to obtain equal rights.

KEY TERMS

accommodation: recognition of and respect for both similarities and differences between majority and minority (p. 48)

assimilation: taking on the values and practices of the majority group (p. 47)

discrimination: negative actions taken against a minority group (p. 44)

gender roles: the socially approved ways of behaving as males and females (p. 30)

mainstreaming: integrating children with exceptional needs into regular classrooms (p. 34)

majority: the group in a society that is the largest in number or has the most power (p. 44)

minority: any social category that offends against the norms of society (p. 44)

passing: trying to hide the fact that one is a member of a minority group (p. 47)

prejudice: a negative attitude toward a minority group that is not based on fact (p. 46)

stereotype: portrayal of all members of a group as having similar fixed, often unfavourable qualities (p. 39)

stigma: any quality that is seen as offensive by the majority (p. 45)

visible minority: persons, other than Aboriginal peoples, who are non-Caucasian in race or non-white in colour (Hou & Picot, 2004) (p. 38)

CLASS ASSIGNMENTS

Complete one or both of the following assignments, as directed by your instructor:

1. For one week, track the topics discussed on one or two talk shows that often deal with family variations. What differences were featured? What appears to be the norm against which they are measured? Is this norm widely held by society? Explain.

2. Look at an occupation that involves working with people. What changes have occurred already and may occur in the future because of changes in families, the racial and ethnic makeup of your community, or both?

PERSONAL ASSIGNMENTS

The following assignments are designed to help you think about your own experience:

1. In what ways have people you know experienced difficulties because they did not fit regulations? How would you like to see these regulations changed? What effect do you think this change will have on the organization involved? Consider staffing, hours of operation, location, funding, and anything else you think is relevant.

2. List the areas in which you consider yourself part of a minority. Have you experienced any discrimination because of this? Explain. How might this experience help or hinder you as you interact with others?

Part Two

THE COUPLE RELATIONSHIP: MERGING DIFFERENCES

© Monica Lau/Photodisc/Getty Images

Chapter 3

Getting Together

OBJECTIVES

- *To point out variations in how families are formed*
- *To locate mate selection in the family life cycle*
- *To present arranged and love matches in social and historical perspective*
- *To explain factors affecting present-day mate selection*
- *To look at the lifestyle of the never-married*
- *To explore how love relationships develop*
- *To outline some problem areas in relationships before marriage, and to describe methods of marriage preparation*

As the king's son came up to the forest, the thorn branches burst into bloom and parted to let him pass. He climbed the tower stairs as the legend told him he should. Then he opened the door to the chamber where Briar Rose lay sleeping, still as lovely as the day she fell under the witch's spell. Immediately he loved her and gently kissed her. As soon as his lips touched hers, Briar Rose opened her eyes and smiled. As soon as the wedding festivities could be arranged, Briar Rose and her prince were married in royal splendour. The witch's curse was forgotten and they lived happily ever after.

In the story of Briar Rose we have all the essentials of romance—the beautiful princess who needs to be rescued, the handsome prince who rescues her, and above all something magical, including love at first sight and living happily ever after. This story and those of Snow White, Cinderella, and their sisters in spirit colour our imagination of love and **courtship.** In North American society, according to popular myth, man meets woman, they fall passionately in love, and, after a suitable interval, fade into the misty shadows to the tune of *The Wedding March.* Yet for many people, "happily ever after" is just an illusion. The reality is both more ordinary and more complex.

In our society, marriage is the norm—most people marry at some point in their lives. Society encourages marriage in a number of ways. Relatives and friends may ask, "Why aren't you married yet?" and may try to find you a suitable mate. More subtle pressures are those in advertising and popular culture. And, when most of the people you know are married, social life is organized around couples. If you are unattached, you may not fit in.

However, the greater acceptance of differences that we now see throughout society also affects marriage. Many people recognize that marriage may not meet a person's needs. Nevertheless, there is great variety among ethnic groups in how much an unmarried person is accepted (Hamon & Ingoldsby, 2003). Traditional marriage encourages women to put the needs of husband and children before their own. Men are encouraged to take on primary financial responsibility for wife and children. Even with the trend toward two-income families, parents find their activities limited both by the care that children need and by the cost of providing that care. One benefit of remaining single is personal freedom (Kingston, 2004).

Acceptance of relationships that do not include marriage is also growing. The number of people living together without marriage or before marriage (cohabitation) is increasing (Statistics Canada, 2002a). Individuals are becoming more open about homosexual relationships, and these are consequently more visible (Lahey & Alderson, 2004). A person no longer has to be married to have children. Women can adopt a child, use artificial insemination or other reproductive technologies, or find a man willing to father a child (Johnson & Colucci, 1999). Single men do not have as many options if they wish to raise a child, but a few adopt or raise a child they have fathered. These parents are invisible because they cannot be distinguished from those who become single parents through divorce or widowhood.

SETTING THE FAMILY CYCLE TURNING

In spite of these variations, mate selection, often referred to as courtship, is still the most common way of starting the family life cycle. Pairing may be heterosexual or, less frequently, homosexual. Both go through a process in which a partner with whom to share one's life is chosen. The next steps vary: some couples begin living together and never marry; others marry first; and many begin with cohabitation and then move to formal marriage.

According to psychiatrist Erik Erikson (1982), the most important developmental task in young adulthood is the establishment of intimacy, in the sense of a close emotional relationship, with another. One of the key aspects of intimacy is the ability and freedom to disclose one's innermost self to another. This ability can be expressed in friendship, or in a sexual-romantic relationship with an individual of the same or opposite sex. In order for intimacy to develop, it is important to know oneself and to be able to trust the other person not to inflict harm because one has been open (Regan, 2003). In much of North American society, development of intimacy is considered a prerequisite for marriage. Of course, not all intimate relationships, or even all formal engagements, lead to marriage.

A second developmental task is for a couple to establish the foundation for their relationship (Carter & McGoldrick, 1999b). A relationship has so many shadings that even the language we use cannot be exact. Communication, for example, can be verbal or nonverbal; it can carry information or emotional messages; it can be used to exert power or to be submissive. A trusting relationship may be one in which each partner's individuality is respected, or it may be one in which a submissive partner implicitly trusts a dominant partner to decide what is best for both. The pattern of relationships, if we follow symbolic-interaction thought, is established from even the earliest interchanges between partners. For example, when professionals counsel women who have been assaulted by their husbands, they often discover that the abusive relationship began during courtship. The same pattern holds true for other aspects, both good and bad, of a couple's relationship. The way a couple interacts while they are "going together" often continues into longer-term cohabitation and marriage.

In societies where couples do not have free choice of a partner, the basis of the relationship is also established before marriage. The shared experiences of the couple include the expectations of their families and of society at large. Personal aspects of their relationship, such as intimacy, may not develop until after marriage.

MATE SELECTION AND SOCIETY

Despite the diversity in individual experiences, courtships can be divided into two basic streams—those decided on by the couple and those decided on by the families of the couple. Both forms are closely tied to the values and traditions of the cultures that support them. Families are not isolated, but each lives in an ecological niche. That is, each family lives in a specific social, cultural, and physical environment in which it functions on a day-to-day basis (Huston, 2000).

In many societies, families provide the principal social security system. Family membership and the rights and responsibilities of individuals are key to such a system. In Asian Indian families, for example, men are expected to provide financial support for their families of procreation as well as other needy relatives. If a father dies, his oldest son or his brother will assume responsibility for his widow and children. Because they are not regarded as wage earners, women are seen as a financial liability and are devalued. In this culture, one person's behaviour affects many family members. The well-being of the family as a whole takes priority over individual happiness. In addition, a traditionally rigid system of social and occupational status has existed for centuries. It should be no surprise that marriages are arranged, both to maintain appropriate status and to increase family economic well-being through the bride's dowry (Medora, 2003).

In contrast to Asian Indian society, mainstream North American culture values individual achievement. Each person is responsible both for his or her own success and for the well-being of his or her family of procreation. Both males and females are valued as individuals. In this system, "family" tends to be defined narrowly in contrast to Asian Indian society. When the individual social security system fails, there is little formal expectation that extended family members will step in. Rather, society as a whole is expected to fill the gap. This expectation is part of a longstanding trend of shifting responsibility from the family to society—for example, for education and policing (Axinn & Thornton, 2000). Picking one's own mate fits into this culture of individuality and self-sufficiency.

In these two societies, as in any other, there are close links between the macrosystem or culture and the exosystem, mesosystem, and microsystem. Cultural values, norms, and roles are maintained through socialization, as pointed out by structural functionalists. From the symbolic-interaction perspective, socialization occurs in day-to-day transactions with those around us. Change in social practices occurs in a variety of ways. For example, Asian Indian society is affected by the development of new technologies and the greater acceptance of education for women. There are some reports of couples falling in love and then having their marriages "arranged" by their families.

THE COURTSHIP CONTINUUM

Usually, arranged and self-chosen marriages are treated as if they are quite different. However, they lie along a continuum, with completely arranged marriages at one end and completely self-chosen unions (with or without marriage) at the other. Most fall somewhere in between, although they tend to be toward one side or the other. For instance, most individuals who choose their partners do take some account of their parents' feelings about their prospective mates. In arranged matches, the couple often will not be forced to marry if either is opposed.

There is also a continuum for the idea of marriage as exchange and marriage as shared emotion. This is related, but not identical to the arranged–free choice continuum. Arranged marriages tend to pay more attention to how each party will benefit from the union, while free choice tends to emphasize shared emotions, such as love and companionship. The latter is related more closely to symbolic interaction, as the couple creates their own unique relationship.

In North America, most individuals are at the romantic love end of the scale (Goode, 1968). This is encouraged in many ways. We are socialized from childhood to fall in love. Adults tease children about their "girlfriends" or "boyfriends." There is also the constant media and advertising message—love is the mountaintop of experiences. Yet people tend to fall somewhere between the two extremes, often using both exchange values and emotional appeals to attract a mate. Love, apparently, isn't blind (Ingoldsby, 2003). Couples often wait until they are financially and educationally ready to marry (Holman & Li, 1995). Several studies demonstrate exchange theory in action during courtship, when individuals display their assets. Men are more likely than women to show off their "material" assets, such as an education, a job, or a car, as a way of attracting a mate. Women tend to emphasize their physical appearance (Regan, 2003). Increasingly important, however, is the ability of women to contribute financially because of young men's difficulties in finding stable well-paying work (Cherlin, 2000). On the emotional side, both men and women display sympathy, kindness, and helpfulness. They also use good manners and humour as methods of attracting one another (Regan, 2003).

MATCHMAKER, MATCHMAKER—ARRANGING MARRIAGES

For centuries children were considered a family asset. They were expected to aid the family through their work or, especially in the case of wealthy or titled families, to help preserve or improve their social standing through marriage. In some societies, such as in India, social class and family descent are very important. If love is allowed free play, social classes might be ignored. Such societies consider both love and the choice of a husband or wife too important to be left to mere children. Instead, marriages are arranged by parents and matchmakers. They may consider eligibility, similarity of background, horoscopes, financial and social position, and, if the couple is fortunate, the personalities of the prospective bride and groom. Some lucky couples grow to love each other after marriage (Medora, 2003).

Strict rules can outline whom a person could marry. For example, the former caste system in Hindu India allowed marriage only to one at the same social level. This is referred to as **endogamy,** or marriage within the group. Systems of this kind may allow some choice of the marriage partner. Often parents seek approval of the young people before final plans are made and select another candidate if the first fails to please the prospective bride or groom (Medora, 2003).

Arranged marriages were and continue to be considered unions of whole groups; thus the extended family is involved in the couple's relationship. In the case of European royalty, marriages arranged for political benefit affected their countries, since a wedding often sealed a treaty. Some couples, already married by proxy (with someone else saying vows for them), met for the first time at the borders of the groom's country. A number of these marriages were successful. Other pairs produced the necessary heir to the throne and then lived separately, and some, at least, engaged in extramarital affairs.

Arranged marriages have taken place in Canada and still do. In New France young people were encouraged by their wealthy landowner parents to marry not for love but for family and property (McKie et al., 1983). This also occurred in Upper Canada (Kieran, 1986). The government in France wished to make the society in New France a copy of French society. However, since there were few marriageable women in the colony, men formed long-term relationships with Aboriginal women. To curb this trend, about 1000

French women, known as "Daughters of the King," were persuaded to sail to North America, for which they received a dowry and the essentials for starting farm life. Marriage became compulsory in New France, and those who refused to marry lost privileges. These marriages were not arranged in the strict sense of the term, but the prospective grooms had relatively little choice (Huck, 2001; Landry, 1992).

In the early part of the 20th century, Sikh immigrants to British Columbia were not allowed to bring their wives and children with them. Given that a good deal of prejudice was against them, unmarried Sikh men could not seek out white women for wives. Following changes in immigration laws in 1951, many Sikh men depended on relatives in the Punjab to arrange marriages for them; others advertised in Indian newspapers (Das Gupta, 2000).

These customs are not confined to other times and other places. For example, relatives still advertise in newspapers published for Indians living in North America or on the Internet, hoping to find spouses for the young people in their family (e.g., BharatMatrimony.com). Usually an exchange of benefits is involved. In many cases, the bride or groom sees marriage as a route to immigration; in return they offer their ability to earn a living or to fit into North American society while keeping up religious and cultural traditions. Ethnic Indians see such marriages as a way of preserving their heritage (Bhargava, 1988).

Even when families do not arrange marriages, there may be extreme pressure on children of new Canadians to marry within their ethnic group. The potential for conflict is high, as the young people may want to follow customs they have learned in Canada instead of those of their ethnic group. In some cases, young people go to social service or mental health agencies because they have become isolated from their families and social group; others may suffer physical or extreme emotional abuse, even death, as parents insist on obedience (Bhandari, 2005; "Dad guilty," 2005).

THE SHIFT TOWARD FREE CHOICE

European-based society has gradually shifted away from arranged marriages and toward free choice. But this has not been a smooth progression, and movement has occurred in parts of the population and not in others. Also, some rapid shifts in attitudes have been followed by periods of reaction. Many changes, including attitudes toward premarital sexual experience, reflect changing social conditions and even increases in scientific knowledge. Earlier practices still affect us today because some members of older generations find it hard to accept that values have changed since they were young.

Early Years of Settlement

The conditions on the North American frontier were ideal for choosing one's mate. Actual practices were related to three phases: the exploration of the wilderness, the establishment of new settlements, and the growth of larger towns and cities. Dates are hard to attach to the phases, since they occurred at different times in different places. For example, European settlements were established earlier in the East than on the Prairies, and earlier near major waterways than in the hinterland.

In the exploration phase, and this would include the era of the early fur traders, survival depended on an individual's initiative and resourcefulness. Added to the harsh conditions was an extreme shortage of white women. Many men formed temporary or permanent unions with Aboriginal women. These unions were often established on the basis of an exchange of goods for expertise in wilderness travel and survival or to cement trading or military alliances (Ray, 1996). It is difficult to know what part, if any, romantic love played in such unions.

This phase was followed by a transitional period during which settlers moved into areas that had been explored and mapped by the traders and explorers. Although many travelled in extended family groups, many also left behind their relatives. The frontier saw an influx of unattached males since it provided opportunities for energetic and enterprising young men. In mate selection, practical matters were important. Was the prospective partner, male or female, strong and healthy? Was he or she a hard worker? Life in the remote parts to which they would be going was not easy. Both partners would have to put in long, hard labour to make their new farm productive (Azoulay, 2001). The choice of partners was limited, especially for men.

Yet it was also in the New World that romantic love came into its own. Many people came to the new colonies to make their fortune or to escape tyranny and to express their freedom to worship as they chose. This individuality was also found in the choice of marriage partners. Even when families were present, young people had a good deal of freedom in selecting a mate. Although everyone worked long hours, there were occasions to meet, such as after church or at community events, such as barn raisings. The appropriate place for courting was the parlour, and often young couples would be left alone there to become acquainted (Rothman, 1987; Ward, 1990).

Life in cities also tended to encourage individuals to choose their own husbands or wives. As young people became less dependent on their parents for financial survival, they had more freedom of choice. On the family farm, which was worked by father and sons, parents had a relatively high level of control over marriages, whether or not they wished to exercise it, since they controlled their children's income. This is still true when a person works in a family business, especially in times when jobs are scarce. In the cities, where a greater variety of jobs was available, such control became weaker, and young people could please themselves more (McKie et al., 1983; Ward, 1990).

A NEW CUSTOM—DATING (AND BEYOND)

Dating

In the years leading up to World War I, when a young man came calling on a young woman, his attentions were assumed to be serious. Courtship took place mainly at community activities and in the parents' home. World War I transformed Canadian society. In 1914, Canada was mainly a country of farms and small towns; by 1918, it had become an industrial nation. Society was forced to change. One of the changes was the invention of dating by young people. For the first time, single men and women would go out alone together without any particular intention of marrying each other. In most cases, the young man would pay the costs for the date.

Dating serves four functions. First, it can add to a person's status if the date is the "right" person, such as the football hero. It can be a form of socialization, because it provides opportunity for members of both sexes to learn how to get along with each other. Dating is also a form of recreation, engaged in just for fun. Finally, dating can be a part of courtship, with the purpose of marriage.

Power in relationships, including dating, has long interested researchers. If a man and a woman date each other for different reasons, their relationship may be in trouble. The person who has the least to lose in the relationship can usually control the relationship. For instance, in the 1960s student nurses in one study were hoping for marriage, but many young men were dating them just for recreation. Thus, the nurses had much more to lose if the relationship ended; so the males were more likely to persuade the nurses to have sex than the nurses were to persuade the men to marry them (Skipper & Nass, 1968).

In societies that allowed individuals some choice in selecting a marriage partner, steady dating frequently became a part of courtship. It was often attractive to women since it combined love and permissible sex (Rothman, 1987). In the 1940s, however, "going steady" took a new turn—people far too young to be planning marriage started "going" with each other. Part of this custom came through a desire for security in social life. If you didn't have someone you could rely on, you might be left sitting at home while all your friends were at the social event of the year. It felt much safer to date just one person who had made a commitment of sorts to you. As dating crept into the social life of younger teens, so did going steady (Herman, 1963).

Currently, the traditional dating pattern, in which a young man asks a young woman out and pays the expenses of the entertainment, seems to be moving to a more egalitarian approach. One-on-one dating also seems to be disappearing among teenagers. They tend instead to move in clusters of friends with similar interests in fashion and music, and with similar values (Bibby, 2001). In these groups, they can learn how to relate to members of the opposite sex in a safer environment than on the individual date. Eventually, though, the young people pair off.

Same-sex dating may be difficult for high school and postsecondary students. Some delay coming out because they fear their parents will disown them. **Homosexual** youth are often harassed and sometimes physically abused at school. There are few rituals of the "boy-meets-girl, boy-dates-girl" type available to **gay male** and **lesbian** individuals. Often dating is postponed until adulthood. Heterosexual couples have more opportunity to let others know about even very new relationships. Because of social expectations and stigma, it is rarely acceptable outside gay and lesbian society to bring a date of the same sex. In addition, if one partner is not sure of his or her homosexual identity or wishes to remain **closeted,** it is quite risky for the other partner to tell relatives and friends (Ambert, 2003; Hillier & Harrison, 2004; Slater, 1995).

Now that there are increasing numbers of unattached people over 40, researchers are starting to look at their dating behaviour. Do they sit primly at some seniors' centre and hold hands? A few do, perhaps. One American study looked at mid-life singles (aged 40 to 69). Nearly a third (31 percent) were in exclusive dating relationships and another third (32 percent) were dating nonexclusively. Only one in ten was not interested in dating at all. Seven percent of men and 3 percent of women reported same-sex dating partners. Most looked for companionship. Men were more interested in sexual activity than women and had more permissive attitudes. This gender gap was widest among the oldest individuals (Montenegro, 2003). Among older widowed people, both men and women interested in dating are looking for companionship. Those who are close to family and friends are less interested in finding a romantic partner (Carr, 2004).

Living Together

Moving in together has become increasingly common for couples of all ages. A small American study found that over half of cohabitors had moved in with partners by the time their romance was six months old. The main reasons they gave were finances, convenience, and housing needs (Sassler, 2004). There seem to be two forms of **cohabitation,** or living together. In one of them, the couples do not see it as a way of forming a family, and children are not part of their plan. For these people, living together seems to be a trial run at marriage. Many, in fact, eventually have traditional weddings (Regan, 2003). Some couples, however, do see children as having a place in their relationship, even if they are not married. This form of cohabitation is more like marriage than courtship. Predictions for the future see even more couples living together before marriage or without marriage. We will consider unmarried cohabitation in more detail in Chapter 4.

Living Apart Together

A type of relationship described quite recently is non-resident partners, often referred to as "living apart together" (LAT). LAT partners regard themselves as a couple, and so do others. About 8 percent of Canadians are in such a relationship. While most are under 30, 45 percent are older. Often a LAT relationship leads to cohabitation or marriage. However, many, especially older individuals, do not have plans to move in together. Some have responsibilities to care for children or parents. Others may receive social subsidies like the Guaranteed Income Supplement for seniors. They may also be set in their ways and value their independence (Levin, 2004; Milan & Peters, 2003).

FREEDOM OF CHOICE?

Theoretically we can marry almost anyone we choose. We are, however, limited in many social and psychological ways. Most of these factors apply to both heterosexual and homosexual couples.

To begin with, there are legal barriers such as being in no more than one marriage at a time. In many parts of the world, people must marry someone of the opposite sex. Other restrictions are based on the **incest taboo,** which appears in some form in every society, and which prohibits mating between people who are too closely related. Thus we are barred from marrying certain relatives, such as parents, grandparents, brothers, and sisters. Society does not, however, know exactly how to deal with the "irregular" relationships that occur in adoptive and stepfamilies. The situation of brothers and sisters by adoption was only clarified in 1991—they cannot marry each other. (See Box 3.1.) Stepsiblings are not legally related, but society frowns on marriages between them, especially if they have been raised together.

BOX 3.1

A QUIZ: CAN YOU MARRY ME?

Here is a list of relatives, extended family members, and other closely connected people. According to Canadian law, which ones can you marry?

I am your

1. Adopted child or parent

2. Former husband's or wife's parent

3. Stepbrother or stepsister

4. Aunt, uncle, niece, or nephew

5. Adopted sister or brother

6. First cousin

7. Deceased spouse's aunt or uncle

8. Half-brother or half-sister

9. Grandfather or grandmother

10. Former stepchild

At Confederation, the federal government was given responsibility for marriage. However, no new law was enacted. Rather, the rules of the various provinces were allowed to continue. Although these varied somewhat, all but Quebec's were based on English law. In 1563 (during the reign of Henry VIII), Archbishop Parker of the Church of England drew up a table of prohibited marriages. This list was adopted by the Church of England and later, in 1835, became law. So Canadian regulations were based on the 1563 list, with only a few changes. Quebec's rules were similar.

continued

BOX 3.1 *(continued)*

Although there had been some changes, the law (or lack of law) led to confusion about a number of relationships. You could marry your deceased spouse's brother, sister, niece, or nephew, but not his or her aunt or uncle. The situation following divorce wasn't at all clear. However, you could marry an adopted brother, sister, or even a child. Every year a few individuals petitioned the Senate to pass a private member's bill so that they could marry a closely related person—an uncle, for example, or a niece.

A new law, *Marriages (Prohibited Degrees) Act* (1990, c. 46), came into effect on December 17, 1991. It does not permit marriage between people who are closely related biologically (grandparents, parents, children, grandchildren, siblings). It treats adoptees as if they had been born into their new family, and therefore bans marriages between an adopted person and adoptive grandparents, parents, and siblings. Half-brothers and half-sisters also are not allowed to marry. But aunts and nieces or nephews, and uncles and nieces or nephews are, as are relatives of former spouses. First cousins and stepbrothers and stepsisters were able to marry even before the 1990 legislation.

Therefore the answers to the quiz are (1) no, (2) yes, (3) yes, (4) yes, (5) no, (6) yes, (7) yes, (8) no, (9) no, (10) yes.

Sources: Hurley, 2005; *Marriage (Prohibited Degrees) Act*, 1990; Standing Committee on Justice and Solicitor General, 1987; "Some notes on prohibited degrees," 1984; Standing Senate Committee on Legal and Constitutional Affairs, 1987; Vienneau, 1990.

Much as we might like to deny it, our families have both direct and indirect influence on our mate selection. In fact, approval by people important to them, like family and friends, has been found extremely important in young adults' decision to marry (Holman & Li, 1995). Parents (and other relatives) can and do let young people know what they think of their choice of partner. Sometimes the approval or disapproval is openly stated; at other times it is communicated through the attitudes and nonverbal messages of relatives. Families may also introduce us to the people we eventually marry. When there are a number of brothers and sisters close in age, for example, one of the girls may fall in love with one of her brother's friends, or vice versa.

The influence of families can be more subtle. Our parents choose where the family lives; this in turn determines who our neighbours are, where we go to school, and the proximity of people our own age. Parents may influence whether we continue our education and where we do so, either through their direct influence or through factors such as income level.

We select our mates from a field of eligible people, who usually live in roughly the same geographical area (Ingoldsby, 2003). It is easier to get to know people who live nearby than those who live far away. In part because many immigrants live in **enclaves,** or groups within the larger society, they tend to marry people of the same ethnic origin. One of the great mixing places is the postsecondary institution. Here people with similar interests from a variety of places have an opportunity to socialize with one another. Internet relationships, of course, can occur over vast distances (Merkle & Richardson, 2000). Sociologists have discovered that we are likely to marry those similar to ourselves in intelligence, education, physical attractiveness, age, religious and ethnic background, and personal habits (Ingoldsby, 2003). In recent years, women's earnings have become more important to their marriage prospects. As a result, partners are becoming more similar as to income (Sweeney & Cancian, 2004). This tendency to marry someone similar to oneself is called **homogamy.**

Geographical and social factors outside our control also influence our selection of mates. Ask anyone who lives in a small community and they will tell you that the choice of a partner is quite limited, as only a few people in the community are of a suitable age. In the metropolitan areas of southern Canada, one can be far more selective because so many more people live there. In many cities, for example, there are gay/lesbian communities. Often same-sex partners meet through introductions by friends. Many young gay men or lesbians cannot court openly in smaller communities, particularly if they live with or are dependent on their parents for support. As a result, homosexual individuals often enter serious courtship later than heterosexual people (Huston & Schwartz, 1995). When a city becomes too big, however, it may become difficult to find someone with similar values. That is one reason for the growing use of advertisements or dating services to locate a partner.

If the male/female ratio is not balanced, one sex may have a much wider choice of partners. "Daughters of the King," for example, had available a number of potential partners because of the shortage of women in New France. One woman broke engagements to two men before marrying a third, all within a few days (Landry, 1992). In modern times, Yukon Territory, Nunavut, and the Northwest Territories have the reputation of being good places for marriage-minded women to go because more men live there than women. According to the 2001 census, men outnumbered women in the Territories in most age groups under 65 years (Statistics Canada, 2001a, 2001b). Individuals usually partner with someone about the same age. When there is a substantial age difference, women tend to be younger rather than vice versa (Boyd & Li, 2003). When the first members of the baby-boom generation reached marrying age, women were at a disadvantage because there were fewer men a bit older than themselves from whom the women could choose. However, as the last of the baby boomers matured, men found that they outnumbered eligible younger women (Kettle, 1980).

The values we have learned from our families and from our friends and acquaintances also affect whom we marry (Pines, 1999). Most people prefer to marry someone from their own racial group. Racial differences are much more conspicuous than religious and ethnic differences. Prejudice, of course, plays a part in this preference. Often individuals also choose someone of the same religious and ethnic origin. The larger the group in the area, the less likely people are to intermarry, since they have a wide choice among people of similar background and only a limited choice of people with different backgrounds. People with an ethnically diverse set of friends are more likely to marry across ethnic and racial lines (Clark-Ibañez & Felmlee, 2004; Herberg, 1989). Some groups intermarry more often than others. For example, among visible minorities, those of a Japanese background are more likely to marry someone from another ethnic or racial group than Blacks or Asians. This is probably related to the long history of Japanese in Canada as well as their relatively small number (Milan & Hamm, 2004). Similarly, in the United States, the Arab-American population is small and far-flung. Among those who are American-born and acculturated, intermarriage is common (Kulzcycki & Lobo, 2002).

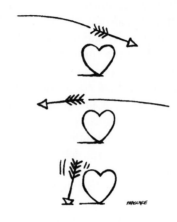

Love can be an elusive target.

Source: Reprinted by kind permission of Barrie Maguire.

THE DISADVANTAGED IN ROMANCE

Some people have difficulty finding partners because they do not fit the accepted standards of eligibility promoted through popular fiction—whether in books, advertising, movies, or television. Desirable men and women are portrayed as young, slim, good-looking, and in control of their bodies and their lives. People who differ substantially from this stereotype may not even be able to establish an intimate relationship.

One such disadvantaged group has been referred to as "people of size." Especially when their weight exceeds 150 kilograms (unless, of course, they look like a football hero), they may be regarded as somewhat obscene, and as objects of curiosity and even ridicule, rather than as romantic partners. In Internet relationships, appearance need not be mentioned or may be misrepresented (Cornwell & Lundgren, 2003). There may, however, be a problem if online friends agree to meet face-to-face.

Another group includes those with visible physical differences such as a facial deformity or a crippling disorder requiring the use of a wheelchair. In addition to the disadvantage of physical difference, these individuals are too often seen as little more than their "disability" and thus as not being full participants in society, as Megan reported in the introduction to Chapter 2. Since they are often regarded as only marginally employable, they also have difficulty finding jobs that would allow them to support family life (Statistics Canada, 2003b).

Besides, they are not "supposed" to be interested in such activities as sex, marriage, or child-rearing (Royal Adelaide Hospital, 1999). Thus, in the competition for partners, such individuals are multiply disadvantaged.

A third disadvantaged group is older people, especially older women. The chance of marrying for the first time drops off dramatically after a person reaches 30 years of age (Bélanger, 1999). There are a number of reasons for this. Since most people are married by their early 30s, their choice of partners becomes more limited after that age. Often women who have devoted themselves to their careers are viewed as being aggressive and unfeminine (Kingston, 2004) and have to either overcome this stereotype or find someone who is not threatened by their success.

The number of eligible over-30s is swelled by the growing number of people who are divorced. These people tend to have problems getting back into the stream of searchers. The social networks of younger people are organized so that meeting eligible individuals is quite easy. Since most people over 30 are married or cohabiting, social life has a couples basis. Meeting someone is therefore more difficult. Women have the hardest time meeting eligible people. Men usually have more economic and social power than women, which makes up for their age. This fact is reflected in the popular notion that women grow old, but men become distinguished. In addition, women, more than men, have custody of children after divorce, and many men do not wish to accept the economic disadvantage and emotional complication of a stepfamily. Some choose younger women without encumbrances, with whom they can renew a sense of their youthfulness. Women usually do not have this option because society looks down on the older woman–younger man relationship. In addition, men die younger than women; the older a woman becomes, therefore, the fewer the men her age. In 1991, for example, there were only 62 unattached men aged 50 to 64 for every 100 women. The ratio was even more unequal for seniors (Riordan, 1994). In 2001, about twice as many women as men over 65 lived alone (Statistics Canada, 2002d).

THE NEVER-MARRIED

Overall, there has been a decrease among 20- to 29-year-olds living as couples. Fewer are marrying. The increase in common-law unions has not made up for the drop in formal marriages (Statistics Canada, 2002d). While many of these singles will eventually marry, many will not. Indeed, marriage statistics are boosted by those marrying for the second time or more (Bélanger & Martel, 2003).

In spite of these trends, our society believes in marriage. Wedlock is seen as a natural and necessary state if individuals are to reach their full development. A stigma is particularly attached to being an unmarried woman, which is reflected in expressions like "old maid" and "left on the shelf." Unmarried people are seen both as defective in personality and as leading tragic lives. The stigma is greater because singlehood is seen as a chosen status rather than as involuntary; it also tends to increase with age (DePaulo & Morris, in press). The truth is, however, that unmarried women tend to have a higher level of educational and professional success than their married sisters, although not as high as men (Schwartzberg, Berliner, &

TABLE 3.1

NEVER-MARRIED MEN AND WOMEN (SELECTED AGE GROUPS), 2001

Age Group	Male	Female
15–19 years	99.6%	99.2%
35–39 years	32.7	24.0
55–59 years	8.3	7.0
75–79 years	6.2	6.1

Source: Adapted from Statistics Canada, "Legal Marital Status (6), Age Groups (19) and Sex (3) for Population, for Canada, Provinces, Territories, Census Metropolitan Areas and Census Agglomerations, 1996 and 2001 Censuses—100% Data," 2001 Census, Catalogue 97F004, October 22, 2002.

Jacob, 1995). In part this is because it is assumed that women will put their husband's and children's interests before their own; thus those who have not married are free to concentrate on their careers.

The degree of pressure to get married also depends on relatives, ethnic background, and personal circumstances. Parents and grandparents may want to see another generation. As an ethnic group, the Irish, for instance, accept singleness fairly readily, but Asian Indians do not. How comfortable an unmarried person feels with his or her state also depends on circumstances. Is remaining single a personal decision or forced on one? If individuals hope to marry, they may feel doubly disadvantaged; they are alone and they do not feel in control of their fate (Schwartzberg et al., 1995).

At each stage, the single person has to deal with particular life-cycle issues. How can one form satisfying relationships apart from the family of origin in a world catering to couples? How long should plans for financial stability be put on hold? How can a childless person develop relationships with young people? Should one have a child even if marriage is not in the picture? How will one be cared for when health fails? Unattached gay and lesbian individuals face many of the same issues as heterosexual singles. In addition, they may have difficulties developing close family-like relationships with friends. This is the result partly of social stigma and partly of limited opportunities, especially in small towns (Schwartzberg et al., 1995).

A special group of the unmarried includes those who choose to be celibate, who choose to make "an honest and sustained attempt to live without direct sexual gratification" (Sipe, 1990, p. 58). Often **celibacy** involves a vow made by people with religious vocations so that they can serve others better. The Roman Catholic Church, in particular, requires celibacy for priests and for members of religious orders. For many, the life is satisfying and these individuals may come to regard members of their religious community as family members. Some individuals, however, do not keep their vows of celibacy (Abbott, 1999). Recently, of course, there has been considerable publicity in Canada concerning sexual abuse in schools and other institutions run by religious organizations, especially when staff members face criminal charges and trials.

We must not assume that unmarried means uncoupled. The unmarried may include homosexual and heterosexual cohabiting couples. A number of these relationships are both longstanding and satisfying.

SEXUALITY

Historically, there have been four approaches to sexual relations among unmarried people: the marital, double, sex-with-affection, and sex-for-pleasure standards (Reiss, 1960). Attitudes toward sexuality and practices have both changed over time.

In the early period of European exploration, values regarding sexuality were often contradictory. Men living among the Aboriginal people often adopted their customs. In settled communities the attitude, at least officially, was much stricter. Many of the early European settlers of North America brought with them a puritan outlook—anything that is fun is probably sinful, especially sex. This attitude is reflected in the "marital standard" for sexual behaviour: sex is permissible only in marriage, and only to produce children (Reiss, 1960). One of the chief advocates of this stance has been the Roman Catholic Church. Actual practices may have been more permissive.

The double standard, whereby men are allowed more sexual freedom than women, has been common at various times among different cultures. During the late 1800s, women were idealized as being pure and sexless (Reiss, 1960). One account tells of a young 19th-century English bride who asked her mother how she should act on her wedding night. Her mother replied, "Lie still and think of the Empire" (Degler, 1974, p. 1467). Victorian women may have been more interested in sex than this story suggests, however (Sprecher & McKinney, 1993). At this time, there was an increase in pornographic material among men. They were also permitted much greater sexual freedom than women. This double standard has continued for a long time. Parents, especially among immigrants from countries with conservative values, still tend to allow sons more freedom than daughters, and to see sexual activity among boys as "natural," but regard girls who have sexual partners as "promiscuous."

Opinions based on faulty science were responsible for some restrictive ideas about sex. For example, around the turn of the 20th century, many people believed that semen was a life force, and that men were weakened if they "spilled" too much. Red meat was blamed for inciting sexual passions. One Michigan doctor set up a spa where men could recuperate their strength. Since he wanted to provide a balanced diet that would not arouse sexual appetites, he invented a vegetable product that is still around today: Kellogg's Corn Flakes (Money, 1986). Although Kellogg's view might seem quaint to most people, some coaches (especially soccer coaches) still encourage athletes to avoid sex so that they will have the energy to win important contests (Abbott, 1999).

During the 1960s and 1970s, sexual experience among dating couples increased. Not surprisingly, studies conducted during the 1960s found that younger people had more permissive sexual attitudes than their parents. Many college students considered premarital sex acceptable for engaged couples, not as acceptable for people in love, and not very acceptable on a casual basis. In general, this attitude corresponds with what Ira Reiss (1960) calls "permissiveness with affection." A major shift in attitudes toward sexuality occurred in Canada for men between 1968 and 1971, and for women between 1971 and 1974 (Barrett, 1980). In general, attitudes became more egalitarian. The sex-for-fun standard, which had already been accepted for men, became more permissible for women (Rothman, 1987). Part of the change came from the general rejection of parents' values during the 1960s. In addition, the availability of the pill in the 1960s reduced the risk of pregnancy.

Attitudes toward premarital sexual activity continued to become more permissive until the 1980s and then have stayed at about the same level (Bibby, 2001). The percentage of grade 11 students who have had sexual intercourse, however, decreased between 1989 and 2002, especially among males. Sexual activity among teenagers appears related to a number of factors. Parents' attitudes have some effect, but this influence wears off with age. Individuals with more permissive attitudes, as might be expected, engage in more sex, as do teens who drink alcohol. Peer group attitudes are also important (Boyce, Doherty, Fortin, & MacKinnon, 2003).

When young couples first have sex, women tend to do it to express love and men do it for physical satisfaction. As they mature, women tend to be more interested in the physical aspects and men in the emotional. The differences, though, are not large. Young men, for example, also have sex for love, and women get physical pleasure from sex (Regan, 2003). About one-third of grade 9 students have experienced oral sex and 23 percent of boys and 19 percent of girls have had intercourse at least once. By grade 11, over half have engaged in oral sex, and 40 percent of boys and 46 percent of girls have experienced intercourse. This is a drop since 1989. Many more boys than girls had had four or more partners (Boyce et al., 2003).

Like women and men in general, lesbians and gay men tend to move into relationships in different ways. Since women tend to be taught that sex is all right in a love relationship, while men are taught that it is fine to have sex for the sake of sex, lesbian couples usually begin by forming an emotional connection and gay men start with a sexual relationship. Traditionally, gay males are thought to emphasize nonmonogamy—short-term and multiple sexual relationships. Nevertheless many form long-term exclusive partnerships. The matter of AIDS has complicated the issue: one partner's affairs may be life-threatening to the other (Johnson & Colucci, 1999).

Problems in sexuality may result from mistaken cues. Men, more than women, are likely to see women's behaviour through "sexual glasses" (Regan, 2003). Thus what women regard as friendliness, men may take to be sexual interest. There are also other forms of miscommunication around sex. In spite of the "no means no" campaigns, the belief that women offer token resistance to sex—that they say no even though they really mean yes—is still common. Studies have found that about one-third of women have actually engaged in this kind of token resistance. The most frequent reason they gave was that they did not want to appear promiscuous. Men also say no when they mean yes. In other cases, individuals may do the opposite—agree to sex even when they do not want it. In one U.S. study, for example, 44 percent of women and 33 percent of men had unwanted sex (Sprecher & McKinney, 1993). In a Canadian study, 6 percent of boys and 11 percent of girls in grade 11 reported having sex when they had not wanted it (Boyce et al., 2003).

There are signs that social attitudes are swinging toward more control of sexual behaviour. Some sex education programs for teens advocate, with varying degrees of success, no sex until the individual is in a committed relationship (Abbott, 1999). Others promote "safe sex" to avoid **HIV** (human immunodeficiency virus), the virus causing **AIDS** (acquired immune deficiency syndrome), and other sexually transmitted diseases. Indeed, both men and women theoretically prefer sexually inexperienced partners over experienced ones, and the less experienced the better (Regan, 2003).

There are questions, however, over how much young people's behaviour has been influenced by these trends. Instances of sexually transmitted diseases have increased among both males and females. The total number of people in Canada infected with HIV, including AIDS, is estimated at about 56 000. New cases have increased at about the same rate for several years. The largest group consists of men having sex with men, though the number is increasing among heterosexual individuals (Health Canada, 2004).

Risk-taking, that is, not using condoms during intercourse or using them inconsistently, was more likely among young people with multiple partners, those who had a poor relationship with their parents, belonged to a sexually active peer group, and used alcohol or drugs. Individuals involved in prostitution were less likely to use protection if they were street youth or male. It is disturbing that many teens believe they are unlikely to be infected with HIV and that they, as well as many adults, do not know there is no cure for HIV/AIDS (Boyce et al., 2003; Health Canada, 2003, 2004).

The changes in attitudes toward sexual behaviour that have occurred in the past 100 years are not purely historical. People now in their 20s and worried about "safe sex" may have parents who believed in sex during engagement, but not just for fun. Grandparents and great-grandparents grew up with still stricter values. Given this large shift in attitudes, the potential for misunderstanding and conflict between the generations is high.

THE LOVE IDEAL

If marriages are not arranged by their families, then couples need some basis for selecting their own partners. In European and North American society, romantic love has become the standard. It may be defined as a strong emotional attachment between adolescents or adults, or as a mixture of sexual desire and tenderness, and of comradely affection and playfulness (Regan, 2003). Psychologists define the criteria for love as physical arousal, the presence (real or imagined) of someone to love, and the belief that you are in love.

The Road to Romantic Love

The idea of romantic love has its roots in the tradition of "courtly love." This was developed by the troubadours in Provence, in what is now southern France, during the 12th century. Some of their ideas were drawn from Roman and Arabic traditions, but the feudal nobility gave courtly love its special flavour. At that time, many of the young knights who served a lord did not have the financial backing to be married, especially if they were younger sons. They diverted their sexual energy through adoration of the lady of the manor and through doing deeds to prove themselves worthy of love. This emotion was spiritual rather than sexual. Thus true love, they felt, was impossible within the arranged marriages of the time. Courtly love, therefore, served to contain the sexual desires of the many young single men and to safeguard the marital rights of the husbands (Beigel, 1951; Lee, 1975).

Over the next centuries, there was a gradual linking of sex and romantic love. At first, sexual favours for gallant deeds occurred outside marriage. Then the language of courtly love came to be used between engaged couples. Thus, for the first time, the notion of love was attached to an unmarried woman. During the Industrial Revolution, emphasis on individuality grew. Young people began to demand the right to choose their own mates. Since love had been associated with courtship, using it as the basis for marriage seemed natural (Beigel, 1951). The earliest settlers from Europe brought this tradition with them to North America, where emphasis on it has been combined with the emphasis on individual achievement.

The Wheel of Love

How can we combine the evidence about homogamy in marriage with the ideal of romantic love? Sociologist Ira Reiss (1980) described what he called the "wheel of love" theory (Figure 3.1). According to this theory, all forms of love and friendship develop through four processes. The first is a feeling of rapport. When people feel comfortable with each other, they reveal aspects of themselves such as their experiences, hopes, desires, and fears. The second phase, self-revelation, can be broad. It can cover many areas of life, or it can be deep, in that it exposes more private feelings and ideas. Usually only close relationships involve deep revelation, and these are likely to involve sexual activity. The third phase is the development of mutual dependencies. Individuals begin to rely on each other to share ideas, jokes, and intimate feelings. Thus the fourth process, personal-need fulfillment, comes into play. Growing trust is also an important aspect of the developing relationship (Regan, 2003). This is a circular process. If needs are fulfilled, there is a feeling of rapport, and the cycle is renewed. Since women are more attuned to relationships, they may be more ready than men to move quickly to the intimacy stage.

These four processes are related to the various factors involved in mate selection. If a couple has similar experiences and values, they are more likely to have a rapport. Cultural background helps determine what each individual feels is proper to reveal. Some topics may be taboo. Certain types of sexual activity may be approved of or discouraged. The needs of one partner may fit the strengths of the other and vice versa, in what is referred to as a complementarity of needs. Thus, a woman who needs to look up to her mate will be most comfortable with a man who needs this type of relationship. Needs can be influenced by social values. In the example just mentioned, for instance, there are signs of a double standard. Often such influence takes place as a result of our social scripts for men's and women's roles (Pines, 1999).

OBSTACLES TO LOVE RELATIONSHIPS—THE COMMUNICATION GAP

Many difficulties in intimate relationships are related to the gender-role socialization of men and women, especially because of the different "communication cultures" they have learned. Men tend to use communication to achieve goals, establish authority, and compete for atten-

Figure 3.1

THE WHEEL OF LOVE THEORY

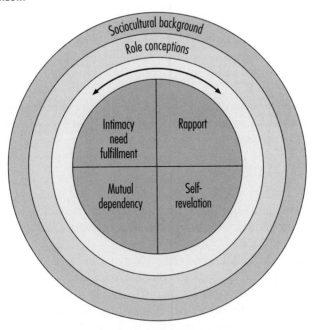

Source: From *Family Systems in America*, 3/e, by Ira Reiss. © 1980. Reprinted with permission of Wadsworth, a division of Thomson Learning (www.thomsonrights.com). Fax 800-730-2215.

tion and power. Women, on the other hand, are more likely to use communication to build connections and to solve problems. For them, closeness is built on communication. For men, however, closeness comes more from shared experiences than personal talk. Thus, both can become baffled and hurt by the lack of understanding they perceive in their partner. When conflict occurs, women more often want to discuss problems, while men are likelier to deny them or to leave the relationship either physically or psychologically (Driver, Tabares, Shapiro, Nahm, & Gottman, 2003; Wood, 1996b).

There are other snags possible. Communication about feelings more often occurs non-verbally than verbally. In fact, we never stop sending nonverbal messages. Because people rarely receive direct education in nonverbal communication, misunderstandings are common (Nowicki, 2003). As we saw in the last chapter, women are more skilled than men at inter-preting nonverbal messages. Often we are afraid to reveal personal information or our inner-most feelings to others for a number of reasons. We may not want to risk being misunderstood or having our emotions used against us; we may also fear making others uncomfortable.

Individuals come to new relationships with expectations that are based in the past. They may have learned these in their families of origin or through relationships with friends or lovers. Some of the expectations can result in warped communication and crippling relationships. One example is the person who treats another as property. In other cases, one partner may see the other as someone from the past, such as a parent or previous lover. Others try to make the partner fit a fantasy ideal. During courtship people may deliberately present themselves as something they are not because they are afraid the person they are seeing will not like the real person. In other relationships, one partner tries to absorb the other and allows no room for individuality, sometimes even telling outsiders the partner's "real" feelings (Sieburg, 1985).

The quality of a relationship during the process of mate selection and the communication on which it is based are important for the marriage that follows. Once they have been established, patterns of communication tend to endure and are difficult to change.

THORNS IN THE RELATIONSHIP

Two major problem areas in relationships are "love gone bad" and "sex gone bad" (Regan, 2003, pp. 39, 90). Both types suggest a failure to achieve the kind of intimacy Erikson (1982) describes. As with communication, patterns set during dating and cohabitation may well continue into marriage if the relationship survives.

Problems with love include unrequited passionate love and obsession with the loved person. The latter may include spying and stalking. Couples may break up because they have mismatched love styles. For example, a partner who is expressive sexually may feel unfulfilled by someone who shows love through sharing activities. Passion normally fades over time, with the result that some individuals may feel they have "fallen out of love" rather than entering a new dimension in their relationship (Regan, 2003).

Sex gone wrong includes sexual dissatisfaction, which may result from poor communication about sexual needs and desires, or from incompatibility. Infidelity breaks the trust and commitment that are expected in a love relationship. In dating relationships it can range all the way from flirting and kissing to sexual intercourse. Infidelity can also include emotional rather than physical involvement. For example, Internet relationships can become so intense as to interfere with face-to-face ones (Merkle & Richardson, 2000). The reasons given for infidelity in premarital relationships are similar to those for infidelity in marriage—dissatisfaction, revenge or jealousy, desire for variety, and sexual incompatibility. Adolescents who were studied also cited a sense of insecurity, immaturity, and a lack of communication. One difference in premarital and marital infidelity is that people are more likely to consider ending a premarital relationship than a marriage because of infidelity, perhaps because they have not committed themselves as strongly to it (Roscoe, Cavanaugh, & Kennedy, 1988).

A more serious problem is premarital violence. The forms it takes are similar to those in marriage. The only exception is that date rape is reported more often than marital rape, perhaps because sexual relations are regarded as the right of husband or wife. Sexual aggressiveness is more common among single men than single women. For men, it is related to their acceptance of rape myths, especially the belief that women control sexual activity and that, even when raped, they enjoy it (Christopher, Madura, & Weaver, 1998). A more subtle form of sexual abuse is discussed in a study of teen mothers. A substantial proportion of young mothers reported verbal sabotage of their use of birth control (e.g., "You want to use the pill so you can sleep around"). Some also reported physical sabotage (e.g., forced sex, flushing pills down the toilet). Such sabotage was more likely to occur in a physically abusive relationship (Center for Impact Research, 2000). Violence also occurs in lesbian and gay relationships. The little evidence available suggests that such violence is similar in both frequency and type to that between heterosexual partners (Chesley, MacAulay, & Ristock,

BOX 3.2

FINDING THE COURAGE TO BREAK FREE

When I was 17 I had a boyfriend who was abusive. I was abused many times over the two years I stayed with him. This was not a live-in arrangement; I was living at home at the time. I had a father, a mother, and four younger brothers aged 16, 15, 14, and 13. At first the abuse was "mild," as in slaps or being pushed or tripped by "accident" on the street. The remorse felt by him afterwards and the attention he gave me were enough to smooth things over. Of course, I told no one of the incidents. Gradually the abuse increased. Over the two years I received a fractured cheekbone, many bruises and scrapes, and I was made to feel that I was worthless. Despite this I stayed because a mutual friend, who had known him before he met me, told me that when his last girlfriend tried to leave, he tried to burn her family's house down. Of course, I knew nothing of this when I first met him. In retrospect, however, it probably wouldn't have made a difference because the initial attraction was too great. However, I was afraid to leave when I wanted to leave.

One day a friend of my brother saw my boyfriend kick me and trip me on a public street. He told my brother, then 16, who told my father. My father asked my boyfriend if he had done this. When my boyfriend said no, my father left it at that and went back to reading his paper. All those months I had suffered abuse to "protect" myself and my family and I felt as if my father couldn't or wouldn't help me. At that time I knew if things were to change, it would be up to me.

Finally I did leave the relationship and only after did I find out my brother, then 18, had been chumming around with my boyfriend, picking up other girls, and laughing at me and the situation. Even after I received the courage to leave, despite what could have happened to my family, my brother brought him home to our house. Again, I felt that nobody cared about how I felt; my parents allowed him in and my brother brought him home.

As to how it affected me, I felt my father had let me down and was a weakling. As for my brother, I decided he was a selfish, unfeeling, poor excuse for family, since up to then I felt we had been very good friends. I have never felt the same about him.

I thank God I had the wisdom and courage to wake up before it was too late.

Source: Written by a nursing student, Cambrian College (1990).

Chapter 3   Getting Together   ■

1998; National Coalition of Anti-Violence Programs, 1998). We will be looking at violence against partners in more detail in Chapter 14. Some of the topics discussed there include why men and women are abusive and why victims remain in violent relationships.

GET READY, GET SET …

Marriage preparation has taken different forms over the years. Two basic approaches reflect two different views of family life. The first, akin to the structural-functional theory, is an emphasis on traditional roles in marriage. In the past, men were trained to be breadwinners, often receiving their education outside the home. The physical care of both the household and family members was entrusted to the women. Traditionally women's education for marriage took place in the home; for generations, girls learned how to keep house from their mothers and other female relatives. If women expected to marry into a middle-class or wealthy family, they would probably also learn how to manage a servant or staff of servants. In a less affluent family, they would learn to perform all the practical aspects of housekeeping and childcare. Sex education was often limited, although many women learned about childbirth from helping others. How much education concerning relationships took place is difficult to know, since this aspect was largely unrecorded.

In Canada, the government became involved in marriage preparation early in the 20th century. In 1903 the Agricultural College in Guelph, Ontario, began what was popularly known as the "Diamond Ring Course." This one-year course was started by reformer Adelaide Hunter Hoodless, whose son had died from drinking unpasteurized milk. She got funding from the province to teach young farm wives subjects such as nutrition and health care (Kieran, 1986). Thus, in part, marriage preparation was regarded as a public health matter. Obviously, the emphasis was on the traditional role of woman as caregiver.

In more recent years, especially since the 1970s, preparation has taken more of a symbolic-interactionist approach. As the divorce rate spiralled, religious organizations and family professionals became alarmed at the number of marriage failures. They started to suggest, and some eventually insisted, that couples complete marriage preparation or premarital prevention courses. The focus in these courses is not the physical care of the family, but rather the relationship between husband and wife. They provide couples with information on potential problems and ways to prevent or limit such problems. Couples may look at key issues such as communication skills, expectations they bring from families of origin, adjustments that need to occur during marriage, conflict management, sexuality, and financial management. The rationale behind current premarital prevention courses is that couples who have been helped to explore these areas will have more firmly based relationships. Thus organizers hope that marriages will endure rather than end in separation or divorce. Such programs, especially those that look at how to negotiate conflicts, are generally useful. They help improve communication, conflict management, and overall satisfaction, at least for the short term; no long-term follow-up has been done (Carroll & Doherty, 2003).

BRIAR ROSE REVISITED

We have come a long way from Briar Rose, the symbol of romantic love. Relationships between couples are far more complex than her story would have us believe. They involve the impact of our society and its values and norms. Families influence our choice. Relationships are a mix of our past history and our ability to communicate. They bring intimacy and conflict. For most couples, the relationship patterns developed during mate selection form the basis for the rest of their family life.

SUMMARY

STARTING FAMILIES. Despite the growing variety in family types, most begin with mate selection. This is related to the developmental task of forming an intimate relationship, and builds a foundation for marriage.

MATE SELECTION AND SOCIETY. The forms that mate selection take are closely related to the values and traditions of the societies of which they are part. This holds true for both traditional cultures and Western industrialized societies. Courtship practices fall along a continuum between arranged and self-chosen marriages, and another between those based on value exchange and shared emotion.

At one end of the scale are arranged marriages, which are planned by parents to link two families. In North America, there has been a shift toward choosing one's own mate. Although in the early years of settlement by European immigrants, choice was limited, choosing for oneself suited the individuality of many newcomers. During the 1920s, the practice of casual dating emerged. It served the functions of status, socialization, recreation, and courtship.

We do not have complete freedom in mate selection. Laws, family influences, availability of potential partners, and the tendency toward homogamy all limit our choices. Some people, such as those with visible disabilities and older women, are at a particular disadvantage.

Often, never-married women are regarded as objects of pity or contempt. Generally, however, they have a higher level of educational and professional achievement than married women. Some people choose to be celibate, sometimes as part of religious vows.

Attitudes toward premarital sexuality were, at times, contradictory. Although official attitudes stressed sex only within marriage, practices may have been more permissive. A double standard, allowing men more freedom than women, was common. The period since the 1960s has been marked by greater sexual freedom, especially among young people, and by more premarital cohabitation. Risk-taking sexual behaviour and misconceptions about HIV among some individuals are worrisome.

THE LOVE IDEAL. The idea that romantic love is the basis for marriage developed gradually from the "courtly love" tradition celebrated by the court poets of the 12th century. The growth of love develops through a series of stages—rapport, self-revelation, mutual dependency, and personal-need fulfillment—that lead to greater levels of intimacy. This process has been referred to as the "wheel of love." The growth of intimacy and love is dependent on open communication. Problems in this area may arise because of difficulties in interpreting nonverbal messages and because of unrealistic expectations.

PROBLEMS DURING COURTSHIP. Many problems that arise during the period of mate selection are similar to those in marriage and cohabitation. Men and women may have different expectations for communication and may misinterpret both verbal and nonverbal messages. Unrequited love and obsession with the beloved can also cause difficulties. Infidelity may occur out of dissatisfaction, desire for variety, sexual incompatibility, or lack of communication. The causes of premarital violence are similar to those in marriage, except that date rape is reported more often than marital rape. Violence may occur in both heterosexual and same-sex couples. Often violence is used to exert power over the partner.

MARRIAGE PREPARATION. Emphasis in marriage preparation has shifted: instead of the practical requirements of running a household, the focus now is on emotional and communication aspects of marriage. Also, training in the home has been replaced by religious organization sponsorship.

KEY TERMS

AIDS (acquired immune deficiency syndrome): a sexually transmitted disease (p. 71)

celibacy: living without sexual gratification (p. 68)

closeted: keeping one's homosexuality secret (p. 61)

cohabitation: living together, usually referring to a couple with a sexual relationship (p. 62)

courtship: a process of mate selection (p. 55)

enclave: people of a minority culture who live as a group within the larger society (p. 64)

endogamy: marriage within one's social group (p. 58)

gay male: homosexual man (p. 61)

HIV (human immunodeficiency virus): the virus causing AIDS (acquired immune deficiency syndrome) (p. 71)

homogamy: the tendency to marry someone similar to oneself (p. 65)

homosexual: being attracted sexually to someone of the same sex (p. 61)

incest taboo: social ban on marrying someone who is too closely related (p. 63)

lesbian: homosexual woman (p. 61)

CLASS ASSIGNMENTS

Complete one or both of the following assignments, as directed by your instructor:

1. Many people live together before marriage. Explain the advantages and disadvantages of this practice. Think about the relationship of the couple, family and community attitudes, as well as financial and legal factors. You may discover information through library research, through interviews with couples and experts, and possibly through TV talk shows.

2. In a group, plan and conduct a survey concerning students' attitudes toward premarital sex. Be prepared to report the results and to discuss what factors might have affected the answers you received.

PERSONAL ASSIGNMENTS

The following assignments are designed to help you think about your own family experiences and expectations:

1. Make a list of the qualities you would like in a partner. Which ones are most important? Explain.

2. Do you and your parents have the same attitudes about relations between men and women? How are they similar, and how do they differ? How do you handle differences of opinion about a boyfriend or girlfriend?

Chapter 4

Wedding Bells ... And After

Photo courtesy of Ramandeep and Inderjit.

OBJECTIVES

- To present economic, legal, and historical aspects of marriage in Canada
- To place marriage in the family life cycle
- To examine the functions of marriage
- To consider the roles of husband and wife in marriage
- To learn about family relationships of heterosexual and homosexual cohabiting couples
- To look at the impact of two careers on marriage
- To explore factors involved in marital happiness
- To consider the future of marriage

It's the big day! The sunny warmth entices guests to chairs ranked before a floral arch. Soon, to the side, the groom swings off his white horse, the image of the imaginary cowboy in his boots, black pants and vest, white shirt, and black hat. He fidgets in front of the arch. Finally the bride arrives and is carefully lifted from her side saddle by friends. Her white gown, her flower girl throwing rose petals, and her maid of honour in green whisper of "traditional wedding." The wedding march does not. The bride walks down the aisle, holding her father's arm, to guitar music and a romantic cowboy song. After their vows, bride and groom mount their matching horses and ride off into the sunset. They soon return, however, for a barbecue dinner and dancing to a popular western band. After their honeymoon, they will return to the house they have shared for the last two years, determined that this marriage will last longer than their first ones.

Weddings are big business. One estimate puts the value at 4.5 billion dollars annually in Canada, with the amount to grow with the addition of same-sex marriages (Atkinson, Ermter, & Velasco, 2003). In late July 2003, a window at a downtown Hudson's Bay Company store in Vancouver sported a wedding cake decorated with same-sex couples—and a sign advertising their gift registry. One writer estimated in 1987 that the average, moderately priced wedding meant nearly $22 000 in business if you included the engagement ring, wedding gifts, and honeymoon, along with the cost of the wedding itself (Maynard, 1987). (For a breakdown of possible expenses, see Box 4.1, "What Does a Wedding Cost?") Often families and friends spend much more. Since many couples are marrying at an older age, they have more money to spend on their weddings. Some cohabiting couples delay marrying until they can have the celebration of their dreams (Oppenheimer, 2000).

SOCIETY AND MARRIAGE

Both government and society at large have a stake in marriage. In the past few years, amid debate, there have been a number of government initiatives in the United States to promote "healthy" marriage. In part, these arise from concern over divorce, over high rates of poverty among single parents, and over child well-being (Ooms, 2002). For example, some states have established the option of "covenant marriage," which requires marriage preparation and limits a couple's ability to divorce (Amato, 2004).

The wedding ceremony itself has two serious functions. It is the public acknowledgment that a new family has been created legally and a ritual organized by the family, marking the change in status and roles among all family members (Kalmijn, 2004).

Many "standard Western wedding" customs are reminders of earlier practices. Does the father give the bride away? Does the groom give her a ring? Both are leftovers from arranged marriages where a daughter was considered a financial asset who could be purchased. The wedding ceremony still contains the traces of property transfer and the bride price. Does the bride wear white? This colour symbolizes virginity, which was valued in arranged marriages. Do we throw rice or its substitute, confetti? We are wishing the couple fertility. In the past,

BOX 4.1

WHAT DOES A WEDDING COST?

It is impossible to give actual prices for a wedding. These vary from place to place. They also depend on the size and style of the wedding, as well as cultural and religious traditions. Here are some costs to consider.

FOR ANY WEDDING

License, ring(s), officiator's fee, and possibly prenuptial agreement.

FOR A TRADITIONAL WEDDING

- *Engagement.* Ring, photographs, party, newspaper announcement.

- *Pre-wedding.* Consultant, invitations, thank-you cards, postage.

- *Clothing and related items.* Wedding dress, veil, lingerie, shoes, formal wear for groom, going-away out-fits, flowers (bouquets, boutonnières, corsages), hairdresser, makeup, fragrance.

- *The ceremony.* Fee for church, synagogue, or other venue, music, decorations, custodian or extra cleaning.

- *Reception.* Cost for hall, hors d'oeuvre and dessert tables, catered dinner and serving staff, alcoholic and nonalcoholic beverages, bartender, wedding cake and knife for cutting it, slicing and wrapping cake, favours or bonbonnières, music, decorations, guest book.

- *Transportation.* Limousine, horse and carriage, or other method.

- *Honeymoon.* Hotel room for wedding night, travel, accommodation, new clothes, luggage, spending money.

- *Related parties.* Rehearsal dinner, post-wedding breakfast.

- *Other.* Photographer, videographer, newspaper announcement, gifts for bride, groom, attendants.

OUTDOOR WEDDING AT HOME (LIKE THE COWBOY WEDDING IN THE INTRODUCTION)

- *Rentals.* Arch, tent, chairs and tables, dishes, glassware, eating utensils, tablecloths, portable fireplace for cool evening, portable dance floor, portable toilets, inflatable play castle for children.

- *Other.* Costs for clothing, food and drink, music, photography, and the like may be similar to those of a formal wedding.

ELOPEMENT

Travel and accommodation, new clothes, photos.

Sources: Editors of *Bride's Magazine*, 1999; "A Handy Budget Checklist," n.d.; "How Much Does a Wedding Cost?" n.d.; Wilson & Hickman, 1999.

the production of children, especially an heir, was one of the reasons marriages were arranged (Nett, 1988).

In pioneer-era North America, weddings were often much simpler than they are today, partly because of financial constraints. Many families were isolated, and marriages occurred when a travelling clergyman came by, often without much prior warning. In some cases, the minister or priest would marry the couple, and at the same time baptize the first child, or even two or three children. Even when the engaged couple lived in a town or city and could plan a more elaborate ceremony, they might have little choice in church or clergyman. In Upper Canada (later to become Ontario), there was a further complication. Until 1797 only Anglican and Roman Catholic clergy could conduct legal marriages. Permission to perform weddings was later given to the clergy of several other denominations. Marriages performed by Methodists (and these included many of the circuit-riding clergy who visited remote communities) were not made legal until 1831. Over the years, many people were married in their own faith, although the marriages were not recognized by the government (Kieran, 1986).

Even the time of year weddings occur is related to social factors. In 1939, for example, there was a double peak in marriages during June and September. This phenomenon reflects the agricultural basis of Canadian society at the time. In June, crops had been planted and farm work temporarily slackened; in September, the harvest was in. During this period, the number of marriages in Quebec was particularly low in March because the Roman Catholic Church discouraged marriages during Lent. In 1985, weddings showed only one peak, during the summer. This was probably a reflection of vacation patterns in an industrial society (Dumas & Peron, 1992).

Economic and political factors are related to the age at which individuals marry for the first time. During the Great Depression, for example, marriages were delayed. In the early years of World War II, marriages of younger people increased spectacularly. One explanation is that young men fearing the uncertainty of war hurried to get married before they were sent overseas. During the prosperous times following the war, the ages of both men and women marrying for the first time reached a low for the century. Now, first marriages are once again occurring later in life. Indeed, since 1991, first marriage rates have closely followed economic upswings and downturns. Three factors may be involved: women's greater involvement in postsecondary education, poor opportunities for young workers, and an increase in couples living together before marriage (Bélanger & Martel, 2003; Gaughan, 2002; Oppenheimer, 2000).

There are also regional and cultural differences. For instance, fewer people have always married in Quebec than in Ontario. One reason, perhaps (according to researchers at Statistics Canada), is the celibacy rule for Roman Catholic priests and nuns, a greater number of whom live in Quebec than in Ontario (Dumas & Bélanger, 1996). Recently, however, the lower marriage rate in Quebec reflects the fact that more couples live in common-law unions in Quebec than in the rest of Canada (Bélanger & Martel, 2003).

LAW AND MARRIAGE

Because marriage is a legal contract, it is governed by law. There are rules about who can marry. For example, brothers and sisters cannot marry in Canada, although such marriages were popular among Egyptian royalty. Marriage to more than one person at a time is not allowed. A divorce or annulment is necessary before a married person can be married again. The law governs who may perform a legal marriage, and also states what happens to property if the marriage is dissolved through death or divorce.

Until recently, same-sex marriages were barred in Canada. Under pressure, several provinces enacted a "registered domestic partnership" law, giving each partner the status of "spouse" for many purposes, regardless of sex. Alberta went further, passing the *Adult Interdependent Relationships Act,* effective in June 2003, which applied to unmarried same-sex and opposite-sex partners but might include other close relationships, such as parent and child. Same-sex couples argue that denying them the right to marry, even though they can register their partnerships, is discriminatory. Court rulings, first in Ontario, British Columbia, and Quebec, then in other parts of Canada, allowed same-sex marriages under the anti-discrimination clause of the Charter of Rights and Freedoms. In response, the federal government drafted legislation legalizing same-sex marriage, and referred the proposed law to the Supreme Court of Canada for an opinion on four questions: (1) Can Parliament alone pass laws concerning marriage? (2) Is the section of the draft bill that permits same-sex couples to marry consistent with the Charter of Rights and Freedoms? (3) Does the freedom of religion guaranteed by the Charter protect religious officials who refuse to perform same-sex marriages? (4) Is the opposite-sex requirement for marriage consistent with the Charter? If not, explain why (Bala, 2004). In December 2004, the Supreme Court answered yes to the first three questions and chose not to answer the fourth. In early 2005, the federal government introduced legislation to permit same-sex marriages. The bill became Canadian law on July 20, 2005.

A marriage brings with it both rights and duties. Each partner has the right to sexual access to the other; they have the right to be treated kindly and not to be abused; they have the right to expect faithfulness from their partner. A divorce can be granted if one partner refuses sex, if he or she has sexual relations with someone other than the spouse, or if he or she is cruel toward the other. Laws against assault apply to spouses as much as to unrelated individuals. Both partners have the right to use family assets, although the individual who owns a car or cottage may sell it without the consent of the other. They have a right to the matrimonial home, which is usually treated in law as a special case. They have a responsibility to support each other and any children they might have. They also have the right to decide the kind of upbringing they want for their children, for example, which schools they should attend and in which religious faith they should be raised (Cochrane, 1999).

Some couples draw up a **marriage contract** (sometimes called a prenuptial agreement)—that is, a legal document that alters the effect of the law, usually as it applies to property. Some couples go as far as to include the number of children they will have and who will take out the garbage. One lawyer suggests that if couples need to include such details, their relationship may well be in trouble. A contract including such details may have little effect if the couple goes to court, because it cannot be enforced (Cochrane, 1999).

Most contracts are drawn up because of financial reasons and are used when one partner (or both) wishes to opt out of the provisions of family law. Talking about law and contracts in general terms is difficult, since legislation differs from province to province. In most provinces, legally married spouses have an equal share in the family home and in assets gained during the marriage. When an individual remarries, a contract may be used to protect the interests of the children from the first marriage. The new spouse may be barred from inheriting property, such as a house, that was acquired during the first marriage. In one case, a woman who had been in extreme poverty following a divorce saw the marriage contract as a sign of love from her second husband. Under the contract, her new husband has no legal right to the house she bought with her own money; thus she is assured that she will not lose financially as a result of her second marriage. When a wealthy spouse marries someone with little money, a contract may be drawn up limiting the share the poorer one can get if the marriage breaks up. Owners of businesses may draw up contracts excluding the business from the assets of the marriage, because under equal-sharing rules the spouse would be entitled to half of the business assets if the marriage ends. This might jeopardize the business if there are several partners. A contract can head off such difficulties (Cochrane, 1999).

Though not as common, a cohabitation agreement may be drawn up by common-law spouses, either of the same or opposite sex, outlining partners' rights and responsibilities. The most important aspects concern property and support rights. Property is not automatically shared, and untangling who is entitled to how much can lead to costly legal battles. Not every province provides for support for common-law partners. Those that do vary in the length of time the couple must live together. Unlike in marriage, one partner's will does not become void when a couple cohabits. Thus, a former spouse or other person may inherit if rights are not clarified by contract or will. A final reason for a cohabitation agreement is to protect partners from future changes in the law. For example, if common-law spouses are granted the same property rights as legally married couples, a contract could exempt them from these provisions (Bala, 2004; Cochrane, 1999).

A marriage contract can create problems. If the financial situation of one or both partners changes, it may impose an unfair settlement on the couple. For instance, both partners may be working when they marry. If they have a child and one spouse stays home to care for the child, that person may not be in a good position to support himself or herself if they split up. It may also be difficult to negotiate a contract during the marriage, for reasons such as a new business partnership, since contracts may involve giving up certain financial rights. Contracts may be set aside in court if they are clearly unfair or if deception was involved (Cochrane, 1999).

MARRIAGE IN THE FAMILY CYCLE

In the past, marriage was a rite of passage, which marked the fact that an individual had reached adulthood. With marriage came approved sexual relations, cohabitation, and parenthood (Kalmijn, 2004; Levin, 2004). Marriage was closely related to the economic and social organization of society; for example, in traditional Aboriginal cultures men and women had different roles based on sex and family status. The same is true of **patriarchal** cultures, where men work to support the family and women provide physical and emotional care for members. However, marriage is changing. It is no longer the official signal that an individual has adult status. In fact, marriages are being delayed until later in life, and individuals are not waiting for the ceremony in order to have sexual relations or to live together. The ability to support oneself financially has become a more common criterion of adulthood. Since more women are now in the workforce, they are not necessarily dependent on men for support. Widely available contraceptives mean that parenthood can often be postponed indefinitely (McGoldrick, 1999a).

Finding a spouse is hard work.

Source: Reprinted by kind permission of Barrie Maguire.

In mainstream society, marriage involves a commitment to the new family system, which is separate from that given to families of origin (McGoldrick, 1999a). This sense of being a couple has been called "we-ness" (Driver et al., 2003). The couple needs to learn to depend first on each other for satisfaction of their needs. This task involves emotional separation from the family of origin, learning to accept the roles of husband and wife, and gaining a sense of identity as a family. Even couples who have lived together before marriage report that their relationship changes after marriage. Many find this fact surprising, but in fact men and women often bring to marriage expectations learned in their families of origin that they did not have of the living-with relationship. They may for the first time have the security to act naturally. Each spouse brings a history of traditions and expectations. The couple must decide which of these they will keep, change, or drop altogether (McGoldrick, 1999a).

The wife and husband have individually been members of various microsystems—family of origin, friends, fellow employees. Now they must renegotiate as a couple their relationships with these groups. This may not have been done prior to marriage. Even if they have been living together, the partners may not have related to the extended families as a couple; each may have visited their family alone. Changes that couples make in visiting patterns, in social activities such as a night out with same-sex friends, or in family rituals and traditions affect others. Some may become hurt or angry. Often the new marriage partner is the first new member of the extended family system in many years. The stress of change may lead the players, including the new couple, to see the situation in terms of villains and victims; thus there may be conflict with in-laws and friends. Some issues may be put on hold by the couple. For instance, they may not deal with sex-role–related issues, such as the responsibility for childcare, until they become parents (McGoldrick, 1999a).

Ethnic couples may face additional adjustment stresses, since the media, schools, and other institutions of the white majority society give off messages about what families should be (Hernandez & McGoldrick, 1999). They are also influenced by the values of their ethnic group. Minority groups may have family boundaries different from those of the majority. For example, many Italian families put more emphasis on the extended family and less on the nuclear family. In traditional East Indian culture, the well-being of extended families takes precedence over individual or couple happiness. A couple may not separate from one or both families of origin to the same degree as in the dominant North American culture. Nevertheless they also need to deal with issues to do with "we-ness" and their relationship with extended family members. Conflict over the definition of sex roles may also exist. Immigrants from Muslim countries, for example, may expect more subservience in women than is usual in English or French Canada. If women begin to accept new values, serious conflict may arise between spouses. Standards among cultures over the degree of emotional intimacy between spouses also vary. In cultures where marriages are usually arranged, less intimacy may be expected than in the dominant culture, with its emphasis on the self-sufficient nuclear family. Intermarriage may make adjustment more difficult for the couple, since they will have to reconcile the expectations brought from their separate cultures (Hines, Preto, McGoldrick, Almeida, & Weltman, 1999).

WHY MARRY?

Although fewer individuals in their 20s are marrying now than even 15 years ago (see Table 4.1), most people will be married at some time during their lives; thus, there must be reasons for its continuing popularity. Over the centuries, marriage has served a number of purposes, most of which are still background reasons for marrying.

Status

Marriages have been arranged for status reasons, both economic and social. Although this is usually not considered a purpose in most of modern North America, it does occur in many parts of the world. Arranged marriages need not be unhappy. Divorce rates are low among

TABLE 4.1

TOTAL FIRST-MARRIAGE RATE,* 1981–2000 (PER 1000)**

	1981	1986	1991	1996	1997	1998	1999	2000
Males								
Canada	645	558	548	512	504	505	516	515
Canada, less Quebec	682	603	604	571	559	563	576	570
Quebec	546	430	381	327	329	317	319	336
	1981	1986	1991	1996	1997	1998	1999	2000
Females								
Canada	651	589	594	548	539	538	548	547
Canada, less Quebec	685	640	648	605	542	595	608	600
Quebec	560	442	427	363	362	350	352	371

Source: Adapted from Statistics Canada, "Report on the demographic situation in Canada, 2001–2002." Catalogue 91-209, December 22, 2003, p. 21.

Notes:

* The first-marriage rate is the number of people who marry for the first time in a given year for every 1000 single people.

** Males aged 17 to 49 and females aged 15 to 49.

such marriages, perhaps because couples face many social pressures to remain together. Unlike those who marry for love, those in arranged marriages cannot be disappointed if love fades. The partners may have common interests, affection, and concern to make the marriage pleasant. Although most Canadians do not marry for money or position, they do consider whether their prospective partner earns enough money so that they can have the lifestyle they want, and if that person will fit into that lifestyle. Marriage continues to give couples a legal and social status they do not gain by cohabitation (Cherlin, 2004).

Various religions, such as Islam, permit multiple marriages. Is it right for a government that is now out of the religion business to continue a law rooted in Christianity? In fact, many people currently practise "serial polygamy," that is, marriage or cohabitation after divorce or separation (Macdonald, 1999). In addition, Canada needs to look at existing polygamous marriages of immigrants. Should the multiple spouses be entitled to the same benefits as single wives (or, less likely, husbands) (Bala, 2004)?

Critics say that polygamy encourages patriarchy and devalues women (Bala, 2004). Supporters, however, dub the practice "the ultimate feminist lifestyle." One plural wife suggests that being one of several not only lightens the burden of housework and childcare, but also provides co-wives with an exceptionally skilled husband (Joseph, 1997). The issue is clouded by a number of allegations: failure to provide adequate support for wives and children, and spouse and child abuse (Bala, 2004). Recently, authorities have investigated the

In the reign of James the Second
It was generally reckoned
A rather serious crime
To marry two wives at one time
　　　—W. S. Gilbert (1875/1996, pp. 33, 35)

It is illegal in Canada to be married to more than one husband or wife at once. The case of the Bountiful community in Lister, B.C., challenges the law. The group, part of a sect that broke away from the Mormon church, openly practises polygamy. The former leader, Winston Blackmore, was speculated to have 30 wives and 80 children. Among other responsibilities, religious leaders approve, even arrange, marriages for all group members.

Officials are concerned over reports of sexual and physical abuse of women and children in Bountiful. They also worry about the potential cost of government programs, such as Canada Pension Plan benefits, if polygamy is legalized. In 1992, British Columbia authorities decided not to prosecute sect members for polygamy. They believed the law banning it could be challenged under the guarantee of religious freedom under the Charter of Rights and Freedoms. More recently, federal authorities stated that the Charter does not protect polygamists (Bala, 2004; Dawson, 2000; "Hunting Bountiful," 2004; Oziewicz, 2000).

Bountiful commune, along with other communities of the sect in Utah and Arizona, over charges that underage girls have been married to members without their parents' consent ("Hunting Bountiful," 2004).

Economics

Marriage can ensure physical and economic survival. When homesteaders went west, both men and women had to put in long hours clearing stumps and breaking the soil; with luck, relatives and neighbours helped. After their children were born, the wife's responsibilities centred more on the small house they had built. Once the children were old enough, they helped out with farm chores. This pattern continued into the 20th century in rural Canada. A study of a Quebec parish in the 1930s found that for a farm to be productive, the labour of all family members was required (Miner, 1939/1974). In current Canadian family law, the two partners have a duty to support each other financially, either by making money or by caring for the home and children (Cochrane, 1999).

Nowadays, marriage is not necessarily of financial benefit. For example, the Old Age Security pension is given by the federal government to individuals rather than to families. Because they can cut costs by sharing accommodation, married and cohabiting couples are less likely to be poor than a single person. Marriage does, however, grant rights to support and to property division. The flip side is the corresponding responsibility. Thus, whether marriage is a benefit financially or a drawback depends on a person's perspective.

Sex

Marriage is designed to regulate sexual behaviour. Usually marriage limits sexual relations to an exclusive partner (or in the case of polygamy, to a group of partners). This expectation is reflected in Canada in divorce law in which **adultery** is grounds for divorce. In the past, it was considered important that a bride be a virgin, and that she have sexual relations only with her husband. This demand ensured that land and titles were passed on only to biological descendants of the husband. It didn't matter, however, if he had sexual experience before and outside marriage. With improved contraception, however, childbearing can be separated from sexual activity. Although sexual access to the partner is presumed, it is not always present in marriage, such as when illness prevents it or when one or both partners do not choose to have sexual relations. When this occurs, divorce may be granted on grounds of cruelty or marriage breakdown (Cochrane, 1999; Rubin, 1996).

Children

Marriage is also designed to care for children. Since they need parents' care for so many years, the stability of the marriage relationship allows them to survive physically and to become socialized and productive members of society (Ooms, 2002). In Canada, children are entitled to financial support regardless of the marital status of their parents (Department of Justice, 2004b). Higher levels of female employment and family benefits have made it possible for single parents to raise children, although usually not in luxury.

Identity

Particularly for women, marriage has over the years provided an identity. In the traditional family, the wife takes her husband's name. Since she has no paid occupation, she takes her status from her husband as well. During daily living the couple forms a unique family culture and worldview. These aspects of the family identity also provide a sense of purpose and meaning for the individual. With current opportunities to build a career, women no longer need to depend on a husband for identity.

Love and Support

Finally, marriage serves to look after the emotional needs of the partners. Obviously this requirement arises from the idea of romantic love. No matter how wrong things are in the rest of the world, people expect their husband or wife to be loving, sympathetic, and encouraging. In marriage a person expects to find unfailing love and support (Lasch, 1979). As we can tell from the levels of marital violence and divorce, however, not all partners are kind and loving. The unmarried can also have their emotional needs met by extended family members, friends, and lovers.

Why Marry?

Most of the functions traditionally considered part of marriage can be met in other ways. So why marry? Obviously, marriage has appeal, as witnessed by the drive to legalize same-sex unions.

First, marriage provides what one theorist calls an "enforceable trust." That is, the legal provisions for support and sexual fidelity provide the couple a degree of security (Cherlin, 2004). Because marriage assumes a long-term contract between spouses, they may feel secure enough to incur short-term costs for long-term benefits (Waite, 2003). For example, one partner may support the other during postsecondary schooling because he or she expects family income to eventually be higher. Married partners also have greater financial rights if their union is dissolved (Cochrane, 2002).

Second, marriage has been regarded socially as superior to other kinds of adult relationships, such as nonsexual friendships, domestic partnerships, long-term cohabitation, and single-parent families (Ellison, 2004). Marriage, more than cohabitation, connects individuals to other individuals and social groups, which can be a source of informal help, such as job referrals (Waite, 2003).

Most of us have been socialized to believe that marriage is the "natural" state for adults. Also, a good deal of pressure is put on couples who are dating or living together to get married. Often parents and grandparents see marriage as a desirable step toward parenthood, and they wish to be grandparents and great-grandparents. Once the majority of a particular age group, or cohort, are married, social life tends to be organized on a couples basis, thereby putting further pressure on individuals to marry. In Sweden, marriages tend to occur in waves. Once a couple has attended several weddings, they may marry as a way to repay social obligations (Le Bourdais, Seltzer, & Trost, 2003).

The whole romantic view of love may also be involved in individual decisions to marry. For those who are having problems such as loneliness or difficulties with their family of origin, marriage may beckon as an instant cure (McGoldrick, 1999a). As we can see by the present high rate of divorce, such hopes are often dashed. Indeed, the first same-sex partners granted a divorce in Canada spoke of their unrealistic expectations that marriage would "fix" their problems (Makin, 2004).

In spite of the pressures to marry, the marriage ideal has changed. It is no longer seen as the principal career for a woman, where she finds her greatest fulfillment, or solely as a financial partnership, with the roles of husband and wife clearly defined. Nor is it seen any longer as mainly a setting in which to raise children. Rather, individuals come to marriage looking for self-fulfillment and for emotional growth and satisfaction. Ideally, each partner is willing to work at making their relationship worthwhile. The result is a greater emphasis on equality and sharing (Simmons & Wright, 2002).

MARRIAGES YESTERDAY

In the past, there was a fairly clear division of men's and women's roles, with some overlap. In some societies, for example, all family members were involved in trapping or fishing. The actual assignment of roles differed across societies.

Aboriginal Societies

There was considerable variety among the Aboriginal peoples in Canada, depending partly on the environment. All engaged in hunting and food collecting, most fished, and some developed simple agriculture. Their lives were attuned to the seasons. For example, Stadaconans planted fields in the spring, then went to the Gulf of St. Lawrence to fish and hunt sea mammals, and returned to their villages to harvest their fields. Subarctic groups, such as the Swampy Cree, hunted caribou, trapped fur-bearing animals during the winter for both fur and meat, and joined other groups for spring freshwater fishing. Most activities were cooperative, with the entire community benefiting (Ray, 1996).

Ordinarily men were responsible for most of the large game hunting, though women and children helped kill buffalo trapped in buffalo pounds. Men also made durable equipment, such as canoes and snowshoe frames. They were responsible for protecting the group from enemies and for waging warfare. Women, whose mobility was limited by the demands of bearing and caring for children, gathered foods and, in Iroquoian nations, engaged in agriculture. They prepared and preserved food, clothing, and household equipment. In fact, women were so valuable in preparing buffalo hides that Plains people took several wives to expand trade in hides with white settlers (Ray, 1996). Worldwide, women in hunter-gatherer societies controlled the actual sharing of food. Indeed, they provided 60 to 90 percent of the calories consumed by the group (Coontz, 2000). The same may have been true in parts of Canada, where Iroquoian women provided half to three-quarters of the calories (Ray, 1996). Women and children without husbands or fathers could survive well in societies with a tradition of sharing food and childcare (Coontz, 2000).

When the reserve system was established, it became impossible for Aboriginal peoples to follow their seasonal migratory traditions. This was especially true near urban and farming settlements. Thus, survival depended on adopting the ways of the colonists or accepting handouts. Men, more than women lost their roles. Women, at least, retained their traditional caregiving activities and, in many cases, became the primary providers, since welfare was often given to women and their children (Brodribb, 1984; Castellano, 1989).

Victorian Ontario

Middle- and upper-class 19th-century British and English-Canadian society seems far removed from the hunting-fishing-gathering Aboriginal societies. One obvious difference is that Victorian society was money-based: families did not move to follow game or gather food, except as recreation. Instead they lived in houses and often accumulated elaborate furnishings that would be difficult to shift from one place to another. Men worked outside the home to earn money or managed inherited wealth. If the family was comfortable financially, the wife had servants to cook, clean, make clothing, and even raise children. Poor women were paid to do these jobs for those with money.

The money basis for society shaped the balance of power in the family. The husband controlled the money. The wife's dowry and any money she inherited were under her husband's control from the moment of marriage. He could gamble it away or refuse to allow her to spend any. His vow at marriage to endow her with all his worldly goods really worked in reverse.

In Upper Canada, women gained some property rights in 1859. From then on, a woman had rights to all property brought into the marriage or inherited after marriage, but she had no right to any money earned during the marriage. This meant that the husband who drank up all his own wealth could by law relieve her of any money she had earned. For the first time a woman could make a will, but she could leave her property to her husband and children only. In 1884, a married woman gained the right to all property she brought into the marriage, whether inherited or earned, and she could bequeath it to anyone she chose (Kieran, 1986).

Since the early 19th-century husband had a right to all the money in the family, and since he was considered "owner" of his wife and children, he had exclusive right to custody of their children if the couple separated. A woman in an unbearable marriage, where she was humiliated and beaten, for example, could leave only at the risk of extreme poverty and the complete loss of her children. Few women found freedom worth the price (Kieran, 1986).

Rural Quebec

Like the Aboriginal and Victorian Ontario families, those in early 20th-century rural Quebec had a clear division between men's and women's roles (Miner, 1939/1974). Men spent their time growing crops, raising large animals, and maintaining buildings and equipment. Women cared for the daily needs of family members; they cooked, sewed, cleaned, spun, and knit, and were responsible for the vegetable and flower gardens. Without modern appliances, tasks like dishwashing required a lot of time; it may have taken three women over an hour to do the dinner dishes for the 10 to 20 people who sat down at meals. Women waited on the men, and often ate after they were finished.

The wife joined the husband's family. The son who would inherit the farm brought his wife to live with his parents. Although the marriage contract usually specified that both parties had an interest in any property, the husband was the administrator and could make whatever arrangements he wished, as long as he provided for his wife. Men managed family finances. Married women rarely had any way of earning much money (Miner, 1939/1974).

Marriage Pros and Cons in Past Societies

Despite their differences, these three forms of society had in common their ability to meet the basic functions of families. From the structural-functional viewpoint, the family was a unit that ensured survival of its members through separate roles for men and women. Exchange theorists point out tradeoffs in these roles. For example, men's big-game hunting was important in providing protein. In return, women prepared and preserved the meat for extended family use. Feminists add that, in societies where status and power are granted to men, women are exploited. This was particularly true of Victorian society. Women traded services in childbearing, and household and family care (as well as their own money) for financial support and status provided by men. This pattern was also present in rural Quebec and in at least some Aboriginal societies.

THE "MODERNIZATION" OF MARRIAGE

Today, couples look forward to a much more democratic marriage. The wife usually plans to keep working following marriage, since her pay is important in maintaining the couple's standard of living. In turn, many husbands do more housework.

This change has been gradual. Sociologists point to the effect of two world wars, in which women had to replace men in the factories and offices. After the war, most women returned to their traditional role, for the ideal of the breadwinner husband and homemaker wife and mother was still strong. One measure of the acceptance of the "traditional" family was the baby boom; it was as if the couples were making up for lost time, and more. This period has been called the "golden age of the nuclear family" (Cheal, 1991). Yet the principle that respectable women could work outside the home had been established.

Women who continued to work after marriage did so in order to help buy houses or new furniture. Once children were born, mothers stayed home, at least until the children were in school. Since women often worked part-time, their pay was seen as an extra, something to help buy luxuries; their real business was looking after the family. By the 1970s, income was not keeping pace with inflation. A wife's pay prevented the family's purchasing power from declining. In many cases, two incomes are now necessary for a family to survive economically. In 1986, 62 percent of marriages had incomes from both spouses; this figure had almost doubled since 1967. In 2003, about 57 percent of all women aged 15 and over had jobs, making up 47 percent of the workforce. Among those aged 25 to 44, the majority of both men and women were employed (Statistics Canada, 2004k). (See Table 4.2.)

In this shift from single-income to dual-income families, many have experienced conflicts concerning men's and women's roles in the family. Values and expectations about what their roles should be have not changed as fast as families have. Women traditionally have been the caregivers in our society. Often they are expected, and they themselves expect, to be

TABLE 4.2		
EMPLOYMENT RATES OF WOMEN AND MEN, BY AGE, 2003		
	Women	Men
All ages	57.2%	67.7%
15–24 years	58.2	57.4
25–44 years	76.1	86.1
45 years and over	42.1	56.0

Source: Adapted from Statistics Canada, "Women in Canada: Work chapter updates, 2003." 89F0133. March 25, 2004, Table 3, p. 12.

responsible for the physical and emotional well-being of the family. An American study found that men reduce the amount of housework time when they begin to live with a woman, while women increase theirs when living with a man (Gupta, 1999). Many women spend more hours per day working, in combined paid employment and family care, than men or homemaker wives (Luxton, 1998). When the demands of paid work and family care conflict, women often feel in a bind. If they go to work when a child is ill, for instance, they may feel guilty no matter what quality of care they have arranged. If no one else can care for a sick family member, women are usually expected to stay home. On the other hand, if a woman stays home from work because she has a sick child, or to see the school principal, she feels guilty for not attending to work responsibilities. A number of women experience burnout because they try to do everything.

Since men traditionally have not had to concern themselves with family care responsibilities, some view housekeeping chores as unmasculine. Thus they feel demeaned if they do traditional "women's work." There appears to be a hierarchy of tasks, with men doing lower-level ones more often than higher ones. In rising order, these are doing dishes, buying groceries, cleaning house, doing laundry, and preparing meals. Men involved in higher-level tasks like meal preparation are more likely to do other housework as well (Twiggs, McQuillan, & Ferree, 1999). Men do take on more responsibility when their wives are employed, but often do more enjoyable tasks like playing with children (Luxton, 1998). Husbands tend to do the highest share of housework (about 35 percent) when partners' earnings are equal (Greenstein, 2000).

ROLES IN MARRIAGE

As might be expected, at present no one pattern of roles in marital couples exists. In fact, four have been described by sociologists.

Conventional Roles

The first role pattern, usually referred to as **conventional roles** (Nett, 1988), is based on the structural-functional notion that men and women have separate spheres of action, and that the home is the proper place for women, just as the labour force is for men. This pattern originated among the middle class in the 19th century. Since the man held the power base in the family, the woman gained her status from her husband. Such a view in an extreme form is represented by the expectation that a wife should be "barefoot, pregnant, and in the kitchen."

As long as the marriage lasts and employment is secure, the conventional pattern has distinct advantages. The specialization in tasks allows the partners to become expert in particular areas. A particular strength is that it provides for care of children and home. Women also have the time and energy to provide the emotional support men need in order to cope with the work world. This division of labour reflects the organization of society, where paid employment tends to become more and more specialized. It also fits in with the socialization children receive in most families concerning gender roles—that girls and boys are expected to behave in different ways. As we saw in Chapter 2, boys are supposed to be more interested in activity and in things, while girls are supposed to be more interested in people, human relationships, and ultimately the family.

However, there are disadvantages to the conventional model. With only one wage earner, families have less security in poorer economic times as well as a lower standard of living. In addition, there is little security for women if partners separate (Beaujot, 2000). Also, the role for women is very isolating, since housework tends to be done alone. Wives' hunger for adult companionship may lead to demands on husbands, and perhaps to marital dissatisfaction and conflict (Armstrong & Armstrong, 1987). It may also be difficult for a woman to move from the workforce to being a homemaker. She may miss the companionship and challenges she had on the job. Also, instead of having her own work identity, she now takes her status from her husband.

Shared Roles

More common now than conventional roles in marriage are **shared roles,** where both partners work and share household responsibilities (Nett, 1988). Since more women work, more are sharing the provider role. Some dual-earner families, however, resemble conventional families, because wives, either through choice or through job availability, only work part-time. In the past, women were able to supplement family income in ways not available now, for example, by selling produce or doing laundry. Modern appliances and city living make such options less feasible, although some women do care for others' children while the parents work, or do paid work at home, often at low wages (Armstrong & Armstrong, 1987). Now that women are sharing the provider role, men should be expected to do day-to-day chores. Instead, they tend to specialize in home repairs and garden work—things that are not done routinely every day (see Table 4.3). Although women work full time, the general notion that men help with housework and women help with the provider role persists. We will look at the relationship between family and workplace more fully in Chapter 12.

TABLE 4.3

TIME USE OF ADULTS AGED 25 TO 44 (AVERAGE HOURS PER DAY), 1998

	Single		Married, No Children		Parents	
	Women	Men	Women	Men	Women	Men
Paid work/education	5.4	6.0	5.2	6.6	3.6	6.4
Unpaid work (e.g., housework)	2.5	1.9	3.4	2.2	6.1	3.5
Leisure	6.0	6.2	4.9	5.4	4.3	4.4
Personal care, including sleep	10.1	9.9	10.5	9.8	10.1	9.8

Source: Adapted from Statistics Canada, "Canadian Social Trends," Catalogue 11-008, Winter 2001, p. 22.

Dual-Career Roles

A third pattern is **dual-career roles,** or marriage in which both partners are committed to their careers (Beaujot, 2000; Nett, 1988). This is sometimes difficult to distinguish from shared roles because there is no clear dividing line. In addition, some women start working to help out financially, and what was originally just a job becomes a career. The difference is the priority set on the career. By definition, careers exclude interrupted or part-time work; so the proportion of women employed in them is very small. Dual-career couples are more likely to share equally both household responsibilities and power, but this balance does not occur invariably. In a small study of such families, couples often shared chores on a basis other than gender (e.g., who likes to cook). Neither partner seemed to be in a better bargaining position (Risman & Johnson-Sumerford, 1998). The arrangement may work very well until the couple has children, often later than other families because of the desire to get careers established. The presence of a child makes long workdays and business trips much harder to schedule. These couples may thus be faced with sacrificing one career, at least for a while, or purchasing household services and nanny care for children. In fact, men often become more involved with their careers and women with child and household (Luxton, 1998). They may also face difficulties such as deciding whose job has priority in the event that the transfer of one partner and not the other comes up. Such decisions may be made on the basis of income earned or availability of jobs in the two fields.

Reverse Conventional Roles

A fourth pattern, in which there is a breadwinner wife and a homemaker husband, is referred to as **reverse conventional roles** (Nett, 1988). The househusband appears in popular culture in the comic strip "Adam @ Home" (Bassett, n.d.) and on the Internet. This arrangement is often temporary. Some couples opt for the husband to stay at home with young children because the wife's pay is higher or more secure. In other cases, wives are forced to become primary breadwinners if their husbands are laid off, forced into temporary or consulting work, or are injured or recovering from an illness. Many men report how rewarding it is to develop a close relationship with their children. Nevertheless, they may encounter social stigma for being freeloaders (Tyre & McGinn, 2003). In some families, when wives earn the bulk of the money, husbands actually do less housework than when both earn about the same. Researchers suggest that such couples accept traditional gender roles. Wives, then, behave to make it appear that men are in control partly to save their husbands' self-esteem. Only when the husband highly respects his wife's work or when the couple strongly believes in equality is the relationship more balanced (Greenstein, 2000; Tichenor, 1999).

MARRIED, BUT NOT MARRIED

Many couples live together before marriage or in place of it. Unmarried cohabitation is not new. In some parts of the world, especially in Africa, Latin America, and Sweden, it has been common for centuries (Cunningham & Antill, 1995). In many countries, it has society's partial blessing as a stage in couple formation and courtship, but one that should lead to formal marriage.

Cohabitation falls somewhere between lifelong marriage and furtive affairs—more stable than an affair, but not as solid as marriage (Béjin, 1985). It is increasingly accepted, especially among younger people. A survey of more than 24 000 Canadians in 2001 found that men were more willing than women to live common-law. Young adults, francophones, those who do not attend religious services, and Canadian-born individuals are more likely than others to approve of cohabitation. In addition, those who had lived through family disruption as children were more apt to be in favour. Among people aged 15 to 29, students were less inclined to want cohabitation (66 percent) than those already employed (76 percent; Milan, 2003).

There has been a marked increase in cohabitation since 1981, especially among younger people. In the 1970s, living together was seen as a step toward marriage undertaken by only a few. Quebec had pulled ahead of the rest of Canada by 1991. In 2001, nearly 30 percent of Quebec couples were cohabiting compared with about 12 percent for the rest of Canada. This appears related to culture because it is Quebec francophones who are most likely to enter a **common-law union** and least likely to choose marriage as a first union (Le Bourdais & Lapierre-Adamcyk, 2004). (See Table 4.4.) For those between 25 and 29 years of age, there was an increase from 17 percent to 20 percent between the 1996 and 2001 censuses. The percentage had nearly doubled since 1981. For cohorts born before 1960, the proportion of

TABLE 4.4

PROPORTION OF COMMON-LAW FAMILIES AS A PERCENTAGE OF ALL FAMILIES, 2001

Canada	13.8%
Newfoundland and Labrador	9.6
Prince Edward Island	9.4
Nova Scotia	11.4
New Brunswick	12.9
Quebec	25.2
Ontario	9.4
Manitoba	9.8
Saskatchewan	9.5
Alberta	11.6
British Columbia	11.1
Yukon	23.0
Northwest Territories	26.3
Nunavut	31.3

Source: Adapted from Statistics Canada, "Profile of Canadian families and households: Diversification continues, 2001 Census." Catalogue 97F0030, October 22, 2002, p. 24.

cohabiting couples is also increasing. This fact suggests that many people are choosing this lifestyle instead of remarrying after divorce or widowhood (Bélanger & Martel, 2003). In addition, those who have cohabited before marriage are more likely to do so after the marriage ends, especially when they are separated or divorced (Wu, 1995a).

Living Together and the Law

Even though couples living together may behave as if they are married, for instance by calling each other "husband" or "wife," and may be considered married by relatives and friends, in law they are not married. Their legal position varies from one province to the next. Federally, if they have lived together long enough, they count as spouses for income tax purposes. They can insure each other's life and qualify for pension benefits, for example, through the Canada Pension Plan. Provincially, there is variation in the responsibility to support each other financially, for example once they have lived together for a specified time or have a child and a relationship of some permanence. Through various court cases, same-sex couples have gained the same rights as other cohabitors (Lahey & Alderson, 2004). Yet in most cases, cohabiting couples do not have the same property rights as married couples (Cochrane, 2002). This is especially true in Quebec, where "persons living in common-law unions may as well be strangers to each other, as far as the Quebec Civil Code is concerned" (Dumas & Bélanger, 1997, p. 126). Whoever owns something—house, car, or business—keeps it without sharing if the couple separates. Former partners may be able to claim a share, however, if they are able to prove that they made a contribution to gaining the asset. In one case heard by the Supreme Court of Canada, for example, a couple that had lived together for about 20 years had in that time built up a successful farm and beekeeping business, which was registered in the man's name. The Court decided that the woman had contributed equal work and effort and gave her half the property and business assets. Yet she had trouble collecting what she was owed. In protest, she killed herself (Cochrane, 2002). There have been other such cases, and in each of them the cohabiting partner needed to prove his or her contribution. As we have seen, some of these difficulties can be overcome by making a cohabitation agreement.

Cohabitation and Marriage

In some ways, cohabitation and marriage are alike. Both involve romantic relationships in which individuals live together. They can pool their income and expenses, and generally benefit in emotional and social ways. Their psychological well-being is similar. Part of the growing similarity is the result of changes in marriage in that women are less financially dependent. In addition, cohabitation is becoming accepted as a setting in which to raise children (Smock & Gupta, 2002). As for housework, women do most. Men least committed to the cohabiting relationship do least (Ciabattari, 2004). In some places, for example, Sweden and Quebec, cohabitation is becoming accepted as a substitute for marriage (Le Bourdais & Lapierre-Adamcyk, 2004).

There are, of course, differences between marriage and cohabitation. Marriage tends to be more permanent. There is no waiting period for legal rights and responsibilities to apply, as when couples live common-law. Cohabitation is not governed by the same social expectations as marriage (Smock & Gupta, 2002). In general, cohabitors report poorer-quality relationships than married couples. Fewer report high levels of satisfaction, and violence is more common. There is little difference in satisfaction, however, between couples who are planning to marry (more than three-quarters of cohabitors studied) and those who are already married. Married and cohabiting couples are affected in the same ways by the presence of biological children and children from past unions, as well as by past-partner relationships. Those who have no plans to marry their partner are more likely to have lived with or been married to someone else than those who are planning to marry. These facts suggest that those not planning marriage may have problems either in making a long-term relationship work or in making a commitment (Brown & Booth, 1996; Cunningham & Antill, 1995).

It is difficult to make general statements about the happiness of cohabiting couples. This is because cohabitation covers a wide range of relationships from steady dating, through trial marriage, to a substitute for marriage, including a setting for raising children. The social context has also changed. In the 1970s, many couples living together were free-thinkers who did not accept social norms. These norms are now changing (Le Bourdais & Juby, 2002).

Earlier studies found that cohabiting partners were often not as committed to their relationship as married couples were and saw fewer barriers to leaving. In fact, fewer than half married their first partner (McDaniel, 1994). Their sexual commitment, too, was more like dating than marriage and thus more open to sexual encounters with other people. It seems that people who were less committed chose to cohabit rather than to marry (Cunningham & Antill, 1995; Forste & Tanfer, 1996; Nock, 1995; Treas & Giesen, 2000). If a couple has children, they are less likely to separate than childless partners (Wu, 1995b). Now that cohabitation is more common, the older research about such unions may not apply. In areas where cohabitation is more accepted, common-law relationships appear more stable. Recent studies show that cohabiting-couple families are more prone to break down than married families—two and a half times more likely in Quebec and five times in the rest of Canada (Le Bourdais & Juby, 2002). Gay and lesbian couples are also at higher risk of separation (Ambert, 2003).

Does living together before marriage affect the quality of the marital relationship? Early studies suggested yes. Some sociologists thought that cohabitors were less traditional in their beliefs and thus less committed to marriage. Others thought cohabitors might be less skilled in keeping relationships going over a long period of time. Recent research results are mixed. One theory argues that cohabitation changes people and their relationships so that they are not as committed to their later marriage. Thus spouses who had cohabited before marriage are less likely to be happy and more likely to divorce than those who had not cohabited. There is some evidence for this theory (Dush, Cohan, & Amato, 2003). A related study, which looked at the first two years of marriage, found that couples who had cohabited prior to marriage were less skilled in problem-solving and were not as supportive of each other as those who had not cohabited (Cohan & Kleinbaum, 2002). The overall divorce rate may have been even higher than it has been because a number of mismatched couples would have separated without having been married. Married heterosexual couples with children and cohabiting same-sex partners have similar levels of marital happiness. Although same-sex couples are more likely to separate, many report being a bit happier (Kurdek, 2004).

Other recent studies suggest that premarital sex and cohabitation have become part of normal courtship. Women who had sex or cohabited only with their future husbands were no more likely to divorce that those who married without premarital sex or cohabitation. Only if they had had more than one such relationship was there greater risk of separation (Teachman, 2003). In Quebec, marriages following cohabitation are at the same risk of disruption as those entered directly (Le Bourdais & Juby, 2002).

There is a major difference between homosexual and heterosexual cohabitation. Until recently, lesbians and gay men had no further stage possible in their relationship, since they were not allowed to marry. Commitment or covenanting ceremonies offered by some churches did not have the legal status of marriage.

Are Married Couples More Faithful Than Cohabitors?

Whether a person is sexually unfaithful depends on individual and group values and on opportunity. If the individual or his or her social group condemns infidelity, it is less likely. If there is opportunity for an undiscovered encounter, infidelity is more likely. One study found that 94 percent of married individuals reported no extra-partner sex in the previous year, compared with 75 percent of cohabitors. Over the life of the marriage, 15 percent of women and 25 percent of men reported being unfaithful. The longer the marriage, the less likely are women to have an affair. With men, the likelihood drops, then rises after middle age. Gay men report many more sexual encounters than women or heterosexual men. In committed gay and lesbian relationships, however, sexuality is similar to that in long-term heterosexual unions. Married individuals are more emotionally satisfied with sex than are cohabitors, though pleasure in sex is about the same for both. Dissatisfaction with the relationship is connected with recent infidelity. Internet infidelity has been investigated only slightly. One study of sexually explicit computer bulletin boards found that 72 percent of those answering an online questionnaire had a spouse or significant other. Although actual physical contact does not occur, absorption with an Internet lover may lead to emotional withdrawal from a partner. There is, of course, no research yet on the effects of sex-enhancing drugs on either long-term relationships or the likelihood of unfaithfulness (Ambert, 2003; Christopher & Sprecher, 2000; Rust & MacPhee, 2001; Treas & Giesen, 2000; Waite & Joyner, 2001).

LESBIANS AND GAY MEN IN HETEROSEXUAL MARRIAGES

Many lesbians and gay men are or have been married to members of the opposite sex. According to older studies, this includes about one-quarter of lesbians and one-fifth of gay men. Women are less likely to be aware of their homosexuality than men at the time they marry. They often get married for the same reasons heterosexual couples do: they are in love with their husband, and friends and relatives expect them to marry. When husbands learn their wives are lesbian, they are usually totally shocked and even ashamed. These men will very likely ask for a divorce and, if they are angry, may threaten to take their children away from their wives. The marriages of homosexual men are usually short, but some last for many years. Some men know of their homosexuality before their marriage, but may try to deny it by forming a "normal" family. Often couples with a gay husband have separate and different activities that keep the family functioning. In many marriages, however, there are growing sexual problems. Wives may feel cheated and resentful when they learn of their husband's sexual orientation. If they have no children, they often separate. A number, however, stay married, some with no sex in marriage, some with the husband involved in bisexual activity. Men who have never told their wives about their gay orientation worry that their homosexuality will be discovered and that they will be shunned (Coleman, 1990; Ross, 1990).

ONE FAMILY, TWO INCOMES—THE NEW REALITY

The idea of marital and partner roles has changed since the first half of the last century. Most married women now work outside the home, even during a recession. In 2003, most men and women aged 25 to 44 held jobs. This number does not include those who were job-hunting at the time (Statistics Canada, 2004k). (See Table 4.2, page 95.) As a result of the number of two-income families, couples have new issues that they need to settle in their marriages. In most cases, both partners in heterosexual and homosexual cohabiting unions are employed.

Role Choice

Often circumstances rather than choice dictate family roles. According to studies by Kathleen Gerson (1987), women followed four different life paths. The first group chose homemaking. These women tended to have a stable marriage and less exciting opportunities in the workplace. In contrast, a second group of women planned a traditional marriage, but ended up in the paid workforce. They were more likely to be influenced by unstable relationships, economic problems, and job opportunities. A third group always wanted to have careers and were reluctant to become mothers and homemakers. Finally, some women planned to have careers, but circumstances prevented this. The paths chosen seemed to depend on the stability of the marriage, on job opportunities, on the ability of a woman's partner to earn enough so that she could stay home, and on how rewarding she considered homemaking. Similarly, men did not depend only on early socialization for their career and family choices. Workplace opportunities and experiences with their partners and children also influenced their decisions (Gerson, 1993). Many couples expect that both partners will need to work.

Role Overload

Individuals must now fill more roles than was expected of them in the past, since a clear-cut separation of men's and women's domains in family life no longer exists. They need to juggle two careers, children, a marriage, and household responsibilities. This fact is especially reflected in two areas of life. First, the individual, family, and work worlds overlap, and one may interfere with the others. Often, time for personal interests is sacrificed because of the time needed for work and family responsibilities. There are also differences according to sex. Men, more than women, allow work to intrude on family activities. Some bring work home. Others develop a camaraderie with men at work, and their social activities after work hours can cut into family time. Women, on the other hand, are more likely to let family responsibilities interfere with work (Beaujot, 2000; Duxbury & Higgins, 2003). Second, couples need to relieve the stress from role overload. Many use extra money to buy timesaving products such as permanent-press fabrics or microwaves, or they pay for household aids such as takeout food, housecleaning, or childcare. When wives make a larger share of the income, the family is more likely to hire outside help (Palameta, 2003).

Expectations about traditional roles can affect a couple's relationship. When a wife's pay catches up to or passes her husband's, men who value themselves as providers may see their marriage as less satisfying. Pay changes do not have the same effect on women, though they report happier marriages if husbands assume more childcare (Brennan, Barnett, & Gareis, 2001).

Both married men and women do more household work than single people. The most serious time crunch comes, however, when children are added to the family. Both parents assume more unpaid work; mothers gain about two hours a day, compared with fathers' one hour. To allow for childcare and housework, mothers cut back on paid work, leisure, and personal care, while fathers reduce leisure activities (Fast & Frederick, 2004a.) (See Table 4.3, page 97.) One study from Australia suggests that the share of unpaid work is even more if volunteer activities and helping others outside the home are included (Hook, 2004). In general, couples do not need a fifty-fifty division of paid and unpaid work to be happy. They do, however, need to regard that division as fair (Stevens, Kiger, & Riley, 2001).

Role-Cycling Problems

One method of dealing with overload is to stagger work and family periods of stress. Just as families go through a life cycle, careers also have a cycle. The most stressful stages in the family cycle are often considered to be child rearing and adolescence. In the career cycle, getting established in a job or a promotion are the most demanding periods. Couples may set different priorities at different times of life. For example, some couples try to establish their careers before they have children in order to avoid having high levels of stress both at home and at work. The theory may break down in practice, however. Once both partners are employed, it may be difficult for one to leave the workforce, because they may have accumulated debts and other obligations based on their higher income; for example, they may have bought new appliances or an expensive car (Hertz, 1987). For some workers, shift work may allow partners to juggle job and family demands (Elquist & Hilton, 2003).

Balancing Partners' Careers

In many occupations, individuals are expected to be single-minded if they are to gain promotion. People who choose to take time off to raise a child or to work part time often are not considered to be serious about work. There can also be a conflict between careers. Some companies need an employee who is willing to relocate in order to be promoted; others require a person to stay in one place to get established. Couples more often favour the husband's career, but this trend is not as strong as in the past (Pixley & Moen, 2003). Some partners have commuter marriages, but such arrangements often make communication and sharing much more difficult. When one partner has to be away a great deal in his or her job, for instance a sales representative who is responsible for a large territory, difficulties with communication and sharing can result. The same holds true for couples who work in different cities (Lang, 1988). If one spouse works long hours or is often out of town, it can be difficult for the other to have his or her own career, especially if they have young children (Fowlkes, 1987).

The Working Couple and Their Social Network

Given the many demands on their time, dual-earner couples often spend relatively little time with friends and extended family. This places a greater demand on the nuclear family to meet all the social and emotional needs of its members. When social networks are limited, families may experience lower levels of social support, and thus may feel higher levels of stress. Support systems assume that give-and-take occurs. One person cannot expect to be helped all the time without helping in return (La Gaipa, 1981). If the relationship remains one-sided for too long, the social support may be cut off. When this occurs, families may become isolated.

MARRIED HAPPINESS

In spite of worries that marriage is going downhill, there has been little change in the level of happiness of married people since 1980. Nevertheless, the level of interaction between husbands and wives has declined (Amato, Johnson, Booth, & Rogers, 2003). There are problems with measuring the success of marriage. What criteria do we use? Do we consider the number who stay married? Some researchers have done just that and have identified risk factors associated with higher levels of divorce (McGoldrick, 1999a); yet not all unhappy marriages end in divorce. Do we ask couples how satisfied they are? Researchers found that most people report being happily or fairly happily married. Do we look for signs of conflict? Couples who do not fight may be avoiding almost all interaction with each other. In spite of these research difficulties, it is possible to consider several aspects of happiness. Although there is scant research about the happiness of long-term heterosexual and same-sex cohabitors, probably many of the same factors are involved. We will look at three influences on marital satisfaction: what individuals bring to marriage, how couples interact, and how extended families and neighbourhoods affect couples (Bradbury & Karney, 2004).

Individual Qualities and Marital Happiness

When we enter a relationship, we bring our personality and past history with us. These shape how we approach interactions with others. Expressiveness, or the ability to show one's feelings, can increase satisfaction when a newlywed's behaviour is affectionate. This behaviour tends to bring out the best in the partner. These good feelings, started early, extend many years into marriage (Miller, Caughlin, & Huston, 2003). Perfectionism, especially if an individual is trying to live up to his or her notion of others' opinions, can be destructive (Haring, Hewitt, & Flett, 2003). If a person has a negative outlook on life, that is, the view that a glass is half empty rather than half full, the level of happiness of both partners is reduced. When a partner has an insecure attachment, needing constant reassurance, the stability of the marriage is higher, but satisfaction declines (Bradbury & Karney, 2004).

Sex-role identity appears to be associated with adjustment in marriage. **Masculine** persons of either sex tend to have high levels of drive and ambition. In the past these qualities have been associated with men, especially as they compete in the workforce. **Feminine** people usually have a strong sense of responsibility and are attuned to interpersonal relationships. Both men and women have different blends of the two characteristics. They can be high in one, high in both, or low in both. Those who are either masculine or feminine have a range of qualities that they can bring to solve marital problems. An **androgynous** individual, one high in both characteristics, has even more to offer, while an undifferentiated individual low in both has the least to offer. Androgynous individuals rate highest in marital adjustment and undifferentiated individuals rate the lowest. The researchers explain this in terms of exchange theory; that is, androgynous partners bring more resources to help solve problems than either masculine or feminine individuals. The undifferentiated bring the fewest (Baucom, Notarius, Burnett, & Haefner, 1990).

Partners who are emotionally healthy have better person skills, which help them maintain their marriage and increase their happiness (Goodwin, 2003). The levels of empathy and interpersonal skills an individual brings have long-term effects on marriage. Those who are high in both establish conflict resolution styles early in marriage that lead to a strong relationship. Those who are low in both empathy and interpersonal skills are more likely to have a troubled marriage (Schneewind & Gerhard, 2002).

Interaction between Partners

The relationship style of couples, that is, the combination of both partners' level of empathy and interpersonal skills, is related to both problem-solving and marital satisfaction. It appears that the pattern of interaction first developed by a couple tends to continue (Schneewind & Gerhard, 2002). The perception of partners is also important. For example, if wives think their marriage is good, they are more likely to consider low-level anger as due to a bad day or some other neutral cause. Those who rate low on their marital bond are apt to think such negativity is personal (Driver et al., 2003).

As we saw in Chapter 3, the quality of communication is important to a relationship, since it directly affects the way in which couples make decisions and solve problems. Couples with a high level of communication with each other are less likely to have problems and are more likely to solve those they experience than couples with less communication. This is especially true concerning husband–wife relations and problems to do with child rearing. For instance, couples who decide together to have children are more likely to remain happy with their marriages than those marriages in which the pregnancy was an accident or where the partners disagreed over having a child (Cowan & Cowan, 2003). Couples in two-career families, especially when one or both travel a great deal, also depend on frequent and clear communication to keep their marriages healthy (Lang, 1988).

Spending a long time talking, however, does not necessarily mean that a couple's communication is effective. When emotions such as anger get mixed up with factual messages, there may be a great deal of misunderstanding. Couples can get caught in a vicious cycle where ambiguous messages are seen as negative or threatening. In turn this leads to further emotional distance between the partners (Driver et al., 2003). Therefore it is important for a person to concentrate on what his or her spouse is saying, rather than planning his or her response. Also important is thinking about how one's words will affect a partner's feelings (Lang, 1988; Cowan & Cowan, 1992).

Nonverbal communication may be more important than what a couple actually says. If a person can read his or her partner's nonverbal messages, the marital quality is probably high. This may be because the person is aware of what his or her spouse is feeling, since nonverbal messages often communicate emotion more accurately than words (White, 1989).

Communication is not a one-time event. Rather, it depends on continued use of maintenance strategies like being positive or being helpful, when one's partner is tired, cross, or otherwise negative. Such sensitivity helps promote resilience in a marriage, the ability to successfully overcome difficulties (Canary, Stafford, & Semic, 2002).

Generally we expect that couples who agree with each other are less likely to break up. Researchers have found that the more agreement there is between spouses, the greater the stability of the marriage. Disagreement in marriage is probably reduced by homogamy. If we marry someone with a similar cultural background, educational level, religion, and values, we are more likely to agree on major issues. Agreement also tends to be greatest when the couple has to coordinate its activities to look after the tasks around home and children (White, 1989).

If one spouse views the other positively, both feel more satisfied. Fondness, admiration, and trust all help to create a climate where marital satisfaction can grow (Driver et al., 2003; Goodwin, 2003). These arise from both individual personalities and established ways of interaction.

Conflict in Marriage

As we might expect, verbal disagreements tend to be higher when the couple is having problems in their marriage. It is difficult to be sure, however, which is cause and which is effect (White, 1989). Are they having problems because they fight? Or are they fighting because they have basic problems in their relationship? Conflict occurs in every marriage—it is a sign that something in the relationship needs attention. What is important is the way the couple deals with conflict. Relationship personality, that is, level of interpersonal competence and empathy of both partners, leads to positive or damaging solutions (Schneewind & Gerhard, 2002). In addition, couples need to recognize whether a problem is solvable. If it is unsolvable, they may work out a system that allows their marriage to continue, even if they disagree (Driver et al., 2003).

Individuals have different conflict styles. Some are nonassertive; that is, they do not defend their own position but give in to the other person. Others go to the opposite extreme and use direct aggression or violence to force their opinions on their partners. Still others use indirect means of communication. Some appear to agree but manage to make things turn out wrong, a strategy called passive aggression. Others hint or use nonverbal messages, and expect to be understood. In other cases, when the wife tries to fight and the husband withdraws, marriage satisfaction is often low (Kurdek, 1995). Those who are most successful in dealing with differences are those who de-escalate their conflict instead of feeding anger. Those who trade anger for anger are more likely to set off a vicious cycle (as pointed out by family systems theorists). As a result, such couples are more likely to divorce (Driver et al., 2003). In dealing with conflict, couples face the challenge of striking a balance between emphasizing their own individuality and togetherness. They need to understand as well that each of them can see the situation only from their own point of view.

The balance between conflict and the pleasant aspects of marriage is also important. Researchers have found, for example, that every negative interaction is balanced by four or five positive ones in stable marriages (Gottman, 1993). The level of conflict and satisfaction appear related to how couples perceive their relationship. In particular, wives who are happy and committed to their husbands are more likely to work actively to keep their marriage positive (Weigel & Ballard-Reisch, 1999). This is especially true if they believe their efforts will work (Myers & Booth, 1999). Men and women, according to a Quebec study, are happier in relationships where they idealize each other (Bouchard, Lussier, & Sabourin, 1999).

Influence of Others

Extended family members can have an impact on a couple's marital happiness in several ways. First, family-of-origin experiences affect both husbands' and wives' satisfaction, probably as a result of the ways they have learned to communicate (Sabatelli & Bartle-Haring, 2003). More directly, parents can create stress in their children's marriages. An Ontario study identified five areas of possible conflict: first, balancing time spent with nuclear and extended families; second, changing family roles and rules; third, pleasing parents or spouse; fourth, struggling with power; and fifth, fearing future obligations to older relatives (Beaton, Norris, & Pratt, 2003). Conflict with in-laws can erode happiness, even in long-term marriages (Bryant, Conger, & Meehan, 2001). Extended families may have a greater effect on minority group members. Relationships with in-laws are more important for some racial or ethnic groups than others (Goodwin, 2003; Root, 2001). Relatives of gay and lesbian individuals may accept negative social stereotypes and completely reject their child and his or her partner. Others are more accepting (Johnson & Colucci, 1999).

The social niche in which couples find themselves is also influential. Couples in interracial marriages and gay and lesbian partners may have to rely for social support more on friends than on families (Johnson & Colucci, 1999; Root, 2001). Thus, the area in which these couples live can affirm or devalue their relationship. Couples who live in areas with high levels of welfare and poverty may suffer from chronic stress. In good times, their marriages may be satisfying. When a crisis occurs (for example, a transit strike with no other means of transportation, or a day-care failure), their relationship may suffer. It is hard to be kind and loving when you are under acute stress (Bradbury & Karney, 2004).

Married Happiness through Life

The initial adjustment and commitment to the marriage does not last. This is true even of those who have worked out a good relationship with each other and with their extended families and circles of friends. People, families, and their situations change over the years. The marriage relationship must also change if the partners are to remain satisfied.

A number of sociologists have tracked marriage across the life span and report similar findings. For example, Lupri and Frideres (1981) studied married couples in Calgary. They found that levels of happiness were high early in the marriage, rose at the birth of the first child, then dropped to an all-time low when there were teenagers in the family. Gradually, satisfaction with the marriage rose as the children left home and the couple were by themselves again. However, happiness never again quite reached the level experienced early in marriage. Another study suggested that parents got a respite between preschoolers and adolescents, when marital happiness rose slightly before dropping again (Walker, 1977).

A number of explanations are given for this satisfaction curve. The birth of the first child usually is experienced as a high, in many ways similar to a honeymoon. New parents, however, soon need to face the realities of day-to-day living with an infant. Family life changes with each new child, whether through birth or adoption. Relationships become more complex as first-time parents make the transition to a threesome. If there is more than one child, sibling relationships are also involved. Furthermore, one parent may be jealous of the baby's relationship with the other parent. The couple may become so tied up with the new daily tasks, especially if both are working outside the home, that they have less time to know what the partner is thinking and feeling (Belsky & Kelly, 1994; Cowan & Cowan, 2003). In fact, having children early in marriage is related to marriage breakdown (McGoldrick, 1999a). This is probably because the couple have not yet consolidated their own relationship. On average, parents are not as happy with their marriages as nonparents—the more children, the lower the satisfaction. Mothers of infants are the least satisfied (Twenge, Campbell, & Foster, 2003).

The demands the new child puts on the parents can affect their relationship. In the first months, sleep is often interrupted, so that parents do not get adequate rest. If both partners work, time demands are more extreme. They may be so tired that they either do not have the energy to spend on each other or may become extremely irritable. If they do not take time to keep lines of communication open, their intimacy, including their sexual relationship, may suffer. For example, couples report decreased sexual responsiveness in women for a year after the birth of the first child (Elliott & Watson, 1985). Marital satisfaction and sexual satisfaction go hand in hand. If either partner is both energetic and happy with life, men are happy with their sexual relationship (Gossman, Julien, Mathieu, & Chartrand, 2003). Exhaustion and a baby's continuing demands can reduce a mother's energy and responsiveness. If that happens, the husband may feel that he isn't appreciated for the effort he puts into helping around the house and supporting the family. Dissatisfaction is higher if there is a combination of risk factors. These include depression after the birth, an unplanned pregnancy, the birth of a daughter, and poor problem-solving abilities (Cox et al., 1999).

Children can have other effects on the marriage. Conflicts over child rearing may arise, especially if one parent is more permissive than the other. One babysitter, for instance, reported that a mother found it cute that her children tied her pantyhose together to make a rope for lowering a basket up and down stairs, while the father forced the sitter, as well as the children, to eat two helpings of vegetables before any of them could have dessert.

The presence of children significantly influences decisions about jobs or careers, about where the family lives, as well as the nature of the husband–wife relationship. If, for instance, one of the children has serious medical problems, the parents may refuse job relocation to remain near an excellent children's hospital or a trusted physician, even if such a choice limits the chance of promotion (Day, Kirk, & Gallagher, 1985). In less extreme circumstances, the family may think about the volume of traffic on the street and distance from the school when they are considering buying a new house or renting an apartment.

Lowest levels of marital satisfaction are reported when children are teenagers (Lupri & Frideres, 1981). A number of explanations are possible. Parents now have children who are keeping adult hours, so that privacy takes some planning. Teenagers, especially when parents disagree on how to deal with the challenges they present, can strain a marriage. Pubescent maturation among girls and early maturation among boys, for instance, are associated with more conflicts between adolescents and mothers, but not with fathers (Steinberg, 1987). Some families taking part in a study of marital stability in large adopting families reported that their marriages had been in danger of failing because of the stress placed on them by one or more very difficult children. For example, if a girl defied and challenged the mother and acted like a sweet innocent around the father, the parents often disagreed about the best way of handling her. In extreme cases, this disagreement resulted in such serious marital difficulties that the parents considered separation (Ward & Tremitiere, 1991). Children may impose a financial strain if they go on to postsecondary education. At this time, a couple's parents may require more assistance if their health is failing; thus further strains are placed on the family. These have sometimes been called the "sandwich years" because couples are squeezed by both the older and the younger generation (Williams, 2004).

Once children have left home, couples are probably in better financial health than they have been for many years. In these years, couples are required to adjust to living without children again. Frequently they must rebuild common interests. Yet, once the adjustment is made, husband and wife can develop a closeness that was lost when they had children at home; thus marital satisfaction increases.

Homosexual couples probably go through periods of adjustment similar to those of heterosexual married and cohabiting couples. There has, however, been little study of how their relationships change over time. These couples also have additional challenges. Most same-sex relationships do not have the same marker events as marriages, for example a wedding ceremony or the birth of a child (Johnson & Colucci, 1999), though this may be changing.

There are a number of criticisms of the life-cycle view of marital satisfaction. Some of these are based on the fact that the surveys were conducted by asking people of different ages about their feelings, rather than following the same couples over the years. There may thus be differences in what different generations consider satisfaction. For example, older generations are shyer discussing sex with their partners than younger couples. It may also be that more older couples report happiness than couples with children because those with unhappy marriages have separated or divorced, and more of the satisfied ones are still together.

LONG-LASTING MARRIAGES

Researchers have been studying marriages that have lasted for a long time and have found some differences between older and younger married couples. There are few similar studies of cohabiting or same-sex relationships. Following retirement, older couples spend more time together. Gender differences are less marked. Older husbands tend to do more housework. If the wife still continues to be employed, there may be role reversal. Sometimes work and housework issues cause marital difficulties (Carstensen, Gottman, & Levenson, 1995; Dickson, 1995). Support for the marriage by friends and relatives is connected to the success of long-term relationships. The pattern may be circular: happy marriages receive more approval and the approval encourages happiness (Bryant & Conger, 1999).

One study looked at why couples stayed together for 50 years. Happy couples spoke of the importance of respecting each other and treating each other with dignity. They agreed on a comfortable level of closeness; for some, there was a lot of togetherness, for others a lot of individual activity. They had a shared vision of what their life together should be, although they may not have put it into words. Unhappy couples married for 50 years, like the happy ones, believed that divorce was not an option for them, and that they just had to make their marriages work. They did this by doing many things on their own and keeping enough distance to avoid conflict. The pattern for long-term marriages was probably set in the early days of their relationship. Couples who were happy in the beginning were more likely to stay happy. Unhappy people remained unhappy (Dickson, 1995).

Another study compared heterosexual couples with same-sex relationships that had lasted for at least 15 years. Sexual orientation apparently was not important for satisfaction with their relationships. The factors that mattered most were ability to contain major conflicts and to develop psychologically intimate communication. The two factors are related. Openness and honesty between partners helps them find ways of talking about conflict so that negativity is kept to a minimum. For those who had difficulty showing affection openly, loyalty, kindness, faithfulness, and sharing counted with their partners (Mackey, Diemer, & O'Brien, 2004).

DOES MARRIAGE HAVE A FUTURE?

Whether marriage has a future depends on the viewpoint you take. From one perspective, marriage is on the decline. Those who believe this point to alarm signals—the growing rate of cohabitation and divorce, the increasing employment of mothers, the raising of children outside marriage, and the pressure to legalize same-sex marriage. These are signs that marriage is becoming deinstitutionalized; that is, that there are fewer norms and values in society telling married people how they should behave (Cherlin, 2004; Coontz, 2004). If we look at the figures, marriage rates are dropping. In part, this is likely the result of delayed marriages, partly because of tighter economic times, partly because of the increase in cohabitation before marriage (Bélanger & Martel, 2003).

From another perspective, marriage is changing to meet the needs of a changing society (Cherlin, 2004). It is moving from a patriarchal, husband-led system to a more egalitarian partnership between husband and wife. Both wage-earning and home and childcare are being shared by more couples. This trend has come about partly in response to economically hard times. In part, however, it also reflects a movement in society to preserve the rights of minorities, including women. The same proportion as in the past eventually get married. The high divorce rate does not necessarily mark the end of marriage itself. Many divorced persons, like the couple in the cowboy wedding, remarry (Bélanger & Martel, 2003). If anything, marriage is valued more highly now than in the past. If there is a marriage crisis, it may arise from valuing it too highly, rather than not enough. Part of the delay in marrying comes from the desire to have everything just right before making a commitment. Part comes from the desire to avoid divorce (Edin, Kefalas, & Reed, 2004; Ellison, 2004; Smock, 2004).

Do the changes in families mean that marriage is on the way out? What of the increase in cohabitation and the demand for same-sex marriage? Marriage still is favoured in law above other relationships (Ellison, 2004). Same-sex marriage is unlikely to undermine marriage as a whole. First, the numbers are relatively small. Second, most same-sex couples choosing to marry are in stable, long-term relationships little different (apart from sexual orientation) from heterosexual married couples (Ambert, 2003; Kurdek, 2004). Cohabitation, because of the many couples involved, has had, and probably will have, a much greater impact on marriage. However, there is little sign, except perhaps in Quebec, that cohabitation will become an alternative to marriage in the near future (Le Bourdais & Lapierre-Adamcyk, 2004; Seltzer, 2004).

Marriage has changed and is changing. The love revolution (marriage for love rather than to meet family and clan needs) started the shift by altering rules and making marriage more satisfying. There is no going back to older ways (Coontz, 2004). Yet, because of the value placed on marriage, there is every likelihood that it will survive.

SUMMARY

MARRIAGE AND SOCIETY. Marriage is not merely a private event. It marks both the legal creation of a family and changes in social status and role. It has been influenced by social factors, such as the availability of clergy, and economic and political factors, such as the Great Depression and World War II. Laws govern whom we can marry and when we can dissolve a marriage. Marriage itself is a contract with implied rights and responsibilities. Formal marriage contracts can be drawn up to modify the financial provisions of family law.

MARRIAGE IN THE FAMILY CYCLE. In the past, marriage marked the transition to adult status; now the change is not so clear. It involves commitment to a new family system and accepting the roles of husband and wife. Couples must renegotiate their relationships with other microsystems of which they are members, such as their families of origin. The degree of separation varies with ethnic group. Over the years, marriage has served a number of functions. It can give both economic and social status, help physical and financial survival, provide both a socially approved sexual relationship and a setting in which children can be raised, and be a source of love and support. We are socialized to believe that marriage is the natural state for adults, and experience social pressure to be like others.

ROLES IN MARRIAGE. Historically, there has been a clear division between men's and women's roles. Among Aboriginal peoples, for example, men were hunters and protectors, and women provided personal care for family members. Among the European settlers, men provided for the family's economic needs, either through wages or farming, and women cared for the household and children. The change to greater equality in roles has been gradual. Married women gradually formed a large part of the paid workforce, especially since the 1970s when many families found two incomes necessary for economic survival. Families usually fall into one of four role patterns: conventional, shared, two-career, and reverse conventional. Both the conventional and the reverse conventional patterns have a clear division of roles between spouses, while shared and two-career role patterns do not make such a strong distinction. In many of these families, however, women are still expected to assume the major responsibility for family care.

UNMARRIED COHABITATION. This is becoming more approved and practised as a lifestyle, especially among younger people and Quebeckers. Although cohabitation resembles marriage, partners have fewer legal rights. Cohabiting couples, on average, are not as satisfied with or committed to their relationship as married couples. Cohabitors tend to share chores more equally than married couples. Although most cohabitors choose not to have children, when they do they are less likely to separate. Couples who lived together before marriage are more likely to divorce, perhaps because they are less traditional in their beliefs. The relationship between same-sex couples is similar to that between heterosexual couples. Same-sex couples who have been in heterosexual marriages may have more complicated relationships.

MARRIAGE AND WORK. The majority of families are two-earner families. Women's choices to be homemakers or have careers depend on the stability of their marriages, on job opportunities, on the ability of their partners to earn enough to allow them to stay at home, and on the level of satisfaction they find in careers and homemaking. Men, however, are not seen as having a similar choice. With two earners, couples may experience the stress of role overload as they juggle jobs, children, marriage, and household responsibilities. Many find that work and family worlds interfere with each other. Some couples try to ensure that the most stressful periods of job and family do not occur simultaneously; in other words, they try to avoid having children as they get established in careers. Difficulties may also arise in balancing the demands of both careers. Particular problems occur when one partner must travel, works long hours, or is transferred. Since dual-earner couples often have difficulty keeping up ties with friends and relatives, they may have low levels of social support.

MARRIED HAPPINESS. Several methods are used for measuring success in marriage, for instance, levels of agreement between husband and wife or positive and negative communication. Marital satisfaction is affected by personal qualities of the partners, by their interactions, and by their extended families and wider society. Happiness appears greatest early in marriage, drops with the arrival of children, is at its lowest point when adolescents are in the house, and increases with the empty nest. Some reasons given for this pattern are the added stress of having more family members and the greater opportunities for disagreement. Long-lasting marriages are not necessarily happy. When they are, couples usually respect each other and have common goals.

KEY TERMS

adultery: the act of having sexual relations with someone other than your spouse (p. 91)

androgynous: being high in characteristics of both masculinity and femininity (p. 106)

common-law union: a union of two partners in a lasting relationship resembling marriage (p. 99)

conventional roles: a marriage with a homemaker wife and breadwinner husband (p. 96)

dual-career roles: a marriage in which both partners are committed to their careers (p. 98)

feminine: a type of personality with a high level of responsibility and concern for interpersonal relationships (p. 106)

marriage contract: a legal agreement between a couple in which they agree to their rights and obligations during marriage or at its end (p. 85)

masculine: a type of personality with a high level of drive and ambition (p. 106)

patriarchal: social organization in which the man is dominant (p. 87)

reverse conventional roles: a marriage with a breadwinner wife and homemaker husband (p. 98)

shared roles: a marriage in which both partners work and share household responsibilities (p. 97)

CLASS ASSIGNMENTS

Complete one or both of the following assignments, as directed by your instructor:

1. Select two television shows that present family life. What roles do men and women play in them? Do you think these roles are typical of society today? Explain.

2. Interview two individuals about the division of responsibilities, chores, and privileges in marriage. Do you feel that their answers are related to their age or cultural background? Why or why not? Compare your information with that gained by your classmates.

PERSONAL ASSIGNMENTS

The following assignments are designed to help you think about your own family experiences:

1. Describe the kind of marriage your parents have, if indeed they are currently married. How has this affected your ideas about the role of husbands and wives in marriage? Why?

2. If you had a marriage contract or prenuptial agreement, what would you choose to include? Why? Would you want such a contract? Give your reasons.

3. What do you think are the greatest challenges marriage faces today? What are the greatest opportunities? Give reasons for your answer.

Part Three

THE EXPANDING FAMILY

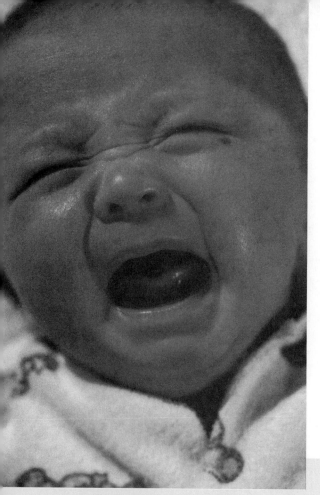

© Comstock IMAGES

Chapter 5

Children—Yes or No?

OBJECTIVES

- To place the decision to have or not have children in the family life cycle
- To look at the historical background of the choice to have children
- To examine possible choices for those who do not want the children they conceive
- To explore options available to those who are childless involuntarily and to consider ethical issues around these options

Daddy and I wanted a little boy so much. We tried and tried, but we couldn't start a baby growing. Then we went to see Dr. Mason. He did lots of tests. He found Daddy didn't have the special seeds that make babies grow and that I didn't have the eggs. We were very sad. So Dr. Mason borrowed seeds from another man and eggs from another woman. He started a baby growing from them in a dish. Then he put that baby inside Mommy in a special operation so it could grow until it was big enough to be born. Mommy and Daddy were very happy. And you know what? That baby was you!

Does this scenario seem farfetched? Not something we talk about, especially with children? We are much more comfortable with the more usual method of producing children, through sexual relations between a husband and wife. This has been the ordinary course of events for millennia. Often in the past, the first child was one of many. Sometimes the success of a marriage was calculated by the number of children a couple had, sometimes by the number of sons.

ENLARGING THE FAMILY CIRCLE

Having a child is a **marker event.** In present-day Canadian society, many of the negotiations of relationships that used to occur at marriage are postponed until the birth of the first child. This may be the first time the parents have to take full responsibility for another person. In a conventional-role marriage, husband and wife have clearly defined roles. When both partners are employed, however, the household and work responsibilities are shared. Once a child is born, husband and wife roles often need to be renegotiated to allow for the child's care (Carter & McGoldrick, 1999b). For young single parents, the transition may mean a shift from childhood to adulthood, from being looked after by parents to looking after a child.

The Social Script

There is still a great deal of social pressure to have children, or to follow the social script. One of the pressures is the myth of motherhood. According to the myth, motherhood is an instinct that can fulfill a woman in a way no other experience can. Of course, much of the notion is true. Bearing and raising a child can provide satisfaction unlike any other life experience. This notion is supported by society in many ways. For example, women who choose not to have children are often considered antisocial or psychologically defective in some way (Douglas & Michaels, 2004). Their marriages are expected to be unsatisfying. An older study of teenagers' hopes for the future found that boys were not worried about possible conflicts between career and family roles; careers came first. Girls, however, wanted children, but felt they would have to do it all alone as wife, mother, and employee, whether or not they were married; they were already worried about priorities (Archer, 1985).

Another part of the myth is the importance of having a child of each sex for a well-rounded family. This expectation is similar to the structural-functional concept of four role types in families—adult male and female, and child male and female. Without all four, the family is felt to be incomplete. This belief accounts for a number of families who have a string of boys or girls before one of the other sex is finally born or adopted.

A minority of unmarried women in their 30s or 40s hear their biological clock ticking and decide to have a child while they still can physically, even if they do not have a husband. Some seek out a temporary partner for the sole purpose of becoming pregnant; others resort to artificial insemination; still others adopt.

Childfree through Choice

In view of the strength of social pressure to have children, why do some couples choose to remain childless? About 7 percent of women and 8 percent of men make this choice. As they approach their mid-30s, only 27 percent of the childless still plan to become parents (Stobert & Kemeny, 2003).

First, they may fear that the husband–wife relationship will be damaged. Once the couple introduces another person into the family, they may not be able to remain as close as they wish. Women may also fear having to give up the equality they have established in their marriage relationships if there are children who require care. Second, some women do not wish to sacrifice a career to which they are dedicated. Having children may mean a conflict between family responsibilities and long hours, travel, or moves for work. Some individuals wish to keep their options open, to be able to change to a job they will enjoy more but that will pay less. The financial commitment a child demands can remove this freedom. Third, some couples want to keep their options open for new experiences of all sorts. Some may look at parenthood as such an experience, but reject it because of the commitment involved. Fourth, the voluntarily childless are more interested in learning about the world than in rearing the young. Finally, some do not have a partner with whom they want to have children. In spite of the growing acceptance of family differences, however, women choosing not to have children do face disadvantages. For example, workplace scheduling may favour those with children. In addition, outsiders may become intrusive, wanting to know why someone remains childless (Burkett, 2000; Stobert & Kemeny, 2003).

THE SHRINKING FAMILY

Before the days of old age and disability pensions, family allowance, and welfare, the family provided almost the only social security system. If it failed, people were dependent on charity. Since many children died, it was important to have a large family so that two or three might survive to look after the parents when they were old or disabled. Feminists add that, until recently, women's economic survival depended on marriage. Men's power over women's sexuality and the resulting children were the price women paid for economic security.

Although the pressure on couples to have children is almost as strong as ever, the size of the Canadian family has been shrinking. The change has not been constant. There have been periods in which the birth rate dropped, during the Great Depression, for example. These were followed by increased levels of childbearing, as in the "baby boom" from 1946 to 1964. Yet the birth rate for women born in the 20th century showed a drop from almost four children to an estimated 2.5 children for those born in 1943 and completing childbearing in the 1980s. The birth rate is continuing to fall (Bélanger & Martel, 2003).

In order to replace the population, each woman must have 2.1 children. Canada has been below this level since 1977. (See Figure 5.1.) The total fertility rate in Canada (i.e., the total number of children a woman is expected to have) dropped to 1.49 per woman, the lowest ever. This followed a slight increase in births in the early 1990s as women who had postponed children gave birth (Bélanger, 1999). The sharpest decline is for women aged 20 to 24, followed by those in their later 20s. The teenage pregnancy rate has also varied. It rose to 44 per 1000 (i.e., 44 of every 1000 teenage girls became pregnant) in the mid-1980s (Klein, 1986). By 2000, it had dropped below 20 per 1000, less than any other under-40 group (Bélanger & Martel, 2003).

The National Longitudinal Survey of Children and Youth, mentioned in Chapter 1, is following children of different ages. Of those born in 1983–1984, 15.4 percent had unmarried parents; the figure for children born in 1993–1994 was 29.1 percent. The greatest increase came for children born to common-law partners. Quebec stands out. In 1993–1994, nearly half the babies were born to unmarried parents (49.3 percent). However, most of these (43.1 percent of all births) were the children of common-law partners, more than double the figure for Canada as a whole (Marcil-Gratton, 1998). As we saw in Chapter 4, the cohabitation rate is higher in Quebec and the relationships more stable than in the rest of Canada.

A number of approaches to increasing the birth rate to replacement levels have been tried or suggested. For example, in the past Quebec offered incentive payments to parents with three or more children ("Baby bonus program works," 1990), but the birth rate showed only a slight increase before dropping again. Others suggest that encouraging immigration of young people who are of an age to have children will help shore up the sagging birth rate and offset the aging population of Canada (Samuel, 1990). In fact, immigration is helping maintain the Canadian population (Bélanger & Martel, 2003). Yet, the birth rate among immigrant women tends to resemble the Canadian-born, the longer they are in Canada (Bélanger & Gilbert, 2003).

Why Is the Family Shrinking?

A number of factors have led to couples choosing to have smaller families, including medical advances, general economic trends, and various psychosocial reasons.

Medical Advances

Medical science has had two major effects on the birth rate. First, infant mortality (i.e., the death of a child under one year of age) declined steadily in Canada since the early 1960s, tapering off recently. Currently the rate is one of the best in the world, lower than that of the United States but higher than that of a number of other developed countries (Statistics Canada, 2004b; Public Health Agency of Canada, 1999). As a result, it is no longer necessary to have a number of children to ensure the survival of two or three. Most children born today in Canada will live to adulthood, if there are no wars or major natural disasters. Second, contraceptives have become more effective since the birth control pill became available in 1961.

Figure 5.1

FERTILITY RATE BY AGE GROUP, CANADA, 1972–2000

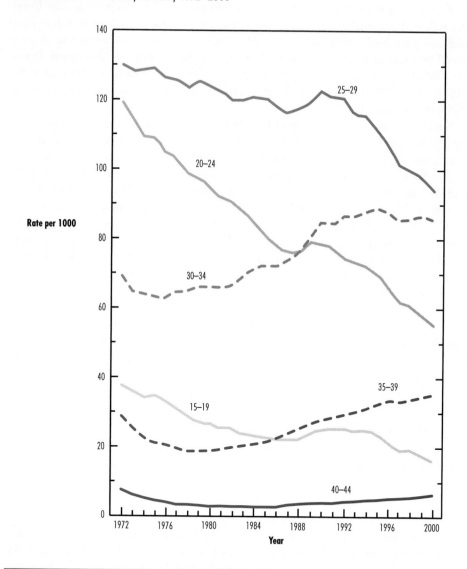

Source: Adapted from Statistics Canada, "Report on the demographic situation in Canada, 2001–2002." Catalogue 91-209, December 23, 2003, p. 34, Figure 6.

Changes in Law

Until July 1, 1969, contraception was illegal in Canada. Under the 1892 Criminal Code, birth control was thought obscene and likely to corrupt morals. In fact, a Toronto druggist was jailed in 1960 for selling condoms. The first family-planning clinics in Canada operated illegally. Many women relied on folk recipes and illegal abortion to control fertility. Since it was perfectly legal, however, to use contraceptive devices to prevent illness or to treat disorders, sympathetic doctors provided many prescriptions (McLaren & McLaren, 1997). The birth rate showed its sharpest drop following the legalization of birth control (Dumas, 1987). The availability of abortion, when a woman's life or health (including mental health) is in danger, was also legalized in 1969. In 1998, the Supreme Court of Canada found the complex procedure required to obtain an abortion was unconstitutional. As a result, abortion was, in effect, no longer criminal (Health Canada, 1998). This change has made it possible to avoid having children after birth control failure. Although the pill was very popular in the 1960s, many couples now use sterilization once they have as many children as they want. Among Canadian married couples, where the wife is over 35, nearly two-thirds are protected by sterilization (Balakrishnan, Lapierre-Adamcyk, & Krotki, 1993).

Religious groups, in particular, have taken positions concerning the morality of these methods of preventing births. Part of the controversy surrounding abortion has been expressed in repeated demonstrations over the past years outside abortion clinics.

Economic Trends

The change in Canada from that of a resource-based economy to a manufacturing-based one has had an impact on the birth rate. Family farms traditionally have depended on child labour. Children were also employed in other resource industries. In the mid-19th century, for example, boys as young as eight years old worked in the coal mines of Nova Scotia and British Columbia. They were important both as a source of cheap labour and as contributors to family income (McIntosh, 1987/88). With time, a combination of cheap immigrant labour, better technology, and school-attendance laws made it difficult for children to participate in manufacturing. Increasing mechanization has further reduced the need for unskilled labour in both food production and manufacturing. Thus children have become a financial liability instead of a resource (Zelizer, 1985).

The birth rate is also connected to national and global economics. During the Great Depression, families became smaller (but see Box 5.1). The economic boom following World War II saw an increase in the birth rate that lasted until the 1960s and produced the baby boom. The inflation and recession of the 1970s and 1980s, with the greater number of women in the workforce, led to smaller families once again (Martel & Bélanger, 1999). Part of this variation in fertility is related to the age at which women have their first child; in boom times it is earlier, and in bust times later. Since women have a limited number of years in which they can bear children, the total number they have is related to the age at which they have the first child and the gap between first and second children (Bélanger & Oikawa, 1999).

BOX 5.1

THE GREAT STORK DERBY

The Great Depression wasn't all doom and financial gloom. In Toronto (and eventually around the world) those years were enlivened by the "Great Stork Derby." On Halloween, 1926 (appropriately), Charles Vance Millar—bachelor, lawyer, and practical joker—died, leaving an eccentric and controversial will. After several smaller bequests, he left the bulk of his estate to the Toronto woman who gave birth to the most children in the 10 years following his death. What had, perhaps, started as a curiosity became vital for two reasons. First, the Depression left many unemployed; those lucky enough to work might make $25 a week. Second, Millar's 100 000 shares in the Windsor/Detroit tunnel project, valued at only two dollars when he died, boosted his estate to $750 000 by the end of the Derby.

The 10 Stork Derby years provided a variety of entertainments. There were updates on the frontrunners, and those mothers became household names. A whole series of court cases added to the suspense. Was the bequest legal? Did the Stork Derby encourage immorality? What exactly were the boundaries of "Toronto"? What about children who hadn't been legally registered? Did stillborn children and those born out of wedlock count? Distant relatives tried to invalidate Millar's will and claim the estate. Ontario proposed using the money for University of Toronto scholarships.

The Derby continued. In the end, the funds were split four ways. Annie Smith, Kathleen Nagel, Lucy Timlock, and Isabel Maclean had each given birth to nine children during the vital years. When two others (Lillian Kenny who had two stillborn children and Pauline Clarke who had several children fathered by a man not her husband) threatened to sue, they were given a settlement of $12 500 each. The Toronto welfare department demanded a slice to repay support given some of the families. Although most winners used the money to benefit their families, Pauline Clarke lit out for Detroit, abandoning her children, and has not been seen since.

Sources: Evasiuk, 1987; Mikkelson, n.d.; Orkin, 1981; Picton, 1989.

The relationship between the economy and the birth rate, however, is far from simple. The recent drop in the birth rate is also connected to women's participation in the workforce. Part of the phenomenon of working wives and mothers is related to the need of families to have two incomes, and to the growth of single-parent families. Since education is more important for employment than in the past, many individuals put off having children until they are through school and able to support them. An American study found that women with college degrees, who had postponed parenthood until after age 30, eventually had more children than similar women with lower educational levels (Martin, 1999). Some career women delay having children until they are well into their 30s and have few childbearing years left. A Calgary study found that women delayed childbearing because they wanted financial independence and economic stability (Altucher & Williams, 2003; Bélanger & Martel, 2003; Benzies, Tough, Tofflemire, Faber, & Newburn-Cook, 2003).

Children are expensive. Including housing and daycare, families spend from 10 percent (Quebec) to 15 percent (Ontario) of their income on the first child (Douthitt & Fedyk, 1990). According to one estimate, it cost nearly $167 000 in 2004 to raise a child to age 18 (Manitoba Agriculture, Food, and Rural Initiatives, 2004). Costs vary across regions. For example, Ontario has higher prices for goods and services and a greater proportion of married women who work. Some of the variation between regions may be accounted for by different standards of what families feel they ought to provide for their children. The increased need to educate children for the technically demanding workplace also places demands on family income.

Psychosocial Reasons

A number of psychosocial reasons are offered in favour of small families. Some of the arguments are similar to those for having no children at all. Having large families places stresses on husband–wife relationships. The potential conflict and stress that arise from dealing with the complexity of relationships can threaten the marriage. As we have already seen, the child-rearing years in a marriage are often the least happy. Socially, having children at a later age has become more acceptable. Such factors are, however, counteracted by the desire of parents for grandchildren and the ticking of the biological clock (Benzies et al., 2003).

Having many children too close together in age may also place a child at a disadvantage. Studies have shown that children in large families tend to have lower intelligence and possibly more emotional problems than children in small families (Parcel & Dufur, 2001). In addition, if resources must be spread among many family members, providing them with the same opportunities as children in small families is difficult.

Individuals who work with people all day may not want to come home to deal with more people. According to the literature on burnout, emotional exhaustion at work leads to irritability and inability to cope with family stresses (Pines, 1996). One former high school teacher explains that she changed occupations because she found it too stressful to deal with teenagers at work, and then go home to more teenagers.

UNWANTED CHILDREN

Many pregnancies are unwanted, including those of both single and married individuals. Basically, an expectant mother has three options: not having the baby, giving the child to someone else to raise, or raising the child herself. Most of the discussion here is concerned with choices made by unmarried women because little information about married women is available.

Until the mid-1970s, unmarried women who became pregnant had to live with the shame of being labelled promiscuous. Few choices were available for so-called fallen women. Life was difficult for both mother and child. Unmarried parenthood was stigmatized. Abortion was illegal, costly, and often dangerous. Often adoption was offered as a form of rescue for both mother and child. The mother could keep her secret and the child did not have to bear the stigma of illegitimacy (Cole, 1984). Due to medical, legal, and social changes, women today have more choices.

Not Having the Baby

The first choice available is not having the baby, in other words, having an abortion. The number of abortions in Canada has increased slowly in recent years (see Table 5.1). In 2000, there was one abortion for every three or four live births. Most were performed on women in their late teens and 20s. In Quebec, there were more than two abortions for every five births, the highest rate in Canada (Bélanger & Martel, 2003). In 2002, both the total number and rate fell slightly (Statistics Canada, 2005c). It is too early, however, to know whether this is a trend or just a slight variation.

Like other aspects of reproduction, abortion has raised many questions. First, the morality of the procedure is related to the moment human life is presumed to begin. Is it at the moment of conception, the moment the child breathes on its own, or some point between these extremes? Second, whose life is to have priority—the woman who is alive now or the fetus that has the potential of living as an independent being? The answer to this is related to the first issue. Third, does a woman have the right to control her own reproductive system? This question has many related issues. Should an adolescent require her parents' consent before having an abortion? Should a wife have her husband's consent? A fourth area involves the timing of abortion. With medical advances in helping premature infants to survive, the time gap between the last date an abortion could be performed safely and the date at which a fetus could survive is becoming shorter. How late should an abortion be permitted? Should access be restricted to the first trimester when abortions are safer and do not raise the question of the potential survival of the child?

Some women are selective about which child they want to give birth to and raise. With greater sensitivity of prenatal diagnosis, it is possible to tell if a child will be born with a chromosomal or genetic disorder. For example, Down's syndrome, a chromosomal disorder that results in low intellectual functioning, can be diagnosed through **amniocentesis,** a procedure in which some of the fluid surrounding the fetus is drawn off through a large syringe and examined under a microscope. We will look in more detail at prenatal diagnosis later in the chapter.

TABLE 5.1

INDUCED ABORTIONS, 1999–2001

	Number of Abortions	Rate per 1000 Women
1999	105 666	15.4
2000	105 427	15.4
2001	106 418	15.6

Source: Adapted from Statistics Canada, "The Daily." Catalogue 11-001. March 31, 2004.

Giving the Child to Someone Else

In the 19th century, when children could be a financial asset, one option for children who were orphans or whose parents could not care for them was to be placed with foster families. In exchange for room and board and some education, the children were expected to assist in the foster household. Many children went from orphanages to these homes, often on farms where boys helped with farm work and girls helped indoors. Usually the families were not well screened, and unfortunate placements occurred. There was very little supervision once the children were in homes. *Anne of Green Gables*, by Lucy Maud Montgomery, is based on a mix-up that occurred when orphanage staff acted on a request sent through a third party. They did no checking up themselves and sent a girl rather than the boy Matthew and Marilla wanted to help with the farm work. Although Anne is a fictional character, many young people in Canada went to work in homes. A large group were sent from England to Canada. The practice of fostering was praised for providing opportunities for young people who had no prospects in England. In reality, however, many children were exploited (Bagnell, 1980).

In such a society, infants were a liability. Abortion was expensive and required connections. Women could get only poor-paying jobs, and welfare was usually reserved for the "deserving poor." In New France during the 1700s, a number of women gave their illegitimate babies to Aboriginal people to raise because they felt this was preferable to exposing them to the elements and thereby allowing them to die (Moogk, 1982). Many children were abandoned. Foundling homes, which were set up to care for abandoned children, had mortality rates of between 85 and 90 percent, partly because of problems with contagious diseases before the days of immunization and the development of modern medicines, and partly because people did not understand the importance of attachment and stimulation to infant development and survival (Rooke & Schnell, 1983). There is continuing concern over abandonment and infanticide. Most states in the United States have enacted "safe haven" laws, naming places where newborn babies can be abandoned, with the hope they will live (Appell, 2002).

Some women, often referred to as "baby farmers," would take unwanted children for a one-time fee and try to place them for adoption. Many of these children died. This led to accusations that baby farmers killed the babies in their care so that they would be able to charge fees over again because they had space for more babies (Zelizer, 1985). More recently, in what has been called the "butterbox babies scandal," a maternity home in Nova Scotia was criticized for selling some babies and letting others die (Cahill, 1992).

By the turn of the century, **foster homes** were seen as the best substitute for the natural home. There was a gradual start of payments to foster parents for children who were hard to place—the very young, the sickly, and those with mental and physical challenges. Eventually, virtually all foster parents received boarding payments to help meet the costs of providing for the children in their care.

Providing foster care until a child was grown used to be possible, but child welfare laws now require early planning and/or periodic review of the child's status, with a view to returning the child to his or her biological parents or finding a permanent substitute family

(Bass, Shields, & Behrman, 2004). Adoption provides such a family. In **adoption,** legal rights and responsibilities are transferred from the birth parents to the adoptive parents. Given improved contraception and greater social acceptance of single mothers, fewer babies are now being placed for adoption. Those single mothers who keep their babies are more likely to come from situations where raising such a child is not stigmatized. In fact, some mothers experience considerable pressure from their peers to raise the child. They also tend to have a deep need for a close relationship, and a desire to demonstrate their love for the child's father or their ability to raise a child. Those who surrender a child for adoption are less likely to come from single-parent homes, are more likely to have professional parents, and are more likely to see adoption as giving their baby a better chance in life (Moore & Davidson, 2002).

Mothers who do make this choice are now offered various degrees of openness in adoption. Often they are able to select adoptive parents. Some agencies arrange meetings; others offer the mother descriptions of several suitable families and allow her to make a choice (Sobol, Daly, & Kelloway, 2000). Usually the decision to give up a child for adoption is extremely painful for the birth mother. Many experience a continuing sense of loss and desire for contact with the adoptee (Fravel, McRoy, & Grotevant, 2000). Extended family members may also experience a similar loss (Ward, in press).

Many children are raised for part or all of their lives by members of the extended family. Although their biological parents may be unable or unwilling to care for them, they may be very much wanted by other relatives. This practice is more common among some ethnic groups than others; for example, Aboriginal people have customarily used the extended family for childcare and informal adoption.

Raising the Child Oneself

The numbers of people who resort to abortion, foster care, or adoption are relatively easy to discover since many are involved with hospitals and social service agencies. But the number who keep and raise unwanted children themselves is impossible to discover. There are several reasons for this. Any child born within a marriage is assumed to be wanted. In fact, though, married women do have abortions and do place their children with other families. But there is a stigma attached to those who do not raise their biological children. In addition, many children who were unplanned and initially unwanted eventually become much loved.

Even knowing the number of unmarried mothers who raise their own children does not provide us with an accurate count, since some women in their 30s or 40s with no opportunity or no desire to marry choose to have a child rather than never experiencing the pleasures of motherhood. Included among these are lesbians who adopt or use new reproductive technologies. In her study of lesbian mothers in Alberta, Fiona Nelson (1996) learned that many women assumed they would have children and being lesbian did not change the situation. The real decision involved how to go about having a child because they could not become pregnant as simply as heterosexual women. Many additional decisions were involved, for example, which partner should have the baby (Chabot & Ames, 2004). Because of stigma against lesbian women in many fertility clinics and because of the cost of having one of the few willing doctors perform artificial insemination, which was not covered under Alberta's health plan, many chose self-insemination. Some lesbians, hiding their sexual orientation, adopt as single women (Slater, 1995). In these cases the child is very much wanted even though the mother is single.

A group virtually ignored are the unmarried fathers who wish to raise their children. Until 1970, they usually had no rights at all, and even today only 2.7 percent of children live with only their father (Dubeau, 2002). Gay men have fewer options for parenthood than women. A few adopt. Some may father a lesbian's child through artificial insemination and become actively involved in parenting, or they may enlist the help of a surrogate mother (Barret & Robinson, 2000).

The unwanted child who is raised by a parent is at risk for physical or emotional abuse (Duffy & Momirov, 1997). In Chapter 14, we will look at this and other factors involved in child abuse.

Single-parent families, who now make up a growing proportion of the population, are discussed in more detail in Chapter 9.

"DESPERATELY SEEKING BABY"

While some parents have children they don't want, others cannot have the children they do want. Infertility can pose a major crisis for a couple. Since our society has as a norm that married couples have children, infertile couples may have a sense of being defective, which reduces their overall sense of self-worth. The medical investigation of infertility is intrusive and often uncomfortable. The couple is asked intimate questions about their sexual activity. Sex may lose spontaneity as the couple plans intercourse when the woman is most likely to be fertile. If the treatment is successful, the woman may experience a very anxious pregnancy because she is afraid to believe she is really going to end up with a baby. If the treatment is unsuccessful, the couple mourns not being able to have children. Often the people around them may not be supportive, because they do not understand the severity of the loss. After all, no one has died. They just didn't exist. The couple is forced to rethink what parenthood really means to them. Should they plan a life without children or find some other way to become parents? (Peoples & Ferguson, 1998).

Usually women feel the lack of children more than men, because they have been socialized to believe that they achieve full worth as human beings only if they are mothers. Their feelings of loss are made worse by others' unthinking questions about childlessness (Peoples & Ferguson, 1998). Men may see their own infertility as an assault on their manhood. Many experience a temporary impotence when they first learn that they are infertile. Many wives experience rage at their husbands. The balance of power in the family may change (Berger, 1980). Fertile partners may feel that if they were married to someone else, they could have children; thus childlessness is part of the price of monogamy. The knowledge that the spouse might have children in another union further undermines the self-esteem of the infertile partner (Butler & Koraleski, 1990). The tests and procedures a couple undergo during a fertility investigation, such as keeping track of when and how intercourse occurred and undergoing tests after having sex, can make them feel as if the doctor is watching them over their bedpost. Sex life can suffer (Pawson, 2003).

In the past, the only choices available to infertile people were to find a child someone else did not want to raise or to remain childless. The options are wider now. They still include foster care and adoption; added to these, however, are the new reproductive technologies.

Foster Care

In the past, families who wanted a child or more children sometimes would turn to foster care. Many children would enter care because of the death of a parent or dire poverty. They would remain in foster care until they reached adulthood; thus fostering involved providing a long-term home for a child. The foster family would receive support payments for the child, who often became a well-integrated member of the family. For many people, this was a satisfactory way of increasing a family. One foster mother, for instance, stated that she and her husband could afford to care for only four children. Once their oldest was independent, they adopted a little girl they had fostered for five years. She was the last of a stream of infants and toddlers who had lived with them.

The trend in foster care, however, is now away from baby care and long-term placements. Advances in medical science mean that children are unlikely to be orphaned, and with the improvement in benefits available for single parents, they are also less likely to enter care because of their parents' deaths or extreme poverty. Instead, they are more likely to be in foster care because they have behavioural problems or because they are victims of neglect or abuse. Children entering care tend to be older than before, and to have many more emotional and physical problems. Foster parents are required to have special therapeutic and child-management skills as well as the ability to be a good parent (Bass, Shields, & Behrman, 2004). Given the problems foster children can bring into the family, and given increased employment of mothers outside the home, foster families are in short supply.

Since foster care is seen as a temporary stop away from home, contact between the children and their birth parents is encouraged so that the move home will be smoother. It is therefore difficult for foster parents to feel that the child is theirs. There is also an emphasis on adoption planning for children who cannot return home. If they want the child to stay, foster parents may have to adopt him or her themselves.

Adoption

For many years, the comfort offered the childless was, "You can always adopt." Unlike foster care, adoption involves the legal transfer of the parent–child relationship to another set of parents.

But adoption was not always seen as a solution. In fact, adoption in early 20th-century North American society was regarded with suspicion. It was feared the child would have inherited "bad blood" from his or her inadequate parents. At this time, adopting children who were somewhat older was considered safer because you could better judge their character. In 1873, New Brunswick became the first Canadian province to pass adoption legislation, followed in 1896 by Nova Scotia. The remaining provinces passed such laws between 1920 and 1930 (MacDonald, 1984). Before that time, birth and adoptive parents might sign an indenture of adoption; this document was not binding and the child could be returned to the biological parents at any time if he or she proved unsatisfactory to the adoptive parents. Frequently, adoptions were informal and without legal protections.

In the 1930s, adoption became more respectable. Agencies tried to place children like those the adopters might have had, matching them for race, religion, and hair and eye colour. Babies were at a premium; there was apparently little demand for older children. During the 1950s, adoption specialists stated that it was in the children's best interests to completely sever ties with birth parents. By 1980 all but two provinces had passed laws declaring that adopted children became for all purposes the children of their adoptive parents (MacDonald, 1984). Original birth records and court records were sealed, even to adoptees, to protect confidentiality (Samuels, 2001).

Environment was felt to be more important than genetics for the development of children. There was also a growing realization that infants need a constant caregiver for the healthiest development. At first agencies tried to place "guaranteed" babies with "ideal" adopting couples; if there was some defect, the child could be returned. Soon, however, parents were forcing changes in agency assumptions and policies. Families might discover that their child had developed severe allergies or had other health problems. Since the parents had already come to love the child, they refused to return the child. Then agencies cautiously began placing children with minor correctable physical problems, then those with more severe difficulties. Now, the definition of an adoptable child is one who is able to benefit from a permanent home (Reid, 1963).

As older children and more children with mental and physical challenges began being placed, it became obvious that nice, childless, middle-class parents sometimes had problems coping with their behaviour. One agency director stated, "We have weird kids, so we need weird parents." The notion of who would make suitable adoptive parents began to change.

Blindness, paraplegia, and unmarried status are no longer barriers. Along with these trends, adoption was advocated as a way of reducing overpopulation. Couples were urged by many articles in the popular press to have only two children to replace themselves and then adopt if they wanted a larger family (Cole, 1984). (See Box 5.2 on multiple sibling adoption.)

While these developments took place, adoption was overtaken by the same factors that helped reduce family size—easy and legal contraception and legal abortion. In addition, unmarried parenthood became more acceptable as the numbers of separated and divorced parents grew. Suddenly in the late 1960s, the supply of adoptable babies dried up, just as adoption was reaching new heights of popularity. Now, couples wanting to adopt a healthy, white baby are in a position of extreme competition, with waiting periods of five years in some places. Due to reduced supply and increased government control, the temptation is high for desperate would-be parents to buy a baby illegally in a black-market adoption (Freundlich, 2000).

During the 1950s and 1960s, intercountry adoptions grew in popularity, especially in Ontario and British Columbia. More recently, foreign adoptions increased from 320 children in 1991 to 2180 in 2003. Most came from China, almost all of them girls, but also some from India, Russia, and other countries. The majority came to Ontario, British Columbia, and especially Quebec, which recorded 918 foreign adoptions in 2003 (Adoption Council of Canada, 2004). Individuals choose intercountry adoption partly because they want to be parents, and because babies are often available from abroad. But many are also concerned about the welfare of children in danger because of war or extreme poverty. Some people, however, see such adoptions as exploitation and imperialism. They also fear political repercussions

BOX 5.2

MULTIPLE SIBLING ADOPTION

Our saga started quite innocently. We thought we needed another boy; we had three daughters and only one son. Adoption looked good. We were delighted with the one girl we had adopted as an infant, and were ready to try a boy a little younger than she was, perhaps aged 5 or 6. We submitted to the usual procedures for approval.

Mother's Day changed everything.

"Let's get them!" said our son as he opened the paper to see "Today's Child," a publication column presenting children needing adoption. Sure enough, there was our little boy, 4½ years old. As a bonus, he would bring his four older brothers.

In about 2 months we were parents of six sons and three daughters, acquiring our first teenager, looking forward to a glorious year with eight teenagers, [and] explaining [to people] our three 7-year-olds, our lifestyle completely transformed.

Source: Margaret Ward, "Full House: Adoption of a Large Sibling Group," *Child Welfare* (1978). Reprinted with permission of the Child Welfare League of America.

from Third World governments that perceive they are being robbed of a valuable human resource (Cole, 1984). In practice, the situation is quite changeable: as some countries have banned foreign placements, others have become new sources of children. Many countries, including Canada, subscribe to the Hague Convention on Protection of Children and Co-operation in Respect of Intercountry Adoption. The Convention sets out principles to protect children and parents and to eliminate profiteering (Duncan, 2000).

Like foster care, adoption still carries a stigma. The blood tie in our society is seen as indissoluble and of a mystical nature. Also, there are numerous accounts of children adopted as infants later finding their "real" parents. It is as if society considers the adoptive parents who have raised them as somehow unreal. One belief in society that devalues adoption has it that the biological tie is important for the bonding of mother and child; therefore, attachment in adoption is regarded as second-best. Adopted children are also seen this way because their genetic heritage is unknown (Erera, 2002). This notion of adoption being second-best makes some adoptive parents feel they are not fully entitled to the child they are raising (Ward, 1979). As a result, they have problems functioning like real parents in areas such as discipline. This emphasis on blood ties and genetic heritage also underlies the recent flood of adoptees seeking contact with their birth parents.

In the 1970s and 1980s, the numbers of all adoptions—of older children as well as of infants—dropped off. In part, this trend parallels the number of children in care (Lipman, 1984). It is also a reaction to figures concerning adoption disruptions (or breakdowns) where the child is removed from the new home. In addition, theories of the importance of early attachments for the child have led to a reluctance to sever birth ties (Steinhauer, 1991). Thus children can be left in foster care, moving from home to home, but retaining contact with a biological parent who cannot raise them. Yet, in spite of the resulting baby shortage, adoption remains an alternative for individuals and couples desiring children.

THE NEW TECHNOLOGY

Some would-be parents dream of having a child who has their own genes. Others do not qualify for adoption. Still others want a child who won't inherit a lethal gene they carry, such as the one for Tay-Sachs disease, which leads to progressive brain deterioration.

Assisted Reproductive Technologies

Such individuals may turn to one of the three basic forms of assisted reproductive technology (ART): artificial insemination, surrogacy, and in vitro fertilization. These have many variations and can be used alone or together.

Artificial Insemination

This new-old method has been around for many years. **Artificial insemination** (AI) involves placing the male's sperm inside the woman's vagina or uterus with a syringe so that she can become pregnant. Donor sperm is used when the husband is infertile or carries a genetic disorder. It has also been used for unmarried women who wish to have children. Since insemination is relatively simple, there are reports of do-it-yourself efforts. For example, in pre-AIDS days, some lesbians wishing to have children used sperm donated by gay men. The technology to freeze sperm allows it to be stored before use, sometimes for years. Some men preserve sperm before undergoing chemotherapy or when they have a terminal illness so that they can father children after treatment or death. In some cases, sperm has been removed from men who are in a coma or even after death (Andrews, 1999; Gosden, 1999). The development of sperm banks allows prospective parents to screen potential donors for qualities they want in their child. One extreme example was the Repository for Germinal Choice in California (now closed), which preserved sperm from outstanding scientists and professionals, including Nobel Prize winners. More than 230 children were born from these donors by women who had been prescreened for intelligence (Goodwin, 2000).

Surrogate Mothers and Host Wombs

When the wife cannot conceive or carry a child to term, some couples turn to **surrogate mothers.** In the simplest form of surrogacy, a fertile woman is impregnated with the husband's sperm and signs over the resulting baby at birth. Historically, surrogacy involved actual sexual intercourse, but nowadays artificial insemination is routine. Surrogacy also permits single men, gay males for instance, to become fathers. In more complex procedures, an embryo is introduced into the surrogate's uterus. This may have developed from the egg of the prospective mother or a donor, fertilized by her husband's or a donor's sperm. In such cases, the situation is called a "host womb" (Gosden, 1999). One much-publicized case involved a mother giving birth to her daughter and son-in-law's triplets (Levin, 1987). More recently, a surrogate mother provided a host womb for quintuplet boys (Fehr-Snyder & Cieslak, 2005).

In Vitro Fertilization

In vitro fertilization (IVF) became news with the birth in 1978 of Louise Brown in England, the first "test-tube baby." This procedure involves removing ripe eggs from the woman's body and fertilizing them with the man's sperm in the laboratory. Two or three embryos are then placed in the woman's uterus with the hope that one will be implanted and the couple will produce a baby. This procedure is usually used when the fallopian tubes leading from the woman's ovaries to her uterus are blocked. Unfortunately, the success rate is only 25 to 30 percent at best. Excess embryos are routinely frozen so that they can be thawed and implanted later if the first try is unsuccessful. Donor eggs have been used when the woman is infertile (following menopause, for example) or is carrying a genetic disorder (Cowan, 2003; Gosden, 1999).

Designer Babies

When prospective parents use reproductive technologies, they can try to create a child with some wished-for characteristics or avoid having one who fails to match their hopes. They may do this by selecting a donor with particular characteristics. For instance, one couple offered $50 000 (U.S.) for a tall, athletic, clever college student to be an egg donor (Kolata, 1999). Or they may try sperm-sorting techniques prior to artificial insemination to improve their chance for a child of the "right" sex (Gosden, 1999).

Diagnosis for Embryo and Fetus

Because the embryo used for IVF develops in a lab dish for the first few days, it is open to examination. With advances in DNA technology, it is possible to test embryos for sex and for a variety of inherited diseases (Gosden, 1999). Several couples have used pre-implantation genetic diagnosis not only to ensure that the child would be free of the disease inherited by their first child, but also would be a tissue match so as to save the life of the first through tissue donation (Verlinski et al., 2004). Scientists are also studying ways to determine which eggs, sperm, and embryos are healthiest. Once a woman is pregnant, with or without assistance, the fetus's development can be monitored through ultrasound, amniocentesis, examination of cells from the placenta, or tests of the mother's blood. The assumption is that a child with a defect of the spinal cord, for example, can be aborted (Gosden, 1999). A few parents have sued when they bore a child with disabilities because they had not been warned of the risk nor offered prenatal diagnosis (Nelson & Robertson, 2001). In cases where the use of fertility drugs or IVF has resulted in a multiple pregnancy, parents may opt for selective reduction, a procedure that destroys "excess" fetuses to allow one or two a better chance to develop. Some couples, when they learn the child is the "wrong" sex, will go to another doctor for an abortion (Gosden, 1999).

Experimental Technologies

In 1997, Scottish scientists announced that they had made a **clone** (i.e., genetically identical copy) of a sheep, which they named Dolly, using a cell from the udder of a six-year-old ewe. Other animals have also been cloned. Theoretically it is possible to clone a human being using the same technology. It may also be possible to combine the cells of two individuals of the same sex to create a child (Howard, 2000). Although laboratory clones are rare, naturally occurring ones (i.e., identical twins) are not. One practical use suggested for clones is to create potential twins for IVF parenthood.

Another technology in the wings is called **germ-line therapy.** Its purpose is to substitute a healthy gene for a defective one, not only to prevent a disorder in one individual but also to pass the healthy genes to his or her descendants. In order to advance knowledge and techniques like cloning and germ-line therapy still further, it is necessary to experiment on animals. If the techniques are to be used for people, human cells and embryos must also be used for experiments (Gosden, 1999).

Social Issues

As McGill University professor Roger Gosden says, "Reproduction is something that individuals do and the rest of society cares about" (1999, p. 5). Conceiving a child is usually a private matter; however, assisted reproductive technologies have opened it to public scrutiny.

Attitudes in society range from condemning all such technologies as unnatural to accepting them wholeheartedly as progress. Most people care to some degree about the ethics of their use. Questions focus on several overlapping concerns.

The Financial Side

ART procedures are expensive and often not covered by medical insurance. Is it right to allow better-off people to have children and deny them to the poor? Will the cost widen the gulf between super-advantaged children (those who have been enhanced) and those who are not? (Gosden, 1999). Also, will payments widen the gap between families with the money to pay and women who provide reproductive services? In some places, large payments are made to egg and sperm donors and to surrogate mothers. Does this amount to baby selling? Some individuals regard paying a surrogate's fee as a type of prostitution because she is paid for the use of her body for sexual purposes. Even if donors and surrogates are banned from making large profits, are they entitled to compensation for their time and discomfort? (Freundlich, 2001). Even in infant adoptions, money can be an issue. In private adoptions, prospective parents must pay for services like home studies. It is also very expensive to adopt a child from abroad (Freundlich, 2000).

Contracts

Lawyers question whether a surrogacy contract can be enforced. Fortunately, such cases rarely arise. In Canada, a birth mother cannot consent to the adoption of her child before a specified time following its birth. This may hold when the surrogate is also the genetic mother of the baby. One well-publicized case was that of "Baby M" in the United States. The surrogate decided to keep the child. The matter was finally resolved, based not on contract law, but on the best interests of the child. Custody was granted the biological father and his wife, who adopted the baby. The surrogate-biological mother was given visiting rights (Freundlich, 2001). What should be the position when the surrogate provides only a host womb and not the egg? Can she be forced to follow certain health restrictions (e.g., no alcohol)? If she doesn't, can she be held liable for damage to the baby? Can contracting parents be forced to assume responsibility if the child fails to satisfy them? In one case, the father and his wife claimed only one of a set of twins—a girl—and refused to take the boy ("Surrogate mother furious," 1988).

Consent

Problems with surrogacy contracts may also involve consent. Did the surrogate truly understand what she was agreeing to? Consent issues arise in other areas. Is it legal, for example, to use sperm or eggs taken from comatose or dead individuals? They are in no position to consent. What of frozen embryos? How long should they be kept? Storage facilities have become overcrowded. Can embryos be destroyed or donated to others without permission from the contracting individuals? What should be done with embryos if the prospective parents both die? Or if the couple divorces and one ex-partner, as has happened, no longer wishes to have a child (Maranto, 1996)? Pro-life advocates insist that embryos are potential human beings and should not be destroyed. Who owns embryos, eggs, and sperm?

Splitting the Parent

In a bizarre case, a California judge ruled in September 1997 that a two-year-old girl had no legal parents and was thus not entitled to child support. She was born following egg and sperm donation and growth in a host womb. The husband, however, did not sign the contract until the surrogate was already pregnant. The couple separated shortly after the baby's arrival. When the mother sued for child support from her ex-husband, he argued he should not be held responsible. The judge's decision was the result. A later decision freed the husband from support obligations and required the wife to adopt the little girl (Freundlich, 2001). This case poses the question, Just who are the parents? In order to discuss the issue at all, we need to develop a new vocabulary, because ARTs have separated conception and pregnancy from parenthood. One proposed set of terms is: (a) *intentional mother and father*, the woman and man who want to have a child; (b) *genetic mother and father*, the woman and man who supply the egg and sperm; (c) *gestational mother*, the woman who carries the embryo and gives birth to the baby; and (d) *nurturing mother and father*, the woman and man who actually raise the child (Hinman, n.d.). In ordinary situations, these different types of parenthood are combined in just one man and one woman. In cases like Baby M or the child without legal parents, where various parent figures are involved, the matter becomes crucial to the well-being of the child. A side issue concerns inheritance rights of children born using frozen sperm or embryos (with or without his consent) following the death of the father (Andrews, 1999).

The Vanier Institute of the Family also raises concerns over the growing use of DNA testing to determine a child's biological father, and refers to a "Genes 'R' Us" attitude. Under Canadian divorce law, an adult who has acted as a parent and treated the child as his or her own is regarded as the child's legal parent, whether biologically related or not. Provincial laws may, however, differ in cases of unmarried and separating parents (Knoppers, 2000). In such cases, as well as those involving ARTs, it is important to protect the welfare of the child. How best to do so depends on the answer to the question, Who is the parent?

The Dream Child

Scientific know-how originally helped couples overcome infertility. Now it can let them choose the kind of baby they want to have through genetic testing of embryos and prenatal diagnosis of disabilities. Questions arise, however, over prenatal diagnosis solely for purposes of sex-selection, as is reported in China and India where males are valued and female fetuses often aborted. There are also concerns about how severe a disability needs to be in order to justify abortion. For instance, does cleft palate, a correctable defect, qualify? There is a danger that what a good life consists of will become narrower. It follows that society may become less tolerant of disability and underachievement (Taylor & Mykitiuk, 2001).

Making designer babies is uncertain in any case. Although there is no scientific follow-up of people conceived through the Repository for Germinal Choice, at least one child experienced learning difficulties (Goodwin, 2000). We all carry genes that, in the wrong combination, can produce surprise disabilities. Genetic accidents and mutations lurk as well. From conception our development is also affected by the environment in which we are set.

Tampering with DNA

In the quest for designer children, scientists have looked ever closer at human genes and the DNA sequences they contain. Now that the human genome has been mapped, even more techniques may become possible. Should cloning be permitted? If so, what will it do to family relationships? Will it put a new twist on the song, "I'm My Own Grandpa"? Germ-line therapy promises to eliminate genetic disorders from a family line. Should this be allowed? Is such manipulation preferable to abortion following prenatal diagnosis? If science is to advance along these lines, it will need to engage in experiments with eggs, sperm, and embryos. Should human ones be used? (Gosden, 1999).

Genetic Information

Although we are not solely our genes—even identical twins differ—most of us value genetic information. For some, it involves life and death. How much information should individuals resulting from ART receive and how best should it be stored? Should donors be warned about being a carrier of a genetic disorder that turns up in a child? For a long time, parents were advised to keep the fact of artificial insemination secret. Some may also hide use of donor eggs or embryos out of a desire to conceal their infertility. Providing genetic information was hampered both by secrecy and by poor record-keeping in the past. Yet social workers point out that family secrets are bad for children. Telling children they are adopted, for instance, is related to better adjustment later in life. Other individuals are concerned that children may grow up without valuable genetic information (Freundlich, 2001; Levy-Warren, 2001).

Individual Rights versus Social Policy

Finally, where should the line be drawn between individual rights and what is good for society as a whole? For example, should the government or some other body decide who can be a parent? Should IVF be available for women aged over 55 years? Life expectancy is increasing and many seniors raise their grandchildren. Should sexual orientation matter? Should payment for procedures be made legal? How should contracts be interpreted? The questions multiply. It is essential to protect family relationships, especially those of children (Shanly, 2001).

The Royal Commission on New Reproductive Technologies and the *Assisted Human Reproduction Act*

As a result of concerns over the many problems and ethical issues surrounding the new reproductive technologies, the federal government created the Royal Commission on New Reproductive Technologies in 1989 to look into these technologies and to make recommendations for policies and safeguards. The Commission issued its report, which contained 293 recommendations, in November 1993. Its major conclusions were that unethical use of reproductive technologies should not be permitted, that regulations are needed to protect all individuals involved as well as society as a whole (Health Canada, 1999). After two attempts, when a proposed law died because an election was called, Parliament passed the *Assisted Human Reproduction Act* (Bill C-6). (See Box 5.3 which provides more information.) Most of the law came into effect on April 22, 2004, with the exception of some provisions that depended on the drawing up of new regulations. It also established the Assisted Human Reproduction Agency of Canada to oversee the whole area (Hébert, Chenier, & Norris, 2004).

INSTANT PARENTHOOD

In the past, before antibiotics were developed, many men and women died young. Stepfamilies were formed as widowed parents remarried. Nowadays such families more often follow divorce than death, with the complication that the children still have a living parent not in the household. With more unmarried parents and divorces than ever before, more people are becoming instant parents when they marry someone with children. The number can be expected to grow in the future.

Being a stepparent has its own particular problems. Although a fuller discussion occurs elsewhere in this book, a few points need to be made here. In some cases, the new partner does not particularly want the children, but is willing to take them for the sake of getting married. In other cases, while the stepparent is willing, the child is loyal to the birth parent and feels that he or she cannot love the stepparent. Stepparents are also hampered by their lack of legal authority over the child, while in some situations they are legally responsible for supporting the child and are considered parents in cases of sexual abuse. Thus society regards them as both parents and nonparents.

SOME ISSUES

A number of issues are common to the following routes toward parenthood: becoming parents of adopted and foster children and of children conceived by birth technologies, and becoming parents in stepfamilies and single-parent families.

The first question is whether a person has a right to genetic information. Such information is denied in many artificial insemination cases. It may also be denied to some children in single-parent families, stepfamilies, adoptive families, and foster families, depending on the will of the parents and the availability of information. For example, an unmarried mother may be unsure of the identity of the father of her child if she had sexual relations with more than one person. On the other hand, she may know his identity but be unwilling to tell the child.

Second, does the individual have a right to have contact with the birth or genetic parent(s)? When divorce has occurred, contact is usually maintained through visiting, or more often nowadays through joint custody. Less often, children whose parents never married have contact with the noncustodial parent, usually the father. At the moment, adoptees

REGULATING REPRODUCTIVE AND GENETIC TECHNOLOGIES

Bill C-6, the *Assisted Human Reproduction Act,* is based on several principles: It is important to protect the health and well-being of children and of women. The use of reproductive technologies must involve free and informed consent. There should be no discrimination based on sexual orientation or on marital status. These technologies should not be commercialized. Finally, the human genome must be protected.

Certain activities are banned; these include

1. human cloning;

2. combining human and animal genetic material;

3. germ-line therapy;

4. use of cells of embryos, fetuses, anyone under 18 years of age, or a corpse, to create an embryo, fetus, or person;

5. sex-diagnosis for sex-selection, except for purposes related to the health of the embryo or fetus;

6. maintenance of an embryo outside the human body after the 14th day following fertilization (excluding time spent in the frozen state);

7. implantation of a human gamete, embryo, or fetus in an animal, and vice versa;

8. advertising and commercialization of any of the above practices; commercialization of surrogacy;

9. commercial transactions involving human genes, cells, embryos, and fetuses.

Source: Reproductive and Genetic Technologies Overview Paper, Health Canada, 1999. Reproduced with the permission of the Minister of Public Works and Government Services Canada, 2005.

and birth parents have no legal right to contact one another. However, voluntary contact once the adopted individual is an adult through provincial adoption-reunion registries is possible. Alberta, British Columbia, and Newfoundland and Labrador now permit adoptees and birth parents to receive identifying information on request, unless either has formally stated that they do not want this information given out. Ontario is also proposing such legislation (British Columbia Ministry of Children and Family Development, n.d.; Canadian Council of Natural Mothers, n.d.; Government of Newfoundland and Labrador, 2005; Legislative Assembly of Ontario, 2005). It is possible to arrange adoptions with varying degrees of openness or contact, but such agreements cannot be legally enforced. For children in foster care, the situation varies. Some children may have frequent contact with biological parents, while others may have none at all. Since artificial insemination is often kept secret, contact rarely if ever occurs. In surrogate motherhood, there may be contact between the surrogate mother and the child. Although some attempts have been made to treat surrogate arrangements as though they were simple adoption cases, this approach tends to break down because of the biological relationship of the father and child. Later contact is probably a matter for the surrogacy contract or the courts.

A third, and important, issue is protection for the child. While some protection exists, it is probably weakest in black-market adoption arrangements and surrogacy contracts. In the former, there is no regulation as to the suitability of the adoptive parents, especially if they choose never to legalize the adoption. In the latter, most surrogacy contracts do not spell out who has responsibility for the child should it be born with mental or physical challenges, or should it not be of the desired sex. A further issue to do with screening prospective parents concerns ensuring that the child enters a reasonably healthy family. Yet any such policy may be discriminatory because similar screening is not required of parents who produce a child in the usual way.

A factor that affects all atypical families is the lack of a social script. Society still considers a married couple and their biological children the norm. From early childhood we learn how biological mothers and fathers ought to act. Yet few norms exist for adoptive parents, foster parents, stepparents, and surrogate mothers. Since these relationships are not the standard ones, there are some areas where social expectations of families do not fit. Consequently, families may feel considerable discomfort that may interfere with their ability to parent the child. They may feel, in fact, that they are not entitled to be parents to the child.

Psychologically, members of these families have all suffered significant losses of some kind. Children have been separated from one or both genetic parents, even if this separation occurred before birth. Infertile parents have lost the ability to have their own biological child. Even fertile parents who have resorted to the new technologies have not been able to conceive in the "normal" way, through sexual intercourse. All members of the family have some degree of pain and a sense of being different with which they must come to terms. There may also be ambiguity about who is considered a family member. For example, is an adoptee considered part of the birth mother's family? Such ambiguity can be a source of continuing stress (Boss, 2002).

THE FUTURE

Experts predict a continuing drop in the birth rate, as more women enter the workforce. They also predict that more couples than ever before will have children because of the new birth technologies available to previously infertile couples. We cannot predict, however, what impact economic factors will have on family size, or what the effects of possible wars and other disasters in the future will be, so any prediction is at best only an educated guess.

SUMMARY

ENLARGING THE FAMILY CIRCLE. Having a child is often regarded as the mark of adulthood. There is much pressure on couples to have children. Since motherhood is considered necessary for personal fulfillment, those who choose not to have children are stigmatized. In fact, these women often have higher levels of career achievement.

THE SHRINKING FAMILY CIRCLE. In the earlier rural economy in Canada, children provided labour for the family enterprise and social security for the elderly. For a variety of reasons, the birth rate has dropped markedly in the past few decades. First, medical advances have reduced infant mortality and provided more effective contraceptives. Second, despite opposition on moral and religious grounds, both contraceptives and abortion have been legalized. Third, economic factors encourage smaller families. Child labour is no longer a part of manufacturing. Poor economic times and women's growing participation in the workforce, as well as the cost of raising children, also foster smaller families. Finally, couples argue that large families may damage the marital relationship and have an adverse effect on child development.

UNWANTED CHILDREN. There are three basic approaches to the unwanted child. First, a woman may choose not to have the baby; that is, she has an abortion. This choice has produced controversies on moral grounds. Second, a parent may give the child to someone else to raise. Often such a child is cared for within the extended family. During the 1800s, many children were placed in work homes, orphanages, and private homes. In time, foster care in which parents were given board payments for the child became more common. Adoption, which involves the permanent transfer of parental rights to other adults, became accepted during the 20th century. A third choice is to raise the child oneself. There is stigma against married people who give up a child. Single-parent families have recently gained wider acceptance.

THE INVOLUNTARILY CHILDLESS. If a couple cannot have children, they may experience stress and loss of self-esteem, both because of their childlessness and because of the investigation and treatment of their infertility. They have several options if they wish to have children. Foster care is still possible, although now it is not usually intended as long-term care and the children are generally older and have more behavioural problems. If a couple wishes to adopt, they face a long wait for a baby; they may choose to parent an older child, one with physical or mental challenges, or one from another country. There is growing openness in adoption, which allows continuing contact with birth parents and the possibility of later contact with adult adoptees. Birth technologies, such as artificial insemination, in vitro fertilization, and surrogate motherhood, offer other choices, although some procedures have a low success rate. Both assisted reproductive methods and genetic technologies have been challenged on moral grounds.

ISSUES. All families in which children are not raised by both biological parents face a number of issues. Does an individual have the right to genetic information about and contact with biological parents? What legal protections are in place for children? What effect does the lack of social script have on these families? What significant losses have family members suffered?

KEY TERMS

adoption: the legal transfer of rights and responsibilities from one set of parents to another (p. 128)

amniocentesis: a procedure in which some of the fluid surrounding the fetus is drawn off and examined under a microscope (p. 126)

artificial insemination: the practice of using sperm from a donor to fertilize an egg (p. 133)

clone: genetically identical copy of a cell or an organism (p. 135)

foster home: a home that provides temporary care for children (p. 127)

germ-line therapy: a genetic technology whose purpose is to substitute a healthy gene for a defective one, not only to prevent a disorder in one individual but also to pass the healthy genes to his or her descendants (p. 135)

in vitro fertilization: the technique of fertilizing a woman's eggs with her partner's sperm in a lab dish, and later placing the embryo(s) in her uterus (p. 134)

marker event: an event that signals a change in status (p. 119)

surrogate mother: a woman who agrees to artificial insemination, usually for a fee, with a view to turning over the resulting child to the biological father and his wife (p. 134)

CLASS ASSIGNMENTS

Complete one or both of the following assignments, as directed by your instructor:

1. Discuss in small groups different options for dealing with an unwanted pregnancy. Design questions for a brief survey. Interview 10 people each and compare your results. Were there any surprises?

2. For a month, keep a scrapbook of stories that appear in newspapers and/or magazines about having children. You may also wish to keep a log of any news stories you hear on the radio or television. What were the main issues?

PERSONAL ASSIGNMENTS

The following assignments are designed to help you think about your own family:

1. If you had your wish, how many children would you have? Why? Would your answer be affected by your marital status? Explain.

2. If for some reason you could not have a biological child, what options would you consider using? Why would you choose to use or not use particular methods of having children? If you would decide not to have a child, give your reasons.

Chapter 6

Bringing Up Baby

© Ryan McVay/Getty Images

OBJECTIVES

- To explain the place of socialization in the family life cycle

- To consider the key role parents play in the socialization of children, both through their own involvement and through their control over children's environments

- To look at the influence of other family members on the socialization of children

- To examine the interplay of society and the family in the area of socialization

The "pacifier" habit—the habit of sucking a rubber nipple—is an inexcusable piece of folly for which the mother or nurse is directly responsible. The habit when formed is most difficult to give up. The use of the "pacifier," thumb-sucking, finger-sucking, etc., make thick boggy lips, on account of the exercise to which the parts are subjected. They cause an outward bulging of the jaws, which is not conducive to personal attractiveness.

Source: Department of Public Health, *The Care of the Infant and Young Child* (Toronto: 1922), p. 30. Reprinted with permission.

A pacifier is helpful for fretfulness or to prevent thumb-sucking.... A baby who has periods of mild irritability can often be entirely quieted by having a pacifier to suck. We don't know whether this is because the sucking soothes some vague discomfort or simply keeps the baby's mouth busy.... Most of the babies who use a pacifier freely for the first few months of life never become thumb suckers, even if they give up the pacifier at 3 or 4 months.

Source: Reprinted with permission of Pocket Books, a division of Simon & Schuster, from *Baby and Child Care* by Dr. Benjamin Spock. Copyright © 1945, 1957, 1976, 1992 by Benjamin Spock, M.D.

Over the years, there has been little change in the physical development of children. All newborn babies need care if they are to survive. Most children sit up before they stand, and stand before they walk. But society has changed in what it thinks is important, and in the kind of behaviour it expects of its members. The use (or nonuse) of a soother is one minor example.

SOCIALIZATION IN THE LIFE CYCLE

Socialization, as was said in Chapter 1, is the process of passing on to new members a culture's ways of thinking and acting. It occurs mainly in childhood. By the time they are adults, people are expected to share the values and norms of society. However, the process does not stop in childhood. Individuals assuming a new role, such as parenthood, or entering a new group, such as a company, are also socialized to some degree. Parents and children shape each other through their interaction (Maccoby, 2003). As infants and children we learn rules for behaviour, for example, that we must not bite our little sister. As young people, we learn how to behave in school and college, and what is expected of us on the job. We learn to be married people and parents. We learn what behaviour is thought suitable for the middle-aged and elderly, and for the separated or widowed. Socialization is, then, a cradle-to-grave process affecting us all.

This learning can occur through explicit instruction, but it occurs most often through the assumptions by which parents and others treat children and adults, and through observation of other people's behaviour. Through learning, individuals develop a sense of their identity, status, and roles in society. They acquire the basic knowledge needed to survive physically in that society, and the skills needed to take part in social life. These differ from one society to another. To take a very simple example, the proper distance to stand from another person varies. In North America, it is farther apart than in Latin American countries. There, people cannot talk comfortably with each other unless they are at about the distance that would be seen here as talking with either sexual or hostile feelings (Hall, 1973).

Socialization of children occurs first in families, beginning with one or both parents, and soon includes other close family members. The circle expands to include more distant relatives, babysitters, daycare personnel, other children, school, television, and many other aspects of society. In this chapter, we will look at family and other social influences on the development of children.

Most theories of the family look at how values and norms of a culture are passed on to new members of the society; in other words, they are concerned about how society reproduces itself. Predictably, some take a macro view. Structural-functional thinkers are interested in how transmission of cultural norms ensures the stability of both families and the society of which they are a part. On the other hand, conflict theorists and feminist thinkers look at the way inequities in society are maintained from one generation to the next. Others approach the topic from a micro perspective, looking at the way family relationships shape individual experiences. This occurs, according to symbolic interactionists, in the day-to-day relationships of the individual members. Systems theorists point to the importance of the family subsystems and boundaries in shaping children.

THE SOCIALIZATION SMORGASBORD

Socialization experiences are something like a buffet. You can eat only what is placed on the table, but you don't need to take everything. Thus the child is presented with a variety of experiences out of which he or she forms an individual identity and value system.

Socialization does not take place in a vacuum. The child participates actively in the process. The levels of physical maturation, intellectual development, and social experiences help determine whether a child can understand and comply with socially approved behaviour (Hall, 1987). For example, toilet training depends on the ability of the child to understand what is expected, as well as on nerves and muscles sufficiently mature to control elimination. Similarly, if a child cannot "read" social cues, he or she cannot respond appropriately to them. This failure may be the result of a problem such as impaired vision or hearing, or delayed intellectual development, or because of a lack of familiarity with the particular cultural norms. The child's developmental stage also affects his or her ability to profit from experiences. In general, a child needs to move from a close relationship with one or two people to interaction with a widening social circle. The ability to profit from peer relations or school experiences will depend on the child's developmental stage (see Table 6.1). Children also make choices about their behaviour. This fact helps explain why children from the same family can turn out to be so different.

WHAT ARE CHILDREN WORTH?

How we socialize children reflects what we expect of their future. It also reflects the value we place on them. If we feel children are an economic resource for the family, child labour makes sense, especially if the family needs the money to survive. If we value the closeness and love

TABLE 6.1

CHILDREN'S DEVELOPMENTAL STAGES AND EXPANDING WORLD STAGES

Developmental Stages	Psychosocial Crises	Radius of Significant Relations
Infancy	Basic trust vs. basic mistrust	Maternal person
Early childhood	Autonomy vs. shame, doubt	Parental persons
Play age	Initiative vs. guilt	Basic family
School age	Industry vs. inferiority	Neighbourhood, school
Adolescence	Identity vs. identity confusion	Peer groups

Source: *The Life Cycle Completed: A Review* by Erik H. Erikson. Copyright © 1982 by Rikan Enterprises, Ltd. Used by permission of W. W. Norton & Company, Inc.

children can bring to parents, we will emphasize the emotional development and sensitivity of the children.

In Canada's early years, children were often employed. Those living on farms shared in daily chores and other farm labour. In cities, children helped in home-based businesses such as boarding houses. They also delivered laundry and meals. Boys worked in street trades: polishing shoes or selling newspapers and fruit. Some were their parents' only support (Bullen, 1992). One report showed that as recently as 1882 many children aged 5 to 15 were still working in manufacturing, and some as young as 2 had been hired in the past (Kieran, 1986). These were not safe and easy jobs. One twelve-year-old lost his arm and leg in a mill accident; his employer gave him $10 compensation and paid his hospital bill but not his doctor's bill. Gradually fewer children were hired. Better technology, cheap immigrant labour, and compulsory school attendance combined to reduce paid child labour (Gaffield, 1982).

The 20th century saw the arrival of the economically worthless but emotionally priceless child, who was expected to provide emotional satisfaction for the parents (Zelizer, 1985). Being a mother was seen as "the greatest duty allotted to womankind" (Department of Public Health, Toronto, 1922, p. 3). As medical science advanced, experts offered advice to mothers on how to raise healthy children. The idea that the scientific method could be applied to human behaviour produced experts on child rearing. Most of the experts' theories were based on observations of white middle-class children. In the past, women had sought advice from their mothers and other women experienced with children; now, traditional methods were devalued by professionals who claimed to know better. Parents' anxiety over child rearing has also increased (Stearns, 2003).

This intrusion into family life by experts affected poor and minority families, especially those receiving welfare. Professionals would visit such families to ensure that funds went only to the deserving poor. If childcare methods did not conform to "scientific" standards, families were subjected to often unwanted advice. If they did not comply, they could lose their children. This still holds true in cases of child abuse and neglect. The case of the Dionne family and their quintuplets was one of the most publicized examples of intrusion by professionals (Nihmey & Foxman, 1987). The children were made wards of the province, were separated from their parents, and were raised according to the best standards known to experts in Toronto. These standards, however, went counter to all the traditions of the rural French-Canadian society to which the family belonged. Eventually the children were returned to the care of their parents, but there was a gulf between their early socialization and the values and customs to which they were now expected to conform. Only quite recently has the public focused on the thousands of minority, especially Aboriginal, children separated from their biological families in boarding schools and foster and adoptive homes (Waterfall, 2003).

Childhood came to be regarded as a special time, and was increasingly differentiated from adulthood. This process led eventually to the development of specialized children's institutions. Children attended school regularly to help provide a much-needed skilled and educated labour force. Special recreational and medical facilities were created for children. The training school, a combination prison and educational facility, was established to teach out-of-control and criminal children socially approved behaviour. Children were given their own courts. Increasingly, children were segregated by age group. For example, the one-room school gave way to larger institutions with one or more rooms for each grade. Since it was recognized that children could not easily protect themselves, pressure was put on the government to protect children from exploitation by adults and mistreatment by parents. Currently, there seems to be a reversal of this trend, especially in the United States, in the thrust to try children who have committed serious crimes in adult court.

PARENTS—THE FIRST SOCIALIZERS

Parents are the single most powerful influence in the socialization of their children (Tesson, 1987). This is especially true during the early stages of development. They directly influence their children both by who they are and through day-to-day interaction. They also exert indirect control over a great deal of their children's environment. For example, by selecting the neighbourhood in which they live, they will affect who will form their children's peer groups.

Family Structure

The number, marital status, sex, sexual orientation, and age of a child's parent-figures help to shape the child. So do the relationship of the person acting as a parent, and the stability of the family over time. The traditional husband-wife family, as we have seen, is becoming more the exception than the rule. A parent at home with a child may be father instead of mother. With the increasing rates of both divorce and remarriage, more children are growing up with one parent, or with an unrelated parent-figure, in the home. The majority of married women work for pay and may depend on others to care for their children. Thus, more and more, the adults who care for children may not be their biological parents. A significant number of children have only one caregiver. Children who grow up in two-parent families, one-parent families, and stepfamilies have different socializing experiences. So do children with same-sex parents. We will look at single-parent, divorced, and remarried families in later chapters.

Several cross-sectional studies give us a snapshot of children's families at one point in time. For example, the General Social Surveys of 1995 and 2001 show us how family composition has changed from one point to the next (see Table 6.2). However, they do not show us the changes individual families go through. For example, we can track the number of children living through their parents' divorce. But if we ignore the formation and breakup of cohabiting families, we do not get a true picture of the family instability some children experience (Raley & Wildsmith, 2004).

How Well Are the Children Doing?

A growing number of studies have looked at how children fare in different types of families. Researchers have used a variety of criteria to determine how well children do. These include school performance and plans for higher education, level of delinquency, early first sexual experience and teen parenthood, risk of later divorce, and relationship with parents (Davis & Friel, 2001; Jeynes, 2002; Parke, 2003; Teachman, 2002).

TABLE 6.2

FAMILIES BY FAMILY STRUCTURE, 1995 AND 2001

Family Structure	1995	2001
Couples with no children	36.4%	37.9%
Couples with children	49.8	48.6
Intact families	44.6	42.9
Married	41.9	39.1
Common-law	2.7	3.8
Stepfamilies	5.1	5.7
Married	2.6	2.9
Common-law	2.5	2.9
Blended families (his/hers/ours)*	1.9	2.3
Her children	2.6	2.9
His children	0.6	0.6
Total married couples with children	44.5	42.0
Total common-law families with children	5.3	6.6
Lone-parent families	13.8	13.5
Male parent	2.0	2.4
Female parent	11.7	11.1

Source: Adapted from Statistics Canada, "General Social Survey Cycle 15: Family history, 2001." Catalogue 89-575, July 11, 2002, p. 5, Table 1.

*Blended families can consist of children in common or no children in common (his and hers).

On average, children living with both biological parents who are married to each other do the best, with adoptees with married parents coming a close second. Children have more difficulties if they grow up with never-married, divorced, or remarried parents. (See Box 6.1.) Cohabiting families, whether with both biological parents or a stepparent, also tend to have more problems. Children living with neither biological parent (not counting adoptees) have the most difficulties (Brown, 2004; Carlson & Corcoran, 2001; Feigelman, 2001; Le Bourdais & Lapierre-Adamcyk, 2004; Manning & Lamb, 2003; Parke, 2003; Sun, 2003). A few small studies have looked at the well-being of children with lesbian parents; they do at least as well as those in single-parent families. While they may be more open to sexual exploration, they are not more likely to be homosexual than the general population (Laird, 2003). Yet, most children in nontraditional families grow up without major problems. According to one calculation, about 10 percent of children living with married biological parents have serious problems, while 20 percent of those in single-parent or stepfamilies do—twice the level. Looking at it another way, 80 percent manage quite well (Greene, Anderson, Hetherington, Forgatch, & DeGarmo, 2003).

BOX 6.1

PARENTS AND THE SHAPING OF A CHILD

Caleb had several strikes against him when he was born. His parents weren't married and had an on-again, off-again relationship. The pregnancy was diagnosed late, only two months before his due date, and was an unwelcome surprise.

He weighed just 2.5 kilograms when he was delivered three weeks early. Right away, medical staff detected problems. He sucked poorly and showed no persistence in feeding. Even months later, he snacked frequently rather than settling down to a regular schedule of meals. He was more irritable than most newborns and hard to comfort. His nose and ears looked a little odd. These were clear signs he had been hurt by his mother's binge drinking during her pregnancy. His development would probably be filled with problems, including learning and behavioural difficulties.

The local child protective services were called in. They allowed Caleb to go home with his parents only on the condition that his mother stop drinking. Before long, however, a surprise checkup visit caught her with alcohol on her breath, so Caleb was taken to a foster home. Though he was soon sent back home again, within a few months his parents' relationship had fallen apart and Caleb was once more in foster care.

The search for a home with relatives was futile. His grandmother felt she was too old: she would be in her 80s before he was an adult. Caleb's aunt already had a baby just a month older than Caleb, and felt she couldn't do justice to her own daughter and a child who needed special care. Finally, the family court terminated the rights of Caleb's parents, and child welfare services found an adoptive family who could meet his needs and would be willing to care for him despite his uncertain future.

What Accounts for Differences in Child Well-being?

No single explanation accounts for differences among families. In part, this comes from the fact that families in a single category are actually quite different. For example, single-parent mothers vary by age, by the route to single parenthood (unmarried, separated, divorced, widowed), by life experiences before and after becoming a parent, and by the length of time single parenting lasts. A number of explanations are suggested by scholars. Risk factors for children include conflict between parents, poor parenting quality, separation of parents when young, lack of contact with nonresidential fathers, and the mother's psychological health. In addition, boys tend to have a harder time than girls (Carlson & Corcoran, 2001; Leon, 2003; Parke 2003). Let's look at some of these factors.

Being male brings risk in childhood. We considered some differences in Chapter 2. In addition to those, more boys die in infancy and childhood, and more are involved in delinquent behaviour than girls. Women also tend to live longer than men (Fitzgerald, 2003; Statistics Canada, 2004b; Statistics Canada, 2004g). Boys are more vulnerable to life changes as well (Parke, 2003).

Children who experience a great deal of conflict between their parents also fare poorly. This is true for families where biological parents are married as well as for cohabiting and stepfamilies. Adolescents with divorced parents, for example, do not do very well if they are caught in the middle of parents' battles or tugs-of-war. In fact, children often do better once high-conflict parents separate (Johnston & Roseby, 1997; Parke 2003). One study found that interactions within families have greater impact than family structure by itself (Lansford, Ceballo, Abbey, & Stewart, 2001), reflecting a symbolic-interaction rather than a structural-functional perspective.

The quality of parenting children receive affects their well-being (Parke, 2003). This is partly related to conflict levels within the family and partly to the mother's psychological health (Carlson & Corcoran, 2001). One notion is that children are better monitored if they live in two-parent families. There is no evidence, however, that the degree of supervision is related to the well-being of children in different types of families (Lansford et al., 2001). Parenting style, which we will consider in more detail later, is also important. Because of the lack of social script, nonbiological parents may have difficulties with discipline. Issues concerning the relationship of children with biological and nonbiological parents have been studied most thoroughly in adoptive families. Because adoptive parents are perceived as somehow not as genuine as birth parents, they may have difficulty believing that they are really entitled to be parents to their adopted child. As a result, they may have difficulties with discipline. Some are very strict and authoritarian because they feel they must be extra-good parents. Others are very permissive, or sometimes inconsistent, because they are afraid of losing their child's love (Ward, 1979). One adolescent adoptee, for example, regularly threatened her mother with, "If you don't get me those expensive boots (or let me go out with the kids, or …), I won't love you anymore." Her mother almost always gave in. Divorced parents tend to spend less time with their children. They also tend to have fewer rules but use harsher discipline than parents who stay married. In addition, when mothers confide financial problems and complain about their ex-husbands to their daughters, the children have more difficulties (Amato, 2000; Koerner, Jacobs, & Raymond, 2000; Simons, Lin, Gordon, Conger, & Lorenz, 1999).

The history of the current relationship affects children's development. Is this the first family the child has known? The second? Or more? Is the parents' relationship stable? Have there been repeated separations and continuing fights? When children become attached to parents and then have to move, they need to mourn the separation. Separation can also lead to acting-out behaviour. One study found that adolescents who were particularly satisfied with the relationship with their same-sex parent before separation were more likely to become delinquent after that parent moved out (Videon, 2002). Lack of contact with nonresidential parents also can result in problems (Parke, 2003). Separation and lack of contact with the same-sex parent affects more boys than girls because custody is more often granted the mother. If there are too many separations, children may fear becoming attached again. This is one of the problems with repeated moves in foster care and adoption (Fahlberg, 1981; Reitz & Watson, 1992). The impermanence of relationships can also affect children who belong to one stepfamily after another (with the parents either married or cohabiting).

Children in poor families and those living in disadvantaged neighbourhoods do not do as well as those in better-off families and communities. Single parenthood, separation, and divorce often mean a loss of income. As a result, families may be forced to move away from friends and other social supports into areas with poorer quality housing and higher crime. Children experience less favourable peer influences in such areas (Carlson & Corcoran, 2001; Crowder & Teachman, 2004; Sun, 2003). Poverty, stressful life events like unmarried motherhood or separation, and low quality of parental functioning all work together to create less favourable environments for children (Anderson, 2003).

Although not as well studied as risk factors, there are also factors that protect children from the disadvantages of nontraditional families and family disruption. Home and school environments that are warm and have structure and clear rules help children flourish. So does a parenting style that is warm and structured, while allowing for the child's individuality. Peer support is also important when children are going through family crises (Kelly & Emery, 2003; Leon, 2003; Rodgers & Rose, 2002).

Parents' Age

The age at which parents have a baby has a strong influence on the child's development. Two extremes—very young parents and "late" parents—will illustrate.

Adolescent Mothers

Very young single mothers face a high degree of stigma (Erera, 2002). Many studies have shown that, while individual adolescent mothers may manage quite well, their children are at risk for developmental problems. First, pregnancies of young teens are highly risky: babies are more likely to be premature and small. Second, very young mothers may not have the financial and social resources to overcome the physical disadvantages. Third, to develop best, a child needs a stable, loving relationship with two parents, or a parent and grandparent, as well as attention by other caring adults. Adolescent development in many ways is the opposite of what is needed for good parenting. Teens are finding their own identity and, in the process, may become impatient with limits on their activities. Babies are very limiting (Zabin & Hayward, 1993). Many adolescent mothers live with their parents. In some cases, grandparents are understanding and helpful. In other cases, disagreements may arise concerning authority and control as grandparents take over infant care out of concern for the baby's well-being. The question then becomes "Whose child is this?" The young mother either gives in or rebels. If she rebels, she may pull out of looking after her baby or she may move out, taking her child with her (Anderson, 2003; SmithBattle, 1996). In either case, the baby loses a parent figure. Living with parents can be conflict-filled and poor for both the young mother's development and her child's. Teen mothers living in romantic relationships are less harsh with their children than other young mothers. It may be that more competent and well-adjusted young mothers live with a male partner (Abell, Dorr, & Guarino, 2003).

"Late" Parents

More women are now having their first children after they are 30 years old (Bélanger & Martel, 2003). According to one American study, childbearing delayed until after age 30 increased most for university graduates; more also had a second or third child. These women were more likely to be in stable marriages and to be employed (Martin, 1999). Thus their children had the advantages of a stable home, and favourable income and neighbourhood environment. Because older women are less fertile than younger ones, they are more likely to turn to reproductive technologies. As a result, they are at risk for multiple births. Such babies are often premature and more likely to have problems in development like cerebral palsy (Luker, 1996). Others have "caboose" or "afterthought" children through carelessness or as a child of a second marriage.

How does older parents' child rearing differ from that of younger parents? Studies of children and fathers suggest that such parents are less physically active. Instead, they are likelier to spend time reading and playing pretend. Because mature parents are more apt to be financially stable, they can often take the time for outings, to museums or football games, for instance. Children in such families may fear their parents will die. Yet, they enjoy both having money for luxuries and spending fun time with their parents (Morris, 1987; Pruett, 2000). Some late-born children may actually have much more adult attention than children in the family born earlier. (See Box 6.2.) One mother reports that her caboose son thought he had six parents, including his four older siblings. One day he asked why his oldest sister called their mother "Mom," and was shocked to discover that his mother was his sister's mother too. It is possible that with more women delaying childbearing, having older parents will not be regarded as being so different in the future.

Day-to-Day Interaction

Parenting Style

The day-to-day treatment of children has long-term effects on the child's development. Diana Baumrind (1980, 1996) describes three types of parenting styles: authoritarian, permissive, and authoritative. **Authoritarian** parents are the drill-sergeant type. Children are expected to obey without question. These families are strong on obligations and responsibilities, but weak on recognizing children's individuality or their need to learn to make decisions for themselves. Often authoritarian parents rely on a punitive discipline style, where they scold, yell at, or physically punish children. Punitive discipline leads to children's aggressive behaviour (Thomas, 2004). Such parents also tend to believe that misbehaviour comes from their children's nature rather than from other causes (Coplan, Hastings, Lagacé-Séguin, & Moulton, 2002). Children growing up in such families tend to become either submissive and unable to make decisions for themselves or defiant and rebellious. A vicious cycle can arise in some families whereby children are defiant, parents become punitive, children hang out with a delinquent or drug-using group, parents become harsher, and so on (Simons, Chao, Conger, & Elder, 2001). It is difficult to know which came first—the defiance or the discipline. Adolescence will probably be a particularly difficult time for such families.

Permissive parents are at the other end of the scale. They recognize children's individuality and their right to make decisions for themselves, but they do not set limits or assign responsibilities and obligations. Children from these families may fail to recognize rights of others and may not develop self-discipline. As a result, they may live aimless and disappointing adult lives.

Finally, **authoritative** parents take a middle position. They have high expectations of their children, but they are also aware of their children's needs and are willing to adjust demands to their interests and abilities. Children from these families are often described as achievers, and as being competent and friendly (Baumrind, 1980). Positive interaction between parents and children, combined with consistent parenting (the hallmarks of the authoritative parent), improve children's social relationships. This is especially true for children who experience risk factors like poverty, lone-parent families, or divorce (Kelly & Emery, 2003). Regardless of family structure, high standards for behaviour and monitoring children's activities, combined with warm supportiveness and avoidance of harsh punishment, result in the most positive child well-being (Amato & Fowler, 2002). Indeed, when parents switch from punitive to nonpunitive parenting, children become less aggressive (Thomas, 2004). Nevertheless, authoritative parenting is not the only style that leads to children's social success. In certain societies, Asian for example, authoritarian parenting, combined with high levels of interest and encouragement, is the norm, and parents in such cultures who use this style do raise children who do well (Chao, 1994; Harris, 1995).

Recently, spanking has drawn attention and criticism. In Ontario, at least, a parent who spanks a child in public is at risk of being charged with child abuse. On the other hand, some popular authors advocate spanking, often based on strict religious beliefs. Research shows that spanking is probably less effective in changing children's behaviour than nonviolent forms of discipline. In fact, spanking, as part of a punitive parenting style, can increase behavioural problems (McLoyd & Smith, 2002). In addition, it teaches children that hitting is the way to solve problems. At its worst, spanking can escalate into child abuse (Pitzer, 1997).

An interesting approach to parenting is Ada Alden's (2004) concept of "red yellow green." The colours are based on traffic lights: red signals indicate "stop" and "danger," yellow "caution," and green "go ahead." All are related to parents' expectations and children's behaviour. Both red and green areas are parent-controlled. Red areas are no-nos and include safety issues, such as playing in supervised areas, as well as unchangeable family rules, like no name-calling and no drug use. The green area marks parents' approval. It provides guidance to children and reassures them that they have done well. Yellow is child-controlled and involves areas where the child makes decisions. At first this is rather limited, as in the choice between two outfits, but increases as the child matures. Parents can emphasize red (authoritarian) or green (permissive). The best outcomes for children occur when the three areas are kept in balance (authoritative).

Family Atmosphere

The general atmosphere in families vitally affects child development and socialization. For example, researchers could predict how well children would manage socially by the degree to which parents expressed their feelings (Boyum & Parke, 1995). Most studies, however, have looked at conflict levels in the family. The amount of conflict between parents and teenagers is related to how warm and supportive parents are. If they are hostile and authoritarian, the conflict tends to escalate. If parents are supportive, family relations improve over the teen years (Rueter & Conger, 1995). Part of family atmosphere is created by the parents' own relationship. Conflict between parents increases children's risk for adjustment problems in several ways. Destructive tactics during conflict, such as yelling, name-calling, threatening, and withdrawal, distress children. Children in families with negative tactics may feel more threatened by disagreements and are more likely to blame themselves for their parents' problems than those whose parents use more constructive tactics. In addition, parents with high levels of conflict are more likely to use harsh discipline and less likely to be involved with their children, for example, by reading or playing (Buehler & Gerrard, 2002; Cummings, Goeke-Morey, & Papp, 2003; Grych, Harold, & Miles, 2003). Parents who discuss issues calmly and show support and affection for each other may actually increase their children's sense of security. The chance of behaviour problems is therefore reduced (Cummings et al., 2003). Parents' conflict style seems to affect children both through parents' actual behaviour and the way children perceive and interpret that behaviour (Buehler, Krishnakumar, Anthony, Tittsworth, & Stone, 1994).

Family Routines, Rituals, and Traditions

Socialization comes from both everyday aspects of living and special occasions. Routines usually involve little conscious thought and occur frequently, often daily (Fiese et al., 2002). These include bedtime routines like tooth-brushing. One research project done some time ago discovered that middle-class families used dinnertime as an opportunity for teaching acceptable social behaviour such as manners. Democratic values were, to some degree, also demonstrated, as children and parents alike talked about their experiences during the day (Dreyer & Dreyer, 1973). Families that have extremely limited space or are so involved in outside activities that members are rarely all home at the same time will have quite a different view of proper mealtime behaviour.

Rituals are events that tell families, "This is who we are." They can be individual family events, like all sitting down together for Sunday dinner. Rituals that occur less frequently around some particular event, such as Hanukkah or Thanksgiving, are called traditions. Both rituals and traditions can weave families and kin together (Fiese et al., 2002; Kirkwood & Engelbrecht, 2002). Unfortunately, because they have so much meaning for families, traditions can also be the source of conflict between generations or between ex-partners.

Family story traditions also help shape children. The events that are remembered and retold often encourage family values by emphasizing heroes or villains (Stone, 1988). Sometimes themes are repeated. For instance, one family told again and again the story about all the young men who ran away from home to make their fortunes in another country. This has given permission to youth in successive generations to move away from their family of origin, yet they keep their family identity because of the story traditions.

Family time has declined. As a result, some routines and rituals, such as family dinners, are disappearing. Studies have found that reduced family time results in poorer child adaptation (Doherty, 1997).

Parents' Education and Employment

The jobs parents hold affect the home in several ways: hours worked, work demands, and income. Parents in occupations requiring a higher education are more likely to be employed and have fewer breaks in work (Parcel & Menaghan, 1994). They also tend to receive higher pay. Parents' income can affect the area in which a family lives. Canadian children in affluent neighbourhoods, it has been found, score higher on tests of school readiness than children living in poorer areas (Kohen, Herzman, & Brooks-Gunn, 1998). The school, recreational facilities, and peer groups are different from one part of a city to another, and from one part of a province to another. Income also determines, in part, how children are dressed and what activities they might take part in. For example, music training or competitive sports requires lessons and/or expensive equipment as well as additional transportation costs. Clothing and activities can affect the peer group with which a child associates. Children from poorer families do not do as well in school, on the average, as children from wealthier families. The difference does not show up during the school year. Rather, when school is closed, children from homes with greater economic resources make more progress than others. This is probably the result of the enrichment activities available (Entwisle & Alexander, 1995). Differences also extend to television use. When parents have a lower educational level, their preschool children tend to watch more entertainment programs and have less contact with books than when parents have more education. Later school performance is related to early experiences with books (Huston & Wright, 1996).

The impact of jobs does not stop at income. When parents, both mothers and fathers, have complex occupations, children do better in school. Complex work provides a variety of tasks and involves qualities such as people skills, knowledge, and the ability to deal with changing circumstances—teachers, doctors, and business managers rather than dishwashers and low-level data entry clerks. American researchers have also found that employed mothers tend to be authoritative with their children, a parenting style leading to academic and social success. The advantages of having parents in more complex occupations are less when money and time are stretched to care for a large family or a new baby (Hoffman & Youngblade, 1999; Parcel & Menaghan, 1994).

ETHNIC AND RACIAL GROUPS

Issues concerning parent–child and other family relationships of immigrants and minority groups have been discussed elsewhere (see Chapter 2 and other sections of this chapter). As for Canada's two major cultural groups, apart from language, what differences are there between francophone and anglophone families? What have been the experiences of Aboriginal families?

How Different Are English Canadians and French Canadians from One Another?

Few studies have compared the way English Canadians and French Canadians raise their children, and most of these are old. One group of researchers did look at families of both cultural groups in Montreal (Smith & Grenier, 1975; Taylor, Frasure-Smith, & Lambert, 1978), but their findings may not be typical of the rest of Canada. They discovered that the families were more alike than different. However, they did find that English-speaking Montrealers encouraged their children to be more independent in solving problems than French-speaking Montrealers did. Anglophones also tended to restrict their children's contact with friends and to treat their children more harshly. French Canadians encouraged in-group ties (i.e., ties with their own social and family group) and tried to develop their children's reliance on the extended family. Since these studies are over 20 years old, however, they do not reflect the recent strength of the nationalist movement in Quebec and any effect it may have on family relationships.

One study looked at the language children learned at home when parents had different mother tongues. Outside Quebec, 79 percent of children with English- and French-speaking parents learned English first. In Quebec, 49 percent with French- and English-speaking parents learned French first, 34 percent learned English first, and 17 percent learned both. Thus both the language spoken by parents and the language used in the community affected children's learning (Turcotte, 1993).

A 2004 survey by the research company Ipsos-Reid, with CTV and *The Globe and Mail*, found that Quebec parents are less likely to spank their children than parents in other provinces (25 percent in Quebec versus 60 percent in Alberta). About 60 to 70 percent of parents in most of Canada believe using flashcards will make their babies smarter, while only 25 percent of Quebec parents agree (Anderssen & McIlroy, 2004; Ipsos-Reid, 2004).

Aboriginal Families

In Chapter 2 we have already discussed a number of factors that affected the family life of Aboriginal peoples. Boarding schools broke up families and eroded traditions. This disruption has been blamed for many problems. Welfare dependency became the only way of survival for many families. The loss of their children to non-Aboriginal families and institutions added to their despair. Alcohol, which was introduced by white traders, became a way of temporarily escaping the hopeless situation. In turn, however, alcohol made matters worse. The growth of a new Aboriginal awareness is helping create family health (Castellano, 2002; Ward, 1988; Waterfall, 2003).

THE WIDER FAMILY CIRCLE

Parents have considerable control over the relationships of children with other family members. For example, parents decide how many children to have. They influence how often children see grandparents and other relatives. Of course, their control is greater for younger than for older children.

Brothers and Sisters—Friends, Foes, and Teachers

Sibling relationships are the least studied of nuclear family relationships (Feinberg, McHale, Crouter, & Cumsille, 2003). Yet they are important to children because they are unique. Brothers and sisters are family members, but they do not have the kind of authority parents have over younger children, unless they are much older or the parents have failed in the care-giving role through neglect, illness, substance abuse, or some other physical or emotional absence. In many ways the sibling relationship is similar to the peer relationship in that it is more egalitarian than that between parents and children. There are, of course, wider age spans in sibling relationships than usually occur among friends. Unlike peer relationships, the sibling relationship is **ascribed,** that is, it is given to a person and is not optional. For practical purposes, the sibling relationship can only be broken by death or by one or more children leaving the family and having no contact.

Birth-Order Effects

The number of siblings, their age, and their sex affect the socialization of a child. An only child, for example, does not have the same experiences in getting along with children as the middle child among nine brothers and sisters. Families with all boys differ from families with all girls or from those with a mix. One aspect of sibling relationships that has captured imaginations recently is the effect of birth order on personality development. For example, the eldest child is described as conscientious and an achiever and, often, as bossy; the middle child as a hellion or mediator; and the youngest as a charmer (McGoldrick, Watson, & Benton, 1999). If there are more than three children in the family, the roles may become quite specialized. Bossard (1975) identifies a variety of roles: the responsible one, the butterfly, the rebel, the princess, and sometimes the scapegoat. Since we usually feel comfortable in the roles we have grown up with, we try to repeat them in adult life. For example, the younger brother of sisters will probably be happier with an oldest sister of brothers. In their relationship, they will thus continue the familiar patterns (McGoldrick et al., 1999).

Birth-order effects are not inevitable: for example, a younger child may take over the role of an older one. This might occur in families where the older child is physically or mentally challenged. Personality is another factor. The eldest may be temperamentally unassertive and allow a younger sibling to be the leader. Such patterns are also influenced by what parents expect of a particular child (McGoldrick et al., 1999). For example, boys in Asian Indian families are favoured, regardless of birth position (Hines et al., 1999).

Siblings as Socializers

Older brothers and sisters help socialize younger ones in many ways. They act as role models. Many children have learned the use of makeup, how to smoke or drink, or how best to get around parents, from brothers and sisters. They teach skills. If they live in an isolated community in the bush, for example, children may learn to identify edible plants and animal tracks from older siblings. Older brothers and sisters can shape younger ones' attitudes. For example, when siblings have a good relationship, they influence attitudes toward safe sex, especially for girls with older sisters (Kowal & Blinn-Pike, 2004). Role models are not always favourable. Both brothers and sisters have similar levels of delinquent activity, especially when combined with the older sibling's hostile and bossy behaviour. Younger brothers who have good relationships with older ones are also drawn into delinquency (Slomkowski, Rende, Conger, Simons, & Conger, 2001).

The early writings on sibling relationships tended to stress rivalry between brothers and sisters. Yet even conflict has a positive side: given that sibling relationships are obligatory, brothers and sisters must learn how to resolve conflict issues (Bank & Kahn, 1982). For example, they need to know when to stand up for their rights and when to give in. When asked by researchers, parents stated that the biggest problems with sibling relationships were anger and conflict, as well as attempts to control the brother or sister. Parents also expected their children to be fond of each other. In fact, difficulties in their children's relationships arose not so much out of conflict and rivalry as out of lack of warmth and affection (Kramer & Baron, 1995). Siblings learn the importance of social context: their behaviour may differ depending on whether a parent is present. Junior may hit little sister over the head to get a toy if mother is out of the room, but not when she is there. They also learn bargaining skills—for example, "If you let me use your stereo for a week, I won't tell Dad you came in drunk on Saturday morning." Sibling relationships can affect relationships with friends as children put to use the social skills they learned with brothers and sisters (McCoy, Brody, & Stoneman, 1994; Downey & Condron, 2004). Having a warm relationship with an older sister can help even those girls with difficult temperaments learn to avoid discord in friendships (McCoy, Brody, & Stoneman, 2002).

Later investigators have pointed out that there can also be great warmth and affection between brothers and sisters. The closeness differs, however, across cultural groups. The sibling relationship can be one of the most enduring in a person's life; for example, elderly women who live with someone other than a husband are most likely to live with a sibling, usually a sister (McGoldrick et al., 1999). Siblings have a store of memories in common and have been socialized in similar ways.

Affection between brothers and sisters depends on access. Siblings in rural areas may spend more time together than city children because nearby peers are few (Brody & Murry, 2001). Access can be limited if the children are widely separated in age, because their interests are too different. Children from large families also comment that the younger ones do not really know the older ones, since they did not live in the same house for long. Access also depends on parents. If they feel it important that their children know and like each other, they will encourage such relationships.

Sometimes when parents abdicate authority, and the children have access to one another, siblings may develop extreme loyalty to one another. Since the parental subsystem is not functioning, the children try to make up for the lack. One of the oldest may become a "parental" child, trying to fill a role for which he, or more often she, is unequipped. In such a case, the younger children are often parented inadequately and the parental child fails to achieve a normal adulthood. Once the younger children are no longer dependent on the older child, he or she may feel lost, unneeded, and depressed (Jurkovic, 1997). Social workers often see these characteristics in brothers and sisters from neglected or abused families, or in children who have moved together from one foster home to another.

Family Size

The number of brothers and sisters also affects development. As family size increases, resources need to be spread among more people. These include financial resources and parents' time and attention. Parents of smaller families can spend more time interacting with each child and monitoring his or her activities. They are also more likely to know their children's friends and their families, thus creating an interconnected social network. In general, children from smaller families do better in school and have fewer problems in behaviour (Parcel & Dufur, 2001). In part, these effects may be the result of residing in a particular neighbourhood. Larger families may not have the financial ability to live in an area with resources such as excellent schools and recreational facilities.

One study looked at the impact of parents' jobs on today's smaller families. The researchers were surprised that even in such families, the timing and number of children affect both behaviour and learning. A new baby leads to more social problems. Having either a number of older siblings or closely spaced younger ones reduces a child's school performance. The effect on learning is long term (Parcel & Menaghan, 1994).

The Physically or Mentally Challenged

Having a brother or sister with exceptionalities also affects socialization. Children in such families may have to adjust to a change in the family rhythm as parents and other family members have to pay attention to the special needs of the exceptional child. Children also need information about the exceptionality, especially if they fear they might "catch" it. Parents may be stretched thin by the demands of the exceptional child, and may not have the time and emotional resources necessary for the other children. Indeed, brothers or especially sisters may be expected to help with childcare, and may be asked to include the sibling in their social activities. Some youngsters feel they have to make up to their parents for what the sibling cannot achieve. Often parents impose a double standard on their children, expecting less from the exceptional child because of his or her limitations. Sometimes these standards are unreasonable, for example, expecting a higher standard of consideration from the "normal" child than from the one who is exceptional in some way. Shared stress can improve family communication and closeness. If, however, the stress is very great, the family can experience extreme tension, blocked communication, and possibly family breakdown (McGoldrick et al., 1999; Seligman & Darling, 1997).

Impact of Parents on Sibling Relationships

Parents influence relationships among their children. For example, parents' no-nonsense (authoritative) parenting style is linked with older siblings' social competence, which is linked in turn to younger siblings' competence (Brody & Murry, 2001).

Negative effects have been studied more than positive ones. Siblings often emphasize their differences to reduce conflict. If parents treat them as a single group, however, without individual qualities (e.g., "the kids"), children engage in more rivalry and conflict (Feinberg et al., 2003). On the other hand, favouritism also creates problems. Parents, especially when under stress, were found to treat children differently as to the degree of warmth and conflict shown and time spent (Tucker, McHale, & Crouter, 2002). The greater the differences in how a mother treats her children, the greater the children's maladjustment, especially if she subjects one child to more anger, harshness, and disapproval than the others. In such families, all children tend to be aggressive and disruptive. The picked-on child is resentful, and the others insecure (Boyle et al., 2004).

Parents have yet another impact on children's relationships. The role of siblings in the socialization of children may be decreasing. Since families are becoming smaller, the present generation of children will have only one or two, if any, brothers or sisters to help socialize them. Some sociologists speculate that in the future peers may become more influential in socialization than they already are because they will fill some of the vacuum in sibling relationships (McGoldrick et al., 1999).

Extended Family Members

The extended family consists of relatives such as grandparents, aunts, uncles, and cousins. Families vary in the number of extended family members they keep in contact with and in the amount of contact they have with one another. Most is known about grandparent–grandchild relationships.

How important are relatives? According to some current theories, the extended family has been weakened by increased mobility. In fact, more children probably know their grandparents now than in earlier generations because of the increased life span. According to estimates, fewer than one-fourth of children born in 1900 had four living grandparents. By 2000, two in three children began life with four grandparents, more if we count step-grandparents (Connidis, 2001). In 2001, nearly half a million Canadians lived in the same household as at least one grandchild. Some children were being raised by their grandparents (Milan & Hamm, 2003). Many children grow up with a warm, continuing relationship with grandparents.

The closeness of the grandchild–grandparent relationship depends on a number of factors. It is usually closer with preteen children. Those who live nearer each other visit more often and phone more frequently. Grandmothers and granddaughters on the mother's side of the family tend to have warmer relationships, especially when parents and grandparents get along. Children in stepfamilies, first-born, and only children are also closer to their grandparents. Often one grandchild is considered special. There are also cultural differences.

For example, Aboriginal cultures in Canada have assigned an important role to the extended family in child rearing. Even if grandparents or other relatives did not actively care for a child, they advised parents on the child's welfare (Connidis, 2001; Kennedy & Chang, 2003; Rosenthal & Gladstone, 2000).

Grandparenting styles are described by scholars as ranging from companionship without parenting, involvement with parent-like responsibilities, and remoteness. Of course, there are variations and combinations of the three styles (Connidis, 2001). Young adults describe grandparents' roles in four ways: as a friend and confidant, as an influential figure, as an indulgent caregiver, and as an intergenerational kin keeper. The traditional respect for elders seems to be replaced by a more equal relationship (Brown, 2003).

A particular point of contact between generations is the observance of rituals and traditions. Christenings, bar mitzvahs, birthdays, first communions, and many other events bring families together. Shared traditions both increase family solidarity and transmit family and cultural values.

SOCIETY AT LARGE

Parents and other family members are not the only people who affect the socialization of the child. Society as a whole is involved, even in small details. As children move out of the home, parents do have some control over their environment. This control is, however, limited and decreases as children become older (Rowe, 1994).

Childcare

The choices parents make about childcare for the time that they are at work affect a child's development. According to one estimate, young children in full-time childcare typically spend nine hours a day, 250 days a year, away from their parents. They thus spend more waking hours with substitute caregivers than with their parents (Doherty, 1996). As a result, the quality of the care they receive is important. The atmosphere in a grandparent's home is different from that in homes where one woman may care for three or four children, and is different still from a babysitter coming into the child's home or from a daycare centre.

According to one study, nearly half of Canadian children cared for by non-relatives received informal home care (Krashinsky, 2001–2002). Because many homecare arrangements are informal and not supervised by the government, it is impossible to look at their impact on children. This is not the case for daycare centres. Such centres differ in their effects on children, with quality of care being critical. Quality childcare goes beyond merely protecting a child's health and safety. It also helps the child's physical, emotional, language, and intellectual development. Centres that do this have caregivers who are sensitive to children's needs and understand child development. Each caregiver is responsible for a limited number of children and the whole group is relatively small. In addition, children are less anxious when their caregivers do not come and go. Caregivers are more likely to be warm and supportive if they are satisfied with their jobs. Children in high-quality care tend to be readier for school and to have better social skills. Those in poor-quality care lag behind. Yet even high-quality daycare cannot completely make up for neglectful or cruel parenting (Cleveland & Krashinsky, 2003).

The School

Once a child has reached the age of four or five years, large blocks of his or her time are turned over to the school, which takes over much of the socialization process. At school, children learn to interact with new authority figures and with children about their own age. They are introduced to many new ideas by the people with whom they interact. These may agree or conflict with the values they have already learned in the family. For example, some immigrant parents object to nonacademic activities. They see a good education as a way for their children to get ahead and object to what they consider a waste of time (Anderson, Waxler-Morrison, Richardson, Herbert, & Murphy, 1990).

The first years of formal education are important to children's self-esteem. Many begin school feeling they are worthwhile individuals. Studies have shown, however, that within a few years their self-esteem drops. In part, this is related to the amount of negative feedback children receive in school, in the form of criticism, comparison with other children, and poor marks. Children from low-income and some minority-group families often do not have as much expected of them as children from middle-class families. Since youngsters are aware of differences in treatment, these expectations result in both lower achievement and lower self-esteem (Santrock, 1992). On the other hand, warm and supportive teachers can partly make up for parents' deficiencies (Parcel & Dufur, 2001).

In school, children also learn about other families through their peers, through books and stories, and through teachers' attitudes. This learning can include family and gender roles. One class assignment that has been criticized by a number of parents is the family tree. This is all very well if children are members of a traditional nuclear family. It is difficult, however, to fit members of divorced, stepparent, and foster or adoptive families into a conventional family tree (Shreck, 2001). In addition, some children may still be experiencing some of the trauma of separation, so this assignment is very painful for them.

Minority Children in School

The interplay between family, school, and society as a whole is perhaps the most obvious with minority-group children. In general, children tend to be more successful in school if their parents are well educated and they do not live in poverty. Two groups more likely than others to be poor are recent immigrants and Aboriginal peoples (Campaign 2000, 2004). Their school experiences differ, however.

As with other groups, Aboriginal parents' higher levels of education and income, especially for non-reserve families, is related to greater success in school (Turcotte & Zhao, 2004). Many families live in rural and remote areas. Reliance on the extended family provides both assistance for the individual and the obligation to help others. Because there may be no high schools or colleges nearby, students must leave home and live in what is, for many, an alien environment. Being separated from their communities deprives them of social support and also limits their ability to fulfill their own family responsibilities. In addition, Aboriginal parents have traditionally adopted a permissive parenting style, which allows children to make many of their own decisions. Negative labels applied to Aboriginal peoples, such as "lazy" or "unreliable," mean that their school experience may be marred by prejudice (Armstrong, 1999; Das Gupta, 2000). Recently, larger numbers of Aboriginal peoples are graduating from high school and are undertaking postsecondary studies, although their rates are still low in comparison to those of the general population. Those who live in cities are most likely to earn a university degree (Tait, 1999; Turcotte & Zhao, 2004).

Recent immigrants, on the other hand, tend to be well educated, one factor in favour of their being granted admission to Canada. Poverty is often a new experience for them, and one they regard as temporary. Education, they feel, is the way for their children to move up socially and economically. Children who do not have English or French as a mother tongue begin school at a disadvantage, but catch up by age 11 or 12. Those who speak an official language make up the difference much faster. Children whose parents have higher levels of education tend to do better (Beiser, Hou, Hyman, & Tousignant, 1998; Statistics Canada, 2002g).

Peers

Once children start daycare or school, peers begin to take on increased importance. When children are young, parents have some power over the peers children spend time with. This control grows less, however, as children become older and move more freely around the neighbourhood. Often parents think of the peer relationship as being negative and blame friends for being bad influences on their children. For example, children tend to try alcohol or drugs or become involved in delinquent behaviour when they are with their friends. Friends also influence children's desires as consumers—what the leader of a group has everyone wants, even if it conflicts with family standards. Children gravitate toward those with similar interests, such as photography or vandalism, and may move through several peer groups before adulthood. In the process, they learn to conform to group cultures.

Friendship has its good aspects. Peers can make up for some of the negative experiences a child has at home. They also provide a dose of reality for the children who are the centre of their parents' lives. Through friends, children come to recognize that instead of being unique they have interests and desires in common with others. The relationship is far more cooperative than that with parents and allows a different kind of development (Youniss, 1980).

Even as children mature, parents influence peer relationships. For example, mothers tend to know their daughters' friends and to be involved in their children's activities, such as coaching a team (Updegraff, McHale, Crouter, & Kupanoff, 2001). When parents are supportive toward their teenagers, the teens are supportive in turn to friends, thus developing close ties (Cui, Conger, Bryant, & Elder, 2002). On the negative side, ineffective parenting is linked with a teen's choice of deviant peers and delinquent behaviour. It is not clear, however, which comes first—parenting quality or defiance (Simons et al., 2001). Adolescent groups come in two general types: socialized and oppositional. Socialized groups tend to accept positive values like training for a job. Oppositional ones choose dangerous activities like drug use and sexual promiscuity. Oppositional teens reject the usual messages about delinquency (Goddard, Goff, Dennis, & Melancon, 2002). Thus, parents may be able to influence socialized teens but have little control over oppositional ones.

As children become older, the peer group assumes greater importance. Most adolescents, for example, rely more on friends than on parents. Yet the growing independence of young people from their parents does not begin in adolescence; rather, it is a long process that starts early in life. It is the peer group that provides much of the opportunity for this gradual separation from the family of origin.

The Media

The media are important socializing agents. Indeed, one study refers to children's "media saturated lives" (Roberts, Foehr, & Rideout, 2005, p. 57). An American study found that children under six spend about two hours a day with screen media, that is, with television, videos and DVDs, video games, computers, and even the **Internet.** Although two-thirds of children under two use such media, usually a parent is in the room with them (Rideout, Vandewater, & Wartella, 2003). School-aged children watch television an average of 25 hours a week, play video and computer games for 7 hours, and use a computer or surf the Internet for 3 hours, not counting school use (Walsh, 2001). Still another study found that 8- to 18-year-olds spend nearly 6.5 hours a day using media, often more than one at a time (e.g., television plus video game plus radio), a practice that researchers call "media multi-tasking" (Roberts et al., 2005).

There are benefits, of course. Children learn from educational television programs or garner information from the Internet. Cell phones, pagers, and e-mails keep family members connected and allow working parents to monitor their children's after-school activities. In addition "tech-talk" can help build relationships between parents and children (English-Lueck, 2001; Magid, 2004b).

There are also concerns. Television watching has been blamed for promoting aggression in children and for teaching gender and role stereotypes (Children Now, 2004; Kaiser Family Foundation, 2003). The growth in specialized channels and the increase of television sets and video games in children's rooms may reduce the time available for family activities (Walsh, 2001).

These criticisms are true in part. Large doses of television violence seem to increase aggression, especially in boys. Yet one study found that experiencing violence in the home is more likely to produce aggressive and delinquent behaviour (Curtis, 2001; Kaiser Family Foundation, 2003). Heavy viewing can also interfere with school performance, especially reading, because it takes the place of homework and reading for pleasure (Roberts et al., 2005; Strasburger, 1993). There is also the problem of stereotyping. Studies of American media, much of which are available in Canada, have looked at the images of men, women, and minorities presented. Since 1999, prime-time shows have increased the number of minority characters, especially African-Americans and Latinos; however, there are fewer

Asians, Pacific Islanders, and Aboriginal people. White people tend to appear in high-status jobs, while Latinos are more often shown as doing lower-status work, and Asians and people from the Middle East are more likely than others to appear as criminals. Both male and female characters occupy high-status careers such as physician, lawyer, or elected official. However, men outnumber women in these roles, while women outnumber men as domestic workers, nurses, and homemakers. The diversity of young people is not reflected in prime-time television. Thus young people from minority groups see few positive role models with whom they can identify (Children Now, 2004). Some shows present variations in family structure. These shows are usually unrealistic, however, because the constraints of programming demand resolution of problems in either half an hour or an hour. Life, of course, does not work that way. The exception to the instant solution is the daytime drama, whose characters are shown with continuing problems. Although daytime talk shows discuss many family variations, some of the situations presented are bizarre. Few programs reflect ordinary, humdrum existence (Spears & Seydegart, 1993).

Whether television is a good or bad influence on children depends greatly on their age and on their families. Although many preschoolers watch considerable television, most view it with other family members (Rideout et al., 2003). The way children handle what they see depends on their stage of development. By the age of eight, they understand that television is not the real world. In addition, the more children think and talk critically about television, the less it affects them (Josephson, 1995). Parents and older siblings can help youngsters learn from and about television through their explanations and comments. Unfortunately, many parents do not make the time to do this (Huston & Wright, 1996). In fact, many parents are impatient of interruptions when they are watching their own programs. Thus, television can interfere with parent–child communication (Mirabelli, 1995). Most school-age children report that there are no family rules about television watching (Roberts et al., 2005). On the positive side, parents encourage children to watch programs the parents think are suitable. They can also regulate viewing, although they are more likely to control the programs their children watch rather than the actual time in front of the set (Huston & Wright, 1996). Recent technical innovations may help parents exert more control over television watching. The **V-chip** is a device designed to allow parents to block unsuitable programs. Parents can also get "lockboxes" to prevent children from viewing any channel with objectionable programming. The joke is that often children must show their parents how to program such devices. Rather than relying on technology many parents monitor their children's viewing themselves (U.S. Federal Communications Commission, 2004; Hazlett, 2004).

A fast-growing form of media use among children, as well as adults, is browsing the Internet. The percentage of Canadians using the Internet is increasing daily, and this country has one of the fastest growth rates in the world. Although boys and girls go online in equal numbers, boys spend more time there (Rotermann, 2001). The Internet provides many benefits to children, especially access to educational materials and the opportunity to get to know people from around the world (Magid, 2004b). But there are concerns as well. Teens may access "cyberporn" sites either intentionally or accidentally (Buerkel-Rothfuss, Buerkel, &

Gray, 2001). Children are also sometimes subject to harassment or bullying online and, if they give out personal information or agree to meet a stranger, may be putting themselves at physical risk. Because teenagers are supervised less than younger children, they may be in greater danger. As with television, parents' interest and involvement with what their children do online is crucial. It is also important for parents to set down guidelines for Internet use. For example, they should instruct children not to give out personal information like an address or a telephone number or agree to meet someone face-to-face without their parents' approval (Magid, 2004b). However, monitoring Internet use is more difficult for parents than monitoring television use. Some screening software is available, but its value is limited since it will block acceptable websites along with pornography, but not material like intensive advertising. With technological advances, cell phones provide many of the features of the Internet. In addition, phone numbers may be shown by caller ID. If phones are equipped with geo-location systems, users can be located by unscrupulous people (Magid, 2004a).

Okay, honey, you can scroll down now.

Source: Reprinted by kind permission of Barrie Maguire.

FACES OF SOCIALIZATION—THE CASE OF GENDER ROLE

No single influence shapes children's socialization. Rather, there is an interplay among the influences of parents, school, media, peers, and other people and institutions. As an example, let us look at various ways children learn about gender roles.

Parents

Parents play a key part in gender role socialization. Boys tend to receive more attention from parents than girls, both negative, such as punishment, and probably also positive. When fathers interact with sons, they stress achievement and the cognitive aspects of what they are doing. With daughters, they emphasize interpersonal relations through encouragement and support. Boys are also more pressured than girls against behaviour felt to be inappropriate for their sex (Golombok & Fivush, 1994). As adults, children of nontraditional parents are more likely than others to have nontraditional attitudes about gender roles (Cunningham, 2001).

The objects that surround children also affect their socialization. Girls' toys, such as dolls and sets of dishes, encourage caring and serving behaviours, while boys' toys, such as cars, are more active and complex, and help develop such abilities as spatial relations. In addition, it is usually more acceptable for girls to play with toys that are designed for boys than vice versa. Even very young boys are aware of fathers' disapproval if they play with girls' toys (Raag & Rackliff, 1998). Sex-typing is related more to fathers' attitudes than mothers' (McHale, Crouter, & Tucker, 1999). In these and other ways, girls are encouraged to conform to the stereotype that women are passive, dependent, and nurturing. Boys, on the other hand, are encouraged to be more independent, active, and aggressive (Golombok & Fivush, 1994). Children who grow up in homes with single mothers or same-sex parents follow gender-typing as much as children with parents of opposite sexes (Stevens, Golombok, Beveridge, et al., 2002).

Schools

In the past, education was very strongly related to gender stereotypes. For example, industrial arts classes were for boys only and home economics classes for girls only. Boys traditionally have done better than girls in mathematics and science, and girls have done better than boys in language skills. Although attempts have been made to desegregate subjects and encourage women to continue math and science into the higher grades, success has been somewhat limited. Studies of schools have shown that role models in these subjects, such as science teachers, are primarily men. Science also tends to be taught using examples from typical male interests, such as competitive sports, an example of earlier gender-role socialization (Golombok & Fivush, 1994).

Peers

Starting in daycare, children are aware of girls' and boys' play materials and some boys already refuse to play with girls' toys (Raag & Rackliff, 1998). By middle childhood, children tend to play in groups of their own sex. Boys and girls develop contrasting peer cultures, with boys more active in large groups and girls quieter in pairs or small groups. Children are encouraged to conform to their peers through teasing and other sanctions (Gurian & Henley, 2001). Sex typing is stronger in boys' time with peers. Girls' activities are more evenly divided between "masculine" and "feminine" activities (McHale, Kim, Whiteman, & Crouter, 2004).

The Media

As we have already seen, the media tend to stereotype male and female behaviour. In television, for example, males are more active and aggressive than females, and are focused on their jobs or on sports activities. Women, though also shown in the workplace, are portrayed more than men in providing care to others. Female characters are more concerned with relationships than males (Children Now, 2004).

FAMILY TRENDS AND SOCIALIZATION

Given that society changes, every age group grows up in a different world. These age groups are called **cohorts.** Their family experiences are also different; for example, individuals born during the Great Depression, like children born now, have fewer brothers and sisters and somewhat older parents. One cohort that has received a great deal of attention is the baby-boom generation, those born between about 1946 and 1964. Their experiences in growing up differ markedly from those of both earlier and later cohorts. In fact, the baby boom is really made up of two groups whose experiences differ from each other. The older group formed the cutting edge of change and the younger were born once change had already taken place. French-Canadian youth had different issues from English Canadians (Owram, 1996).

A number of factors affected the socialization of the baby-boom generation. First, the country was in prosperous times, and the general affluence led people to expect that life would be easy. Second, there was a mushrooming of technology. Third, institutions were weakened, and a loss of respect for authority resulted. The early baby boomers produced social protests and the hippie movement that rejected parents' values. Fourth, parents made Dr. Spock's *Baby and Child Care* a bestseller. His advice was for a much more permissive kind of care than that recommended in earlier years. An example is given at the beginning of this chapter concerning the use of soothers. Some parents, however, took his advice to the extreme, and provided very little structure for their children. Fifth, the effect of being born into a large family meant that more of the process of socialization was carried on by children, and that teamwork and social skills were emphasized. These children also experienced more family instability because of an increasing number of broken marriages. Sixth, this is the first generation that never knew what it was to live without television. Seventh, the period after World War II saw a swift migration from farm to town, and from town to city. Small towns tend to set and enforce standards more than cities do, but they are also much more supportive to families. Finally, advances in medicine meant a rapid drop in infant and child mortality and a reduction of physical suffering (Hicks & Hicks, 1999; Kettle, 1980). There are problems with generalizations such as these; the baby-boom generation encompasses a wide age group, and it is rash to equate people now nearing 60 with those in their 40s. In addition, such statements ignore the many variations in life experience.

As the big generation moved through the school system, they were subjected to more crowding and a greater number of young, hastily trained teachers. Added to the effect of numbers was the fact that more young people were staying in school longer, partly because they could not find jobs, and partly because the jobs that were available required a higher level of technical skill. A number of experimental plans were introduced to try to cope with the many more students who did not plan to go to university. It was for this generation that the community college system was developed.

According to Kettle (1980), the effect of these factors on many individuals in this cohort is that they tend to live by their feelings and tend to be suspicious of obligations. They tend to be concerned with personal development first and then with family happiness. Many have little loyalty except to themselves. As young adults, they had difficulties finding and keeping jobs. By the 1980s, most had abandoned their protests and concentrated instead on getting ahead financially. Positions of responsibility opened up as their parents retired. Many have become more conservative in their outlook on life. Later members of the generation had greater difficulties with employment. Positions were held by older members of the cohort and economic times were less favourable (Owram, 1996). Although the early baby boomers were sometimes rather casual about raising their children, later ones are more attentive parents (Hicks & Hicks, 1999).

In contrast to the baby boomers, Generation X is much smaller and includes those born between 1965 and 1979. This cohort has grown up in more difficult financial times than the baby boomers. Parents responded by having fewer children. They were less likely to be raised in traditional families. The divorce rate of their parents increased dramatically. X-ers are the first generation to grow up with many of their mothers in the workforce. A combination of factors has blocked their careers. Until recently, the economy made jobs harder to find. When positions that matched their qualifications came up, baby boomers, who had been in the workplace longer, snapped them up. Many X-ers have shifted from job to job or become self-employed. As a result, they have become flexible and self-reliant, but not loyal to any single company (Hicks & Hicks, 1999). Indeed, poverty in families with parents aged 25 to 34 rose from 12 percent in 1981 (the baby boomers) to 18.9 percent in 1997 (Ross, Scott, & Smith, 2000). Although poverty rates have fallen recently, there are still a greater number of poor families than in 1989, the year before the last recession (National Council of Welfare, 2004). Many put family needs above job demands. Their focus on relationships is also expressed in their definition of "family" as including those who provide each other emotional commitment and support, regardless of their legal relationship (Clack, 2004; Hicks & Hicks, 1999). It is too early to tell, of course, how the Generation X cohort will change as they age. We can expect, however, that they will differ from the baby boomers because their experiences growing up have been different. Generation Y (born between 1979 and 1994) is the first generation to grow up with computers at home, instant messaging, and cellular phones. They are also the most closely watched generation in history (*Wikipedia*, 2004).

SOME ISSUES

Concern is growing over the amount of control in the socialization process parents have given up or have lost. With both parents working, nonfamily socializers, including babysitters and daycare staff members, influence children at a younger age than in the past. Children are also introduced earlier to the influence of peers who are not chosen by their parents.

There is some controversy over whether this lower level of control is neutral or harmful for children.

Also, older children have less supervision. Once they are beyond the age at which they require a babysitter by law, many are left to fend for themselves; these children have been popularized as "latchkey kids." Some are without adult control for several hours between the end of the school day and parents' return from work. Some adolescents are also left unsupervised in their homes. There are concerns over the influence of television on such children and the opportunities allowed for experiments with drugs or for sexual activity.

Another concern is over the reduced interaction between parents and children when both parents work outside the home. Does this affect the attachment and emotional development of children? Research results have been mixed, with some studies showing that children who are in daycare full time during their first year experience insecure attachment, higher levels of aggression, and lower school performance. Other findings suggest that children suffer no ill effects. The results appear to depend on the quality of the care children receive (Cleveland & Krashinsky, 2003).

The recognition of physical and emotional abuse of children raises another issue. Should parenting education be compulsory? In the past, women have learned how to raise children from their mothers and other female relatives. Systems theorists point out that this practice results in the repetition of harmful patterns of interaction from one generation to the next. What an individual learns in his or her original family is often repeated in the family of procreation. If parenting education is considered essential, who should be entrusted with it? Should it be a compulsory school subject? If individuals do not receive it, will child protection agencies be allowed to step in to ensure that parents are adequately trained before they are allowed to raise their children?

Since socialization helps produce new members of society, it is a target for any group that feels that the family or society itself is threatened. As well, any who feel that the present society is unjust look for changes in the way children are raised. Thus, socialization provides a focus for conflicts over many social issues.

SUMMARY

SOCIALIZATION AND SOCIETY. Socialization is the passing on to new members of society a culture's ways of thinking and acting. It is strongest in childhood, but takes place at each role or status change through life. Although all aspects of society are involved in socialization, the family plays a key role. Every society provides distinct socialization experiences. Each individual, however, remains free to accept or reject the values and norms of society. The roles people are expected to fill have changed over time. In earlier times, children were involved at a young age in the family's livelihood, until prevented by labour and school attendance laws. In the 20th century, the child became a source of emotional satisfaction. A scientific approach to child rearing was stressed by child development experts. Often this meant going against the traditions of minority groups such as those of Aboriginal peoples and immigrants. Childhood came to be considered a special time, and services and institutions arose to meet its needs.

PARENTS AS SOCIALIZERS. Parents are the single most powerful influence on children. The number, marital status, sex, sexual orientation, and age of parent-figures are important in shaping children's environments. Parenting styles (authoritarian, authoritative, or permissive) are important in day-to-day interaction. Families also affect the development of children through their routines and traditions, their educational and occupational levels, and cultural differences.

THE WIDER FAMILY. Other relatives also affect the socialization of children:

Siblings. Brothers and sisters affect socialization in many ways. The number, ages, and birth order influence development. Siblings also provide role models, give information about peer values and interaction, provide opportunities to practise solving conflicts, and offer affection and support. A sibling's exceptionalities can also affect the development of other children in the family.

Extended Family. Extended family members can provide affection and teach the child family traditions. The extended family is important among Aboriginal peoples, but its prestige has been damaged by the influence of white society.

SOCIETY AT LARGE. Children are also socialized by institutions and individuals who are not related to them. Babysitters and daycare personnel provide a variety of environments. In school, children learn social values about families, which help shape their self-concept and values. Peers are a source both of individual development and of potential conflict with families. The media provide models of gender roles and present popular ideas about families. The impact of the media on socialization is influenced by family factors such as supervision. Family trends also affect socialization; for example, cohort size can affect opportunities and expectations about education and employment.

ISSUES. One concern is parents' shrinking control over the socialization of children, since both parents work outside the home in many families. Many theorists also recognize the problems arising from poor parenting and advocate compulsory education for parenting.

KEY TERMS

ascribed: a relationship that belongs to a particular role rather than being a matter of choice (p. 160)

authoritarian: a parenting style that requires unquestioning obedience (p. 155)

authoritative: a parenting style that sets expectations for children, but adjusts them to the individual (p. 156)

cohort: a group of people, roughly the same age, living in the same historical time (p. 171)

Internet: a worldwide network of computers allowing easy communication and exchange of information (p. 167)

permissive: a parenting style that allows children to make their own decisions without providing firm guidelines (p. 155)

sibling: a brother or a sister (p. 159)

V-chip: a device designed to allow parents to block unsuitable television programs (p. 168)

CLASS ASSIGNMENTS

Complete one or more of the following assignments, as directed by your instructor:

1. Some parents have difficulty letting go of their children. Discuss some of the reasons this might be so. What might be done to avoid this difficulty?

2. Look at five recent books written for preschool children that show family interaction in some way. What messages does each give about family and gender roles? Do these messages reflect the reality of present-day family life?

3. Do you think there should be a law that requires people to take a parenting course before having children? What do you see as the advantages and disadvantages of such legislation?

PERSONAL ASSIGNMENTS

The following questions are designed to help you look at your own family experience and its influence on your life:

1. How have brothers and sisters affected your socialization? Consider their age, sex, number, and personalities. If you have no siblings, what effect has this had on you? Why?

2. What family stories were you told? What messages did they give you? How did these affect your development?

Part Four

© Tery Dixon/Getty Images

Chapter 7

Middle Age and the Empty Nest

OBJECTIVES

- To show the place of the middle years as a transition in the family life cycle

- To explore the transitions that occur for both children and parents during the middle years

- To describe the stresses on the parents from both the child and grandparent generations

When I was in my 20s, 40 seemed ridiculously far off—a venerable middle age at which I envisioned myself taking a crash course in bridge and migrating south to avoid the cold. Now, having rocketed to that age zone with astonishing speed, it seems the archetypal middle age about which I was so patronizing isn't quite so venerable after all.

For one thing, the much hyped decline of the body, while not exactly welcome, is neither devastating nor inevitable. Sure, I've had to make the acquaintance of the color technician at the hairdresser and I sport some lines on my face that surprise me every time I pass a mirror. But the overall physical plant is holding up just fine. Good genes may play a part here, but they don't tell the whole story. A better explanation is that I'm representative of the "new middle age," a generation that has radically changed what the 40s look and feel like. I exercise—something I never did in my 20s or even 30s—I eat sensibly and slather on the sunscreen. Happily, I can report that all these efforts really pay off. Without question, I'm in better shape now than I've ever been before.

Source: Barsky (1990, January), p. 34. Reprinted by permission of the author.

The middle years of life—usually considered the years between the ages of 40 or 45 and 64—are for men a time of fulfillment, of reaching the pinnacle of their careers. For women, on the other hand, the period is seen as one of physical deterioration and uselessness, since they have accomplished their mission of bearing and raising children. Any meaning left for their lives is in caring for their husbands and living out their hopes in their grandchildren. This double vision is the result of the traditional view of marriage and family.

In fact, though, the middle age of this view is a fairly recent idea. For example, Robert and Ann Miller, who lived in the Niagara Peninsula in the 1800s, had 14 children. The oldest was born when Ann was 20, the youngest when she was 45. By the time her youngest daughter was married, Ann Miller was in her 60s. Child rearing consumed about 45 years of her life. Robert died at the age of 62 when the youngest child was 15. A busy middle age came for the Miller parents somewhere between the last birth and the time most of their children were independent.

With their smaller nuclear families, parents nowadays are usually finished active child rearing earlier in their lives. Since longevity has increased, people can expect to live longer than their ancestors did. Thus, many years of life (about 13 years) remain after the children have moved out and before retirement (Blacker, 1999). Population projections show that the number of middle-aged people, aged 45 to 64 years, will increase by about 30 percent from 2001 to 2011 (Statistics Canada, 2002d). (See Table 7.1.) Just as other attitudes about family relations have changed over the past few decades, so have attitudes about the post-child years. Lesley Barsky's (1990) comments on turning 40 reflect these new values.

THE FAMILY STRESS BOMB—THE MIDDLE YEARS

The middle years have now joined child rearing as the longest stages in life. The midlife group is very diverse. Since their ages span 20 to 25 years, they may include first-time parents as well as great-grandparents (Allen, Blieszner, & Roberto, 2000). At the beginning of

TABLE 7.1

POPULATION AND GROWTH RATE, AGES 35 TO 44, 1991, 2001, 2011

	35–44 Years	45–64 Years
Population (millions)		
1991	4.37	5.37
2001	5.10	7.29
2011 (estimate)	4.51	9.47
Percentage Increase		
1991–2001	16.7%	35.8%
2001–2011	−11.5%	29.9%

Source: Adapted from Statistics Canada, "Profile of the Canadian population by age and sex: Canada ages, 2001 Census." Catalogue 96F0030, July 16, 2002, p. 28.

the midlife period, many will be approaching the peak of their careers, while those at the end will be nearing retirement. Women in this group may have been employed outside the home throughout their adult lives, they may be entering the workforce for the first time, or they may be reentering the workforce after a long interval devoted to child rearing. Therefore, any generalizations about this group will fit only parts of the population. In addition, gay men and lesbians vary as to the age they come out, the types of families they form, and the kinds of communities they live in (Laird, 2003). Because there is so little information on same-sex couples, this discussion will focus on heterosexual ones.

These years of the family life cycle are transitional. For those with children, there is a shift from active child rearing at the beginning of this stage to the post-child family at the end. This period often marks the splitting of one family into two or more, as children form their own nuclear families. The process involves a major readjustment of the family system. New boundaries must be drawn as to who is a family member. Relationships need to be worked out between the family of origin and the new families of procreation. New roles need to be established to reflect these changes.

Like all major life changes, family adaptation in the middle years contains a series of stressors. A **stressor** is a life event that can produce change in the family system (Boss, 2002). Examples are parenthood or death. Losing family members, gaining family members, and any new responsibilities that fall on family members can all act as stressors. How families cope with the stress will probably set the pattern for the quality of the remainder of their lives (Kingsmill & Schlesinger, 1998).

Tasks of the Parent Generation

The tasks that confront the parent generation at this stage fall into three groups, all of which involve redrawing the family boundaries and redefining individual roles. First, the relationship with their children changes as the children move from adolescence into young adulthood. Parents need to allow their children the freedom to grow up and move out. Once the children have become independent, parents need to learn how to relate to the children as adults rather than as children. As the members of the younger generation begin to form their own families, the parents need to accept new individuals into their extended families. These may include sons- and daughters-in-law, grandchildren, and perhaps step-grandchildren. With these new members come new roles—those of parents-in-law and grandparents (Blacker, 1999).

Second, there is a new focus on the couple relationship. Now that the pair is alone, they must renegotiate their couple system as a *dyad*, or pair, rather than as part of a larger family system. This process may give rise to new sources of conflict. The role patterns they assumed as a young couple or as parents of young or adolescent children may not reflect their needs in maturity. For instance, they may have avoided talking about problems in the marriage by becoming involved with their children. This buffer is now lost. There may be friction over the reallocation of the functions that were filled by children; for instance, the wife may object to assuming those household tasks that were previously looked after by children, and the husband may feel that the household is her domain. Couples who have stayed together for the sake of the children may now separate, or continue unhappily together because they feel stuck in the relationship (Weinstein, 1996).

Third, if any members of the grandparent generation are in ill health, the parents may need to deal with their disability and possible death. At this time, there may be a shift in focus for caregiving activities from children to parents. Boundary and role difficulties may arise if the middle-aged adults take over decision-making for their parents (Connidis, 2001).

Tasks of the Child Generation

While these adjustments are taking place in the parent generation, corresponding changes are occurring in the child generation. They need to differentiate themselves from their family of origin and develop their own values and goals for life. This is the period for developing close peer relationships with both sexes; these may be either friends or potential mates. Young adults also need to establish themselves in the work world so that they can attain financial independence (Fulmer, 1999).

Several things can interfere with this process. For example, when young people cannot find employment, it is obviously difficult for them to support themselves. If parents divorce or one is chronically ill or dies while there is an adolescent or young adult in the home, the child may feel obliged to stay and care for one or both parents and siblings in the home. This sense of obligation may hold the young person tightly to the family, instead of allowing the mutual separation of parents and children that is the major life-cycle task (Rolland, 1999; Weinstein, 1996). The degree of separation varies with ethnic cultural values.

THE PARENT GENERATION AT MIDLIFE

As we saw in Chapter 1, when families try to solve problems, they first use methods that have worked in the past. For example, when children are no longer present to do certain household chores, the wife may extend her caregiving activities to include these chores. If the workload becomes too unbalanced, especially if she is newly employed out of the home, she may make demands on her husband to help. If this solution is not effective, the couple may fall into a vicious cycle, or develop some new method of handling household tasks through the process of morphogenesis (Broderick, 1993). The same process holds true for both practical difficulties and problems in relationships.

One characteristic common to the middle years is the reexamination by the individual of his or her life course and family relationships. Just as men's and women's experiences differ, so also do their processes of self-evaluation.

Men at Midlife

For most men, there are two main areas on which their lives focus: family and work. The middle years are often transitional in both areas. For some men, the strain is so extreme that the period has been dubbed the **midlife crisis**. Daniel Levinson and his colleagues, who studied middle-aged men, describe this period as one of the major transitions of life, along with the early-adult and late-adult transitions (see Figure 7.1). As we have seen, the three generations experience these transitions at about the same time (Levinson, 1978).

Figure 7.1

DEVELOPMENTAL PERIODS IN EARLY AND MIDDLE ADULTHOOD

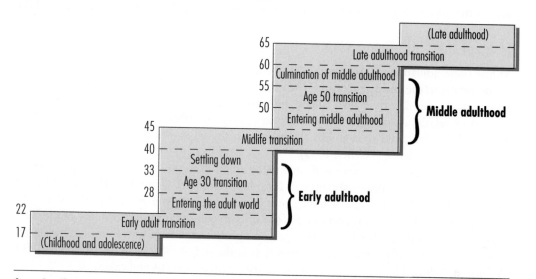

Source: From *The Seasons of a Man's Life* by Daniel Levinson, Copyright © 1978 by Daniel J. Levinson. Used by permission of Alfred A. Knopf, a division of Random House, Inc.

Men and Work

According to Levinson (1978), a young man forms a dream of what he wishes to accomplish in life. By midlife, it should be apparent whether that dream is attainable. If he has not achieved it, he must alter his plans to fit reality. If he has achieved it, he needs to find another goal to give his life direction. For many in the baby-boom cohort the dream may be an illusion. The members of that generation were socialized to expect that they would achieve more than their parents. The likelihood of their making it into management positions, however, is 10 to 25 percent less than those of people a little older than themselves because of the many people competing for the few available positions. On top of that, downsizing in large companies may bring layoffs instead of promotions. As a result, this group may have experienced considerable frustration and anger because their dreams have been delayed (Kettle, 1980).

Often parents have looked forward to having their children become independent so that they will have some financial freedom. This may allow them the option of a new job or career. When young people have problems finding work, however, they remain dependent longer, and the parents' hopes do not come to pass.

Men and Their Families

Due to frustrations and disappointments in the realm of work, many men look for satisfaction from their families. Yet these relationships are also undergoing shifts during the middle years. As children become independent, move out, and establish their own families, men are confronted with three dimensions of change in family relationships.

First, they are now moving up one generation. This fact is emphasized if they become grandparents. If their parents die, they become the senior generation. They are obviously becoming older physically. This is underlined by the fact that a number of men die in these years. So men begin realizing that their lives too will end some day, and that day may not be far off. For gay men, the sense of coming death may be sharpened as a result of the death of friends from AIDS. In contrast, in spite of some minor complaints, most still feel vigorous. Some men express this tension in lifestyle changes. Fitness and other aspects of healthy living may concern them. They also may change their style of dress, or acquire the proverbial sports car (Blacker, 1999; Levinson, 1978).

Second, they are faced with the prospect of spending the rest of their lives alone with their partners, without having children as a buffer between them. In addition, their partners too are growing older and remind them of their own age. Some men conclude that this relationship is not rewarding, and choose to separate or divorce. Many find new partners, often selecting someone younger than the first. Others choose to remain in their relationship. Often, as they adjust to the childless household, there is a shifting of roles of both men and women toward greater androgyny, or a balance between the masculine and feminine characteristics in each of their personalities. Men at this age often become more concerned with relationships and the masculine trait of competitiveness may recede in them. Women, on the other hand, become more interested in achievement. Those couples who stay together and modify their relationship usually experience an increase in marital satisfaction (Blacker, 1999). This is not surprising, because, as we saw in Chapter 4, androgynous couples tend to be the happiest. Gay men may also be committed to their relationship and face many of the same issues as heterosexual couples (Blacker, 1999).

Third, men's relationships with their children are in transition as they separate from each other. This process may be made more difficult both by the characteristics of the young person, and by pressures from a man's relationship with his parents. Often during the midlife transition, a man's children are adolescents. Their vitality is more likely to arouse envy and resentment than delight and forebearance by their contrast with his own aging process. A man may also be preoccupied with unresolved grievances against his own parents that have resurfaced with their increasing dependency. He may therefore be even more intolerant of the grievances of his children. Some men do maintain contact with youth by becoming mentors; that is, they act as a close adviser for someone younger whom they help achieve their life dream. In this way, they make a contribution to society and are involved in a young person's achievements (Levinson, 1978). Erikson (1982) sees the mentor relationship as an expression of the generativeness of adulthood.

At midlife, many men enter the stage Erik Erikson (1982) calls **generativity,** when they become concerned about what they are doing for future generations. Over half of a group of men aged 53 years had achieved generativity (Westermeyer, 2004). Those who did were most likely to be happily married, to have been successful at work, and to have close friendships. As young adults, these men had experienced both mentor and good peer relationships. During this phase, many men become more involved with their children and grandchildren. Childless men may fulfill these needs by working for political or social reform. They may also interact with young people, for instance, through their work, by volunteering as a mentor for a youth group, or through closer involvement with younger relatives (Bergquist, Greenberg, & Klaum, 1993). One gay man, for example, became a favourite uncle for his nieces and nephews.

Women and Transitions at Midlife

The study of women's transitions at midlife came later than that of men's. Most of the research deals with homemaker wives. However, most people currently in middle age are employed outside the home. In 2003, about 75 percent of women aged 45 to 54 had jobs, and 45 percent of those between 55 and 64 (Statistics Canada, 2004k). One important issue for these women is the shift in social expectations for women that has occurred during their lifetime. When they were young, it was usual for women to remain in the home. If they worked at all, they did so before children were born, and some worked after children were grown. Thus they did not have careers in the same way as their husbands. With the increase today in the number of working wives, there is both pressure on these women to find a job, and a sense of the opportunity to become more independent. The women's movement has made women more aware of new possibilities for fulfillment, both within marriage and in the wider world, through work and volunteer activities (McGoldrick, 1999b). Maturity often involves integrating the earlier emphasis on social relationships and intimacy with independence and self-determination (Campbell, 1989).

Complicating the issue is the woman's age. Menopause is a marker event with no parallel in men's lives. For those who see a woman's primary fulfillment as motherhood, menopause signals an end to her most rewarding years. In general, women are considered to be old at a younger age than men (Kite & Wagner, 2002). This can affect both their employment and their remarriage prospects. Since middle age is sometimes considered to last from about the age of 40 to 55 and old age from 65 and beyond, individuals in their late 50s and early 60s are in a never-never land between the two. This fact itself is stressful (Campbell, 1989). Nevertheless, many women experience the energy of "menopausal zest" (Blacker, 1999).

Like men, women's transitions also involve job and family, but the emphasis is different. In most families, it is the woman who has had the major responsibility for household duties, even if she has been in the workforce. As children move out and she is not involved in active child rearing, she may feel liberated. Yet she may also feel a sense of loss. Women have been socialized to concentrate on family needs, often at the expense of their own needs (Blacker, 1999). If this has been the centre of their lives, children's growing independence leaves them feeling lost and dislocated. The resulting depression and sense of uselessness that women experience is often referred to as the **empty nest syndrome.**

Women, especially mothers, need to find a new centre for their lives. There are three possible areas for the new focus: the extended family, marriage, and work.

Some women seek to maintain their traditional caregiving roles by either having a last-chance child or by looking after others within the extended family. They may do this through involvement with their children and grandchildren, for example, by providing childcare while the young parents are at work. Although this arrangement often works well, it can also lead to conflict over child-rearing standards and other control issues. Some women care for their parents or other relatives. In all of these cases, problems may arise over where boundaries should be drawn between families.

This may be a time for renewal in marriage. As we have already seen, if the union survives the transition, it is often happier than in the child-rearing years. Women, however, are more likely than men to suffer in the case of family breakup. Given the increase in the divorce rate over the last few years, more middle-aged women will suffer from personal loss due to rejection. Some, of course, will themselves leave marriages that have been unsatisfactory since they no longer have children to hold them there. In addition, about half of all widows are under the age of 60; the majority of these are in their 50s. Thus a woman in midlife is in danger of finding herself without children, a husband, sex, and the social and financial support she has been accustomed to (Campbell, 1989).

A third option is to begin or resume a career. Researchers have found attitudes toward careers differ between mothers and nonmothers. The latter appear to have a life pattern more similar to that of men. Mothers, however, find the 40s a liberating time since they no longer need to be absorbed in child-rearing activities. For them it is a time for career changes or returning to school (McGoldrick, 1999b). Unlike younger women, those in their 50s have difficulty finding jobs, unless they have recently been involved in the workforce. They may lack marketable skills or recent experience and are at an age when extensive training or education may no longer be practical (Campbell, 1989).

Marriage and Sexuality

Once all the children have left home, the marriage relationship becomes more important. Couples need to review their marriages and often also need to work out new arrangements. This is especially true if children have been the centre of the marriage. If strains have existed between the partners, they are more obvious when children are no longer there to distract attention from them. There can be an imbalance in the marriage as a result of the developmental stages the husband and wife are going through. For example, the husband may want to change the relationship to fit his new values after midlife and the wife may be excited about a new job. If the wife has been a family caregiver, the husband may have difficulties adjusting to the fact that she now wants to concentrate on a career rather than on just the family (Blacker, 1999).

The sexual relationship of the couple may change. For some couples, interest in sex increases. Now that children are grown, more private time is available with fewer interruptions. After menopause, there is no need to fear pregnancy. Men's slowed response time allows a more relaxed approach, and often more pleasure for the woman (Blacker, 1999). On the other hand, interest may drop off through boredom. One couple who swore off sex spoke of how "the habit of sex" interfered with the companionship they both enjoyed in their marriage (Amiel, 1987). Some couples accept the social stereotype that older people are asexual beings (Greenberg, Schimel, & Martens, 2002). This goes hand in hand with the idea that sexual relations are intended only for procreation. According to this notion, once a woman has passed menopause and no possibility exists for more children, there is no reason for continuing sexual relations. In addition, biological aging and illness also affect the frequency of sex and, in fact, are the major factors in its decline after midlife (Call, Sprecher, & Schwartz, 1995).

THE YOUNGER GENERATION—MOVING OUT AND THE REVOLVING DOOR

While parents of families are experiencing the transitions of midlife, their children are also going through the early-adult transition. The period from early adolescence to the early 20s is marked by growing independence until finally the young person lives independently and perhaps establishes his or her own nuclear family. During adolescence and early adulthood, major changes occur in four areas: sexuality, identity, autonomy, and attachment/separation (Preto, 1999).

The young person changes physically. The upsurge in sexual thoughts can produce confusion and even fear in all family members. To younger siblings, the adolescent suddenly is no longer the familiar brother or sister they grew up with. Parents may be disturbed by their children's interest in sexual activity. Many mothers have become upset when they discover their daughters have bought contraceptives. Sometimes the opposite-sex parent has incestuous feelings toward the child. In order to protect against these impulses, conflict with this parent increases. Conflict with the same-sex parent may arise out of competition. If parents are not open about sexuality or if they themselves are experiencing conflicts and anxieties about their own sexuality, they are likely either to be too permissive with their children or to set unreasonably strict limits (Preto, 1999).

During adolescence, young people must shape their own identity (Erikson, 1982). They no longer accept others' views of who they are. The process of identity formation can be very exciting, but it may also be a source of conflict with parents. During the process, young people often question and challenge their parents' rules and standards for behaviour. At times, they may criticize parents for being hypocritical, since the standards they set out for their children are different from the way they have actually lived. This challenge from their children may come at the same time as the adults are evaluating their own lives and questioning their own values, and can be an added source of conflict and stress (Preto, 1999).

Adolescents need to learn to be responsible for their own decisions. Many parents have difficulty achieving a balance between trying to control the young person and allowing them to make their own decisions, even if they are wrong. This is especially hard if they feel they are supporting their children and also being judged by them (Fulmer, 1999).

The young person's move away from the family and toward the peer group, and eventually toward an intimate relationship with another individual, is often felt as a loss by the family. The other members are no longer needed in the same way they were when the child was younger. Some families respond to this sense of loss by being overprotective and overcontrolling. In others, the young person may be forced to leave before he or she is really ready so that this stage can be over and done with. Parents must learn to relate to their grown children as adults. The parent generation also needs to develop flexible family boundaries to allow young people to leave, and to welcome their sons' and daughters' partners and children into the extended family (Blacker, 1999).

The Not-So-Empty Nest

In the recent past, young adulthood was almost synonymous with moving out and living on your own. This was part of growing up. The situation has changed in the past 20 years. From

1981 to 2001, the number of unattached young adults aged 20 to 29 who continued to live with their parents increased from 27.5 percent to 41.1 percent. Younger adults are more likely to remain home than older ones, although ages have been gradually creeping upward (Statistics Canada, 2002d).

There seem to be a number of reasons for this change. One is related to the fact that young people are now cohabiting or getting married later. Single young adults can either live with their parents or live somewhere else. More are choosing to continue to live with their parents or to return home after a period of being on their own. Thus there is a longer transitional period from child rearing to the empty nest. Another reason young adults are choosing to live at home is that more of them are in full-time postsecondary education now than was the case in the mid-1970s. Still another is that finding and keeping a job that pays enough to allow independent living has been more difficult recently, both because of slow economic growth and the numbers of the baby-boom generation who are still employed (Beaujot, 2004). In addition, the cost of establishing a separate household can be extremely high, especially in urban areas like Toronto or Vancouver. Cultural influences are also at work. Some ethnic and immigrant groups encourage young adults to live with parents until they are married.

Different life courses may produce similar effects in the late teens and early 20s. Some young adults continue their education; during this period, they may continue living at home. Others become pregnant at a young age, and continue to live at home with their children. In either case, the young adult does not move out of the parents' home until his or her middle or late 20s (Kliman & Madsen, 1999).

Some young people move away from home and come back again repeatedly, a phenomenon that has been called the **revolving door.** Returns may be the result of job loss, poor employment prospects, or marriage breakdown. In the latter case, both the child and grandchildren may move in, and the grandparents are often faced with renewed child-care responsibilities to allow their adult child to enter the workforce (Kingsmill & Schlesinger, 1998; Ward & Spitze, 1996b; White & Peterson, 1995). Both adult children and the parents with whom they live can benefit from the arrangement. The young person has the opportunity to complete an education or to find a job that will allow him or her to live independently. The parent can benefit from having someone to share both the work and the expenses of the household (Boyd & Norris, 1995). The financial and housework contributions of children tend to be quite modest, however. Daughters usually help more with chores and sons are more likely to pay room and board. Children tend to do more housework in one-parent than in two-parent households. In most cases, though, the arrangement is designed to help children rather than parents (Spitze & Ward, 1995; Ward & Spitze, 1996a, 1996b). An American study found that parents and young adult children differed over the amount of financial help the younger generation should receive. Children, especially sons, expected more assistance than parents felt they should give. Which children should receive help depended on both the parents' financial situation and their values (Goldscheider, Thornton, & Yang, 2001).

Living with parents has recently become more acceptable (Alwin, 1996). Nevertheless, having children continue living at home or returning home as young adults can be stressful for parents and means a new adjustment of roles, since the old parent–child ones may now be inappropriate. This situation may interfere with parents' own plans. If their marriage is difficult, the return may create extra strains, which might be the last straw before a complete breakdown. Nevertheless, many Canadian parents studied were quite satisfied with both the living situation and their marriages. More important than actually having children at home was how the situation agreed with what the parents expected about having their children move out. Parents who were unhappiest with their own marriages had children who left and returned three or more times through the revolving door (Mitchell & Gee, 1996).

Many practical issues arise when parents and adult children live together: privacy for both parents and children, the use of the family car, family rules and regulations, the sharing of expenses, and the use of the house for parties and other forms of socializing. The whole situation is ambiguous. On the one hand, parents feel the need to maintain control of their own home. On the other, the adult "children" have a need to control their own lives (Kingsmill & Schlesinger, 1998). In fact, the revolving door has become so common that how-to books and pamphlets for parents on coping with adult children who return home are now available. For example, the B.C. Council on Families offers a sample contract outlining privileges and responsibilities of the young person (Usher, n.d.).

THE SANDWICH GENERATION

At the same time as middle-aged individuals are experiencing pressure from their in-and-out children, they may also be trying to cope with the fact that their parents are aging and need assistance. As we shall see in the next chapter, the conflict between the need for help on the part of infirm elderly parents and their desire for independence is similar in some ways to adolescent–parent conflicts. Thus the middle generation is subject to stress from both the younger and older generations. This is often called the **sandwich generation** (Williams, 2004). See Table 7.2.

TABLE 7.2		
THE SANDWICH GENERATION		
Population aged 45 to 64	7 325 000	
No children at home	4 680 000	
Children at home	2 645 000	
No elder care	1 933 000	
Plus elder care (sandwiched Canadians)	712 000	
Employed	589 000	(83%)
Not employed	123 000	(17%)

Source: Adapted from Statistics Canada, "Perspectives on Labour and Income." Catalogue 75-001, Summer 2004, p. 6.

Although most elderly people live by themselves or with a spouse, they tend to live near relatives. As their age increases and their health declines, they become more dependent on their children for assistance. The burden of caring for elderly parents tends to fall on women. Middle-aged and older women provide most of the home health care. In contrast to earlier generations, many of these women have jobs. In some ways the daughters of sick parents are needed at home almost as much as the mothers of preschool children. Women also provide part-time health care to aged relatives living elsewhere. In addition, many families provide assistance such as shopping, home maintenance, and home care. Even when adult children do not provide many actual services for a parent, they may be involved in the time-consuming and often frustrating task of locating required help. Caring for both children and elderly relatives can be stressful, especially for those with several children or those caring for more than one older person. Those who spend more than eight hours a month caring for elders are more likely to have health problems and to experience work-related pressures. Sandwiched workers may feel stressed, but 95 percent are satisfied with life in general (Williams, 2004).

THE SOCIAL TIME CLOCK

In our society, many aspects of life are governed by age. For example, there are minimum ages at which one can begin school, drive, drink alcohol, or vote. Marriage and family life are also affected by legal restrictions. For example, individuals wishing to marry have to reach a certain age to do so without their parents' consent. People who wish to adopt usually have to be over a given age, and children being adopted must consent to their adoptions at ages varying from 7 to 12, depending on the jurisdiction.

There are also social norms for the timing of life events. People say things like "I was young when I had my first baby" and "I was pretty old when I graduated from school" or "She was widowed very early." These statements indicate that we expect certain events to occur at particular times in life. This socially approved timetable has been called the social time clock.

Distinctions between life periods have become blurred (Neugarten & Neugarten, 1986). It is very difficult, for example, to define when middle age begins or when old age takes over. Yet people are more likely to experience a crisis if life events occur "off time" (McGoldrick & Gerson, 1985). There are social scripts, that is, expected patterns of behaviour, for these events. People can anticipate them and think about what they will do when the time comes. For instance, parents can look forward to and plan for the "empty nest." If, however, the children do not leave home at the socially appropriate time, both parents and adult children experience stress. Widowhood at age 35 is more of a crisis than at 65. Becoming a grandmother at 27 may be a crisis, but becoming one at 60 may be impatiently anticipated. (See Box 7.1.)

STRAINS OF THE MIDDLE YEARS

The major theme of the middle years is the triple transition within the extended family. The main focus in young adulthood is separation from the family of origin; in late adulthood, there is increasing dependence on their children; the middle-aged generation is pulled

BOX 7.1

A GRANDMOTHER AT 27

Most women don't expect to become grandmothers until they are in their 40s or 50s. But some women become grandmothers in their late 20s or early 30s when their daughters, products of teenage pregnancies themselves, become teenage mothers.

To see how young grandmothers handle their out-of-sync roles, sociologist Linda Burton interviewed mothers, grandmothers and great-grandmothers from black working-class families in Southern California. Eighteen of the grandmothers were in their late 20s through their late 30s; 23 were "on-time" grandmothers in their 40s and 50s.

Burton compared the responses of the early grandmothers with the "on-time" grandmothers and found that women who became grandmothers later in life were happier with their roles. They were more likely to have established careers, as well as the time and money to spend on their grandchildren. Most of those who became grandmothers at a youthful age felt that they were too young to be grandmothers, did not like the "old" connotation it bestowed on them and resented being saddled with a grandchild when they wanted to get on with their lives.

One 28-year-old grandmother told Burton, "I could break my daughter's neck for having this baby. I just got a new boyfriend. Now he will think I'm too old. It was bad enough being a mother so young—now a grandmother too!"

Since many of the teenage mothers were too immature to care for their babies, they turned them over to their mothers, as their mothers had done with them. But quite a few of the young grandmothers refused to care for their grandchildren and instead handed them over to their mothers. So these great-grandmothers—the youngest was 46 years old—found themselves caring for the babies of the granddaughters they had also raised.

Not surprisingly, some great-grandmothers were unhappy with this situation. One 56-year-old told Burton, "My daughter and granddaughter keep making these babies and expect me to take care of them. I ain't no nursemaid; I ain't old; and I ain't dead yet." The burden was especially hard on great-grandmothers in five-generation families who were also caring for their ailing parents.

Burton did find a few young grandmothers who were content with their roles. One 38-year-old mother who was caring for seven children at home felt that the addition of a grandchild was no burden at all. "This baby has only added joy to my life. . . . I take pride in being a grandmother."

And a 91-year-old great-great-great-grandmother, who gave birth to her first child at age 14, likes the idea of being able to meet and know the many generations of her family that followed her. "Then you have more people to look out behind you when you [are] old like me."

Source: Stark, 1986, p. 18. Reprinted with permission from *Psychology Today* © 2000 (Sussex Publishers, Inc.)

between separating from the young and accepting more responsibility for the old. In the process, family boundaries must be redrawn and family roles redefined. For many, it is a time of extreme stress.

With the need for both greater education and reduced opportunity for employment, young people are remaining in their parents' homes for longer periods. There is no prescribed role for these young people and no specific marker event to label them as adults; therefore, stress on all family members is increased. Society as a whole needs to rethink the place of young adults within the family.

Another issue is how to make the middle years fulfilling, especially for women. This issue is particularly relevant for those who have never, or have only temporarily, been in the workforce. The number of single women, especially those separated and divorced, is increasing. They may not have families who require their attention. Psychological and financial independence can be an important issue during the middle years. Since many younger women are now employed outside the home, problems in this area may not be as pressing in coming years.

To conclude, the transitions of the middle years are a source of stress. However, they open the possibility of building more satisfactory relationships on which to base the rest of life.

THE MIDDLE YEARS. The middle years are a time of transition, marked by a shift from active child rearing to the post-child family. This life stage has emerged fairly recently as the result of smaller families and the shorter time span devoted to raising children. The major task facing adults is the formation of new family boundaries and redefinition of roles for both the parent and child generations.

THE PARENT GENERATION AT MIDLIFE. During this time, middle-aged adults often reexamine their life course and family relationships. Men tend to focus on two areas. In the realm of work they may question whether they can achieve their goals, or if they should change them. In relation to the family, they realize that they are moving up one generation and have a sense that they are aging, especially as they look at their maturing children. They also face the prospect of spending the rest of their life alone with the same wife. As a result there is a greater concern with relationships. Middle-aged women experience the shift of changing social expectations for women away from homemaker toward career person. It is a source of both pressure and opportunity. Some of those who mourn the end of their child-rearing days, in the so-called empty nest syndrome, continue caregiving in other ways. This is also a time of either renewal of the marriage or its dissolution through divorce or death. If the couple relationship survives, the couple's sexual relationship may change, either becoming more satisfying or diminishing.

THE YOUNGER GENERATION. During the adolescent and early adult years, members of the younger generation are moving away from their parents. This occurs in a variety of ways: by seeking to establish an identity, by being responsible for their decisions, by shifting toward the peer group and away from the family of origin, and by forming an intimate relationship. There are obstacles, however, to living independently, such as later marriage, employment difficulties, single parenthood, and marriage breakdown with a return to the parents' home. When young people move back home, there may be friction over rules, privacy, and appropriate roles.

THE SANDWICH GENERATION. Middle-aged adults may become caught between the continuing dependency of their children and the increasing disability of their parents. The pressure may be increased by off-time events such as the pregnancy of an adolescent daughter. The burden of providing care for both young and old tends to fall on women. The middle years are marked by triple transitions within the extended family, which may produce high levels of stress as the members attempt to adjust.

empty nest syndrome: the depression and sense of uselessness some women experience when the last child leaves home (p. 185)

generativity: concern at midlife over one's contribution to future generations (p. 184)

midlife crisis: extreme strain as a person reevaluates his or her life in middle age (p. 182)

revolving door: young people's repeated moving in and out of their parents' home (p. 188)

sandwich generation: middle-aged adults who experience the stress of continuing dependency of their children and increasing disability of their parents (p. 189)

stressor: a life event that can produce change in the family system (p. 180)

CLASS ASSIGNMENTS

Complete one or both of the following assignments, as directed by your instructor:

1. Explore the opportunities for education and retraining available in your community for women in their 40s and 50s. How likely are they to find employment? In what fields? Explain.

2. How is midlife different for people who have children when in their late 30s or 40s? Think about couples with "afterthought children," remarried couples wanting a child of the second marriage, and single parents who become pregnant or adopt.

PERSONAL ASSIGNMENTS

The following assignments are designed to help you look at your own family experiences:

1. Thinking about your experience or that of someone you know, explain both the advantages and disadvantages of the "revolving door"—of children moving in and out of their parents' home.

2. Who looks after older relatives in your family? Describe both the frustrations and the rewards.

Chapter 8

Grey Power and the Sunset Years

Courtesy of the Dobson family.

OBJECTIVES

 To look at aging and death in relation to the family life cycle

 To examine the lifestyle and family relationships of younger and older elderly people, including variations among minority groups

 To discuss the implications of terminal illness and death for family members

 To explore policy issues concerning services for the elderly

Lock Up Your Moms!

Get used to the idea: one day your widowed mom might knock on your door arm-in-arm with a man you've never seen before. They'll both have a tan. And she'll say:

"Hey, kid, meet your new dad."

It's happening all the time. As women outlive their husbands, a whole generation of Canadians face the possibility of "re-patriation," usually by way of Florida....

They're stealing our women. And not just any of our women. They're stealing our moms!

Florida is where it's all happening for Canada's "rocker, walker and shawl" set. And it may be where your future "father" is living right now, at least for six months of the year.

Source: Jeff Mahoney, *The Hamilton Spectator*, September 30, 2000, p. W2. Reprinted with permission of The Hamilton Spectator.

WHAT IS OLD?

The elderly—almost immediately the popular image springs before our eyes: we see Granny in a rocking chair; she is plump and soft; her hair is pulled back into a bun; and she spends her time knitting for family members. Popular mythology paints a picture of the three-generation family of the past, where parents, children, and grandparents lived together in a large cooperative family. Both these stereotypes are deceptive.

In fact, these images do not and never did fit the realities of most Canadian families and their older members. We need only look at statistics to understand why. In the past, many people did not live to old age, that is, to what we usually consider normal retirement age—65. Those who did usually chose to live near, not with, other family members. Three-generation families have always been a minority in Canadian society. When such households existed, they resulted either from the control the oldest generation kept over land or from the financial and physical dependence of the aged on their children (Connidis, 2001). Both are situations where there can be extreme conflict. In fact, past generations were aware of this potential for conflict, as we can tell from the will of Robert Miller of South Grimsby Township, Ontario. In it, Miller carefully outlined just what rights his widow would have in the house she would share with their youngest son (see Box 8.1).

The image of Granny in the rocking chair is also deceptive. Most societies, as was discussed in Chapter 7, have what is referred to as a social time clock (Neugarten & Neugarten, 1986). This reflects the age range in which certain life events are "supposed" to happen. The time clock for becoming old is less clear-cut, but it still exists. As a result, life events that occur "on time" usually seem less traumatic than those that come too early or too late. For example, widowhood is probably less of a crisis for the woman who is 65 than for the one who is 30. When events such as retirement and grandparenthood come at expected ages, they can be prepared for mentally.

THE ELDERLY IN THE PAST

The following is an excerpt from the will of Robert Miller, a farmer from South Grimsby Township, Ontario, dated February 1, 1871. He died March 26, 1871, aged 63 years, 11 months.

I give and bequeath unto my Wife Ann Miller, in addition to Her legal claims of Dower all my household furniture of every kind including beds and bedding, Stoves and pipes, wearing apparel, including the Geese, the fowl, the bees and Two Cows, Two Sheep, and Two Hogs to choose any She likes, and feed for them through the Winter. I also give unto her One half of the growing Wheat to be given to Her in clean grain, One third of the Apples and also all the wood She wants for house use, To have free access to the well at all times and to any or all the buildings about the premises. My said wife to have the free and exclusive use of the front door, Yard, and Three rooms in the front part of the House.

Sixty acres and the building were left to Robert Miller's youngest son, with the understanding he would support his two youngest sisters, aged 15 and 17, until they were married or of age.

DIMENSIONS OF AGING

Our society recognizes several aspects of becoming old: chronological, biological, psychological, and social (Baker, 1988). All are involved with our notions of the social time clock.

Chronological Age

Chronological age is the number of years a person has lived. Certain privileges and responsibilities go along with age, such as receiving a pension or having to take an annual driving test.

Does old age begin at retirement? If so, does that mean we now become old sooner than in the past? Retirement age has been decreasing over the last few decades. In 1998, 20.6 percent of both men and women aged 45 to 69 were retired (Fast & Frederick, 2004b). The change can be credited mainly to improved pension plans, which make it financially possible for people to retire younger (Williams, 2003). With options for early retirement now available, many people leave their employment between the ages of 55 and 64. Obviously, most people in this age range are not ready for the rocking chair or the nursing home.

Many people who write about old age use 65 as the starting-off mark. In fact, 65 is a relatively new standard. For example, in 1952 the government old age pension was given to all residents over the age of 70. It was not until 1966 that the age was lowered to 65. Prior to the establishment of pension plans, many aging people worked as long as they could. For many, to admit that they were so old and weak that they could not work meant becoming dependent on their children or on charity (Williams, 2003).

Physical Age

Physical changes occur during the aging process. White hair, wrinkles, and slowing movement are often equated with old age. These changes affect how we perceive ourselves and how others treat us; as a result they also affect our self-esteem. There are sex and class differences in how physical changes are regarded. Men in professional and managerial positions are considered to have greater knowledge based on experience; grey hair is thus a mark of distinction. On the other hand, men who do manual labour or play sports professionally see **physical aging** as a sign of failing ability. Aging can be an even greater crisis for women, especially if they have depended on physical attractiveness to fill esteem needs (Baker, 1988).

Some social scientists suggest that old age begins when physical disability sets in. If we use this standard, we would have to exclude many people in their 70s or even 80s because they still remain vigorous (Neugarten & Neugarten, 1986).

Psychological Age

Other people believe in the idea of **psychological age,** arguing that old age is a frame of mind. They point to "old" behaviour such as Granny sitting in a rocking chair, knitting. Attitude differences between the elderly and the not-so-old can be explained in part, of course, by the experience the former have gained by moving through the life cycle. Some characteristics are cohort effects (Baker, 1988); that is, they are most likely the result of being raised during particular historical events such as the Great Depression and World War II, and of the values that were prevalent during their early lives. Yet, it is difficult to find qualities that are characteristic of most elderly. They show more differences than similarities, as do younger people.

Social Age

Aging also has a social aspect. **Social age** is based on cultural norms, which specify how we should act when we are a certain age and how we should interact with people older and younger than ourselves (Baker, 1988). The boundaries between periods of life are, however, becoming blurred. The timing of marker events such as grandparenthood, widowhood, and retirement are changing. Today, women have first children as early as 12 and as late as 45, so that the age at which they become grandparents ranges widely. Women born during the 1800s could expect to be widows in their late 50s; the corresponding age today is almost 70 (Gee, 1987; Neugarten & Neugarten, 1986). With these changes, our expectations of appropriate behaviour are also shifting. Retirement, for example, has lost its link with physical frailty. Granny is probably not in her rocking chair; she is more likely to be actively involved with her family and in the community or wintering in Florida. Attitudes toward timing changes are not unanimous. For example, while on the one hand, many people see earlier retirement as a desirable goal, on the other, there are attacks on mandatory retirement at a specific age.

Increased Longevity

Since people are now living longer than they used to, they are more likely to survive to ages at which they can experience later life-cycle stages. When the average person died at the age of 60, many did not experience retirement or grandparenthood. More generations have the opportunity to know each other now than in the past. This fact can also create problems over who is eligible to fill certain age-related roles. One older study of five-generation families found there was confusion as to who had the rights and privileges of old age (Hagestad, 1986). Was it the very oldest, who were in their 80s and 90s? If so, where did it leave their children, who were in their 60s and 70s (an age often considered "old")? Traditionally children keep an eye out for their parents and provide assistance to them, even if they do not live together. In these five-generation families, elderly people were looking out for still more elderly parents and were missing out on the benefits of old age themselves.

Increased longevity has resulted in new terminology to describe the older members of our society. Sociologists are beginning to describe individuals over 65 as young-old (65–74 years), middle-old (75–84 years), and old-old (85 years and over).

THE AGING OF CANADA

In spite of some vagueness as to when old age really begins, one fact is clear: the population of Canada is becoming older. This is the combined effect of a number of factors. As we have seen, people are living longer. In a few years, the oldest members of the baby-boom bulge will be starting to retire and will swell the number of seniors. According to Statistics Canada (2002e), seniors, who made up 13 percent of the population in 2001, will make up 15 percent of the population by 2011. (See Table 8.1.) The fastest-growing age group is the old-old, which gained 41 percent from 1991 and is expected to grow by another 43 percent by 2011. Nearly 4000 were aged 100 or older, an increase of 21 percent since 1991 (Statistics Canada, 2002e).

Since the birth rate is down, there are fewer young members of Canadian society to offset the increase among the elderly. Obviously, the increasing proportion of older people in Canada will have far-reaching effects on our social and political institutions. Nevertheless, these effects will not be felt equally by all parts of the country. Certain areas have an unusually high proportion of older people. Some, like the Okanagan Valley and southern Vancouver Island in British Columbia, have had an influx of the elderly, probably because of their mild climate. The "oldest" municipality in Ontario is the former mining town of Elliot Lake, which has turned itself into a retirement centre (Statistics Canada, 2002d).

DEVELOPMENTAL TASKS OF OLD AGE

As members age, the family faces important changes and adjustments in both family systems and roles. The key task for older people is accepting the shift of roles to allow the next generation to take over leadership in various areas of private and public life. This task involves a

TABLE 8.1

THE ELDERLY IN CANADA, 1991–2011

	65–69 Years	70–79 Years	80+ Years
Population			
1991	1 070 000	1 440 000	660 000
2001	1 130 000	1 820 000	930 000
2011 (estimate)	1 149 000	1 990 000	1 330 000
Percentage Increase			
1991–2001	5.6	26.9	41.2
2001–2011 (estimate)	31.3	8.9	42.7

Source: Adapted from Statistics Canada, "Profile of the Canadian population by age and sex: Canada ages, 2001 Census." Catalogue 96F0030, July 16, 2002, p. 28.

number of smaller changes. As people retire, they make room for younger employees to take over management jobs. Grandparents usually do not have the primary responsibility for raising the new generation of children. Nevertheless, older people have a vital role in providing both moral support and practical help to the middle generation as its members take over the central position. Their children, however, must in turn value the wisdom and experience of the elderly without taking over the day-to-day tasks of living that their parents and grandparents can still manage. The older generation must also adapt to their own physical decline. They must deal with the loss of spouse, brothers and sisters, and friends and acquaintances. Ultimately they must prepare for their own death (Carter & McGoldrick, 1999b).

Erik Erikson (1982) describes the psychosocial task of old age as integrity versus despair. As individuals look back on their lives, they look for order and meaning. Every society has its own definition of what makes a good life; thus the kind of meaning a person finds in his or her life may differ from one society to another, but the attempt to find meaning is common to all. Without a sense that life has had meaning and purpose (in other words, integrity), an individual sinks into a final despair. Time is now too short to start another life in order to make some mark in the world. With a sense that life has had meaning, on the other hand, a person need not fear death.

There are apparently few differences in adjustment to old age between homosexual and heterosexual men and women. They face many of the same issues around shifts in their relationships as they retire and as their health deteriorates. Relatively little is yet known about how gay men and lesbians age because many older individuals have remained in the closet. This is likely because when they were young, there were high levels of stigma against homosexual individuals. As a result, the older adults may be unwilling to discuss their homosexuality (Connidis, 2001).

THE "YOUNG" OLD

Any division of people into categories of old age such as young-old or old-old is artificial. Many of the variations among individuals have more to do with functioning than with age itself. Decisions and events that occur earlier in life can also make major differences in the lifestyles of the elderly and in their options for the future. For example, a man who has a first child at the age of 25 may well be a grandfather, and possibly even a great-grandfather, at 65. On the other hand, a man who has a child when he is in his 50s will have parenting responsibilities that will continue into his old age.

Economic Factors

In the past, pensions were often not available. Even when employers offered contributory plans, they were often optional. Under such circumstances, men continued to work as long as they were able. If they had a large enough income, they were able to put aside money for retirement. Otherwise, they were dependent on the support of their children or, at the extreme, of the community. In 1951, the *Old Age Security Act* provided for pensions for all Canadians aged at least 70. From 1966, most workers have also been covered by either the Canada Pension Plan or the Quebec Pension Plan. In addition, many employers now offer private plans and individuals can set up their own registered retirement savings plans (Williams, 2004). It has become economically feasible for larger numbers of the population to enjoy travel and other leisure activities following retirement. In fact, they are sometimes referred to as "Woopies"—well-off older people (Royal Bank, 1989).

The age at which people retire has fallen over the years. Men aged 60 to 64 are retiring in much greater numbers: in 1971, 68.3 percent of them were employed, and by 1981, only 58.3 percent were still in the workforce. Many pension plans are set up so that the employee may take early retirement and still have an adequate income (Schellenberg, 1994). Some individuals making this choice go on to second careers or to fulfilling forms of humanitarian service, including volunteer work. A number of people retire, however, because they are laid off or their job was downsized. Some take early retirement deals because they fear future lay-offs (Schellenberg & Silver, 2004).

In spite of these changes, there are still many inequities in pensions, and it is women who are disadvantaged (Lindsay, 1999). Most pensions are related to the individual's earnings. Women usually do not work as many years as men; they may take time off to care for children. Many retire at the same time as their older husbands (Schellenberg, 1994). More women than men work part time or in service occupations where there are no pensions. Women often earn less when they do work. Pensions continue the inequities in pay. The Old Age Security Pension and its accompanying income supplement were never designed to be the sole source of income in old age. Yet many women live at about the poverty line because the government pension is the only one they have. Even with Canada and Quebec Pension Plans added in, many remain poor (National Council of Welfare, 2004).

Activities and Interests

State of health is an important factor in the amount of activity people undertake. Most of the young-old are still in good health. In fact, the older man who feels he is reasonably healthy is more likely to be satisfied with his life. Although good health is also important for women's outlook on life, they tend to put more value on the relationship with their children; if it is satisfying, then life is satisfying (Koropeckyj-Cox, 2002; Mehlsen, Platz, & Fromholt, 2003).

Retirement usually marks a major change in activities. This can be a problem for those who define their value as individuals by their occupations (Walsh, 1999). Most retirees, however, are happy and busy. They substitute active recreation, time with friends, caring for others, and volunteer work for paid work (Fast & Frederick, 2004b). Working women may not feel as much displacement as men, since many of them continue the homemaking role for which they have been responsible during their working years. On the other hand, many individuals feel that working is a burden, but that it is necessary for survival. For these, retirement is a welcome opportunity to spend their time in more enjoyable activities.

A husband's retirement can mean important changes for a woman. Some homemaker wives complain of having a man underfoot all day when they have been used to being alone and directing their own time. The couple needs to renegotiate their areas of responsibility. If they do not work out a comfortable arrangement, marital conflict may increase. In his search for something to do, for instance, a man may start to take over household responsibilities that have been an important source of his wife's self-esteem (Walsh, 1999). Some working wives also choose to retire early when their husbands do, so that retirement demands a double adjustment.

Family Relationships

For older people, as for younger, family relationships depend on a number of factors. First, a person must have relatives in order to have any interaction. Obviously, a man cannot have a spousal relationship if he has no wife. Second, the frequency and variety of contact matter. Does a woman see her children once a week or once every six months? How often do they phone each other? Third are the possibilities for providing, receiving, and exchanging services and aid. If an individual has no money or is in poor health, providing financial help or physical assistance in cleaning or babysitting is difficult. Finally, the quality of family relationships is important. This aspect can include mutual affection and shared opinions and values. It is possible for relatives who see each other on a daily basis to spend the time fighting or belittling each other. There may actually be a closer relationship with someone who has less frequent contact (Beaulieu & Spencer, 1999).

Relationships with Spouses

The majority of older people live with a family member, especially a spouse. Many of those who are married report a high level of marital satisfaction (Connidis, 2001). Marriages that

have survived to this point may have fewer pressures on them—no teenagers in the house, more time for each other, a more relaxed attitude toward life, and men's desire for greater emotional connectedness. The sexual aspect of a relationship remains important in old age. We looked at the qualities of long-lasting marriages in Chapter 4. Aging gay and lesbian couples may have an increased desire for a long-term monogamous relationship (Connidis, 2001).

More men than women over the age of 65 are married. This fact results mainly from women's longer life span. In 2001, 35.4 percent of women aged 65 and over were living with a spouse or partner compared with 61.4 percent of men. For those aged 85 and over, 7.2 percent of women and 39.5 percent of men were partnered (Statistics Canada, 2002b). An increasing number of women are divorced. For a number of reasons, more widowed and divorced men than women remarry. Men more than women depend on their spouse for social and emotional support. Women have more close relationships with others since they are the ones who usually keep up contact with relatives. Thus they are not as dependent on a spouse for emotional support. It is also easier for men to find a new partner. More eligible women are available than men because men tend to die earlier (Connidis, 2001). Homosexual individuals are affected like other aging adults by the imbalance between males and females, but in an unexpected way. According to one researcher, "A common complaint for older gay men is that they are vigorously pursued by older heterosexual women who are looking for mates and husbands" (Quam, 1993, paragraph 15). Adult children may also play a role in remarriage. Some may actively discourage remarriage because they see it as disloyalty to the deceased parent or because they are worried about their inheritance. The easing of attitudes toward cohabitation may also contribute to the increase of older as well as younger people living together without marriage (Connidis, 2001).

Relationships with Children

Most older people (80 percent) have at least one living child. Like people now in their child-rearing years, a sizable proportion of older people have just one or two children (Connidis, 2001). Usually at least one of these children lives quite close to the parents, so that most older people see one of their children about once a week (Bess, 1999b). Contact is most often made by telephone, followed in frequency by personal visits and letter writing. Those who live nearby have shorter but more frequent visits than those who live at a distance. The closest relationship is usually between mothers and daughters (Connidis, 2001), partly because women are seen as "kin-keepers"; that is, they have the responsibility of keeping up contacts with relatives (Hagestad, 1986).

The parent–child relationship is not one-sided; rather, they help each other. For example, adult children may provide practical assistance in house and yard maintenance. When adult children have crises such as divorce, widowhood, or the birth of a child with health problems, parents are key providers of support (Connidis, 2001). Financial aid can flow in either direction.

Relationships with Grandchildren

The relationship between grandparents and grandchildren is often considered special because it is not complicated by the responsibilities and conflicts of being a parent. More than three-quarters of those aged 65 or over have at least one grandchild. On average, they have nearly five apiece (Milan & Hamm, 2003). Unlike the relationship with grown children, the emotional closeness is affected by how near grandchildren live to grandparents and how often they see one another. It is also influenced by the relationship between parents and grandparents (Connidis, 2001). Being grandparents or great-grandparents can give the elderly a new lease on life since they see a part of themselves that will survive. Having grandchildren is also an opportunity to come to terms with both the satisfactions and disappointments of raising one's own children, and adds the pleasure of seeing them experience the fulfillment of being parents (Walsh, 1999).

Some grandparents raise their grandchildren on either a full- or a part-time basis. Because the arrangements are so varied, generalizing about their experiences is impossible. For some there is little choice. One grandmother, for example, heard a knock on her door at 3 a.m. She found her two-month-old grandson in a basket on her doorstep. "What choice did I have?" she said. "My daughter was back on the street" (Kornhaber, 1996, p. 133). A grandparent with full custody has both total responsibility and authority for the child. If the arrangement is informal, neither grandparent nor grandchild may have the security of knowing that the arrangement will last. In such cases, grandparents may not have authority to register the child for school or to sign for medical care (Milan & Hamm, 2003). Some grandparents have a live-in child and grandchild (e.g., a young unmarried mother and her baby) and must constantly supervise care. On the other hand, those who provide daycare while a parent works get a break at the end of the day. Taking in a teenager who is having problems with his or her parents in still another variety of grandchild care. If a grandchild has behaviour problems, the grandparent caregiver may feel burdened and overstressed, especially if he or she provides full-time care (Guzell, Landry-Meyer, & Gerard, 2002). In spite of potential exhaustion and problems, caregiving grandparents find satisfaction in looking after their grandchildren. Many grandchildren do thrive under grandparents' care. According to one study, most children raised by grandparents are less rebellious and more grateful than children raised by parents (Kornhaber, 1996).

The impact of divorce on grandparents has only recently received much recognition. Grandparents' divorces can result in more distant relationships with grandchildren. In part, this depends on the quality of ties with their adult children (King, 2003). The relationship between grandparents and their adult children is important, because the latter control access to the grandchildren. This connection is doubly important if the child's ex-spouse has custody of the grandchildren. Grandparents can have both positive and negative effects on grandchildren in these circumstances. They can provide support and a haven for grandchildren when problems at home are too difficult to live with (Connidis, 2001). The expectation that they be a resource for the family but at the same time not interfere can be a burden for some seniors. Often family counselling ignores grandparents, although they may play a vital role in family interactions. It is not clear what rights of access to grandchildren grandparents have, even if their relationship has been close and its continuation is in the child's best interests (Landau, 1997). If access is cut off, both grandparents and grandchildren may lose an important emotional resource (see Box 11.1, page 263). With the increase in remarriages of both older divorced parents and divorced adult children, the number of step-grandparents is growing. In some cases, these relationships are close (Connidis, 2001).

Relationship with Siblings

Most older people have at least one living brother or sister. Sibling ties among adults have received little attention, especially those of gay men and lesbians. Usually, there is less interaction with siblings than with children and grandchildren, although sisters seem to have a special relationship. As might be expected, those who have never married and the childless widowed are especially dependent on siblings. When they do associate, they seem drawn together partly by shared family history and partly by interest rather than by the sense of obligation that is true for parents and children (Connidis, 2001).

THE "OLD" OLD

Health and Self-Care

As people grow older, physical well-being and concern about possible or actual illness become more important. This is realistic. Those over the age of 75 are more likely than younger people to have a chronic health problem or disability. Most common are mobility and memory problems (Cossette & Duclos, 2002). Physical and mental deterioration can be made worse if an individual becomes depressed, feels helpless, and fears losing control over his or her life. Loss of hope can lead an individual to give up (Walsh, 1999).

Elderly people who live in senior residences or nursing homes may first have lived with other family members. Often overlooked are the number of seniors caring for others—a spouse, friend, or neighbour. Often the caregiving ends when the mental or physical health of the older person makes it impossible for the family to cope any longer. Some aspects of chronic illness can be extremely difficult to live with. For example, taking care of a person who has sleep disturbance and roams the house during the night, is incontinent, makes delusional statements, or behaves aggressively are very stressful. When an elder enters an institution, it does not mean that family contacts are cut off. Some women go to the nursing home every day to feed or provide other care for a parent (Connidis, 2001; Stobert & Cranswick, 2004).

Whether seniors live in their own homes, with a child, or in an institution, family members, especially daughters, feel a duty to provide care, even if they have other responsibilities such as children or a job. This can result in very mixed feelings. Some women are afraid they are neglecting their husbands or children; some feel they can never do quite enough to satisfy their elderly relative. They may feel guilty for not doing enough, and become overprotective and interfere unnecessarily with their parent's independence. In spite of the difficulties, many woman caregivers find looking after an older relative rewarding. Adult children who provide the most demanding care have reported that it is stressful and emotionally satisfying at the same time. Caregivers are most likely to see the rewards if they have enough practical help and financial aid (Connidis, 2001; Stobert & Cranswick, 2004).

THREE KEY ISSUES

There are three key areas of conflict involving older people and their family members: independence versus dependence, connectedness versus separateness, and openness versus privateness.

Independence versus Dependence

Life satisfaction of older people is related to the degree to which they can control their own lives. Stress may come from two sources: frustration at not being able to do accustomed tasks and a shift in their social roles. Giving up control means that older people must also change their social roles.

The ability to remain independent is related to both the financial status and the physical and mental condition of the older individual. For many seniors, independence means having a car and being able to drive, especially in small towns and rural areas (Bess, 1999a). These factors work alone or in combination. For example, older people who cannot manage to do repairs to a house or clean an apartment can still live on their own if they have enough money to pay someone to do these things for them. A number of older people move to smaller houses or apartments that require less care. Some maintain independence by finding housing with special aids like bathroom modifications or a lift (Che-Alford & Stevenson, 1998).

Most men are helped by their wives. Women, who are more likely to be widowed, receive assistance from their daughters, followed by friends and neighbours, then from extended-family members (Maurier & Northcott, 2000). The more assistance a person needs, the more independence and decision-making power is given up (Connidis, 2001). Increasing disability can change the husband–wife relationship, especially when one partner must make decisions for the other. Perhaps the most difficult adjustment comes when a partner needs to enter a nursing home. The institutionalized spouse is often angry, resentful, and depressed, while the other feels both relief and guilt (Machir, 2003). Government services can help keep older people in their own homes, for example, through the provision of grants to help finance renovations to make homes accessible to disabled persons, and through the provision of homemaker and home nursing services that reduce the need for institutionalization. Of course, living in a seniors' residence or a nursing home greatly reduces independence. Due to rules and routines, there can also be problems practising the traditions and rituals of one's cultural background, which tend to become more important as one ages (Maurier & Northcott, 2000). In fact, relatively few older people live in an institution. In 2001, 9.2 percent of senior women and 4.9 percent of senior men were living in health-care institutions, rising to 35.4 percent of women and 22.6 percent of men aged 85 and over. These rates have declined since 1981, and will probably continue to decline further in the future (Statistics Canada, 2002b).

Dependence can also be related to the attitude of relatives or nursing-home staff. If they see a person's condition as being worse than it is, and think that he or she is incompetent, they will try to make decisions for the older person and discourage any independence he or she might show. As a result, the older person is taught to be helpless (Walsh, 1999).

Connectedness versus Separateness

The struggle for independence often reflects tension between the desire for connectedness and separateness. In many ways this is reminiscent of adolescent-parent conflicts, except that this conflict occurs between adult child and older parent. Older people value their relationships with their children and grandchildren, yet they also wish to maintain their own unique lifestyle. As parents become older and frailer, their children may worry about them and try to limit their independence unnecessarily. For example, some children will be afraid that a

---

BOX 8.2

NOT A TEASING MATTER

Aunt Martha began acting strangely a year ago, after her husband's death following a long illness. Not only would she refuse invitations to go out but was very reluctant to allow us to visit any more. While she was downstairs, I saw she had replaced her twin bedroom set with a gigantic king-size bed!

I teased her about it: "What is a 74-year-old widow doing with a new king-size bed?" She got very angry and said she didn't think it was any of my business. She was sick and tired of the family's moral judgments which she had endured all her life! Then she calmed down and told me. The man next door, a retired physician whose wife had died several years before, had begun "calling" on her. She felt so good about it. "I was a loyal wife for 53 years and it wasn't no picnic, believe me, especially when Andy got sick. Now I'm having some fun for a change."

Source: National Advisory Council on Aging, "Family Role and the Negotiation of Change for the Aged," 1983, pp. 24–25. Reprinted with permission.

parent will fall or become ill and lie helpless for hours, or even days, without being able to call for help. As a result, they will urge their parent to move in with them or to move to an institution where they can be supervised more closely, rather than working to arrange a checkup system or a method of summoning help. Since many older people resist being managed to this degree, the result is family conflict (Kingsmill & Schlesinger, 1998).

Openness versus Privateness

Privacy may become precious in the face of retirement, widowhood, sickness, and institutionalization. In some cases, the older person may fear family members' disapproval of new ways of behaving and become secretive. Living in a nursing home makes a private life virtually impossible. Shared rooms and bathrooms make it difficult to discuss confidential topics or even to be private about matters like elimination (Maurier & Northcott, 2000). For another example, husbands and wives sometimes do not share the same room. Even if they do, it is difficult for them to engage in any sexual activity without fear of interruption, or even in safety, if they are not provided a double bed. The situation is even more difficult for couples who meet at the home (Hammond, 1987).

MINORITY GROUPS AND AGING

Immigrants

Cultures differ greatly in their views regarding how responsible the middle generation should be for looking after the elderly. Certain groups, such as Italians and Chinese, have strong beliefs about not "abandoning" relatives to nursing homes (Radina, 2003). Older people may feel isolated and shamed both because they are away from family and community and because elders are traditionally cared for within the family (Parker, 2004). Families that arrived earlier are more likely to consider seniors' residences and care homes. Nursing homes designed for a specific ethnic group help reduce the feeling of being cut off from one's culture. The waiting lists may, however, be very long (Basavarajappa, 1998; Maurier & Northcott, 2000).

Recent immigrants are more likely to live in three-generation households than those born in Canada. This is especially true of those coming from Asia and Central and South America (Glick & Van Hook, 2002). Such households are most common in British Columbia and Ontario where there are areas with high concentrations of newcomers. Many older individuals have come to join their younger relatives. They are not eligible for welfare or government pensions for a considerable time after arrival. If they do not have financial resources, they may have no choice where to live. Nearly half (48 percent) of recent immigrants aged 65 and older live with relatives, compared with only 5 percent of the Canadian-born (Thomas, 2001). Many three-generation families include someone with a disability. The elder may be cared for within the family or may help care for a younger member (Basavarajappa, 1998; Che-Alford & Hamm, 1999). Because many do not know English or French, they may be afraid to go out on their own and cannot make use of many community resources for seniors (Martin-Matthews, 2000).

Aboriginal Peoples

Traditionally, the grandparent generation among Aboriginal peoples in North America was responsible for socializing the children. They had both practical knowledge and a wealth of cultural information they could pass on. Much of their teaching of core values and survival techniques was transmitted through storytelling. In return, their grandchildren had the honoured responsibility of helping them to remain independent. If they had no grandchildren themselves, they became informal grandparents to other children, who filled the grandchild role (Vanderburgh, 1987).

The elder role was eroded through the coming of Christian missions, with their accompanying boarding schools, which removed children from their homes and cultures. In addition, during the 1960s and 1970s, many children were apprehended by child welfare authorities and placed with white foster and adoptive families. As a result, elders were no longer vital members of society because the socialization of children had passed to other people. Since children were no longer available to provide practical assistance, it also became more difficult for the old to retain their independence. The role of the family is being taken on by the community through services like home support for the elderly and on-reserve nursing homes (Castellano, 2002; Vanderburgh, 1987).

In recent years there has been a renewal of interest in traditional Aboriginal ways. Elders are once again valued as transmitters of culture. In the Far North, attempts are being made to reinstate the role of elders as advisers (Brunes, 2004). Elders may, however, be filling a role that is somewhat different from the traditional one. They no longer act only within the confines of their family, but also in the context of voluntary groups such as elders' circles. For example, elders are included in school and college programs both to provide encouragement for education and to strengthen ties to Aboriginal traditions. One example is the Aboriginal Elder/Outreach Program established in Saskatchewan in 1999 (Saskatchewan Education, n.d.). Valuable life experience has been redefined to include how to deal with schools, social service agencies, health-care facilities, and the legal system. Indeed, such knowledge may be just as important for survival as traditional methods of hunting, fishing, or agriculture. In addition, elders are seen as custodians of the traditional culture, from which the younger generations have been alienated (Vanderburgh, 1987).

DEATH OF FAMILY MEMBERS

There has been a shift in the social time clock for dying. In the past, death lurked around every corner and could occur at any age. With medical advances and increased life expectancy, death is now regarded as belonging mainly to old age. Serious illness and death that occur earlier are seen in terms of an incomplete life. The death of the last member of the oldest generation now more clearly marks a shifting of generations, so that the next generation becomes the oldest and next in line for death. As life expectancy has increased, so has the incidence of long and debilitating illnesses such as cancer and Alzheimer's disease. As a result, when we talk about death, we need to distinguish between the actual death and the events leading up to it. Both have a profound but different impact on families (Rolland, 2003).

Terminal Illness

The final illness can be very stressful for families. First, both the dying person and his or her relatives must face the deterioration of physical or mental powers (Mills & Wilmoth, 2002). Elderly people tend to fear prolonged illness and dependency more than death itself. This fear is related to the desire for independence, and in extreme cases may be expressed by refusing treatment. With illnesses like Alzheimer's disease and others like it, the marriage relationship is totally destroyed. The caregiving spouse becomes widowed for all practical purposes long before the partner dies (Berardo, 2001). Part of the stress involved in terminal illness comes from the changes in lifestyle needed to deal with the illness. These affect the older person and his caregivers alike. For example, if a person cannot control his or her bladder or bowels, someone has to clean and change the person. A key stress factor for relatives is the time needed for the physical care of the dying person or for repeated hospital visits. One of the major problems with dying in a hospital, however, is the fact that the individual dies a social death before he or she dies physically. This happens because staff members may treat the patient as a dying body rather than as a person (Lopata, 1996).

Second, the family, especially the husband or wife, has to prepare for the actual death and for the changes that must occur in lifestyle and relationships. Individuals who know they are dying have the opportunity to look over their lives, to make plans for their families, and to say final goodbyes and make peace with people they have been alienated from. Family members also have a chance to say farewell. Such preparation for a spouse's death can aid the long-term adjustment of a husband or wife (Rolland, 2003). This is more likely if friends have also been widowed and provide role models. The ability to prepare for death is affected by the information the family is given and by their degree of openness in talking about it. Sometimes, of course, death comes suddenly. While there may be little physical suffering, there is no opportunity for goodbyes. By the 1980s, most doctors treating patients with a terminal illness said it was generally their policy to tell the patient that he or she was dying. Even though family members know how serious the illness is, however, they may not give up hope until the moment of death (Giboney, 2001). Some who do accept the fact may still not communicate freely, pretending that the family member is not dying (McGoldrick & Walsh, 1999).

Lack of openness may also affect the ability to talk about such matters as prolonging life once the quality of life is destroyed. Most people now feel that a person has a right to die with dignity rather than being subjected to painful or humiliating treatments, which may prolong life by a matter of days or weeks. The growing hospice movement has also encouraged humane care for the dying. In these institutions or at home, the concern is to make the patients' last days as comfortable as possible. Staff are trained to be supportive to both the dying and the members of their families (Giboney, 2001).

The Fact of Death and Its Aftermath

There are ethnic and class differences in the way people deal with death. Many in the majority culture prefer death to occur in hospitals. This is part of the North American tendency to deny death, as is seen in the transfer of responsibility for looking after the body to a funeral home. For other ethnic groups, however, to die away from one's home and family compounds the tragedy (McGoldrick & Walsh, 1999).

Funerals are family times. Often these events, even more than weddings, are occasions when all the relatives gather together. Until the funeral is over, family members often forget their differences and offer assistance to one another (Baker, 1988). A funeral is also the occasion for formal leave-taking of the person who has died. As such it is an important aspect of mourning. North American culture, however, tends to minimize everything that has to do with death. This is reflected in the preference for the hospital as the place for dying, in the control of the ceremonies by the funeral industry, and in the short time allowed for bereavement leave from work. Such practices make it difficult for some cultural groups to retain their traditional customs (McGoldrick & Walsh, 1999). They may also interfere with the grieving process by encouraging family members to distance themselves from the death.

During a serious or terminal illness, a homosexual partner may not be recognized as a family member by medical professionals. When a partner dies, grieving heterosexual spouses are recognized as suffering deep grief. The understanding and support they receive helps them move through the grieving process. Lesbians and gay men have often been denied this recognition and support (Johnson & Colucci, 1999).

Adjustment to Widowhood

Widowhood initially involves a sense of loss, disorientation, and loneliness. This is also true for cohabiting and same-sex couples. The discussion here will focus on married couples since these are the most common. Women who have centred their lives on their husbands and families often feel a loss of identity. They may also feel a loss of status. Over the years, the couple has built up a family identity with shared customs and habits. As married people, they have a recognized status within society. With the death of the spouse, all that is gone. Those who have looked after their partner during a long illness may feel they have lost their purpose in life. For some, however, the death comes as a relief, for example, when one's partner has suffered for a long time or the relationship has been unhappy or abusive. Women tend to manage better than men after the death of a spouse, probably because they depend on children and friends for social and emotional support. Men fare worse, since they usually have depended on their wives for emotional support. In the crisis of death they are often left isolated. Especially in the first year following the death of a spouse, men more than women suffer an increase in death and suicide rates (Connidis, 2001; McGoldrick & Walsh, 1999).

The psychological task confronting widowed people is grief over the loss, and then commitment to their own continuing life. Typically they go through three stages. First, they need to loosen their bonds to their spouse and accept the fact he or she is dead. Second, they must pay attention to day-to-day living such as job and household management. Finally, they shift to new activities and interest in others. During this period, family relationships must be reworked to create a new balance. For example, a widow may now tell her worries to a daughter, when in the past she confided in her husband. The process of mourning and adaptation to the new life typically takes one to two years (McGoldrick & Walsh, 1999). Because death in modern society has become concentrated in the later years of life, some older people may experience a series of bereavements and thus go through extreme grief. They may also have limited time and energy to form new attachments (Berardo, 2001).

The Economics of Death

Often the death of a spouse means a drop in family income (Li, 2004). This is especially true when an employed partner dies. As has already been discussed, long-term hardships tend to be greater for women, since they often have limited financial resources such as pensions and are less likely to find a new marriage partner. There are also the costs surrounding death itself. There may be a drop in income during the final illness because the sick person cannot work and the partner may need to take a leave of absence from his or her job. Funeral expenses may run very high because the family may try to show their love and respect to the deceased by making elaborate arrangements. Add to these the cost of cemetery plot and grave marker.

Often a period of uncertainty follows death as financial affairs are sorted out. If one partner has handled all the finances, the survivor may not even know what resources are available. A widow may not know for some time to what income she is entitled. Some survivors' pensions, for example, are based on the widow's age. If a person dies intestate—that is, without making out a will—there is much greater delay and confusion. Common-law partners may be shocked to find they are not entitled to property rights they expected (Cochrane, 2002). As a result, survivors may experience continuing distress until financial affairs are settled.

WHAT DOES THE FUTURE HOLD?

In coming years, we will probably see a great but temporary increase in the proportion of the elderly in the Canadian population. In part, this increase will be the result of a gradually increasing life expectancy. Since much of the change will, however, be due to the aging of the baby-boom generation, the numbers of old people will decrease again once the wave has passed.

The greater number of elderly in the population will call for changes and create conflicts in society. Many of our myths about aging and the elderly will be challenged. Older people are remaining vigorous and independent much longer as a result of health care advances (Gilbert & Bélanger, 2001). Because of improved pensions, fewer elderly people are now living in poverty. In fact, the number of poor seniors has declined even as the total numbers of the elderly have risen sharply (National Council of Welfare, 2004). Thus we can expect an increase in "grey power." It is already reflected economically in the increasing number of television commercials aimed at older people. We can also expect pressure on governments to maintain, or even improve, services like pensions and health care.

Along with such pressure, there have been repeated alarms over the ability of coming generations, especially since the birth rate is lower, to shoulder the tax burden for services to the elderly. In recent years, however, the governments have increasingly shifted costs for present and future care to individuals. Let's look at some examples. In 1952, the Old Age Security (OAS) pension was given to all Canadians aged 65 years and over. The OAS is no longer a universal benefit. Rather, since 1989, it has been subject to a **clawback.** That is, it is counted as income and taxed. Over a certain income level, part or all of the pension is reclaimed by the federal government. In 1998, the Canada Pension Plan (CPP) was reformed by increasing the contributions of both employers and employees and by limiting some benefits (Maurier & Northcott, 2000). Some provinces have reduced the health services they provide beyond the minimum required under the Canada Health Act. A number of services such as drug benefits are based on income. Provinces also vary on how much (or little) help they provide in buying assistive devices like wheelchairs. There may also be a lack of information on how to get financial assistance (Fawcett, Ciceri, Tsoukalas, & Gibson-Kierstead, 2004).

Mythical and stereotypical portraits of persons such as the ones mentioned in Box 8.3 continue to be an integral part of the general images the young and old have of one another. These images have given rise to the popular concept of a "generation gap."

BOX 8.3

MYTHS

Ageism and resulting age biases are the result of myths and stereotypes that have their root more in fiction than in fact.

For example:

For many younger people, most older people are:

- Inflexible, rigid and set in their ways
- Over-conservative in dress, conduct, politics and popular viewpoint
- A homogeneous group of persons 65 years of age and older
- Weak, feeble, in poor health, institutionalized, dependent and lonely
- If not senile, definitely declining in intelligence and the ability to learn
- Non-productive

On the other hand, many older persons see the majority of younger persons as:

- Immature, lazy and playful
- Disrespectful of authority and property
- Careless, impulsive and irresponsible
- Extreme in dress, manners, behaviour and popular viewpoint
- Loud, boisterous and irritating
- Lacking in experience and general knowledge

Source: "A Guidebook for Intergenerational Planning" (Toronto: Ministry of Tourism and Recreation, 1983), p. 11. Reprinted with permission.

Can Canada continue to provide services at the present level, or even improve them? It depends on whom you ask. Some look only at the cost of services and demand cutbacks to control these costs. Others look at sources of income and suggest that no cutbacks are needed. They point to the recent budget surpluses and those expected both federally and provincially over the next few years. Some of the costs will also be offset by lower expenses in services for the dwindling number of younger people, such as education and correctional services. Some programs can reduce costs in other areas. For example, seniors can be kept out of hospital or their stays made shorter through expanding care at home by nurses, physiotherapists, homemakers, and others, and by providing assistive devices like lifts and wheelchairs (National Advisory Council on Aging, 2000).

One major concern in providing services to older people is "generational equity." That is, can each generation get a fair share of resources? One fact remains: our society will be faced with major adjustments as we adapt to the increasing numbers of older people. Legislators and service providers will need to come up with innovative plans if the needs of all citizens are to be met (Maurier & Northcott, 2000).

THE AGING POPULATION. The population of Canada is growing older as a result of the aging baby-boom generation and a low birth rate. Old age is, however, difficult to define because it consists of several dimensions. Chronological age refers to the years an individual has lived; physical age to changes in the body; psychological age to emotional and cognitive aspects of aging; and social age to social norms. The developmental tasks of old age include allowing the next generation to take over leadership, and finding order and meaning in life as its end approaches.

THE "YOUNG" OLD. People in their early retirement years now enjoy better pensions than in the past. There are, however, many inequities. Women, in particular, are disadvantaged because of their lower employment rate and lower pay with fewer benefits. The interest of older people shifts from employment to other activities. When men are at home, family roles change. Family relationships are an important source of social support. Men are more likely than women to be married. Women live longer, and widowed or divorced men are more likely to remarry. The relationship with children is often based on mutual help. The relationship with grandchildren can be close, but it is affected by distance or by custody following divorce. The unmarried and childless tend to have the closest ties with brothers and sisters. Gay men's and lesbians' adjustment is similar to that of heterosexual adults.

THE "OLD" OLD. Health and self-care become issues as people grow older. Chronic illness becomes more of a concern to both the elderly and their children, who may have to care for their parents. Life satisfaction is related to the degree older individuals can control their own lives. Their ability to do so is affected by financial, physical, and mental factors, as well as by the attitudes of family members and professional helpers. Most older people wish to maintain their lifestyle while keeping up relationships with their relatives. Privacy may become precious as individuals become more dependent on the care of others.

MINORITY GROUPS. Cultural groups differ greatly in their attitudes toward the elderly. Immigrants are more likely than other Canadians to live in three-generation families. Among Aboriginal peoples in the past, elders held an important role in transmitting cultural values to the young. This has been eroded through the colonialism of the majority culture. Recently, however, elders are becoming more valued.

DEATH OF FAMILY MEMBERS. Often a prolonged illness and dependency is feared more than death itself. If possible, both the dying person and family members need to prepare themselves and say their farewells. Although funerals draw family members together, the trend toward minimizing death may make ethnic observances difficult. The adjustment to widowhood involves dealing with the loss of identity and status, grieving the loss of one's partner, and then commitment to continuing one's own life. Economic hardship may result from death, both because of funeral costs and because of a drop in income.

THE FUTURE. A large but temporary increase of elderly people is predicted for the future. This will temporarily place more political power in their hands. One issue that still needs to be addressed is how to meet the cost of providing care for the growing population of elders.

KEY TERMS

chronological age: the number of years a person has lived (p. 197)

clawback: the practice of defining benefits as income and taxing them and of requiring repayment when income reaches a certain level (p. 213)

physical aging: changes that occur in the body as a result of the length of time a person has lived (p. 198)

psychological age: the attitudes and beliefs one has about one's age (p. 198)

social age: cultural norms that specify appropriate behaviour for people of a given age (p. 198)

CLASS ASSIGNMENTS

Complete one or both of the following assignments, as directed by your instructor:

1. Discover what facilities and services are available in your community for senior citizens. Did you find any gaps? What are the difficulties in acquiring needed services?

2. Three options for the care of frail elderly people are going to an institution, living with relatives, and receiving services in their own homes. Describe the advantages and disadvantages of each of these options for older people and their relatives.

PERSONAL ASSIGNMENTS

The following assignments are designed to help you explore your own family experiences and your expectations for the future:

1. Among the people you know, whom do you think of as old? What characteristics, in your opinion, distinguish between old and not old? Why?

2. Even though it seems far in the future, describe what you feel would make life worthwhile once you are retired. Be realistic. What steps can you take beforehand to make these plans attainable?

Part Five

CHANGES IN THE FAMILY

Chapter 9

The Lone-Parent Family—The Future Majority?

OBJECTIVES

- *To look at the place of single parenthood in the family life cycle*

- *To consider variations in single parenthood*

- *To examine the quality of life of single-parent families, including that of the children*

- *To explore two special groups of single parents— the very young mother and the single father*

Rose is an accountant and an executive in her firm. When she was 37 and still single, she decided not to put off motherhood any longer. She considered adoption, but learned she would probably receive an older child, not the baby she wanted. A divorced friend of her brother's, a man whom she regards as extremely intelligent and good-natured, agreed to help Rose. Because she receives an excellent salary, she doesn't expect him to pay child support. Eighteen-month-old Alec spends days with a nanny and evenings with his mother. On weekends, he and his mother visit his uncle, Rose's brother, and sometimes see his father.

After living with Jason for nearly a year, Suzanne, now aged 35, became pregnant. In spite of their stormy relationship, they married. After ten years, she and the children left after Jason assaulted her. She lived with her widowed mother until she could find a full-time job. As long as she's careful, she can make ends meet with her salary and the child support Jason pays. She's grateful her three children can go to their grandmother's before and after school. She doesn't know how she'd manage without her mother's help.

Cassie, 24 years old, has moved from one live-in relationship to another since she dropped out of school when she was 17. She has held many jobs as a store clerk or waitress, but usually loses them when she becomes angry with the boss. She has two sons, aged five and three. She hopes her new baby will be a girl so that she can give her a better life than she herself has had. All her children have different fathers. Her latest boyfriend is threatening to leave. He doesn't want a child and resents spending money on Cassie's boys. She has applied to welfare for help.

As a whole, North American society expects adults in the family to come in pairs, one of each sex—husband and wife, mother and father. Single parents offend against what Dr. Ben Schlesinger (1990) calls the "Noah's ark syndrome": they don't come two by two.

In the past, sociologists, social workers, and other concerned individuals referred to "broken," "incomplete," or "atypical" families, as if something were missing or faulty (Lessa, 2003). For example, Imber-Black (1989) tells of two male caseworkers who kept telling a single mother that her son needed a male role model without asking about her extended family support system. In fact, an uncle was available and willing to be involved. Indeed, many individuals in society nowadays still feel there is an oddness to single-parent families. Single mothers tend to be blamed for their own poverty and for damaging their children (Erera, 2002). Reactions may vary depending on whether the lone parent is considered a victim of circumstances or is blamed for the situation. "Innocent" victims usually do not experience as much stigma as people who are considered responsible for their situation. Thus a woman who left her husband may be seen as more to blame than a widow. One American study found that premarital childbearing was higher in communities that were tolerant of single parents (Butler, 2002).

For many years, the single-parent family was the fastest-growing family type in Canada. In the 25 years from 1966 to 1991, the number of lone-parent families in Canada increased 269 percent, while the number of husband-wife families rose only 147 percent (using figures from McKie, 1993). In 2001, such families made up over 13 percent of all Canadian families. This is a sex-related phenomenon: as we can see in Table 9.1, nearly all—more than 82 percent—single parents were women (Statistics Canada, 2002b). More children are experiencing single-parent families, and at younger ages. By the age of 16, one in five children born in the early 1960s lived in a single-parent home. This "milestone" occurred by age 12 among children born in the early 1970s, by age eight among those born in the early 1980s, and for those born in the 1990s, by age five. (See Figure 9.1.) According to the National Longitudinal Survey of Children and Youth (started in 1993–94), all signs indicate that children born later will experience lone-parent family living even earlier. Often, lone parenthood is temporary. Many families spend some time as one-parent families before, after, or between two-parent episodes (Juby, Marcil-Gratton, & Le Bourdais, 2001). Numbers can be deceptive, however. Many single-parent families are that in name only. There may be live-in partners and others who act as parents (Anderson, 2003).

Several factors are involved in the trend toward single parenthood. Both the pregnancy and the birth rates among teens were considerably lower in 2000 than in 1974. Even the increase reported in the late 1980s and early 1990s did not reach the 1974 level (Dryburgh, 2000; Statistics Canada, 2004h). Nevertheless, fewer teens are married now and fewer of the unmarried place their babies for adoption. In 1931, less than half of 1 percent of lone-parent families were the result of births to unmarried women, in contrast to 22 percent in 1996 (Milan, 2000). Since the late 1960s, unmarried mothers have met with less prejudice, although they are still subject to a certain amount of criticism. The growing number of divorces has increased their acceptance, because divorced and never-married single parents are virtually indistinguishable. Working mothers have become commonplace, and family benefits are still available to help them support their children; therefore many more unmarried mothers are choosing to raise their children themselves. The divorce rate has also increased dramatically during the same period, partly as a result of changed legislation. In addition, cohabitation has increased, and these relationships are not as stable as marriages. Underlying all these factors is the waning of the emphasis on the traditional nuclear family and the growing acceptability of family variations.

TABLE 9.1

LONE-PARENT FAMILIES IN CANADA, 1995 AND 2001

	1995		2001	
	Number	**Percentage**	**Number**	**Percentage**
Total families	8 363 000	100.0	8 790 000	100.0
Total lone-parent families	1 151 000	13.8	1 185 000	13.5
Male parent	168 000	2.0	209 000	2.4
Female parent	982 000	11.7	976 000	11.1

Source: Adapted from Statistics Canada, "General Social Survey—Cycle 15: Family history, 2001." Catalogue 89-575, July 11, 2002, p. 5, Table 1.

Figure 9.1

CUMULATIVE PERCENTAGE AT EACH BIRTHDAY OF CANADIAN CHILDREN BORN INTO A TWO-PARENT FAMILY WHO HAVE EXPERIENCED PARENTAL SEPARATION, BY TYPE OF UNION INTO WHICH THEY WERE BORN (1983–84 COHORT)

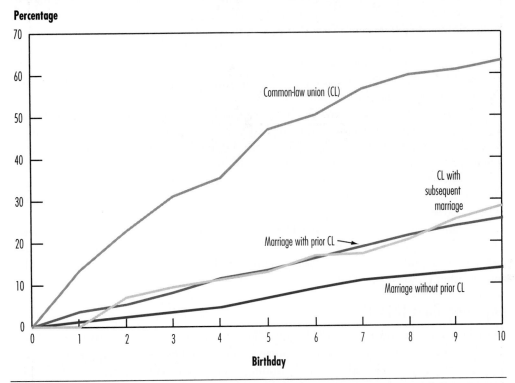

Source: Adapted from Statistics Canada, "Growing up with Mom and Dad? The intricate family life courses of Canadian children, 1994–95." Catalogue 89-566, July 1998.

Most of the figures on lone parenthood are based on numbers for the total population in Canada or on studies of the white majority. Relatively little information concerning minority groups exists. Most immigrants come to Canada as single individuals or married families; comparatively few come as lone parents. How many become lone parents after their arrival is unknown. Aboriginal families are more likely than others to have just one parent. Nearly twice as many Aboriginal families are headed by single parents, including fathers, than in the Canadian population as a whole. In addition, Aboriginal families tend to be larger; thus more of their children live in lone-parent families (Statistics Canada, 2003a).

THE PATH OF SINGLE PARENTHOOD

As we can see in the stories of Rose, Suzanne, and Cassie, with which this chapter opened, there is no one road for women to reach lone parenthood. The percentage of lone-parent families was only slightly higher in 2001 (13.5 percent) than in 1931 (12 percent). The reasons differed, however. In 1931, three-quarters resulted from the death of a parent. Now many are the result of divorce. In addition, a larger number of women now have children outside marriage. History and changes in law have helped produce these changes. The number of widows may have been so high in the 1940s partly because many husbands and fathers of young children died during World War II. More recently, as we shall consider in greater detail in the next chapter, divorces have increased following changes in the law in 1981 and 1986, making them both much easier to obtain and more acceptable.

The life patterns of never-married, divorced, and widowed female lone parents vary in a number of ways, and may have less in common than is usually imagined. They include poor, never-married women with several children, like Cassie; older professional women who have chosen to be parents, like Rose; widowed men and women; and a growing number of the divorced, like Suzanne (Anderson, 2003). These differences in life patterns include the age at which the woman became a single parent, the likelihood of marriage and remarriage, current life circumstances, and the impact of the life-cycle stage when single parenthood began. Many of these factors are interrelated. Because the majority of lone parents are women, most of the discussion will focus on their experiences.

Current living circumstances vary. The parent can live on her own; have a live-in friend, either male or female with or without a sexual relationship; have a live-in weekend friend; have an out-of-the-house heterosexual or homosexual relationship; or live with her mother and/or father (Anderson, 2003).

How Long Does It Last?

Several patterns are noticeable in the length of lone parenthood and in the way it ends. These are related to both the age at which a woman becomes a single parent and the way it happens. According to some older research findings, those who had children out of wedlock began parenting alone at the youngest age. They also spent the shortest time as lone parents, and were most likely to marry or enter a common-law relationship. Lone parenthood for separated or divorced mothers began later because most had been in a marriage for some time. It lasted longer and was less likely to end because mothers entered a new union. For some, lone parenthood ended because they gave up custody of the children or the children became independent. As a group, widows were the oldest when they became single parents. They remained lone parents the longest, and were least likely to remarry. These findings are predictable since, in our society, younger women are far more likely to find husbands or partners than older women. Widows and never-married mothers whose children were younger than two years were more likely to enter a union than divorced women. This may reflect the fact that fathers were involved with their young children following divorce, a situation that would complicate any new relationship. A few women, more commonly those who had a child before marrying, had more than one lone-parent period (Le Bourdais, Desrosiers, & Laplante, 1995; Moore, 1988). According to Dr. Zheng Wu (1994) of the University of Victoria, the likelihood of remarriage for divorced and widowed individuals depends on how desirable they think marriage is, how eligible they themselves are, what barriers like children or religion exist, and how many eligible individuals are available.

For most children, the first experience in lone-parent families lasted less than five years. By the age of six, 10 out of 100 children from broken unions have had a second experience of living in a single-parent family (Marcil-Gratton, 1993). Less is known about men's experience as lone parents than of women's. This may be because there are far fewer male lone parents than female. Also, lone fathers are more likely to marry or cohabit than mothers; so they are lone parents for shorter periods.

Single Parenthood and the Life Cycle

Differences in women's experiences are related to life-cycle issues. Let's first look at those women who became pregnant outside of marriage. Those who have never married or cohabited begin their families, not through couplehood, but through parenthood. The parent–child relationship differs fundamentally from the couple relationship. There is usually a much greater age and power difference between parents and children than there is between partners. In addition, children need a different kind of nurturing from that needed by a husband or wife. According to traditionalists, the couple union in marriage is a necessary first stage in healthy family formation. Otherwise, the family is considered defective (Gleason, 1999).

Age is also extremely important to the experience of single parenthood. Pregnancy during adolescence comes at a point when most young women are struggling with the issues of independence from their family of origin. They often do not have realistic plans for future employment or, if they do, they have not completed the necessary education or training. The later pregnancy occurs, the more likely a woman is to have completed her education and to have become established in a career, and the more likely she is to be able to support herself and her child above the level of poverty. For males, many of the same factors are true. Those who are younger are less likely to be able to contribute in a meaningful way financially and socially to the rearing of their children (Carter, 1999; National Council of Welfare, 2004).

The age factor also affects older women. They may feel they are not likely to find a husband before they are past childbearing age. Older single women, according to one study, tended to have mixed feelings about marriage, with high ideals of what marriage should be and an unwillingness to settle for anything less. In fact, some single mothers did not even search very hard for "Mr. Right" before deciding on lone parenthood (Siegel, 1995). Some women seek out a man to father a child or make use of artificial insemination. In this case, pregnancy is not accidental, but is the result of a woman's wish to include parenthood in her experience.

The divorced and widowed both must deal with the pain and anger that surrounds the end of marriage. For such individuals, age is once again a significant factor in the single-parenting experience. Did the breakup or death occur within two to three years of marriage, or as part of the midlife reassessment? What were their roles within the marriage? Long-term homemakers may not have the job skills necessary to support themselves at the level the family had enjoyed. Divorced couples share family assets (Cochrane, 2002). However, early in the family life cycle there may be more debts than assets. Widows have a greater chance than divorced women of being financially stable, partly because they do not share resources with an ex-spouse, and partly because generally the family has had more time to acquire assets.

The situation for the formerly married or partnered is complicated by the age of the child at the time single parenthood begins. The impact of single parenthood varies according to whether the child is a new baby, a school-aged child, a teenager, or a young person on the brink of leaving home. Since children's needs and developmental tasks correspond to the different stages, they will make different emotional and financial demands on their parents (Anderson, 1999).

THE QUALITY OF LIFE

To better understand how the many single-parent families in Canada—most of which are headed by females—manage, it is important to look at their economic circumstances, housing, and social life.

Single Parents and Economic Survival

Female lone parents are at risk of living in poverty. In 2000, lone-mother families were far more likely to be poor than other families, with nearly half below the poverty line. This was especially true for those below the age of 25, like Cassie, who had not graduated from high school and had more and younger children. Many of these were dependent on family benefits or welfare (National Council of Welfare, 2004). Widows are probably the best off financially, since they benefit from pension plans and usually do not have children as young as those of other single parents to care for.

A study of childcare needs of Canadian parents found that only 52 percent of single mothers were employed. In contrast, 81 percent of single fathers worked. Women with preschool children were less likely to be employed or to be serious students than others. So were those with two or more children. Those under the age of 25 and those with lower levels of education were also less likely to be working or in school (see Table 9.2). This is the group most likely to be receiving social assistance and most likely to be living in poverty. When asked why they did not want or have a job, about 30 percent said they wanted to stay home to look after their children; 19 percent were in school; and 10 percent had difficulty finding and paying for childcare (Lero & Brockman, 1993). A study of incentives to help long-term welfare recipients become self-sufficient found that childcare and transportation problems, as well as physical and emotional disabilities, were barriers to employment (Michalopoulos et al., 2002).

Working lone mothers experienced a great deal of tension in juggling work, family, and daycare. More single than married mothers reported that the stress was severe. They felt more tired and overloaded and had more trouble balancing the demands of home and work. In addition, single mothers were concerned about daycare costs and worried more that their childcare plans would fall through (Lero & Brockman, 1993). During classroom discussions,

TABLE 9.2

COMPARISON OF POOR AND NON-POOR LONE-PARENT MOTHERS

	Non-poor	Poor
Total (thousands)	396	375
Average number of children < 7 years	0.23	0.69
Average number of children < 18 years	0.97	1.50
	100%	100%
Age:		
< 35	18.0	48.7
35–64	82.0	51.3
Education:		
Less than high school graduate	15.8	39.9
High school graduate/Some postsecondary	29.8	32.0
Postsecondary certificate, diploma/University degree	54.4	28.1
Weeks employed:		
Full year	80.4	18.6
Some	10.5	25.8
None	9.1*	55.6

Source: *Canadian Fact Book on Poverty—2000* by Ross, Scott, & Smith (2000, p. 70). Used with permission from The Canadian Council on Social Development (www.ccsd.ca).

*Estimate less reliable due to small sample size.

college students (many of whom are single parents) complained about problems in finding care for children during vacations, before and after school, and on teachers' professional development days. In addition, lone parents in the daycare study felt that they would have fewer opportunities for promotion (Lero & Brockman, 1993). For example, single parents are unable to travel much for business or work much overtime because of their family responsibilities. Even when they are employed, many single mothers find dead-end jobs with low pay and little possibility for promotion.

In spite of its drawbacks, government assistance is often the only reasonable alternative to paid employment for single parents, especially when their children are young. It does not, however, provide the means for an adequate standard of living, since benefits fall well below the **poverty line** (National Council of Welfare, n.d.). Stigma is also attached to receiving benefits. People who stay home with their children are often regarded as freeloaders. If they are on welfare, they are open to invasion of privacy and judgments on the part of professionals who administer the system. Some places have established "snitch lines," which neighbours can call anonymously to report suspected welfare cheaters. Sometimes these are used maliciously. There is growing pressure on mothers to seek employment, especially in times when governments are cutting social welfare spending.

Some ways of getting off social assistance are through upgrading or completing one's education, or by finding an adequate job. Whether a woman follows these paths depends in part on what she hopes for herself and for her children. If she wants badly to get off welfare or family benefits, or wants her children to go to university or college, she is more likely to go back to school herself or get a job. This is especially true if her friends and relatives approve of such moves and help her in practical ways. She is less likely to make the effort if she has several children and has spent a length of time on welfare (Gorlick & Pomfret, 1993). The effect of recent programs to move people off welfare is still unclear. While governments claim success, there are concerns that lone parents and their children may be actually worse off than when they were on welfare (Yoshikawa, Magnuson, Bos, & Hsueh, 2003).

Housing

Housing is the single largest expense for most single mothers and may be difficult to find. Low- and moderate-cost housing has largely been provided by nonprofit groups. Recent funding cuts have meant that fewer units are being built. In addition, in many inner-city neighbourhoods, older buildings, which had contained cheaper apartments, are being converted into luxury apartments and condominiums. Because they are more likely to be poor, single mothers are often caught in a financial squeeze. They cannot afford a car, so they need to live near transportation routes or within walking distance of jobs and services. Thus, employment and housing choices may be limited by lack of transportation (Spector & Klodawsky, 1993). A study of poor families living in mid-size Alberta cities found that they spend a larger percentage of their income on housing than those better off (Lee & Engler, 1999). Single mothers are more likely than others to live in low-income areas for longer periods of time (Frenette, Picot, & Sceviour, 2004).

In order to raise children, parents need enough space, preferably with a suitable play area, and they need to be able to reach schools, stores, medical care, and other services. Most cannot buy a house. They tend to live in apartments, row housing, or co-op housing. Many of these kinds of accommodation, especially where rent is geared to income, have large groups of female-headed single-parent families living in them. Problems with privacy arise when so many families with young children are clustered together (Spector & Klodawsky, 1993). There can also be prejudice against families and children who live in low-rent housing complexes. For example, children may be stereotyped as troublemakers and other youngsters may not be allowed to play with them.

Social Life

What kind of social life does a single parent have? According to an older survey of social services agency staff, many parents lack emotional support and social activities. The majority of single parents, on the other hand, reported adequate contact with others, although a minority reported being lonely. Half the parents were involved in leisure activities at least once a week.

Source: *Custody of Dad.* Reprinted by kind permission of Barrie Maguire.

When asked what problems they encountered regarding leisure activities, they cited lack of money as significant. This is easy to understand if you add up the costs, for example, of going to a movie—namely, movie admission, snack, babysitting, and transportation. Some found that timing was inconvenient. There can be scheduling conflicts with a job or with the need of children to have a parent home after school (City of Calgary, 1985).

Social support can be separated into two areas: how supportive society is as a whole and the immediate sources of emotional and practical help. Most single mothers have informal networks made up of children, parents, other relatives, and friends who provide information and assistance, support mothers emotionally, and bolster their self-esteem. Most support comes from females—friends, mothers, and relatives. A mother's satisfaction with the support she receives is related to its level; the higher the level, the more satisfied she is. A few single parents cannot count on friends or relatives to help them out at all. Some members of their networks are so critical or demanding that they add to the parent's stress level (Anderson, 2003). Parents with poor support systems may not have the resources to cope with emergencies or long-term stress. As a result, they may become clients of social service agencies in order to get the kind of backup that informal networks provide for other single parents.

In Chapter 2, we looked at some of the problems minority groups face. Single parents meet with some of these same problems. Often criticism is greater if the individual is considered to be responsible for his or her circumstances. Never-married mothers are seen as more responsible for their situation than abandoned wives or widows. For example, one grocery-store cashier cashed a government cheque for a young woman. She complained to her next customer about unmarried parents getting taxpayers' money. Even worse in her eyes was the fact that the mother had not had the good taste to choose a white man; the child's father was obviously Black. Victims who are perceived as playing no part in their own misfortune usually do not experience such stigma.

In the past, the one-parent family that needed financial aid was seen as having personal rather than more general economic problems, and was regarded with some suspicion by official helpers. The original Ontario legislation establishing **Mothers Allowance** in 1920 made only mothers who were widows, wives of permanently disabled men, and deserted wives eligible, provided they were fit and proper to have care and custody of children. This followed similar legislation in Manitoba (passed in 1916) providing for payments to morally upright women with dependent children (Lessa, 2003).

ARE CHILDREN IN LONE-PARENT FAMILIES AT RISK?

In view of the difficulties many single mothers face, an important question is the effect on children of growing up in such a family. This aspect of lone parenthood has probably attracted the most research. Nevertheless, the findings are anything but definite. Children who grow up in lone-parent families are stereotyped as being likely to become problem children who are emotionally disturbed or delinquent. There is a grain of truth in this, but the facts are much more complex than this stereotype suggests. Although children growing up in a lone-parent family are at greater risk for developing problems, in fact most do not have unusual difficulties (Anderson, 2003). We will look at three aspects of adjustment: school achievement and employment, family life, and personal adjustment.

School Achievement and Employment

On average, children from single-parent families do not do as well in school as children in two-parent families. By their early 20s, they are more likely to have dropped out of school and are less likely to have technical qualifications or to have or be pursuing postsecondary education than those from two-parent families. The number of years of schooling is affected by the length of time spent in a lone-parent family, the number of children in the family, and the cause of lone parenthood. Those who spend less time with a single parent and have fewer brothers and sisters are more likely to stay in school. So are those who have only one parent because the other one has died (Parcel & Dufur, 2001; Parke, 2003). Dropping out of school affects other aspects of life, such as getting a job and living on one's own (Aquilino, 1996). Employment prospects are, of course, affected by education. Generally, adults who grew up in a single-parent family have a lower income, are more likely to have lived on welfare at some time, and are less likely to own their own home (Gee, 1993). Those growing up in divorced homes are likely to start work earlier than those from a two-parent family or from a home where the father has died (Ambert, 2002).

Family Life

Two aspects of family life are affected by lone parenthood: relationships within the single-parent family and relationships within families formed by adult children of single parents. In divorced families, parents and children may not be as close as in other families (White, 1994). When mothers use a hostile parenting style, children have more difficulties in both school and relationships (Ross, Roberts, & Scott, 1998; Thomas, 2004). Young women tend to leave home earlier, possibly because of friction in the family, especially if their parents have remarried (Anderson, 2003). Some of the factors involved will be discussed in more detail in the next two chapters.

Individuals who grew up in lone-parent families because their parents had divorced are more likely to have formed partnerships at an early age, through either marriage or cohabitation. They are also more likely to have a child before they are 20. Once they have married, they are more likely to divorce. The reasons are difficult to untangle, but besides growing up in a lone-parent family, other possible influences are early age at marriage and cohabitation before marriage, both of which are connected with a higher divorce rate (Ambert, 2002).

Personal Adjustment

Young adults whose parents separated before they were five are more likely than others to have long-term emotional difficulties, to have committed a serious crime, or to have had a child outside marriage. They are more disruptive, more unhappy, and seem more worried as teenagers than those whose parents did not divorce. However, many such children showed similar kinds of behaviour before their parents had separated. So it is difficult to sort out how much has been caused by divorce and how much by factors like family conflict (Ambert, 2002).

Explanations for Difficulties

Two basic explanations are used to account for the differences between children from single-parent and two-parent families. The first states that children in single-parent families are not properly socialized. According to this point of view, having anything less than both a mother and father in-house is deficient, because children do not have both male and female role models. This argument ignores the influence of other adults, siblings, friends, and the media. Critics of lone-parent families also suggest that parents provide poor role models for children because they have chosen not to marry. If they have left a marriage, they may not teach their children how to manage interpersonal conflict (Gee, 1993). A second view states that any negative effect of single-parent families on children results from the higher levels of poverty in female-headed families. When mothers work, they cannot supervise their children closely. In addition, children may work full time or help care for brothers and sisters, activities that can interfere with schooling and may lead to dropping out (Dodson & Dickert, 2004).

A major difficulty with both types of explanations is the huge variety in lone-parent families. Some of the studies have followed children from such families until they were adults. At the time they began living in them, single-parent families were not as common or as acceptable as they are today. Young people now growing up in such families may not be affected in the same way those from earlier cohorts were. While one explanation may apply to some families, it may not account for the experience of many others.

A SPECIAL WORRY—THE TEEN MOTHER

There is a great deal of concern over the "epidemic" of adolescent mothers, "children having children," as some put it. Adolescents, we are told, are not yet developed physically. They also need to mature emotionally before they can adequately parent a child, and they have no partner to help them. Because teen mothers have not completed their education, the story goes, they are doomed to life on welfare, or at best in near poverty. As a result, their children are likely to have serious problems in their development and are at risk of being abused

(Lessa, 2003). There is, of course, some truth in these generalizations. However, they do not capture the variety in the experiences of many young mothers.

First, there is no new epidemic of teen births. In 2002, the proportion of births to women under 20 was, in reality, quite low, at only about 5 percent of all births. Just 120 babies were born to girls under 15. Of the rest, most were born to women aged 18 and 19, an age individuals are considered adults for many purposes. In fact, there are fewer teens giving birth now than in the 1970s, partly because more turn to abortion, especially at younger ages; partly because fewer become pregnant in the first place. What has changed, however, is that fewer are married by time the baby is born. Thus most teen mothers are now single mothers (Dryburgh, 2000; Statistics Canada, 2004g, 2004h, 2004j). The concern over teen births is focused on the fewer younger rather than the older ones who are in the majority. These younger mothers have not finished growing physically and have just embarked on the developmental tasks of adolescence. They have the least education and seem likeliest to spend most of their lives in poverty. They are also more likely to be known to social service agencies than older mothers. Most of the discussion will focus on younger teens.

Why do teenagers have children? There is no simple answer. It is not usually a reasoned decision; few actually plan to have a baby. Those who really do not want to become pregnant are less likely to have a child because they are more likely to use contraceptives and, should pregnancy occur, resort to abortion. Many pregnant teens do not see very strong reasons not to have the baby, even if they do not see many advantages in motherhood. Often they already feel that their life prospects are not too promising. Many, for example, have school difficulties even before they become pregnant. Where young mothers have suffered emotional deprivation, a baby may seem to promise emotional closeness. For some, having a child marks the beginning of adulthood. Cultural factors may also be involved (Bissell, 2000). These factors do not affect teenagers alone, but may also be involved in pregnancies of older women.

Low birth weights are most common at both ends of the reproductive span, that is, among women under 15 or over 44 years. There is no increased risk for most teen births. Low birth weight, usually the result of prematurity, can result in more deaths among newborns and higher levels of both physical and learning problems.

Young parents, married or not, are more likely to be poor than older ones (National Council of Welfare, 2004). They are less likely to have advanced education and have fewer years' work experience. Although many fathers in their teens and early 20s care about their children, they may be hard put to support just themselves. Once the baby is born, the teen mother may have difficulty returning to school. She is less likely to do so if she has dropped out prior to becoming pregnant (Bissell, 2000). Daycare centres attached to schools do help such mothers complete their education. If a teen mother finds a job, daycare costs may make it difficult for her to make ends meet (Michalopoulos et al., 2002).

The kind of support the young teen receives from her own parents and other relatives may prove crucial for her future, for example, allowing her to complete her education or hold a job. The younger the teen, the more likely the grandparents (the teen's parents) will help with baby care and financial support. Mothers receiving such help usually have better mental health and, thus, are better parents (Anderson, 2003).

Yet support can bring conflicts. If single parents live with their parents or depend on them for babysitting, disagreements may arise over how children should be raised or over areas of responsibility. In the worst cases, the child is used as a weapon in the parent–grandparent relationship. In one situation, an unmarried mother who lived with her parents expected her mother to provide unlimited childcare and laundry services. If the mother complained about her daughter's irresponsibility or about how often she went out, the daughter would threaten to move out and cut off any contact between grandmother and adored grandchild.

These problems are symptoms of boundary and role confusion. Ordinarily the individual has established an adult identity separate from her family of origin before becoming a parent. Pregnancy and childbirth make her more dependent. Yet she is called on to solve problems concerning her own and her baby's future for which she often does not have the knowledge or skills. Before she knows her own identity, she must define her role as mother. When three generations live together, confusion about who should fill parent and child roles may result, since the division of responsibilities may not be clear. Is the single mother an adult or is she a child? Since she has not separated from her parents, she is filling the role of a child in the family. However, her motherhood marks her as an adult. Should the grandparents act as parents to the grandchild? If so, what position does the mother hold?

An American study of low-income teen mothers found that the most successful and least successful children (in terms of school readiness) were raised quite differently. Many of the mothers who provided less support for children's learning had themselves had problems during their own childhoods. They had few personal strengths and little family support, especially from a male partner. They had lower education, were less likely to be employed, and lived in less desirable neighbourhoods. They seemed to spend most of their energy in just surviving. The mothers of the most successful children had mothers who were less likely to have been teen mothers themselves. These young mothers tested higher on intelligence tests and were more successful in school. Those who beat odds against them also seemed to have qualities like street smarts and determination that let them make the most of even limited opportunities (Luster, Bates, Fitzgerald, Vandenbelt, & Key, 2000; Luster, Perlstadt, McKinney, Sims, & Juang, 1996).

The well-being of adolescent mothers and their children depends both on the characteristics of the mother herself and on the family and community of which she is a part. If she wants an education, has support from her family, and lives in a safe community, she and her child are more likely to overcome the disadvantages of her early parenthood.

THE SINGLE FATHER

In general, little information is available about the single father beyond a few statistics. In 2001, only 17.64 percent (less than one in five) of single parents were men (see Table 9.1, on page 220). This proportion has remained about the same since 1986, even though the actual numbers of lone fathers have increased. Men tend to become single parents in the middle and late years of the life cycle. Few are in their teens or 20s. This is partly the result of the increase in divorce and the granting of custody to fathers (McKie, 1993).

There are a number of reasons why relatively few fathers have custody of their children. Since women tend to live longer than men and are usually younger than their husbands, they are more likely to become single parents through widowhood. At divorce, custody of children is usually granted to the mother. Now that fathers are increasingly involved in the daily care of their children, they try more often to gain either sole or **shared custody** of their children. If this trend continues, we can expect to see more single fathers in the future. At this point, only in unusual circumstances does an unmarried father gain custody of his child.

According to Kyle Pruett (2000), a psychiatrist at Yale Medical School, there are five myths about men who have custody of their children. First, there are few single fathers. Second, most divorced fathers remarry. Third, many single fathers are widowed and only a few have never married. Fourth, single fathers do well economically. Fifth, divorced fathers receive custody mostly of boys. Although these stereotypes fit many lone fathers, there are numerous exceptions (Pruett, 2000).

When we compare lone mothers and lone fathers, there are more similarities than differences. These arise from the child's need for care and from conflicting demands of the workplace, school, and family. Fathers experience many of the same stresses and frustrations as mothers (Pruett, 2000). As we shall see in the next chapter, both men and women face economic problems following separation or divorce. Mothers, however, experience greater financial disadvantages because they are less likely to have as high an education or as well-paying a job. The little research available about parenting by single fathers reflects what is known, in general, about parenting styles. Adolescents in more permissive families show higher levels of delinquent activity and substance abuse. Those in families showing low levels of warmth experience more emotional distress, but not acting-out behaviour. Teens in warm, democratic families fare best (Matjasko, 2002).

WHAT OF THE FUTURE?

All statistical forecasts suggest that the number of single-parent families will increase, especially as the result of divorce. Many young people will spend part or all of their childhood in such families. This fact raises a number of issues for all of us.

First, the level of poverty is high among single parents. As we shall see in more detail in Chapter 15, it has far-reaching effects on children's physical and intellectual development. In addition, children from low-income families tend not to stay in school. Thus they are more likely to end up in lower-paying jobs, with the prospect of raising poor families themselves. Ultimately this cycle will affect all of us through the cost of providing the income support programs or other services many of these families will need.

Second, fathers are important to children's development. We need to look at ways to encourage the greater involvement of fathers with children in female-headed single-parent families. This will include looking at the appropriateness of contact with particular fathers. For example, a violent individual may not be a beneficial presence in a child's life. There may be some need to overcome the resistance of mothers who may want no contact with the father, or who fear that he will attempt to gain custody.

Third, many single parents receive much emotional and practical support from their extended families. It is important for agency personnel to encourage this support. Too often they devalue or undermine it (Anderson, 2003). Relatives will be around long after the agency has bowed out. The future well-being of the family may depend in part on the continuing involvement of relatives and friends.

Finally, it is important, especially for the sake of the children, to eliminate the stigma against single-parent families that remains in society. If society as a whole recognizes that single parents are for the most part as concerned and competent as the majority of other parents, we will have come a long way toward that goal.

SUMMARY

LIFE PATTERNS OF LONE PARENTS. The lone-parent family is the fastest-growing family type in Canada. Members now experience less stigma than in the past. Life patterns vary among the never-married, divorced, and widowed as to the duration of lone parenthood and the likelihood of marriage. Differences in experiences are also related to life-cycle issues. Individuals who become lone parents during adolescence have quite different experiences from those for whom it begins in middle age. The ages and needs of the children also affect the parents.

CHILDREN IN LONE-PARENT FAMILIES. Children in single-parent families are often expected to have emotional or behavioural problems. They tend to leave school earlier and have lower-paying jobs than individuals raised in two-parent families. Their families of procreation may be less stable. However, many difficulties can be explained by financial hardship and family conflict rather than by the number of parents in the household.

QUALITY OF LIFE. Many lone parents have limited emotional support and social activities, partly because of the cost of entertainment, and partly because of the lack of time. Most single parents receive emotional support and practical help from relatives and neighbours. A few must depend on social agencies. Many female lone parents, especially young ones, live below the poverty line. They are more likely to receive family benefits or welfare than husband-wife families with children. Those who are employed often have dead-end jobs or face barriers such as childcare difficulties. The quality of housing is related to income levels.

THE TEEN MOTHER. Many adolescent mothers live below the poverty line, since they have limited education and job skills. Babies of younger mothers may be at greater risk for health and psychological problems. Mothers who receive support from older relatives are more likely to complete school and enter employment. Such support, however, may bring conflict.

THE SINGLE FATHER. There are relatively few single fathers. Following divorce, custody is usually given to the mother, and only rarely do unmarried fathers raise their children. Although their circumstances vary, single fathers are usually older than single mothers, are more likely to be employed and to have a higher level of education, and to have more income.

KEY TERMS

Mothers Allowance: government monthly support program originally provided to mothers who were widowed or abandoned or to wives of disabled men (now called Family Benefits and available to parents of either sex) (p. 227)

poverty line: a level of income below which an individual or family is considered to be living in poverty (p. 225) shared custody: custody of children shared by both parents (p. 232)

social support: practical assistance or emotional backup provided by others (p. 227)

CLASS ASSIGNMENTS

Complete one or more of the following assignments, as directed by your instructor:

1. Some individuals believe that being a single parent is a handicap in our society. Others point out that it has its advantages. What arguments can be made for each side?

2. A large percentage of single-parent families headed by women live below the poverty line. What effects might this have on the development of children raised in such families? Consider both short- and long-term physical, psychological, and social aspects.

3. How does single parenthood differ for men and women? Consider work, childcare, school, extended family relationships, and any other aspects that seem relevant.

PERSONAL ASSIGNMENTS

The following assignments are designed to help you think about your own family experience.

1. Do you think it is ethical for a woman to choose to become pregnant if she is not married? What factors affected your answer? Does it make any difference if a single person who chooses to adopt a child is male or female?

2. On the basis of your own experience or that of someone you know, what practical suggestions can you make for developing a satisfying family life for both the single parent and his or her children? Consider relationships within the family, and between the family and the rest of society.

© Monica Lau/Photodisc Green/Getty Images

Chapter 10

Coming Apart—The Divorce Experience

OBJECTIVES

- To place the current situation of divorce in historical perspective

- To consider causes for divorce

- To look at the developmental stages of divorce and its relationship to the family life cycle

- To describe the three crises of divorce—emotional, economic, and parental

- To examine the effects of divorce on children

- To consider issues around the custody of children

Public Announcement

John and Jane Smith announce an amicable divorce.

Their friends and relatives are asked not to take sides and to please keep in touch with both.

For the time being they are both still at home:

1234 14th Street,

Western City,

Prairie Province, Canada

Source: Excerpted from Statistics Canada, "Divorce: Law and Family in Canada." Catalogue 89-502, 1983, p. 159.

The most common deviation from the traditional family life cycle is **divorce,** or the legal dissolution of a marriage. It is becoming so common, in fact, that it may in time come to be considered a "normal" family event. Divorced families add two or three phases to the life cycle: separation, perhaps remarriage, and finally, stabilization in a new family pattern.

A SHORT HISTORY

Divorce has not always been so common. As we have seen, for much of history marriage was considered a way of uniting families, and of providing stability for society. Therefore, divorce was seen as an exception to be undertaken for only very grave reasons. For example, when biological descent for inheritance of property or titles was important, illegitimacy was considered a threat; therefore adultery by a wife once carried much social stigma and was grounds for divorce. Cruelty, on the other hand, was considered part of family life and usually was not considered a reason for breaking up the marriage.

Laws were, at first, influenced strongly by the Church of England in Upper Canada and the Roman Catholic Church in Lower Canada. Since neither church recognized divorce, no divorce law existed. New Brunswick allowed divorce in 1758 on the grounds of adultery and desertion. In 1787, Nova Scotia allowed divorce on the grounds of adultery. There is little indication, however, of how many divorces were granted. The situation in the Northwest (what is now British Columbia, Alberta, Saskatchewan, and Manitoba) from 1800 to 1837 was somewhat different. Since the area was owned and administered by the Hudson's Bay Company and the North West Company, there was little concern about marriage and divorce laws. Eventually the companies, for financial reasons, introduced a marriage contract in which a husband agreed to support his family that was formed *à la façon du pays* (i.e., according to the custom of Aboriginal people) and to marry as soon as a clergyman was available (McKie et al., 1983).

With Confederation in 1867, the federal Parliament gained exclusive authority in matters of divorce; yet all it did was allow existing provincial laws in Nova Scotia, New Brunswick, and British Columbia to stand. Anyone living in a province without a divorce court could submit a private member's bill to Parliament; when it passed, the person was granted a divorce. The process was long, public, and expensive. The rules differed depending on the petitioner. Men had to prove adultery on the part of their wives. Women, on the other hand, also had to prove either desertion for two years or longer or extreme physical or mental cruelty. It was easier to desert your family (often called "the poor man's divorce") than go through a legal divorce (McKie et al., 1983; Snell, 1992). From 1925 on, women could sue for divorce on the same grounds as men. They had only to prove adultery, not adultery and another cause. By 1968, all provinces except Quebec and Newfoundland had divorce laws with adultery basically the sole grounds for divorce (Allen, 1999).

Immediately after World War II, the divorce rate jumped. During the war, many women replaced men in the workforce, since the latter were in the military. The freedom and financial independence these women experienced undoubtedly encouraged some divorces, as did hasty wartime marriages and prolonged separations.

Soon, however, the divorce rate dropped off. In the postwar years the idea of family was attractive to many. In the stability following the war, people married in increasing numbers. Churches opposed change in divorce law. Neither the Roman Catholic nor the Anglican Church recognized divorce or remarriage, and the United Church opposed any broadening of the grounds for divorce. The few bills that were introduced in the House of Commons or the Senate regarding divorce in the 1940s did not pass (McKie et al., 1983).

The 1960s saw much change in divorce legislation. Parliament was still handling divorces for Quebec and Newfoundland. Two senators blocked all divorce bills coming before Parliament in order to force a change in the law. In 1966, a Special Joint Committee of the Senate and House of Commons on Divorce held many hearings on the subject. By this time, the churches had changed their position. The Roman Catholic Church stated that its members could vote according to their conscience, and the Catholic Women's League stated that Roman Catholics should not make other Canadians live by their beliefs. Both the Anglican Church and the United Church briefs included marriage breakdown as an advisable cause for divorce. Bill C-187 proposed wider divorce grounds and the transferring of jurisdiction for all divorces to the courts. On July 2, 1968, the new divorce law received royal assent (McKie et al., 1983). The divorce rate increased dramatically as a result of the wider grounds for divorce. (See Table 10.1.)

In 1986, the law was amended further. Parties to the divorce no longer had to show fault. The waiting period for divorce on the grounds of marriage breakdown was reduced to one year. Once again the divorce rate jumped in response to the shorter waiting period. The number of divorces reached their peak, at 96 200, in 1987, but dropped to 67 408 in 1997. Although there was a slight increase since then, the numbers were still well below the 1987 level. The length of marriage before divorce also increased recently. The decrease in divorces since 1987 may be partly due to the older age at marriage and to the greater number of people who choose to cohabit. The separations of cohabitors are not included in divorce statistics (Bélanger & Martel, 2003; Statistics Canada, 2005b). In the 1970s, although divorces were increasing, there were relatively few divorced people in the population. Now, more women between the ages 40 and 54 and men between 45 and 54 have been divorced than the women and men in these age groups who have never married (Beaujot, Gee, Rajulton, & Ravanera, 1995).

TABLE 10.1

DIVORCES IN CANADA

Year	Number of Divorces
1921	558
1941	2 462
1961	6 563
1968*	11 343
1969	26 093
1981	67 671
1985**	61 980
1986	78 304
1987***	96 200
1998	69 088
2000	71 144
2002	70 155

Source: Adapted from Statistics Canada, "The Daily." Catalogue 11-011. May 4, 2004.

* Reform of divorce laws.
** Divorce Act ("no-fault").
*** Peak year for divorces.

WHY PEOPLE DIVORCE

There are two ways of looking at why people divorce: we can examine either situations people regard as reasons to divorce or underlying causes.

In a study of Canadians' attitudes to divorce, researchers have looked at three kinds of reasons: fundamental issues like infidelity and abuse, experiential issues like disagreements and unsatisfactory sex life, and fertility issues like infertility and the presence of children. (See Table 10.2.) Almost all Canadians feel that divorce is justified when one partner abuses the other, fails to show respect, or is unfaithful. Experiential issues and fertility issues rated lower. Interestingly, it is older people (aged 50 and over) who have the most lenient attitude about divorce. This may reflect their greater experience of married life (Frederick & Hamel, 1998).

Another way of looking at reasons for divorce involves cultural and demographic factors. Culturally, there has been a shift away from a sense of duty and toward personal fulfillment. As a result, divorce law changed, making it easier. Expectations for marriage increased, so that negative interaction like contempt and blaming became reasons for divorce (experiential reasons). Demographic reasons include such things as early marriage, premarital cohabitation, and having divorced parents. So are lower levels of education and higher rates of poverty (Ambert, 2002; Greene, Anderson, Hetherington, Forgatch, & DeGarmo, 2003).

Still another approach is using the perspective of family theories. The structural-functional view regards marriage as an efficient way of organizing family responsibilities.

TABLE 10.2

ELDERS MORE LIKELY THAN YOUNGER CANADIANS TO AGREE WITH REASONS TO DIVORCE

	Gen-Xers 15–29 (%)	Boomers 30–49 (%)	Elders 50 and Over (%)	Total (%)
Fundamental Issues:				
Abusive behaviour from the partner	95	95	94	95
Unfaithful behaviour from the partner	89	85	89	88
Lack of love and respect from the partner	86	87	87	88
Partner drinks too much	68	73	80	74
Experiential Issues:				
Constant disagreement about how family finances should be handled	28	40	49	40
Unsatisfactory sexual relationship with partner	21	37	45	35
Unsatisfactory division of household tasks with partner	12	16	21	17
Conflict about how the children are raised	14	17	21	17
Fertility Issues:				
Inability to have children with the partner	8	12	17	13
Disagreement about the number of children to have	3	6	11	7
Would stay for the children	44	39	52	43

Source: Adapted from Statistics Canada, "Canadian Social Trends." Catalogue 11-008, Spring 1998, p. 8.

Men provide economic support and women provide personal care. The basis for this "contract" has been eroded through economic uncertainty and demands for personal freedom (Oropesa & Gorman, 2000). Canadians believe that fundamental issues like abuse are a breach of the implied contract.

The exchange perspective considers the value each partner finds in marriage and divorce. When there are many costs, divorce is less likely than when there are fewer. Such costs can be both economic (e.g., drop in disposable income) or social (e.g., stigma). For example, divorce is more likely if there are more possible new partners available, as when a wife has many male colleagues (South, Trent, & Shen, 2001). The costs of divorce have recently become lower. Women have greater economic independence; thus they are better able to support themselves. When they earn about half the family income, dependence of one partner on the other for support is less and divorce is likelier (Rogers, 2004). As we saw in Chapter 4, men's ability to earn a living has become less reliable. Having fewer children results in fewer ties to break. Finally, no-fault divorce has reduced penalties for those previously assigned blame. Also, there is now less stigma against divorced people. As a result of these factors, divorce has increased (Allen, 1999; Hiedemann, Suhomlinova, & O'Rand, 1998; Previti & Amato, 2003).

According to feminists, traditional marriage supports the unequal division of power between husbands and wives. Now that women have more opportunities, they no longer need to depend on men to support them and can leave oppressive relationships (Rogers, 2004).

Symbolic-interaction theorists focus on the patterns of interchange between husband and wife. Individuals' expectations affect their behaviour. There has been a shift in emphasis from finding security in marriage to reaching one's highest potential. Thus, an unhappy spouse feels justified in leaving an unsatisfying marriage and searching for fulfillment elsewhere (Ambert, 2002; Greene et al., 2003).

None of these factors is by itself sufficient to explain the changes in divorce rates; together, however, they go a long way.

THE ROAD TO DIVORCE

Divorce is rarely a sudden event; the process takes place in several phases. These involve both active and emotional aspects.

The Decision to Divorce

The decision to divorce does not usually occur in a single phase. In the first step, one or both individuals come to realize that something is wrong with their marriage; this often follows a period of denial (Ahrons, 1999). Many couples who divorce appear to follow what John Gottman (1994) calls the "divorce cascade." That is, they seem to follow the same downhill path: first, increasing conflict, then serious consideration of divorce, then separation, and finally divorce. The further along they are in this sequence, the harder it is to avoid divorce. It is as if the couple was caught in a strong river current that sweeps them into the rapids and finally over the waterfall of divorce. This does not mean that all couples who have conflicts go the same route. Many do work out their problems and have satisfying relationships.

People may delay separation until a time they consider suitable. Women may find a job or go back to school. Often the couple will decide to delay the divorce until the children leave home. During this period, they may become involved in activities outside the family, in a kind of emotional withdrawal. For some families, this period is one of great uncertainty and stress. The old husband-and-wife roles are disappearing and new ones, for example those of divorced **co-parents,** have not yet been developed. Eventually, the couple needs to move past the tendency to blame each other and accept the fact that the marriage cannot be saved and that both individuals have played a part in its failure (Ahrons, 1999; Carter & McGoldrick, 1999a; Hetherington, 2003).

Some minority groups emphasize family ties and responsibilities above personal satisfaction. Recent immigrants from these cultures are less likely to approve of divorce. The longer they live in Canada, however, the more likely they are to adopt the values of the majority (Oropesa & Gorman, 2000).

Planning the Breakup

In the second stage, the couple must plan the breakup of the system. They need to work cooperatively to settle issues such as **custody** of children, visitation, and finances. They also need to tell extended family members and deal with their reactions. The planning process often does not run smoothly. Many couples separate and reconcile again, sometimes repeatedly. During these temporary separations, the family can be under a great deal of stress since its members do not know whether the separation will become permanent and, so, they are uncertain about who is actually part of the family and whether roles should be reorganized. This kind of stress is called "boundary ambiguity." At this stage, the family may also face the reality of what a divorce will mean economically (Ahrons, 1999; Boss, 2002; Carter & McGoldrick, 1999a).

Separation and Family Reorganization

The third phase is the separation prior to divorce. A separation changes the relationship between husbands and wives, but does not automatically redefine it. If only one partner wishes to separate, boundaries may be particularly uncertain. This uncertainty frequently leads to conflict, perhaps centred on the children. Such a dispute may be an attempt to punish, to maintain contact with, or simply to get a rise from the former partner (Emery & Dillon, 1994). The couple now need to restructure the family by separating the marital and parental relationships. Such restructuring may be orderly, or disorderly and marked by conflict. Parents need to work out new rules for the continuing relationship between the child and each of the parents. They also need to decide how they will coordinate their responsibilities as co-parents. An important aspect of the separation is deciding custody arrangements for children. Many people feel that **joint custody** is best for children, with both parents sharing responsibility and decision-making. Others question their ability to share decision-making if they cannot get along well enough to live together. Couples also need to work out their relationships with the extended family, including the spouse's relatives, so that the children do not lose touch with them (Ahrons, 1999; Carter & McGoldrick, 1999a).

Only when the parent without custody fades out of the picture do we have a true one-parent family. When both parents are involved, the children act as links between two connected households. Thus both parents continue to be part of the child's family in an arrangement sometimes referred to as a **binuclear family.** This arrangement can reduce the stress of divorce for children; they do not suffer so extreme a loss. One parent is not cut off from the children, with the other burdened with parenting overload. Occasionally the parents remain good friends; more usually they are only able to focus on the children's welfare without open conflict (Ahrons, 1999).

THE CRISES OF DIVORCE

The breakdown of a marriage or cohabitation brings with it three crises: the emotional crisis, the economic crisis, and the parenting crisis. A bitter court battle makes all of these crises worse (Payne, 1986). Divorce produces what is called a **transitional state**; that is, it creates a temporary imbalance as a result of the changes in relationships, routines, assumptions, and roles. Often new patterns of behaviour are needed. Since separation and divorce interrupt the usual family developmental tasks, they create a series of adjustments that throw all family members off balance. This **disequilibrium** lasts for a period of one to three years. The distress surrounding the change is a "normal" short-term stress response. Many factors influence the individual's reaction to divorce: the circumstances of the separation, the quality of life after separation, the person's sex, the length of the marriage, the family's life-cycle stage, the acceptance of their ethnic or religious group, and past experience with stress. One area needing research is how same-sex couples adjust to breakup (Ahrons, 1999; Boss, 2002; Hetherington, 2003).

The Emotional Crisis

During and after the separation process, individuals suffer the loss of an important relationship. Often it has served as a centre for their lives, whether it was seen as satisfactory or unsatisfactory. The breakup is more painful for a person who does not expect or want it, and easier if the two partners have made the decision together. The emotional loss felt in divorce is akin to that felt on the death of a loved one, except that the ex-partner is still around. This continuing presence can lead to a recurring sense of loss, as well as renewed bitterness or anger. Often it takes considerable time for an individual to become emotionally divorced from a partner. Both yearning for the lost relationship and anger over the breakup are signs that this emotional divorce has not occurred. When children are involved, total emotional separation is usually impossible, since the former partners must deal with each other as parents and grandparents of their children and grandchildren (Ahrons, 1999). Friendship is healthy; preoccupation with the lost marital relationship is not (Madden-Derdich & Arditti, 1999). Often both spouses experience an emotional roller coaster. Just as they weather one emotional crisis, another confronts them.

Separation and divorce usually mean that individuals have to redefine themselves as people. The roles they have filled within the marriage are now lost, and to lose a role is to lose part of oneself. One of the difficulties with divorce is that our society has no readily defined roles for the formerly married. They must work out new ones for themselves as unmarried people, but also often as people with children. There is also little social guidance for how one should behave in a "normal" divorce (Ahrons, 1999).

Divorced and separated individuals are often socially isolated at first. The relationship with extended family members changes. Although they may maintain a connection, they are no longer related to their ex-spouse's relatives. They may have limited support from their own relatives. Families that have dealt with divorce before are often more comfortable in dealing with the issues that arise. Some individuals cut themselves off from the extended family to avoid criticism. By doing this, they isolate themselves further. Women from minority groups that do not condone divorce may also face alienation from and shunning by extended family members and their ethnic community (Anderson et al., 1990).

Divorced women may find social life limited by their lack of a "single" identity. They do not fit into the social pattern of a married person and are not comfortable with being single. Many isolate themselves because they feel overloaded with tasks; others do so because they feel the sense of failure common after divorce. There is often a sharp decline in support for women from married friends. Divorced men often have an easier time socially than divorced women. Although they usually do not have the circle of intimate friends that women have, they often have a social network at their place of employment. Men tend to remarry sooner than women, often to partners much younger than themselves (Brinig, 1999).

By about two years post-divorce, many people are adapting. Within six years, most have built a reasonably satisfying life. There are six patterns of adjustment. "Enhancers" blossom. They become more competent and fulfilled. Some have the new experience of living alone. The "goodenoughs," the largest group, manage quite well. About six years post-divorce, their lives are similar to pre-divorce. "Seekers" are anxious for a new mate and may not be careful in their choice. One woman said, "I wanted a man so badly, anyone looked good." "Swingers" dress youthfully, go to singles bars, use more alcohol and drugs, and are involved in more casual sex. They tend to be men rather than women because it is hard to have a self-indulgent lifestyle when you have custody of children. Then there are "competent loners," similar to "enhancers," but not wanting a long-term partner. Finally the "defeated" are mired in despair long after the divorce. Some had problems before divorce; others couldn't escape poverty (Hetherington, 2003).

Thus there are three aspects of the emotional crisis of divorce. First, the ex-spouses must accept the loss of the marriage and mourn its passing. They must also become emotionally detached from the other person as a spouse, but maintain a relationship as co-parents if they have children together. Second, they must deal with identity issues. Previously they had defined themselves in terms of their roles in the marriage; now they must take up new roles as single people. Unfortunately, they receive little guidance from social norms. Third, they must build new social networks as single people to replace those that supported the marriage. In successfully accomplishing these tasks, they will find that divorce can provide an opportunity for growth.

The Economic Crisis

Divorce is called "the most expensive life event" (Investors Group, 2004). It usually means a drop in the standard of living, especially for the **custodial parent,** that is, the parent who has custody of any children of the marriage. Even if both spouses have been working outside the home, the income now has to cover the costs of running two homes. Since women are usually granted custody of children, their financial needs following divorce are greater than their husbands'. Yet, as we have seen, they often do not have the ability to earn as much as men (Ambert, 2002).

Both parents are responsible for the support of their children. In the past, amounts paid by the **noncustodial parent** varied widely. In 1997, the federal government passed the Federal Child Support Guidelines, which take into account the costs of raising a child, the parents' income, and the number of children. The custodial parent is assumed to pay a similar percentage of his or her income. Opting out of the federal child support system is possible, but the judge will ensure that the agreement will meet the child's needs (Cochrane, 2002). If the noncustodial parent, usually the father, does not have a steady job or has disappeared, the family may be reduced to living on welfare. This is especially true if the mother has few or no marketable skills. Chapter 15 looks in more detail at the serious implications of poverty for the development of children. In general, private arrangements between separated parents (whether they had been married or cohabiting) result in both more regular visits and child support payments (Marcil-Gratton, Le Bourdais, & Lapierre-Adamcyk, 2000).

The division of family property was, in the past, often obviously unfair. The case of Irene Murdoch is an example. Jim and Irene Murdoch of Turner Valley, Alberta, separated in 1968 after they had been married 25 years. Mrs. Murdoch had done the usual farm chores such as milking, caring for small animals, and household care. She had also done so much heavy farm work that her husband did not need to hire a labourer, even during his frequent illnesses.

If she were not married, Mrs. Murdoch would have been granted compensation for all the work she had done. The courts, however, including the Supreme Court of Canada, stated that she had done what any farm wife would have done, and refused to grant her any share in the farm. As a result of the outrage prompted by this case, the various provinces passed laws to give an equal share of property to partners who had contributed work rather than money to the family economy (Kieran, 1986). In spite of changes in legislation, women may still be at a disadvantage when we consider the benefit package attached to men's employment. For example, should a spouse's future earnings be taken into account? Should there be compensation for loss of benefits like health or life insurance and pensions?

The Parenting Crisis

When a family separates, new boundaries must be drawn. Much of the confusion and stress during the separation process arises from an absence of clear boundaries. The old family with its old rules and rituals no longer exists, but new ones have not yet taken their place. This is especially true for parenting. Both authority and responsibility concerning the children need to be renegotiated. To do this successfully, parents need to separate spousal roles from parental roles; only the former are ended by divorce. They also need to establish new rules. For example, who does the child ask for money or help with homework? How much participation is expected of a noncustodial parent? Each parent needs to establish a relationship with the children separate from the other parent. How much authority will she, or more usually he, have over the children? If joint custody is decided upon, how will the responsibility for the children be shared? Parents' communication is an important factor as to whether each parent will allow the other to relate to the child without prejudice or interference. If there is no clear understanding of the new rules of the relationship, the child is likely to become the victim of conflicts between the parents (Ahrons, 1999). Adolescents can also manipulate parents who do not communicate with each other (Manning, 2003).

Divorcing parents may be unable to respond to their children's emotional needs. There are several reasons for this. The initial sense of shock may paralyze them. Later on, parents may be too absorbed in their own crisis to be aware of how the divorce is affecting their children. They may also feel that very young children cannot understand what is going on, and may ignore their distress. Often a parent becomes depressed. One aspect of depression is that the individual becomes less sensitive to the feelings of others. For all these reasons children may be emotionally neglected at a time when they need special care (Amato, 2000; Ambert, 2002).

CHILDREN AND DIVORCE

Parents' divorce transforms children's lives forever. Childhood, adolescence, and adulthood all become different. Divorce touches all aspects of children's lives—where they live, how they interact with parents, if and how they can continue relationships with friends. Some come through the experience and flourish. Others do not.

Few children want their parents to divorce, no matter how much tension there has been in the marriage. For them, it means changing the relationship with each parent. Many children cling to a fantasy that their parents will be reunited and the family will be whole again (Thompson, 2000).

Children from divorced families are at greater risk than children from two-parent families of developing problems like delinquency, early sexual intercourse, emotional distress, and school difficulties. Most, however, do not (Hetherington, 2003). The impact of divorce on children depends on a number of factors. First, the age of the child is important. Children aged over about nine or ten years are able to understand divorce in a realistic way, though they do not need to hear all the details of the breakup. Preschool children often feel responsible for the family breakup. They also believe that they have the power to bring parents back together. This is part of the magical thinking of childhood. They feel that the world revolves around them, and that all that happens is a result of their actions. Most children of divorce are less attached to their parents than those from two-parent families. It was generally thought that preschoolers would suffer most short-term but would soon recover. More recent research suggests that, regardless of age, children who had warm relationships with parents prior to the divorce do as well as children from intact families. If parenting is upset by the divorce, then children have problems (Leon, 2003).

If divorce occurs when children are adolescents, some may feel relieved at the end of continuing conflict (Ahrons, 1999). Others experiment with sex or drugs and may separate prematurely from their family. If, however, a parent turns to them for support or if they feel the need to look after a devastated parent, they may have difficulty getting on with their own lives. This is especially true in a high-conflict divorce when the child is expected to take sides. Teens and young adults may show similar reactions if they have lived for years in an angry divorce. Researchers describe what they call a **sleeper effect,** in which a problem emerges only long after the divorce. Young adults whose parents divorced when they were children may display a fear of intimacy or betrayal that will interfere with any attempts to form intimate relationships. Serious problems are, however, the exception (Jacquet & Surra, 2001; Johnston & Roseby, 1997; Kelly & Emery, 2003; Wallerstein, Lewis, & Blakeslee, 2000).

Second, divorce may affect boys and girls differently. Research results are mixed. Some show gender differences. Most, however, have found that effects are similar for both boys and girls (Leon, 2003).

Third, the level of parental conflict both before and after separation is critical and probably has more impact on children's post-divorce adjustment than the absence of a parent. Children openly exposed to conflict do less well, especially if violence is involved or if children feel caught in the middle (Amato, 2000; Ambert, 2002).

Fourth, life changes after divorce are also important. The number and degree of changes affect the children's ability to adapt. For example, a child who moves from a house to a small apartment in a new neighbourhood and experiences a dramatic lowering of his or her standard of living will probably have more difficulties adapting than a child who stays in the family home and continues to go to the same school with his or her friends. Father absence, as we have already discussed, is related directly to economic instability. The absence will also affect the children's relationship with other relatives, especially grandparents. Without his active participation, the children may have limited access to the extended family members of the **nonresidential parent.** Parents may form one or more new relationships. If these are disrupted, children have multiple losses and adjustments. It is suspected that the connection between divorce and greater rates of delinquency, underachievement, and promiscuity in children depends more on stress-inducing changes, including changes in the relationship with parents, than on the divorce itself (Butler, Scanlan, Robinson, Douglas, & Murch, 2003; Connidis, 2001).

Finally, the nature of the new parenting arrangements is important to the children's adjustment. Children want and need an ongoing relationship with both parents. This is most likely to happen if fathers are well educated and live quite nearby, and the children are young. Many children, however, have little contact with the noncustodial parent one year after the divorce, especially if the parent has remarried (Greene et al., 2003).

Social supports are important for children, just as they are for adults. Grandparents, friends, teachers, and others may provide the emotional and practical help children need to help them cope with the emotional fallout of divorce. Children need accurate information about the separation and custody arrangements. Grandparents can soften some of the stresses of divorce. Since the grandparent–grandchild relationship remains stable when the parent–child relationship is undergoing structural changes, it teaches children that not all relationships are temporary and unhappy. In order to be effective supports to children, grandparents must show their concern and involvement without interfering or taking sides (Butler et al., 2003; Wallerstein et al., 2000).

A useful way of looking at the impact of divorce on children is to consider both risk and protective factors. Stressors and risks include the actual separation, conflict between parents before and after separation, poorer quality of parenting after divorce, loss of important relationships (including friends), and financial hardship (Kelly & Emery, 2003). Even before their parents separate, teenagers have more school, emotional, and behavioural problems (Sun & Li, 2002). Protective factors include effective parenting by both parents and reduced conflict after divorce. Those with serious problems tend to have more risk factors and few protective ones. Those with more protective factors often cannot be distinguished from other children. Many adults with divorced parents have painful memories, but these do not interfere with day-to-day living (Kelly & Emery, 2003).

CUSTODY AND PARENTING

Who Gets Custody?

As we have already seen in the chapter on single parents, mothers are usually granted custody after divorce. This was not always so. In English common law, which was also followed in English North America, fathers had automatic right to custody of their children. Mothers had few legal rights. During the 19th century changes began to take place. Mothers were gradually given custody, first of young children, then of older children. This shift was partly the result of the Industrial Revolution, during which the workplace and the home became separated. Men had to be free to earn an income and women were expected to stay home and raise their children. Power passed from the father to the family court judge, who could decide if the mother deserved to have custody of her children. Custody could be denied her if she was considered at fault in the divorce by committing adultery or by leaving the home (Arnup, 1989; McKie et al., 1983). The current standard used is that of the best interests of the child. This still means that mothers are usually granted custody. There may be reluctance to grant custody to a lesbian mother, however, especially if she is very open in her lifestyle or is a gay activist, on the grounds that living with her might be harmful for the child (Arnup, 1989). When parents can agree on custody and visiting arrangements, nonresidential parents see their children more often and also provide support more regularly (Marcil-Gratton et al., 2000).

Source: *Custody of Dad. Reprinted by kind permission of Barrie Maguire.*

Although the actual numbers are still relatively small, more fathers are now gaining custody of their children following divorce. This is more likely to happen when children are older, especially when the oldest is a boy (Fox & Kelly, 1995). Most often fathers gain custody when the mother consents. Frequently, however, her consent is not wholehearted. Since court cases are often costly, some women cannot afford to hire a lawyer. Others believe that the father can offer the children more stability immediately following the divorce. Still others want to avoid the emotional stress for themselves, and especially for their children, that comes with a contested custody case. Men seek and obtain custody for a number of reasons: some have a strong sense of family or believe that they are a better parent than the mother; others seek custody out of revenge; and still others are granted custody against their will because they have been deserted by their wives. Fathers with custody who do best tend to be those who have higher incomes; they are also those who wanted custody and were involved with child rearing before the marriage breakup; they do not place the entire blame for the failure of the marriage on either partner; and their ex-wives are also involved with the children on a regular basis, so that the fathers do not carry the full burden of parenting (Edwards, 1989; Greif, 1985).

There is a growing move to joint custody following divorce. The principle of shared parenting is in theory good for the child, since both parents are involved in decision-making and care. The definition of joint custody, however, is still being argued. Does the child have to live an equal amount of time with each parent? Does joint custody mean that both parents have the right to make decisions concerning their child, even if the child lives most of the time with one of them? Joint custody works best if the parents can lay aside their personal disagreements to act together in the best interests of their child. Unfortunately, this does not always happen. Children can and do become pawns in the angry fighting between parents. One study found that adolescents with dual residence were especially likely to feel caught between parents when conflict levels were high. When conflict levels were low, however, they felt close to both parents (Buchanan, Maccoby, & Dornbusch, 1991; Greene et al., 2003). Although research findings are still scarce, it appears that children do adjust to moving back and forth between homes.

Problem Areas

Two major problem areas arise out of custody conflicts—failure to comply with support orders and with custody provisions. Some parents fail to pay child support. Sometimes this occurs if the parent thinks the settlement was unjust or custody arrangements unfair. Sometimes non-payment is a method of harassing an ex-partner or trying to exert control over decisions affecting children. Provinces are responsible for enforcing child support orders. In British Columbia, for example, if parents do not pay their child support, it can be deducted from their paycheque or bank accounts (Ministry of Attorney General, 1998). In addition, the Federal Child Support Guidelines grant provinces the power to deduct payments owing from federal pensions and to use Revenue Canada records to find a missing parent. In extreme cases, the parent's passport can be suspended (Department of Justice Canada, 2004b).

BOX 10.1

OTHER TIMES, OTHER CUSTOMS

In 18th-century England, a man who couldn't afford to vanish could dispose of his wife by selling her to another man.... A 1772 source explains that the husband "puts a halter about her neck and thereby leads her to the next market place, and there puts her up to auction to be sold to the best bidder, as if she were a brood mare or a milch-cow." Since she is now someone else's, she obviously isn't his, so he goes home and marries again. (This was probably less appalling than it sounds. Historians figure it was often by prearrangement, with buyer, seller and merchandise all in agreement, providing a swift and amicable closure.)

Women had fewer alternatives, although a man's impotence was always fair grounds for annulment. To prove impotence in certain jurisdictions, "seven honest women" were appointed to labor diligently over the poor embarrassed fellow, noting his reaction. No reaction, no marriage, with both parties free to roll the dice again.

British social custom demanded that one party be innocent and want a divorce and the other guilty but, mysteriously, not want a divorce. If both parties were sleeping with someone else, both were guilty so they had to stay married forever. If both wanted a divorce, that was collusion, so they had to stay married forever.

Source: B. Holland, "The Long Good-bye," *The Smithsonian*, March 1998, pp. 91, 92.

Some parents try to prevent visits if support is not paid. This breach of the terms of custody can backfire since the noncustodial parent can request change of custody because access has been denied. Occasionally a noncustodial parent takes the law into his or her own hands and kidnaps the child. Often abductions are discovered when the parent does not return the child after a visit. One of the most urgent steps in abduction cases is locating the child, especially if there is a danger that he or she will be taken out of the country. The Hague Convention on the Civil Aspects of International Child Abduction, which has been accepted by many countries, tries to ensure that an abducted child is returned promptly to the custodial parent. It also attempts to ensure that rights of custody and access of one country are respected by other countries. If a child is taken to a country that has signed the Convention, steps are taken to return the child. When the child is taken to a country that does not recognize the Convention, especially one where fathers normally get custody and mothers have few rights, getting the child back is much more difficult. In such cases, parents can spend large sums on detectives and foreign lawyers in attempts to find and reclaim their children. Long-term abductions can be particularly damaging to children (Chiancone, Girdner, & Hoff, 2001).

In both noncompliance with child-support orders and kidnapping cases, the main victim is usually the child. Regardless of the parents' intentions, the child suffers in these cases through the consequences of poverty, deprivation of a parent, being uprooted from a home, and being forced to live on the run.

Parents without Custody

Most noncustodial parents are men. Divorce often means for them a loss of a sense of home and family. Women traditionally have been expected to provide for the emotional needs of their families. When the marriage is broken, men are sometimes at a loss as to how to manage the father–child relationship on their own. Often visits are seen as playtime, with very little discipline involved. Sometimes the father will increase his time at his parents' home, especially if it is conveniently located. Visits tend to become fewer and further apart if the ex-spouses are hostile toward each other or if the father does not make support payments regularly (Greene et al., 2003).

There is a great deal of pressure in society for mothers to assume custody of their children following breakup of a marriage. The title of Harriet Edwards's book, *How Could You?* (1989), reflects the stigma experienced by mothers who do not have custody. These mothers, however, often feel that it is in their children's best interests to stay with their father since he can provide a stable home at a time when they cannot. Regardless of their motives, noncustodial mothers are blamed by society for being "unnatural," even though in a few cases courts awarded custody to the father against the mother's wishes. This often occurred after she had left the children with him temporarily until she could establish her own home. By the time she could take them, the ex-husband could argue that it would be better if the children were not uprooted. Some mothers felt a custody battle would be too damaging for their children. Many women had no choice in the custody matter; they simply could not afford to raise the children, since their earning power was so much less than that of their former husbands. Often the children lived with the mother for some time before the custody shifted to their father (Edwards, 1989; Eicher-Catt, 2004).

DIVORCE AND THE FAMILY LIFE CYCLE

Divorce has a different impact at different stages of the family life cycle. The least disruption occurs with the newly married couple with no children. Fewer people are involved and fewer family traditions need to be dropped. Since each partner has been single fairly recently, they are able to slip back into single roles and lifestyle more easily than those married for a long time. As more people are added to the family and the family has a longer history together, divorce becomes more difficult. Many plans and hopes—vacation, new house, children—have to be cancelled. Traditions build up through years of interaction. Part of the dislocation of divorce with a longtime marriage is the loss of these rituals (Ahrons, 1999).

Divorce is increasingly common at midlife (Wu & Penning, 1997). When children leave home, couples have the chance to reassess their marriages. Many divorces are initiated by women. Although some are frightened about being on their own financially, most feel relief at leaving a dead relationship. Divorce can be difficult for a homemaker wife who is suddenly faced with finding a job when she has been out of the workforce for many years. Some women may see divorce as a personal failure because they did not make their marriages work (Blacker, 1999).

THE FUTURE

Divorce shows no signs of going away. In fact, there are predictions that in the future at least half of all marriages will be dissolved. As a society, this phenomenon presents us with a crucial issue: how best to ensure the healthy development of children living in divorced families.

Children tend to do best when they have a continuity in their relationships. This means that they need regular contact with both parents, unless there are overriding reasons to deny it, such as serious abuse. They also need contact with both extended families. For this to occur, all the adults involved must cooperate. Children also need to be assured of adequate financial support. This demands the serious commitment of both parents to the welfare of the children. It also needs to be backed up with effective enforcement laws. This will happen only if the courts, and society at large, take the matter seriously. Finally, children's interests are best served if their parents receive adequate backup from their extended families and from society as a whole. If single parents are left to do everything alone—earn a living and raise children—without any assistance, the phenomenon of single-parent burnout will continue to occur. In the end, it means that society at large must be concerned about the well-being of these families.

HISTORY OF DIVORCE IN CANADA. New Brunswick and Nova Scotia were the earliest provinces to have a divorce law, with very limited grounds. After Confederation, in provinces without divorce courts, individuals had to resort to private members' bills in Parliament. Following World War II, divorces increased as a result of prolonged separations, hasty wartime marriages, and women's growing independence as a result of joining the workforce. Under pressure for change, a new divorce law, which established wider grounds for divorce, came into effect in 1968. In 1986, a new law allowed for no-fault divorce and a shorter waiting period. Following each legal change, the number of divorces increased dramatically.

REASONS FOR DIVORCE. Most Canadians believe divorce is justified when a partner is unfaithful or abusive. Theorists point to a number of underlying causes for the increase in the divorce rate. Fewer people believe in the traditional idea of marriage and its responsibilities. Women's employment enables them to leave oppressive relationships. Costs of divorce are no longer as high, both socially and economically, as in the past. People now value individual happiness over family duty.

THE ROAD TO DIVORCE. There are several phases in a divorce. The decision to divorce comes with the realization that the marriage cannot be saved. Often it follows continuing conflict and temporary separation. Then couples must plan the breakup: they need to settle custody and financial issues. Finally, following separation, the family must reorganize. They need to separate marital and parental roles in order to allow the children to be part of the families of both parents.

CRISES OF DIVORCE. There are three crises of divorce—the emotional crisis, the economic crisis, and the parental crisis. In the emotional crisis, the ex-spouses need to mourn the loss of their marriage, establish new identities as single persons, and form new social networks. If these tasks are accomplished, opportunities for personal growth will result. Economically, a divorce usually means a drop in the standard of living, especially for the parent with custody of the children. Both parents are responsible for supporting the children. Any unfairness this might cause is tempered by the fact that property is divided equally. In addition, the parents need to work out new guidelines for authority over and responsibility for the children. Children fare best if parents can cooperate to ensure their welfare.

CHILDREN AND DIVORCE. The impact on the children depends on several factors. Younger children tend to adjust better in the long run. A few children of divorce suffer serious long-term effects. The parents' level of conflict is probably more important to the adjustment of children than the divorce itself. Lifestyle changes are also significant, including the quality of parenting and the social supports available to the children.

CUSTODY. Mothers are usually granted custody, although joint custody and father custody are increasing. There are two major problem areas regarding custody. One is the failure to comply with support orders; provinces now have support-enforcement programs in place. A second problem area is the failure to comply with custody and visiting provisions. If the custodial parent refuses to allow court-ordered visits with the other parent, this may be grounds for a change in custody. Some parents kidnap their children. The main victim in support, visitation, and custody violations is the child. Many parents without custody lose the sense of home and family. In these cases, visiting and support may taper off. Mothers who give up custody of their children often face stigma, even if they feel they are acting in the best interests of the children.

FAMILY LIFE CYCLE AND DIVORCE. The least disruption occurs when newly married couples divorce. Individuals who divorce after long-term marriages and who have school-aged children usually experience the greatest difficulty. Homemaker wives have problems rebuilding their social lives and looking for a job if they have to do so.

KEY TERMS

binuclear family: an arrangement where both father and mother act as parents to their child(ren) following divorce, while they maintain separate homes (p. 242)

co-parent: a divorced person who shares the responsibility for his or her child (p. 241)

custodial parent: an individual who has custody of his or her child (p. 244)

custody: the legal right and responsibility to care for a child in one's own home (p. 242)

disequilibrium: a lack of balance in the family system (p. 243)

divorce: the legal dissolution of a marriage (p. 237)

joint custody: the legal right and responsibility of both parents to make decisions and care for their child (p. 242)

noncustodial parent: the parent who does not have custody of the child (p. 245)

nonresidential parent: the parent who does not live in the home with the child (p. 247)

sleeper effect: a problem that emerges only long after an event such as divorce (p. 247)

transitional state: a state of temporary imbalance resulting from changes in relationships, routines, assumptions, and roles (p. 243)

CLASS ASSIGNMENTS

Complete one or both of the following assignments, as directed by your instructor:

1. In some communities, mediation is available for couples seeking divorce. How does mediation differ from using the court to solve differences over custody and support? Explain the factors that make mediation most effective. Find out if mediation services are available in your community.

2. Imagine a family with a seven-year-old boy. The parents are planning to divorce and would like joint custody of their son. Working in pairs, draw up a plan for co-parenting. Take into account schooling, residence, holidays, transportation, and any other factor you think is relevant.

PERSONAL ASSIGNMENTS

The following assignments are designed to help you think about your own experience and opinions:

1. Following some divorces, custody of children is split: one child will stay with the mother and another with the father. What do you feel are the advantages and disadvantages of this arrangement? Do you feel that it is all right for children to be separated in this way? Or do you think they should be kept together? Explain.

2. Do you feel grandparents should be given the legal right to have access to their grandchildren or either sole or joint custody following the divorce of the parents? Why or why not?

Chapter 11

The Second Time Around

OBJECTIVES

- ■ To look at historical changes in remarriage patterns
- ■ To consider the process of forming a new family system and its relationship to the family life cycle
- ■ To examine factors leading to success and failure in stepfamily relationships
- ■ To look at the relationship of the stepfamily and society at large

Once upon a time there lived a man with a wife and a beautiful daughter. While his child was still young, the man's wife died. The man was at his wit's end trying to make a home for his child.

"I must find a wife," he told himself. "Then we will have a proper home."

So he did as he said, and found a widow with two daughters. They were soon married. His new wife happily moved in, along with her children.

Soon, however, both she and her daughters had turned his child into a servant. The girl had to do all the heavy cleaning, and was at their beck and call all day and all night. Sometimes she crept into the fireplace to rest from the demands of her stepmother and stepsisters, so she was always covered in ashes.

"You're just a cinder girl," they taunted her.

And that is how she came to be called Cinderella.

REMARRIAGE—A NEW TREND?

The divorce rate is increasing. As a result, predictions have been made that the remarriage rate will also increase. A survey, undertaken by Statistics Canada in 1990 to gather information that wasn't available in census reports, discovered that only a small minority of all adult Canadians had been married more than once. If we consider only those Canadians who have actually been married, fewer than one in ten had been married more than once. Third and fourth marriages were rare (McDaniel, 1994). More recent figures show that in 2000, 34.7 percent of marriages involved at least one partner who had been married before. In almost half of these, both spouses had been married at least once (Bélanger & Martel, 2003). Divorced people accounted for most of this number. The numbers of remarriages more than doubled from 1971 to 1996, but have remained at about the same level since then (see Table 11.1).

TABLE 11.1		
REMARRIAGES, CANADA, 1971–2000		
	Percentage of Marriages with at Least One Spouse Previously Married	Percentage of Remarriages with Both Spouses Previously Married
1971	16.6	40.8
1981	27.5	40.8
1991	32.1	42.8
1996	34.1	45.0
2000	34.7	45.5

Source: Adapted from Statistics Canada, "Report on the demographic situation in Canada, 2001–2002." Catalogue 91-209, December 22, 2003, p. 19.

Until the end of World War II, remarriage tended to follow the death of a spouse. Now it is likelier to follow divorce. Of the marriages that ended in 1970–72, widowhood was the cause for 58 percent of women and 23 percent of men. Divorce ended marriages at a rate of about 19 percent for both women and men (Adams & Nagnur, 1988). Thus, the numbers of the widowed eligible to remarry outstripped the numbers of the divorced. Divorce is far likelier now to mark the end of marriage. In addition, widowhood adds one person to the pool eligible for remarriage; divorce returns two. Divorced people are more likely to remarry because they are younger and more eager for a new relationship (Milan, 2000). Complex factors lie behind the shift from remarriage after widowhood to remarriage after divorce. First, life expectancy has increased; thus there is less likelihood a person will be widowed at a young age when he or she is more likely than someone older to marry again. Second, as we saw in the last chapter, following changes in the law in 1968 and 1986, there has been an enormous increase in the number of divorces, and this probably affects younger rather than older people (i.e., an age group more likely to remarry). Other factors that may affect remarriage rates are improved pensions, which may allow older people to live independently if they choose to, and a greater social acceptance of common-law unions and single living.

Many families in which one or both parents are remarried are stepfamilies (see Figure 11.1). According to the National Longitudinal Survey of Children and Youth, about one-fifth of children born in 1983–84 had already experienced family breakup by time they were 10. Thirteen years after separation, 85 percent of children had a new "parent." These events were likelier if children were born in a cohabitation union than in marriage. As time passes, the numbers can only increase (Juby, Marcil-Gratton, & Le Bourdais, 2001). Obviously there are generational differences. Younger people are more likely to get divorced. As they age, and as more divorces occur among the coming generations, sociologists expect an increase in the total number of divorced individuals and, as a result, an increase in people marrying for a second or third time.

A small proportion of stepfamilies result when a gay or lesbian partner brings along a child conceived in an earlier heterosexual relationship. A few adopt as single parents or bear a child through artificial insemination before the step-relationship begins. Such families face all the problems of heterosexual remarried families. In addition, they must deal with issues around coming out. Will it affect their jobs? Could there be a demand for change in custody? How will officials at the child's school react? Will other children harass the child? On the other hand, will openness build a more supportive partner relationship and encourage step-parent-stepchild bonds? (Laird, 2003).

Stepfamilies are more likely to involve cohabiting partners; these relationships are less stable than marriages (Juby et al., 2001). Remarriage is not a guarantee of happiness. Although most second marriages are stable, they still show a higher rate of divorce than first marriages. One does not have to look far to find explanations. In some cases problems like family violence, alcoholism, or psychiatric disorders, such as neurosis or schizophrenia, that led to the breakup of the first marriage continue, and create similar difficulties in a later marriage. Another reason lies in the fact that many remarriages include children. Such marriages involve many additional relationships: with the former spouse or spouses (the parents of the

Figure 11.1

PERCENTAGE OF CHILDREN AGED 0–11 YEARS IN STEPFAMILIES, BY BLOOD RELATIONSHIP

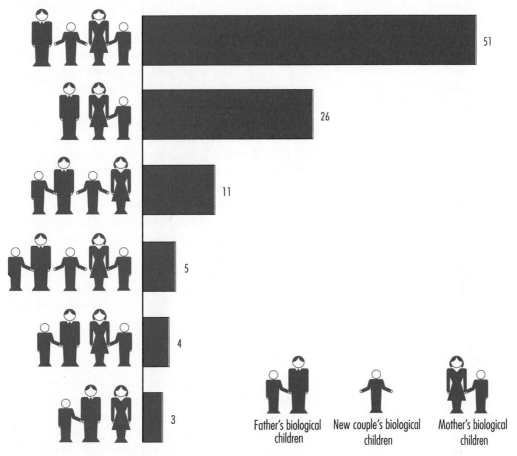

The majority of children in stepfamilies lived in blended families in 1994.

Source: Adapted from Statistics Canada, "Canadian Social Trends." Catalogue 11-008, Spring 1997, p. 9.

children), with extended-family members, and especially with the children themselves (Coleman, Ganong, & Fine, 2000; Kaufman, 1993). About half of stepfamilies become blended families; that is, they have an "ours" child (Juby et al., 2001).

FORMING A NEW FAMILY SYSTEM

Unlike nuclear families, **reconstituted families,** or remarriage families, have few norms to guide their formation. If they try to mimic first-marriage families, there can be serious difficulties. They just do not fit the expected patterns.

Stages of Remarriage-Family Formation

There are three distinct stages in entering and adapting to a second marriage: entering the new relationship, planning the new marriage and family, and forming the remarriage family (Carter & McGoldrick, 1999a).

Before people can successfully enter a new marriage, they need to recover from the loss of the first. Often a great deal of anger is directed toward the ex-spouse. If it continues, a divorce will not take place emotionally. This is because anger provides a powerful link to the former partner. The new couple must also commit themselves to forming a new family and be ready to deal with all the complications that will arise.

The second phase involves planning the new marriage. The couple needs to work at open and honest communication. They also must accept that difficulties will not be ironed out overnight. It is important for them to deal with relationships with relatives outside the household. The relationship with the ex-spouse involving co-parenting and financial support needs to be maintained. Extended family members must establish relationships with the new spouse and any children he or she brings into the marriage. Plans have to be made for the children to stay connected with the extended families of both ex-spouses. Throughout this phase, the partners must accept their own anxieties and those of the other family members about the new family.

Finally, the new family is formed. This involves renegotiating boundaries and roles, and making room for all the children to keep up their relationships with their biological parents, grandparents, and other relatives. The new family has to share their memories and make new rituals so that they will develop a sense of belonging.

Boundaries

One of the main differences between first marriages and second or later ones involves family boundaries. As we saw in Chapter 1, boundaries mark out who belongs to the family. They must be open enough to allow interaction with the outside world, yet clear enough so that the family feels some sense of unity. Establishing traditions and rituals, for example, connected with holidays and events like birthdays, helps build family solidarity (Visher, Visher, & Pasley, 2003).

In first-marriage families, boundaries are relatively well defined. Members live in the same place and are supported by household adults. Authority and responsibility rest with the married couple, who are also the parents of the children (Kaufman, 1993).

Remarriage families do not fit the non-divorce two-parent pattern. First, parents and children do not all stay in the same residence. Custody arrangements determine whether the children live with one parent and visit with the other, or live at times with one and at times with the other, and whether brothers and sisters share the same household. In addition, if both adults in the remarried household have children, the custody and visiting arrangements of the second set further complicate the situation. The number of people living in the home can vary from week to week. Financial support for children is often provided, in part, by non-household members. The parent paying support may have little control over how this money is used. Authority over and responsibility for the children rest in two households. Often the rules vary depending on where the children are currently living. Boundary ambiguities like these can increase stress (Visher et al., 2003).

Some families respond to this complex and ambiguous situation by attempting to become as much like a first-marriage family as possible. They may, for example, try to draw a tight boundary of loyalties around the remarriage family, and try to cut off contact with the nonresidential parent and his or her relatives. Such an approach is unrealistic. It may throw children into a conflict of loyalties in the face of demands to belong exclusively to one parent's family. In fact, keeping boundaries permeable usually provides the most workable solution; in other words, the new family needs to allow members, such as visiting children, to move in and out, and yet establish its own stable lifestyle. It also needs to allow for necessary contact between households of current and former spouses, at least with respect to the children. **Permeable boundaries** also permit children to move back and forth between households for either custody changes or visits, with the least amount of strain (Church, 2004; McGoldrick & Carter, 1999; Visher et al., 2003).

Roles

The lack of clarity in family boundaries has its counterpart in confusion over roles. Roles in nuclear families are complementary, that is, they travel in pairs—husband and wife, parent and child. There are also social expectations for the person who fills a role. Role strain occurs if there is a misfit between the individual and the role he or she is expected to fill, or if no recognized role exists for the individual. Also, as was pointed out in Chapter 1, for example, stepmothers have only two social scripts to follow—the biological mother and the stereotypically wicked stepmother—neither of which fits most families.

One of the main difficulties in remarriage families is that there are too many candidates for the available roles. This fact affects the stepparent in particular. The children already have two biological parents and are not usually interested in replacing them. If the new spouse tries to take over the role of the parent of the same sex, he or she will meet resistance and resentment from the children. Loyalty issues are involved. Conflict can break out over many issues, from meals that are too different from what the children are used to eating, to discipline. A key time for discomfort is any special event involving the child. At graduations and weddings, for example, families have the potentially awkward task of including at least one extra parent figure. Usually such issues underline the fact that the stepparent is not the "real" parent (Kaufman, 1993). Similarly, there are "extra" grandparents and other kin.

Traditional gender roles (in which women are expected to take responsibility for the emotional well-being of the family, including rearing the children, and men are expected to manage finances) work against stepfamilies. These roles are unrealistic when some of the children are virtual strangers to the wife and some of the family's income and expenditure is outside the husband's control. Families seem to work best if the responsibility of raising children is established in a way that does not exclude either biological parent. Stepparents need to work out what role is appropriate for them. Often in successful reconstituted families, this involves being an adult friend rather than a parent to the stepchildren (Preece, 2003–2004; Visher et al., 2003).

A difficulty facing some children is the loss of accustomed roles. This can occur in at least two ways. First, when the new family includes stepsiblings, unless they are widely separated by age, one oldest child loses his or her position, and so does one youngest child. Second, the only boy or girl may gain a same-sex stepsibling and forfeit his or her special status.

Renegotiating family boundaries and roles may take place over a prolonged period of time. Even when the family achieves a comfortable working arrangement, members should expect that it will need continuing adjustment. As children mature and visiting and custody agreements are altered, the relationships will need to be reworked.

ESTABLISHING NEW FAMILY RELATIONSHIPS

The Marital Relationship

As in any other marriage, partners in remarriages have the task of commitment to the new family system. They too need to realign relationships with extended family and friends to include the new spouse. In addition, however, they must also adjust the relationship with their children and ex-spouse.

Often couples in second marriages are less romantic and more realistic, honest, and willing to discuss difficulties in the marriage. Remarried couples may be particularly sensitive to conflict following the breakup of an earlier marriage. This sensitivity can result in more open expression of differences of opinion and greater awareness of the feelings of the spouse. Some couples, however, are so afraid that disagreements will lead to another divorce that they avoid them; this approach leads to difficulties in their relationship (Allen, Baucom, Burnett, Epstein, & Rankin-Esquer, 2001; Coleman et al., 2000).

The fact that the parent–child bond began before the marriage, not following it, can create difficulties in the relationship between the new spouses. Stepparents may compete with stepchildren for the attention of the spouse/parent. In addition, privacy and time alone for the couple may be lacking. Frequently, couple time cuts into children's time at a point when the latter are already feeling left out and confused following the remarriage (Preece, 2003–2004; Visher et al., 2003).

The ex-spouse can also affect the new marriage. The fact that he or she has a continuing relationship with the children means that there is also a continuing relationship with the former partner. Some contacts are necessary to arrange for visits and to discuss issues related to the children's welfare. Ann Crytser (1990) has coined the expression "wife-in-law" to refer to the relationship between current and ex-wives. This relationship is usually unchosen, unwanted, without rules or traditions, and is emotional and permanent. If a will is poorly drawn up, the connection can even last after the death of the man they both married.

The influences of ex-spouses can vary widely. Last-minute cancellations of or requests for visits can disrupt the couple's plans or deprive them of needed privacy. Failure of the ex-spouse to meet support obligations on time or requests for additional money can play havoc with financial planning. Occasionally an individual continues to call on an ex-partner to solve daily problems like household repairs and day-to-day discipline; a new spouse can resent such intrusions. Some of these difficulties involve boundaries and appropriate roles and are part of the issues to be resolved during system reorganization. Others are a necessary

BOX 11.1

DO GRANDPARENTS HAVE RIGHTS?

The story is sad, but too common. When Mattie and Brad divorced, Mattie was granted primary custody of their two children. Brad had visiting rights. On weekends the children were with him, he brought them to his parents' home. After three years, Brad was transferred out of the province. About the same time, Mattie remarried. She now refuses to let Brad's parents visit their grandchildren. She believes that visits should take place on Brad's time. Besides, she argues that his parents are critical of her and her new husband, and that their attitude will harm her relationship with her children. Brad's parents think about suing for visiting rights.

Following divorce, grandparents tend to be cut off from grandchildren in two situations. The first is when their former child-in-law has custody, and when their own child has little contact with the children, especially when grandparents have mixed into the marital dispute. The second occurs when there is conflict between grandparents and their former child-in-law's new partner. The father's parents are at particularly high risk of losing contact if the mother has custody. Some grandparents try extra hard to get along with the custodial parent. Others lose touch with grandchildren. A few go to court.

Provinces vary in rights granted to grandparents. Quebec is most far-reaching in its Civil Code. A father or mother cannot deny access or interfere with grandchild–grandparent relationships unless there is a grave reason. When there is a dispute, the court decides. In other provinces a relative can apply for access. Some, such as Alberta, specifically mention grandparents in their laws. Courts in most provinces rely on the best interests of the child in making a decision. In Quebec, parents need to show that contact will harm the child. In most other provinces, grandparents need to prove that having contact is in the child's best interests. It is presumed, unless proven otherwise, that parents will make the best choices for their children. Courts tend to place more weight on grandparents' claims if they have lived with their grandchild or have had a great deal of contact, for instance by providing daycare. If there is a high level of conflict between parents and grandparents, then courts usually decide that cutting off visits is better for the child's family and thus for the child.

In some cases, the conflict is settled with the help of a mediator. This is what happened with Mattie and Brad's parents. The grandparents can have six visits a year. Mattie will decide the time and place.

Sources: Atkinson, 1999; Connidis, 2001; Department of Justice, 2004a; Goldberg, 2003; Kruk, 1995.

point of contact for the well-being of the children. Often current and ex-spouses must interact in public places, for instance, at times of crisis (like funerals) or celebration (like graduations and weddings); such situations add to the stress (Church, 2004).

The most common difficulty between spouses, however, is conflict over children. Since the stepparent role is not clearly defined in our society, parents, stepparents, and children alike may have unreasonable and contradictory expectations. Conflict may develop out of parents' differences in attitudes about discipline, or out of children's attempts to play their parents against each other or to appeal to the loyalty of the birth parent. Occasionally conflict takes a different form in families where there are teens or young adults. The biological parent may become jealous of the developing affection between stepparent and stepchild, especially if he or she interprets it in sexual terms (Bray & Kelly, 1998; McGoldrick & Carter, 1999).

Partners usually become aware of insurmountable difficulties early in the remarriage; thus most divorces occur quickly. If the marriage is not dissolved quickly, it is likely to be as stable as any first marriage (McGoldrick & Carter, 1999).

Residential Parent–Child Relationships

The parent-child relationship often suffers in the early post-divorce period. Given that the **residential parent** is adjusting to the loss of a spouse as well as restructuring his or her life, often little emotional or even physical energy is available to deal effectively with the child. The child, who is also having difficulty, often takes bad feelings out on the parent through defiance and rebellion or other forms of obnoxious behaviour (Greene et al., 2003).

Some children face the parent's disorganization by becoming a **parentified child,** that is, by accepting an unusually high degree of the parent's responsibilities of care and nurturing. With this role comes greater decision-making power. Often the single parent and child will close ranks and become more dependent on each other. The child may become a confidant(e). This is especially true of a single mother and daughter. When the parent remarries, the child often has to give up some of the responsibility and closeness to the new adult in the family. Naturally, the child often feels a sense of both loss and resentment. As a result, the child may try to maintain power by becoming more demanding toward the birth parent, with attention-seeking behaviour, or he or she may become depressed and withdrawn (Kaufman, 1993). Often, however, the residential parent, especially the mother, continues to act more or less as a single parent following remarriage; that is, he or she continues to take the main responsibility for the child (Boxnboim & Erera, 1995; Visher et al., 2003).

Nonresidential Parent–Child Relationships

The relationship between the child and the nonresidential parent varies a great deal from family to family. Some parents have little or no contact with their children. Others are very involved in decisions about the child and in his or her physical care. Variations are related to distance between homes, the length of time since the divorce, the age of the child, and the amount of support paid. If the parent is depressed or feels guilty, he or she may avoid visits because they only aggravate these feelings. More frequent contact is associated with higher income and education, and with reasonably friendly relations with the ex-spouse. Nonresidential mothers are much less likely to stop visiting children and are more likely to keep up regular, frequent visits. If either parent remarries, visits with the nonresidential parent tend to drop off (Greene et al., 2003).

Often children's contact with nonresidential parents involves social and fun activities such as going to movies or on trips, while the residential parent is involved in day-to-day activities such as helping with homework and maintaining discipline. Thus, noncustodial parents are seen as the source of pleasure, but they are cut off from the mainstream of daily living. However, custodial parents may become resentful at being forced into the role of disciplinarian and "bad guy."

Even though the residential parent may have negative feelings about arranging visits, contact between the children and nonresidential parent is valuable. As we saw in the last chapter, the well-being of children depends on the maintenance of ties with both biological parents. Yet keeping up connections may be a source of conflict. Children in stepfather families see more conflict between parents than other children. This happens not so much because there is an unusually high level of disagreement inside their home or between their biological parents. Rather, the two types of conflict added together produce the higher levels (Hanson, McLanahan, & Thomson, 1996).

The Stepparent–Stepchild Relationship

The relationship between stepparent and stepchild is important for two reasons. First, many marriages founder because problems in this relationship eventually destroy the marriage. Second, adolescents in stepfamilies are at high risk of developing behavioural problems.

To be successful stepparents, adults need to accomplish two tasks: develop an appropriately affectionate relationship with the child and establish themselves as legitimate parental authorities and disciplinarians. Unfortunately, the tasks are somewhat contradictory. Many families fall short of these goals. A barrier to working out problems is the relative impermanence of the stepparent relationship; it lasts only as long as the marriage does. If the marriage founders, the stepparent generally no longer has any relationship with the child. One factor works in favour of stepfamilies: most children prefer to live in a two-parent family.

Developing a Relationship

Stepparents tend to be more successful with younger children, who may transfer their attachment from their biological parent to the stepparent. Both stepfathers and stepmothers report more positive relationships with boys than with girls. The stepmother–stepdaughter relationship suffers from the most severe problems. Often daughters feel responsible for the emotional relationships in the family. Since stepmothers also believe they should nurture these relationships, their stepdaughters feel displaced and resist sharing this role (McGoldrick & Carter, 1999).

Some of the problems in stepfamily relationships arise from myths and unrealistic expectations, which place unnecessary burdens on all members. Let's take a look at some of these misconceptions.

1. *"One big happy family."* In order to prove to themselves and to the world that the new family is a success, some stepparents feel the need to keep all family members happy and contented (Church, 2004; Visher et al., 2003). Even in first-marriage families satisfying everyone is impossible because needs and desires conflict. It is even more difficult for stepfamilies to achieve this ideal.

2. *"Instant love."* Often stepfamily members are expected to feel immediate attachment to, or even love, one another. Parents and children who accept this myth have a vision of the ideal child or parent that no human being can fulfill. What makes this situation harder is that the child's ideal is often the nonresident biological parent, who is used as a glowing example of parenting. Both stepparent and child are bound to be disappointed or resentful in this situation (Church, 2004; Visher et al., 2003).

3. *"The rescuer."* This fantasy comes in two versions—making up for what the poor child has been through or straightening the kid out. Neither works. Taking away past pain from family upsets or making up for it is impossible. If the stepparent tries to "correct" what he sees as past failures in discipline with a view to turning the child into a productive member of society, he will in all likelihood arouse this child's resentment, which can lead to conflict with the biological parent (Church, 2004; Visher et al., 2003).

4. *"The wicked stepmother."* Stepmothers have had bad publicity from way back. The wicked stepmother is a folk figure who stars in the traditional tales, like the Cinderella story. Real stepmothers often strive to overcome this handicap by trying to be extra nice. Sometimes the "rescuer" or "happy family" fantasy is the result. The problems the stepmother experiences may partly be the result of her persistence in trying to become a nurturer. When she isn't appreciated, she may become angry or resentful, truly a "wicked" stepmother. If she did not try so hard to counteract the myth, she might actually be more successful (Church, 2004).

If people believe the myths, they go into stepfamilies with unrealistic expectations, which may produce disappointment or undeserved suspicion. As a result, they interfere with the development of working relationships.

The degree of acceptance of stepfamily members is often affected by loyalty issues. The child may see the stepparent as an intruder trying to take the "real" parent's place. If attachment does begin to grow, the child may feel that he or she is being disloyal to the same-sex biological parent. In either case, the child may be anxious and resentful enough to ward off the new parent by trying to drive a wedge into the marriage (Preece, 2003–2004). Stepparents may also feel disloyal if they become attached to their new spouse's children. Men who left their children from a former marriage in the custody of their ex-wife do not relate as well to stepchildren as do men who were bachelors. Part of the reason, some researchers believe, is that the father's sense of guilt over leaving his own children interferes with the new relationship (Bray & Kelly, 1998).

Another complication that may arise between opposite-sex stepparent and stepchild has to do with there being no explicit incest taboo surrounding this relationship. Stepfathers may find it easier to express affection either verbally or through granting special privileges than physically. Sometimes conflict is used to keep a safe distance, since showing fondness may arouse sexual feelings (Bray & Kelly, 1998; Kaufman, 1993).

Discipline

Discipline is another potential area of conflict. One of the difficulties is that stepparents are not seen as "real" parents, since they are not the children's birth parents. Only "real" parents, in the minds of many children, are entitled to be disciplinarians. The issue can be complicated by differences in child-rearing styles and strategies, or by the failure of the residential birth parent to act as a disciplinarian. Discipline is also a key area in which a jealous birth parent may undermine the position of the stepparent. The most successful stepparents are those who first develop a friendly relationship with the child and then assert their authority. Adolescents tend to do best when stepparents are supportive and are not very controlling. The secret to success lies with the birth parent. He or she must legitimate the role and authority of the stepparent (Brandes, 2003; Coleman et al., 2000).

Relationships between Stepbrothers and Stepsisters

A marriage between divorced parents creates stepsiblings. Many stepsiblings do not live together since the most common pattern is for children to live with their mothers. Unless visits are arranged so that only one set of children is in the house at one time, there is periodic interaction between resident and visiting children. With more fathers being granted custody of their children, the likelihood of two sibling groups being combined in one household has increased. For these children, adjustments have to be made on a more permanent basis (Kaufman, 1993).

Children expect their birth parents to consider them special; thus when there are conflicts, children expect their own parent to side with them. Any differences in treatment between stepsiblings are usually interpreted by children as favouritism. A key ingredient in this mix is a sense of loss and jealousy because the birth parents are spending time with the other children, often at the expense of time with their own (Kaufman, 1993).

If one set of children visits or moves into the family home permanently, problems may arise over turf. When children are expected to share space and toys, opportunities for friction increase greatly. These may centre on both the use of space and possessions. The conflict is made worse if the two sets of children have different attitudes toward such aspects of daily life as tidiness or the use of others' property (Visher et al., 2003).

Children's roles in families may conflict. Two only children, for example, may have difficulty getting used to having another child around, especially if they are the same age and sex. Also, adjusting to the fact that there can be only one oldest and one youngest in a family may be hard. Often parents discount the sense of loss a child experiences if he or she has to give up an important role.

When adolescents of both sexes are in a family, conflict may be adopted as a way of maintaining a safe distance between them. The incest taboo between stepsiblings ranges from weak to nonexistent, and such conflict provides a safe buffer against sexual attraction (Kaufman, 1993).

On the positive side, stepsiblings can provide one another with emotional support, for example, if visits with the nonresidential parent fall through. Since they have all had similar experiences of losing their original family and having to adjust to living in a new blended family, they can form a mutual self-help group (Kaufman, 1993).

The Child Born into a Stepfamily

Almost half (48 percent) of stepfamilies have a child born to them. This is most common when the mother and existing children are younger. Such children change the family because they are related to everyone as biological child or sibling. Having a baby is related to stepfamily stability, either because the baby strengthens relationships or because couples choosing to have a child are more likely to have a strong bond. There have, however, been few studies of relationships in these families or of the effect on both stepchildren and children of the remarriage (Juby et al., 2001).

EFFECTS OF STEPFAMILY LIVING ON CHILDREN

Recently, researchers in many countries have studied the effects on children of living in a stepfamily. Most compared stepchildren to those living with both biological parents and those in single-mother homes. Stepchildren fared much like children raised by single mothers. They had more educational, emotional, and behavioural difficulties than children growing up in their original nuclear families. The differences, however, were small. Many did as well as those living with both biological parents (Coleman et al., 2000).

We have already seen most of the reasons suggested for these differences in Chapter 9. First, children in stepfamilies experience more stress. The more life changes children experience, the more stress they will feel. Parents are not as competent because they too are under stress. There may be conflicts between households and between stepfamily members. There are also few healthy role models for stepchildren and stepparents to follow. Second, parenting may differ in stepfamilies because stepfathers show less affection and supervise children less. However, parenting styles (i.e., authoritative, authoritarian, permissive) have similar results whether used by biological or stepparents. Finally, stepchildren's problems may reach back before the new family was formed. For example, difficulties may arise because of their parents' psychological problems or as a result of poverty. None of the explanations succeed in fully accounting for stepchildren's disadvantages (Coleman et al., 2000).

REMARRIAGE AND THE FAMILY LIFE CYCLE

The experience of remarriage differs according to the life-cycle stage of each partner. If they are in the same phase, they share common problems. Their greatest strain involves responsibilities to their children. This is especially difficult when they have adolescents. Some issues are common in families with adolescents. For example, the family's need to form attachments often conflicts with the adolescent's normal need to separate from the family. Also, difficulties arise out of the teen's ability to manipulate parents and out of adolescent sexuality. In later life-cycle stages, grown children may complain about having to shift their "normal" image of parents and/or grandparents to one that includes a stepparent. They may also have concerns about inheritance. Particular problems arise if one spouse is considerably older than the other, and their life-cycle stages differ. For instance, some men marry women roughly the same age as their children. In general, the greater the difference in life-cycle stage, the harder it is to adapt to the new family because husband and wife are dealing with different life-cycle issues (McGoldrick & Carter, 1999; Visher et al., 2003).

THE STEPFAMILY AND THE WIDER SOCIETY

The relationship of the stepfamily to society is somewhat confused. In some ways these families are indistinguishable from first-marriage families. They have two parents in the household, for instance, living with their children. This invisibility helps the family blend in, at least superficially. Yet the fact that they seem the same leads to the expectation that they will be like other families. Some of the differences seem almost petty, yet they can create problems. For example, school officials may not think to send duplicate report cards and school notices to each biological parent (Olsen, 1997).

Stepfamilies also experience role ambiguity. They do not receive clear messages from society about norms for dealing with the complex relationships in their families. The stepfamily is sometimes called an "incomplete institution" because it does not come with the kind of ready-made norms and roles surrounding first-marriage families (Coleman et al., 2000; McGoldrick & Carter, 1999). On the one hand, they are expected to have something wrong with them. In part, this is realistic since many children in these families do display problems in relationships with peers and authority figures because of unresolved anger; yet expecting problems often becomes a self-fulfilling prophecy. On the other hand, society often expects the stepfamily to act like "one big happy family."

Given the number of children involved, it is important for all of us to develop a model of stepfamily health rather than stepfamily disturbance. With such a model, we will be able to support parents in creating a stable and nurturing environment.

SUMMARY

HISTORICAL CHANGES. The nature of remarriage has changed in recent years. In the past, most stepfamilies were formed after one spouse died. Now they more commonly follow divorce. As a result, the remarriage is complicated by the existence of a living ex-spouse.

FORMING A NEW FAMILY SYSTEM. Forming a reconstituted family occurs in several stages. First, the couple needs to recover from the loss of their first marriages and commit themselves to their new one. Second, anxiety about remarrying and arrangements for children's continued contact with the other parent and his or her relatives need to be worked out. Third, boundaries and roles need to be renegotiated. Since the children belong in two households, boundaries need to be flexible enough to allow for their coming and going. In addition, financial support and parental authority are also divided. There is often lack of clarity over roles in stepfamilies, in particular, over the stepparent role. Same-sex stepparents face the same problems as other stepparents. They also have to deal with social attitudes concerning homosexuality, which may complicate stepparenting.

ESTABLISHING NEW FAMILY RELATIONSHIPS. Members of reconstituted families must work out relationships with old and new family members:

The Parental Relationship. Often the resident parent cannot respond to the child's needs immediately after the divorce. As a result, some children take on the parent's responsibilities for care and nurturing of other family members. When the parent remarries, the parentified child experiences both a loss of power and feelings of resentment. The relationship with the nonresidential parent may vary from no contact to frequent visiting. Continuing contact, in most cases, improves the well-being of the children. Stepparents need to accomplish two tasks: to develop an appropriately affectionate relationship with the child, and to establish themselves as legitimate disciplinarians. They are hampered by myths that suggest either that everything will work out smoothly or that stepparents are cruel. Children often resist becoming attached to their stepparent because of loyalty to the same-sex birth parent. Discipline is another area of conflict, since children may not accept the stepparent's authority.

Stepsibling Relationships. Often stepsiblings do not live in the same household, but have contact during periodic visits. Whether they visit or share a home, there may be conflict over space, possessions, rules, and attention from parents. Little is known about the effect of having a child born into a stepfamily.

EFFECT OF STEPFAMILY LIVING ON CHILDREN. Children in stepfamilies, like those in single-mother families, have, on average, more problems than children living with both biological parents. Explanations include increased stress levels, stepparents' parenting styles, and problems from the past.

REMARRIAGE IN THE LIFE CYCLE. As in divorce, the impact of remarriage depends partly on the life-cycle stage of the new partners. For example, the age of the children has an effect on family life. Additional pressures may exist if the new partners are in different life-cycle stages.

STEPFAMILIES AND SOCIETY AT LARGE. Since stepfamilies superficially resemble first-marriage families, they are often expected to be like them. On the other hand, they also are expected to have something wrong with them. Society still needs to develop positive models of step-family roles.

KEY TERMS

parentified child: a child who takes on an unusually high degree of a parent's role (p. 264)

permeable boundaries: family boundaries that allow members to move through them (p. 261)

reconstituted family: a remarriage family (p. 259)

residential parent: the parent with whom the child lives (p. 264)

CLASS ASSIGNMENTS

Complete one or both of the following assignments, as directed by your instructor:

1. Many of the problems of remarriage families centre on power issues. Identify areas where power or control might be a problem. What difficulties can these issues cause and how might they be avoided?

2. One issue that sometimes arises is the possibility of a stepparent adopting a stepchild. What is the law in this regard? Explain the advantages and disadvantages of stepparent adoptions.

PERSONAL ASSIGNMENTS

The following questions are designed to help you reflect on your own experience:

1. In stepfamilies you are acquainted with, what factors made for relatively harmonious relationships? Explain why. How do you think such relationships can be encouraged in other families?

2. Often little things, or hassles, are a major source of friction in families. Identify some of these apparently small difficulties that you feel can cause serious problems in step-families. Explain your answer.

© ChipPix/ShutterStock

Chapter 12

The Family and the World of Work

OBJECTIVES

■ *To consider the history of daycare and its relation to women's work*

■ *To examine sources of stress in the interactions between work and family life*

■ *To explore the effect of unemployment on the family*

■ *To look at the impact of worker burnout on the entire family*

What a shock when I went back to work! My reason was the usual one: our growing family needed more money. Teenagers are more expensive than toddlers and my husband's pay hadn't kept pace with inflation, so I got a job filling in for a teacher on maternity leave.

I knew it would mean major changes for my family. A stay-at-home mother does chores and deals with family problems during the day. No more! We assigned chores and planned schedule changes. These took hold after early resistance. What none of us had counted on was that my work almost paralyzed me as a family member. I came home exhausted and didn't have the physical energy to deal with the many hassles and concerns that crop up in any family. Even more trying was the fact that I worked with teenagers and when I came home I couldn't escape them. I wasn't much good as either a wife or a parent.

More and more families are affected by the conflict between work and family responsibilities. From the ecological perspective, individuals are members of two microsystems—family and work. These microsystems interact through the work-family mesosystem. The influence, or spillover, can be either positive or negative and can occur from work to family or vice versa (Roehling, Moen, & Batt, 2003). As we saw in Chapter 4, a major trend in our society is the increase in the number of women employed outside the home. See Table 12.1.

In 1941, less than 4 percent of married women had paid jobs, in contrast to 45 percent of the single, divorced, separated, or widowed. Since 1984, married women have been more likely to be employed than the unmarried (Crompton & Vickers, 2000; Statistics Canada,

TABLE 12.1

PERCENTAGE OF ADULTS AGED 25 AND OVER WHO ARE EMPLOYED

	25–44 Years		45–54 Years		55–64 Years	
	Women	Men	Women	Men	Women	Men
1976	49.9	90.9	45.6	88.9	30.4	72.8
1981	60.2	90.1	51.7	88.5	31.0	70.7
1986	66.2	86.2	55.8	85.9	30.3	62.6
1991	70.4	83.5	64.3	84.2	32.4	57.1
1996	70.9	82.9	66.2	82.4	33.6	53.7
2001	75.3	85.9	72.2	84.2	39.4	57.6
2002	75.8	85.7	73.8	84.3	41.3	59.8
2003	76.1	86.1	74.9	84.5	45.0	61.4

Source: Adapted from Statistics Canada, "Women in Canada: Work chapters updates, 2003." 89F0133. March 25, 2004, Table 4, p. 13.

2004k). The number of women in the paid workforce has grown sharply since the 1970s, especially in cities. The greatest increase has been among those aged 25 to 44, in other words, among women most likely to have children at home. See Table 12.2. Over two-thirds of mothers with children aged three to five are in the paid labour force, including nearly 60 percent with children under three. Over three-quarters of those with school-aged children are employed (Curto & Rothwell, 2003; Statistics Canada, 2004k). This trend has produced two major problem areas: care for young children and older family members and, for dual-earner families, juggling two jobs along with household responsibilities.

CARE FOR FAMILY MEMBERS

The care of children, the disabled, and the elderly makes demands on family members. In the next chapter, we will look at families with chronically ill and disabled members. There has been relatively little consideration of the interplay between family work responsibilities and the care of aging family members. Much more attention has been paid to childcare.

Childcare

Daycare in Canada is closely tied to social attitudes toward women's work. There has long been the assumption that children are best off at home, looked after by their mothers. Daycare centres were established only when it was seen to benefit society, either from the desire for better supervision of children or from the need for the mothers to join the workforce.

TABLE 12.2		
EMPLOYMENT OF WOMEN WITH CHILDREN UNDER 16, PERCENTAGE EMPLOYED		
	Female Lone Parents	Women with Partners
1976	48.3	38.4
1981	54.4	48.9
1986	51.7	57.4
1991	52.2	64.6
1996	53.3	66.8
2001	66.6	71.0
2002	66.9	72.3
2003	67.9	72.3

Source: Adapted from Statistics Canada, "Women in Canada: Work chapters updates, 2003. 89F0133. March 25, 2004, Table 6, p. 15.

Note: In 2003, 46.9 percent of single mothers with a child under age three and 60.7 percent of those with children aged three to five were employed. The figures for women with partners were 64.9 percent and 70.2 percent respectively.

The first daycare centres were established under various auspices, such as schools and children's hospitals, in response to problems experienced by lone mothers. Most, however, were developed by religious organizations, such as the earliest day nurseries in Montreal, or by volunteer women's organizations. These services were never planned from the user's point of view, and they were always seen as an emergency service to meet the needs of society. As a form of welfare, they allowed mothers to work to support themselves and their children. Children in these centres received training to turn them into productive members of society. The emphasis was on manners, cleanliness, obedience, and religion. There was a continuing sense, however, that such care was second-rate, lagging far behind care at home (Schulz, 1978).

Although provinces have responsibility for social programs, the federal government has from time to time encouraged the development of specific programs through conditional grants of money. During World War II, for example, there was an urgent need for women, including those with children, to join the workforce. In 1942, the federal government agreed to enter cost-sharing agreements with the provinces to provide daycare primarily for the children of mothers working in essential industries. Only Ontario and Quebec took advantage of this arrangement. In these provinces, there was an enormous expansion of daycare services. Once the war was over, federal funding was discontinued and led to the closing of many daycare centres. In Ontario, the public outcry was so great that in 1946 the province passed the *Day Nurseries Act,* which provided funding and established minimum standards (Schulz, 1978).

Childcare can be formal or informal (see Figure 12.1). Informal arrangements are not subject to government regulations. Formal arrangements are covered by regulations and include family daycare and daycare centres (Connor & Brink, 1999). According to the National Longitudinal Survey of Children and Youth, over one-half of all children aged six months to five years were in some form of childcare. Only one-quarter of these attended daycare centres (Statistics Canada, 2005a). In 2001, there were regulated childcare spaces available for only 12 percent of all children with working mothers (Lauzière, 2004).

Today, the levels and types of childcare provided vary. There are several reasons for such differences. First, the current attitude in society toward such care is mixed. Some people point out that high-quality daycare should be a right granted to working parents and their children. It is seen as remedial, or as an aid to the development of children with special needs, including those who are developmentally challenged. In addition, subsidized daycare is part of the welfare system. On the other hand, daycare is seen as a cost to the parent (especially the mother) that allows the "indulgence" of a job, since the tax credit provided by the government does not equal the actual cost of care (Cleveland & Krashinsky, 2003).

Second, there is no national policy regarding daycare because daycare is a provincial responsibility. In addition, there is the belief that families should take on full responsibility for raising their children; therefore, subsidized daycare is seen as an exception rather than something all families should have. To add to the confusion, because care of children is considered a private rather than public affair, little information has been collected in the past on either the need for or quality of daycare in Canada (Lero & Kyle, 1991).

Figure 12.1

CHILDCARE IN CANADA

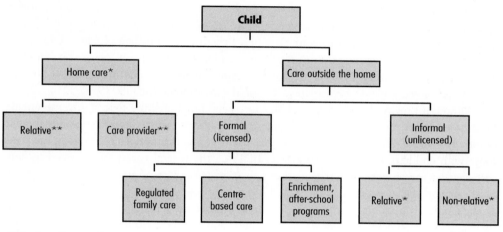

* May be paid or unpaid.
** Could be a licensed care provider.

Source: Adapted from "The Impacts of Non-Parental Care in Child Development," August 1999, p. 68. Reproduced with permission of Her Majesty the Queen in Right of Canada 2005.

From the 1960s on, federal governments have promised increased funding for childcare, but little money has materialized. The year 1995 was a critical point. In Ottawa, there was anxiety about Quebec separatism as well as pressure from other provinces for less federal influence in social policies. There was also concern over budget deficits and the national debt. For the first time, the federal government announced actual spending cuts. In 1996, tax money transferred from Ottawa to the provinces and territories was combined into a single grant, the Canada Health and Social Transfer. In these ways, the federal government reduced its ability to shape social programs (Mahon, 2004).

The growth and continuing existence of childcare programs depends both on available money and on political viewpoint. Any reduction in federal funding reduces the ability of provinces to pay for social programs. This is especially true for Newfoundland and Labrador, the Maritimes, Saskatchewan, and Manitoba. In some provinces, like Alberta and Ontario, governments believed in reducing provincial control over some social programs, leaving responsibility to municipalities and families. Such provinces did not provide additional funds for childcare (Mahon, 2004).

In most parts of Canada, families have problems with the cost of childcare. Fees have increased and subsidies are limited. Because fewer parents can afford formal daycare, a number of centres have laid off staff, further reducing places available. As a result, informal childcare has probably increased. The quality of care in daycare centres may have declined because few monitoring standards exist. In fact, most children are now in unregulated care (Lauzière, 2004; Mahon, 2004).

Because so many parents of young children work, they and their children need "reliable child care arrangements that are affordable, reasonably convenient, available when needed, and of high quality" (Lero, 1993, p. 4). They also need to have backup plans if children are ill or if something out of the ordinary happens, like a family emergency or a school holiday. In the Ottawa area, many parents have access to emergency care through the National Capital Region Emergency Child Care Consortium. This service is supported by employers, unions, and other groups (Short Term Child Care, n.d.). Finding care that meets family needs is complicated by the fact that nearly half of employed parents do not work from nine to five. Many work weekends, late afternoons, evenings, or irregular hours. Schedules like these are the result of the growing number of jobs in service occupations—stores, transportation, and recreation. Unfortunately, most daycare is still based on the nine-to-five schedule (Lero, 1993). In addition, care during school vacations is important. An American study found that many children are in self-care while parents work (Cappizano, Adelman, & Stagner, 2002).

There are several factors for the kind of childcare parents choose. First, the age of the child matters. Parents of infants and toddlers are most likely to care for children themselves, either by having a full-time at-home parent or by staggering work times. The next choice is relatives. Second, parents' ideas about child development are important. Do they believe attachment to the mother is primary? Or do they believe the child will benefit from the programs and social interaction of a centre? Third is income and job type. Both higher income parents and poor families use daycare centres the most. Middle-income parents have trouble affording the fees and receive no subsidies. If parents work shifts or hold two jobs, they may find daycare centre hours do not match their own. Fourth, family characteristics affect the care chosen. Better educated parents and single mothers are more likely to use daycare centres. Parents of larger families are apt to care for children themselves, probably because the cost of childcare outstrips possible earnings. If they do use outside care, they often choose less expensive forms. Finally, the community itself has an effect. Places vary as to the supply of affordable, accessible care. Parents may also choose a care centre near their home or work (Connor & Brink, 1999). The actual care parents use may differ from their first choice. In one study, more than half who preferred a daycare centre or a babysitter in their own home were using other forms of care. If they wanted to leave their child with a babysitter or a relative, about 70 percent did so (Beaujot, 2000).

Changes in availability and cost of daycare affect women more than men because they provide the bulk of care. As parents, women may have to choose between full-time or part-time employment. If they do have paid work, they may have less choice in the childcare they can afford. Working mothers are more likely to be under stress if they have less confidence in the care their children receive. Lack of childcare subsidies for students on top of increased fees may rule out further education. Childcare providers, mostly women, are also affected. They may have lower job security and poorer working conditions (Doherty, Friendly, & Oloman, 1998).

Hi-ho, it's off to work we go!

Source: Reprinted by kind permission of Barrie Maguire.

Quebec is an exception. The provincial government shifted money from other social programs to subsidize new childcare spaces in its Early Childhood Care and Education. The program was implemented in stages; in the fall of 2000, all children up to age 12 became eligible. The province also reduced the cost to five dollars per day per child (raised to seven dollars in 2003). Only parents who cannot find a seven-dollar spot can claim a Quebec income tax credit for childcare. In addition, children from low-income families may be subsidized (Gouvernement du Québec, 2004; Tougas, 2002).

Elder Care

"The new leaner, meaner era of tightened budgets, hospital closures, early discharges, and day surgery" (Kingsmill & Schlesinger, 1998, p. 139) has thrown increased responsibility for the care of the elderly onto family members. In recent decades, there has been a 100 percent increase in days taken off work for personal and family reasons. Over one-third of this increase is spent caring for an elderly relative. Help with personal care, such as bathing, toileting, and dressing, is more demanding than help with shopping or home maintenance. Taking elders for medical appointments and dealing with social service agencies can be time consuming and frustrating, and usually must occur during working hours. Women are more likely than men to miss work-related social events and to lose out on promotions as a result of elder care responsibilities. In addition, during 2002 about 20 percent of women caregivers aged 45 to 54 cut back on work hours. Some quit. Flexible work arrangements can reduce the work–family tug-of-war (Cranswick, 2003). Federal compassionate care benefits are available to people who leave work to care for a family member who is likely to die within 26 weeks (Stobert & Cranswick, 2004).

WORK AND FAMILY STRESS

Families and work are interrelated in many other ways. One of these is the stress that results from the conflicting demands of job and home. This is a two-way street. The tensions from paid work carry over to the home, and the family issues affect the job (Roehling et al., 2003).

Expectations

One of the major stressors in dual-income families is the expectations of family members and the people around them. Social values affect individuals. For instance, women complain that if they stay home, they are seen as failing to live up to their potential. If they work outside the home, they fear being criticized for neglecting their children. In addition to pressure from social expectations, individuals are affected by their own expectations. Some, for example, are perfectionists who place themselves under unnecessary stress because they want to do everything well. Traditional ideals of family togetherness and quality time with children may also lead to dissatisfaction with the balance of work and family responsibilities. Such ideals cannot be met by dual-earner parents (Daly, 2001).

The expectations of employers and fellow employees may be anti-family. Employers frequently expect employees to work more than eight hours a day and five days a week, especially if they want to advance in their careers. Job transfers, part of the cost of promotion, disrupt relationships with relatives and friends. If a spouse refuses to move, he or she can be blamed for holding the partner back (Duxbury, Higgins, & Coghill, 2003).

Some researchers suggest that shift work creates problems for marriages. Others think that this type of stress is related to expectations. If relatives and friends work shifts, this work pattern may appear normal (Elquist & Hilton, 2003).

Work and Marital Happiness

An American study that looked at working mothers found there was little connection between the fact that mothers had jobs and the marital satisfaction they and their husbands felt. When fathers were more involved with their children, both spouses tended to rate their marriages happier. The only exception was possibly husbands in dual-earner families with traditional ideas about gender roles (Hoffman & Youngblade, 1999). When men work long hours and have high levels of job-related stress, relationships with their wives and children suffer (Crouter, Bumpus, Head, & McHale, 2001; Fraenkel, 2003).

Another American study looked at partners' work schedules. Researchers found that when individuals worked night or rotating shifts, their marriages were at greater risk for separation. The researcher suggests that both physical and social stress are involved for those working after midnight. One spouse needs to sleep during the day. When there are children, that parent may go short on sleep. In addition, some of the occupations requiring night shift work produce high stress levels themselves—nurses, emergency personnel, police, or on-call workers. In 1995, at least one parent had an atypical schedule in 40 percent of families with children (Le Bourdais, Marcil-Gratton, & Juby, 2003). In contrast, a study of blue-collar workers found that shift work was not related to marital happiness. Rather, women's perception that they carried unfair household responsibility in addition to their jobs was connected with marital dissatisfaction (Elquist & Hilton, 2003). As we move toward 24-hour, 7-day business hours, more workers will probably have night and rotating shifts.

Juggling Time and Energy—The Time Crunch

Many individuals have problems balancing the demands of work and family. First, there never seems to be enough time and energy for individuals to accomplish all they wish to in either their work or family roles. This may result in short-term difficulties in getting day-to-day work completed or it can result in failure to achieve overall goals. Second, there can be difficulties over scheduling of time. Shift work, frequent travel, and long hours may mean that family members get to spend little time with one another. The situation is made worse when people believe that everything can be solved through more efficient time management rather than through compromises between ideals and real life (Daly, 2001; Fraenkel, 2003).

Among the most time-crunched are dual-earner couples, especially those with young children. In such families, women are under more stress than men. In families with children under five, 30 percent of women are severely time-crunched, in contrast to less than 26 percent of men. One explanation for this difference is that, even in dual-earner families, women are still mainly responsible for children and household. It is women, most often, who shop for groceries, take children to doctors' appointments, arrange for daycare, and see to all the many other responsibilities of a family. Parents with children living at home—women more than men—report time stress more often than the childless. To make matters worse, women usually have less flexibility at work than men. It is thus more difficult for them to come in late or leave early (Statistics Canada, 2003e).

Family and Work Interference

Conflict between work and family has two aspects. First there are practical factors such as the time crunch and scheduling conflicts. These are sometimes referred to as role interference or role **spillover.** Second are perceptions an individual has of being stressed or overwhelmed by the pressures of multiple family and work roles. These are known as role overload and role strain. In general, workers report negative work-to-family effects, although positive influences are possible (Duxbury & Higgins, 2003; Grzywacz, Almeida, & McDonald, 2002). The influence may be circular. Stresses at work can lead to less time and emotional energy for home. The worker's partner may then feel overburdened and resentful, leading to marital upset. This in turn may distract the individual from his or her work, thereby increasing work-related stress (Fraenkel, 2003).

A large study of Canadians working for big companies, governments, or institutions like schools and hospitals learned that work-to-family interference is a serious problem for one in four employees. Almost 40 percent report moderate levels of interference from their job in meeting family responsibilities. This is most likely to occur when home demands are high.

Business managers, professionals, workers in hospitals and schools, and those with children and elder care responsibilities experience highest levels of interference. Many people, however, feel they can separate work and family, and that work does not affect family life (Duxbury & Higgins, 2003).

Negative work-to-family spillover occurs most often when individuals, especially women, have heavy workloads and little control at work. It is also common among parents of young children and among single parents (Duxbury & Higgins, 2003; Lero & Kyle, 1991; Voydanoff, 2004). Stress at work rather than actual hours worked probably is the most damaging. Among police couples, the husband's stress at work is related to separation and divorce, while exhaustion does not appear to be (Roberts & Levenson, 2001).

Although it is reported less often, family-to-work spillover does occur. Just over one-tenth of workers report interference with work responsibilities by family demands (Duxbury & Higgins, 2003). About one-tenth of workers aged 45 to 54 caring for elderly relatives lost income because of family responsibilities. About 2 percent quit paid work (Cranswick, 2003). One study estimated that men in unhappy marriages lost about 38 days a year of work time. Their absenteeism was higher than happier men, partly because of stress-related illnesses. They also did not accomplish as much when they were at work (Forthofer, Markman, Cox, Stanley, & Kessler, 1996).

Some studies have found that the more family-friendly the workplace is, the less strain there is in juggling work and family roles. This was especially true if the supervisor was flexible about work scheduling. If parents could take phone calls at work from or about children, if they could come in late or leave early to keep appointments, or take occasional days off without pay, they could manage both family and work responsibilities (Warren & Johnson, 1995). However, using strategies like telecommuting or flextime, which are discussed later, may cut into family time and increase a sense of spillover, especially for wives (Roehling et al., 2003).

Childcare Responsibilities

Working parents are concerned about the possible negative effects of their employment on their children. More attention is paid to the impact of mothers because it is often assumed that all men work and that women are responsible for the care of family members. Although quality time is generally seen to be more important than the actual hours spent with a child, it is difficult to both define quality time and to make it happen on schedule (Daly, 2001).

Two facts are clear—childcare consumes a great deal of time, and it is usually women's work. Mothers of young children working full time spend an average of 2.8 hours per day solely caring for their children. Men spend less than two. This does not count the time that parents supervise activities such as watching television or playing (Statistics Canada, 2003e). Fathers are more likely to care for children if they work different hours from their wives, especially if they have preschoolers. Most often this happens when men work afternoon or evening shifts (Brayfield, 1995).

Children now require more time and attention from their parents than ever before. There are not as many adults to share childcare responsibilities, such as grandparents or unmarried female relatives. Families are also smaller, so that there may not be older siblings to care for younger ones. Even though parents working outside the home do use various childcare resources, when they are home they still must spend time with the children. When there are children in the home, employed women aged 25 to 44 extend the time spent each day in unpaid work (e.g., childcare, housework) by over an hour and a half, and men by an hour. Even when a husband helps with childcare, he may take over the enjoyable tasks, like playing with the children, and the mother may not feel any relief (Statistics Canada, 2003e).

Household Responsibilities

Housework is not the hard labour it once was. One needs only to consider the appliances now available. The microwave is a real advance over the wood stove that was once used for cooking. There are dishwashers, automatic washers and dryers, and central vacuum cleaners. For those who do not want to cook, there are restaurants, and takeout and delivery services. Advances in household technology, it is said, have made it possible for women to enter the workforce in ever-increasing numbers. The same could be said for technology like contraception and the baby bottle (Cowan, 1991, 1992). The situation is not that simple, however.

Technology and Housework

Much of the hard physical labour of housework has been reduced through the introduction of utilities like electricity and running water. Chopping wood and pumping water to cook meals and wash dishes are no longer necessary. The "lady of the house" no longer starts her day by "emptying ashes from the messy wood stove, carrying wood, building a fire to cook the meal and heat the house" (Hamilton, 1971, p. 49).

Appliances have made tasks like laundry quicker and easier, especially for women who cannot afford servants. The fact is, however, that technology has made household work different for women rather than having lessened it. Some has been eliminated, but most of this kind of work, like chopping wood, was done by men and boys. Some work is easier, but the quantity has increased. One reason is that standards of cleanliness have increased. To take an everyday example, people usually change their underwear more often now than in the 1900s. Some work that used to be done by servants, like cleaning, is now done by the woman with the help of her appliances. She also has taken over tasks that used to be sent out—laundry, for instance (Bose, Bereano, & Malloy, 1991; Cowan, 1992; MacDonald, 2001; Silva, 1999).

Certain kinds of household work have been brought about or increased by technology. Assembling, cleaning, and maintaining appliances require time. In addition, the noise they make can add to housekeeping stress levels. Some work increases are partly invisible, for example, planning and provisioning for meals and transportation. In order to prepare meals, someone must do the shopping. This means checking on supplies, looking at advertisements to see what is on sale, planning meals, and buying and storing food. In the past, the grocer, butcher, and other tradespeople brought food to the door. Now, of course, someone does the shopping at the supermarket, and often that person must drive there. Someone must also drive children to activities and appointments. Coordinating these activities calls for management skills. In 1850, the stove signified woman's workplace; today it is often the car (Bose et al., 1991; Cowan, 1992; DeVault, 1991; Orrange, Firebaugh, & Heck, 2003).

How much time is spent on household work is related to such factors as income levels, age and quality of the housing, and personal standards for meal preparation and cleanliness. Older houses and apartments usually require more effort in cleaning, as do crowded quarters and those with inadequate storage. Not everyone can afford modern appliances. Those with low income levels must spend more time in planning and in finding bargains to make ends meet without the transportation resources of wealthier families. Buying meals out or hiring help are beyond the reach of those living near the poverty line (Armstrong & Armstrong, 1987; DeVault, 1991).

Women's Work, Men's Work

Someone needs to do household work. In most cases, the "someone" is a woman. As we saw in Chapter 4, the shift from wage-earner husbands to dual-earner families has not meant an equal shift in household responsibilities. Rather, it has led to conflicts over just how household work and childcare should be divided. Use of the time left over after paid work and personal care (such as sleep and dressing) differs between parents and those without children. Single adults use the time for leisure, childless couples split it between household work and leisure, and parents tend to use it for unpaid work like childcare and housework. (See Table 4.3, page 97.) Parents have increased their workday by nearly an hour since 1986 by cutting back on personal care and leisure. Mothers, rather than fathers, reduce paid work in order to care for children. The difference has narrowed, however, as mothers spend more time in paid work and fathers are more involved in childcare, household maintenance, and meal preparation (Fast et al., 2001). In general, women have reduced time spent on housework during the last 10 years, whether they are married, single, or have children at home (Artis & Pavalko, 2003).

Paid Work, Household Work, and Women

For women, since they have such a heavy responsibility for child rearing and household work, paid and unpaid work can be similar. Often the jobs available to women take for granted that they will be caregivers—waitress, shop clerk, nurse, teacher, and daycare worker all fall into this category (Kiecolt, 2003). Women's work in the marketplace is thus mainly geared to ensuring the well-being of others. This kind of responsibility is related to **burnout,** which is the physical and emotional exhaustion caused by prolonged stress from trying to live up to impossible goals (American Psychological Association, 1997). Burnout is discussed in more detail later in this chapter.

LOSING A JOB—THE EFFECTS OF UNEMPLOYMENT

A different kind of job-related stress comes with unemployment. Of course, whether expected or sudden and unpredicted, unemployment has a financial impact on the family, even if it does not result in outright poverty. This is especially true if the family has only one income or if two or more members are unemployed. If a family lives in an area with one major industry that drastically reduces its workforce or even closes, there may be widespread layoffs or business closures (Boss, 2002). Other jobs may be difficult to find, forcing the worker to relocate. A study of fishery workers in Newfoundland describes the effect of widespread unemployment. Fishing has been part of the cultural identity of the province for over 500 years. When people lose a job, they also lose a traditional way of life. In addition, many people, especially young ones, move away from outport communities to find work. Thus they lose both social life and emotional support (Borgen, Amundson, & McVicar, 2002).

Family well-being depends on the degree and type of stress related to job loss. It also depends on the way family members think about unemployment and the strategies they use to deal with both practical and emotional needs (Waters, 2000). We will look at stress and coping in more detail in the next chapter.

Most recently unemployed people go through a series of reactions to job loss. The first stage is usually shock and denial, especially if the layoff is unexpected. Often they feel anger next, followed by worry and anxiety. When they start a job search, they frequently feel a sense of anticipation. Depending on its success, the person may go through a yo-yo of emotions—fear, anger, frustration. If the job search is unsuccessful for a long time, an individual can give up. Families also bear the brunt of the emotional roller coaster because the feelings and behaviour of the unemployed member become unpredictable (CMHA, n.d.).

Work serves many functions beyond the financial. It structures time—sleeping and eating times, weekdays and weekends, work and vacation. With unemployment, this framework suddenly disappears, not only for the unemployed individual but also for the rest of the family. Deprivation of time structures is connected with psychological distress (Waters & Moore, 2001). Work also provides for regular contact outside the family. Often one of the first ways families cut back financially is in the area of recreation, thus reducing social contact still further (Waters & Muller, 2003). Finally, work provides a person with status and identity. For young people, in particular, having a job means being counted as an adult (CMHA, n.d.).

Often unemployment undermines an individual's sense of self-esteem (Waters & Moore, 2001). If a man or his family holds the traditional value that a man provides financially for the family, losing a job means that he has failed as a person (Waters & Moore, 2002). The individual whose personal identity depends on his or her profession (a police officer or a surgeon, for example) may also feel a deep sense of loss. A common response to the need for income is for the spouse of the unemployed individual to find a job or to increase work hours. This strategy further alters the power of family members.

Families may have problems in knowing how to cope with the practical aspects of unemployment. Sometimes their difficulties are psychological and social rather than due to lack of knowledge about money management. They may make costly decisions out of panic (National Endowment for Financial Education, 2002). In families where a manager husband loses his job or has to take a lower paying position, the partners often try to carry on almost as if nothing has changed. Eventually they can no longer hide what has happened. Loss of the family car, for instance, limits the activities in which children can participate. If the family has to sell their home, there is usually some financial relief, but the money is commonly earmarked for debt payment. Often older children help out. They also want some say in family decisions because of their financial contribution. Thus, downward mobility affects not only lifestyle but also parent–child relationships (Newman, 1992).

BURNOUT AND THE FAMILY

Although many families manage to juggle work and family responsibilities, others find the task extremely stressful. One danger is the possibility of burnout. Burnout, as has been mentioned, is a state that occurs when a person, often in a helping profession, experiences prolonged stress without learning how to cope with it. Women more than men experience burnout, especially those in management and professional positions, and those who have heavy caregiving responsibilities (Duxbury & Higgins, 2003).

Burnout produces physical and emotional exhaustion because of the excessive demands placed on the individual. People may impose extremely high standards on themselves; their families, employers, and friends, or society itself may impose high expectations. For example, if an employed woman with young children is a perfectionist at work, and her husband expects her to keep the house spotless and take the children to numerous recreational activities in which they are involved, she may be a candidate for burnout. Her first response probably will be to try harder, but she will find that she still cannot keep up with the many demands on her time and energy. As a result, she is likely to become exhausted and depressed, a condition that makes it difficult for her to respond to the emotional needs of her husband and children or to be productive at work (Freudenberger & North, 1985; Pines, 1996). In police families, for example, both exhaustion and job stress are damaging to family

---

BOX 12.1

SUDDEN STRESS

Ralph Brown was numb, barely able to comprehend that after 10 years he was suddenly indefinitely laid off from his job. Sure, he had heard rumors of impending layoffs, but he had reasoned that certainly 10 years of seniority would prevent him from being affected. Soon he would have to face his family with the word. What would happen to all of their plans—the addition he was going to build on the house, skis for his daughter, camp for his son, the new freezer for his wife? How could he explain that he had no job, no plans for getting one, and no knowledge as to whether or when he would be called back to his old job? What would they think? What would they say? Of course, they knew times were tough. Several friends and neighbors had already been laid off. But that was different. What would happen to him, his family? What if his wife were laid off too?

Source: From "Underemployment . . . Stress and the Family," 1983 adaptation by Patricia Voydanoff, in *Stress and the Family* 1983, vol. 2, p. 90. Charles R. Figley and Hamilton I. McCubbin, eds. (New York: Brunner/Mazel). Reproduced with permission. All rights reserved.

life, but stress has worse effects (Roberts & Levenson, 2001). Among Protestant clergy, the more demanding the pastor regards the congregation, the lower his or her sense of well-being. The effect may, however, be worse if spouse and children are resentful of the unpredictability and time demands of the pastor's work (Lee & Iverson-Gilbert, 2003).

Indirect Effects

Some of the effects of burnout on the individual have an indirect impact on the family. Often emotional exhaustion goes hand in hand with physical exhaustion. As a result the individual becomes susceptible to illness. Stress is a direct factor in some illnesses, such as heart disease and ulcers. The individual may also suffer psychologically. The reduced sense of accomplishment and self-esteem that goes with burnout and the loss of one's zest for life are the main characteristics of depression. In attempts to deal with the emotional effects of burnout, the individual may take to alcohol or drugs. Suicide is an extreme response. These physical and emotional disorders affect the family if the burned-out member cannot take part normally in family life (American Psychological Association, 1997; Morton & Saulis, 1994). We will look, for example, at the effects of chronic illness and alcoholism on family members in Chapter 13. In the extreme, of course, death completely deprives the family of one of its members.

Direct Effects

Burnout also directly affects the family. The overstressed individual's growing dislike of interacting with others may lead to irritation with and anger at family members. When they are emotionally drained, individuals cannot calmly handle everyday hassles at home. They are less able and willing to spend time or become emotionally involved with family members. Instead they want to be left in peace. Because they feel bad, they may demand extra attention and understanding by the family and then feel ashamed of needing such attention. If other family members expect them to interact as they did in the past, the burned-out person may withdraw out of a sense of hurt and neglect. This reaction may lead in turn to injured feelings on the part of a spouse or children. Sometimes the desire for a hassle-free home leads to pressure on other family members to be perfect. The burden may be particularly difficult for children of police and correctional officers, judges, and clergy (Freudenberger & North, 1985; Morton & Saulis, 1994; Pines, 1996; Texas Medical Association, 2001).

Burnout may reduce individuals' ability to cope with stress or to use proven methods of stress reduction. Some are resistant to therapy. This reaction seems to occur especially among doctors and mental-health workers who do not want to admit to the same kinds of problems their patients and clients display. Often they are too tired to make active efforts, such as exercising, to reduce stress, especially if their schedules require them to work 10- or 12-hour shifts (which is the case for some correctional officers and nurses). Many are unable to open up emotionally to their spouses. Some may feel that to do so may be a breach of professional confidentiality. Others may wish to protect their family from the grim realities of the job. Some may also be trying to protect themselves (Maslach, 1982; Texas Medical Association, 2001).

What is the effect of burnout on the family? As we saw in our discussion of family systems, a change in the behaviour of one member affects the rest of a family's members. The increased irritability and lower levels of patience and tolerance of the burnout victim may lead to squabbling and bickering, which escalate into serious marital and family conflict. The resulting separation or divorce may be blamed on problems in the marital relationship rather than on job stress, the real cause. Burnout may also be catching. Some partners may be nurturers; they will respond to the obvious distress on the part of their spouse by increased nurturing. In spite of this, the burned-out person does not feel better. The partner then tries harder. But the burnout victim's apathy and unwillingness to communicate eventually tend to make the spouse feel rejected. If the situation continues for some time, the partner may burn out too (Freudenberger & North, 1985; Pines, 1996).

FLEXIBLE WORK ARRANGEMENTS

One way employers and families have tried to address the problem of competing work and family demands is by setting up alternative work arrangements. There are benefits for both (Hill, Hawkins, Ferris, & Weitzman, 2001). Alternative arrangements take three forms: flexible time, or flextime, which was referred to earlier in this chapter; flexible workplace; and reduced hours of work. In addition, some large firms provide daycare and elder care services. Flextime and flexible workplace arrangements are more common in small to medium-sized businesses (Comfort, Johnson, & Wallace, 2003; Pohlman & Dulipovici, 2004).

Flexible Time Arrangements

A number of employers have established alternatives to the traditional eight-hour day. One arrangement is **flextime.** In one variation, all employees are expected to be at work during a core period in the middle of the day but may decide for themselves when they will arrive or leave, provided they work the usual number of hours (Comfort et al., 2003). Theoretically this allows parents to better meet family needs as well as workplace responsibilities. Indeed, women with flexible work schedules feel less stressed by family responsibilities than those with more rigid schedules and can work longer hours (Hill et al., 2001).

Some people prefer longer periods off work. Their needs may be met by a **compressed workweek,** in which they work 10- or 12-hour shifts for three or four days, and then have several days off. The long hours can, however, contribute to exhaustion and burnout. In addition, the hours may make it more difficult to look after family needs on working days (Gottlieb, 1999; Saskatchewan Women's Secretariat, n.d.).

Flexible Workplace

Computers and communications technology make it possible for people to work outside the office, an option sometimes referred to as the virtual office or **telecommuting.** This type of arrangement appeals to people who commute long distances every day, who do not want their children to spend 10 hours or more a day in childcare, and who want flexibility to schedule their daily work. This is not a magic solution, however, for work–family problems. Some do find that the flexibility is helpful because having the parent at home solves daycare problems. However, the increase in information technology such as wireless computing and instant messaging makes juggling work and home responsibilities more difficult (Fraenkel, 2003).

Reduced Hours of Work

Part-time work allows individuals to fulfill care responsibilities for children or older relatives. It may, however, be feasible only for those whose partners earn a good income (Hill, Märtinson, & Ferris, 2003). Labour unions are also concerned with the trend to converting full-time jobs into part-time jobs without benefits. Cutting back on hours can hurt a career. Part-time workers tend to be paid less and to be passed over for promotion (Comfort et al., 2003). Protected part-time work occurs when salaries and benefits are prorated according to the hours worked. The arrangement can be either permanent or temporary. Another plan is **job sharing,** in which two employees share one full-time job, with prorated salaries and benefits. Reduced work hours do not appeal to everyone since few can afford to live on less than a full-time salary (Ontario Women's Directorate, 1991).

Who Uses Family-Friendly Work Arrangements?

Full-time workers in two-parent families with children under 16 have most access to family-friendly benefits. Flextime and telecommuting are, however, used more by men than women. Managers and those in professions are more likely to be offered flexible work arrangements. Women, more than men, are likely to work part time to allow for family responsibilities. Some jobs don't lend themselves to telecommuting, such as manufacturing, sales, or nursing (Comfort et al., 2003). An American study suggested that those who most need family-friendly benefits are the least likely to get them (Holcomb, 2003).

THE FAMILY, WORK, AND SOCIETY

Some of the tensions between family and the workplace can be better understood using Garbarino's ecological model of interacting systems (discussed in Chapter 1). In the macrosystem, we find conflicting values. For example, women are felt by some to find their greatest fulfillment as wives and mothers. Others consider that women can best achieve their potential in the work world through careers. Thus no matter what choice women make, someone will tell them that they are wrong. Another source of tension in families is the unequal value placed on men's and women's work. This can be seen, for instance, in levels of pay, and in the concern over the effect of working mothers, but not working fathers, on their children's development.

In the exosystem, institutions such as the workplace and daycare centres also seem to present conflicting values. On the one hand, women are encouraged to find employment. On the other, many employers are unfriendly toward families. Daycare centres are planned as a service for working parents, yet it is difficult to find one with hours that will accommodate shift work.

Some of these conflicts are played out in the mesosystem. Teachers, for example, may feel that children's failure to do homework arises from inadequate supervision when two parents are employed out of the home. Parents, for their part, may feel that the expectations of the school are unrealistic. All of these pressures work together to produce stress in the family microsystem over such matters as childcare and household chores. In turn, the marital and parental subsystems are also affected.

Many individuals feel that the only real answer to some of these problems is a shift in values in our society. There are signs, small and slow though they are in coming, that norms are changing to accommodate the needs of two-earner families.

SUMMARY

FAMILY CARE. Family care is closely tied to social attitudes toward women's work. When mothers' paid employment has been seen as important for society, daycare for children has been provided. Current attitudes reflect concern over government spending and a belief that families are responsible for their own members. Some parents have problems finding affordable daycare that matches their work hours, especially if they work shifts. Elder care has not received as much notice as daycare, yet families are increasingly called on to provide services for older relatives.

WORK AND FAMILY STRESS. An important way in which work and families are interrelated is through conflicting demands. One of the major stresses for families comes from expectations of society and of employers. Women get conflicting messages about motherhood and work. Not all workplaces are responsive to family needs. Often family and employment demands need to be juggled. Family responsibilities may be handled on work time. Yet family or personal well-being, especially leisure time, is frequently sacrificed to the job. Parents must care for children outside daycare hours and also look after the household. Modern appliances have changed the nature of housework rather than the amount that is done. These duties still consume a great deal of time, with women usually assuming the major responsibility for them. Many women experience stress because their jobs also require caregiving activities.

UNEMPLOYMENT. Unemployment affects families, not only through loss of income, but also through changes in time management and family roles, which may affect the unemployed individual's self-esteem.

BURNOUT. Burnout is the result of extreme stress, often job-related. It results in physical and emotional exhaustion, poor job performance, and a reduced ability to deal with the demands of others. As a result, it has serious effects on the family. Indirectly, an individual's stress-related illness or substance abuse creates additional stress for the family. Directly, individuals may withdraw from family life or be much less tolerant of family-related stressors.

FLEXIBLE WORK ARRANGEMENTS. One solution for the conflict between family and employment is adapting work hours so that they meet family needs. These alternative arrangements include flexible work hours, flexible workplace, and reduced hours of work. While all permit individuals more leeway in handling family needs, all have drawbacks. In addition, many workers do not have access to family-friendly arrangements. Full-time work, regardless of hours or workplace, still produces high levels of stress among parents of young children. Income levels and promotion opportunities may be reduced with flexible work arrangements.

FAMILY, WORK, AND SOCIETY. Some of the tensions between family and the workplace can be understood using the ecological model, in which social values, institutional attitudes, and family needs all interact.

burnout: a state of physical and emotional exhaustion resulting from prolonged stress from trying to live up to impossible goals (p. 283)

compressed workweek: a full-time job in which a workweek is concentrated in three or four days, allowing for several days in succession off work (p. 287)

flextime: an arrangement in which full-time employees can determine when they arrive at and when they leave work (p. 287)

job sharing: the sharing of one full-time job by two employees (p. 288)

spillover: a situation where family and work role or time demands interfere with each other (p. 280)

telecommuting: working outside the office (often at home) using a computer and telecommunications technology (p. 287)

CLASS ASSIGNMENTS

Complete one or both of the following assignments, as directed by your instructor:

1. Explore in more detail different options, such as flextime and job sharing, that might help individuals manage both family and work responsibilities. What are the advantages and disadvantages of each?

2. What are the various daycare options available in your community? Who offers them? How are they supervised? What advantages does each of the various choices offer children? What are the potential problems?

PERSONAL ASSIGNMENTS

The following assignments are designed to help you reflect on your own experience:

1. Students often experience high levels of stress, especially if they have family responsibilities. What do you consider the main sources of stress? Describe the effect they have on families. What suggestions can you offer for reducing such stress?

2. Select an occupation in which you are interested. What do you feel may be the main sources of stress in this occupation? How might these particular stressors affect a family?

Part Six

SOCIAL PROBLEMS IN THE FAMILY

© Zigy Kaluzny/Getty Images

Chapter 13

The Family Beleaguered— When Problems Come

When the police charged my son and his friend with break, enter, and theft, we were angry but didn't realize how difficult the whole experience would be for us. Since he was a young offender, at least one parent was expected in court. And it wasn't just the one time. There was a preliminary interview with the lawyer. There were repeated returns to court over the next several months because there was a second charge pending and it would be to his benefit to have both tried together.

I kept having to ask for time off work. It got pretty awkward after a while to explain where I needed to be. My husband could just as easily have taken time off, but he argued that he would lose more pay than I would, so I was the one who had to go to court.

It was a real worry when our son broke the conditions of his probation, such as the curfew that was imposed. When it appeared that he was dealing drugs out of the house, we asked him to move out. After all, we were worried about the effect on our other children if we overlooked his behaviour. He quit school. That was a further violation of his probation. I can't understand how he got away with it, but his probation officer never called him to task.

In all those months, we didn't talk about it with our friends or relatives. It was embarrassing to say the least. We also felt some guilt. After all, parents are supposed to control their children, aren't they?

Families have problems. Since many problems are related to deviance or being different in some way, they have a social dimension to them. We have already considered many aspects of minority and majority relationships (Chapter 2). In this chapter, we will look at when being different becomes a problem.

What exactly is a social problem? A useful definition is that "a social problem exists when a significant number of people believe that a certain condition is in fact a problem" (Coleman & Kerbo, 2002, p. 4). Yet this definition raises a number of issues. When there are competing views, who decides what is a problem? For whom is it a problem? How do social problems affect families? We will look at each of these issues in turn.

WHO DECIDES WHEN A PROBLEM IS A PROBLEM?

The simplest answer is that the public decides what is a problem. Public opinion does not always remain the same, however. For example, harsh physical discipline of children has at times been encouraged so that they may grow into law-abiding adults. Sayings like "Spare the rod and spoil the child" (which many people wrongly assume is a quotation from the Bible) are used to justify such practices (Greven, 1990). In contrast, a major concern nowadays is the damage that can be done to children as a result of physical violence.

Similarly, over the years, homosexuality has been seen as a sin, a crime, a mental illness, or simply a variation on family living. As a sin, it was linked with other forms of sex, such as masturbation and **bestiality,** in which reproduction was not a goal. Originally, homosexuality was dealt with by the church rather than criminal courts. In 1535, England passed a law making male sodomy (anal intercourse between men) a crime. There were later laws established against gross indecency (i.e., all sexual acts between men not covered under sodomy). Convicted homosexuals were often referred to psychiatrists, who undertook research to learn more about what they considered a psychological and sexual disorder. Early researchers also suspected that "self-abuse," in other words, masturbation, could produce homosexuality. This is probably the source of the myth, popular in the early 1900s, that masturbation leads to insanity (Kinsman, 1987). Even though many gay and lesbian individuals argue that homosexual couples are a form of family, many people still feel that such relationships are abnormal (Laird, 2003).

Obviously, a problem is something that is undesirable in some way. Behaviour that would tend to cause physical harm to oneself and, more important, others is almost always seen as a problem. Yet some individuals are not felt to deserve as much protection as others.

For example, in the past, Aboriginal peoples have been treated as an exploitable resource to aid the economic development of a dominant society. Their traditional livelihood has been destroyed and their ancestral lands taken over so that newcomers to the land might prosper. The British, for example, believed that whites were destined to rule large parts of the world. During early contact with Aboriginal peoples, charters gave Aboriginal lands to traders and settlers and spoke of waging war on the barbarians. One of the results was the destruction of the Beothuk Indians. Through the residential schools, the newcomers taught Aboriginal children the values of white society, in the process telling them that **indigenous** peoples were savage and incompetent. By destroying Aboriginal culture and values in this manner, the newcomers attempted to gain control of both people and resources (Ray, 1996; Shewell, 2004).

The public is made up of many groups that often have competing interests. One or more groups in society usually have been quite successful compared with others. They are often referred to as having **vested interests,** since they have a stake in keeping society as it is. These powerful groups tend to have the greatest influence in defining problems. Since they tend to be among the wealthiest and thus pay more taxes, they may be concerned with the cost of problems to society (Bogenschneider, 2002; Coleman & Kerbo, 2002). For example, child abuse can be very expensive. If the abuse is left undetected and untreated, victims can become a continuing financial burden on society. They may have to receive repeated medical treatment. If they are severely damaged, they may need lifelong care. Adults who were abused as children may require psychiatric services or welfare assistance because of emotional damage that prevents them from becoming productive members of society. They may also emotionally or physically damage their own children, thus extending the cost to another generation (Barnett, Miller-Perrin, & Perrin, 2005).

Gatekeepers control access to important people or services. In the case of social problems, they are individuals recognized as having special expertise in identifying problems and often given the authority to label individuals or groups as being the source of a problem. Some of the gatekeepers in Canadian society are doctors, police officers, judges and juries, and social workers. For example, doctors decide whether an individual's mental condition is dangerous enough to require confinement. They are the ones who decide whether a person is sick or injured enough to be admitted to hospital. The actions and decisions of police officers, judges, and juries determine whether to label an individual as a criminal. Child welfare workers are entrusted with deciding whether children are in sufficient danger to remove them from their homes. All of these people work within laws, regulations, and guidelines that they are held responsible for following, even if they personally disagree with them. In this way they support the power of the dominant group in society.

Not everyone in society defines problems in the same way. Two groups may see a particular situation as containing a problem, but they may differ drastically as to just what the problem is (Coleman & Kerbo, 2002). In the case of homosexuality, for instance, many in society (such as conservative religious groups) see homosexual behaviour as bad or sick. On the other hand, gay-rights activists see the problem not in their own behaviour, but in the intolerance of society. Groups like those advocating gay rights, rights for the physically or mentally challenged, or rights of fathers to have custody of their children are referred to as special-interest groups. Often they want regulations or laws supported by vested interests to be changed. When the special interests of two groups are similar, they may work together to force change. For example, although they disagree on some issues like trapping fur-bearing animals, conservationists and Aboriginal peoples have cooperated in trying to prevent lumber companies from cutting old-growth forests in Northern Ontario.

THE IMPACT ON FAMILIES

When society or the family itself decides a situation is a problem, for example, unemployment, individuals and families as a whole are affected. The social definition of a problem can create internal problems for the family; for example, when the father in a family is charged by the police, this may affect the relationship of spouses and of parents and children.

Dealing with a New Problem

Families differ in the way they respond to a stressful situation. We have all met those who seem to handle far more than their share of misfortune and still keep a positive outlook on life. Other families seem to fall apart at the slightest difficulty. Reuben Hill (1958) proposed what he called the *ABCX model* of response. In this model, "A" refers to the stressor event, the arrest of the family breadwinner, for example. See Figure 13.1, next page.

The impact of the stressor is affected by the family's resources—the "B" factor (Patterson, 2002). Do they have money for day-to-day living? Can they afford a lawyer? Do they know how to go about finding one with some expertise in the particular sort of crime? They probably want someone who has specialized knowledge of criminal law, as opposed to business or family law. Do they know anyone they can ask for advice? Usually a family will try to solve problems in ways that have worked before. Some families may have a good deal of experience in dealing with the justice system; thus they have a level of practical know-how other families do not

The response of the family is also affected by the way the family members view the event—the "C" factor (Boss, 2002; Patterson, 2002; Walsh, 2003b). For instance, does the wife see herself as a social outcast if her husband is charged with a crime? Or does she see him as the victim who needs to be defended from a racist society? Or does she feel that he no longer deserves to be a family member? The viewpoint of the children in the family may differ from the parents' viewpoint. They may consider a father's exploits an interesting

Figure 13.1

A SCHEMA FOR DEPICTING THE INTERPLAY OF STRESSOR EVENT, CONTRIBUTING HARDSHIPS, AND FAMILY RESOURCES IN PRODUCING A FAMILY CRISIS

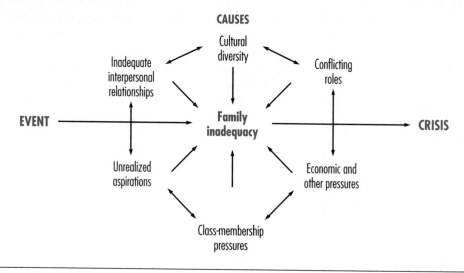

Source: Hill, 1958, p. 145. Reprinted with permission from Families in Society (www.familiesinsociety.org), published by the Alliance for Children and Families.

adventure, and plan to avoid the same pitfalls with the law. On the other hand, they may be ashamed and try to hide or even deny a connection with him.

These three factors interact to produce the "X" factor—the **crisis.** When a family is in crisis, it means that there is an imbalance in the demands placed on the family and their ability to meet the demands. Once the familiar problem-solving methods fail, the family boundaries are loosened enough to allow for new information, rules and roles become confused, and tension between family members increases. At times like this, the family is open to try new ways of finding solutions. These solutions may be **functional** or **dysfunctional;** that is, they may increase the family's ability to solve new problems (functional) or they may temporarily reduce family tensions but create new problems in the future (dysfunctional) (Boss, 2002; Patterson, 2002). Functional solutions might involve a stay-at-home spouse finding a job, learning of sources of practical help such as counselling services, or developing skills in dealing with the justice system. Dysfunctional solutions may involve blaming the husband and father for all the family's difficulties, or centring all interactions on his needs. Thus the couple might not talk about their own conflicts, but only about his court appearances and defence.

Long-Term Problems

Usually a family does not experience a problem as a single, "bolt from the blue" stressor. Family crises evolve over time, and pressures from various sources accumulate. This fact led to an expansion of the ABCX model into the double ABCX model, as shown in Figure 13.2 (McCubbin & Patterson, 1983).

According to this expanded model, five general types of stressors can pile up. First, there is the initial stressor and its hardships: for example, a breadwinner in the family is charged and convicted. Second, there are normative stresses in the family, that is, changes that most families go through and that can be expected. The growing independence of an adolescent or young adult is one of these "ordinary" stressors. If the mother has relied on one of her children for emotional support after her husband was charged, she may become very anxious if that child wants to move away from home. Timing may be important. If stressful events occur at the same time as other important life events, then stress may be greater. Third, families may also experience strains that began before the particular stressor. Perhaps the husband had been involved with earlier criminal activities for which he had not been charged. Perhaps the wife is alcoholic, or there has been a pattern of continuing family violence. Fourth, there are the efforts of the family to cope. If they deny the problem, for example, they may cut themselves off from outside help or may be unable to discuss the situation in order to come up with a concrete plan for dealing with it. Fifth, there may be **ambiguity;** that is, the situation within the family or within society may not be clear. Some convicts' wives, for example, have been propositioned by "friends" of their husband who think they must be lonely and anxious for a new sexual relationship. The stigma toward criminals within society may also affect the family by virtue of their association with a convict. Ambiguity can also be

Figure 13.2

THE DOUBLE ABCX MODEL

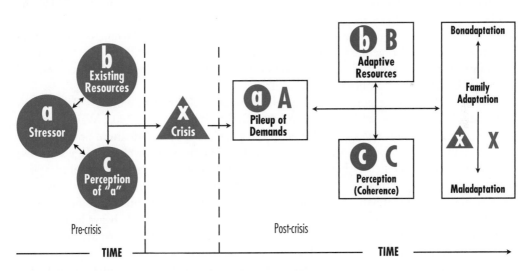

Source: From Yoav Lavee, Hamilton McCubbin, and Joan M. Patterson. (1985). "The double ABCX model of family stress and adaptation: An empirical test by analysis of structural equations with latent variables." *Journal of Marriage and the Family, 47,* p. 812.

the result of not knowing how long the problem, for instance, the chronic illness of a family member, will last. All these stressors work together to cause *pileup*—the "aA" factor (Boss, 2002; McCubbin & Patterson, 1983; Walsh, 2003b).

The resources that help the family adapt to the situation make up the "bB" factor. These can include personal resources of individual family members, such as education, health, money, and, most important, self-esteem and a sense of mastery. Having an optimistic outlook on life is also a resource. As well, the "bB" factor includes the resources of the family system, such as flexible role relationships and the ability to share power. If the family breadwinner, for example, is sent to a penitentiary, is the partner able to find a job to support the family? Finally, it includes social support, which can provide practical help and emotional support, and can foster a sense of self-esteem in family members. As time goes on, the resources available may change as some are used up and new sources of help are found (Moore, Chalk, Scarpa, & Vandivere, 2002; Patterson, 2002; Walsh, 2003b).

The meaning a family finds in an event is important to how members cope with it. First, they may see it as having nothing to do with them, as favourable, or as threatening. Second, they evaluate what might and can be done and how likely any strategy is to work. Third, hey may change their perception of the event as a result of new information they gain. Families may also have **snag points,** or areas of difficulty, that interfere with constructive efforts to cope with problems (Patterson, 2002; Walsh, 2003b). Some families may have rules about open communication; for example, talking about the convict father may be taboo, or lies may be told about why he is no longer present. Another snag point may be related to the level of intimacy in the family. In some families, members are so distant that no one feels involved in anyone else's life. Thus family members might not stand behind one another. In other families, members are so enmeshed in one another's lives that it is unclear who really has the problem. In such families, everyone feels as disgraced as if they themselves had been convicted. When families are very rigid about roles, for example, men's and women's duties, there may be a crisis when someone is imprisoned or absent and cannot fulfill the role. Sometimes a family's unrealistic goals and values fail to make allowances for changed circumstances, and therefore interfere with problem-solving ability.

Some of these snag points are also related to the "cC" factor, which is the family's appraisal of the situation and the meaning they find in it (Patterson, 2002; Walsh, 2003b). For example, goals and values are reflected in the assessment of the situation. Some families feel it is a disaster if they cannot meet a cherished goal because of the chronic illness or disability of a family member. Others see it as a challenge, or give the crisis a special meaning. Parents of children with severe mental challenges, for instance, sometimes say they have learned the value of human life and love through knowing their child. One father commented, "No matter what else goes wrong with my life, I know he will always be the same. He creates a calm centre." However, a healthy attitude does not deny the reality of the situation or minimize what needs to be done to meet the situation.

All these factors combine to create the "xX" factor, the family's adaptation to the problem (Patterson, 2002). Family efforts need to be coordinated so that members can create a new lifestyle to suit the changed circumstances. Strategies may include activities that are meant to change the situation. Some coping strategies control the meaning of the problem, for instance, by saying it is the will of God, or that a child was born with a disability because he or she has a special mission on earth. Other strategies, like finding relief help or learning relaxation techniques, help manage stress.

Recently, researchers have focused on family **resilience,** the ability to do well in the face of adversity. For example, some families fall to pieces when they give birth to a disabled child. After the initial shock, others go on to manage the difficulties well. Resilience does not, however, mean making the best of a bad situation. Rather it involves change, sometimes drastic, to produce a stronger and healthier adaptation (Boss, 2002; Patterson, 2002; Walsh, 2003b).

TWO SPECIFIC FAMILY PROBLEMS

The double ABCX model describes the way families respond to many crises and ongoing problems. As we saw in Chapter 8, for instance, the death of a husband or wife is an event that requires fundamental changes in lifestyle and in relationships. The eventual adaptation of survivors depends not only on their own resources but also on the social support they receive and the interpretation they place on their loss. As we shall see in the next chapter, the same factors hold true for family violence. In this section, we shall look at two situations that both society and families define as being problems.

Chronic Illness and Disability

Many people experience chronic illness or a disability. In 2001, 12.4 percent of Canadians had some sort of disability. The numbers ranged from about 3 percent of children under 15 to over half of adults over 74 years of age. Developmental delays were most common among young children and mobility and memory problems among older adults (Cossette & Duclos, 2002).

Chronic illness or disability usually starts in one of two ways—suddenly, or over a period of time. Although in many ways the effect on the family is similar in the two situations, there are also differences.

The Initial Shock

Sudden awareness of the problem may come about as the result of an accident or the birth of a child with obvious problems. One parent described the birth of such a child as learning that she had arrived in Holland when she had planned a wonderful trip to Italy (Kingsley, 2002). For some people, the way they are given the bad news is a problem, especially when there are long waits for information. Most prefer to be told sooner rather than later and to be given all the facts fully and clearly, thus reducing the stress of ambiguity (Boss, 2002). After the initial shock, the first concern may be with the individual's survival. Soon energy increases, which is indicated by visiting the family member in the hospital perhaps, taking him or her for tests, providing the new care that is necessary, or taking over the responsibilities the ill member used to look after. The "A" factor includes the acute illness, the diagnosis, the first attempts at medical treatment, and the energy rush used to meet the new demands on the family (Walsh, 1998).

Later, a period of assessment will determine just what level of functioning is likely. Sometimes this cannot occur until there has been time for healing and for extensive testing. During this process, the problem becomes a chronic one, extending over a period of time.

During the initial phase of illness, the needs of other family members are often ignored. Meals may become "catch as catch can." Laundry may pile up. Children may receive very little attention and supervision. If the illness lasts more than a few days, one or more family members may get burned out. They no longer have the energy to respond to the physical and emotional demands placed on them. As a result, they become irritable and tend to withdraw from others. They may in turn become ill themselves. The family system itself starts to break down as family resources can no longer meet the demands of illness. The family goes into crisis.

In other cases, the onset of illness is gradual. Little by little the family, or others, come to believe that something is wrong. This may take place when an older member is showing memory loss and changes in personality, a baby is not meeting developmental stages, or an individual has a series of illnesses. At the point when the disorder is diagnosed as chronic—for example, Alzheimer's disease, a chromosomal disorder leading to physical and mental delays in development, or AIDS—the family faces a crisis similar to the acute onset of an illness. In addition, these families have a history of living with the long months or years of worry and fear that have created other stressors as members have tried to cope.

In both cases, the meaning the family attaches to the illness is important; this is affected by a variety of factors. What is their script for what family relationships should be like? Do they have experience with a similar disorder? If so, do they feel their experience has given them the power to cope or do they dread living through the problem once again? How do they see the prognosis? Do they feel that an individual can live a rewarding life if he or she is confined to a wheelchair or is facing death? Or do they dread the process? The reason they give for the illness or disability is also important. Do they blame themselves because they were not more careful, or do they see an accident or a genetic disorder as occurring in spite of all their precautions? Do they blame the sufferer? This may be important with an illness like AIDS that is often stigmatized by society and can lead to fear and even hysteria (Coleman & Kerbo, 2002; Power & Dell Orto, 2004).

The Long Haul

As an illness becomes chronic, stressors on the family pile up (Patterson, 2002). These can come from many sources. The nature of the illness is a continuing stress, especially if there are unpredictable episodes or it is progressive (Rolland, 2003). If the prognosis is uncertain, then ambiguity produces further stress (Boss, 2002). Within the family itself, members may approach burnout and no longer be able to handle the everyday hassles of family living. Relationships with other family members can become strained. Chronic illness or disability can place enormous stress on the marital subsystem (Rolland, 2003). There may also be resentment over the demands of the ill member and often a feeling of guilt about not being more patient. Sometimes the needs of well family members are felt to be a burden. Overall, tension and conflict may increase.

Family activities and goals may need to be changed. These changes may, in part, be due to financial limitations, as a direct result of either the needs of the patient or the impact the illness has on other members' employment options. If an illness is unpredictable, like asthma for example, it may be difficult to count on family rituals and customs since they may be interrupted by the medical needs of the individual. When a parent is emotionally disturbed, the family environment may also be unpredictable. Sometimes family members will fill their roles well. At other times, the family will be thrown into chaos when the parent's disorder flares up. In a progressive illness, such as multiple sclerosis, the family has the strain of repeatedly adjusting to new care and role demands. Shifting from one role to another or adding roles is stressful. Planning for the future may also be difficult if the prognosis is uncertain. Will the patient recover? If not, when is death likely to occur—tomorrow or five years from now (Rolland, 2003)? Social activities may also change. If the behaviour of the person with a chronic illness or disability is unpredictable, or if the illness demands a great deal of time from the caregiver or if it carries stigma, such as disfigurement or AIDS, the family may become socially isolated just when they need other people most.

Added to all these stressors are **normative family changes**—the changes expected as part of the family life cycle. These include puberty, the growing independence of young people, finding a mate, having children, and retiring. Chronic illness can have a different effect, depending on the stage of the family life cycle of either the parents or children (Rolland, 2003). For instance, a young person's chronic illness or disability may influence his or her decision (or even opportunity) to marry and, if the person does marry, whether to have children. Illness can also interfere with the growing independence of a young person. If the adolescent or young adult is ill, he or she may remain dependent on the family of origin long past the time most young people are living on their own. If a parent is ill, the young person may feel duty bound to stay home and help with care. In later life, illness of a partner can disrupt plans made for activities such as travel after retirement. Middle-aged children, often referred to as the sandwich generation, can also feel trapped by their parents' need for care.

As already mentioned, the resources an individual can call on affect the ability to cope. Some resources, however, create their own demands and difficulties. Dealing with the medical system, especially if it is not very sensitive to the needs of family members, can be an added source of stress (Neufeld, Harrison, Stewart, & Hughes, 2003). Supplementary health insurance can help relieve the financial burden of chronic illness. At times, however, it is unclear whether the plan will cover all or even some of the costs, thus increasing anxiety among family members (Jacobs, 1991). Similarly, friends and relatives can play a key role in protecting children from the periodic neglect of a mentally ill parent. If, however, they take responsibility for areas the parent can still manage, they may undermine the individual's position in the family and push the person to the sidelines (Walsh, 1998). On the other side, the care receiver can also provide support for the caregiver by encouraging a discussion of frustrations and by being appreciative (Wright & Aquilino, 1998).

Over time, families may change their perception of the illness. For example, one family with a child with severe physical challenges started out by blaming one another for his

DOING PRETTY WELL

She's not the woman I remember. My competent, dependable mother is gone. She can't manage her own money, even if she could see to sign a cheque. She's surprised every time she's wished "Happy Birthday," and asks her age over and over, then queries, "How did I get so old?"

My father looked after her as long as he could. He lived with her endless repetitions and her need to have everything explained again and again. And he did it with a patience beyond mine. He tried to allow her the dignity of shaping her routines, even past her ability to decide if she needed a bath or change of clothes. Finally he could cope no longer, and they entered a home together.

My mother still has memories. Some are false. For a time she imagined my father died from a wild animal attack, though he slipped away in his sleep. She does recall childhood places and events. She remembers her children's names, and recognizes the ones who visit most often. But she doesn't remember the stroke that consigned her to a wheelchair some months ago.

And yet her old humour and spunk still sparkle through her dimness. She informed one grandson, "My, how you've grown—in both directions!" And recently she announced, "I'm doing pretty well for a 94-year-old."

problems. Eventually, they came to see him as a force that pulled them together because he was so dependent on them for survival. Some couples who have had a mentally or physically challenged child born to them, or who nurse a chronically ill child, have adopted other children with similar problems because they feel that the skills they have gained in dealing with their birth child should not be wasted but used for the welfare of others (Sandness, 1983).

As a result of the interplay of these factors, family coping patterns emerge. Dysfunctional coping can include overprotection of the ill or disabled member, denial of the reality of the illness, and anger and resentment toward the ill person or toward other family members. In general, the family feels out of control and victimized. Functional coping, on the other hand, helps the family feel in control of the situation. They try to understand the medical situation through communicating with others in a similar situation and with medical personnel. They work at keeping the family together and emphasize cooperation. They do not cut themselves off from social support. As a result of their sense of control, their self-esteem is high and they remain psychologically stable. Counselling and support can help families cope. Often this is given only at the time of diagnosis but not when it is needed later on. In the case of a disabled child, parents may not have the energy to deal with psychological issues at first. In addition, if the problem is diagnosed when the child is an infant, the "differences" the parents have to deal with may not be obvious until the child enters school or even later. It is at this point that parents may benefit most from counselling (Patterson, 2002; Power & Dell Orto, 2004; Rolland, 2003; Smith & Soliday, 2001).

The Alcoholic Family System

Like other problems, alcohol and other substance abuse is defined by society; the acceptance of alcohol use varies among cultures. There are also variations in the drug of choice (Hudak, Krestan, & Bepko, 1999). About 17 percent of Canadian drinkers, men more than women, are considered high-risk drinkers (Canadian Centre on Substance Abuse, 2004).

Why do we refer to an alcoholic family system rather than to a family with an alcoholic member? One of the difficulties with alcohol abuse, as we shall see, is the fact that so much of family life focuses on the alcohol abuse that it becomes the main organizer; that is, the entire family system is involved with alcoholism (Brown & Lewis, 1999).

Alcoholism has a number of factors similar to chronic illness. Given his or her physical condition, and in the case of alcoholism his or her behaviour, one family member cannot fill the usual family roles and responsibilities. Others have to adjust their behaviour to account for this. Alcohol abuse itself adds stresses in terms of changed behaviour, physical state such alcohol-related illness, income difficulties if drinking interferes with work, and social isolation (Stewart & Wall, 2004). As with chronic disease, further stresses are also created by developmental demands on the family and attitudes of society. (See Figure 13.3, next page.)

But alcoholism and chronic illness also differ in important ways. Unlike many chronic illnesses, alcoholism does not start suddenly; rather it develops over a period of time. Society considers it **discreditable,** and considers the alcoholic as too morally weak to stop drinking (Hudak et al., 1999). The family, along with the alcoholic member, often goes to great lengths to avoid acknowledging the problem. As a result, family members often assume stereotyped roles in alcoholic families. One or more may be **enablers.** Enablers are persons whose behaviour allows another to act in a certain way; in the case of alcoholic families, the behaviour allows the individual to continue drinking without suffering the most extreme consequences (Copans, 1989; Roberts & McCrady, 2003). This can include a wife phoning her husband's workplace to say that he is sick, or young children looking after their drunk or hung-over mother. The concept of a "drinking partnership" is useful. Both members work out norms about alcohol use for their household. Each shapes the other's beliefs and behaviours about drinking (Roberts, 2005). The partner or child of an alcoholic may be codependent. **Codependence** (the tendency for nonalcoholic members of an alcoholic family to display a variety of psychological symptoms as a result of the alcoholic member's behaviour) is one effect of the drinking partnership. Originally, it was viewed only as it affected the alcoholic. Now, however, it is recognized as a psychological problem in its own right. Symptoms of codependence are quite characteristic. The individual has little sense of self-worth and needs continuing approval from others. This need has several results. First, the **codependent** person does not have clear personal boundaries and takes on the drinker's problems. Eventually the entire life of the family begins to revolve around the alcoholic member. Second, the codependent finds meaning and worth in caretaking. By becoming indispensable, he or she also makes it easier for the alcoholic to become and remain dependent. Third, the codependent believes that he or she is responsible for whatever happens to the significant other. Thus, as the situation becomes more chaotic, the individual tries to exert more

Figure 13.3

DOUBLE ABCX MODEL APPLIED TO ALCOHOL ABUSE

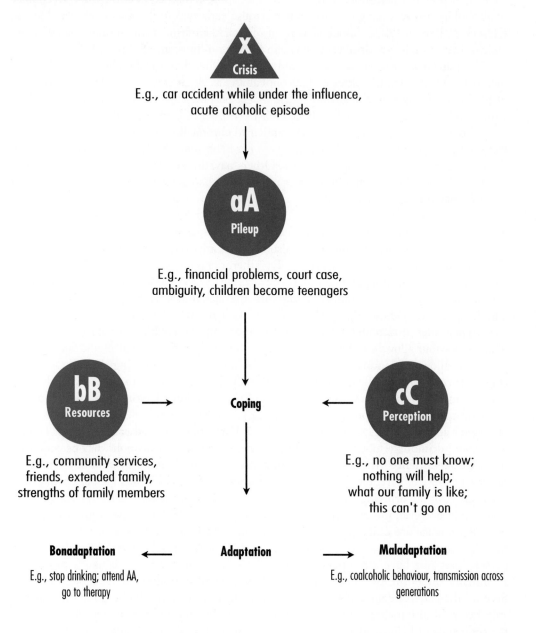

X
Crisis

E.g., car accident while under the influence,
acute alcoholic episode

aA
Pileup

E.g., financial problems, court case,
ambiguity, children become teenagers

bB
Resources

Coping

cC
Perception

E.g., community services,
friends, extended family,
strengths of family members

E.g., no one must know;
nothing will help;
what our family is like;
this can't go on

Bonadaptation   **Adaptation**   **Maladaptation**

E.g., stop drinking; attend AA,
go to therapy

E.g., coalcoholic behaviour, transmission across
generations

and more control, perhaps by watching every move of the drinking partner. Fifth, as pressures increase, the codependent partner is at risk of developing stress-related illnesses, such as ulcers and high blood pressure. All these characteristics are the result of trying to maintain the image of normal family life, not signs of a basic personality disorder (Brown & Lewis, 1999; Hudak et al., 1999; Loukas, Piejak, Bingham, Fitzgerald, & Zucker, 2001; Schaeff, 1986).

Alcoholism can have a profound effect on the marriage relationship, in addition to the development of codependence. Irritability during drinking bouts may alternate with excessive kindness during sober spells. The kindness, however, feels unnatural, as if the alcoholic is playacting and exaggerating the role of the good spouse and parent. The husband or wife of the drinker may, however, use sober periods to express anger that has been festering by being cold, sarcastic, and complaining. Sometimes the anger escalates into violence. Conversation can disappear when husbands refuse to talk during periods of heavy drinking. Meals may be missed and joint recreation spoiled by embarrassing behaviour. Sex may disappear completely. Sometimes the nondrinking partner will refuse sexual relations to punish the alcoholic (Hudak et al., 1999; Wiseman, 1991).

Members of alcoholic families learn a number of lessons about family life (Copans, 1989). In such families, individuals spend their time worrying about whether the alcoholic member will come home drunk, covering up drinking behaviour, or not inviting friends home because a parent may be drunk. The first lesson, then, is that alcohol is the centre of family life (Schaeff, 1986; Wiseman, 1991). A second lesson is that alcohol can make things better. In some cases, the alcoholic member is more loving and warm while drinking than while sober. Also the drinker will demonstrate that alcohol will make unpleasant withdrawal symptoms go away. A third lesson is that alcohol abuse is a family secret to be denied and covered up.

This pattern of coping has its costs. It may lead to a variety of symptoms in the nonalcoholic member, including anxiety, depression, shame, and anger. Children of alcoholic parents, especially if the parents have antisocial behaviour, are more likely to display behaviour problems themselves. In part, this occurs because the nonalcoholic parent may use coercive or other ineffective parenting methods (Loukas et al., 2001). On the positive side, some adult children of alcoholics are drawn to the helping professions where they can care for others in a socially approved manner. Yet they may have difficulty with particular kinds of clients or patients as a result of their early experiences. For example, one psychiatrist, who as a teenager was sent to find his alcoholic father and bring him home, found that he was impatient and ineffective when he tried to treat an alcoholic patient.

Often the alcoholism is not admitted until a decisive event makes denial impossible, such as criminal charges for drunk driving (Brown & Lewis, 1999). This event may differ for the alcoholic and family members. For example, the alcoholic may not experience drinking as a problem until his wife leaves him. Obviously an earlier event or series of events created a crisis for her.

When the alcoholic member stops drinking, however, there may be a "crisis" of sobriety. The family still has its old patterns, and has to learn new ones. The period of adjustment typically lasts from six months to two years. All family members may need to have counselling or be involved in mutual support groups, such as Alcoholics Anonymous, Alanon, and Alateen. The irresponsible family member needs to learn to take responsibility for his or her behaviour, and overly responsible members need to learn how to stop taking on responsibility that is not theirs. Both lessons may be extremely difficult because they involve creating a completely different family pattern (Brown & Lewis, 1999; Hudak et al., 1999).

COMMUNICATION AND PROBLEM-SOLVING

As families encounter problems, they must find solutions if they are to cope. As we have seen, communication helps couples and families change their system in order to find solutions. In families where there is less positive communication, there is also less change and lower levels of adaptability than in families with more balanced communication (Olson, 1990). Families who can talk openly about their feelings adapt relatively well to chronic illnesses and other disabilities. By doing so they provide valuable emotional and practical support to each other (Walsh, 2003b).

Families with more effective problem-solving skills usually communicate clearly. This occurs both in words and through a wide range of interpersonal messages. When they encounter a problem, they try out a variety of patterns of interaction that have already worked in an attempt to solve the problem. If they are unable to do so right away, they do not feel helpless. Instead they look for new solutions. On the other hand, families that are less effective in solving problems often have more limited patterns of interpersonal communication and

Help Wanted ... make that Help *Needed* !

Source: Reprinted by kind permission of Barrie Maguire.

often seem to be talking at cross-purposes. Since they also attempt to keep things the same and resist change, they are unable to adapt to new circumstances (Walsh, 2003b).

THE LONG VIEW

All families are changed by the problems they experience. The way they change is shaped by what they themselves, and society as a whole, believe about the situation. Old patterns of problem-solving, the resources available, and other pressures all contribute to striking a new balance. Some families break under the stress; others develop strengths they never dreamed possible.

SUMMARY

WHAT IS A PROBLEM? A social problem exists when a significant number of people believe it is a problem. What is considered a problem has changed over the years. For example, homosexuality has been described at different times as a sin, a crime, a mental disorder, and an alternative lifestyle. Often the dominant group in society has the greatest influence in deciding what a problem is.

THE ABCX MODEL. The way families respond to a problem depends on the stressor itself ("A" factor), the family's resources ("B" factor), and their interpretation of the situation ("C" factor). These factors work together to produce a crisis ("X" factor), which calls for new ways of solving problems. If the problem is long term, stressors can pile up. Again family resources and interpretation affect the outcome—the eventual adaptation of the family to the problem. This second pattern has been called the double ABCX model.

TWO FAMILY PROBLEMS. Two long-term problems that affect families are chronic illness or disability and alcoholism.

Chronic Illness. Chronic illness can have either a sudden or a gradual onset. In either case, the illness and the diagnosis create stress, which is affected by both the coping resources of the family and the meaning they attach to the illness. Often members respond to the crisis with high levels of activity. When the illness is prolonged, other stressors are also involved, such as changes in family lifestyle and ordinary life-cycle changes. Different resources may be required to cope in the long term, and the family's interpretation of the situation may change over time. These combine to produce new coping patterns.

Alcoholic Family. Like chronic illness, alcohol abuse is a family stressor. As in chronic illness, the family's coping resources and the meaning members place on alcohol abuse will affect the severity of the crisis. Various attempts at coping may combine with other stressors to produce a pileup. Eventually the family may adapt by making alcohol abuse part of the family pattern through enabling behaviours. The husband or wife of an alcoholic may become codependent. Often the marriage suffers. If the alcoholic member stops drinking, the family may go through a further crisis because the old coping patterns are no longer appropriate.

COMMUNICATION AND PROBLEM-SOLVING. Positive communication is important for helping families change in a positive way. Often those who are less effective at solving problems have limited or negative patterns of communication.

KEY TERMS

ambiguity: lack of clarity (p. 299)

bestiality: sexual relations between a person and an animal (p. 295)

chronic illness: prolonged illness (p. 301)

codependence: the tendency for nonalcoholic members of an alcoholic family to display a variety of psychological symptoms in response to the alcohol abuse. These arise from lack of self-worth and include lack of clear personal boundaries and assumption of responsibility for the alcoholic behaviour. (p. 305)

codependent: the spouse of an individual who abuses alcohol or other substances (p. 305)

crisis: an imbalance in demands placed on an individual or family and their ability to meet the demand (p. 298)

discreditable: damaging to one's reputation (p. 305)

dysfunctional: decreased ability of family to solve problems (p. 298)

enabler: a person whose behaviour allows another to act in a certain way; often used in reference to nonalcoholic members of alcoholic families (p. 305)

functional: increased ability of the family to solve problems (p. 298)

gatekeepers: individuals recognized as having special expertise in identifying problems (p. 296)

indigenous: Aboriginal (p. 296)

normative family changes: changes that are expected as part of the family life cycle (p. 303)

resilience: the ability to do well in the face of adversity (p. 301)

snag points: areas of difficulty that interfere with constructive efforts to cope with problems (p. 300)

vested interests: group of people who have a stake in keeping society as it is (p. 296)

CLASS ASSIGNMENTS

Complete one or both of the following assignments, as directed by your instructor:

1. By reading newspapers and/or watching television, discover two current issues that present the family with problems. Explain what stresses they place on the family and solutions that have been proposed. What are the advantages and disadvantages of these solutions?

2. Explain why an individual in a helping profession would find the double ABCX model useful. Illustrate your answer by applying the model to a specific problem.

PERSONAL ASSIGNMENTS

The following assignments are designed to help you think about your own experience:

1. What problems has your family experienced? How have they affected family relationships and roles? Did they change the day-to-day organization of family life? Explain.

2. When you have personally experienced problems, what methods have you used to try to resolve them? Did these methods work? Why or why not? What other means might you have used?

Chapter 14

Home Dangerous Home—Abuse and Violence in the Family

OBJECTIVES

 To place family violence in historical perspective

 To look at child abuse, characteristics of victims and abusers, and the response of society

 To look at partner abuse, characteristics of victims and abusers, reasons people stay in abusive relationships, and the response of society

 To look at elder abuse, characteristics of victims and abusers, and the response of society

 To consider theories about abuse

 To think about ways of preventing family violence

Jannie, I'll call her, was my neighbour—a pretty, thirtyish woman. I was young and naive when we met. Within a month, she started telling me the troubles of her marriage. She provided the main family income as a secretary and struggled to keep atop their debts. When her husband worked, he made good pay, but soon after taking up a new job, he found some grievance against his boss and quit. They'd moved often, as he looked for more opportunities. He enjoyed fine things. He had the latest in stereo and television equipment, all charged to credit cards. Jannie found out about the bills when the cards were cancelled. When she dared challenge him, he beat her. This wasn't the first time, either. It had been much worse during her two pregnancies. In between, he told her how stupid, how ugly she was. Jannie feared for their children. Her husband flew into a rage if they touched any of his electronics. I wondered why she stayed with him. She said she couldn't leave. After all, she had made her marriage vows. He threatened to keep the children if she left. Besides, he treated her like a princess afterwards to make up for beating her. Why didn't she get her parents to help? Her family had warned her she shouldn't marry him. All they'd say was, "I told you so." What about her priest or the police? They'd tell her it was her job to make the marriage work—she should try harder to please her husband. There was nowhere else for her to go anyway. Her husband usually commandeered her paycheque and she couldn't afford her own apartment. Why, you ask, didn't she go to a shelter, call an abuse hotline? This was 1958, long before wife abuse was publicly acknowledged. You either rescued yourself or made do. Or told your neighbour your woes.

"A haven in a heartless world" (Lasch, 1979) is how the family is described. Home is the one place of all places where we are protected and safe. Yet for too many people, the family home is the most dangerous of places. They are the victims of family cruelty and violence.

WHAT IS FAMILY VIOLENCE?

Family violence wears many faces. It is the baby who is battered, the child who is sexually assaulted, the woman who is punched and kicked by her husband, the elderly man who is attacked and exploited by his children.

We all recognize these individuals as abused. Yet the whole area of family violence and abuse suffers from confusing definitions. Violence can refer to many actions, ranging from throwing things, to shoving and punching, to using a knife or a gun. Although common and not usually recognized as violent, verbal abuse, consisting of yelling, screaming, and/or swearing, is intimidating. Some people make a distinction between "normal" violence (such as pushing and slapping) and "abusive" violence (such as beating up a person). The same act, however, may have an entirely different effect depending on who does it and against whom it is directed. For example, a small woman may shove a large man without any particular damage. On the other hand, a strong man's shove may send someone smaller (e.g., a child or a woman) slamming into a wall. Abuse is similarly subject to differences in definition. Some people may feel that any physical punishment is child abuse. Others go by the saying "Spare the rod and spoil the child" (Barnett, Miller-Perrin, & Perrin, 2005; Frankel-Howard, 1989).

Definitions are important. Levels of reporting depend on what one considers abuse. Does one count explicit sexual language or walking about naked in front of a child as a form of sexual abuse? Does slapping a child rate as child abuse? Is belittling a person a form of abuse? A broad definition would mean earlier involvement of authorities. As a result, more families could face social or legal intervention and agencies would need to provide more services. Definitions determine who is counted as abused and who is eligible for services. They also decide the type of help offered and how well it stops the abuse (Malley-Morrison & Hines, 2004).

For our purposes, **violence** is defined as an act intended to physically hurt another person. **Abuse,** a more general term, refers to a situation in which a person takes advantage of a less powerful person. Thus abuse can include neglect, sexual and emotional abuse, and financial exploitation, as well as physical violence (Frankel-Howard, 1989).

Although family violence has been around for a long time, concern about it is relatively recent. Historically, the first type of abuse to catch public attention was child abuse, followed by wife beating and elder battering.

CHILD ABUSE

History of Child Abuse

For centuries, children were considered the property of their parents, especially of their fathers. Not only were fathers able to decide, as we saw in the chapter on mate selection, who their children could marry, they also often had the power of life and death. **Infanticide,** the killing of babies, and the killing of young children, have occurred from early times. Some cultures have viewed the practice as a form of birth control or of ensuring the survival only of strong and healthy individuals who could contribute to society. Sometimes babies were used as religious offerings. There are records of young children sealed in the foundations of buildings or bridges to ensure a strong structure (Frankel-Howard, 1989; Tower, 1989).

Both parents and teachers have in the past been encouraged to punish children physically. The saying "Spare the rod and spoil the child" was often quoted as a guideline. This belief is reflected, among other places, in nursery rhymes. The old woman who lived in a shoe with her many children, for example, "whipped them all soundly and sent them to bed." Children were seen as basically bad. Through punishment they could be transformed into God-fearing individuals (Frankel-Howard, 1989; Tower, 1989). The result was that many children were not only whipped but also physically injured, all in the name of turning out good citizens.

Sexual exploitation of children was also common. In ancient times, fathers often arranged the marriages of their young daughters to gain some financial advantage. These marriages were sometimes consummated before the girls reached puberty. In ancient Greece, it was common for men to use boys for sexual pleasure. In fact, most boys of noble families had to take adult lovers who would train them to be soldiers. Finally, in 1548, England passed a law protecting boys from forced **sodomy** and, in 1576, passed another prohibiting forcible rape of girls under the age of 10 (Tower, 1989).

In spite of laws and social criticism of the sort found in Charles Dickens's novels (e.g., *Oliver Twist*), most abuse of children was overlooked. A man's home was his castle. Outsiders had no business poking their noses into what went on in the privacy of his four walls.

In 1874, the case in New York of Mary Ellen, a child battered by her foster parents, caught popular attention in North America. Initial attempts to remove her from the home failed because no law against child abuse existed. Eventually advocates argued that laws against cruelty to animals also referred to children, since children are also part of the animal kingdom. Following the Mary Ellen case, Societies for Prevention of Cruelty to Children were formed in New York State and child abuse legislation was passed (Barnett et al., 2005).

In Canada, the first Children's Aid Society was formed in Toronto in 1891. "An Act for the Prevention of Cruelty to and Better Protection of Children" was passed in Ontario in 1893. As in New York, the initial concern of reforms centred on child employment and substitute caregivers rather than on neglect and abuse by parents, although the latter was covered by the legislation. For many years, Canadian legislation changed little. For example, British Columbia kept most of the wording of its 1893 act into the 1970s (Kieran, 1986; Wachtel, 1989).

Following popularization of the term "battered child syndrome," coined by C. Henry Kempe in the early 1960s, mandatory reporting laws were passed. By the late 1970s, 9 of the 12 provincial and territorial jurisdictions had passed such laws and the remainder had set up monitoring programs (Wachtel, 1989).

What Is Child Abuse?

The area of child abuse, like all aspects of family violence, suffers from some confusion over its definition. The most obvious forms—battering that produces serious physical injuries, severe neglect, and flagrant sexual abuse—are generally recognized as abusive. As attention to abuse grew, definitions became broader and more inclusive. For example, a child who witnesses parents' violence is now considered abused (Moss, 2003). All definitions assume appropriate standards of behaviour for parents exist and that abusive acts violate these standards. The problem is that these standards vary over time, for example, those concerning appropriate discipline. They also vary across cultures and between social and cultural groups. Thus what is seen as abusive or neglectful by one group is considered responsible parenting by another (Malley-Morrison & Hines, 2004).

Since some forms of abuse are difficult to detect or prove, they may not be included in official definitions. Emotional abuse or psychological aggression, for example, can be just as damaging to a child as physical abuse. Yet it is difficult for an outsider to prove that a parent is rejecting, cold, or inconsistent enough to be abusive; thus few cases of emotional abuse are reported (Straus & Field, 2003). There are other grey areas. Most laws, for example, allow parents to use "reasonable force" against their children. When does force stop being reasonable and become abusive? Is exhibitionism included in sexual abuse? In one police report, for example, 46 percent of sexual abuse cases concerning children involved indecent exposure (Kempe & Kempe, 1984).

How Many Parents Abuse or Neglect Their Children?

The true level of child abuse is unknown. Reporting of cases has increased since the 1970s (Pottie Bunge & Locke, 2000). The most common type of child maltreatment investigated by child welfare authorities is neglect. In 2002, 94 police departments reported 34 048 cases of assault against those under age 18, including 8755 cases of sexual and 25 293 cases of physical assault (Brzozowski, 2004). This increase is usually attributed to publicity about abuse, to changes in definitions, and to compulsory reporting laws (Barnett et al., 2005).

Usually, only the most extreme cases of abuse are reported to police or child protection agencies. A variety of explanations are given for low reporting and recognition rates. First, since child abuse is frowned on by society, it is often a secret. For this reason, it may not come to anyone's attention. Second, children may be too afraid or too young to disclose abuse. Third, professionals who see signs of abuse may not report the incident. They may not admit to themselves that abuse is really happening or that it is serious enough to report. Fourth, a parent's or caregiver's explanation for injuries may seem plausible, so that no one becomes suspicious. Fifth, people may feel it isn't their business, and therefore fail to report the abuse they know about (Hay, 1997).

There are many variations in estimates of abuse. The differences are the result of definitions used, of reporting laws, and of the attitudes of service providers (Cabrera, 1995). In the area of sexual abuse, for example, estimates vary widely. A figure that is commonly cited comes from the Badgley Report on the Sexual Abuse of Children (Trocmé et al., 2001): one in two girls and one in three boys will be the victims of unwanted sexual acts by the time they are 18. These numbers are the result of a wide definition of sexual abuse, ranging from indecent exposure to forced intercourse. Re-analysis of the Badgley Report data suggests instead that one in five girls and one in ten boys are victims of sexual abuse (Wachtel, 1999). More recent studies have found that for every 1000 children, sexual abuse was confirmed or had a high level of suspicion for 1.2 children, a much lower rate than suggested by the Badgley Report. About four times as many girls as boys are victims (Brzozowski, 2004). In both Canada and the United States, reports of sexual abuse have declined (Brzozowski, 2004; Jones & Finkelhor, 2001).

The huge growth in the reported cases of abuse has strained the resources of social service agencies (Wachtel, 1999). For the most part, the increase in staff (if any has occurred at all) in no way matches the increase in reported cases.

Which Children Are at Risk of Abuse or Neglect?

Many abused and neglected children are doubly disadvantaged. The abuse itself, of course, endangers them. Children at risk of being abused include unwanted children, children living with a lone parent, those born either prematurely or suffering from **perinatal** complications, those with physical or mental challenges, or those in poor health. Often seriously abused children are very young. Most deaths from physical abuse occur in children aged three and younger. Thus, abused and neglected children are often particularly helpless (Barnett et al., 2005; Brzozowski, 2004).

Children who are particularly vulnerable to sexual abuse are often emotionally deprived and socially isolated. They usually know and trust the adult who abuses them and have a special fondness for that person (usually a male). Sometimes the **perpetrator** (i.e., the abuser) is the only person who shows the child affection, and is often someone who is expected to be protective. Girls, in particular, are sexually abused by family members (Barnett et al., 2005).

Early writers in the field of abuse mentioned other characteristics of abused children. The physically abused, they said, often behaved in a provocative manner in order to get parents' attention, no matter how brutal. Sexually abused girls behaved in a seductive manner (Barnett et al., 2005). More recently people have come to realize that such behaviour is described from the perspective of the abuser rather than the victim, and point out that many children with similar behaviour are never abused. Indeed, such ideas blame the victim rather than the culprit for the abuse.

Is Spanking Child Abuse?

In the summer of 2001, seven Ontario children were removed kicking and screaming from their home by police and child welfare authorities. Their parents believed that the Bible ordered them to discipline their children with objects rather than their hands, which were to be used only for love. Eventually the children were returned to their parents (Moore, 2002). This incident highlights a current argument about whether spanking is child abuse. Facts about spanking are scarce. Researchers state that most parents spank their children, if only occasionally. An American study found that younger, less well-educated mothers tended to spank children more often than fathers and older, better educated mothers. Spanking tapered off as children became older. The researchers suggest that mothers have most responsibility for day-to-day care of children. As youngsters age, they are easier to reason with. In addition, older mothers have probably learned a wider range of ways to manage children's behaviour (Day, Peterson, & McCracken, 1998).

Those who argue that spanking is not abuse state that their parents spanked them and it did them no harm. The use of corporal punishment also has roots in literal interpretations of Bible passages like Proverbs 33: 13–14. ("Withhold not correction from the child, for if thou beatest him with the rod, he will not die. Thou shalt beat him with the rod and deliver his soul from Hell."—*King James Version.*) On the opposite side, child development experts point out that parents who spank often tend to spank a lot and that the severity usually increases. Children disciplined this way are at risk, when they are adults, of becoming abusers themselves. Others, taking a more moderate view, suggest that occasional, mild spanking does no harm, but that there are more effective forms of discipline (Baumrind, 1996; Day et al., 1998; Goldberg, 1996; Robinson, 2001). In January 2004, the Supreme Court of Canada took the moderate view, ruling that minor force, occurring once in a while, is allowed for children aged 3 to 12. Objects used to administer physical punishment are barred, as is any force used on a child's head (Brzozowski, 2004).

What Kinds of People Abuse or Neglect Their Children?

We have problems drawing a composite portrait of the child abuser or neglecter. There can be no single picture (see Figure 14.1). Perpetrators can be male or female. They differ in their ages, and in their relationship to the child, and can be mothers, fathers, siblings, stepparents, babysitters, and others who have contact with the child. They come from all parts of society. Originally it was thought that abusers were mainly from the lower socioeconomic level of society. This view, however, was probably based on the fact that people who are on welfare, who come in contact with social agencies, and who live in apartments rather than houses are more open to observation and are thus more likely to be reported. If this is so, many middle-class abusers are probably not identified (Maidman, 1984).

Figure 14.1

THE MOST FREQUENTLY ACCUSED IN ASSAULTS AGAINST CHILDREN AND YOUTH COMMITTED BY FAMILY MEMBERS, 1999[1,2]

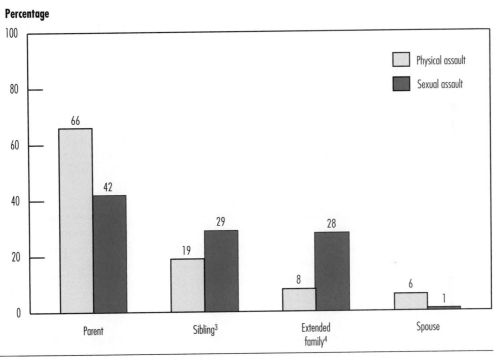

Source: Adapted from Statistics Canada, "Family Violence in Canada: A Statistical Profile, 2004," Catalogue 85-224, July 6, 2004.

Notes:
Percentages may not total 100% due to rounding.
[1]Data are not nationally representative. Data are based on a sample of 164 police departments, representing 46% of the national volume of crime in 1999.
[2]Includes victims under the age of 18 years where sex of the victim is known.
[3]Sibling includes natural, step-, half-, foster, or adopted siblings.
[4]Extended family includes others related by blood, marriage, adoption, or foster care.

Physical Abuse

Early studies produced a stereotype of the abusive mother based on these biased findings. Those at particular risk of abusing children were felt to be disadvantaged and to have poor self-esteem. Particular groups that were identified were the young (under 20 years) and the unmarried. Often the child was unwanted. A mother whose parents separated before she was 15 years old, or who lived in a foster home because she or her siblings were neglected or abused, was considered to be at particular risk (Frankel-Howard, 1989).

Nevertheless, abusive parents seem to have some characteristics in common, which can be explained in terms of the ABCX model (discussed in Chapter 13). Often they are under high levels of stress. Stressors may be of many kinds; examples are problems in the marriage, unemployment, and illness or disability of a family member. Often the coping resources of abusive parents are poor; for example, many abusive families are isolated from relatives and have few close friends. Some live in areas with little community feeling. Others lack financial resources. Abusive parents often perceive parenting as very stressful. For instance, they may believe they have little control over the situation. They also have difficulty seeing the relationship from the children's point of view; that is, they are not aware of the age-appropriate emotional states and needs. When there is a crisis, they give first claim to their own needs, with the children's needs sometimes not considered at all. In addition, many believe that their children deliberately set out to defy or sabotage them. Often they also have standards for children's behaviour well beyond their developmental level. These negative attitudes toward their children help feed the parents' feelings of stress and loss of control, and thus act as a trigger for aggression (Acton & During, 1990; Barnett et al., 2005).

Neglect

Neglected children also tend to live in families under stress. Often they have single parents and/or parents who depend on welfare. Children in larger families are also more likely to be neglected. They are endangered by their parents' failure to provide for them or protect them. Neglectful mothers are often isolated. They may view their neighbours or relatives as unsupportive and are less involved in social activities (Barnett et al., 2004; Trocmé et al., 2001).

Sexual Abuse

It is difficult to get a clear picture of the parent who sexually abuses his or her child because known cases are probably only the tip of the iceberg. Most of the studies on sexual abuse have looked at father-daughter incest; even less is known about other forms, such as father-son abuse. What has appeared in the research so far is not a single picture, but rather a series of pictures. Abusers can be male or female from any background. They can be macho or saintly, extroverted or introverted (Cabrera, 1995).

Sexually abusive families have two features in common. For an adult to abuse a child, he or she must be sexually aroused by children and must be likely to act on that arousal. When these preconditions are in place, other factors increase the likelihood of abuse. Many families are isolated. Therefore, they have little relief from a poor marital relationship and relatively few opportunities for sexual activity, such as having an affair or going to a prostitute. Second, the marital relationship is often emotionally and sexually unsatisfying. Frequently the wife is not interested in sex or is ill, disabled, or absent. Third, the oldest daughter is often at risk, especially if she has become a parentified child. Her father may regard her as a partner in a sexual as well as a parental sense. Often abusive fathers interpret young daughters' normal attachment to them and their curiosity about physical differences in an inappropriate sexual way. Fourth, many believe they are promoting their children's welfare rather than hurting them. Yet the love and caring such fathers express for their children is contradicted by their lack of concern for the effect the incest will have on the victims (Barnett et al., 2005; Faller, 1993; Gilgun, 1995; Waterman, 1986).

Contrary to popular notions, women do sexually abuse both boys and girls, but figures are nonexistent. Greater stigma is attached to mother-child incest than the father-child. Women do not initiate this abuse themselves in all cases. Sometimes they do so to go along with the idea of their male partner, or they comply because they fear being abused themselves. Child sexual abuse by women has many long-term effects similar to abuse by men (Jennings, 1994; Ogilvie, 2004).

BOX 14.1

JONATHAN'S STORY

The day my son received his black graduation cap and diploma from preschool was one of the happiest days of my life. It was more than a milestone for Jonathan, it was a celebration of his life and our togetherness, despite our experience with domestic violence. As I watched him, my eyes welled with tears. There was my Jonathan; he had made it out alive.

From the moment Jonathan was conceived, his biological father subjected Jonathan and I to physical and emotional abuse. Throughout my very difficult pregnancy, the father pushed, shoved, slapped, and kicked me, hoping I would miscarry the child he publicly crowed about.

When Jonathan was an infant his so-called "father" yelled and threw things at him. On Jonathan's first birthday, his father threw an electric typewriter at him. At two and a half, his father slashed Jonathan's pet cat Caley with a knife, while hissing, "That's what I'd like to do to your mother."

This little boy saw his father beat and rape me. He heard my screams and couldn't do anything about it. Those screams will stay with him for the rest of his life. Later, during a court-ordered access visit, this man managed to slam Jonathan's foot in a door, spraining his ankle—an "accident" of course. The incidents of abuse go on and on. You cannot imagine the torture I felt seeing my little boy being hurt like that.

continued

BOX 14.1 *(continued)*

Jonathan was fortunate in connecting with two great counsellors, people who believed him and supported him through this ordeal. The preschool Jonathan attended took the time to listen. They showed him it was okay to talk about the abuse. The teachers knew the violent pictures he drew were his way of dealing with his anger and fear; they did not tell him the pictures were unacceptable. The teachers also made me feel better and they did not blame me or think that I was crazy.

Other things could have made it easier for Jonathan. It would have helped if the police had been better trained to work with children. The police felt Jonathan was not able to tell the difference between truth and fiction, even though our lawyer felt otherwise. Judges also need to be trained about domestic violence. Even with the evidence of extreme abuse, Jonathan's father was granted supervised access. (If it had been me up on the abuse charges, Jonathan would have been taken away from me.) There were times I couldn't take Jonathan with me to my various appointments with police or court personnel, because they didn't have any place for him to play. It would also have helped Jonathan to have a support group to join. He would have realized that he was not alone, that other children are also abused.

Yes, Jonathan has survived the experience, but at what cost to his young life? As they called his name at his preschool graduation, I smiled. In spite of everything, we are the lucky ones. At least we are together here tonight, and we have each other.

Source: *Vis-à-Vis*, 1994/95 Winter, p. 10. Reprinted with permission from The Canadian Council on Social Development (www.ccsd.ca).

Figure 14.2

ILLUSTRATION BY "JONATHAN," AGE FIVE

I hide under my bed when Daddy hits Mommy. I am scared.

Source: "To Make a Difference." Reprinted with special permission of The London Coordinating Committee to End Woman Abuse.

Other Forms of Abuse

Child Witnesses of Domestic Violence

Children are seriously affected by violence directed at other family members. According to the National Longitudinal Survey of Children and Youth, one in twelve (8 percent) of children aged four to seven had witnessed at least one episode of violence at home. A few (5 percent of witnesses) had seen it often (Moss, 2003). Children are affected by what they see and hear. All are terrified. Some become withdrawn and anxious. Others act out through aggression and delinquency. Children learn, in addition, that violence is part of a close sexual relationship between adults (Bancroft & Silverman, 2002; Hotton, 2003; Moss, 2003; Onyskiw & Hayduk, 2001; Pepler, Catallo, & Moore, 2000).

Emotional Abuse in Child Custody and Access Cases

When a woman leaves an abusive relationship, the only way the husband may be able to control her is by terrorizing her through their children. He may use anti-mother conditioning to alienate the children from his partner. Some tactics include grilling the children for information about their mother; attempting to undermine the children's respect for their mother through name-calling, for example, "stupid bitch"; blaming the mother for the family breakup; saying she does not love the children; or threatening to hurt or kill the mother (Taylor, 1993). While there are few accounts of similar abuse by mothers, undoubtedly some try to undermine the relationship between fathers and children.

Children and Adolescents as Abusers

Only quite recently has attention turned to children and adolescents as abusers. While researchers have taken some notice of adolescent sexual offenders, abuse within the family has been largely ignored.

Sibling Abuse

Violence between siblings is often considered part of the normal experience of growing up. As Pagelow says, "Violence by children is seen, but it is not seen as violence" (1984, p. 341). She suggests this is the reason little research is done on either its **incidence** (i.e., the percentage of the population that is affected) or aftereffects. What evidence is available is contradictory. Some researchers find boys are more aggressive; others that girls are; and still others that levels for both sexes are about the same (Duffy & Momirov, 1997). Part of the reason for the lack of research can be found in society's generally complacent attitude about sibling rivalry in general and boys' aggression in particular (Pagelow, 1984). Although some suggest that brother–sister sexual abuse, for example, is more common than father–daughter incest (Wiehe & Herring, 1991), fewer cases are reported to police than abuse by parents (Brzozowski, 2004). Often physical, emotional, and sexual abuse occur together. Parents may encourage children to settle their own conflicts and may not be aware of damage done. They also may be unaware of sexual activity among their children or not recognize the signs it is occurring (Duffy & Momirov, 1997).

Sibling abuse can be distinguished from non-abusive sibling interaction using the following questions. Is there a marked difference in power between the siblings? How often and how long does the behaviour take place? How much pressure is involved, and how much secrecy? How harmful are the interactions? Does the behaviour fall outside levels of typical sibling rivalry or normal sex play? Do parents stop the behaviour appropriately? (Barnett et al., 2005).

Parent Abuse

Even less is known about parent abuse than sibling abuse. Because there is no Canadian research, there is no clear idea of the numbers involved. Often parents do not admit such abuse except in extreme cases. Estimates suggest that 7 to 13 percent of children attack their parents. Parent abusers are usually children between the ages of 10 and 24. They live with their parents and depend on them for support. Of known cases, older children tend to be more violent toward parents than younger ones, with a peak in the late teens. Yet abusers are not necessarily the largest or strongest. Parent abusers often have little interest in school and are involved with the police or with child welfare authorities. They are likely to have friends who are delinquent and who may also assault their parents. Substance abuse is common. Some researchers suggest that parent abuse may be retaliation for earlier abuse by a parent. Such aggression may be aimed at the less powerful parent rather than the one who was the abuser. Parent abusers probably use assault to gain power and control in the family (Cottrell, 2003; Denham & Gillespie, 1999; Duffy & Momirov, 1997).

Effects of Abuse on Children

All abuse is harmful to children. The actual form of the effects may vary by type of abuse. Some effects are long term. Physical difficulties often occur in physical and sexual abuse and neglect. These include, for example, death, broken bones, genital bleeding, and failure to thrive. Children suffering any form of abuse may have learning problems, the result of either physical or emotional damage. Problem behaviours are common. These include physical aggression and delinquency, seductive behaviour among the sexually abused, apathy and withdrawal, and substance abuse. As a result, many have difficulty getting along with other children and forming satisfying relationships as adults. Often they have difficulty trusting others. In addition, victims may suffer from serious depression and, among the physically and sexually abused, from posttraumatic stress disorder. Not all abused children, fortunately, suffer serious or long-term effects from maltreatment (Barnett et al., 2005; Hyman, 1995; Luster & Small, 1995; Preece & Busby, 1995).

Official Responses to Child Abuse

As we have seen, child protection laws are in place at both the national and the provincial level. These require cases of child abuse to be reported. However, problems arise because there is no standard definition of child abuse. If the abuse is severe, the abuser is prosecuted. In less severe cases, social service agencies, such as Children's Aid Societies or provincial child welfare departments, deal with the matter. They may remove the child permanently, or temporarily until the home can be made safe. They may provide counselling and treatment to the various family members, teaching them proper parenting methods or ways of dealing with the aftereffects of abuse. Treatment for survivors is not a priority, however, among many medical service providers (Cabrera, 1995).

There are contradictory pressures on protection agencies. On the one hand, they are expected to prevent abuse from recurring. If a child is returned home and then is severely abused or killed, the public is outraged. On the other hand, these agencies may be accused of child snatching and intruding unjustifiably on family life. It is impossible to predict in every case whether the child will be safe at home. Children who are removed from their homes may be damaged further by the system designed to protect them. Many children are moved repeatedly while they are in foster or residential care. Many are further physically or sexually abused, either by caregivers or by other children in the same placement (Cabrera, 1995).

Child welfare policies have also been insensitive to cultural differences and destructive to minority families. This is particularly true of Aboriginal children and their families. The current thrust to establish Aboriginal-run child welfare agencies and services underlines the importance of providing culturally appropriate services to all minority families (Malley-Morrison & Hines, 2004).

Many programs for abusive families emphasize reeducating abusive parents so that children can be raised safely at home. Parent education programs pay attention to the social aspect as well—the parent's isolation and the development of social competence and self-esteem. Many of the services have, however, been developed as small-scale programs or demonstration projects and are not available to all families needing them. With current concerns about deficits and funding levels, whether such programs can be expanded or even continued is uncertain. There is also concern that overemphasis on preserving families might endanger children (Barnett et al., 2005; Gelles, 2000).

ABUSE BETWEEN PARTNERS

Abuse between partners can take many forms, all the way from emotional abuse to murder. Often different kinds occur in combination. Abuse comprises physical assault (hitting, punching, kicking), psychological abuse (belittling, threatening, destroying possessions), restriction of movement (locking in or out of the dwelling), economic deprivation, sexual abuse, and homicide (Bala, 1999). The focus of research and service provision has primarily been on violence against women by their male partners. Little research has been done on abuse by same-sex partners, although roughly the same proportion of homosexual individuals are abused as heterosexual (McKenry & Serovich, 2002). Abused men are beginning to be recognized.

Like child abuse, woman abuse is rooted in history. Women have long been seen as possessions of men. In England, women and children were considered the property of the husband and father, who had the obligation to control and discipline them. A man was allowed to beat his wife as long as the stick he used was no thicker than his thumb. This law was not repealed until 1820. From 1909 to 1960, the Canadian Criminal Code included the separate offence of wife battering, in which the victim had to demonstrate a greater degree of bodily harm than was required in cases of assault by a stranger. Abused children received protection under the law earlier than did abused wives. The latter had to wait for the women's movement to publicize their plight. In 1983, a man could finally be charged with raping his wife. Since then, procedures and programs have become more sensitive to the needs of the victims of crime (Ad Hoc Federal-Provincial-Territorial Working Group, 2003; Bala, 1999; MacLeod, 1989).

How Many Spouses Are Assaulted?

Since violence against a female partner was considered a private family matter and was tolerated for centuries, it has largely been a hidden crime. Figures are usually based on estimates and, as in child abuse, vary according to the definition used. In the following discussion, there is usually no distinction made between married and cohabiting couples since violence in these relationships is similar.

In 1993, Statistics Canada conducted a survey to determine the degree of violence against women. This study was followed by the 1999 General Social Survey. Researchers asked both men and women about violence in their current and previous marital and common-law relationships (including same-sex ones) during the past five years. Both men and women reported the same level of violence (4 percent) by a current partner. Women (28 percent) were more likely than men (22 percent) to report violence in a previous relationship. Women, however, were more likely to suffer injury, to require medical treatment, and to fear for their lives (Pottie Bunge & Locke, 2000). In 2000, 85 percent of individuals who reported spousal abuse to police were women. They are more likely to be seriously injured than men and to report more cases to police (Ad Hoc Federal-Provincial-Territorial Working Group, 2003).

Assault against husbands has generally been ignored. Recently there has been controversy about how severe a problem husband abuse actually is. That some wives strike their husbands meaning to injure them is not disputed. The question is, Is husband abuse as serious a problem as wife abuse? The debate began in the United States, where the rates of spousal homicide by women and men are nearly equal; slightly more women than men are murdered by their partners. Indeed, women are more likely to be killed by a partner than by a stranger on the street. The reverse is true for men. Several studies have suggested that women attack men at least as often as men attack women. One of the problems with these studies is that they do not tell whether women use violence mainly as a means of self-defence. If they do, they are still the principal victims of marital violence in spite of their own physical attacks (Brzozowski, 2004; Loseke & Kurz, 2005; Straus, 2005).

Those who believe that wife abuse is more serious than husband abuse point to the following facts. First, women are likelier to suffer more serious injuries than men. Men are, on the average, stronger than women. They are not as likely to be injured by a blow from their partners as vice versa. From 1993 to 2002, women were four times more likely to be killed by husbands than vice versa. Second, men often kill wives after prolonged periods of physical violence; women rarely do. Third, men more than women hunt down and kill partners who left them or were unfaithful. Fourth, men far more often than women kill their children along with their spouse. Finally, women who kill partners often do so as a "defensive" action following years of physical and sexual abuse. Usually they can see no other way out (Anderson, 2002; Brzozowski, 2004; LaViolette & Barnett, 2000; Loseke & Kurz, 2005; Straus, 2005). Because relatively little is known about abuse of husbands and because women are more likely to be injured, much of the remaining discussion will focus on abused women.

Dating Violence

Not much was known about dating violence until recently. Yet, as we saw in Chapter 3, this can be a serious problem between unmarried couples. No national statistics are available, however. A nationwide survey of university and college students found that 13.7 percent of men reported that they had abused their dating partner in the past year. On the other hand, 22.3 percent of women said they had been victims. Violence was also common in high school dating relationships. Many college and university men who abused their partners believed male–female relationships should be patriarchal, that is, that the male should be dominant. Often they had been drinking at the time of the abuse. Many abusers had experienced violence in their families of origin (DeKeseredy & Ellis, 1995). Other studies have shown that dating violence is common among adolescents and young adults. Types of violence include physical and sexual assault, sexual coercion, and emotional abuse. Estimates vary from 20 to 67 percent of couples, depending on whether emotional and verbal abuse are included (Department of Justice, 2003).

The Victims of Woman Battering

Many researchers have concentrated on the battered woman rather than on the violent partner. They have tried to find characteristics that put her at risk of becoming a victim, looking for ways in which she brings violence on herself. For example, some studies of husband abuse suggest that women may be the first to strike out. Husbands then respond with greater violence (DeKeseredy, 1993).

All the studies have failed to find typical characteristics of abused women, with one exception. They have all married or are living with an assaultive man (Frankel-Howard, 1989; LaViolette & Barnett, 2000). The circumstances around the relationship are important. Women in new partnerships are abused more often. These numbers may reflect the fact that many leave before too long. They may also be related to the fact that younger people tend to be more violent. Cohabiting women are assaulted more often than those who are married. In addition, when women leave abusive partners, they are particularly at risk of violence (DeMaris, Benson, Fox, Hill, & Van Wyk, 2003; Hart & Jamieson, 2002).

Women at Special Risk

Although there are no national figures, family violence is reported to be very high in Aboriginal communities. A 1989 study by the Ontario Native Women's Association reported that 8 out of 10 Aboriginal women were abused, and said that there was "growing documentation [showing] that Aboriginal female adults, adolescents and children are experiencing abuse, battering and/or sexual assault to a staggering degree" (LaRoque, 1994, p. 72). Aboriginal peoples point to the destruction of traditional culture by white colonialism. For example, stereotyping of Aboriginal men as violence-crazed "savages" and of Aboriginal women as sexually loose "squaws" encouraged both Aboriginal and non-Aboriginal men to physically and sexually abuse women. In addition, the removal of children from their homes exposed them to abuse in institutions and failed to teach them about normal family life. Thus, they were more likely to become abusers in their turn (Hart, 1997; LaRoque, 1994; Maracle, 1993).

Other problems add to the likelihood of abuse although they do not cause it. Abuse occurs more often among poor people, not because they are poor, but because poverty creates stress (Duffy & Momirov, 1997). More Aboriginal people live in poverty than any other group. Alcohol and substance abuse is tied to violence; using such drugs can loosen usual controls over a person's behaviour. The fact that abuse is pervasive from one generation to the next provides violent role models (Duffy & Momirov, 1997; Health Canada, 1997).

Three other groups of women are at particular risk if they are victims of spousal abuse. The first group consists of those who live in rural or isolated areas, who may have difficulty getting to a shelter, even if one is in the area. Since everyone knows everyone in a small community, it may be hard for the woman to ask for help. This is especially so if the doctor and the police officer are friends of the husband. Safe homes have been set up in some communities, but here too lack of anonymity may be a problem (Hart & Jamieson, 2002; Kirkpatrick, 1993). The second group, immigrant women, may face language and cultural difficulties in getting help (Hart & Jamieson, 2002). Muslim women in Toronto, for example, report that counsellors at mainstream agencies were either prejudiced or uninformed about Islamic cultural practices (Azni, 1999). Immigrant women may also fear that they will be rejected by their communities or even deported. Women with physical challenges make up the third group of those at particular risk. They are twice as likely to be physically and sexually assaulted as the able-bodied. Since they are largely dependent on their caregivers, they may be institutionalized if they complain of abuse. Those who do go for help may find that they cannot even enter the building because it has no wheelchair access, or that they are not believed, especially if they report sexual abuse (Denham & Gillespie, 1999; Hart & Jamieson, 2002).

Abuse in Gay and Lesbian Relationships

Abuse in gay and lesbian relationships is a latecomer to the field of family violence. There are several reasons for the oversight. First, partner violence has received attention only in the past 30 to 35 years. Second, stereotypes of gay and lesbian relationships interfere with recognizing abuse. Lesbians, for example, are regarded as warm and supportive and, thus, nonabusive. When a gay man assaults his partner, the situation may be regarded as a fair fight between equals, an extension of "boys will be boys." Third, some individuals fear that admitting problems in same-sex relationships will only increase stigma against them. Finally, victims doubt that police and other professionals will regard such abuse as a serious issue (Ambert, 2003).

Numbers are almost impossible to come by. One American estimate puts the rate at about the level for heterosexual couples (McKenry & Serovich, 2002). It is possible that the type of abuse differs between men and women. Violence may occur more often among gay men. Men abuse more often than women in heterosexual relationships, and a gay union involves two men (Island & Letellier, 1991). On the other hand, lesbians may abuse emotionally more often than physically (Chesley et al., 1998). Regardless of the numbers and types of abuse, gay men and lesbians are affected in the same way as victims in heterosexual couples. In addition, they have further difficulties, as mentioned, because of antihomosexual prejudice (Ambert, 2003).

Who Abuses Their Partners?

Research on perpetrators has focused on men in heterosexual relationships. Little is known about women or homosexual individuals who assault their partners. However, the following social and psychological characteristics are fairly common among these men. They tend to accept fully the traditional male and female roles and to draw strict lines between what is masculine and feminine. Part of their image of the "ideal" man is someone who is in control of all aspects of his life, including his wife and children. They use violence as a way of solving problems and of controlling others. They have difficulty dealing with emotions. They appear to believe that "real men" do not express soft emotions such as tenderness or fear. All that is left is anger, and this they cannot control. These men have trouble trusting others, including their partners. Often women abusers have poor self-images. A sense of being in control of the people around them makes them feel more adequate. They do not take responsibility for their actions. Instead they blame stress, an alcohol problem, or their partners for the violence (Bancroft & Silverman, 2002). Later in the chapter, we will look more generally at the roots of violence.

Why Do Partners Stay?

Many individuals leave several times and return to an abusive partner before leaving for good. Relatively little is known about why men stay in or return to abusive relationships. There are three basic reasons women stay. First, they are committed to the wife/mother role. Second, they are afraid of the consequences of leaving. Third, they have learned to feel powerless and guilty (Barnett et al., 2005).

Commitment to the Wife/Mother Role

Many women in abusive relationships have fully accepted traditional male and female roles. Some believe they have married "for better or for worse" and must keep their vows. Girls are still taught that it is a woman's responsibility to make an intimate relationship work and to keep family peace. Therefore, asking for help means admitting that they have failed in their main task in life. Since they are ashamed, the victims themselves may also cut themselves off from family and friends to keep the violence secret. Some women also feel that a mother should sacrifice herself for her children and that a single-parent home would harm them. Often the last straw before leaving is a physical attack on the children. Especially if attacks occur only once in a while and are followed by apologies and promises that it will never happen again, many women hope the violence will stop. In addition, many women love the "nice" side of their partners (Barnett et al., 2005; Hart & Jamieson, 2002; Weitzman, 2000).

Fear of the Consequences of Leaving

Abused women fear many things. Some men threaten to severely injure or even kill their partners if they leave. A woman may fear poverty and isolation. Often abused women have been homemakers and have been out of the workforce for some time and feel it is impossible to support themselves or their children on the low wages they can earn, if they can even find a job. Many fear going on welfare. If she has been working, her partner is likely to have controlled the finances. If so, she has no resources and yet is not eligible for social assistance. Immigrant women may fear deportation if they apply for financial aid (Barnett et al., 2005; Hart & Jamieson, 2002).

Some men try to control their partners through their children. They may make threats in regard to the children—either of injury or of custody suits. Some try to undermine their children's respect for their mother by calling her names or telling them that she is stupid. If the woman threatens to leave, or actually does so, her partner may inform the children she does not love them. This indoctrination campaign to alienate the children from their mother has been described as a form of emotional abuse of both woman and children (Taylor, 1993; Toews, 2003).

Men who stay with abusive partners may also fear the consequences of leaving. Having to admit that they are abused may make them afraid others will look down on them because they are unmanly. They may also fear that they will lose their children.

Feeling Powerless

Many abused women feel helpless. After years of emotional and physical abuse, their self-esteem may be so low that they no longer believe they can be successful at anything. When they find that all their attempts to escape violence are unsuccessful, they not only stop trying but also give up all hope of their circumstances changing.

Helplessness may, in fact, be a reality. Many women find no source of help. Some men physically prevent their partners from seeking help by locking them in the house or removing telephones. The victims of abuse might not get social assistance until they have their own address and they cannot get an address without money. If there is no shelter nearby or if it is full, they may literally have nowhere to go. Some women stay with an abusive husband or return to one because they cannot find affordable housing or the means to provide the necessities of life for themselves and their children (Denham & Gillespie, 1999; Hart & Jamieson, 2002).

There is sometimes further victimization by the people the abused woman turns to for help. Clergy, family members, or friends may assume it is her fault if the relationship is not working and may urge her to go home and try harder. The woman then feels guilty for somehow having failed at her proper role. She may also feel guilty for her natural anger and frustration. The insensitivity of those around her fuels her sense of helplessness (Weitzman, 2000).

How Does Society Respond to Spousal Abuse?

In the past, our society has not been very responsive to wife abuse, tending to regard it as a private family matter. Since the late 1970s, however, the demand for spousal assault to be taken as seriously as any other form of violence has increased (Ad Hoc Federal-Provincial-Territorial Working Group Reviewing Spousal Abuse Policies and Legislation, 2003).

Abused women's first need is for protection. This can be provided in two ways: through the police and courts and through places of safety such as shelters. In a survey of partner violence, just 37 percent of cases with female victims and 15 percent with male victims were reported to police. Only half the males notified police themselves, in contrast to three-quarters of females. Most victims reported the incident to police to stop the violence or to receive protection. The differences in reporting probably reflect the more severe violence women experience (Pottie Bunge & Locke, 2000).

In the past, police have not always laid charges in cases of spousal abuse. Three factors for this failure have been suggested: (1) the belief that what happens in the home is private, (2) the belief that couples should try to reconcile rather than expose their problems in court, and (3) the fear that the victim will refuse to testify. Police viewed their task as one of quieting down the situation so that there would be no more violence that day (Bala, 1999).

Since 1982, all provincial and territorial governments have issued directives to police and, in most cases, to Crown attorneys that encourage a more careful investigation and prosecution of spousal-assault cases like any other criminal cases. The growing concern about spousal abuse has resulted in improved training throughout the justice system. Larger police forces have also established special units to respond to family violence (Ad Hoc Federal-Provincial-Territorial Working Group Reviewing Spousal Abuse Policies and Legislation, 2003). In 2002, charges were laid by police in 79 percent of cases reported to them (Brzozowski, 2004).

Often a pressing need for abused women is safe housing. The immediate need is met by transition houses and sometimes by safe homes in isolated communities, but their numbers fall far short of need. **Second-stage housing** provides longer-term accommodation lasting usually from six months to one year. Women who use extended services often have endured serious abuse and need continuing safety. Transition houses offer information, emotional support, and practical resources so that women can plan for their future. Some shelters have expanded services to include follow-up programs, drop-in centres, and support groups for women and children, but receive no additional funds for them (Ad Hoc Federal-Provincial-Territorial Working Group Reviewing Spousal Abuse Policies and Legislation, 2003; Denham & Gillespie, 1999).

The economic cutbacks by federal and provincial governments during the later 1990s have affected the services offered abused women and their children. Whole sections of the safety net (e.g., second-stage housing in Ontario and Nova Scotia) no longer receive public funding. Services must therefore rely on donations. Burnout among those working with abuse victims has always been high. Now, however, more and more experienced staff leave this field of work because of job cuts, overwork, and poor pay. More volunteers are used to fill the gap, but program funders take little account of the time and money needed to train, advise, and emotionally support them. As a result of these factors, fewer services are available (Denham & Gillespie, 1999).

In many large centres, treatment is available for all family members. Women suffer emotional as well as physical damage when they are abused. Children from violent families may be anxious, even terrified. They may also have problems managing their anger. Therapy is offered to abusive men. This focuses on the way they victimize and control their partners in order to stop their violent behaviour. All treatment focuses on the safety and protection of potential victims. However, members of minorities such as gay men and lesbians and recent immigrants may have difficulty finding appropriate help (Ad Hoc Federal-Provincial-Territorial Working Group Reviewing Spousal Abuse Policies and Legislation, 2003; Denham & Gillespie, 1999; Pepler et al., 2000).

ABUSE OF OLDER ADULTS

Abuse of older adults is the most recent kind of family violence to be recognized. The image of old age as a time of peace and serenity probably interfered with the recognition that older people may be at risk (Sacco, 1995). The great increase in the number of older people is partly responsible for the growing incidence of elder abuse. What was a rare event is now much more common in large part because there are now so many more seniors than in the past. Also, more people now are professionally concerned with older people. The 1990s saw growing research into elder abuse (Kinnon, 2001).

There is still no standard definition of abuse of older adults. Most professionals agree on three basic kinds—domestic elder abuse, institutional abuse, and self-neglect or self-abuse. This discussion will focus on domestic elder abuse—maltreatment outside an institution by someone with a special relationship to the senior, such as a spouse, sibling, child, or grandchild. Most studies of elder abuse include physical, psychological, and financial abuse as well as neglect. Financial abuse involves the theft of money or objects of value. This occurs most commonly by cashing pension or Old Age Security cheques and not giving the senior the money, or by misusing a power of attorney. Neglect can be classified as active or passive, depending on whether failure to provide is intentional or unintentional. Some service providers also add abandonment (Kinnon, 2001). There is disagreement about whether elder abuse should include abuse that began prior to old age, such as spousal violence or abuse by children that started years earlier.

The 1999 General Social Survey (GSS) asked 4324 Canadians over 65 not living in institutions about abuse they experienced. The numbers are probably low because some elders do not report abuse or underreport how often it occurs (Pottie Bunge & Locke, 2000). Many older people feel stigma in raising a child who mistreats them (Kinnon, 2001). In addition, a telephone survey like the GSS cannot reach individuals who are confined to their rooms without a phone or who have conditions like dementia. Only 1 percent reported they had been physically or sexually assaulted by a spouse, adult child, or caregiver in the previous five years. Seven percent had experienced emotional or financial abuse, more often emotional abuse like being put down or called names by their spouses. Some had been cut off from family and friends. Men were more likely than women to report being victims of emotional or financial abuse, as were divorced or separated elders (Pottie Bunge & Locke, 2000). Women are more likely than men to be victims of family violence. Of cases reported to police, 64 percent involved female victims. The fact that women suffer from spousal violence more than men largely accounts for the difference in rates. Older men were more likely to be victims of non-family violence (Brzozowski, 2004).

Who Is at Risk?

There are no clear factors predicting abuse of older adults and there is no single cause. In particular, it is impossible to tell who is in danger of financial abuse (McDonald & Collins, 2000). Researchers and people working with the elderly suggest a number of risk factors. First, many, but not all, abusers have a history of psychiatric illness and problems with drugs and alcohol. Second, abusers may have experienced family violence as children. Third, older adults who are dependent on others for care may become too heavy a burden and thus be abused. Or the opposite may be true. The abuser is dependent on the victim and strikes out in words or actions because he or she feels powerless. Fourth, stress can lead to violence. This appears to occur most often when an older person suffers from some dementia, such as Alzheimer's disease, and when the caregiver is clinically depressed. Abusive caregivers tend to have provided care for more years and for more hours a day to a more difficult relative than non-abusive caregivers. Fourth, society tends to hold negative stereotypes of older people. As a result, the elderly may be seen as less human and are thus more susceptible to abuse (Kinnon, 2001; Pillemer, 2005; Steinmetz, 2005). As already stated, there is some evidence for each of these risk factors, but they cannot explain or predict all cases of abuse.

Elder Abuse and Society

A study in Ontario in 1984 found that many professionals were unaware of elder abuse (Moore & Thompson, 1987). Since then, many service providers have been offered training sessions on recognizing elder abuse and helping its victims (McDonald & Collins, 2000). Nevertheless, some professionals may not believe complaints of abuse. Disbelief may be the result of ageism; for example, some individuals cannot imagine an old person being attractive enough to be sexually assaulted. They may also see an older person's symptoms as part of the aging process rather than abuse (Kinnon, 2001).

Some individuals feel that reporting of elder abuse should be mandatory, just as it is for child abuse. Such legislation has already been enacted in British Columbia, New Brunswick, Nova Scotia, and Prince Edward Island. One concern about making reporting mandatory is that such laws may violate the rights of the elderly under the Charter of Rights and Freedoms; that is, they would have little more ability to direct their own lives than children. For example, mandatory reporting may deprive them of the choice of where to live. It might mean that elderly people will end up in nursing homes or other institutions against their will (McDonald & Collins, 2000).

WHY DO PEOPLE ABUSE FAMILY MEMBERS?

Characteristics of Abusers

Most of the theories about violence and exploitation consider individuals and families, and less often society as a whole. Much of the research is based on cross-sectional methods, such as surveys. Thus it ignores how relationships develop and change over time (McDonald & Collins, 2000).

According to Dr. Jane Gilgun (who has interviewed many men who murdered family members), perpetrators want the same things from life that most people want: a sense of safety and security, the ability to influence one's personal world, and a sense of identity. The problem lies in how they go about satisfying these desires (Gilgun, 1999).

Violent behaviour is patterned. That is, perpetrators come in different types. Reactors, the first type, use violence as a means of feeling competent and in control. After the violent act, they often feel guilt and remorse. Soon, however, they start feeling inadequate and powerless again. Tension builds. Then they become violent. Often there is some trigger event that releases the assault (Gilgun, 1999). The victim is frequently blamed for "causing" the violence when all she or he did was unwittingly provide a trigger. One abusive incident occurred, for instance, because the victim cut carrots the wrong way (Island & Letellier, 1991). Sometimes the sequence of violent event, remorse, building tension, and another violent act is referred to as the "cycle of violence" (Women's Issues and Social Empowerment, 1998). However, it is probably better to call it the *violence-relaxation cycle* to distinguish it from intergenerational transmission of abuse, also referred to as a cycle of violence. Often reactors have unrealistic expectations of relationships. For example, there may be role reversal where parents expect their children to provide them with the kind of love, approval, and sense of importance they should really provide their children.

A second type, the entitled, are not driven by the emotional cycle experienced by reactors. They feel no remorse or shame. Rather, they act out of a long-term sense of being entitled to what they want. They use violence because they have learned it works, for example, extorting money from an elderly relative in order to buy drugs. This kind of abuser may rape a partner if he is refused sex. A third type of abuser is overwhelmed by events. Often the violence occurs once only. For example, a woman who has been abused for many years may lash out just once and kill her batterer. Finally, a few are neurologically or psychologically ill (Gilgun, 1999). A rare example is the schizophrenic individual who has delusions that family members are trying to harm him or her (Arboleda-Flórez, Holley, & Crisanti, 1996). Attempts to find genetic or biological causes for abuse have, however, been largely unsuccessful.

Theories of Abuse and Neglect

Situational Theory

The situational or stress theory suggests that abuse occurs when the abuser is under stress. Such situations include a physically frail or mentally incompetent adult or a hard-to-care-for child. This explanation, however, comes dangerously close to blaming the victim. In addition to difficulties inside the family, stressors can also include work problems, poverty, and other environmental factors. The stress model fails to account for the facts that not all abusers are under high levels of stress and that many people who experience high levels of stress are not abusive (McDonald & Collins, 2000). By taking account of individual and family resources and the meanings family members find in the situation, the ABCX model (Chapter 13) provides a fuller explanation than a purely stress model.

Social Exchange Theory

The social exchange theory states that social interaction involves rewards and penalties between at least two people. The abuser will use violence as long as it is rewarding, that is, if the rewards outweigh the costs. Calling the police may tip the balance so that the violence is no longer rewarding. Victims will stay as long as the satisfaction of their needs outweighs the costs of abuse. Because some people hold more power, they expect more rewards. Those with less power have fewer rewards. This theory may explain some abuse. It fails, however, in instances where the abuser is dependent on his or her victim, as in parent abuse by a teenager

(Barnett et al., 2005; McDonald & Collins, 2000). It also does not readily fit the case of child abuse, where a child cannot leave even if its needs are not met.

Symbolic Interaction Theory

The symbolic interaction theory focuses on the interaction between the abuser and abused. It emphasizes both the actual behaviour and the meanings both people find in this behaviour. One example is the abuser who believes that men should rule in their homes and the victim who believes it is her responsibility to keep the family happy. Symbolic interaction theory also includes social learning or modelling one's behaviour on another's. Thus children learn to be violent by observing their parents (Barnett et al., 2005; McDonald & Collins, 2000). One study, for example, found that both males and females who abused children were more likely to have seen one parent hit another and to have been hit by an adult themselves (Heyman & Smith Slep, 2002). Symbolic interaction theory does not take into account, however, any influences outside the family.

Family Systems Theory

According to family systems theory, we learn patterns of interaction within families. These patterns include roles, which are expected patterns of behaviour for family members. These roles become so ingrained that they are difficult to change. Families with an abusive member include violence in the father and husband roles, for example, and victimization in the child and wife roles. Thus when abused children grow up, males may become batterers, living out roles they learned from their fathers, and females become battered women, following their mothers' roles. There is some research supporting this view (Heyman & Smith Slep, 2002; Widom & Maxfield, 2001). This pattern is sometimes referred to as the "cycle of violence," but is better called *intergenerational transmission* of abuse to distinguish it from the violence-relaxation cycle, which, as noted above, is sometimes called by that name. The systems theory fails to explain many cases of abuse or lack of it. In a follow-up study of over 1500 victims of child abuse and neglect, 18 percent had been arrested for violent crimes in contrast to 14 percent in a non-abused group. Not all these crimes involved family violence (National Institute of Justice, 1996). Thus, although their rates of violence are slightly higher than for the non-abused, the majority of child victims do not become abusive adults. In addition, most abusers do not have violent families of origin (Duffy & Momirov, 1997).

Feminist Theories

Feminist theories consider violence the result of patriarchy. Patriarchy allows men more power than women and asserts that it is right for them to have that power. This imbalance leaves women vulnerable to abuse. In an extension, parents, especially fathers, have power over children; thus children are vulnerable. The strict feminist view fails to account for abuse in gay and lesbian relationships or for women's violence against men. The real issue may involve a power imbalance between abuser and abused rather than gender itself (Barnett et al., 2005; McDonald & Collins, 2000).

Societal Perspective

Society itself has been blamed for abuse. Many identified abusers are from lower socioeconomic classes. Their violence may be a response to the stress of social factors such as poverty, unemployment, poor and crowded housing, and often a sense of powerlessness. Yet many abusers are well educated and financially comfortable. In addition, our society is a violent one, as we can see any day of the week on our television screens (Barnett et al., 2005; Josephson, 1995), and thus provides a model for violent behaviour.

Many of the theories about violence in our society are attractive. Although there is evidence to support most of them to some degree, no one theory fully accounts for violence; there is no simple explanation. Rather, violence is probably the result of a complex interaction of many factors: the individual characteristics of the abuser, the stresses resulting from both family relationships and from society itself, and the manner in which people are socialized to accept the values and norms of society.

PREVENTING FAMILY VIOLENCE

Although the forms family violence take differ, there are three basic approaches to prevention.

The most common approach is referred to as *tertiary prevention*. This is treatment or some other intervention to keep abuse from recurring. It includes, for example, services to battered women that empower them to leave an abusive situation, such as shelters, second-stage housing, and skills training. It can also include treatment of perpetrators. Some programs include teaching parenting skills to abusive parents, providing group therapy for violent husbands, and treating behaviour problems, such as aggression, in children from abusive homes. (See Figure 14.3.) These services can be very expensive and show only limited success (Wolfe & Jaffe, 2001).

Secondary prevention programs involve working with groups considered to be at risk for abuse. Some that are aimed at preventing child abuse are prenatal nutrition programs, fetal alcohol syndrome support programs, and remedial schooling (Malley-Morrison & Hines, 2004; Wolfe & Jaffe, 2001). There are also educational programs to teach seniors how to avoid financial exploitation (McDonald & Collins, 2000).

A third approach is *primary prevention,* which aims to keep abuse from occurring at all. One of its principal methods is education. There are many ways this is done. Marriage preparation, prenatal, and parent education courses can include discussion of abuse. Home visits made to new parents are key in child abuse prevention because visitors can spot early signs of abuse or refer stressed parents to educational and support programs. Television has also become important in teaching the public about abusive situations and sources of help. There are also programs targeting children, such as "good touch, bad touch" (Malley-Morrison & Hines, 2004; Wolfe & Jaffe, 2001).

One difficulty with primary and secondary prevention efforts is lack of knowledge about their effectiveness. Since they are broad-based, and since we cannot predict accurately who is likely to abuse a family member, many education or community-based programs may be unfocused. Yet, because they reach so many people, they provide the best hope for making the family home the one place of all places where members are protected and safe.

Figure 14.3

SERVICES TO SUPPORT ABUSED WOMEN AND CHILDREN

Use Justice System $

- family court
- assessments
- criminal court
- legal aid
- victim/witness programs
- probation services
- parole services
- incarceration
- criminal injuries compensation
- men's counselling programs

Contact Police $

- police surveillance/response
- police investigation
- access to reports

Seek Medical Help $

- ambulance service
- emergency medical care
- hospital stays
- X-rays, lab work
- doctors' appointments
- dental treatments
- drug and alcohol centres
- chiropractors
- prescription drugs
- eating disorder clinics
- psychiatric institutions
- community health clinics
- services for children labelled as having attention deficit disorder

Struggle with Employment $

- time off work
- loss of productivity
- retraining programs
- lost tax revenues due to death, injury, or incarceration

Find Housing $

- transition houses
- second-stage shelters
- rent-to-income housing
- volunteer programs
- YMCA
- emergency housing

Seek Educational Support $

- special education
- violence prevention programs
- tutor services
- social work services

Contact Social Agencies $

- counselling programs
- mental health services
- sexual assault centres
- child welfare services
- foster care
- youth services
- education and prevention programs
- volunteer programs
- Kids Help Line
- Aboriginal women's centres
- immigrant and visible minority women's services
- disabled women's services
- daycare

Seek Income Assistance $

- welfare
- mother's allowance
- employment insurance
- enforcement of child support payments

Source: Vis-à-Vis, 13(4), p. 12. © 1996. Reprinted with permission from The Canadian Council on Social Development (www.ccsd.ca).

SUMMARY

WHAT IS FAMILY VIOLENCE? The whole area of family violence and abuse suffers from confusing definitions. In this book, "violence" refers to an act intended to physically hurt another person and "abuse" refers to a situation where a person takes advantage of a less powerful one. Due to problems with definitions and reporting, actual levels of abuse are unknown.

CHILD ABUSE. Historically, child abuse has been part of society. In North America, the first laws against it were passed in the late 1800s. Child abuse is commonly considered to include neglect and physical and sexual abuse. Some people also include emotional abuse. Abused children are often young, unwanted, and physically or mentally disadvantaged. Abusers come from every class in society. Often they are under high levels of stress, are isolated socially or physically, and perceive parenting as stressful. Sexual abusers, in addition, tend to have unsatisfactory marital relations. While sibling abuse is common, little is known about it. Not much is known about children who abuse parents. Victims of child abuse can display a variety of problems both in the short term and as adults. When abuse is reported, the perpetrator may be charged, the child may be removed from the home, and the family may receive therapy.

PARTNER ABUSE. Violence between partners became a social concern more recently than did child abuse. Although there is disagreement about how serious a problem abuse of male partners is, in general men are less likely to be injured than women. Couple violence can begin before marriage, and it occurs more commonly among cohabiting couples than in more casual relationships. Victims of spousal abuse do not fit a single description. Perpetrators tend to accept traditional gender roles and use of violence as a method of control. Some women spend many years in an abusive relationship. They may be committed to the wife/mother role; they may also fear the consequences of leaving. In addition, they may feel powerless, and this feeling can be reinforced by society. Groups at particular risk include Aboriginal, immigrant, physically challenged, and isolated women. Abuse in gay and lesbian relationships appears to be similar to other forms of partner abuse. In the past, spousal assault was often considered a private matter. Now police are directed to charge abusers when there are reasonable grounds to do so. Although they do not meet the demand, shelters are available for abused women and their children.

ABUSE OF THE ELDERLY. Elder abuse has only recently received much attention. In addition to neglect and physical and sexual abuse, it also includes financial exploitation. Both partners and children may be perpetrators. In some families, elder abuse is part of a longstanding pattern of violence. In others, it may result from frustration with the needs of the older person, and the lack of resources and support to help the caregiver meet those needs. There is controversy over whether reporting elder abuse should be mandatory or whether it infringes on the rights of the older person.

WHY DO PEOPLE ABUSE FAMILY MEMBERS? Abusers have the same desires as other people, but use violent means to fulfill them. Four types of individuals using violence are the reactors, the entitled, the overwhelmed, and occasionally the psychiatrically impaired. No theory of abuse and neglect can fully explain family violence. The situational theory points to stress; social exchange theory to costs and benefits; symbolic interaction theory to the meaning given to events; family systems theory to intergenerational transmission of violence; feminists to imbalance of power; and societal theorists to cultural attitudes.

PREVENTING VIOLENCE. There are three basic approaches to prevention. The first is to treat abusers or separate them from their victims to keep the violence from happening again. The second is providing services to groups thought to be at risk. The third is to prevent violence altogether through education, or by encouraging society to be supportive to families.

KEY TERMS

abuse: a situation in which a person takes advantage of a less powerful person (p. 315)

incidence: percentage of cases in the population (p. 324)

infanticide: the murder of a baby (p. 315)

perinatal: around the time of birth (p. 317)

perpetrator: a person who is guilty of a crime, for example, abuse (p. 317)

second-stage housing: longer-term housing for abused women (p. 332)

sodomy: anal intercourse (p. 315)

violence: an act intended to physically hurt another person (p. 315)

CLASS ASSIGNMENTS

Complete one or both of the following assignments, as directed by your instructor:

1. What facilities exist in your community to assist abused women? Are they adequate? Why or why not? Are there gaps in the services available? Explain.

2. There are two basic approaches to dealing with families that abuse children. One is to leave the child in the home while the family receives treatment. The second is to remove the child from the home. Give the advantages and disadvantages of each approach.

PERSONAL ASSIGNMENTS

The following assignments are designed to help you think about your own experience:

1. Do you know anyone who is (was) abused? What effect has the abuse had on the individual, either in the short or the long term? How could the abuse have been prevented or stopped earlier?

2. Do you believe that reporting abuse of the elderly should be compulsory? Why do you think it should or should not be?

© Leah-Anne Thompson/ShutterStock

Chapter 15

Poverty and the Family

OBJECTIVES

- To place poverty in Canada in historical perspective
- To look at poverty among specific groups of the poor
- To consider the characteristics of the poor
- To look at how families in poverty do or do not make ends meet
- To look at homelessness in Canada
- To examine the effect of poverty on children
- To consider ways of combating poverty

In August 2001, Kimberly Rogers of Sudbury, Ontario, took an overdose of medication and killed both herself and her unborn baby. In April, she had been convicted of welfare fraud for receiving both student loans and social assistance. She was sentenced to six months' house arrest, allowed out of her stifling apartment only to go to church and doctors' appointments and for three additional hours a week. She also had to repay more than $13 000 in benefits and lost the right to have part of her student loan forgiven. Finally, she was immediately banned from receiving any further social assistance for three months. She appealed her conviction under the Charter of Rights and Freedoms, arguing, among other things, that she was denied the right to life because she had no income and that the penalty was cruel and unusual punishment. The judge temporarily restored her benefits, but did not alter the house arrest. Once 10 percent of her social assistance was deducted as repayment, she had only $18 a month beyond rent for food and other needs.

Her death raised a furor of controversy. Should she have been cut off from assistance, considering she was pregnant? Were levels of welfare and student loans enough to live on? Is deprivation of basic needs a suitable penalty for any crime? Should people committing welfare fraud be given a second chance like other criminals? How can government stop welfare cheats and use public money responsibly?

There are two further developments concerning Kimberly Rogers and welfare fraud. In December 2002, the coroner's jury at her inquest recommended that social assistance staff be given authority to make exceptions when a person's life could be threatened, and also that a person under house arrest be assured adequate housing, food, and medications. In the meantime, Ontario regulations were changed to ban anyone guilty of welfare fraud from receiving benefits, not for only three months, but for life (Disabled Women's Network Ontario, 2002; Keck, 2002; Sarlo, 2003).

Most poor people do not commit suicide or die of starvation. Yet they may have serious difficulties making ends meet. In general, poverty is defined almost entirely in terms of income. Financial levels alone do not accurately reflect the ability of some people to manage better than others the money they have available. For example, some are able to grow or gather food to supplement what they can buy. Others have developed shrewd management skills. Yet most families require a certain minimum level of income to create satisfying lives in our society.

There are two basic ways of defining poverty. One is to consider what it would take to provide what is absolutely necessary for physical survival. The most extreme definition would apply to the family that uses food banks, hostels, and second-hand clothing to survive, and receives only the most basic health care. Historically this has been the kind of criterion used in deciding whether someone needed social assistance. The other approach to defining poverty is based on social well-being in addition to physical survival. Most measures of poverty in Canada use the latter type of definition (Hunter, 2003).

HELPING THE "WORTHY" POOR

In the early years, the poor depended almost entirely on their families or on other private individuals for help. Until World War I, public assistance was provided by local governments or charities on an emergency basis only. Most of the help involved the provision of grocery hampers, second-hand clothing, and vouchers for fuel. Very little cash was provided, partly because poverty was believed to result from bad budgeting (along with a variety of vices, such as drinking). It was generally felt that help should be at a level lower than the earnings of the most poorly paid labourer, so that handouts were barely enough to survive on. The notion that asking for help should be so unpleasant that a person who did not need it would not ask also prevailed. For example, homeless elderly people were kept in local jails on charges of vagrancy because there was no other place they could go. Some places demanded that people live in a workhouse if they were to receive assistance (Guest, 1985).

Gradually what is called the **social safety net** began to develop. Mothers' pensions (later called mothers' allowances) were set up to help needy children. However, eligibility depended on the mother. The criteria varied from province to province. In British Columbia, for example, mothers were eligible if their husbands were in a tuberculosis sanatorium, mental hospital, or prison, or if they themselves were chronically ill, disabled, or widowed. Applicants had to be of good character (even having to provide letters of reference) and had to pass a strict **means test** to prove that they needed help. Once they received the allowance, such mothers were subject to intrusion into their personal lives—no man could live in the house (except a close relative) and permission was needed to move from city to country or vice versa. In 1927, old age pensions were established for the needy, again subject to a strict means test (Guest, 1985).

Beginning around the time of World War I, the idea of a social security net for all began to take hold, although it developed slowly. By the 1920s, workers' compensation and minimum-wage legislation had come into being. Following World War II, the pace of change picked up—family allowances, universal old age pensions, medical insurance, and the Canada and Quebec Pension Plans were adopted. There continue to be services provided to those with low incomes, for example, the Guaranteed Income Supplement for the elderly and pensions for the disabled. To receive these, individuals or families must pass a means test, administered either by service providers or through income tax returns. The responsibility for providing social programs shifted from the municipality to the provincial and federal governments by means of cost-sharing arrangements (Guest, 1985). Recently the movement has been in the other direction, with more weight placed on provincial and local governments. In order to reduce the cost of providing universal programs, the government has established what is called the clawback, benefits defined as income and then taxed.

POVERTY, OFFICIALLY DEFINED

Currently, poverty is considered in relation to the income of the "average" Canadian. One of the most commonly used definitions is the Statistics Canada low income cutoff point, which is updated annually. This takes into account family size, up to seven members, and community size. The poverty lines are set at a level where a family spends significantly more of its income on food, clothing, and shelter than the average family (see Table 15.1). These cutoff points are artificial (Hunter, 2003). A family with an income 10 percent above the poverty line could afford only a couple of extra bus tickets or cups of coffee per day more than those at the poverty line.

TABLE 15.1

LOW INCOME CUTOFFS (1992 BASE), 2003 AFTER TAX

Community Size

	Rural Areas	Less than 30 000	30 000– 99 999	100 000– 499 999	500 000+
1 person	$10 718	$12 389	$13 558	$13 771	$16 348
2 persons	13 079	15 118	16 544	16 803	19 948
3 persons	16 542	19 120	20 924	21 252	25 230
4 persons	20 603	23 814	26 061	26 469	31 424
5 persons	23 028	26 616	29 127	29 584	35 122
6 persons	25 453	29 418	32 193	32 699	38 820
7 or more persons	27 878	32 220	35 259	35 814	42 519

Source: Adapted from Statistics Canada, "Low income cut offs from 1994–2003 and low-income measures, 1992–2001." 1992–2003, no. 2. Catalogue 75F0002, March 6, 2004.

Two factors that influence the impact of poverty on families are its depth and its duration. Depth of poverty refers to the amount a family or individual income is below the poverty line. The further below, the more difficult it is to provide the basic needs. Duration or persistence refers to how long the poverty lasts. Short-term low income is easier to weather than prolonged periods because individuals usually have some resources to help tide them over a bad period. When poverty is prolonged, however, everyday resources are eventually depleted and need to be renewed. For example, income could initially be used almost entirely for food and living expenses. Eventually it must stretch to cover replacement costs for clothing and for household supplies such as furniture, bedding, and towels. Thus, the longer poverty lasts, the harder it is for the family to make ends meet (National Council of Welfare, 2004; Ross, Scott, & Smith, 2000).

WHO ARE THE POOR?

For several reasons, determining the number of poor people in Canada is difficult. First, the total depends on the definition used. Second, the very poorest of the poor are almost impossible to count because they include the homeless.

Poverty rates have varied with the economy. In the 1960s, the poverty rates were higher than now. In the mid- to late 1970s, they began to fall and reached a low point in 1978. The year 1981 saw the beginning of a recession, and poverty levels rose in the next years; with economic improvement, the rates dropped again to the 1981 levels. Following yet another recession, the economy picked up once more by 1997. Nevertheless, poverty levels remained above those in 1981 and 1989. By 2001, poverty rates fell to about 1980 levels (National Council of Welfare, 2004; Ross et al., 2000).

Poverty rates are lowest for families with two or more earners. They are also relatively low for married or common-law couples. The rate rises, however, for two-parent families with one earner. Single-adult households are even more likely to be poor. Those headed by women are most likely to be poor. Unattached women and women in lone-parent families are more likely than others to remain poor for an extended time. Men in single-adult households also experience long-term poverty, but not to the same extent as women (Lochhead & Scott, 2000).

As far as numbers are concerned, four groups stand out—young unattached people, older women, female-headed single-parent families, and one-earner couples with children. In every working-age group, those most likely to be poor are younger, have lower levels of education, and are less likely to hold full-time jobs. Women, especially young women, are likelier than men to remain poor longer. Those who do move out of poverty tend to go from a one-adult to a two-adult two-earner household. Those who move from a two-adult to a one-adult household risk becoming poor (Lochhead & Scott, 2000; National Council of Welfare, 2004; Ross et al., 2000).

There has been a decrease in poverty among the elderly as a result of improved pensions and government benefits. The majority receive most of their income from public programs. If the individual was employed, Canada or Quebec Pension Plans provide an income. Old Age Security is paid to all seniors, although it is subject to clawback at higher income levels. For those with low incomes, benefits are also provided through the Guaranteed Income Supplement. The combination of these income sources has served to move many older people above the poverty line. A large number, however, are among the near-poor. Many of the elderly poor are women. They are less likely to have contributed to the Canada or the Quebec Pension Plan and are more dependent on the Supplement (National Council of Welfare, 2004; Ross et al., 2000).

Minority Groups and Poverty

In 1995, among Aboriginal people, 43.4 percent were poor in contrast to 19.3 percent of all Canadians. Rates of poverty were highest, over 50 percent, in Saskatchewan and Manitoba (Ross et al., 2000). Their average income was half that of non-Aboriginal families ($12 000 in contrast to $25 000). The 45 best-off Aboriginal communities, mainly in southern Ontario and coastal British Columbia, had educational and income standards similar to those in the poorest regions in non-Aboriginal parts of Canada. A number of factors contribute to their low income—lower levels of education, fewer jobs, and more lone-parent families (Armstrong, 1999; Castellano, 2002).

Immigrants who have been in Canada less than five years have a greater risk of poverty (35.8 percent in 2000), especially in large cities. Entry-level jobs, which many immigrants must take, are usually low paying. In addition, there has been a swing toward self-employment, difficult for newcomers without connections. Those who come from countries with language and customs very different from Canada may have the most difficulty finding well-paying jobs (Chui & Zietsma, 2003; Heisz & McLeod, 2004; Picot & Hou, 2003).

In 2001, 33 percent of Canadians with disabilities aged 15 to 64 had income under $10 000 a year (below the poverty line), compared with 23.5 percent of those without disabilities. Often their costs of living are higher than average because of their special needs. Their employment levels, on the other hand, are lower than for other Canadians. Only 49.3 percent of those aged 25 to 54 held jobs in 2001, in contrast to 82.3 percent of those without disabilities (Statistics Canada, 2003b, with calculations by the author). Studies of the deaf community point to their difficulties in finding employment. Between 60 and 70 percent of deaf people in Canada are functionally illiterate, that is, unable to read or write everyday materials (Griffiths & Cruise, 1999). Because of lower educational levels, they are streamed into jobs with low wages, few benefits, and little opportunity for a better position. In addition, they face stereotypes about deaf persons, which isolate them even further (Canadian Hearing Society, 2002).

What Is Beyond the Numbers?

One of the most striking facts about poverty in Canada is that many people who live in poverty have jobs. In 2001, poor people who received at least half their income from a job accounted for 49 percent of all non-elderly poor families and 57 percent of poor unattached individuals. Who is the typical working-poor family? They most likely live in a city in Ontario; they have not had as much schooling as their more affluent neighbours; they have more children (even the family with one or two children is twice as likely to be poor as a childless couple); they are probably young, with parents aged 25 to 44; and they are likely to have only one employed family member. The non-poor are far more likely to have two or more adult earners. In poor families with one child, even if both parents work full time at the minimum wage, the family will still fall below the poverty line. Obviously single parents are at an even greater disadvantage (National Council of Welfare, 2004; Ross et al., 2000).

Market poverty, that is, poverty based on wages alone, has grown. There are several reasons. First, many jobs do not pay well enough to allow even full-time workers to support families. Adding to the problem is low income from self-employment and part-time work. Second, unemployment has been high, although it has eased recently. The official numbers do not count those who became discouraged, or the ones wanting full-time work but only finding part-time. In 1997, it took longer to find a job than in 1981—an average of 22.3 weeks in contrast to 15.1 weeks. In addition, the eligibility rules for employment insurance became stricter. Third, some individuals experienced special barriers in finding and holding jobs. For many parents, especially women, it costs less to stay home with children once childcare, transportation, and other employment-related costs are taken into account. Many people with disabilities are able and willing to work. The lack of affordable transportation and inability or unwillingness of employers to redesign jobs or provide flexible hours set up barriers. A growing number of older workers aged 55 to 64 are retired or "voluntarily idle."

They may, however, have little choice over early retirement. Others have been laid off. These older people have problems finding employment because they are competing against younger workers with more education and more up-to-date job skills (Cheal, 1998; Ross et al., 2000; Schellenberg & Silver, 2004).

When families do not have jobs and are not eligible for employment insurance, they turn to social assistance. Welfare rates in all provinces are well below the low income cutoff (National Council of Welfare, n.d.). Yet, for some families, add-ons like drug and dental care make welfare preferable to low-paying jobs without such benefits (Sayeed, 1999).

Often income does not cover families' living costs. How do they cope? Many food bank users in the Toronto area did not have a telephone, walked rather than using a bus, relied on charities, borrowed money, and were given money and food by family or friends. Most stated they went hungry at least once a month and half said that their children did too (Michalski, 2003). An American study of single mothers surviving on welfare and low-wage work describes several strategies. First choice was financial help from the child's father or the current live-in boyfriend. Second was asking relatives for help. The amount they could expect, however, was limited because such assistance usually demands a return of favours. Third choice was to take a side job, taking cash and not reporting the income. Some found a "real" job using false ID. In both cases, the extra money was not reported so that their welfare would not be cut. Going to an agency for help was near the bottom of the list. Last of all came selling sex, drugs, or stolen goods. Many women moved between the various strategies, using a new option when another dried up (Edin & Lein, 1997). There has been no study of the same scope in Canada, but undoubtedly people on welfare here use many of the same strategies.

A 1996 study of mid-sized Alberta cities found that poor families tended to pay somewhat less rent than average. Even then, many paid more than 30 percent of their income for accommodation (Lee & Engler, 1999). Cheaper housing near city cores is being "gentrified," that is, renovated into stylish and expensive homes costing far more than what the original residents can afford. Less subsidized housing is being produced. Most of what exists is available to families and seniors, with a small number reserved for those with disabilities. Usually, young unattached individuals are not eligible for such housing. Some people double up to save money. Many of the poor, however, must depend on the "for-profit" rental market (Caragata, 2003; Federation of Canadian Municipalities, 2000).

Since housing is so expensive, people with low incomes have to cut back in other ways. One area is food. Food insecurity is the uncertainty that people can buy enough nutritious food they like, or the actual inability to do so. Less money leads to less food and food of poorer quality. Children with poorer nutrition have more health problems and more school absences, and may have more difficulty concentrating in school. When food runs short, mothers tend to eat less or miss meals altogether so that they can feed their children. To fill the need, families turn to food banks, soup kitchens, and friends and relatives for help. Food banks and soup kitchens are especially common in Ontario, where they seem to be social institutions (McIntyre, Connor, & Warren, 1998). Unfortunately, supplies at food banks are often limited because they depend on donations. Users have little choice about what they will eat.

Sometimes people are limited as to amount or are even turned away when quantities run low. Actual hunger occurs much less often than food insecurity. On the basis of information from the National Longitudinal Survey of Children and Youth, however, researchers estimate that about 57 000 Canadian families occasionally have nothing to eat (McIntyre et al., 1998).

HOMELESSNESS

There are no exact figures for the number of homeless people in Canada. This is in part a result of the difficulty in counting them. It is also due to the fact that the homeless population changes from day to day and so do definitions of homelessness. A head count of people staying in shelters was conducted on January 22, 1987 (during the Year of the Homeless), in which 305 shelters participated. Using the average of these agencies, it was estimated that 10 672 people spent that night in a shelter. Of course, the homeless who did not use a shelter remained uncounted (McLaughlin, 1987). The uncounted include those staying with friends and those sleeping in cars or doorways (Caragata, 2003). Later, Statistics Canada tried unsuccessfully to count the homeless during the 1991 census (Begin, Casavant, Chenier, & Dupuis, 1999).

Who are the homeless? The picture of the 1930s transient, unemployed man is no longer appropriate. Instead, the homeless include two-parent families, single parents and their children, single women, older persons, and young people. Among the homeless are psychiatric patients and individuals with disabilities. Many are receiving social assistance; some have low-paying jobs. There appear to be three different groups among the homeless: those who are chronically homeless and often have problems with drugs and alcohol; those who are cyclically homeless because of job loss, family violence, or release from prison, and may be repeaters; and those who are temporarily homeless for a relatively short time as a result of marital separation or a disaster like a fire (Begin et al., 1999).

About 30 percent of homeless people are women. Mother-headed lone-parent families appear to be most at risk, especially when they have few backup resources. They are usually less noticeable than men partly because they fear child protection services will take their children. Many also remain homeless for shorter periods because they exchange sex or housekeeping for accommodation. Such women have often experienced family breakdown or are escaping abuse. The number of young homeless people is increasing. These include those living in shelters with one or both parents as well as runaways, many of whom are escaping from abuse. Living on the streets, however, is also violent, especially for young people. The number of families needing emergency shelter appears to be growing. People of colour, especially Aboriginal people in prairie cities, are overrepresented among the homeless. Immigrants may also experience problems in finding housing (Begin et al., 1999; Caragata, 2003; Wingard, McCormack, & Neigh, 2003).

Most reasons given for the increase in homelessness are based on educated guesses. The shortage of affordable housing is a key reason, but it fails to explain the whole phenomenon. Changes in employment patterns mean that many men now using shelters found casual and seasonal labour in the past. Some people point to the policy of releasing psychiatric patients

Source: Reprinted by kind permission of Barrie Maguire.

from long-term care without providing adequate community resources. Still others suggest drug and alcohol abuse are factors. Most recently, changes in the eligibility for and levels of welfare are blamed (Begin et al., 1999).

Conditions in shelters do not favour family living. Men's shelters are generally worse than women's. Many of the latter are designed to house abused women. Some men's shelters are in old buildings, including former warehouses and factories. There is little privacy because beds are in dormitories. Lice, dirt, and odour are common. Often shelters lack privacy, and other residents and staff members may interfere with how a parent cares for her child (Anderson & Koblinsky, 1995; Caragata, 2003; Novac, Brown, & Bourbonnais, 1996).

WHAT IS POVERTY DOING TO CHILDREN?

Children make up the largest single group of the poor people in Canada—1 065 000 in 2002, nearly one in six children. In 1989 (when 14.4 percent of children were poor), the federal House of Commons passed a resolution to eliminate child poverty by the year 2000. This has not happened. The rate reached a high of 21.3 percent in 1993 and has hovered around the 20 percent level since then. Although most poor children are members of two-parent families, a growing proportion has single mothers (see Table 15.2). The lack of accessible and affordable housing and high-quality daycare also contribute to the problem. Child poverty in Canada is higher than in most western European countries, though not as high as in New Zealand or the United States (Campaign 2000, 2004; Ross et al., 2000; UNICEF, 2005).

Poverty influences the family and community environments in which a child grows up. Poor children are twice as likely as others to live in poorly functioning families. Parents are more likely to be depressed and to carry the emotional scars of their own parents' divorce, substance abuse, or violence. Since they are under chronic stress from poverty, poor parents are

TABLE 15.2

CHILD POVERTY BY FAMILY TYPE, 2001

	Number of Children	Poverty Rate
All poor children	1 071 000	15.6%
Poor children in two-parent families	611 000	10.8%
Poor children with single parent	386 000	45.4%

Source: National Council of Welfare, 2004, p. 111, Table 8.3. Reproduced with the permission of the Minister of Public Works and Government Services Canada, 2005.

more likely than non-poor to be distracted or hostile in their parenting. Families often move as a result of marriage breakup or as a result of job loss or change. They may also look for better or more affordable housing. Poor children are twice as likely as others to live in substandard housing. Apartments are often crowded and uninviting for play or study (Jones et al., 2002; Pinderhughes, Nix, Foster, Jones, et al., 2001; Ross & Roberts, 1999; Statistics Canada, 2005d).

The community is also important. Children interact with peers and adults, learning values and forming social and helping networks. Poor children are more likely than others to live in neighbourhoods with at least one serious problem. These include drug use and dealing, excessive public drinking, burglaries, youth delinquency, unrest arising from racial or religious prejudice, and littering of garbage and glass. Twice as many poor parents as non-poor feel their neighbourhood is unsafe. When parents believe their neighbourhood is unsafe, children are not allowed out alone to play. Thus, they are limited in their ability to form relationships and learn social skills (Jarrett & Jefferson, 2004; Ross & Roberts, 1999).

Children's behaviour, health, school learning, and recreational activities are all affected by income levels. Behaviour, as we saw in Chapter 6, is shaped by the child's temperament and by the adults and peers with whom he or she interacts. Negative behaviours are signs of trouble ahead. Poor children are more likely than non-poor to be considered troublemakers, to have emotional problems, to be hyperactive and inattentive in school, to engage in delinquent ways (lying, cheating, stealing, vandalizing), and to hang around with children in trouble with the law (Ross & Roberts, 1999).

Children in low-income families also tend to have poorer health. Their health can be affected even before birth. When money is tight, the food budget often suffers and with it the health of children. Babies with low birth weight are more commonly born to low-income mothers than to more affluent ones. This is associated with a greater number of birth defects and higher infant mortality (McIntyre et al., 1998; Tipper & Avard, 1999). The effects of poverty continue into school age. Poor children suffer a wide range of health problems. Often they have inadequate nutrition that lacks essential vitamins. If a family lives in substandard or crowded housing, children may be exposed to more illnesses to which they are less resistant because of their diet. Children in poor families have more problems with hearing, vision, speech, physical mobility and dexterity, and pain and discomfort (Ross & Roberts, 1999).

Poor children are often not as ready for school as others, partly because of limited experiences, partly because of physical and health difficulties (Tipper & Avard, 1999). This shows up in vocabulary development in preschoolers, reading difficulties, and the need for special education. More children repeat grades and drop out without completing high school. Few go on to postsecondary education. There are several reasons for this. Since they are ill more frequently, poor children miss more time from school and may have trouble catching up. If they go to school hungry, they may also have difficulty concentrating on class activities. Crowded homes may mean there is no suitable place for homework and studying. When housing is substandard, poor families tend to move more often. As a result, children lose time having to adapt to new schools and different curriculums. They may be stigmatized if they cannot pay for school outings and activities or if they wear unfashionable clothes. For many children, schooling is so unpleasant that dropping out is a relief. One in six teens from low-income families is neither in school nor employed. Such teens are at much greater risk of getting in trouble with the law, of abusing alcohol and drugs, and of becoming poor adults in their turn (Ross & Roberts, 1999).

Both income and community recreational facilities affect how much children are involved in sports and cultural activities. The cost of sports equipment and fees, of musical instruments and lessons, for example, limit their participation. If there are no free or cheap well-run play or sports facilities nearby, there are further barriers. Fewer children in low-income families play unorganized sports, for example pick-up hockey at a neighbourhood rink. Children in low-income families thus miss out on learning skills and social competence (Ross & Roberts, 1999).

At the bottom end of the poverty scale are homeless children. American studies have found that health, psychological, behavioural, and educational effects are similar to those of other poor children, but more extreme. Many of these children see life as temporary. People, places, and schools come and go. So do families. Many homeless children are separated from parents and/or brothers and sisters. Some stay with relatives; a few are put in foster care. With impermanence a fact of life, there is no urge to complete school projects. Homeless children have not developed a sense of their space or possessions. If they ever had any toys, they have been lost or stolen along the way. Thus many lack the experiences with toys and places that help develop a knowledge of size, colour, and spatial relationships (Anderson & Koblinsky, 1995; Gewirtzman & Fodor, 1987; Maza & Hall, 1988).

WHAT CAN BE DONE?

Providing people with adequate income is clearly the answer to poverty. The question is how this goal should be achieved. We will look at three suggestions.

1. *Create jobs.* The best form of social security is to have a job and support oneself. Recently there has been moderate economic growth but the increase in jobs has been confined only to certain parts of the economy, such as information technology. In an attempt to be globally competitive, companies are using labour outside the country

and/or providing employment for only limited periods (e.g., contract work). Many Canadians are unemployed even though they want to work. No amount of retraining will get them back into the workforce if jobs are not there. Job creation has been a goal set forth by both federal and provincial governments. Many of the jobs for new employees that have been created, however, pay low wages, are often part time or temporary, and offer no benefits like health plans or pensions. To succeed, job training and employment assistance need to be long term and geared to occupations needing workers (Lochhead & Scott, 2000; Morissette & Johnson, 2005).

2. *Increase social assistance.* Some people wish to provide an adequate income through direct grants. This approach has been rejected by provincial governments. British Columbia, for example, has made it harder to qualify for welfare and has placed a two-year limit on receiving it (Michael & Rietsma-Street, 2002). There has recently been a change in focus to providing social assistance. In 1998, the federal government, using funds from other programs, set up the National Child Benefit. All families with incomes less than a specified amount are eligible for the benefit, whether this income comes from welfare or employment. Some provinces deduct the amount from the welfare paid to families in order to fund other programs. Some provide extra money to families moving from welfare into the workforce. Others provide noncash services like school nutrition and "head start" education for preschoolers. It is too early, however, to tell how much this program will reduce family poverty (Sayeed, 1999).

3. *Workfare.* **Workfare** is the policy of requiring able-bodied welfare recipients to train for a job or to work. People who support workfare point out that some families do better financially on welfare than by taking a job. Thus there is no incentive for them to become responsible for themselves financially. Workfare would eventually reduce their reliance on social assistance. For example, both Ontario and British Columbia cut welfare rates and changed eligibility to make working a better deal than welfare. Both provide financial help to low-income working families, especially those moving off welfare (Goldberg, 1999; Ontario Ministry of Community and Social Services, 2000; Snyder, 2003). Those who oppose workfare point out difficulties in such programs. Single parents, one of the largest groups receiving welfare, are considered ready for work when their children are younger than in the past—as early as six months in Alberta. This is not accompanied by adequate childcare subsidies. Job training and placement programs are usually short term and result in low-paying employment, so that families are no better off. Programs punish welfare recipients who do not actively look for or find work by cutting their benefits. On average, people leaving welfare during the 1990s increased their income. Marriage helped single women, in particular, to leave poverty. For about one-third of welfare leavers, however, family income declined. Many people who left welfare returned to the system, usually temporarily (Frenette & Picot, 2003).

Whatever solution or combination of solutions is chosen, moving families out of poverty is a complex and difficult task. Yet it must be tackled, especially for the benefit of children.

SUMMARY

WHAT IS POVERTY? Two ways have commonly been used to define poverty. The first uses as a standard the minimum amount of money required to ensure physical survival. The second is based on the standard of social well-being. In North America, the focus was initially on providing the barest essentials to the deserving poor. Often this was given by charitable groups. Gradually the government provided more income-support services, and today the definition of poverty is closer to the well-being standard. One of the most used definitions is the Statistics Canada low income cutoffs.

WHO ARE THE POOR? There are four principal groups of poor people. Older women often have not been employed and are solely dependent on the government pension. Young adults aged 16 to 24 are affected by the shift of employment from well-paying areas to poorer-paying consumer services. Often these jobs are part time. Young working couples make up a third group. These tend to be single-earner families with several children. The hardest hit are female-headed single-parent families, especially young mothers. Those with low educational levels tend to be the worst off. Other groups with extremely high poverty levels are Aboriginal peoples, visible minorities, and people with disabilities.

COPING WITH POVERTY. Those supported by welfare or low-paying jobs use various strategies: help from family and friends, unreported work, and occasionally illegal activities. The situation of the poor is made worse by the lack of affordable housing. With much of their income going for shelter, individuals have little left for food and other essentials. There has been an increase in the use of food banks during the last several years.

HOMELESSNESS. Estimates of the number of homeless vary widely. Shelter residents are a diverse population. Shelter conditions do not favour family living, both because of the lack of privacy and because some residents have problems that disturb others. Often shelters are a last resort after several moves.

POVERTY AND CHILDREN. Children are the largest single group of poor people. Poverty affects both health and education. Since so much of family income goes for shelter, nutrition may be inadequate and resistance to illness low. Substandard and crowded housing may expose children to more illnesses. Many children from low-income families do poorly in school. This tendency may be linked to both health and living conditions. Many who drop out of school have poor job prospects and continue poverty into a new generation. Children in shelters suffer health, educational, and emotional difficulties more severe than other poor children.

WHAT CAN BE DONE? A number of remedies that address parts of the problem have been suggested. These include job creation, targeting social assistance to special groups of families with children, and workfare.

means test: a method of screening applicants to ensure that only those who need financial assistance receive it (p. 344)

social safety net: basic social security programs needed to support family life (p. 344)

workfare: policy of requiring able-bodied welfare recipients to train for a job or to work (p. 353)

CLASS ASSIGNMENTS

Complete one or both of the following assignments, as directed by your instructor:

1. Many students live in poverty. What strategies do they use to make money go further? Would these strategies work for a family over a long period of time? Explain.

2. What is the minimum wage in your province? If a person works 40 hours per week, what will the take-home pay be after employment insurance, Canada Pension Plan, and taxes (if any) are deducted? How much will have to go for rent (a) for a single person and (b) for a single parent with one child? Draw up a budget to cover other costs such as food, clothing, transportation, and childcare. What occasional expenses may occur? How will they be met?

PERSONAL ASSIGNMENTS

The following assignments are designed to help you think about your own experience:

1. On the basis of your own experience or that of people you know, explain the differences between those living on a low income who manage reasonably well financially and those who have extreme financial difficulties.

2. Describe what you feel are the effects of poverty on the parent–child relationship. Explain your answer.

Part Seven

THE FUTURE OF CANADIAN FAMILIES

CHAPTER 16
The Crystal Ball—
Predicting the Future
of the Family

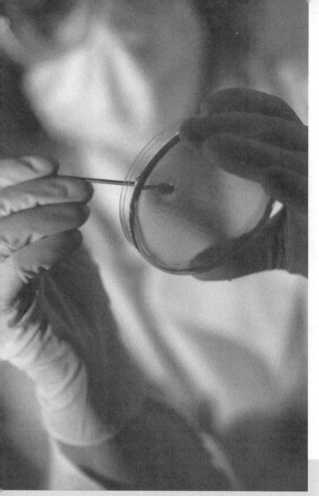

Chapter 16

The Crystal Ball—Predicting the Future of the Family

OBJECTIVES

- *To consider the implications for the future of an aging population*

- *To look at what forms families will likely take in the future and what changes in roles will follow*

- *To consider the impact of technology on the family*

- *To examine the impact of government policies on families*

2025:

[The elderly] now live in the Eaton Centre, which was converted from a shopping centre a few years back. What is left of its open space retains something of the building's original character; it is now the city's central bartamart.

It is spring, and New Class Action is making a last effort to influence the retirement referendum.... The generation of the post-Second-World-War baby boom is the core of this last-ditch move to restore retirement pensions, but now for the first time they are fighting a younger portion of the electorate that is almost as numerous as they are and much brighter and better organized—a population that most definitely does not want to support the millions who could lay claim to a pension.

Source: "The Big Generation," John Kettle, 1980, p. 16. Reprinted with permission of the author.

What will the Canadian family look like in 10 years? In 30 years? Will we be able to recognize it as a family? Will families even exist at the beginning of the 22nd century? Or will the forms we already know survive?

We can make educated guesses about the future of the family by looking at several factors: in particular, statistical trends, recent government policies, and activist hot points. Such predictions are more likely to be accurate one or two years down the road rather than 10, 30, or 40. We can even attempt to explain what these trends may mean in terms of family experiences, but this is shakier ground. There are so many unknowns in the situation that in 20 years predictions made today may seem absolute foolishness. In spite of that risk, let's look into the crystal ball to try to ascertain the future of the family.

AN AGING POPULATION

Unless there is a catastrophe that kills off senior citizens or a massive increase in births, Canadians can expect the population as a whole to become older. Two major factors working together will produce this trend: first, the changing birth rate, and second, advances in medical technology. In the past 50 years, there have been large swings in the birth rate. From the end of World War II until the early 1960s, the rate was high—the so-called baby boom. The older members of this generation are moving out of childbearing age. By 2026, they will be aged 60 to 80, and many will have retired. The boom was followed by a "baby bust." The birth rate has now dropped below the level necessary to replace the population. These trends are working together to push up the average age of Canadians (George, Loh, Verma, & Shin, 2001).

Advances in medical technology have also had their impact at both ends of life. The development of relatively easy and safe contraceptives has made it easier to avoid having children. More women now have children later in life, have fewer than in the past, or have none at all. At the other end of life, people are living longer. The oldest old, those over 80, make up the fastest-growing age group. Combined with the numbers of the big generation, the increased life span will magnify the effects of the dropping birth rate (George et al., 2001).

What Does an Old Population Mean?

The aging of the population will have a number of consequences in the future. There are several practical questions. Who will support the growing number of seniors? As they become frail, who will look after them? What new or expanded services will be needed? How much will the costs of medical care increase as seniors age? How will such costs be covered? In sum, who will care for the elderly as they become frailer and how will this care be paid for?

Private pensions have improved, both in availability and level of benefits. Seniors are also covered by the Canada Pension Plan. Many have saved additional money. Thus many people, especially the "young old," are paying much of their own way. There is no guarantee, however, that this situation will continue. The job market for young people is insecure. Service jobs, like caring for the elderly, have increased but do not pay well. Because many have only temporary or part-time work and others are self-employed, pensions may be low or nonexistent. Taxes pay for other benefits—medical care, Old Age Security, and the Guaranteed Income Supplement. The taxes seniors pay on their incomes do not meet the actual costs of pensions and medical care, especially as they become frailer. Thus, the tax burden will fall increasingly on the smaller working population who can less readily afford the cost.

Personal care, in the past, was primarily provided by families. It still is, although there has been growing reliance on seniors' residences and nursing homes. As the population ages, the demand for housing and residential care for the elderly will increase. There has been a move away from institutional care. Should more facilities be built? After all, the need will be temporary, as was the need for more and larger schools while the baby boom passed through the educational system. Should more services be offered to keep seniors living in the community and to assist family members in their care? Yet with more women—traditionally the caregivers—in the workforce, family members may not be able to provide needed care (Cranswick, 2003; Neysmith, 2003; Williams, 2004).

The aging of the population has had an unexpected benefit for families. More generations are alive now than at any other time in history. Children nowadays are more likely to know their grandparents and great-grandparents than ever before (Connidis, 2001). The multi-generation extended family provides continuity by passing on traditions and family history, but it may also mean more demands placed on younger relatives.

DIFFERENT TYPES OF FAMILIES

The "traditional" family—husband, wife, and their biological children—has been considered the norm in Canadian society, although there have always been variations on the theme, for instance, never-married individuals living alone or with relatives, widowed parents and their children, and childless couples. Since the late 1960s, however, the numbers of these "different" family forms have shown a marked increase, a trend that is expected to continue into the future.

More people live alone now than in the past. The increase has been greatest among older women. Women are outliving their husbands in greater numbers. They are able to live alone rather than with family members because of the improvement in pensions. This trend will probably continue. At the other end, younger people are finding it harder to establish themselves financially. Thus they will probably continue to delay marriage and may continue living with their parents. Or they may return following a job loss or divorce. Unless economic times improve markedly, these trends will also probably continue (Statistics Canada, 2002d).

Marriage patterns are changing. Unmarried cohabitation has increased. Although often this is a prelude to marriage, many of these relationships are temporary. This group also includes relationships between homosexual individuals. The meaning of marriage itself appears to be changing. In the past, it marked the union of one man and one woman, with the purpose (among others) of having and raising children. Bearing children outside marriage has become increasingly common (LeBourdais & Lapierre-Adamcyk, 2004). Divorce and remarriage have increased. Gay and lesbian groups have been successfully pressuring the government to legalize same-sex marriages (Lahey & Alderson, 2004). The ban against polygamy has been questioned (Macdonald, 1999). However, despite the many challenges, the ideal in our society of one relationship at a time (serial monogamy) remains constant.

Children's living situations have changed. Marriages are now occurring later in life and most children are born to married couples. As a result, children have older parents than in the recent past and fewer siblings. This lack is offset by the number of living grandparents. Many children live with just one parent, either because their parents never married or because they have separated or divorced. This is a change from as recently as the 1950s, when most single parents were widowed. More children now live in stepfamilies than in the past (Statistics Canada, 2002b). While it is true that many widowed parents remarried, the children in such families were not faced with the conflicting loyalties of having a parent outside

We're to be married today, today!

Source: Reprinted by kind permission of Barrie Maguire.

of the home. Most children also have both parents in the workforce and are socialized by a variety of caregivers.

Since 1967, immigration patterns have changed. The number of individuals coming from Europe and countries with populations of European origin has dropped, while the number coming from countries in Asia, Africa, the Caribbean, and Central and South America has increased. This trend will probably continue (Bélanger & Malenfant, 2005). The new immigrants have brought different traditions with them, including those involving the family. Some, for instance, rely more strongly on the extended family for social life and for practical and moral support. Also, a number of traditions encourage arranged marriages. Thus these immigrants and their children are contributing to the variety of family forms.

CHANGES IN FAMILY ROLES

A young person can no longer count on going through the "traditional" family life cycle, which includes marriage, having and raising children, the empty nest, and shared retirement and old age, with appropriate roles established for each phase. New stages are added as individuals cohabit, marry, separate, divorce, and re-couple. With second and third marriages, the social time clock is becoming more and more blurred. Parents may have two sets of children widely separated in age. New social scripts that specify behaviour appropriate for the new life stages are already emerging (Walsh, 2003a). A new law deals with legal issues surrounding assisted human reproduction (Hébert, Chenier, & Norris, 2004). In the future we can expect laws or court cases to clarify grey areas surrounding lone parenthood, remarriage, and stepfamilies. Societal pressure to respect the differences in families of racial, ethnic, and sexual minorities will continue. Also, there will be demands for social institutions such as schools and the legal system to be more sensitive to these differences.

There is increasing role flexibility between the sexes. The breadwinner husband and homemaker wife have become a minority of families as more and more women are working outside the home. The increase in the cost of living and high levels of unemployment call for at least two wage earners per family if the family is to avoid poverty. With high levels of separation and divorce, women can no longer depend on a spouse for lifelong financial support. Having a job provides a certain level of insurance. The responsibilities of both earning a living and looking after the home and children are shared by spouses, although often not equally. Advocates call for greater equality both in women's pay and in men's participation in homemaking. There is also pressure for more daycare and a greater variety in the forms it takes to better meet the needs of working parents and their children (Duxbury & Higgins, 2003; Krashinsky, 2001–2002).

Children will have more parent figures in the coming years. These will of course include the biological parents, but parents' lovers, adults with whom the mother or father share accommodation, surrogate mothers, stepparents, babysitters, and daycare personnel may be added. As a result, the socialization of children may be less strongly under their parents' control, even though they may choose many of the socializers. Experts disagree over the effect this trend will have on children.

Although at the moment the two forms exist side by side, there appears to be a basic shift in society from a **patrilineal** to a **matrilineal** family organization (Segalen, 1986); that is, kinship is being counted through the mother rather than the father. In "traditional" families, patrilineal descent is reflected in the wife's taking the husband's name at marriage and in the desire to give birth to a son "to carry on the family name." When parents divorce, custody of the children is now usually awarded to mothers. The number of mothers with custody is swelled by the number of never-married mothers. When mothers remarry, children acquire a new father figure with a new set of relatives; they may even take his name. Through all the family changes the children experience, the connection with the mother's extended family is the most enduring.

TECHNOLOGY AND FAMILY LIFE

In the 1940s and 1950s, forecasters predicted a robot in every turn-of-the-century home to look after all the drudgery—dishes, meals, cleaning, laundry—without the close supervision of the homemaker. In spite of the influx of dishwashers, automatic washers and dryers, central vacuums, and microwaves, this prediction has obviously not been fulfilled. Yet, as we have seen, technology, including contraceptives, reproductive technologies, and other medical breakthroughs, has had and will continue to have a great impact on families. There are reports of advances in genetic engineering that may provide cures for currently untreatable diseases. Yet, these advances raise questions about the ethics of cloning and experimentation on human embryos (Freundlich, 2001).

One of the most profound influences on families is in the area of communications technology. We have already discussed how computers and telecommunications have made it possible for people to work from home, and how children are affected by television and the Internet (Fraenkel, 2003; Walsh, 2001). But there is concern over the effect of these technologies on family relationships. Certainly, some individuals spend long hours surfing the Internet or engaging in discussions, some quite intimate, in online chat rooms. When this occurs, family relationships may suffer and fade through lack of interaction. Indeed, some people escape from their problems by turning to Internet relationships that are not as demanding. In fact, there are even suggestions that Internet sex counts as adultery (Rust & McPhee, 2001). Some individuals are concerned that the growth in computer use in families may undermine parents' authority because many children have gained more expertise than their parents (Bold, 2001; Lindlof, 1992). This situation is similar to that of immigrant families where children interpret the new language for their parents.

Yet, communications technology can also help keep families in touch. Busy working parents use pagers and cellular phones so that they can always be available if their children need them and to check up on their children's activities. Telephones, fax machines, recorded messages; all keep distant family members in contact. E-mail and voice communication over the Internet are also rapidly becoming important ways families communicate. In fact, for many, e-mail is replacing regular mail; it is faster and doesn't require a trip to the mailbox (English-Lueck, 2001). In 2003, nearly 55 percent of Canadian households regularly used e-mail or the Internet and the number is growing rapidly (Statistics Canada, 2004d). Because of its growth, communications technology will continue to affect families into the future. What that effect will be depends on the people who use it.

THE FAMILY IN SOCIETY

All families are affected by laws and government policies. We will look in turn at the impact of governments on changing definitions of the family and on the rights and responsibilities of family members. We will also consider other areas we can expect government influence.

The December 2004 Supreme Court of Canada ruling that same-sex marriage is legal followed a growing number of provincial court decisions that banning such marriage violates the Charter of Rights and Freedoms ("Supreme Court Approves," 2004). Early the next year, the federal government introduced a bill to legalize same-sex marriage. The legislation came into effect on July 20, 2005. Many laws affecting families are based on a marriage model. This standard, however, does not fit many close relationships among adults. Such relationships include parents and adult children, siblings, and close friends, who share living expenses and household responsibilities. Alberta's *Adult Interdependent Relationships Act* is intended to apply to cohabitation, but might also affect a nonconjugal relationship, like that between parent and child. There are concerns, therefore, over the legal responsibilities of such adults (Bala, 2004).

Governments at all levels have changed regulations to increase the self-sufficiency of individuals, for example through changes in eligibility for employment insurance and welfare and through the establishment of workfare programs. Governments have also moved away from universal benefits and have shifted funds to help selected groups of people, such as poor families with children. Some examples are the clawback that reclaims part of the Old Age Security pension from more affluent individuals, and the shift from a family allowance paid for each child to the Child Tax Credit, which provides larger sums to poorer families. There is also increased emphasis on financial responsibility for family members, for example making parents legally liable for their children's vandalism (Cheal, 1998). The responsibility does not end with family breakup. For example, the Supreme Court of Canada found a divorced man liable for supporting a stepchild who lived with him during his marriage to her mother, even after the marriage breakup (*Chartier v. Chartier*, 1999). Cynics suggest that the notion of recognizing a larger range of close relationships comes from a desire to shift further financial responsibility onto relatives and close friends.

The efforts of federal and provincial governments to reduce deficits are placing more responsibility on family members for the physical care of relatives. Since most adults are employed, this need conflicts with workplace demands. If families are to cope, they will need more community services, such as home nursing and relief help (Neysmith, 2003). The price of providing these is much lower than the cost of residential care, but it is still not clear whether governments will provide adequate funding.

There are others areas where we can expect official control. First, in spite of the new law, grey areas in assisted human reproduction will certainly continue to arise. Changes in laws will undoubtedly be recommended to deal with these issues. Second, we can expect society to be more involved in regulating particular family relationships. Increasingly, homes are developing "see-through walls." Children are cared for by non-family members either in or out of the children's homes. Social services are available to seniors in their own homes. Concern that many children and adults alike are receiving substandard care by family members or other caregivers is growing. For example, there is debate over the issue of spanking. Pressure is also being exerted to make reporting of elder abuse mandatory.

THE UNKNOWNS

Any predictions made so far have been based on statistical trends in Canadian society, on current social activism, and on recent government laws and financial policies. These do not take into account many unknown influences that can produce profound changes. These include global factors such as widespread economic recessions, wars, or natural disasters (including epidemics such as AIDS). Political action within Canada has already affected families and will do so in the future. The direction of these changes is difficult to predict many years ahead. Immigration policies influence the age, family composition, origin, and occupation of various segments of the population. Social and economic policies at the federal, provincial, and municipal levels determine what services are available to families and who can benefit from them. Through taxation and income distribution programs like tax benefits and clawbacks, they will also affect the disposable income of families. Finally, it is impossible to predict the decisions of individuals and their families. Such decisions can have an enormous influence on society, as we have already experienced in the case of the baby-boom generation.

WILL THE FAMILY SURVIVE?

The traditional patriarchal extended family system (in which the nuclear family of parents and children are a part of the larger family) is under siege. It has suffered gradual erosion since at least the beginning of the Industrial Revolution. Once the nuclear family left the small community of friends, neighbours, and relatives and moved to the city, it had to rely more on its own resources. The change began in the cities, but spread at different rates to different parts of the country. For example, rural areas and traditional religious groups have been slower to change.

Signs of this movement in current society are numerous. One such sign is the strong emphasis on the couple, rather than on the wider family. In fact, for many there has been a movement away from marriage (a public event that includes the community) toward a pact between individuals (a private event), which does not require legal sanction. If the emotional needs of the partners can no longer be met, the family is dissolved. The family uses rather than produces goods and services. In keeping with this shift, fewer families provide the services that were seen as their responsibility in the past: the care of the sick, the elderly, the disabled, and the mentally ill. This sense of responsibility has never totally disappeared, and is encouraged by lack of services and by specific government policies. Even the functions the family has kept, such as the socialization of children or the financial support of family members, are shared with people and institutions outside the family. Daycare centres, babysitters, and schools all share the responsibilities of raising children; governments provide pensions and family benefits. Analysts suggest we are now questioning the rules governing the social life of society, including marriage, childbearing, and even the entire concept of the family (Dumas & Peron, 1992).

Will the family survive? The answer depends on how we define the family. If we consider the traditional patriarchal family, the answer may well be no. However, its disappearance is by no means certain. At the end of the 19th century, the American press looked with alarm at the state of the family. The concerns sound familiar: the divorce rate was rising; middle-class women were having fewer children; women's position was changing as they attended university and demanded the vote; and morals were declining (Lasch, 1979). Yet following World War II, there was a blossoming of traditional family values (Dumas & Peron, 1992). Indeed, most people hold the traditional family as their ideal, though they may not attain it (Bibby, 2004–2005; Daly, 2004). We cannot be certain whether the changes now occurring in society are the result of a long-term trend or are another swing of the pendulum.

Throughout history the family has taken many forms, but it has never disappeared. The family thus far has been the most efficient way of meeting individual needs. These include economic needs, the need for intimate relationships, and the need for a connection to society through socialization of all members. At different points in time, the family has given up all of these functions, but it has always retained at least one. Currently its primary task is to meet intimacy and care needs, although to some degree it retains both economic and social functions. The balance among them helps shape the form the family takes in different times and places.

Dr. Kerry Daly, of the University of Guelph, suggests that we are caught up in negative stories—that the family is fragile and that it is declining. He encourages us to think of the positive. First, families are a force for justice, for example, openness in adoption and the growing rights of gay and lesbian couples and their children. Second, families act as an anchor of care. Whether they do the actual labour of care themselves or arrange for others to do so, members rely on and take responsibility for each other (Daly, 2004). The family has proven itself highly adaptable. Its varying forms enable us to meet the challenges of a constantly changing society (Erera, 2002). As with animal species, the ability to adapt to new conditions fosters survival.

Although the family of the future may be quite different from what we have known to date—yes, the family will survive.

SUMMARY

Although it is impossible to predict the future, we can make some educated guesses in relation to the state of the family in Canada.

First, we can expect an older population as the result of the aging baby boom, increased longevity, and a reduced birth rate. There may, however, be a financial crisis in providing care and support for the elderly.

Second, family types will probably become, if anything, more varied in the future. More people will live alone. Unmarried cohabitation will likely continue to delay marriage and childbearing. Children will live in varied family settings. Given the number of immigrants from Third World countries, new traditions will be brought to Canada.

Third, family roles will change to accommodate family variety. There will also be greater role flexibility between the sexes as both husband and wife work outside the home. Children will have more parent figures. Due to the high divorce rate and the number of single parents, there may be a basic shift from a patrilineal to a matrilineal society.

Fourth, the explosion in communication technologies will affect families. Whether they loosen relationships or keep family members in closer touch depends on how they are used.

Fifth, society will be more involved in the family by defining rights and responsibilities and by regulating reproductive technologies and supervising family relationships.

However, unpredictable factors, such as economic trends, wars, or natural disasters, may also deeply affect the family. In addition, government actions that affect immigration and income distribution policies cannot be forecast.

Although the traditional patriarchal extended family may not survive, the family will adapt to meet new challenges.

KEY TERMS

matrilineal: counting descent through one's mother (p. 363)

patrilineal: counting descent through one's father (p. 363)

CLASS ASSIGNMENTS

Complete one or both of the following assignments, as directed by your instructor:

1. What solutions are available to increase the proportion of young people in the Canadian population? Explain the benefits and drawbacks of each of the choices.

2. What is meant by "a shift from a patrilineal to a matrilineal society"? Describe the possible impact of this shift on institutions such as schools, daycare centres, or the workplace.

PERSONAL ASSIGNMENTS

The following assignments are designed to help you explore your own feelings and opinions:

1. In the year 2025, what do you expect your family situation will be? Give reasons for your answer.

2. Do you think that the family will disappear? Give reasons for your answer.

3. What use do you (or others you know) make of the Internet? Do you believe it helps or harms the family? Explain.

APPENDIX

Major Sociological Theories

COMTE AS THE FATHER OF SOCIOLOGY

August Comte (1798–1857) has sometimes been called the father of sociology. He was the one who coined the term "sociology" to refer to the study of groups. He believed that, by using scientific means, the laws of society could be discovered. This, he felt, could be done by observation, by comparison of humans and animals, and by studying history.

Following Comte, three major schools of sociology developed: the structural-functional, conflict, and symbolic-interaction. We will look at the main ideas of these theories and at one or two people who helped develop them. Most of the discussion depends on the writing of Klein and White (1996) and of Swingewood (1991). Larson (1986), Lundy and Warme (1990), and Szacki (1979) have been consulted less often.

STRUCTURAL FUNCTIONALISM

Main Ideas

1. Societies are wholes and are made of connecting parts, which function in relation to the other parts of the society.
2. As long as the parts of society are doing unique things to help society, they are indispensable and will survive.
3. The various parts of society never work together perfectly. That is why there are mechanisms for controlling people.
4. Social change occurs slowly, as a response to changed conditions. It is adaptive and evolutionary.
5. People are held together by fundamental values that are shared by most members of society, and these help maintain society as it exists.

Structural-Functional Sociologists

Emile Durkheim (1858–1917). Durkheim, a Frenchman, was the first individual to be made a professor of sociology. Through his efforts to develop research methods, sociology came to be accepted as a scientific discipline. He stated that sociology was the study of what he called *social facts*. These facts come in three groups: (1) the number of people and how close together they live, the organization of their territory, technology, and the like; (2) social institutions, like schools, legal systems, churches, and businesses; and (3) beliefs, opinions, and values. Social facts become internalized by individuals; that is, they are accepted as the person's own and govern his or her behaviour. The milieu or collection of social facts plays a crucial role in people's behaviour. If there is no strong moral centre to society, anarchy and destruction take over. Durkheim saw in European society that there were few norms that showed people how they could meet their biological and social goals. This absence of norms he called *anomie*. In his studies of suicide, he tried to relate suicide to social factors and identified a type related to a lack of meaning in society, "anomic suicide."

Talcott Parsons (1902–1979). According to Parsons, society is made up of a system of interrelated actions. These social actions are built on the rules, norms, and patterns that are central to the particular society. The social milieu, or environment, in which people live is made up of a coordinated set of norms. Roles are stable ways in which people behave and are expected to behave and they are connected to a particular status, for example, "father," "student," and "police officer." Like Durkheim, Parsons believed that the norms of society govern people's behaviour because they are internalized.

CONFLICT THEORY

Main Ideas

1. Human beings are motivated, for the most part, by self-interest.
2. Conflict is always present within social groups and between them. This is the normal state of society.
3. The main concern in studying social groups is to find out how they handle conflict.
4. Conflict is based on the unfairness with which resources are divided between groups and between individuals.
5. Whoever has the most resources can usually negotiate the most rewards during negotiation. Coalitions may be formed to overcome this advantage.

Conflict Theorists

Karl Marx (1818–1883) and **Friedrich Engels** (1820–1895) jointly wrote a book entitled *The German Ideology* in 1846. This was the first book to outline the theory that society develops through stages: from slave societies to feudal ones, and finally to capitalist societies. In his two most famous books, *The Communist Manifesto* and *Wage Labour and Capital*, Marx argued that social change occurs through conflict and struggle. He also stated that labour is the basis of human culture. A worker puts his life into what he makes. Capitalism regards the worker as having something to sell—his work. Once it is purchased by someone else, it is no longer his own. Since it was his life, his life is also no longer his own. Marx saw this process as one of *alienation*: people were alienated from nature, from themselves, and from others. The situation could change only if workers reclaimed their own work through conflict and revolution.

SYMBOLIC INTERACTIONISM

Main Ideas

1. If we are to understand human behaviour, we must look at what it means to the individual. People define for themselves the meaning of each situation and interaction. To do so, they must have minds and be able to think.
2. People learn meanings from society.
3. If people believe they are filling a role well in a relationship, they feel good about the relationship.
4. Others expect individuals to fill roles in certain ways. If these expectations are clear, there is less role strain.
5. The more roles a person fills, the less likely are expectations to be clear, and the greater the role strain is likely to be. This is in part because there is less agreement about how he or she should behave in each situation.
6. The greater the role strain, the harder a role is to get into and the easier it is to get out of.

Symbolic-Interactionist Thinkers

Charles Horton Cooley (1864–1933). Cooley is most famous for his concept of the *looking-glass self*, according to which we imagine how we appear to other people, and imagine what they think of us. We also have our own emotions about these imaginings, for example, pride and embarrassment. We then govern what we do by how we believe others see us. This concept has led to the statement "What humans define as real has real consequences." Cooley also believed that we are nothing without other people, that "I" is impossible without "you." The self develops only as we interact with other people and with society as a whole.

    George Herbert Mead (1863–1931). Mead is most often called the originator of symbolic interactionism, yet he published only a few articles and no books. After his death, his students published his ideas, using their lecture notes as the basis. His central idea was that human beings can adapt to their environment if they have symbols, such as language, in common. Through his interest in how a baby learned the rules of its society, he understood that learning took place through interaction with others, especially through play and games. Because reality exists in people's interactions, it is always changing. People invent new roles and new meanings. Each way they see the situation is real to them. We exist as selves only through interaction with others. Mead also explained that each individual is both "I" and "me," with the "I" who observes and thinks, and the "me" who is aware of being an object to other people.

These three theories have shaped much thinking about the family. For example, the ecological, family systems, and family development theories draw on the system aspect of structural functionalism. The exchange, family systems, and developmental theories also make use of some of the concepts of symbolic interactionism. All are concerned about conflict within the family, though they have different ways of studying it.

GLOSSARY

abuse: a situation in which a person takes advantage of a less powerful person

accommodation: recognition of and respect for both similarities and differences between majority and minority

adoption: the legal transfer of rights and responsibilities from one set of parents to another

adultery: the act of having sexual relations with someone other than your spouse

AIDS (acquired immune deficiency syndrome): a sexually transmitted disease

ambiguity: lack of clarity

amniocentesis: a procedure in which some of the fluid surrounding the fetus is drawn off and examined under a microscope

androgynous: being high in characteristics of both masculinity and femininity

artificial insemination: the practice of using sperm from a donor to fertilize an egg

ascribed relationship: a relationship that belongs to a particular role rather than being a matter of choice

assimilation: taking on the values and practices of the majority group

authoritarian: a parenting style that requires unquestioning obedience

authoritative: a parenting style that sets expectations for children, but adjusts them to the individual

bestiality: sexual relations between a person and an animal

binuclear family: an arrangement where both father and mother act as parents to their child(ren) following divorce, while they maintain separate homes

boundary: an imaginary line marking who belongs to a system

burnout: a state of physical and emotional exhaustion resulting from prolonged stress from trying to live up to impossible goals

celibacy: living without sexual gratification

chronic illness: prolonged illness

chronological age: the number of years a person has lived

clawback: the practice of defining benefits as income and taxing them and of requiring repayment when income reaches a certain level

clone: genetically identical copy of a cell or an organism

closeted: keeping one's homosexuality secret

co-parent: a divorced person who shares the responsibility for his or her child

codependence: the tendency for nonalcoholic members of an alcoholic family to display a variety of psychological symptoms in response to the alcohol abuse. These arise from lack of self-worth and include lack of clear personal boundaries and assumption of responsibility for the alcoholic behaviour.

codependent: the spouse of an individual who abuses alcohol or other substances

cohabitation: living together, usually referring to a couple with a sexual relationship

cohort: a group of people, roughly the same age, living in the same historical time

cohort effect: characteristics or attitudes that result from the period of history in which people have lived

common-law union: a union of a man and a woman in a lasting relationship resembling marriage

communal living: a group of people, who may or may not be related by birth or marriage, sharing financial resources and living arrangements

compressed workweek: a full-time job in which a workweek is concentrated in three or four days, allowing for several days in succession off work

conventional roles: a marriage with a homemaker wife and breadwinner husband

correlation: a mathematical method for showing whether a relationship exists between factors

courtship: a process of mate selection

crisis: an imbalance in demands placed on an individual or family and their ability to meet the demand

cross-sectional research: a method of research that studies individuals of different ages and compares them in relation to the factor under investigation

custodial parent: an individual who has custody of his or her child

custody: the legal right and responsibility to care for a child in one's own home

developmental task: a task that an individual is expected to achieve at a particular stage in development

direct observation: a research method in which the researcher watches and records behaviour

discreditable: damaging to one's reputation

discrimination: negative actions taken against a minority group

disequilibrium: a lack of balance in the family system

divorce: the legal dissolution of a marriage

dual-career roles: a marriage in which both partners are committed to their careers

dysfunctional: decreased ability of family to solve problems

empty nest syndrome: the depression and sense of uselessness some women experience when the last child leaves home

enabler: a person whose behaviour allows another to act in a certain way; often used in reference to nonalcoholic members of alcoholic families

enclave: people of a minority culture who live as a group within the larger society

endogamy: marriage within one's social group

exosystem: institutions and organizations in society in which individuals do not take an active part, but that affect them through the mesosystem or microsystem

experiment: a research method that involves changing conditions deliberately and observing any changes in behaviour that result

extended family: the nuclear family and all other relatives

feminine: a type of personality with a high level of responsibility and concern for interpersonal relationships

flextime: an arrangement in which full-time employees can determine when they arrive at and when they leave work

foster home: a home that provides temporary care for children

functional: increased ability of the family to solve problems

gatekeepers: individuals who control access to services and are often recognized as having special expertise in identifying problems

gay male: homosexual man

gender roles: the socially approved ways of behaving as males and females

generativity: concern at midlife over one's contribution to future generations

germ-line therapy: a genetic technology whose purpose is to substitute a healthy gene for a defective one, not only to prevent a disorder in one individual but also to pass the healthy genes to his or her descendants

HIV (human immunodeficiency virus): the virus causing AIDS (acquired immune deficiency syndrome)

homogamy: the tendency to marry someone similar to oneself

homosexual: being attracted sexually to someone of the same sex

household: a person or group of persons who occupy the same dwelling

in vitro fertilization: the technique of fertilizing a woman's eggs with her partner's sperm in a lab dish, and later placing the embryo(s) in her uterus

incest taboo: social ban on marrying someone who is too closely related

incidence: percentage of cases in the population

indigenous: Aboriginal

infanticide: the murder of a baby

Internet: a worldwide network of computers allowing easy communication and exchange of information

interview: a research method in which the researcher asks questions face-to-face

job sharing: the sharing of one full-time job by two employees

joint custody: the legal right and responsibility of both parents to make decisions and care for their child

lesbian: homosexual woman

longitudinal research: a research method in which the same individuals are studied for a period of time

macrosystem: society's culture and ideology

mainstreaming: integrating children with exceptional needs into regular classrooms

majority: the group in a society that is the largest in number or has the most power

marker event: an event that signals a change in status

marriage contract: a legal agreement between a couple in which they agree to their rights and obligations during marriage or at its end

masculine: a type of personality with a high level of drive and ambition

matrilineal: counting descent through one's mother

means test: a method of screening applicants to ensure that only those who need financial assistance receive it

mesosystem: the relationships between two or more microsystems

microsystem: small groups in which people interact face-to-face

midlife crisis: extreme strain as a person re-evaluates his or her life in middle age

minority: any social category that offends against the norms of society

monogamy: marriage to one person at a time

morphogenesis: development of new forms of behaviour

Mothers Allowance: government monthly support program originally provided to mothers who were widowed or abandoned or to wives of dis-

abled men (now called Family Benefits and available to parents of either sex)

noncustodial parent: the parent who does not have custody of the child

nonresidential parent: the parent who does not live in the home with the child

normative family changes: changes that are expected as part of the family life cycle

norms: ways of behaving that are typical of a certain group

nuclear family: a family consisting of a husband, a wife, and their children

parentified child: a child who takes on an unusually high degree of a parent's role

passing: trying to hide the fact that one is a member of a minority group

patriarchal: social organization in which the man is dominant

patrilineal: counting descent through one's father

perinatal: around the time of birth

permeable boundaries: family boundaries that allow members to move through them

permissive: a parenting style that allows children to make their own decisions without providing firm guidelines

perpetrator: a person who is guilty of a crime, for example, abuse

physical aging: changes that occur in the body as a result of the length of time a person has lived

polygamy: marriage of one person to more than one person of the opposite sex

poverty line: a level of income below which an individual or family is considered to be living in poverty

prejudice: a negative attitude toward a minority group that is not based on fact

psychological age: the attitudes and beliefs one has about one's age

qualitative research: research methods that provide verbal descriptions of behaviour

quantitative research: research methods widely used in the scientific community that present information in the form of numbers

reconstituted family: a remarriage family

residential parent: the parent with whom the child lives

resilience: the ability to do well in the face of adversity

reverse conventional roles: a marriage with a breadwinner wife and homemaker husband

revolving door: young people's repeated moving in and out of their parents' home

role: a function expected of a person who has a particular status

sandwich generation: middle-aged adults who experience the stress of continuing dependency of their children and increasing disability of their parents

second-stage housing: longer-term housing for abused women

shared custody: custody of children shared by both parents

shared roles: a marriage in which both partners work and share household responsibilities

sibling: a brother or a sister

sleeper effect: a problem that emerges only long after an event such as divorce

snag points: areas of difficulty that interfere with constructive efforts to cope with problems

social age: cultural norms that specify appropriate behaviour for people of a given age

socialization: the passing on of the basic knowledge of a culture's ways of thinking and acting, including how to survive and how to take part in social life

social safety net: basic social security programs needed to support family life

social scripts: cultural rules that tell us what, where, when, how, and why we should do something

social support: practical assistance or emotional backup provided by others

social time clock: socially approved timetable for certain life events

sodomy: anal intercourse

spillover: a situation where family and work role or time demands interfere with each other

status: a social position that carries a set of expectations concerning suitable behaviour

stereotype: portrayal of all members of a group as having similar fixed, often unfavourable qualities

stigma: any quality that is seen as offensive by the majority

stressor: a life event that can produce change in the family system

subsystem: smaller groupings within a system

surrogate mother: a woman who agrees to artificial insemination, usually for a fee, with a view to turning over the resulting child to the biological father and his wife

survey: a method of research that involves getting information from many individuals

system: a set of interrelated and interacting parts

telecommuting: working outside the office (often at home) using a computer and telecommunications technology

theory: general framework of ideas that can be used to answer questions about the world

transitional state: a state of temporary imbalance resulting from changes in relationships, routines, assumptions, and roles

V-chip: a device designed to allow parents to block unsuitable television programs

values: social principles that are accepted by society as a whole or by a group within that society

vested interests: group of people who have a stake in keeping society as it is

violence: an act intended to physically hurt another person

visible minority: persons, other than Aboriginal peoples, who are non-Caucasian in race or non-white in colour (Hou & Picot, 2004).

workfare: policy of requiring able-bodied welfare recipients to train for a job or to work

REFERENCES

Abbott, E. (1999). *A history of celibacy*. Toronto: HarperPerennial Canada.

Abell, E., Dorr, K., & Guarino, A. (2003, November). *The effects of different living arrangements on the parenting practices of adolescent mothers*. Poster presentation at annual conference of National Council on Family Relations, Vancouver.

Acton, R. G., & During, S. (1990). The treatment of aggressive parents: An outline of a group treatment program. *Canada's Mental Health, 38*(2/3), 2–6.

Adams, O. B., & Nagnur, D. N. (1988). *Marriage, divorce and mortality: A life table analysis for Canada and regions*. Ottawa: Statistics Canada.

Ad Hoc Federal-Provincial-Territorial Working Group Reviewing Spousal Abuse Policies and Legislation. (2003). *Final report*. Ottawa: Federal-Provincial-Territorial Ministers Responsible for Justice.

Adoption Council of Canada. (2004). *International adoptions up: 2,181 in 2003*. Retrieved November 5, 2004, from http://www.adoption.ca

Ahrons, C. R. (1999). Divorce: An unscheduled family transition. In B. Carter & M. McGoldrick (Eds.), *The expanded family life cycle: Individual, family, and social perspectives* (3rd ed., pp. 381–398). Boston: Allyn & Bacon.

Alden, A. (2004). *Parenting on purpose: Red yellow green framework for respectful discipline*. Plymouth, MN: Crane.

Aldous, J. (1996). *Family careers: Rethinking the developmental perspective*. Thousand Oaks, CA: Sage.

Allen, D. W. (1999). No-fault divorce and the divorce rate: Its history, effect, and implications. In D. W. Allen & J. Richards (Eds.), *It takes two: The family in marriage and finance* (pp. 1–35). Toronto: C. D. Howe Institute.

Allen, E. S., Baucom, D. H., Burnett, C. K., Epstein, N., & Rankin-Esquer, L. A. (2001). Decision-making power, autonomy, and communication in remarried spouses compared with first-married spouses. *Family Relations, 50*, 326–334.

Allen, K. R., Bliezner, R., & Roberto, K. A. (2000). Families in the middle and later years: A review and critique of research in the 1990s. *Journal of Marriage and the Family, 62*, 911–926.

Altucher, A., & Williams, L. B. (2003). Family clocks: Timing parenthood. In P. Moen (Ed.), *It's about time: Couples and careers* (pp. 49–59). Ithaca, NY: ILR Press.

Alwin, D. F. (1996). Coresidence beliefs in American society—1973 to 1991. *Journal of Marriage and the Family, 58*, 393–403.

Amato, P. R. (1987). Family process in one-parent, step-parent, and intact families: The child's point of view. *Journal of Marriage and the Family, 49*, 327–337.

Amato, P. R. (2000). The consequences of divorce for adults and children. *Journal of Marriage and the Family, 62*, 1269–1287.

Amato, P. R. (2004). Tension between individual and institutional views of marriage. *Journal of Marriage and Family, 66*, 959–965.

Amato, P. R., & Fowler, F. (2002). Parenting practices, child adjustment, and family diversity. *Journal of Marriage and Family, 64*, 703–716.

Amato, P. R., Johnson, D. R., Booth, A., & Rogers, S. J. (2003). Continuity and change in marital quality between 1980 and 2000. *Journal of Marriage and Family, 65*, 1–22.

Ambert, A.-M. (1998). *Divorce: Facts, figures, and consequences*. Ottawa: Vanier Institute of the Family. Retrieved July 19, 2000, from http://www.vifamily.ca/cft/divorce/divorce.htm

Ambert, A.-M. (2002). *Divorce: Facts, causes, and consequences* (revised). Ottawa: Vanier Institute of the Family.

Ambert, A.-M. (2003). *Same-sex couples and same-sex parent families: Relationships, parenting, and issues of marriage*. Ottawa: Vanier Institute of the Family.

American Psychological Association. (1997). *The road to burnout*. Retrieved February 2, 2001, from http://helping.apa.org/work/stress6.html

Amiel, B. (1987, June). No sex please, we're British. *Chatelaine*, 147–148.

Anderson, C. (2003). The diversity, strengths, and challenges of single-parent households. In F. Walsh (Ed.), *Normal family processes: Growing diversity and complexity* (3rd ed., pp. 121–152). New York: Guilford.

Anderson, E. A., & Koblinsky, S. A. (1995). Homeless policy: The need to speak to families. *Family Relations, 44*, 13–18.

Anderson, J. M., Waxler-Morrison, N., Richardson, E., Herbert, C., & Murphy, M. (1990). Conclusion: Delivering culturally sensitive health care. In N. Waxler-Morrison, J. M. Anderson, & E. Richardson (Eds.), *Cross-cultural caring: A handbook for health professionals* (pp. 245–267). Vancouver: UBC Press.

Anderson, K. L. (2002). Perpetrator or victim? Relationships between intimate partner violence and well-being. *Journal of Marriage and Family, 64,* 851–863.

Anderssen, E., & McIlroy, A. (2004, April 10). Quebec distinct in nursery too, poll finds. *The Globe and Mail,* pp. A1, A5.

Andrews, L. B. (1999, March 28). The sperminator. *New York Times Magazine,* 62–65.

Appell, A. R. (2002). Safe havens to abandon babies, Part I: The law. *Adoption Quarterly, 5*(4), 59–69.

Appleblatt, A. (1976). *Saskatchewan and the Ku Klux Klan.* Retrieved July 25, 2004, from http://www.usask.ca/education/ideas/tplan/sslp/kkk.htm

Aquilino, W. S. (1996). The life course of children born to unmarried mothers: Childhood living arrangements and young adult outcomes. *Journal of Marriage and the Family, 58,* 293–310.

Arboleda-Flórez, J., Holley, H. L., & Crisanti, A. (1996). *Mental illness and violence: Proof or stereotype?* Ottawa: Health Canada.

Archer, S. (1985). Career and/or family: The identity process for adolescent girls. *Youth and Society, 16,* 289–314.

Armstrong, P., & Armstrong, H. (1987). The conflicting demands of "work" and "home." *Family matters* (pp. 113–140). Toronto: Methuen.

Armstrong, R. (1999, Winter). Mapping the conditions of First Nations communities. *Canadian Social Trends,* 14–18.

Arnup, K. (1989). "Mothers just like others": Lesbians, divorce, and child custody in Canada. *Canadian Journal of Women and the Law, 3,* 18–32.

Artis, J. E., & Pavalko, E. K. (2003). Explaining the decline in women's household labor: Individual change and cohort differences. *Journal of Marriage and Family, 65,* 746–761.

Atkinson, J. (1999). *Grandparent access to their grandchildren: A contemporary issue.* Retrieved February 17, 2005, from http://reliableanswers.com/cps/legal/grandparents.asp

Atkinson, N., Ermter, A., & Velasco, A. (2003, August 14). The *fab* fairy wedding guide. *fab: The Gay Scene Magazine,* 13–15, 17–18, 21–22, 24, 26, 29–30.

Atwood, J. D. (1996). Social construction theory and therapy assumptions. In J. D. Atwood (Ed.), *Family scripts* (pp. 1–33). Washington, DC: Accelerated Development.

Axinn, W. G., & Thornton, A. (1993). Mothers, children, and cohabitation: The intergenerational effects of attitudes and behavior. *American Sociological Review, 58,* 233–246.

Axinn, W. G., & Thornton, A. (2000). The transformation in the meaning of marriage. In L. J. Waite, C. Bachrach, M. Hindin, E. Thomson, & A. Thornton (Eds.), *The ties that bind: Perspectives on marriage and cohabitation* (pp. 147–165). New York: Aldine de Gruyter.

Azni, S. (1999). Wife abuse and ideological competition in the Muslim community of Toronto. In H. Troper & M. Weinfeld (Eds.), *Ethnicity, politics, and public policy: Case studies in Canadian diversity* (pp. 164–189). Toronto: University of Toronto Press.

Azoulay, D. (2001, February/March). Only the lonely. *The Beaver,* 35–41.

Baby bonus program works as Quebec birth rate increases. (1990, July 17). *Toronto Star,* p. A10.

Badr, H. (2003, December). Re-covering Islamic identity in the U.S. after 9/11. *Family Focus,* pp. F13, F15.

Bagnell, K. (1980). *The little immigrants: The orphans who came to Canada.* Toronto: Macmillan.

Baker, M. (1988). *Aging in Canadian society: A survey.* Toronto: McGraw-Hill Ryerson.

Baker, M. (1995). *Canadian family policies: Cross-national comparisons.* Toronto: University of Toronto Press.

Bala, N. (1999). *Legal responses to domestic abuse.* Retrieved June 3, 2000, from http://www.familylawcentre.com/ccbaladomviolence.html

Bala, N. (2004). *Controversy over couples in Canada: The evolution of marriage & other interdependent relationships.* Retrieved July 8, 2004, from http://qsilver.queensu.ca/law/papers/evolutionapril.htm

Balakrishnan, T. R., Lapierre-Adamcyk, E., & Krotki, K. J. (1993). *Family and childbearing in Canada: A demographic analysis.* Toronto: University of Toronto Press.

Balcazar, H., & Qian, Z. (2000). Immigrant families and sources of stress. In P. C. McKenry & S. J. Price (Eds.), *Families & change: Coping with stressful events and transitions* (2nd ed., pp. 359–377). Thousand Oaks, CA: Sage.

Baltes, P. B., Reese, H. W., & Nesselroade, J. R. (1977). *Lifespan developmental psychology: Introduction to research methods.* Monterey, CA: Brooks/Cole.

Bancroft, L., & Silverman, J. G. (2002). *The batterer as parent: Addressing the impact of domestic violence on family dynamics.* Thousand Oaks, CA: Sage.

Bank, S. P., & Kahn, M. D. (1982). *The sibling bond.* New York: Basic Books.

Barnett, O., Miller-Perrin, C. L., & Perrin, R. D. (2005). *Family violence across the lifespan: An introduction* (2nd ed.). Thousand Oaks, CA: Sage.

Barret, R. L., & Robinson, B. E. (2000). *Gay fathers: Encouraging the hearts of gay dads and their families* (2nd ed.). San Francisco: Jossey-Bass.

Barrett, F. M. (1980). Sexual experience, birth control usage, and sex education of unmarried Canadian university students: Changes between 1968 and 1978. *Archives of Sexual Behavior, 9*, 367–390.

Barsky, L. (1990, January). 40 something: The new exciting middle age? *Chatelaine*, 33–37.

Basavarajappa, K. G. (1998). *Living arrangements and residential crowding: The situation of older immigrants in Canada, 1991*. Ottawa: Statistics Canada.

Bass, S., Shields, M. K., & Behrman, R. (2004). Children, families, and foster care: Analysis and recommendations. *The Future of Children, 14*(1), 5–29. Retrieved from http://www.futureofchildren.org

Bassett, B. (n.d.). *Adam @ home*. Retrieved September 29, 2004, from http://www.ucomics.com/adamathome

Baucom, D. H., Notarius, C. I., Burnett, C. K., & Haefner, P. (1990). Gender differences and sex-role identity in marriage. In F. D. Fincham & T. N. Bradbury (Eds.), *The psychology of marriage: Basic issues and applications* (pp. 150–171). New York: Guilford.

Baumrind, D. (1980). New directions in socialization research. *American Psychologist, 35*, 639–652.

Baumrind, D. (1996). The discipline controversy revisited. *Family Relations, 45*, 404–414.

Beaton, J. M., Norris, J. E., & Pratt, W. (2003). Unresolved issues in adult children's marital relationships involving intergenerational problems. *Family Relations, 52*, 143–153.

Beaujot, R. (2000). *Earning and caring in Canadian families*. Peterborough, ON: Broadview Press.

Beaujot, R. (2004). *Delayed life transitions: Trends and implications*. Ottawa: Vanier Institute of the Family.

Beaujot, R., Gee, E. M., Rajulton, F., & Ravanera, Z. R. (1995). *Family over the life course: Current demographic analysis*. Ottawa: Statistics Canada.

Beaulieu, M., & Spencer, C. (1999). *Older adults' personal relationships and the law in Canada: Legal, psychosocial and ethical aspects*. Ottawa: Law Commission of Canada.

Begin, P., Casavant, L., Chenier, N. M., & Dupuis, J. (1999). *Homelessness*. Ottawa: Library of Parliament. Retrieved February 25, 2001, from http://www.parl.gc.ca/information/library/prbpubs/prb991-e.htm

Beigel, H. G. (1951). Romantic love. *American Sociological Review, 16*, 326–334.

Beiser, M., Dion, R., Gotowiec, A., Hyman, I., & Vu, N. (1995). Immigrant and refugee children in Canada. *Canadian Journal of Psychiatry, 40*, 67–72.

Beiser, M., Hou, F., Hyman, I., & Tousignant, M. (1998). *Growing up Canadian—A study of new immigrant children*. Ottawa: Human Resources Development Canada.

Béjin, A. (1985). The extra-marital union today. In P. Ariès & A. Béjin (Eds.), *Western sexuality: Practice and precept in past and present times* (pp. 158–167). Oxford: Basil Blackwell.

Bélanger, A. (1999). *Report on the demographic situation in Canada, 1998–1999: Current demographic analysis*. Catalogue No. 91-209-XPE. Ottawa: Statistics Canada.

Bélanger, A., & Gilbert, S. (2003). The fertility of immigrant women and their Canadian born daughters. In A. Bélanger (Ed.), *Report on the demographic situation in Canada 2002: Current demographic analysis* (Catalogue no. 91-209-XPE, pp. 127–151). Ottawa: Statistics Canada.

Bélanger, A., & Malenfant, É. C., with Martel, L., Carrière, Y., Hicks, C., & Rowe, G. (2005). *Population projections of visible minority groups, Canada, provinces and regions 2001–2017* (Catalogue no. 91-541-XIE). Ottawa: Statistics Canada.

Bélanger, A., & Martel, L. (2003). Current demographic analysis for Canada, 2002. In A. Bélanger (Ed.), *Report on the demographic situation in Canada 2002* (Catalogue no. 91-209-XPE, pp. 9–124). Ottawa: Statistics Canada.

Bélanger, A., & Oikawa, C. (1999, Summer). Who has a third child? *Canadian Social Trends*, 23–26.

Bélanger, A., & Ouellet, G. (2002). A comparative study of recent trends in Canadian and American fertility. In A. Bélanger (Ed.), *Report on the demographic situation in Canada 2001* (Catalogue no. 91-209-XPE, pp. 107–136). Ottawa: Statistics Canada.

Bell, J., & Prokaska, L. (2001, September 17). Fire guts temple; mosque vandalized, *Hamilton Spectator*, pp. A1, A4.

Belsky, J., & Kelly, J. (1994). *The transition to parenthood: How a first child changes a marriage*. New York: Delacorte.

Benzies, K., Tough, S., Tofflemire, K., Faber, A., & Newburn-Cook, C. (2003, November). *Timing of motherhood: Factors influencing women's decisions to delay childbearing*. Poster presentation at annual conference of National Council on Family Relations, Vancouver.

Berardo, F. M. (2001, December). Elder grief. *Family Focus*, F23–F24.

Berger, D. M. (1980). Infertility: A psychiatrist's perspective. *Canadian Journal of Psychiatry, 25*, 553–559.

Bergquist, W. H., Greenberg, E. M., & Klaum, G. A. (1993). *In our fifties: Voices of men and women reinventing their lives.* San Francisco: Jossey-Bass.

Bess, I. (1999a, Autumn). Seniors behind the wheel. *Canadian Social Trends*, 2–7.

Bess, I. (1999b, Summer). Widows living alone. *Canadian Social Trends*, 2–5.

Bhandari, A. (2005, March 12). Guess who's coming to dinner. *The Globe and Mail*, p. F7.

Bhargava, G. (1988). Seeking immigration through matrimonial alliance: A study of advertisements in an ethnic weekly. *Journal of Comparative Family Studies, 19*, 245–259.

Bibby, R. W. (2001). *Canada's teens: Today, yesterday, and tomorrow.* Don Mills, ON: Stoddart.

Bibby, R. W. (2004–2005, Winter). Future families: Surveying our hopes, dreams, and realities. *Transition*, 3–14.

Births. (2000, October 18). *Hamilton Spectator*, C1.

Bissell, M. (2000). Socio-economic outcomes of teen pregnancy and parenthood. *Canadian Journal of Human Sexuality, 9*, 181–190.

Blacker, L. (1999). The launching phase of the life cycle. In B. Carter & M. McGoldrick (Eds.), *The expanded family life cycle: Individual, family, and social perspectives* (3rd ed., pp. 287–306). Boston: Allyn & Bacon.

Bogenschneider, K., (2002). *Family policy matters: How policymaking affects families and what professionals can do.* Mahwah, NJ: Lawrence Erlbaum.

Bold, M. (2001, March). Impact of computer-mediated communication on families. *Family Focus*, F16–F17.

Borgen, W. A., Amundson, N. E., & McVicar, J. (2002). The experience of unemployment for fishery workers in Newfoundland: What helps and what hinders. *Journal of Employment Counseling, 39*, 117–126.

Bose, C. E., Bereano, P. L., & Malloy, M. (1991). Household technology and the social construction of housework. In M. C. LaFollette & J. K. Stine (Eds.), *Technology and change: Readings from Technology and Culture* (pp. 261–290). Chicago: University of Chicago Press.

Boss, P. (2002). *Family stress management: A contextual approach* (2nd ed.). Thousand Oaks, CA: Sage.

Bossard, J. H. S., with Boll, E. S. (1975). *The large family system.* Westport, CT: Greenwood. (Originally published in 1956.)

Bouchard, G., Lussier, Y., & Sabourin, S. (1999). Personality and marital adjustment: Utility of the five-factor model of personality. *Journal of Marriage and the Family, 61*, 651–660.

Boxnboim, S., & Erera, P. I. (1995, November). *Parenting patterns of remarried mothers with their biological children.* Paper presented at the Annual Conference of National Council on Family Relations, Portland, OR.

Boyce, W., Doherty, M., Fortin, C., & MacKinnon, D. (2003). *Canadian youth, sexual health, and HIV/AIDS study: Factors influencing knowledge, attitudes, and behaviours.* Toronto: Council of Ministers of Education, Canada.

Boyd, M., & Li, A. (2003, Autumn). May–December: Canadians in age-discrepant relationships. *Canadian Social Trends* (Statistics Canada Catalogue no. 11-008), 2–6.

Boyd, M., & Norris, D. (1995, Autumn). Leaving the nest? The impact of family structure. *Canadian Social Trends* (Statistics Canada Catalogue no. 11-008), 14–17.

Boyle, M. H., Jenkins, J. M., Georgiades, K., Cairney, J., Duku, E., & Racine, Y. (2004). Differential-maternal parenting behaviour: Estimating within- and between-family effects on children. *Child Development, 75*, 1457–1476.

Boyum, L. A., & Parke, R. D. (1995). The role of family emotional expressiveness in the development of children's social competence. *Journal of Marriage and the Family, 57*, 593–608.

Bradbury, T. N., & Karney, B. R. (2004). Understanding and altering the longitudinal course of marriage. *Journal of Marriage and Family, 66*, 862–879.

Brandes, A. T. (2003, December). From stepfamily to "new-family" [audiotape]. In J. B. Comeau (Ed.), *Family Information Services Professional Resource Materials.* Minneapolis: Family Information Services.

Bray, J. H., & Kelly, J. (1998). *Stepfamilies: Love, marriage, and parenting in the first decade.* New York: Broadway Books.

Brayfield, A. (1995). Juggling jobs and kids: The impact of employment schedules on fathers' caring for children. *Journal of Marriage and the Family, 57*, 321–332.

Brennan, R. T., Barnett, R. C., & Gareis, K. C. (2001). When she earns more than he does: A longitudinal study of dual-earner couples. *Journal of Marriage and Family, 63*, 168–182.

Brinig, M. F. (1999). The effect of divorce on wives. In D. W. Allen & J. Richards (Eds.), *It takes two: The family in marriage and finance* (pp. 36–62). Toronto: C. D. Howe Institute.

Brink, S., & McKellar, S. (2000). NLSCY: A unique Canadian survey. *Isuma—Canadian Journal of Policy Research, 1*(2), 111–113. Retrieved June 12, 2004, from http://www.isuma.net

Brinkerhoff, M. B., & Lupri, E. (1989). Power and authority in the family. In K. Ishwaran (Ed.), *Family and marriage: Cross-cultural perspectives* (pp. 213–236). Toronto: Wall & Thompson.

British Columbia Ministry of Children & Family Development. (n.d.). *Confidentiality and access to information.* Retrieved April 25, 2005, from http://www.mcf.gov.bc.ca/adoption/act/access_info .htm

Broderick, C. B. (1993). *Understanding family process: Basics of family systems theory.* Newbury Park, CA: Sage.

Brodribb, S. (1984). The traditional roles of native women in Canada and the impact of colonization. *Canadian Journal of Native Studies, 4*(1), 85–103.

Brody, G. H., & Murry, V. M. (2001). Sibling socialization in rural, single-parent African-American families. *Journal of Marriage and Family, 63*, 996–1008.

Brown, L. H. (2003, November). *Grandparent-grandchild role expectations as viewed by young adults.* Poster presentation at annual conference of National Council on Family Relations, Vancouver.

Brown, S., & Lewis, V. (1999). *The alcoholic family in recovery: A developmental model.* New York: Guilford.

Brown, S. L. (2004). Family structure and child well-being: The significance of parental cohabitation. *Journal of Marriage and Family, 66*, 351–367.

Brown, S. L., & Booth, A. (1996). Cohabitation versus marriage: A comparison of relationship quality. *Journal of Marriage and the Family, 58*, 668–678.

Brunes, L. (2004, Spring). The seniors of Canada's far north. *Expression*, 1–8.

Bryant, C. M., & Conger, R. D. (1999). Marital success and domains of social support in long-term relationships: Does the influence of network members ever end? *Journal of Marriage and the Family, 61*, 437–450.

Bryant, C. M., Conger, R. D., & Meehan, J. M. (2001). The influence of in-laws on change in marital success. *Journal of Marriage and Family, 63*, 614–626.

Brzozowski, J.-A., (Ed.). (2004). *Family violence in Canada: A statistical profile 2004* (Catalogue no. 85-224-XIE). Ottawa: Statistics Canada.

Buchanan, C. M., Maccoby, E. E., & Dornbusch, S. M. (1991). Caught between parents: Adolescents' experience in divorced homes. *Child Development, 62*, 1008–1029.

Buehler, C., & Gerard, J. M. (2002). Marital conflict, ineffective parenting, and children's maladjustment. *Journal of Marriage and Family, 64*, 78–92.

Buehler, C., Krishnakumar, A., Anthony, C., Tittsworth, S., & Stone, G. (1994). Hostile interparental conflict and youth maladjustment. *Family Relations, 43*, 409–416.

Buehler, C., Krishnakumar, A., Stone, G., Anthony, C., Pemberton, S., Gerard, J., & Barber, B. K. (1998). Interparental conflict styles and youth problem behaviors: A two-sample replication study. *Journal of Marriage and the Family, 60*, 119–132.

Buerkel-Rothfuss, N., Buerkel, R. A., & Gray, P. L. (2001, March). Youth and sexually explicit Internet images. *Family Focus*, F19–F20.

Burgess, E. W., & Locke, H. J. (1960). *The family: From institution to companionship* (2nd ed.). New York: American Book Company.

Burkett, E. (2000). *The baby boon: How family-friendly America cheats the childless.* New York: Free Press.

Butler, I., Scanlan, L., Robinson, M., Douglas, G., & Murch, M. (2003). *Divorcing children: Children's experience of their parents' divorce.* London, England: Jessica Kingsley.

Butler, A. C. (2002). Welfare, premarital childbearing, and the role of normative climate: 1968–1994. *Journal of Marriage and Family, 64*, 295–313.

Butler, R. R., & Koraleski, S. (1990). Infertility: A crisis with no resolution. *Journal of Mental Health Counseling, 12*, 151–163.

Cabrera, N. J. (1995). Violence by and against children in Canada. In J. I. Ross (Ed.), *Violence in Canada: Sociopolitical perspectives* (pp. 126–152). Don Mills, ON: Oxford University Press.

Cahill, B. (1992). *Butterbox babies.* Toronto: McClelland-Bantam.

Call, V., Sprecher, S., & Schwartz, P. (1995). The incidence and frequency of marital sex in a national sample. *Journal of Marriage and the Family, 59*, 639–652.

Campaign 2000. (2004). *One million too many: Implementing solutions to child poverty in Canada.* Toronto: Author.

Campbell, C. (1999, October). Service a safety net for working parents. *Families & Health*, 6.

Campbell, S. (1989). The 50-year-old woman and midlife stress. In T. W. Miller (Ed.), *Stressful life events* (pp. 711–727). Madison, CT: International Universities Press.

Canadian Centre on Substance Abuse. (2004). *Canadian addiction survey: Highlights.* Ottawa: Canadian

Centre on Substance Abuse. Retrieved January 15, 2005, from http://www.ccsa.ca

Canadian Conference of Catholic Bishops. (1980). *Marriage and the family: Working paper*. Ottawa: Author.

Canadian Council of Natural Mothers. (n.d.). *Alberta—Open adoption records November 1, 2004*. Retrieved April 25, 2005, from http://nebula.on.ca/canbmothers/English/ProvincialInfo/AlbertaRecords.htm

Canadian Council on Social Development. (1996). Services to support abused women and children. *Vis-à-vis, 13*(4), 12.

Canadian Hearing Society. (2002). *Employment and employability needs of the deaf community in Peel and Halton Regions*. Mississauga, ON: Canadian Hearing Society—Peel.

Canary, D. J., Stafford, L., & Semic, B. A. (2002). A panel study of the associations between maintenance strategies and relational characteristics. *Journal of Marriage and Family, 64*, 395–406.

Capizzano, J., Adelman, S., & Stagner, M. (2002). *What happens when the school year is over? The use and costs of child care for school-age children during the summer months*. Washington, DC: Urban Institute.

Caragata, L. (2003). Housing and homelessness. In A. Westhues (Ed.), *Canadian social policy: Issues and perspectives* (3rd ed., pp. 67–89). Waterloo, ON: Wilfrid Laurier University Press.

Carlson, M. J., & Corcoran, M. E. (2001). Family structure and children's behavioral and cognitive outcomes. *Journal of Marriage and Family, 63*, 779–792.

Carr, D. (2004). The desire to date and remarry among older widows and widowers. *Journal of Marriage and Family, 66*, 1051–1068.

Carroll, J. S., & Doherty, W. F. (2004). Evaluating the effectiveness of premarital prevention programs: A meta-analytic review of outcome research. *Family Relations, 52*, 105–118.

Carstensen, L. L., Gottman, J. M., & Levenson, R. W. (1995). Emotional behavior in long-term marriage. *Psychology and Aging, 10*, 140–149.

Carter, B. (1999). Becoming parents: The family with young children. In B. Carter & M. McGoldrick (Eds.), *The expanded family life cycle: Individual, family, and social perspectives* (3rd ed., pp. 249–273). Boston: Allyn & Bacon.

Carter, B., & McGoldrick, M. (1999a). The divorce cycle: A major variation in the American family life cycle. In B. Carter & M. McGoldrick (Eds.), *The expanded family life cycle: Individual, family and social*

perspectives (3rd ed., pp. 373–380). Boston: Allyn & Bacon.

Carter, B., & McGoldrick, M. (1999b). Overview: The expanded family life cycle: Individual, family, and social perspectives. In B. Carter & M. McGoldrick (Eds.), *The expanded family life cycle: Individual, family and social perspectives* (3rd ed., pp. 1–26). Boston: Allyn & Bacon.

Castellano, M. B. (1989). Women in Huron and Ojibwa societies. *Canadian Woman Studies, 10*(2/3), 45–48.

Castellano, M. B. (2002). *Aboriginal family trends: Extended families, nuclear families, families of the heart*. Ottawa: Vanier Institute of the Family.

Center for Impact Research. (2000). *Domestic violence and birth control sabotage: A report from the teen parent project*. Chicago: Center for Impact Research.

Chabot, J. M., & Ames, B. D. (2004). "It wasn't 'let's get pregnant and go do it'": Decision making in lesbian couples planning motherhood via donor insemination. *Family Relations, 53*, 348–356.

Chao, P. K. (1994). Beyond parenting control and authoritarian parenting: Understanding Chinese parenting through the cultural notion of parenting. *Child Development, 65*, 1111–1119.

Chartier v. Chartier. (1999). 1 S.C.R. 242, 1999. Retrieved March 4, 2001, from http://www.lexum.umontreal.ca/csc-scc/en/pub/1999/vol1/html/1999scr1_0242.html

Che-Alford, J., & Hamm, B. (1999, Summer). Under one roof: Three generations living together. *Canadian Social Trends*, 6–9.

Che-Alford, J., & Stevenson, K. (1998, Spring). Older Canadians on the move. *Canadian Social Trends*, 15–18.

Cheal, D. (1991). *Family and the state of theory*. Toronto: University of Toronto Press.

Cheal, D. (1998). Poverty and relative income: Family transactions and social policy. In D. Cheal, F. Woolley, & M. Luxton, *How families cope and why policymakers need to know* (pp. 1–26). Ottawa: Canadian Policy Research Networks.

Cherlin, A. J. (2000). Toward a new home socioeconomics of union formation. In L. J. Waite, C. Bachrach, M. Hindin, E. Thomson, & A. Thornton (Eds.), *The ties that bind: Perspectives on marriage and cohabitation* (pp. 126–144). New York: Aldine de Gruyter.

Cherlin, A. J. (2004). The deinstitutionalization of American marriage. *Journal of Marriage and Family, 66*, 848–861.

Chesley, L. C., MacAulay, D., & Ristock, J. L. (1998). *Abuse in lesbian relationships: Information and resources*. Ottawa: Health Canada.

Chiancone, J., Girdner, L., & Hoff, P. (2001, December). Issues in resolving cases of international child abduction by parents. *Juvenile Justice Bulletin.* Washington, DC: U.S. Department of Justice.

Children Now. (2004). *Fall colors 2003–04: Prime time diversity report.* Retrieved November 30, 2004, from http://www.childrennow.org

Christopher, F. S., Madura, M., & Weaver, L. (1998). Premarital sexual aggressors: A multivariate analysis of social, relational, and individual variables. *Journal of Marriage and the Family, 60,* 56–69.

Christopher, F. S., & Sprecher, S. (2000). Sexuality in marriage, dating, and other relationships: A decade review. *Journal of Marriage and the Family, 62,* 999–1017.

Chui, T., & Zietsma, D. (2003, Autumn). Earnings of immigrants in the 1990s. *Canadian Social Trends* (Statistics Canada Catalogue no. 11-008), *70,* 24–28.

Church, E. (2004). *Understanding stepmothers: Women share their struggles, successes, and insights.* Toronto: HarperCollins.

Ciabattari, T. (2004). Cohabitation and housework: The effect of marital intentions. *Journal of Marriage and Family, 66,* 118–125.

City of Calgary. (1985). *A profile and needs assessment of Calgary's single-parents.* Calgary: City of Calgary, Social Services Department.

Clack, E. E. (Ed.). (2004, May 1). Study probes generation gap. *Children's Business.* Retrieved December 1, 2004, from http://www.reachadvisors.com/childrensbusinessarticle.html

Clark-Ibañez, M., & Felmlee, D. (2004). Interethnic relationships: The role of social network diversity, *Journal of Marriage and Family, 66,* 293–305.

Cleveland, G., & Krashinsky, M. (2003). *Fact and fantasy: Eight myths about early childhood education and care.* Toronto: University of Toronto, Childcare Resource and Research Unit.

CMHA (Canadian Mental Health Association, Newfoundland and Labrador Division). (n.d.). *Guide to coping with unemployment.* Retrieved February 2, 2001, from http://www.infonet.st-johns.nf.ca/cmha/resource/publications/gcwu/

Cochrane, M. G. (1999). *For better or for worse: The Canadian guide to marriage contracts and cohabitation agreements.* Toronto: Wiley.

Cochrane, M. G. (2002). *Surviving your divorce: A guide to Canadian family law* (3rd ed.). Etobicoke, ON: Wiley.

Cohan, C. L., & Kleinbaum, S. (2002). Toward a greater understanding of the cohabitation effect: Premarital cohabitation and marital communication. *Journal of Marriage and Family, 64,* 180–192.

Cole, E. S. (1984). Societal influences on adoption practice. In P. Sachdev (Ed.), *Adoption: Current issues and trends* (pp. 15–29). Toronto: Butterworths.

Coleman, E. (1990). The married lesbian. In F. W. Bozett & M. B. Sussman (Eds.), *Homosexuality and family relations* (pp. 119–135). New York: Haworth.

Coleman, J. W., & Kerbo, H. R., with Ramos, L. L. (2002). *Social problems* (8th ed.). Upper Saddle River, NJ: Prentice Hall.

Coleman, M., Ganong, L., & Fine, M. (2000). Reinvestigating remarriage: Another decade of progress. *Journal of Marriage and the Family, 62,* 1288–1307.

Comfort, D., Johnson, K., & Wallace, D. (2003). *Part-time work and family-friendly practices in Canadian workplaces* (Catalogue no. 71-584-MIE No. 6). Ottawa: Statistics Canada.

Connidis, I. A. (2001). *Family ties and aging.* Thousand Oaks, CA: Sage.

Connor, S., & Brink, S. (1999). *The impacts of non-parental care on child development.* Hull: Human Resources Development Canada, Applied Research Branch.

Cook, T. E. (2003). *Separation, assimilation, or accommodation: Contrasting ethnic minority policies.* Westport, CT: Praeger.

Coontz, S. (2000). Historical perspectives on family studies. *Journal of Marriage and the Family, 62,* 283–297.

Coontz, S. (2004). The world historical transformation of marriage. *Journal of Marriage and Family, 66,* 974–979.

Copans, S. (1989). The invisible family member: Children in families with alcohol abuse. In L. Combrinck-Graham (Ed.), *Children in family contexts: Perspectives on treatment* (pp. 277–298). New York: Guilford.

Coplan, R. J., Hastings, P. D., Lagacé-Séguin, D. G., & Moulton, C. E. (2002). Authoritative and authoritarian mothers' parenting goals, attributions, and emotions across different childrearing contexts. *Parenting: Science and Practice, 2,* 1–26.

Cornwell, B., & Lundgren, D. C. (2003). Love on the Internet? In M. Coleman & L. Ganong (Eds.), *Points and counterpoints: Controversial relationship and family issues in the 21st century: An anthology* (pp. 10–14). Los Angeles: Roxbury.

Correctional Service of Canada. (2004). *Private family visiting* (Catalogue no. PS84-1/2004). Retrieved

November 11, 2004, from http://www.csc-scc.ca/text/pblct/visit/index_e.shtml

Cossette, L., & Duclos, E. (2002). *A profile of disability in Canada, 2001*. (Catalogue no. 89-577-XIE). Ottawa: Statistics Canada.

Cottrell, B. (2003). *Parent abuse: The abuse of parents by their teenage children* (Catalogue no. H72-22/25-2003E). Ottawa: National Clearinghouse on Family Violence.

Cowan, C. P., Cowan, P. A., Heming, G., Garrett, E., Coysh, W. S., Curtis-Boles, H., & Boles, A. J., III. (1985). Transitions to parenthood: His, hers, and theirs. *Journal of Family Issues, 6*, 451–481.

Cowan, D. B. (2003). Assisted reproductive technology and the fertility clinic. In J. Haynes & J. Miller (Eds.), *Inconceivable conceptions: Psychological aspects of infertility and reproductive technology* (pp. 11–16). New York: Brunner-Routledge.

Cowan, P. A., & Cowan, C. P. (2003). Normative family transitions, normal family process, and healthy child development. In F. Walsh (Ed.), *Normal family processes: Growing diversity and complexity* (3rd ed., pp. 424–459). New York: Guilford.

Cowan, R. S. (1992). Twentieth-century changes in household technology. In A. S. Skolnick & J. H. Skolnick (Eds.), *Family in transition: Rethinking marriage, sexuality, child rearing, and family organization* (7th ed., pp. 82–92). New York: HarperCollins.

Cowan, R. S. (1991). From Virginia Dare to Virginia Slims: Women and technology in American life. In M. C. LaFollette & J. K. Stine (Eds.), *Technology and choice: Readings from Technology and Culture* (pp. 291–303). Chicago: University of Chicago Press.

Cox, M. J., Paley, B., Burchinal, M., & Payne, C. C. (1999). Marital perceptions and interactions across the transition to parenthood. *Journal of Marriage and the Family, 61*, 611–625.

Cranswick, K. (2003). *General social survey cycle 16: Caring for an aging society* (Catalogue no. 89-582-XIE). Ottawa: Statistics Canada.

Crompton, S., & Vickers, M. (2000, Summer). One hundred years of labour force. *Canadian Social Trends* (Statistics Canada Catalogue No. 11-008), 2–13.

Crouter, A. C., Bumpus, M. F., Head, M. R., & McHale, S. M. (2001). Implications of overwork and overload for the quality of men's family relationships. *Journal of Marriage and Family, 63*, 404–416.

Crowder, K., & Teachman, J. (2004). Do residential conditions explain the relationship between living arrangements and adolescent behavior? *Journal of Marriage and Family, 66*, 721–738.

Crytser, A. (1990). *The wife-in-law trap*. New York: Pocket Books.

Cui, M., Conger, R. D., Bryant, C. M., & Elder, G. H., Jr. (2002). Parental behavior and the quality of adolescent friendships: A social-contextual perspective. *Journal of Marriage and Family, 64*, 676–689.

Cummings, E. M., Goeke-Morey, M. C., & Papp, L. M. (2003). Children's responses to everyday marital conflict tactics in the home. *Child Development, 74*, 1918–1929.

Cunningham, J. D., & Antill, J. K. (1995). Current trends in nonmarital cohabitation: In search of the POSSLQ. In J. T. Wood and S. Duck (Eds.), *Understudied relationships: Off the beaten track* (pp. 148–172). Thousand Oaks, CA: Sage.

Cunningham, M. (2001). The influence of parental attitudes and behaviors on children's attitudes toward gender and household labor in early adulthood. *Journal of Marriage and Family, 63*, 111–122.

Curtis, T. (2001, March). Television violence and aggression. *Family Focus*, F8, F11.

Curto, J., & Rothwell, N. (2003, February). The gender balance of employment in rural and small town Canada. *Rural and Small Town Canada Analysis Bulletin* (Statistics Canada Catalogue no. 21-006-XIE). Retrieved from http://www.statcan.ca/cgi-bin/downpub/freepub.cgi

Dad guilty of stabbing daughter. (2005, March 4). *CNEWS*. Retrieved April 19, 2005, from http://cnews.canoe.ca/CNEWS/Law/2005/03/4/pf 950550.html

Daly, K. J. (2001). Deconstructing family time: From ideology to lived experience. *Journal of Marriage and Family, 63*, 283–294.

Daly, K. (2003). Family theory versus the theories families live by. *Journal of Marriage and Family, 65*, 771–784.

Daly, K. (2004, October 4). *Reframed family portraits*. 40th Anniversary Lecture, Vanier Institute of the Family, Ottawa.

Dannefer, D., & Perlmutter, M. (1990). Development as a multidimensional process: Individual and social constituents. *Human Development, 33*, 108–137.

Das Gupta, T. (2000). Families of Native people, immigrants, and people of colour. In N. Mandell & A. Duffy (Eds.), *Canadian families: Diversity, conflict, and change* (2nd ed., pp. 146–187). Toronto: Harcourt Canada.

Davis, E. C., & Friel, L. V. (2001). Adolescent sexuality: Disentangling the effects of family structure and family context. *Journal of Marriage and Family, 63*, 669–681.

Dawson, F., with Heyman, D. (2000, September 25). Polygamist commune probed for underage marriages. *Calgary Herald* [Online]. Retrieved December 12, 2000, from http://www.calgaryherald. com/news/ stories/000925/4575231.html

Day, R. D., Peterson, G. W., & McCracken, C. (1998). Predicting spanking of younger and older children by mothers and fathers. *Journal of Marriage and the Family, 60,* 79–94.

Day, R. J. F. (2000). *Multiculturalism and the history of Canadian diversity.* Toronto: University of Toronto Press.

D'Costa, R. (1987). Recent immigrants slow down population aging. *Perception, 10*(5), 30–31.

Degler, C. (1974). What ought to be and what was: Women's sexuality in the nineteenth century. *American Historical Review, 79,* 1467–1490.

DeKeseredy, W. S. (1993). *Four variations of family violence: A review of sociological research.* Ottawa: National Clearinghouse on Family Violence.

DeKeseredy, W. S., & Ellis, D. (1995). Intimate male violence against women in Canada. In J. I. Ross (Ed.), *Violence in Canada: Sociopolitical perspectives* (pp. 97–125). Don Mills, ON: Oxford University Press.

DeMaris, A., Benson, M. L., Fox, G. L., Hill, T., & Van Wyk, J. (2003). Distal and proximal factors in domestic violence: A test of an integrated model. *Journal of Marriage and Family, 65,* 652–667.

Denham, D., & Gillespie, J. (1999). *Two steps forward … One step back: An overview of Canadian initiatives and resources to end woman abuse 1989–1997.* Ottawa: Health Canada. Retrieved February 16, 2001, from http://www.hc-sc.gc.ca/hppb/familyviolence/ html/two_steps/ english/

Department of Justice Canada. (2003). *Dating violence: A fact sheet from the Department of Justice Canada.* Retrieved September 11, 2004, from http://canada.justice.gc.ca/en/ps/fm/datingfs.html

Department of Justice Canada. (2004a). *Canadian custody and access provisions: Extended family custody and access.* Retrieved February 17, 2005, from http://canada.justice.gc.ca/en/ps/pad/reports/chart/ chart1-4e.html

Department of Justice Canada. (2004b). *Overview of the Canadian system of support enforcement.* Retrieved September 24, 2004, from http://canada.justice.gc.ca/en/sup/ enforcement_overview.html

Department of Public Health, Toronto. (1922). *The care of the infant and young child.* Toronto: Author.

DePaulo, B. M., & Morris, W. L. (in press). Singles in society and in science. *Psychological Inquiry.*

DeVault, M. L. (1991). *Feeding the family: The social organization of caring as gendered work.* Chicago: University of Chicago Press.

Dickson, F. C. (1995). The best is yet to be: Research on long-lasting marriages. In J. T. Wood & S. Duck (Eds.), *Under-studied relationships: Off the beaten track* (pp. 22–50). Thousand Oaks, CA: Sage.

Disabled Women's Network Ontario. (2002). *Verdict of coroner's jury into the death of Kimberly Ann Rogers.* (2002). Retrieved January 21, 2005, from http://dawn.thot.net/Kimberly_Rogers/kria118.html

Dodson, L., & Dickert, J. (2004). Girls' family labor in low-income households: A decade of qualitative research. *Journal of Marriage and Family, 66,* 318–332.

Doherty, G. (1996). *The great child-care debate: The long-term effects of non-parental child care.* Toronto: University of Toronto, Childcare Resource and Research Unit. Retrieved December 21, 2000, from http://www.childcarecanada.org/ resources/CRRUpubs/op7/7optoc.html

Doherty, G., Friendly, M., & Oloman, M. (1998). *Women's support, women's work: Child care in an era of deficit reduction, devolution, downsizing and deregulation.* Ottawa: Status of Women Canada.

Doherty, W. J. (1997). *The intentional family.* Reading, MA: Addison-Wesley.

Douglas, S. J., & Michaels, M. W. (2004). *The mommy myth: The idealization of motherhood and how it has undermined women.* New York: Free Press.

Douthitt, R. A., & Fedyk, J. (1990). *The cost of raising children in Canada.* Toronto: Butterworths.

Downey, D. B., & Condron, D. J. (2004). Playing well with others in kindergarten: The benefit of siblings at home. *Journal of Marriage and Family, 66,* 333–350.

Doyle, R., & Visano, L. (1987). Toronto social agencies don't meet needs of minorities: Report. *Perception, 10*(5), 12–13.

Dreyer, C. A., & Dreyer, A. S. (1973). Family dinner time as a unique behavior habitat. *Family Process, 12,* 291–301.

Driver, J., Tabares, A., Shapiro, A., Nahm, E. Y., & Gottman, J. M. (2003). Interactional patterns in marital success or failure: Gottman laboratory studies. In F. Walsh (Ed.), *Normal family processes: Growing diversity and complexity* (3rd ed., pp. 493–513). New York: Guilford.

Dryburgh, H. (2000). Teenage pregnancy. *Health Reports, 12*(1), 9–19.

Dubeau, D. (2002). *Portraits of fathers.* Ottawa: Vanier Institute of the Family.

Duffy, A., & Momirov, J. (1997). *Family violence: A Canadian introduction*. Toronto: James Lorimer.

Dumas, J. (1987). *Current demographic analysis: Report on the demographic situation in Canada 1986*. Ottawa: Statistics Canada.

Dumas, J., & Bélanger, A. (1996). *Report on the demographic situation in Canada 1995: Current demographic analysis*. Ottawa: Statistics Canada.

Dumas, J., & Peron, Y. (1992). *Marriage and conjugal life in Canada: Current demographic analysis*. Ottawa: Statistics Canada.

Duncan, M. (2000). The Hague Convention on Protection of Children and Co-operation in Respect of Intercountry Adoption: Its birth and prospects. In P. Selman (Ed.), *Intercountry adoption: Developments, trends and perspectives* (pp. 40–52). London, England: British Agencies for Adoption and Fostering.

Dush, C. M. K., Cohan, C. L., & Amato, P. R. (2003). The relationship between cohabitation and marital quality and stability: Change across cohorts? *Journal of Marriage and Family, 65*, 539–549.

Duvall, E. M., & Miller, B. C. (1985). *Marriage and family development* (6th ed.). New York: Harper & Row.

Duxbury, L., & Higgins, C. (2003). *Work-life conflict in Canada in the new millennium: A status report: Final report*. Ottawa: Health Canada.

Duxbury, L., Higgins, C., & Coghill, D. (2003). *Voices of Canadians: Seeking work-life balance*. Hull, QC: Human Resources Development Canada. Retrieved November 26, 2003, from http://labour-travail. hrdc-drhc.gc.ca/worklife/vcswlb-tcrctvp/tm.cfm

Edin, K., Kefalas, M. J., & Reed, J. M. (2004). A peek inside the black box: What marriage means for poor unmarried parents. *Journal of Marriage and Family, 66*, 1007–1014.

Edin, K., & Lein, L. (1997). *Making ends meet: How single mothers survive welfare and low-wage work*. New York: Russell Sage Foundation.

Editors of *Bride's* Magazine. (1999). *Bride's book of etiquette* (Rev. ed.). New York: Perigee.

Edwards, H. (1989). *How could you? Mothers without custody of their children*. Freedom, CA: Crossing Press.

EGALE (Equality for Gays and Lesbians Everywhere). (1999a, May 20). *M v. H: An EGALE backgrounder*. Retrieved May 19, 2000, from http://www.egale.ca/legal/backgrd3.htm

EGALE. (1999b, May 20). *Supreme court rules: Same-sex couples entitled to equality*. Retrieved May 19, 2000, from http://www.egale.ca/pressrel/990520.htm

EGALE. (n.d.). *Bill C23 and conjugal relationships*. Retrieved May 19, 2000, from http://www.egale.ca/documents/conjugality.htm

Eicher-Catt, D. (2004, March). Noncustodial mothers and mental health: When absence makes the heart break. *Family Focus*, F7–F8.

Eichler, M. (1987). Family change and social policies. In *Family Matters*. Toronto: Methuen.

Elliott, S. A., & Watson, J. P. (1985). Sex during pregnancy and the first prenatal year. *Journal of Psychosomatic Research, 29*, 541–548.

Ellison, M. M. (2004). *Same-sex marriage: A Christian ethical analysis*. Cleveland, OH: Pilgrim.

Elquist, M. J., & Hilton, J. M. (2003, November). *Marital satisfaction and equity in work/family role responsibilities in dual earner shiftworkers*. Poster presentation at annual conference of National Council on Family Relations, Vancouver.

Emery, R. E., & Dillon, P. (1994). Conceptualizing the divorce process: Renegotiating boundaries of intimacy and power in the divorced family system. *Family Relations, 43*, 374–379.

English-Lueck, J. A. (2001, March). Technology and social change: The effects on family. *Family Focus*, F1–F3, F5.

Entwisle, D. R., & Alexander, K. L. (1995). A parent's economic shadow: Family structure versus family resources as influences on early school achievement. *Journal of Marriage and the Family, 57*, 399–409.

Erera, P. I. (2002). *Family diversity: Continuity and change in the contemporary family*. Thousand Oaks, CA: Sage.

Erikson, E. H. (1982). *The life cycle completed: A review*. New York: W. W. Norton.

Evasiuk, S. (1987, September 12). The age of reason: Radio play brings back outrageous baby derby. *Toronto Star*, p. F4.

Fahlberg, V. (1981). *Attachment and separation*. London: British Agencies for Adoption and Fostering.

Faller, K. C. (1993). *Child sexual abuse: Intervention and treatment issues*. Washington, DC: U.S. Department of Health and Human Services, National Center on Child Abuse and Neglect. Retrieved February 12, 2001, from http://www.calib.com/nccanch/pubs/usermanuals/sexabuse/

Fan, X., Miller, B. C., Christensen, M., Park, K.-E., Grotevant, H. D., van Dulmen, M., et al. (2002). Questionnaire and interview inconsistencies exaggerated differences between adopted and non-adopted adolescents in a national sample. *Adoption Quarterly, 6*(2), 7–27.

Fast, J., & Frederick, J. (2004a). *The time of our lives: Juggling work and leisure over the life cycle* (Catalogue no. 89-584-MIE). Ottawa: Statistics Canada.

Fast, J., & Frederick, J. (2004b). *The transition to retirement: When every day is Saturday, 1998* (Catalogue no. 89-584-MIE no. 5). Ottawa: Statistics Canada.

Fast, J., Frederick, J., Zukewich, N., & Franke, S. (2001, Winter). The time of our lives ... *Canadian Social Trends* (Statistics Canada Catalogue no. 11-008), 20–23.

Fawcett, G., Ciceri, C., Tsoukalas, S., & Gibson-Kierstead, A. (2004). *Supports and services for adults and children aged 5–14 with disabilities in Canada: An analysis of data on needs and gaps.* Ottawa: Canadian Council on Social Development. Retrieved December 12, 2004, from http://socialunion.gc.ca/pwd/

Federation of Canadian Municipalities. (2000). *A national affordable housing strategy.* Ottawa: Federation of Canadian Municipalities.

Fehr-Snyder, K., & Cieslak, D. J. (2005, April 27). Oh boy, they're here. *Arizona Republic,* pp. A1, A16.

Feigelman, W. (2001). Comparing adolescents in diverging family structures: Investigating whether adoptees are more prone to problems than their non-adopted peers. *Adoption Quarterly, 5*(2), 5–27.

Feinberg, M. E., McHale, S. M., Crouter, A., & Cumsille, P. (2003). Sibling differentiation: Sibling and parent relationship trajectories in adolescence. *Child Development, 74,* 1261–1274.

Fiese, B. H., Tomcho, T. J., Douglas, M., Josephs, K., Poltrock, S., & Baker, T. (2002). A review of 50 years of research on naturally occurring family routines and rituals: Cause for celebration? *Journal of Family Psychology, 16,* 381–390.

Fitzgerald, R. (2003). *An examination of sex differences in delinquency* (Catalogue no. 85-561-MIE200301). Ottawa: Statistics Canada.

Forste, R., & Tanfer, K. (1996). Sexual exclusivity among dating, cohabiting, and married women. *Journal of Marriage and the Family, 58,* 33–47.

Forthofer, M. S., Markman, H. J., Cox, M., Stanley, S., & Kessler, R. C. (1996). Associations between marital distress and work loss in a national sample. *Journal of Marriage and the Family, 58,* 597–605.

Fowlkes, M. R. (1987). The myth of merit and male professional careers: The roles of wives. In N. Gerstel & H. E. Gross (Eds.), *Families and work* (pp. 347–360). Philadelphia: Temple University Press.

Fox, G. L., & Kelly, R. F. (1995). Determinants of child custody arrangements at divorce. *Journal of Marriage and the Family, 57,* 693–708.

Fox, G. L., & Murry, V. M. (2000). Gender and families: Feminist perspectives and family research. *Journal of Marriage and the Family, 62,* 1160–1172.

Fraenkel, P. (2003). Contemporary two-parent families: Navigating work and family challenges. In F. Walsh (Ed.), *Normal family processes: Growing diversity and complexity* (3rd ed., pp. 61–95). New York: Guilford.

Frankel-Howard, D. (1989). *Family violence: A review of theoretical and clinical literature.* Ottawa: Health and Welfare Canada.

Fravel, D. L., McRoy, R. G., & Grotevant, H. D. (2000). Birthmother perceptions of the psychologically present adopted child: Adoption openness and boundary ambiguity. *Family Relations, 49,* 425–433.

Frederick, J. A., & Hamel, J. (1998, Spring). Canadian attitudes to divorce. *Canadian Social Trends* (Catalogue no. 11-008-XPE), 6–11. Ottawa: Statistics Canada.

Frenette, M., & Picot, G. (2003). *Life after welfare: The economic well being of welfare leavers in Canada during the 1990s* (Catalogue no. 11F0019MIE–No. 192). Ottawa: Statistics Canada.

Frenette, M., Picot, G., & Sceviour, R. (2004). *How long do people live in low-income neighborhoods? Evidence for Toronto, Montreal, and Vancouver* (Catalogue no. 11F0019MIE–No. 216). Ottawa: Statistics Canada.

Freudenberger, H. J., & North, G. (1985). *Women's burnout.* New York: Penguin.

Freundlich, M. (2000). *The market forces in adoption.* Washington, DC: Child Welfare League of America.

Freundlich, M. (2001). *Adoption and assisted reproduction.* Washington, DC: Child Welfare League of America.

Fulmer, R. (1999). Becoming an adult: Leaving home and staying connected. In B. Carter & M. McGoldrick (Eds.), *The expanded family life cycle: Individual, family, and social perspectives* (3rd ed., pp. 215–230). Boston: Allyn & Bacon.

Gaffield, C. (1982). Schooling, the economy, and rural society in nineteenth-century Ontario. In J. Parr (Ed.), *Childhood and family in Canadian history* (pp. 69–92). Toronto: McClelland & Stewart.

Garbarino, J. (1992). *Children and families in the social environment* (2nd ed.). New York: Aldine de Gruyter.

Gaughan, M. (2002). The substitution hypothesis: The impact of premarital liaisons and human capital on marital timing. *Journal of Marriage and Family, 64,* 407–419.

Gee, E. M. (1987). Historical change in the family life course of Canadian men and women. In V. W. Marshall (Ed.), *Aging in Canada: Social perspectives* (2nd ed., pp. 265–287). Markham, ON: Fitzhenry & Whiteside.

Gee, E. M. (1993). Adult outcomes associated with childhood family structure: An appraisal of research and an examination of Canadian data. In J. Hudson & B.

Galaway (Eds.), *Single parent families: Perspectives on research and policy* (pp. 291–310). Toronto: Thompson Educational Publishing.

Gelles, R. J. (2000). Controversies in family preservation programs. In R. A. Geffner, P. G. Jaffe, & M. Suderman (Eds.), *Children exposed to domestic violence: Current issues in research, intervention, prevention, and policy development* (pp. 239–252). New York: Haworth Maltreatment & Trauma Press.

George, M. V., Loh, S., Verma, R. B. P., & Shin, Y. E. (2001). *Population projections for Canada, Provinces and Territories 2000–2026* (Catalogue no. 91-520-XIB). Ottawa: Statistics Canada.

Gerson, K. (1987). *Hard choices: How women decide about work, career, and motherhood.* Berkeley, CA: University of California Press.

Gerson, K. (1993). *No man's land: Men's changing commitments to family and work.* New York: Basic Books.

Gewirtzman, R., & Fodor, I. (1987). The homeless child at school: From welfare hotel to classroom. *Child Welfare, 66,* 237–245.

Ghalam, N. Z. (1996, Autumn). Living with relatives. *Canadian Social Trends,* 20–24.

Giboney, S. K. (2001, December). A visible death. *Family Focus,* F3, F7.

Gilbert, S., & Bélanger, A. (2001). Impact of causes of death on life expectancy at higher ages from 1951 to 1996. In A. Bélanger, Y. Carrière, & S. Gilbert, *Report on the demographic situation in Canada 2000* (Catalogue no. 91-209-XPE, pp. 137–151). Ottawa: Statistics Canada.

Gilbert, W. S. (1996). Trial by jury. In I. Bradley (Ed.), The complete annotated Gilbert and Sullivan. Oxford: Oxford University Press. (Originally published 1875.)

Gilgun, J. F. (1995). We shared something special: The moral discourse of incest perpetrators. *Journal of Marriage and the Family, 57,* 265–281.

Gilgun, J. F. (1999). *Brainstorming: A comprehensive theory of family violence.* Retrieved January 17, 2005, from http://www.mincava.umn.edu/documents/jgilgun/brainstorm.html

Gill, A. (2000, June 10). What are the wages of cybersin? *The Globe and Mail,* R18.

Gleason, M. (1999). *Normalizing the ideal: Psychology, schooling, and the family in postwar Canada.* Toronto: University of Toronto Press.

Glick, J. E., & Van Hook, J. (2002). Parents' coresidence with adult children: Can immigration explain racial and ethnic variation? *Journal of Marriage and Family, 64,* 240–253.

Goddard, H. W., Goff, B. G., Dennis, S. A., & Melancon, M. V. (2002, November). *Value differences in adolescent crowds.* Poster presentation at annual conference of National Council on Family Relations, Houston, TX.

Goldberg, D. L. (2003). *Grandparent-grandchild access: A legal analysis.* Ottawa: Department of Justice Canada.

Goldberg, K. (1996, Fall). Corporal punishment of children: When family issues become public concerns. *Canada's Children.* Retrieved November 20, 2000, from http://www.cfc-efc.ca/docs/00000823.htm

Goldscheider, F. K., Thornton, A., & Yang, L.-S. (2001). Helping out the kids: Expectations about parental support in young adulthood. *Journal of Marriage and Family, 63,* 727–740.

Golombok, S., & Fivush, R. (1994). *Gender development.* Cambridge: Cambridge University Press.

Goode, W. J. (1968). The theoretical importance of love. In M. B. Sussman (Ed.), *Sourcebook in marriage and the family* (3rd ed., pp. 249–257). Boston: Houghton Mifflin.

Goodwin, C. (2000, January 16). "Nobel sperm bank" babies … and how they grew. *The Toronto Star* [Online]. Retrieved January 19, 2000, from http://www.thestar.ca/thestar/editorial/life/20000116BOD016_BS-BRAINS.html

Goodwin, P. Y. (2003). African American and European American women's marital well-being. *Journal of Marriage and Family, 65,* 550–560.

Gorlick, C. A., & Pomfret, D. A. (1993). Hope and circumstance: Single mothers exiting social assistance. In J. Hudson & B. Galaway (Eds.), *Single parent families: Perspectives on research and policy* (pp. 253–270). Toronto: Thompson Educational Publishing.

Gosden, R. (1999). *Designing babies: The brave new world of reproductive technology.* New York: W. H. Freeman.

Gossman, I., Julien, D., Mathieu, M., & Chartrand, E. (2003). Determinants of sex initiation frequencies and sexual satisfaction in long-term couples' relationships. *Canadian Journal of Human Sexuality, 12,* 169–181.

Gottlieb, B. H. (1999, July/August). Flexible work arrangements: The promise and the practice. *CFWW Research News.* Retrieved September 27, 2000, from http://www.uoguelph.ca/cfww/ news_07_99.html

Gottman, J. M. (1991). Predicting the longitudinal course of marriages. *Journal of Marital and Family Therapy, 17,* 3–7.

Gottman, J. M. (1993). A theory of marital dissolution and stability. *Journal of Family Psychology, 7,* 57–75.

Gottman, J. M. (1994). *What predicts divorce? The relationship between marital processes and marital outcomes.* Hillsdale, NJ: Lawrence Erlbaum.

Gouvernement du Québec. (2004). *Childcare services.* Retrieved December 29, 2004, from http://www.messf.gouv.qc.ca/services-a-la-famille/services-de-garde/

Government of Newfoundland and Labrador. (2005). *Accessing records from Vital Statistics under the Adoption Act.* Retrieved April 25, 2005, from http://www.gs.gov.nl.ca/gs/vs/adoption-records.stm

Greenberg, J., Schimel, J., & Martens, A. (2002). Ageism: Denying the face of the future. In T. D. Nelson (Ed.), *Ageism: Stereotyping and prejudice against older persons* (pp. 27–48). Cambridge, MA: MIT Press.

Greene, S. M., Anderson, E. R., Hetherington, M. E., Forgatch, M. S., & DeGarmo, D. S. (2003). Risk and resilience after divorce. In F. Walsh (Ed.), *Normal family processes: Growing diversity and complexity* (3rd ed., pp. 96–120). New York: Guilford.

Greenstein, T. N. (2000). Economic dependence, gender, and the division of labor in the home: A replication and extension. *Journal of Marriage and the Family, 62,* 322–335.

Greenstein, T. N. (2001). *Methods of family research.* Thousand Islands, CA: Sage.

Greif, G. L. (1985). *Single fathers.* Lexington, MA: Lexington Books.

Greven, P. (1990). *Spare the child: The religious roots of punishment and the psychological impact of physical abuse.* New York: Vintage Books.

Griffiths, A., & Cruise, D. (1999). *Hear no evil.* 14th Annual Atkinson Fellowship in Public Policy. Toronto: Atkinson Charitable Foundation. Retrieved January 23, 2005, from http://atkinsonfdn.on.ca

Grych, J. H., Harold, G. T., & Miles, C. J. (2003). A prospective investigation of appraisals as mediators of the link between interparental conflict and child adjustment. *Child Development, 74,* 1176–1193.

Grzywacz, J. G., Almeida, D. M., & McDonald, D. A. (2002). Work-family spillover and daily reports of work and family stress in the adult labor force. *Family Relations, 51,* 28–36.

Guest, D. (1985). *The emergence of social security in Canada.* Vancouver: University of British Columbia Press.

Gupta, S. (1999). The effects of transitions in marital status on men's performance of housework. *Journal of Marriage and the Family, 61,* 700–711.

Gurian, M. & Henley, P., with Trueman, T. (2001). *Boys and girls learn differently! A guide for teachers and parents.* San Francisco: Jossey-Bass.

Guzell, J. R., Landry-Meyer, L., & Gerard, J. M. (2002, November). *Exploring strengths and stressors during a life-course transition: The case of grandparents raising grandchildren.* Poster presentation at annual conference of National Council on Family Relations. Houston, TX.

Haddock, S. A., Zimmerman, T. S., & Lyness, K. P. (2003). Changing gender norms: Transitional dilemmas. In F. Walsh (Ed.), *Normal family processes: Growing diversity and complexity* (3rd ed., pp. 301–336). New York: Guilford.

Hagestad, G. O. (1986). The family: Women and grandparents as kin-keepers. In A. Pifer & L. Bronte (Eds.), *Our aging society: Paradox and promise* (pp. 141–160). New York: W. W. Norton.

Hall, E. T. (1973). *The silent language.* Garden City, NY: Anchor Press/Doubleday.

Hall, E. (1987, November). All in the family. *Psychology Today,* 54–60.

Hamilton, J. (1971). *Progress.* Calgary: Calgary Power.

Hammond, D. B. (1987). *My parents never had sex: Myths and facts of sexual aging.* Buffalo, NY: Prometheus.

Hamon, R. R., & Ingoldsby, B. B. (Eds.). (2003). *Mate selection across cultures.* Thousand Oaks, CA: Sage.

A handy budget checklist to keep track of wedding cost. (n.d.). Retrieved April 6, 2001, from http://www.ataaa.com/budget.htm

Hanson, T. L., McLanahan, S. S., & Thomson, E. (1996). Double jeopardy: Parental conflict and step-family outcomes for children. *Journal of Marriage and the Family, 58,* 141–154.

Haring, M., Hewitt, P. L., & Flett, G. L. (2003). Perfectionism, coping, and quality of intimate relationships. *Journal of Marriage and Family, 65,* 143–158.

Harris, J. R. (1995). Where is the children's environment? A group socialization theory of development. *Psychological Review, 102,* 458–489.

Hart, L., & Jamieson, W. (2002). *Woman abuse* (revised, Catalogue no. H72-22/4-2002E). Ottawa: Health Canada.

Hart, R. (1997). *Beginning a long journey: A review of projects funded by the Family Violence Prevention Division, Health Canada, regarding violence in Aboriginal families.* Ottawa: Health Canada.

Havighurst, R. J. (1952). *Developmental tasks and education* (2nd ed.). New York: Longman's Green.

Hay, T. (1997). *Child abuse and neglect* (Rev. ed.). Ottawa: Health Canada.

Hazlett, T. (2004, February 14). *Requiem for the v-chip.* Retrieved November 30, 2004, from http://slate.msn.com/id/2095396/

Health Canada. (1997). *Family violence in Aboriginal communities: An Aboriginal perspective*. Ottawa: Health Canada.

Health Canada (1998, April). *Induced abortion*. Retrieved November 20, 2000, from http://www.hc-sc .gc.ca/main/ lcdc/web/brch/factshts/inabor_e.html

Health Canada. (1999). *Reproductive and genetic technologies overview paper (1999)*. Ottawa: Health Canada. Retrieved August 20, 2000, from http://www.hc-sc .gc.ca/english/rgt/overview.htm

Health Canada. (2003). *Responding to a changing epidemic*. Retrieved August 26, 2004, from http://www.hc-sc.gc.ca/hppb/hiv_aids/report03/ wad2.html

Health Canada. (2004, May). *HIV/AIDS EPI updates*. Ottawa: Health Canada, Centre for Infectious Disease Prevention and Control, Surveillance and Risk Assessment Division.

Hébert, M., Chenier, N. M., & Norris, S. (2004). *Bill C-6: Assisted Human Reproduction Act*. Retrieved November 3, 2004, from http:// www.parl.gc.ca/ common/Bills_ls.asp?Parl=37&Ses=3&ls=C6

Heisz, A., & McLeod, L. (2004). *Low-income in Census Metropolitan Areas, 1980-2000* (Catalogue no. 89-613-MIE, No. 001). Ottawa: Statistics Canada.

Herberg, E. N. (1989). *Ethnic groups in Canada: Adaptations and transitions*. Scarborough, ON: Nelson Canada.

Herman, R. D. (1963). The "going steady" complex: A re-examination. In M. B. Sussman (Ed.), *Sourcebook in marriage and the family* (2nd ed., pp. 75–79). Boston: Houghton Mifflin.

Hernandez, M., & McGoldrick, M. (1999). Migration and the life cycle. In B. Carter & M. McGoldrick (Eds.), *The expanded family life cycle: Individual, family, and social perspectives* (3rd ed., pp. 169–184). Boston: Allyn & Bacon.

Hertz, R. (1987). Three careers: His, hers, and theirs. In N. Gerstel & H. E. Gross (Eds.), *Families and work*. Philadelphia: Temple University Press.

Hetherington, E. M. (2003). Intimate pathways: Changing patterns in close personal relationships across time. *Family Relations, 52*, 318–331.

Heyman, R. E., & Smith Slep, A. M. (2002). Do child abuse and interparental violence lead to adulthood family violence? *Journal of Marriage and Family, 64*, 864–870.

Hicks, R., & Hicks, K. (1999). *Boomers, Xers, and other strangers: Understanding the generational differences that divide us*. Wheaton, IL: Tyndale.

Hiedemann, B., Suhomlinova, O., & O'Rand, A. M. (1998). Economic independence, economic status, and empty nest in midlife marital disruption. *Journal of Marriage and the Family, 60*, 219–231.

Hill, E. J., Hawkins, A. J., Ferris, M., & Weitzman, M. (2001). Finding an extra day a week: The positive influence of perceived job flexibility on work and family life balance. *Family Relations, 50*, 49–58.

Hill, E. J., Märtinson, V., & Ferris, M. (2004). New concept part-time employment as a work-family adaptive strategy for women professionals with small children. *Family Relations, 53*, 282–292.

Hill, R. (1958). Generic features of families under stress. *Social Casework, 49*, 139–150.

Hillier, L., & Harrison, L. (2004). Homophobia and the production of shame: Young people and same sex attraction. *Culture, Health & Sexuality, 6*, 79–94.

Hines, P. M., Preto, N. G., McGoldrick, M., Almeida, R., & Weltman, S. (1999). Culture and the family life cycle. In B. Carter & M. McGoldrick (Eds.), *The expanded family life cycle: Individual, family, and social perspectives* (3rd ed., pp. 69–87). Boston: Allyn & Bacon.

Hinman, L. M. (n.d.). *Reproductive technology and surrogacy: An introduction to the issues*. Retrieved May 30, 2000, from http://ethics.acusd.edu/ Papers/Introduction%20Technologies.html

Hoffman, L. W., & Youngblade, L. M. (1999). *Mothers at work: Effects on children's well-being*. Cambridge: Cambridge University Press.

Holcomb, B. (2003). Friendly for whose family? In M. Coleman & L. Ganong (Eds.), *Points & counterpoints: Controversial relationship and family issues in the 21st century: An anthology* (pp. 167–169). Los Angeles: Roxbury.

Holland, B. (1998, March). "The long good-bye," *Smithsonian*, 91–92.

Holman, T. B., & Li, B. D. (1995, November). *Premarital factors influencing perceived readiness for marriage*. Paper presented at the Annual Conference of the National Council on Family Relations, Portland, OR.

Hook, J. L. (2004). Reconsidering the division of household labor: Incorporating volunteer work and informal support. *Journal of Marriage and Family, 66*, 101–117.

Hotton, T. (2003). *Childhood aggression and exposure to violence in the home* (Catalogue no. 85-561-MIE). Ottawa: Statistics Canada.

Hou, F., & Picot, G. (2004, Spring). Visible minority neighbourhoods in Toronto, Montréal, and Vancouver. *Canadian Social Trends* (Statistics Canada Catalogue no. 11-008), 72, 8–13.

Howard, R. (2000, September 27). Editorial: Two men and a baby adds up to a heap of controversy. *Hamilton Spectator*, p. A14.

How much does a wedding cost? (n.d.) Retrieved April 6, 2001, from http://www.directweddings.co.uk/costs/

Huck, B. (2001, February/March). Love in another world. *The Beaver*, 12–19.

Hudak, J., Krestan, J. A., & Bepko, C. (1999). Alcohol problems and the family life cycle. In B. Carter & M. McGoldrick (Eds.), *The expanded family life cycle: Individual, family, and social perspectives* (3rd ed., pp. 455–469). Boston: Allyn & Bacon.

Hune, S. (2000). Doing gender with a feminist gaze: Toward a historical construction of Asian America. In M. Zhou & J. V. Gatewood (Eds.), *Contemporary Asian America: A multidisciplinary reader* (pp. 413–430). New York: New York University Press.

Hunter, G. (2003). The problem of child poverty in Canada. In A. Westhues (Ed.), *Canadian social policy: Issues and perspectives* (3rd ed., pp. 29–49). Waterloo, ON: Wilfrid Laurier University Press.

Hunting Bountiful. (2004, July 10). *The Economist*, p. 34.

Hurley, M. C. (2005). *Bill C-38: The Civil Marriage Act* (LS-502E). Ottawa: Library of Parliament, Parliamentary Information and Research Service.

Huston, A. C., & Wright, J. C. (1996). *Television and socialization of young children*. Retrieved August 18, 1996, from http://www.cyfc.umn.edu/Television.htm

Huston, M., & Schwartz, P. (1995). The relationships of lesbians and gay men. In J. T. Wood & S. Duck (Eds.), *Under-studied relationships: Off the beaten track* (pp. 89–121). Thousand Oaks, CA: Sage.

Huston, T. L. (2000). The social ecology of marriage and other intimate unions. *Journal of Marriage and the Family, 62*, 298–320.

Hyman, B. (1995, November). *The economic consequences of child sexual abuse in women*. Paper presented at the Annual Conference of National Council on Family Relations, Portland, OR.

Imber-Black, E. (1989). Women's relationships with larger systems. In M. McGoldrick, C. M. Anderson, & F. Walsh (Eds.), *Women in families: A framework for family therapy* (pp. 451–469). New York: Norton.

Imber-Black, E. (1993). Secrets in families and family therapy: An overview. In E. Imber-Black (Ed.), *Secrets in families and family therapy* (pp. 3–28). New York: Norton.

Ingoldsby, B. B. (2003). The mate selection process in the United States. In R. R. Hamon & B. B. Ingoldsby (Eds.), *Mate selection across cultures* (pp. 3–18). Thousand Oaks, CA: Sage.

Ingoldsby, B., Smith, S. R., & Miller, J. E. (2004). *Exploring family theories*. Los Angeles: Roxbury.

Institute of Canadian Studies. (2002). *Canadian Doukhobors on the Web: An overview*. Ottawa: University of Ottawa, Author. Retrieved on July 25, 2004, from http://www.uottawa.ca/academic/arts/cdn/doukhobor_intro.htm

Investors Group. (2004, July 16). *The most expensive life event according to 61% of those who know*. Retrieved July 20, 2004, from http://www.investorsgroup.com/english/about_us/news_releases/2004/040716divorce.htm

Ipsos-Reid. (2004, April 10). *Parents on parenting: How are Canada's children being raised? Part IV* [Press release]. Toronto: Ipsos-Reid.

Island, D., & Letellier, P. (1991). *Men who beat the men who love them: Battered gay men and domestic violence*. New York: Harrington Park.

Jacobs, J. S. (1991). Families with a medically ill member. In F. H. Brown (Ed.), *Reweaving the family tapestry: A multigenerational approach to families* (pp. 242–261). New York: W. W. Norton.

Jacquet, S. E., & Surra, C. A. (2001). Parental divorce and premarital couples: Commitment and other relationship characteristics. *Journal of Marriage and Family, 63*, 627–638.

Jarrett, R. L., & Jefferson, S. M. (2004). Women's danger management strategies in an inner-city housing project. *Family Relations, 53*, 138–147.

Jennings, K. T. (1994). Female sexual molesters: A review of the literature. In M. Elliott (Ed.), *Female sexual abuse of children* (pp. 219–234). New York: Guilford.

Jeynes, W. (2002). *Divorce, family structure, and the academic success of children*. New York: Haworth.

Johnson, T. W., & Colucci, P. (1999). Lesbians, gay men, and the family life cycle. In B. Carter & M. McGoldrick (Eds.), *The expanded family life cycle: Individual, family and social perspectives* (3rd ed., pp. 346–361). Boston: Allyn & Bacon.

Johnston, J. R., & Roseby, V. (1997). *In the name of the child: A developmental approach to understanding and helping children of conflicted and violent divorce*. New York: Free Press.

Jones, C., Clark, L., Grusec, J., Hart, R., Plickert, G., & Tepperman, L. (2002). *Poverty, social capital, parenting, and child outcomes in Canada* (Catalogue no. RH63-1/557-01-03E). Ottawa: Human Resources Development Canada. Retrieved November 22, 2004, from http://www11.sdc.gc.ca/en/cs/sp/arb/publications/research/2002-002357/

Jones, L., & Finkelhor, D. (2001, January). The decline in child sexual abuse cases. *Juvenile Justice Bulletin*. Washington, DC: U.S. Department of Justice.

Joseph, E. (1997). *Polygamy: The ultimate feminist lifestyle*. Retrieved December 11, 2000, from http://www.polygamy.com/Practical/Ultimate.htm

Josephson, W. L. (1995). *Television violence: A review of the effects on children of different ages*. Ottawa: Health Canada.

Juby, H., Marcil-Gratton, N., & Le Bourdais, C., with Huot, P.-M. (2001). A step further in family life: The emergence of the blended family. In A. Bélanger, Y. Carrière, & S. Gilbert, *Report on the demographic situation 2000: Current demographic analysis* (Catalogue no. 91-209-XPE, pp. 169–203). Ottawa: Statistics Canada.

Jurkovic, G. J. (1997). *Lost childhoods: The plight of the parentified child*. New York: Brunner/Mazel.

Kaiser Family Foundation. (2003). *TV violence*. Menlo Park, CA: Author. Retrieved February 25, 2004, from http://www.kff.org

Kallen, E. (1989). *Label me human: Minority rights of stigmatized Canadians*. Toronto: University of Toronto Press.

Kallen E. (2003). *Ethnicity and human rights in Canada: A human rights perspective on ethnicity, racism, and systemic inequality* (3rd ed.). Don Mills, ON: Oxford University Press.

Kalmijn, M. (2004). Marriage rituals as role transitions: An analysis of weddings in the Netherlands. *Journal of Marriage and Family, 66*, 582–594.

Kaufman, T. S. (1993). *The combined family: A guide to creating successful step-relationships*. New York: Plenum.

Keck, J. (2002). Remembering Kimberly Rogers. *Perception, 25*(3/4). Retrieved January 21, 2005, from http://www.ccsd.perception/2534/kimberly.htm

Kelly, J. B., & Emery, R. E. (2003). Children's adjustment following divorce. *Family Relations, 52*, 352–362.

Kempe, R. S., & Kempe, C. H. (1984). *The common secret: Sexual abuse of children and adolescents*. New York: W. H. Freeman.

Kennedy, G. E., & Chang, J. I. (2003, November). *Over the river and through the woods: Grandparental influences on healthy grandchild development*. Poster presentation at annual conference of National Council on Family Relations, Vancouver.

Kettle, J. (1980). *The big generation*. Toronto: McClelland & Stewart.

Kiecolt, K. J. (2003). Satisfaction with work and family life: The evidence of a cultural reversal. *Journal of Marriage and Family, 65*, 23–35.

Kieran, S. (1986). *The family matters: Two centuries of family law and life in Ontario*. Toronto: Key Porter.

King, V. (2003). The legacy of a grandparent's divorce: Consequences for ties between grandparents and grandchildren. *Journal of Marriage and Family, 65*, 170–183.

Kingsley, E. P. (2002, Spring). Welcome to Holland. *Transition, 3*.

Kingsmill, S., & Schlesinger, B. (1998). *The family squeeze: Surviving the sandwich generation*. Toronto: University of Toronto Press.

Kingston, A. (2004). *The meaning of wife*. Toronto: HarperCollins.

Kinnon, D. (2001). *Community awareness and response: Abuse and neglect of older adults* (Catalogue no. H39-262/2001E, revision). Ottawa: Health Canada, Family Violence Prevention Unit.

Kinsman, G. (1987). *The regulation of desire: Sexuality in Canada*. Montreal: Black Rose.

Kirk, H. D. (1984). *Shared fate: A theory and method of adoptive relationships* (2nd ed.). Port Angeles, WA: Ben-Simon.

Kirkpatrick, S. (1993). Safe homes: The risks involved. *Vis-à-Vis, 11*(1), 5.

Kirkwood, D., & Engelbrecht, J. (2002, November). *Family rituals, routines, and traditions: Building bridges and making memories*. Poster presentation at annual conference of National Council on Family Relations, Houston, TX.

Kite, M. E., & Wagner, L. S. (2002). Attitudes toward older adults. In T. D. Nelson (Ed.), *Ageism: Stereotyping and prejudice against older persons* (pp. 129–161). Cambridge, MA: MIT Press.

Klein, D. M., & White, J. M. (1996). *Family theories: An introduction*. Thousand Oaks, CA: Sage.

Klein, L. (1986, Fall). Our willy-nilly childbearing: Unintended and teenage pregnancy in the United States. *The Pharos*, 27–29.

Kliman, J., & Madsen, W. (1999). Social class and the family life cycle. In B. Carter & M. McGoldrick (Eds.), *The expanded family life cycle: Individual, family, and social perspectives* (3rd ed., pp. 88–105). Boston: Allyn & Bacon.

Knoppers, B. M. (2000, April). DNA profiles put families to test. *Families & Health, 7*.

Knowles, V. (2000). *Forging our legacy: Canadian citizenship and immigration, 1900–1977* (Catalogue no. Ci51-93/2000E). Ottawa: Public Works and Government Services Canada. Retrieved July 26, 2004, from http://www.cic.gc.ca/english/department/legacy/

Koerner, S. S., Jacobs, S. L., & Raymond, M. (2000). When mothers turn to their adolescent daughters: Predicting daughters' vulnerability to negative adjustment outcomes. *Family Relations, 49,* 301–309.

Kohen, D. E., Hertzman, C., & Brooks-Gunn, J. (1998). *Neighborhood influences on children's school readiness.* Hull, QC: Human Resources Development Canada. Retrieved December 17, 2000, from http://www.hrdr.gc.ca/stratpol/arb/publish/bulletin/mydocument/V4N1C03E.html

Kolata, G. (1999, March 3). $50,000 offered to tall, smart egg donor. *New York Times,* p. A10.

Kornhaber, A. (1996). *Contemporary grandparenting.* Thousand Oaks, CA: Sage.

Koropeckyj-Cox, T. (2002). Beyond parental status: Psychological well-being in middle and old age. *Journal of Marriage and Family, 64,* 957–971.

Kowal, A. K., & Blinn-Pike, L. (2004). Sibling influences on adolescents' attitudes toward safe sex practices. *Family Relations, 53,* 377–384.

Kramer, L., & Baron, L. N. (1995). Parental perceptions of children's sibling relationships. *Family Relations, 44,* 95–103.

Krashinsky, M. (2001–2002, Winter). "Are we there yet?" The evolving face of child care policy in Canada. *Transition,* 3–5.

Kruk, E. (1995). Grandparent-grandchild contact loss: Findings from a study of "grandparent rights" members. *Canadian Journal on Aging, 14,* 737–754.

Kulczycki, A., & Lobo, A. P. (2002). Patterns, determinants, and implications of intermarriage among Arab Americans. *Journal of Marriage and Family, 64,* 202–210.

Kurdek, L. A. (1995). Predicting change in marital satisfaction from husbands' and wives' conflict resolution styles. *Journal of Marriage and the Family, 57,* 153–164.

Kurdek, L. A. (2004). Are gay and lesbian cohabiting couples *really* different from heterosexual married couples? *Journal of Marriage and Family, 66,* 880–900.

La Gaipa, J. J. (1981). A systems approach to personal relationships. In S. Duck & R. Gilmour (Eds.), *Personal relationships I: Studying personal relationships* (pp. 67–89). London: Academic.

Lahey, K. A., & Alderson, K. (2004). *Same-sex marriage: The personal and the political.* Toronto: Insomniac.

Laird, J. (2003). Lesbian and gay families. In F. Walsh (Ed.), *Normal family processes: Growing diversity and complexity* (3rd ed., pp. 176–209). New York: Guilford.

Landau, H. (1997). *Grandparents' visitation rights—To grandfather's house we go?* Retrieved April 1, 1998, from http://www.divorcesource.com/NY/ARTICLES/landau1.htm

Landry, Y. (1992). Gender imbalance, les filles du roi, and choice of spouse in New France. In B. Bradbury (Ed.), *Canadian family history: Selected readings* (pp. 14–32). Toronto: Copp Clark Pitman.

Lang, D. V. (1988). *The phantom spouse: Helping you and your family survive business travel or relocation.* White Hall, VA: Betterway.

Lansford, J. E., Ceballo, R., Abbey, A., & Stewart, A. J. (2001). Does family structure matter? A comparison of adoptive, two-parent biological, single-mother, stepfather, and stepmother households. *Journal of Marriage and Family, 63,* 840–851.

LaRoque, E. D. (1994). *Violence in aboriginal communities.* Ottawa: Royal Commission on Aboriginal Peoples.

LaRossa, R., Jaret, C., Gadgil, M., & Wynn, G. R. (2000). The changing culture of fatherhood in comic-strip families: A six-decade analysis. *Journal of Marriage and the Family, 62,* 375–387.

Larson, C. J. (1986). *Sociological theory: From the enlightenment to the present.* Bayside, NY: General Hall.

Lasch, C. (1979). *Haven in a heartless world: The family besieged.* New York: Basic Books.

Laszloffy, T. A. (2002). Rethinking family development theory: Teaching with the Systemic Family Development (SFD) Model. *Family Relations, 51,* 206–214.

Lauzière, M. (2004). Child care for a change! *Perception, 27*(1 & 2). Retrieved November 8, 2004, from http://www.ccsd.ca/perception/2712/overview.htm

Lavee, Y., McCubbin, H. I., & Patterson, J. M. (1985). The double ABCX model of family stress and management: An empirical test by analysis of structural equations with latent variable. *Journal of Marriage and the Family, 47,* 811–825.

LaViolette, A. D., & Barnett, O. W. (2000). *It could happen to anyone: Why battered women stay* (2nd ed.). Thousand Oaks, CA: Sage.

Le Bourdais, C., Desrosiers, H., & Laplante, B. (1995). Factors related to union formation among single mothers in Canada. *Journal of Marriage and the Family, 57,* 410–420.

Le Bourdais, C., & Juby, H. (2002). The impact of cohabitation on the family life course in contemporary North America: Insights from across the border. In A. Booth & A. C. Crouter (Eds.), *Just living together: Implications of cohabitation on families* (pp. 107–118). Mahwah, NJ: Lawrence Erlbaum.

Le Bourdais, C., & Lapierre-Adamcyk, É., with Pacaut, P. (2004). Changes in conjugal life in Canada: Is cohabitation progressively replacing marriage? *Journal of Marriage and Family, 66,* 929–942.

Le Bourdais, C., Marcil-Gratton, N., & Juby, H. (2003). Family life in a changing world: The evolution of the Canadian family in a context of marital and economic instability. In M. J. Kasoff & C. Drennan (Eds.), *16th Annual Reddin Symposium: Family, work, and health policy in Canada* (pp. 21–45). Bowling Green, OH: Bowling Green State University, Canadian Studies Center.

Le Bourdais, C., Seltzer, J. A., & Trost, J. (2003, November). *Cohabitation and marriage in western countries* [videotape]. Panel presentation at annual meeting of National Council on Family Relations, Vancouver.

Lee, C., & Iverson-Gilbert, J. (2003). Demand, support and perception in family-related stress among protestant clergy. *Family Relations, 52,* 249-257.

Lee, J. A. (1975). The romantic heresy. *Canadian Review of Sociology and Anthropology, 12,* 514–528.

Lee, K. K., & Engler, C. (1999). *A profile of poverty in mid-sized Alberta cities.* Ottawa: Canadian Council on Social Development. Retrieved January 12, 2001, from http://www.ccsd.ca/pubs/altapov/report.htm

Leon, K. (2003). Risk and protective factors in young children's adjustment to parental divorce: A review of the research. *Family Relations, 52,* 258–270.

Lero, D. S. (1993). In transition: Changing patterns of work, family life, and child care. *Transition, 23*(2), 4–7.

Lero, D. S., & Brockman, L. M. (1993). Single parent families in Canada: A closer look. In J. Hudson & B. Galaway (Eds.), *Single parent families: Perspectives on research and policy* (pp. 91–114). Toronto: Thompson Educational Publishing.

Lero, D., & Kyle, I. (1991). Work, families, and child care in Ontario. In L. C. Johnson & D. Barnhorst (Eds.), *Children, families and public policy in the 90s* (pp. 25–72). Toronto: Thompson Educational Publishing.

Lessa, I. (2003). Single motherhood in the Canadian landscape: Postcards from a subject. In A. Westhues (Ed.), *Canadian social policy: Issues and perspectives* (3rd ed., pp. 90–107). Waterloo, ON: Wilfrid Laurier University Press.

LeVay, S. (1993). *The sexual brain.* Cambridge, MA: MIT Press.

Levin, E. (1987, October 19). Motherly love works a miracle. *People Weekly,* 39–43.

Levin, I. (2004). Living apart together: A new family form. *Current Sociology, 52,* 223–240.

Levinson, D. J., et al. (1978). *The seasons of a man's life.* New York: Alfred A. Knopf.

Levitt, C., & Shaffer, W. (1987). *The riot at Christie Pits.* Toronto: Lester & Orpen Dennys.

Levy-Warren, M. H. (2001). A clinical look at knowing and feeling: Secrets, lies, and disillusionments. In V. B. Shapiro, J. R. Shapiro, & I. H. Paret (Eds.), *Complex adoption & assisted reproductive technology: A developmental approach to clinical practice* (pp. 251–275). New York: Guilford.

Li, C. (2004). *Widowhood: Consequences on income for senior women* (Catalogue no. 11-621-MIE-2004015). Ottawa: Statistics Canada.

Li, P. S. (1998). *The Chinese in Canada* (2nd ed.). Toronto: Oxford University Press.

Lindlof, T. R. (1992). Computing tales: Parents' discourse about technology and family. *Social Science Computer Review, 10,* 291–309.

Lindsay, C. (1999, Spring). Seniors: A diverse group aging well. *Canadian Social Trends,* 24–26.

Lipman, M. (1984). Adoption in Canada: Two decades in review. In P. Sachdev (Ed.), *Adoption: Current issues and trends* (pp. 31–42). Toronto: Butterworths.

Lipman-Blumen, J. (1984). *Gender roles and power.* Englewood Cliffs, NJ: Prentice-Hall.

Lochhead, C., & Scott, K. (2000). *The dynamics of women's poverty in Canada.* Ottawa: Status of Women Canada.

Lockwood, K. (1994/95, Winter). Jonathan's story. *Vis-à-Vis,* p. 10.

Lopata, H. Z. (1996). *Current widowhood: Myths and realities.* Thousand Oaks, CA: Sage.

Loseke, D. R., & Kurz, D. (2005). Men's violence toward women is the serious problem. In D. R. Loseke, R. J. Gelles, & M. M. Cavanaugh (Eds.), *Current controversies in family violence* (2nd ed., pp. 79–95). Thousand Oaks, CA: Sage.

Loukas, A., Piejak, L. A., Bingham, C. R., Fitzgerald, H. E., & Zucker, R. A. (2001). Parental distress as a mediator of problem behaviors in sons of alcohol-involved families. *Family Relations, 50,* 293–301.

Luker, K. (1996). *Dubious conceptions: The politics of teenage pregnancy.* Cambridge, MA: Harvard University Press.

Lundy, K. L. P., & Warme, B. D. (1990). *Sociology: A window on the world* (2nd ed.). Scarborough, ON: Nelson Canada.

Lupri, E., & Frideres, J. (1981). The quality of marriage and the passage of time: Marital satisfaction over the family life cycle. *Canadian Journal of Sociology, 6,* 283–305.

Luster, T., Bates, L., Fitzgerald, H., Vandenbelt, M., & Key, J. P. (2000). Factors related to successful outcomes among preschool children born to low-income adolescent mothers. *Journal of Marriage and the Family, 61,* 178–187.

Luster, T., Perlstadt, H., McKinney, M., Sims, K., & Juang, L. (1996). The effects of a family support program and other factors on the home environments provided by adolescent mothers. *Family Relations, 45,* 255–264.

Luster, T., & Small, S. A. (1995, November). *Sexual abuse history and problems in adolescence: Exploring the effects of moderating violence.* Paper presented at the Annual Conference of National Council on Family Relations, Portland, OR.

Luxton, M. (1998). Families and the labour market: Coping strategies from a sociological perspective. In D. Cheal, F. Woolley, & M. Luxton, *How families cope and why policymakers need to know* (pp. 57–73). Ottawa: Canadian Policy Research Networks.

Maccoby, E. E. (2003). The gender of child and parent as factors in family dynamics. In A. C. Crouter & A. Booth (Eds.), *Children's influence on family dynamics: The neglected side of family relationships* (pp. 191–206). Mahwah, NJ: Erlbaum.

MacDonald, C. (2001, August/September). Washday: The weekly ritual. *The Beaver,* 16–21.

MacDonald, J. A. (1984). Canadian adoption legislation: An overview. In P. Sachdev (Ed.), *Adoption: Current issues and trends* (pp. 43–61). Toronto: Butterworths.

Macdonald, R. A. (1999). *Perspectives on personal relationships.* Ottawa: Law Commission of Canada. Retrieved December 11, 2000, from http://www.lcc.gc.ca/cgi-bin/repere_en.cgi?tout=polygamy &language=en&range=1&numdoc=4

Machir, J. (2003, September). The impact of spousal caregiving on the quality of marital relationships in later life. *Family Focus,* F11–F13.

Mackey, R. A., Diemer, M. A., & O'Brien, B. A. (2004). Relational factors in understanding satisfaction in the lasting relationships of same-sex and heterosexual couples. *Journal of Homosexuality, 47*(1), 111–136.

MacLeod, L. (1989). *Discussion paper: Wife battering and the web of hope: Progress, dilemmas and visions of prevention.* Ottawa: Health and Welfare Canada.

Madden-Derdich, D. A., & Arditti, J. A. (1999). The ties that bind: Attachment between former spouses. *Family Relations, 48,* 243–249.

Magid, L. (2004a). *Talk to your kids about cell phone use.* Retrieved November 30, 2004, from http://www.safekids.com/cellphone.htm

Magid L. (2004b). *Teen safety on the information highway* (Revised). National Center for Missing and Exploited Children. Retrieved November 3, 2004, from http://www.safeteens.com/safeteens.htm

Mahon, R. (2004, November). *Early child learning and care in Canada: Who rules? Who should rule?* Discussion paper for National Conference on Child Care in Canada, Canadian Council on Social Development, Winnipeg.

Maidman, F. (1984). Physical child abuse: Dynamics and practice. In F. Maidman (Ed.), *Child welfare: A source book of knowledge and practice* (pp. 135–181). New York: Child Welfare League of America.

Makin, K. (2004, September 21). Lesbian divorcées speak out. *The Globe and Mail* [Online edition]. Retrieved September 21, 2004, from http://www.globeandmail.com

Malley-Morrison, K., & Hines, D. A. (2004). *Family violence in a cultural perspective: Defining, understanding, and combating abuse.* Thousand Oaks, CA: Sage.

Manitoba Agriculture, Food and Rural Initiatives. (2004). *The cost of raising a child: 2004.* Winnipeg: Author. Retrieved November 8, 2004, from http://www.gov.mb.ca/agriculture/homeec/coc2004/cba28s02.html

Mann, S. (2001, February/March). Love, gender, and Canadian history. *The Beaver,* 6–7.

Manning, C. L. (2003, November). *Information games: How adolescents exercise power in relationships with nonresident parents.* Poster presentation at annual conference of National Council on Family Relations, Vancouver.

Manning, W. D., & Lamb, K. A. (2003). Adolescent well-being in cohabiting, married, and single-parent families. *Journal of Marriage and Family, 65,* 876–893.

Maracle, S. (1993). Family violence: Aboriginal perspectives: A historical viewpoint. *Vis-à-Vis, 10*(4), 1, 4.

Maranto, G. (1996, April). Embryo overpopulation. *Scientific American* [Online]. Retrieved June 2, 2000, from http://www.sciam.com/0496issue/0496infocus.html

Marcil-Gratton, N. (1993). Growing up with a single parent, a transitional experience? Some demographic measurements. In J. Hudson & B. Galaway (Eds.), *Single parent families: Perspectives on research and policy* (pp. 73–90). Toronto: Thompson Educational Publishing.

Marcil-Gratton, N. (1998). *Growing up with Mom and Dad? The intricate family life courses of Canadian children* (Catalogue No. 89-566-XIE). Ottawa: Statistics Canada.

Marcil-Gratton, N., Le Bourdais, C., & Lapierre-Adamcyk, É. (2000). The implications of parents' conjugal histories for children. *Isuma–Canadian*

Journal of Policy Research [Electronic journal], *1*(2), 32–40. Retrieved June 12, 2004, from http://www.isuma.net

Marriage (Prohibited Degrees) Act. (1990). Retrieved February 17, 2005, from http://laws.justice.gc.ca/en/M-2.1/text.html

Martel, L., & Bélanger, A. (1999). Relative income, opportunity cost and fertility changes in Canada. In A. Bélanger (Ed.), *Report on the demographic situation in Canada 1998–1999: Current demographic analysis* (pp. 123–163). Ottawa: Statistics Canada.

Martin, S. P. (1999). *Fertility trends among U.S. women who defer childbearing past age 30* (CDE Working Paper No. 99-11). Madison, WI: University of Wisconsin–Madison, Center for Demography and Ecology.

Martin-Matthews, A. (2000). Change and diversity in aging families and intergenerational relations. In N. Mandell & A. Duffy (Eds.), *Canadian families: Diversity, conflict, and change* (2nd ed., pp. 323–360). Toronto: Harcourt Canada.

Maslach, C. (1982). *Burnout: The cost of caring.* Englewood Cliffs, NJ: Prentice-Hall.

Mathews, F. (2002). The forgotten child: The declining status of boys in Canada. *Transition, 33*(1), 3–6.

Matjasko, J. L. (2002, November). *Single-father family typologies and adolescent functioning.* Poster presentation at annual conference of National Council on Family Relations, Houston, TX.

Maurier, W. L., & Northcott, H. C. (2000). *Aging in Ontario: Diversity in the new millennium.* Calgary: Detselig Enterprises.

Maynard, R. (1987, June). Here come the brides. *Report on Business Magazine,* 24–30.

Maza, P. L., & Hall, J. A. (1988). *Homeless children and their families: A preliminary study.* Washington, DC: Child Welfare League of America.

McCoy, J. K., Brody, G. H., & Stoneman, Z. (1994). A longitudinal analysis of sibling relationships as mediators of the link between family processes and youths' best friendships. *Family Relations, 43,* 400–408.

McCoy, J. K., Brody, G. H., & Stoneman, Z. (2002). Temperament and the quality of best friendships: Effect of same-sex sibling relationships. *Family Relations, 51,* 248–255.

McCubbin, H. I., & Patterson, J. M. (1983). Family transitions: Adaptation to stress. In H. I. McCubbin & C. R. Figley (Eds.), *Stress and the family: Vol. 1. Coping with normative stress* (pp. 5–25). New York: Brunner/Mazel.

McDaniel, S. A. (1994). *Family and friends.* Ottawa: Statistics Canada.

McDonald, L., & Collins, A. (2000). *Abuse and neglect of older adults: A discussion paper.* Ottawa: Health Canada.

McGoldrick, M. (1999a). Becoming a couple. In B. Carter & M. McGoldrick (Eds.), *The expanded family life cycle: Individual, family, and social perspectives* (3rd ed., pp. 231–248). Boston: Allyn & Bacon.

McGoldrick, M. (1999b). Women through the family life cycle. In B. Carter & M. McGoldrick (Eds.), *The expanded family life cycle: Individual, family, and social perspectives* (3rd ed., pp. 106–123). Boston: Allyn & Bacon.

McGoldrick, M., & Carter, B. (1999). Remarried families. In B. Carter & M. McGoldrick (Eds.), *The expanded family life cycle: Individual, family, and social perspectives* (3rd ed., pp. 417–435). Boston: Allyn & Bacon.

McGoldrick, M., & Gerson, R. (1985). *Genograms in family assessment.* New York: Norton.

McGoldrick, M., & Walsh, F. (1999). Death and the family life cycle. In B. Carter & M. McGoldrick (Eds.), *The expanded family life cycle: Individual, family, and social perspectives* (3rd ed., pp. 185–201). Boston: Allyn & Bacon.

McGoldrick, M., Watson, M., & Benton, W. (1999). Siblings through the life cycle. In B. Carter & M. McGoldrick (Eds.), *The expanded family life cycle: Individual, family, and social perspectives* (3rd ed., pp. 153–168). Boston: Allyn & Bacon.

McHale, S. M., Crouter, A. C., & Tucker, C. J. (1999). Family context and gender role socialization in middle childhood: Comparing girls to boys and sisters to brothers. *Child Development, 70,* 990–1004.

McHale, S. M., Kim, J.-Y., Whiteman, S., & Crouter, A. C. (2004). Links between sex-typed time use in middle childhood and gender development in early adolescence. *Developmental Psychology, 40,* 868–881.

McIntosh, R. (1987/88, December/January). Canada's boy miners. *The Beaver,* 34–38.

McIntyre, L., Connor, S., & Warren, J. (1998). *A glimpse of child hunger in Canada.* Hull: Human Resources Development Canada.

McKenry, P., & Serovich, J. (2002, November). *Major facts about gay and lesbian partner abuse.* Presentation at annual conference of National Council on Family Relations, Houston, TX.

McKie, C. (1993). An overview of lone parenthood in Canada. In J. Hudson & B. Galaway (Eds.), *Single parent families: Perspectives on research and policy* (pp. 53–71). Toronto: Thompson Educational Publishing.

McKie, D. C., Prentice, B., & Reed, P. (1983). *Divorce: Law and the family in Canada* (Catalogue no. 89-502). Ottawa: Statistics Canada.

McLaren, A., & McLaren, A. T. (1997). *The bedroom and the state: The changing practices and politics of contraception and abortion in Canada, 1980–1997* (2nd ed.). Toronto: Oxford University Press.

McLaughlin, M. A. (1987). Homelessness in Canada: The report of the national inquiry [Special insert]. *Social Development Overview, 5*(1).

McLoyd, V. C., & Smith, J. (2002). Physical discipline and behavior problems in African American, European American, and Hispanic children: Emotional support as a moderator. *Journal of Marriage and Family, 64,* 40–53.

Medora, N. P. (2003). Mate selection in contemporary India: Love marriages versus arranged marriages. In R. R. Hamon & B. B. Ingoldsby (Eds.), *Mate selection across cultures* (pp. 209–230). Thousand Oaks, CA: Sage.

Mehlsen, M., Platz, M., & Fromholt, P. (2003). Life satisfaction across the life course: Evaluation of the most and least satisfying decades of life. *International Journal of Aging and Human Development, 57,* 217–236.

Merkle, E. R., & Richardson, R. A. (2000). Digital dating and virtual relating: Conceptualizing computer mediated romantic relationships. *Family Relations, 49,* 187–192.

Michael, H. J., & Reitsma-Street, M. (2002). *A new era of welfare: Analysis of B.C.'s employment and assistance acts.* Retrieved January 21, 2005, from http://web.uvic.ca/spp/

Michalopoulos, C., Tattrie, D., Miller, C., Robins, P. K., Morris, P., Gyarmati, D., et al. (2002). *Making work pay: Final report on the self-sufficiency project for long-term welfare recipients.* Ottawa: Social Research and Demonstration Corporation.

Michalski, J. H. (2003). The economic status and coping strategies of food bank users in the greater Toronto area. *Canadian Journal of Urban Research, 12,* 275–298.

Mikkelson, B. (n.d.). *The great stork derby.* Retrieved December 2, 2000, from http://www.snopes2.com/pregnant/babyrace.htm

Milan, A. (2000, Spring). One hundred years of families. *Canadian Social Trends* (Statistics Canada Catalogue no. 11-008), 2–12.

Milan, A. (2003, Autumn). Would you live common-law? *Canadian Social Trends* (Statistics Canada Catalogue no. 11-008), 2–6.

Milan, A., & Hamm, B. (2003, Winter). Across the generations: Grandparents and grandchildren. *Canadian Social Trends* (Statistics Canada Catalogue no. 11-008), 2–7.

Milan, A., & Hamm, B. (2004, Summer). Mixed unions. *Canadian Social Trends* (Statistics Canada Catalogue no. 11-008), 2–6.

Milan, A., & Peters, A. (2003, Summer). Couples living apart. *Canadian Social Trends* (Statistics Canada Catalogue no. 11-008), 2–6.

Milan, A., & Tran, K. (2004, Spring). Blacks in Canada: A long history. *Canadian Social Trends* (Statistics Canada Catalogue no. 11-008), *72,* 2–7.

Miller, P. J. E., Caughlin, J. B., & Huston, T. L. (2003). Trait expressiveness and marital satisfaction. *Journal of Marriage and Family, 65,* 978–995.

Milloy, J. S. (1999). *A national crime: The Canadian government and the residential school system, 1879 to 1986.* Winnipeg: University of Winnipeg Press.

Mills, T. L., & Wilmoth, J. M. (2002). Intergenerational differences and similarities in life-sustaining treatment attitudes and decision factors. *Family Relations, 51,* 46–54.

Miner, H. (1939/1974). *St-Denis: A French-Canadian parish.* Chicago: University of Chicago Press.

Ministry of Attorney General (1998, April). *What parents need to know about changes to support enforcement measures.* Vancouver: Government of British Columbia, Ministry of Attorney General. Retrieved January 22, 2001, from http://www.ag.gov.ca/public/98093.htm

Ministry of Children and Youth Services, Ontario. (2003). *Relative and step-parent adoption when the child is resident in Ontario.* Retrieved July 1, 2004, from http://www.children.gov.on.ca/cs/en/programs/Adoption/Publications/relativeStepparentAdoptionOntario.htm

Mirabelli, A. (1995). Virtual unreality: Television, families and communities in the nineties. *Transition, 25*(1), 4–6.

Mitchell, B. A., & Gee, E. M. (1996). "Boomerang kids" and midlife parental marital satisfaction. *Family Relations, 45,* 442–448.

Money, J. (1986). *Lovemaps: Clinical concepts of sexual/erotic health and pathology, paraphilia, and gender transposition in childhood, adolescence, and maturity.* New York: Irvington.

Montenegro, X. P. (2003). *Lifestyles, dating, and midlife singles.* Washington, DC: American Association of Retired Persons.

Montgomery, J., & Fewer, W. (1988). *Family systems and beyond.* New York: Human Sciences Press.

Montgomery, L. M. (c. 1935). *Anne of Green Gables.* Toronto: McClelland-Bantam.

Moogk, P. N. (1982). Les petits sauvages: The children of eighteenth century New France. In J. Parr (Ed.), *Childhood and family in Canadian history* (pp. 17–43). Toronto: McClelland & Stewart.

Moore, D. S. (2001). *The dependent gene: The fallacy of "nature vs. nurture."* New York: Henry Holt.

Moore, K. A., Chalk, R., Scarpa, J., & Vandivere, S. (2002). *Family strengths: Often overlooked, but real.* Washington, DC: Child Trends.

Moore, M. (1988, Autumn). Female lone parenthood: The duration of episodes. *Canadian Social Trends,* 40–42.

Moore, N. B., & Davidson, J. K., Sr. (2002). A profile of adoption placers: Perceptions of pregnant teens during the decision-making process. *Adoption Quarterly, 6*(2), 29–41.

Moore, O. (2002, June 29). Lawyers tune final arguments in crucial child hearing. *The Globe and Mail,* p. A3.

Moore, T., & Thompson, V. (1987). Elder abuse: A review of research, programmes and policy. *The Social Worker/Le Travailleur social, 55,* 115–122.

Morris, M. B. (1987). Children's perceptions of last-chance parents: Implications of current trends toward late childbearing. *Child Welfare, 66,* 195–205.

Morissette, R., & Johnson, A. (2005). *Are good jobs disappearing in Canada?* (Catalogue no. 11F0019MIE no. 239). Ottawa: Statistics Canada.

Morton, T. D., & Saulis, M. K. (1994). *Supervising child protective services workers.* Washington, DC: U.S. Department of Health and Human Services. Retrieved February 3, 2001, from http://www.calib.com/pubs/usermanuals/supercps/

Moss, K. (2003). Witnessing violence—Aggression and anxiety in young children. *Supplement to Health Reports* (Statistics Canada Catalogue no. 82-003), *14,* 53–66.

Muslim Women's League. (1999a). *Female genital mutilation.* Retrieved July 11, 2004, from http://www.mwlusa.org/publications/positionpapers/fgm.html

Muslim Women's League. (1999b). *Position paper on "honor killings."* Retrieved July 11, 2004, from http://www.mwlusa.org/publications/positionpapers/hk.html

Myers, S. M., & Booth, A. (1999). Marital strains and marital quality: The role of high and low locus of control. *Journal of Marriage and the Family, 61,* 423–436.

National Advisory Council on Aging. (1983). *Family role and the negotiation of change for the aged.* Ottawa: Author.

National Advisory Council on Aging. (2000). *The NACA position on enhancing the Canadian health care system.* Ottawa: Author.

National Coalition of Anti-Violence Programs. (1998). *Annual report on lesbian, gay, bisexual, transgender domestic violence.* Retrieved October 3, 2000, from http://www.vaw.umn.edu/ FinalDocuments/glbtdv.htm

National Council of Welfare. (2004). *Poverty profile 2001* (Catalogue no. SD25-1/2001E-PDF). Ottawa: National Council of Welfare. Retrieved December 8, 2004, from http://www.ncwcnbes.net

National Council of Welfare. (n.d.). *2003 welfare incomes and estimated poverty lines by province and household type.* Retrieved January 21, 2005, from http://www.ncwcnbes.net

National Endowment for Financial Education. (2002). *Job loss.* Greenwood Village, CO: NEFE.

National Institute of Justice. (1996). *The cycle of violence revisited.* Washington, DC: U.S. Department of Justice.

Nelson, E., & Robertson, G. (2001). Liability for wrongful birth and wrongful life. *Isuma—Canadian Journal of Policy Research, 2*(3), 102–105. Retrieved June 12, 2004, from http://www.isuma.net

Nelson, F. (1996). *Lesbian motherhood: An exploration of Canadian lesbian families.* Toronto: University of Toronto Press.

Nett, E. M. (1988). *Canadian families: Past and present.* Toronto: Butterworths.

Neufeld, A., Harrison, M. J., Stewart, M., & Hughes, K. (2003, November). *Nonsupport and advocacy among family caregivers.* Poster presentation at annual conference of National Council on Family Relations, Vancouver.

Neugarten, B. L., & Neugarten, D. A. (1986). Changing meanings of age in the aging society. In A. Pifer & L. Bronte (Eds.), *Our aging society: Paradox and promise* (pp. 33–51). New York: W. W. Norton.

Newman, K. S. (1992). The downwardly mobile family. In A. S. Skolnick & J. H. Skolnick (Eds.), *Family in transition: Rethinking marriage, sexuality, child rearing, and family organization* (7th ed., pp. 385–398). New York: HarperCollins.

Neysmith, S. (2003). Caring and aging: Exposing the policy issues. In A. Westhues (Ed.), *Canadian social policy: Issues and perspectives* (3rd ed., pp. 182–199). Waterloo, ON: Wilfrid Laurier University Press.

Nihmey, J., & Foxman, S. (1987). *The time of their lives: The Dionne tragedy.* Toronto: McClelland-Bantam.

Nock, S. L. (1995). A comparison of marriages and cohabiting relationships. *Journal of Family Issues, 16,* 53–76.

Novac, S., Brown, J., & Bourbonnais, C. (1996). *No room of her own: A literature review on women and homelessness.* Ottawa: Canada Mortgage and Housing.

Nowicki, S., Jr. (2003, February). The hidden language of relationships [audiotape]. In J. K. Comeau (Ed.), *Family Information Services Professional Resource Materials.* Minneapolis: Family Information Services.

O'Donnell, V., & Tait, H. (2003). *Aboriginal Peoples Survey 2001—Initial findings: Well-being of the non-reserve Aboriginal population* (Catalogue no. 89-589-XIE). Ottawa: Statistics Canada.

Ogilvie, B. A. (2004). *Mother-daughter incest: A guide for helping professionals.* New York: Haworth.

Olsen, C. S. (1997, Summer). Stepping stones for stepfamilies. *CFLE Network, 5.*

Olson, D. H. (1990). Commentary: Marriage in perspective. In F. D. Fincham & T. N. Bradbury (Eds.), *The psychology of marriage* (pp. 402–419). New York: Guilford.

Ombudsman of British Columbia. (1999). *Righting the wrong: The confinement of the Sons of Freedom Doukhobor children.* Retrieved July 25, 2004, from http://www.ombud.gov.bc.ca/reports/Public_Report/PR38_Righting_The_Wrong/

Ontario Ministry of Community and Social Services. (2000). *Making welfare work: Report to taxpayers on welfare reform.* Toronto: Author.

Ontario Ministry of Tourism and Recreation. (1983). *A Guidebook for Intergenerational Planning.* Toronto: Author.

Ontario Women's Directorate. (1991). *Work and family: The crucial balance.* Toronto: Ministry of Community and Social Services.

Onyskiw, J. E., & Hayduk, L. A. (2001). Processes underlying children's adjustment in families characterized by physical aggression. *Family Relations, 50,* 376–385.

Ooms, T. (2002). *Marriage and government: Strange bedfellows?* Washington, DC: Center for Law and Social Policy.

Oppenheimer, V. K. (2000). The continuing importance of men's economic position in marriage formation. In L. J. Waite, C. Bachrach, M. Hindin, E. Thomson, & A. Thornton (Eds.), *The ties that bind: Perspectives on marriage and cohabitation* (pp. 283–301). New York: Aldine de Gruyter.

Orkin, M. M. (1981). *The great stork derby.* Don Mills, ON: General Publishing.

Oropesa, R. S., & Gorman, B. K. (2000). Ethnicity, immigration, and beliefs about marriage as a "tie that binds." In L. J. Waite, C. Bachrach, M. Hindin, E. Thomson, & A. Thornton (Eds.), *The ties that bind:*

Perspectives on marriage and cohabitation (pp. 188–211). New York: Aldine de Gruyter.

Orrange, R. M., Firebaugh, F. M., & Heck, R. K. Z. (2003). Managing households. In P. Moen (Ed.), *It's about time: Couples and careers* (pp. 152–167). Ithaca, NY: Cornell University Press.

Owram, D. (1996). *Born at the right time: A history of the baby-boom generation.* Toronto: University of Toronto Press.

Oziewicz, E. (2000, December 9). Bountiful's troubling tradition. *The Globe and Mail,* pp. F4–F5.

Pagelow, M. D. (1984). *Family violence.* New York: Praeger.

Palacio-Quintin, E. (2000). The impact of day care on child development. *Isuma—Canadian Journal of Policy Research, 1*(2), 17–22. Retrieved June 12, 2004, from http://www.isuma.net

Palameta, B. (2003, August). Who pays for domestic help? *Perspectives on Labour and Income* (Statistics Canada catalogue no. 75-001-XIE), 12–15.

Parcel, D. L., & Dufur, M. J. (2001). Capital at home and at school: Effects on child social adjustment. *Journal of Marriage and Family, 63,* 32–47.

Parcel, T. L., & Menaghan, E. G. (1994). *Parents' jobs and children's lives.* New York: Aldine de Gruyter.

Parke, M. (2003). *Are married parents really better for children? What research says about the effects of family structure on child well-being.* Washington, DC: Center for Law and Social Policy.

Parker, M. (2004, June). Meeting the needs of Southeast Asian elders. *Family Focus,* F10–F12.

Parsons, T., & Bales, R. F. (1955). *Family, socialization and interaction process.* Glencoe, IL: Free Press.

Patterson, J. M. (2002). Integrating family resilience and family stress theory. *Journal of Marriage and Family, 64,* 349–360.

Patton, M. Q. (1990). *Qualitative evaluation and research methods* (2nd ed.). Newbury Park, CA: Sage.

Patton, M. Q. (1996). Preface: A look at the mosaic of qualitative research. In M. B. Sussman & J. F. Gilgun (Eds.), *The methods and methodologies of qualitative family research* (pp. xvii–xxii). New York: Haworth.

Pawson, M. (2003). The battle with mortality and the urge to procreate. In J. Haynes & J. Miller (Eds.), *Inconceivable conceptions: Psychological aspects of infertility and reproductive technology* (pp. 60–72). New York: Brunner-Routledge.

Payne, J. D. (1986). Whither the broken family? *Transition, 16*(1), 4, 10.

Peoples, D., & Ferguson, H. R. (1998). *Experiencing infertility: An essential resource.* New York: Norton.

Pepler, D. J., Catallo, R., & Moore, T. E. (2000). Consider the children: Research informing interventions for children exposed to domestic violence. In R. A. Geffner, P. G. Jaffe, & M. Suderman (Eds.), *Children exposed to domestic violence: Current issues in research, intervention, prevention, and policy development* (pp. 37–57). New York: Haworth Maltreatment & Trauma Press.

Peter, K. (1987). *The dynamics of Hutterite society: An analytical approach.* Edmonton: University of Alberta Press.

Phenice, L. A., & Griffore, R. J. (1996). Understanding ethnic minority families: An ecological approach. *Family Science Review, 9,* 5–12.

Picot, G., & Hou, F. (2003). *The rise in low-income rates among immigrants in Canada* (Catalogue no. 11F0019MIE–No. 198). Ottawa: Statistics Canada.

Picton, J. (1989, February 26). Lawyer's will started baby boom. *Toronto Star,* pp. A1, A6.

Pillemer, K. (2005). Elder abuse is caused by the deviance and dependence of elderly caregivers. In D. R. Loseke, R. J. Gelles, & M. M. Cavanaugh (Eds.), *Current controversies in family violence* (2nd ed., pp. 207–220). Thousand Oaks, CA: Sage.

Pinderhughes, E. E., Nix, R., Foster, E. M., Jones, D., & The Conduct Problems Prevention Research Group. (2001). Parenting in context: Impact of neighborhood poverty, residential stability, public services, social networks, and danger on parental behaviors. *Journal of Marriage and Family, 63,* 941–953.

Pines, A. M. (1996). *Couple burnout: Causes and cures.* New York: Routledge.

Pines, A. M. (1999). *Falling in love: Why we choose the lovers we choose.* New York: Routledge.

Pitzer, R. L. (1997, November). *Corporal punishment in the discipline of children in the home.* Presentation to annual conference of the National Council on Family Relations, Arlington, VA.

Pixley, J. E., & Moen, P. (2003). Prioritizing careers. In P. Moen (Ed.), *It's about time: Couples and careers* (pp. 183–200). Ithaca, NY: ILR Press.

Pohlman, C., & Dulipovici, A. (2004). *Fostering flexibility: Work and family.* Canadian Federation of Independent Business. Retrieved September 9, 2004, from http://www.cfib.ca

Porter, E. (1987). Conceptual frameworks for studying families. In *Family matters: Sociology and contemporary Canadian families* (pp. 41–61). Toronto: Methuen.

Pottie Bunge, V., & Locke, D. (Eds.). (2000). *Family violence in Canada: A statistical profile 2000.* Catalogue No. 85-224-XIE. Ottawa: Statistics Canada.

Power, P. W., & Dell Orto, A. E. (2004). *Families living with chronic illness and disability: Intervention, challenges, and opportunities.* New York: Springer.

Preece, J. C., & Busby, D. M. (1995, November). *Parenting quality and familial stress as mediators of long-term psychological and interpersonal adjustment of incest survivors.* Paper presented at the Annual Conference of National Council on Family Relations, Portland, OR.

Preece, M. (2003–2004). When lone parents marry: The challenge of stepfamily relationships. *Transition,* 7–10.

Prete, C. (2003, June 27). Going to the prom Muslim style. *Hamilton Spectator,* pp. A1, A10.

Preto, N. G. (1999). Transformation of the family system during adolescence. In B. Carter & M. McGoldrick (Eds.), *The expanded family life cycle: Individual, family, and social perspectives* (3rd ed., pp. 274–286). Boston: Allyn & Bacon.

Previti, D., & Amato, P. R. (2003). Why stay married? Rewards, barriers, and marital stability. *Journal of Marriage and Family, 65,* 561–573.

Prince, B. (2004). *I came as a stranger: The underground railroad.* Toronto: Tundra.

Pruett, K. D. (2000). *Fatherneed: Why father care is as essential as mother care for your child.* New York: Free Press.

Public Health Agency of Canada. (1999, June 16). *Infant mortality.* Ottawa: Author. Retrieved November 5, 2004, from http://www.phoc-aspc.gc.ca/meas-haut/mu_c_e.html

Quam, J. K. (1993, June/July). Gay and lesbian aging. *SIECUS Report.* Retrieved November 29, 1996, from http://www.cyfc.umn.edu/Diversity/Gay/gayaging.html

Raag, T., & Rackliff, C. L. (1998). Preschoolers' awareness of social expectations of gender: Relationships to toy choices. *Sex Roles, 38,* 685–700.

Radina, M. E. (2003). Cultural values and caregiving. In M. Coleman & L. Ganong (Eds.), *Points and counterpoints: Controversial relationship and family issues in the 21st century: An anthology* (pp. 265–271). Los Angeles: Roxbury.

Raley, R. K., & Wildsmith, E. (2004). Cohabitation and children's family instability. *Journal of Marriage and Family, 66,* 210–219.

Ray, A. J. (1996). *I have lived here since the world began: An illustrated history of Canada's Native people.* Toronto: Lester/Key Porter.

Regan, P. (2003). *The mating game: A primer on love, sex, and marriage.* Thousand Oaks, CA: Sage.

Reid, J. H. (1963). Principles, values, and assumptions underlying adoption practice. In I. E. Smith (Ed.), *Readings in adoption* (pp. 26–37). New York: Philosophical Library.

Reiss, I. L. (1960). *Premarital sexual standards in America.* New York: Free Press.

Reiss, I. L. (1980). *Family systems in America.* New York: Holt, Rinehart & Winston.

Reitz, M., & Watson, K. W. (1992). *Adoption and the family system: Strategies for treatment.* New York: Guilford.

Rideout, V. J., Vandewater, E. A., & Wartella, E. A. (2003). *Zero to six: Electronic media in the lives of infants, toddlers and preschoolers.* Menlo Park, CA: Henry J. Kaiser Family Foundation. Retrieved February 25, 2004, from http://www.kff.org

Riordan, R. (1994, Spring). Two by two? Sex ratios of unattached Canadians. *Canadian Social Trends,* 26–29.

Risman, B. J., & Johnson-Sumerford, D. (1998). Doing it fairly: A study of post-gender marriages. *Journal of Marriage and the Family, 60,* 23–40.

Roberts, D. F., Foehr, U. G., & Rideout, V. (2005). *Generation M: Media in the lives of 8–18-year-olds.* Menlo Park, CA: Kaiser Family Foundation.

Roberts, L. J. (2005, March). Alcohol and the marital relationship. *Family Focus,* F12–F13.

Roberts, L. J., & McCrady, B. S. (2003). *Alcohol problems in intimate relationships: A guide for marriage and family therapists.* Washington, DC: National Institutes of Health, National Institute on Alcohol Abuse and Alcoholism, Publication no. 03-5284. Retrieved April 22, 2005, from http://www.niaaa.nih.gov/publications/niaaa-guide/

Roberts, N. A., & Levenson, R. W. (2001). The remains of the workday: Impact of job stress and exhaustion on marital interaction in police couples. *Journal of Marriage and Family, 63,* 1052–1067.

Robinson, B. A. (2001). *Child corporal punishment: Spanking.* Retrieved July 8, 2001, from http://www.religioustolerance.org/spanking.htm

Robinson, J. P., & Godbey, G. (1997). *The surprising ways Americans use their time* (2nd ed.). University Park, PA: Pennsylvania State University Press.

Rodgers, K. B., & Rose, H. A. (2002). Risk and resiliency factors among adolescents who experience marital transitions. *Journal of Marriage and Family, 64,* 1024–1027.

Roehling, P. V., Moen, P., & Batt, R. (2003). Spillover. In P. Moen (Ed.), *It's about time: Couples and careers* (pp. 101–121). Ithaca, NY: Cornell University Press.

Rogers, S. J. (2004). Dollars, dependency, and divorce: Four perspectives on the role of wives' income. *Journal of Marriage and Family, 66,* 59–74.

Rolland, J. S. (1999). Chronic illness and the family life cycle. In B. Carter & M. McGoldrick (Eds.), *The expanded family life cycle: Individual, family, and social perspectives* (3rd ed., pp. 492–511). Boston: Allyn & Bacon.

Rolland, J. S. (2003). Mastering family challenges in serious illness and disability. In F. Walsh (Ed.), *Normal family processes: Growing diversity and complexity* (3rd ed., pp. 460–489). New York: Guilford.

Rooke, P. T., & Schnell, R. L. (1983). *Discarding the asylum: From child rescue to the welfare state in English-Canada (1800–1950).* Lanham, MD: University Press of America.

Root, M. P. P. (2001). *Love's revolution: Interracial marriage.* Philadelphia: Temple University Press.

Roscoe, B., Cavanaugh, L. E., & Kennedy, D. R. (1988). Dating infidelity: Behaviors, reasons, and consequences. *Adolescence, 23,* 35–43.

Rosenthal, C. J., & Gladstone, J. (2000). *Grandparenthood in Canada.* Ottawa: Vanier Institute of the Family.

Ross, D. P., & Roberts, P. (1999). *Income and child well-being: A new perspective on the poverty debate.* Ottawa: Canadian Council on Social Development. Retrieved March 25, 2000, from http://www.ccsd.ca/pubs/inckids/

Ross, D. P., Roberts, P. A., & Scott, K. (1998). *Mediating factors in child development outcomes: Children in lone-parent families.* Ottawa: Human Resources Development Canada.

Ross, D. P., Scott, K. J., & Smith, P. J. (2000). *The Canadian fact book on poverty—2000.* Ottawa: Canadian Council on Social Development.

Ross, M. W. (1990). Married homosexual men: Prevalence and background. In F. W. Bozett & M. B. Sussman (Eds.), *Homosexuality and family relations* (pp. 35–57). New York: Haworth.

Rossi, A. S. (1984). Gender and parenthood. *American Sociological Review, 49,* 1–19.

Rotermann, A. (2001, Winter). Wired young Canadians. *Canadian Social Trends* (Statistics Canada Catalogue no. 11-008), 4–8.

Rothman, E. K. (1987). *Hands and hearts: A history of courtship in America.* Cambridge, MA: Harvard University Press.

Rowe, D. C. (1994). *The limits of family influence: Genes, experience, and behavior.* New York: Guilford.

Royal Adelaide Hospital. (1999). *Disability and sexuality: Information for students.* Adelaide, Australia: Royal

Adelaide Hospital. Retrieved September 9, 2000, from http://www.stdservices.on.net/std/social_aspects/disability.htm

Royal Bank. (1989, Winter). *Reporter*.

Rubin, B. A. (1996). *Shifts in the social contract: Understanding change in American society*. Thousand Oaks, CA: Pine Forge.

Rueter, M. A., & Conger, R. D. (1995). Antecedents of parent-adolescent disagreements. *Journal of Marriage and the Family, 57,* 435–448.

Rust, A., & MacPhee, D. (2001, March). Internet infidelity: What research tells us. *Family Focus,* F21–F22.

Sabatelli, R. M., & Bartle-Haring, W. (2003). Family-of-origin experiences and adjustment in married couples. *Journal of Marriage and Family, 65,* 159–169.

Sacco, V. F. (1995). Violence and the elderly. In J. I. Ross (Ed.), *Violence in Canada: Sociopolitical perspectives* (pp. 153–185). Don Mills, ON: Oxford University Press.

Saleem, S. (2003, August 30). Arranged marriages: A proposal I never thought I would consider. *Hamilton Spectator,* p. M3.

Samuel, T. J. (1990, May/June). *Immigration of children as an element of immigration policy*. Paper presented at the Joint meeting of Canadian Population Society and Canadian Sociology and Anthropology Association, Victoria, BC.

Samuels, E. J. (2001). The strange history of adult adoptee access to original birth records. *Adoption Quarterly, 5*(2), 63–74.

Sandness, G. (1983). The miracle of Molly. In L. Dunn (Ed.), *Adopting children with special needs: A sequel* (pp. 33–34). Washington, DC: North American Council on Adoptable Children.

Santrock, J. W. (1992). *Life-span development* (4th ed.). Dubuque, IA: Wm. C. Brown.

Sarlo, C. (2003, February). The Kimberly Rogers case. *Fraser Forum,* 26–27.

Saskatchewan Education. (n.d.). *Aboriginal Elder/Outreach Program*. Retrieved January 6, 2001, from http://www.sasked.gov.sk.ca/k/pecs/community/imed/elder.htm

Saskatchewan Women's Secretariat. (n.d.). *The changing workplace: Flexible working arrangements*. Retrieved July 27, 2000, from http://204.83.176.82/flexible%20working%20arrangements%20new.htm

Sassler, S. (2004). The process of entering into cohabiting unions. *Journal of Marriage and Family, 66,* 491–506.

Sayeed, A. (1999). *Improving the National Child Benefit: Matching deeds with intentions*. Toronto: C. D. Howe Institute.

Schaeff, A. W. (1986). *Co-dependence: Misunderstood—mistreated*. San Francisco: Harper & Row.

Schellenberg, G. (1994). *The road to retirement: Demographic and economic changes in the 90s*. Ottawa: Canadian Council on Social Development.

Schellenberg, G., & Silver, C. (2004, Winter). You can't always get what you want: Retirement preferences and experiences. *Canadian Social Trends* (Statistics Canada Catalogue no. 11-008), 2–7.

Schene, P. (1998). Past, present and future roles of child protective services. *The Future of Children, 8*(1), 54–71.

Schlesinger, B. (1990, June). *The one-parent family*. Paper presented at the 2nd International Rural Mental Health and Addictions Conference, North Bay, ON.

Schneewind, K. A., & Gerhard, A.-K. (2002). Relationship personality, conflict resolution, and marital satisfaction in the first 5 years of marriage. *Family Relations, 51,* 63–71.

Schulz, P. V. (1978). Day care in Canada: 1850–1962. In K. G. Ross (Ed.), *Good day care: Fighting for it, getting it, keeping it* (pp. 137–158). Toronto: Women's Press.

Schwartzberg, N., Berliner, K., & Jacob, D. (1995). *Single in a married world: A life cycle framework for working with the unmarried adult*. New York: Norton.

Segalen, M. (1986). *Historical anthropology of the family* (J. C. Whitehouse & S. Matthews, Trans.). Cambridge: Cambridge University Press.

Seligman, M., & Darling, R. B. (1997). *Ordinary family, special children: A systems approach to childhood disability* (2nd ed.). New York: Guilford.

Seltzer, J. A. (2004). Cohabitation in the United States and Britain: Demography, kinship, and the future. *Journal of Marriage and Family, 66,* 921–928.

Shanahan, L., & Sobolewski, J. M. (2003). Child effects as family process. In A. C. Crouter & A. Booth, (Eds.), *Children's influence on family dynamics: The neglected side of family relationships* (pp. 237–252). Mahwah, NJ: Erlbaum.

Shanly, M. L. (2001). *Making babies, making families: What matters in an age of reproductive technologies, surrogacy, adoption, and same-sex and unwed parents*. Boston: Beacon.

Sherif-Trask, B. (2004, December). Why the study of non-Western families matters. *Family Focus,* F1–F3.

Shewell, H. (2004). *"Enough to keep them alive": Indian welfare in Canada, 1873–1965*. Toronto: University of Toronto Press.

Short Term Child Care. (n.d.). *Short term child care story*. Retrieved December 30, 2004, from http://www.stcc.on.ca/

Shreck, K. H. (2001, September/October). Rethinking the family tree. *Adoptive Families, 39–40.*

Sieburg, E. (1985). *Family communication: An integrated systems approach.* New York: Gardner.

Siegel, J. M. (1995). Looking for Mr. Right? Older single women who become mothers. *Journal of Family Issues, 16,* 194–211.

Silva, E. B. (1999). Transforming housewifery: Dispositions, practices and technology. In E. B. Silva & C. Smart (Eds.), *The new family?* (pp. 46–65). London, England: Sage.

Simmons, L. A., & Wright, D. W. (2002, November). *Does a marriage ideal exist? Using Q-Sort methodology to assess views on healthy marriages.* Poster session presented at annual conference National Council on Family Relations, Houston, TX.

Simons, R. L., Chao, W., Conger, R. D., & Elder, G. H. (2001). Quality of parenting as mediator of the effect of childhood defiance on adolescent friendship choices and delinquency: A growth curve analysis. *Journal of Marriage and Family, 63,* 63–79.

Simons, R. L., Lin, K.-H., Gordon, L. C., Conger, R. D., & Lorenz, F. O. (1999). Explaining the higher incidence of adjustment problems among children of divorce compared with those in two-parent families. *Journal of Marriage and the Family, 61,* 1020–1033.

Sipe, A. W. R. (1990). *A secret world: Sexuality and the search for celibacy.* New York: Brunner/Mazel.

Skipper, J. K., Jr., & Nass, G. (1968). Dating behavior: A framework for analysis and an illustration. In M. B. Sussman (Ed.), *Sourcebook in marriage and the family* (3rd ed., pp. 211–220). Boston: Houghton Mifflin.

Slater, S. (1995). *The lesbian family life cycle.* New York: Free Press.

Slomkowski, C., Rende, R., Conger, K. G., Simons, R. L., & Conger, R. D. (2001). Sisters, brothers, and delinquency: Evaluating social influence during early and middle adolescence. *Child Development, 72,* 271–283.

Smith, D. E. (1993). The standard North American family: SNAF as an ideological code. *Journal of Family Issues, 14,* 50–65.

Smith, N. F., & Grenier, M. K. (1975). English- and French-Canadian children's views of parents. *Canadian Journal of Behavioural Science, 7,* 40–53.

Smith, S. R., & Ingoldsby, B. (2003, November). *The future of the Hutterite family.* Poster presentation, Annual conference of National Council on Family Relations, Vancouver.

Smith, S. R., & Soliday, E. (2001). The effects of parental chronic kidney disease on the family. *Family Relations, 50,* 171–177.

SmithBattle, L. (1996). Intergenerational ethics of caring for adolescent mothers and their children. *Family Relations, 45,* 56–64.

Smock, P. J. (2004). The wax and wane of marriage: Prospects for marriage in the 21st century. *Journal of Marriage and Family, 66,* 966–973.

Smock, P. J., & Gupta, S. (2002). Cohabitation in contemporary North America. In A. Booth & A. C. Crouter (Eds.), *Just living together: implications of cohabitation on families, children, and social policy* (pp. 53–84). Mahwah, NJ: Lawrence Erlbaum.

Snell, G. (1992). "The white life for two": The defence of marriage and sexual morality in Canada, 1890–1914. In B. Bradbury (Ed.), *Canadian family history: Selected readings* (pp. 381–399). Toronto: Copp Clark Pitman.

Snow, J. E. (2004). *How it feels to have a gay or lesbian parent: A book by kids for kids of all ages.* New York: Harrington Park.

Snyder, L. (2003). Workfare. In A. Westhues (Ed.), *Canadian social policy: Issues and perspectives* (3rd ed., pp. 108–127). Waterloo, ON: Wilfrid Laurier University Press.

Sobol, M. P., Daly, K. J., & Kelloway, E. K. (2000). Paths to the facilitation of open adoption. *Family Relations, 49,* 419–424.

Some notes on the prohibited degrees of marriage. (1984, February 22). Provided in 1995 by Raymond L. du Plessis, Q. C., Law Clerk and Parliamentary Counsel, Senate of Canada.

South, S. J., Trent, K., & Shen, Y. (2001). Changing partners: Toward a macrostructural-opportunity theory of marital dissolution. *Journal of Marriage and Family, 63,* 743–754.

Spears, G., & Seydegart, K. (1993). *Gender and violence in the mass media.* Ottawa: Health Canada, Family Violence Prevention Division.

Spector, A. N., & Klodawsky, F. (1993). The housing needs of single-parent families in Canada: A dilemma for the 1990s. In J. Hudson & B. Galaway (Eds.), *Single parent families: Perspectives on research and policy* (pp. 239–252). Toronto: Thompson Educational Publishing.

Spitze, G., & Ward, R. (1995). Household labor in intergenerational households. *Journal of Marriage and the Family, 57,* 355–361.

Spock, B. (1976). *Baby and child care.* New York: Pocket Books.

Sprecher, S., & McKinney, K. (1993). *Sexuality.* Newbury Park, CA: Sage.

Standing Committee on Justice and Solicitor General. (1987). *Minutes of the proceedings and evidence.* Issue no. 22. Ottawa: House of Commons.

Standing Senate Committee on Legal and Constitutional Affairs. (1987). *Proceedings.* Issue no. 21. Ottawa: Senate of Canada.

Stark, E. (1986, October). A grandmother at 27. *Psychology Today.*

Statistics Canada. (1997, Spring). Canadian children in the 1990s: Selected findings of the National Longitudinal Survey of Children and Youth. *Canadian Social Trends* (Catalogue no. 11-008), 2–9.

Statistics Canada. (2001a). *Age and sex, 2001 counts for females, for Canada, provinces and territories—100% data.* Retrieved September 6, 2004, from http://www12.statcan.ca/english/census01/highlight/AgeSex/

Statistics Canada. (2001b). *Age and sex, 2001 counts for males, for Canada, provinces and territories—100% data.* Retrieved September 6, 2004, from http://www12.statcan.ca/english/census01/highlight/AgeSex/

Statistics Canada. (2002a). *Changing conjugal life in Canada* (Catalogue no. 89-576-XIE). Ottawa: Statistics Canada.

Statistics Canada. (2002b). *Family history* (Catalogue no. 89-575-XIE). Ottawa: Statistics Canada.

Statistics Canada. (2002c, October 22). *Legal marital status (6), age groups (19) and sex (3) for population for Canada, provinces, territories, census metropolitan areas and census agglomerations, 1996 and 2001 censuses—100% data. 2001 Census of Canada* (Catalogue no. 97F0004XCB01001). Retrieved September 13, 2004, from http://www12.statcan.ca/english/census01/products/standard/themes/

Statistics Canada (2002d). *Profile of Canadian families and households: Diversification continues* (Catalogue no. 96F0030XIE2001003). Ottawa: Statistics Canada.

Statistics Canada. (2002e). *Profile of the Canadian population by age and sex: Canada ages* (Catalogue no. 96F0030XIE2001002). Ottawa: Statistics Canada.

Statistics Canada. (2002f). *Profile of languages in Canada: English, French, and many others* (Catalogue no. 96F0030XIE). Ottawa: Statistics Canada.

Statistics Canada. (2002g, April). School performance of children from immigrant families. *Update on Family and Labour Studies* (Statistics Canada Catalogue no. 89-001-XIE), 1–2.

Statistics Canada. (2003a). *Aboriginal peoples of Canada: A demographic profile* (Catalogue no. 96F0030XIE2001007). Ottawa: Statistics Canada.

Statistics Canada. (2003b). *Education, employment and income of adults with and without disabilities—Tables* (Catalogue no. 89-587-XIE). Ottawa: Statistics Canada.

Statistics Canada. (2003c). *Ethnic Diversity Survey: Portrait of a multicultural society* (Catalogue no. 89-593-XIE). Ottawa: Statistics Canada.

Statistics Canada. (2003d). *Longitudinal survey of immigrants to Canada* (Catalogue no 89-611-XIE). Ottawa: Statistics Canada. Retrieved September 4, 2003, from http://www.statcan.ca/english/freepub/89-611-XIE

Statistics Canada. (2003e). *Work, parenthood, and the experience of time scarcity* (Catalogue no. 89-584-XIE). Ottawa: Statistics Canada.

Statistics Canada. (2004a). *2001 Census dictionary* (revised, Catalogue no. 92-378-XIE). Ottawa: Statistics Canada.

Statistics Canada. (2004b, September 27). Deaths. *The Daily.* Retrieved September 27, 2004, from http://www.statcan.com

Statistics Canada. (2004c, May 4). Divorces 2000 and 2001. *The Daily.* Retrieved May 4, 2004, from http://www.statcan.ca/Daily/English/040504/d040504a.htm

Statistics Canada. (2004d, July 8). Household Internet use survey. *The Daily.* Retrieved July 8, 2004, from http://www.statcan.ca/Daily/English/040708/d040708a.htm

Statistics Canada (2004e, March 31). Induced abortions. *The Daily.* Retrieved March 31, 2004, from http://www.statcan.ca/Daily/English/040331/d040331c.htm

Statistics Canada. (2004f). *Infant mortality, by age group and sex, Canada, 2002.* Ottawa: Author. Retrieved November 5, 2004, from http://www.statcan.ca/english/freepub/84F0211XIE/2002/tables/html/t002_en.htm

Statistics Canada. (2004g). *Live births, by age of mother, Canada, provinces and territories, annual, 2002, Table 102–4503.* Retrieved December 16, 2004, from http://www.statcan.ca

Statistics Canada. (2004h). *Live births by age and marital status of mother, Table 102–4507 Canada annual, 2002.* Retrieved December 16, 2004, from http://www.statcan.ca

Statistics Canada. (2004i). *Low income cutoffs from 1994–2003 and low-income measures from 1992–2001* (Catalogue no. 75F0002MIE–No. 002). Ottawa: Author.

Statistics Canada. (2004j). *Teen pregnancy, by outcome of pregnancy and age group, count and rate per 1,000 women aged 15 to 19, in Canada, provinces, and territories, 1998–2000.* Ottawa: Author. Retrieved December 13, 2004, from http://www.statcan.ca/english/freepub/82-221-XIE/01103/tables/html/411.htm

Statistics Canada. (2004k). Women in Canada: Work chapter updates 2003 (Catalogue no. 89F0133XIE), Ottawa: Author.

Statistics Canada. (2005a, February 11). Induced abortions 2002. *The Daily.* Retrieved February 11, 2005, from http://www.statcan.ca/Daily/English/050211/d050211a.htm

Statistics Canada. (2005b, February 7). Childcare. *The Daily.* Retrieved February 7, 2005, from http://www.statcan.ca/Daily/English/050207/d050207b.htm

Statistics Canada. (2005c, March 9). Divorces 2003. *The Daily.* Retrieved March 9, 2005, from http://www.statcan.ca/Daily/English/050309/d050309b.htm

Statistics Canada. (2005d, February 21). National Longitudinal Study of Children and Youth: Home environment, income and child behaviour. *The Daily.* Retrieved February 21, 2005, from http://www.statcan.ca/Daily/English/050221/d050221b.htm

Statistics Canada. (n.d.). *Immigrant status and period of immigration (10A) and place of birth of respondents (260) for immigrants and non-permanent residents for Canada, provinces, territories, census metropolitan areas and census agglomerations, 2001 census—20% sample data* (Catalogue no. 97F009XCB01002). Retrieved January 21, 2003, from http://www.statcan.ca

Stearns, P. N. (2003). *Anxious parents: A history of modern childrearing in America.* New York: New York University Press.

Steinberg, L. (1987). Single parents, stepparents, and the susceptibility of adolescents to antisocial peer pressure. *Child Development, 58,* 269–275.

Steinhauer, P. D. (1991). *The least detrimental alternative: A systematic guide to case planning and decision making for children in care.* Toronto: University of Toronto Press.

Steinmetz, S. K. (2005). Elder abuse is caused by the perception of stress associated with providing care. In D. R. Loseke, R. J. Gelles, & M. M. Cavanaugh (Eds.), *Current controversies in family violence* (2nd ed., pp. 191–205). Thousand Oaks, CA: Sage.

Stevens, D., Kiger, G., & Riley, P. J. (2001). Working hard and hardly working: Domestic labor and marital satisfaction among dual-earner couples. *Journal of Marriage and Family, 63,* 514–526.

Stevens, M., Golombok, S., Beveridge, M., & the ALSPAC Study Team. (2003). Does father absence influence children's gender development: Findings from a general population study of preschool children. *Parenting: Science and Practice, 2,* 47–60.

Stewart, S. H., & Wall, A. M. (2004, Summer). Drinking problems in Canada then and now. *Transition,* 8–10.

Stobert, S., & Cranswick, K. (2004, Autumn). Looking after seniors: Who does what for whom? *Canadian Social Trends* (Statistics Canada Catalogue no. 11-008), 2–6.

Stobert, S., & Kemeny, A. (2003, Summer). Childless by choice. *Canadian Social Trends* (Statistics Canada Catalogue no. 11-008), 7–10.

Stone, E. (1988). *Black sheep and kissing cousins: How our family stories shape us.* New York: Penguin.

Strasburger, V. C. (1993). *Children, adolescents, and the media: Five crucial issues.* Retrieved August 18, 1996, from http://www.cyfc.umn.edu/media/crissues.htm

Straus, M. A. (2005). Women's violence toward men is a serious problem. In D. R. Loseke, R. J. Gelles, & M. M. Cavanaugh (Eds.), *Current controversies in family violence* (2nd ed., pp. 55–77). Thousand Oaks, CA: Sage.

Straus, M. A., & Field, C. J. (2003). Psychological aggression by American parents: National data on prevalence, chronicity, and severity. *Journal of Marriage and Family, 65,* 795–808.

Sun, Y. (2003). The well-being of adolescents in households with no biological parents. *Journal of Marriage and Family, 65,* 894–909.

Sun, Y., & Li, Y. (2002). Children's well-being during parents' marital disruption process. *Journal of Marriage and Family, 64,* 472–488.

Supreme Court approves same-sex marriage. (2004, December 9). CTV.ca. Retrieved December 10, 2004, from http://www.ctv.ca

Surrogate mother furious as couple rejects one of twins. (1988, April 24). *Toronto Star,* p. A24.

Sweeney, M. M., & Cancian, M. (2004). The changing importance of white women's economic prospects for assortative mating. *Journal of Marriage and Family, 66,* 1015–1028.

Swingewood, A. (1991). *A short history of sociological thought* (2nd ed.). London: Macmillan.

Szacki, J. (1979). *History of sociological thought.* Westport, CT: Greenwood.

Tait, H. (1999, Spring). Educational achievement of young Aboriginal adults. *Canadian Social Trends,* 6–10.

Taylor, D. M., Frasure-Smith, N., & Lambert, W. E. (1978). Psychological development of French and English Canadian children: Child-rearing attitudes and ethnic identity. In L. Driedger (Ed.), *The Canadian ethnic mosaic: A quest for identity* (pp. 153–168). Toronto: McClelland & Stewart.

Taylor, G. (1993). Child custody and access. *Vis-à-Vis, 10*(3), 4.

Taylor K., & Mykitiuk, R. (2001). Genetics, normalcy and disability. *Isuma—Canadian Journal of Policy Research, 2*(3), 65-102. Retrieved June 12, 2004, from http://www.isuma.net

Teachman, J. D. (2002). Childhood living arrangements and the intergenerational transmission of divorce. *Journal of Marriage and Family, 64,* 717–729.

Teachman, J. (2003). Premarital sex, premarital cohabitation, and the risk of subsequent marital dissolution among women. *Journal of Marriage and Family, 65,* 444–455.

Tesson, G. (1987). Socialization and parenting. In K. Anderson et al. (Eds.), *Family matters: Sociology and contemporary Canadian families* (pp. 87–111). Toronto: Methuen.

Texas Medical Association. (2001). *Physician stress and burnout.* Retrieved January 6, 2005, from http://www.texmed.org/cme/phn/psb/

Thomas, D. (2001, Summer). Evolving family living arrangements of Canada's immigrants. *Canadian Social Trends* (Statistics Canada Catalogue no. 11-008), 16–22.

Thomas, E. M. (2004). *Aggressive behaviour outcomes for young children: Change in parenting environment predicts change in behaviour* (Catalogue no. 89-599-MIE). Ottawa: Statistics Canada.

Thompson, C. J. (2000). Parenting after divorce. In J. K. Comeau (Ed.), *Family information services: Professional resource materials* (pp. FI-P/CD 21–41). Minneapolis, MN: Family Information Services.

Tichenor, V. J. (1999). Status and income as gendered resources: The case of marital power. *Journal of Marriage and the Family, 61,* 638–650.

Tipper, J., & Avard, D. (1999). *Building better outcomes for Canada's children.* Ottawa: Canadian Policy Research Networks.

Toews, M. L. (2003, November). *Gender-role identity in the context of marital separation: A qualitative study of abusive men.* Poster presentation to annual conference of National Council on Family Relations, Vancouver.

Tougas, J. (2002). *Reforming Québec's early childhood care and education: The first five years.* Toronto: University of Toronto, Centre for Urban & Community Studies, Childcare Resource & Research Unit.

Tower, C. C. (1989). *Understanding child abuse and neglect.* Boston: Allyn & Bacon.

Tran, K. (2004, Summer). Visible minorities in the labour force: 20 years of change. *Canadian Social Trends* (Statistics Canada Catalogue no. 11-008), 7–11.

Treas, J., & Giesen, D. (2000). Sexual infidelity among married and cohabiting Americans. *Journal of Marriage and the Family, 62,* 48–60.

Trocmé, N., MacLaurin, B., Fallon, B., Daciuk, J., Billingsley, D., Tourigny, M., et al. (2001). *Canadian incidence study of reported child abuse and neglect: Final report* (Catalogue no. H49-151/2000E). Ottawa: Health Canada, National Clearinghouse on Family Violence.

Tucker, C. J., McHale, S. M., & Crouter, A. C. (2002, November). *Patterns of differential treatment: Links with parental stressors.* Poster session presented at annual conference of National Council on Family Relations, Houston, TX.

Turcotte, M., & Zhao, J. (2004). *A portrait of Aboriginal children in non-reserve areas: Results from the 2001 Aboriginal Peoples Survey* (Catalogue no. 89-597-XIE). Ottawa: Statistics Canada.

Turcotte, P. (1993, Summer). Mixed-language couples and their children. *Canadian Social Trends,* 15–17.

Twenge, J. M., Campbell, W. H., & Foster, C. A. (2003). Parenthood and marital satisfaction: A meta-analytic review. *Journal of Marriage and Family, 65,* 574–583.

Twiggs, J. E., McQuillan, J., & Ferree, M. M. (1999). Meaning and measurement: Reconceptualizing measures of the division of household labor. *Journal of Marriage and the Family, 61,* 712–724.

Tyre, P., & McGinn, D. (2003, May 12). She works, he doesn't. *Newsweek,* 44–52.

Umaña-Taylor, A. J. (2003). Language brokering as a stressor for immigrant children and their families. In M. Coleman & L. Ganong (Eds.), *Points & counterpoints: Controversial relationships and family issues in the 21st century: An anthology* (pp. 157–159). Los Angeles: Roxbury.

Underwood, M. K. (2003). *Social aggression among girls.* New York: Guilford.

UNICEF. (2005). *Child poverty in rich countries, 2005.* Innocenti Report Card No. 6: Florence Italy: UNICEF Innocenti Research Centre.

United Church of Canada. (1989, Fall). A definition of family. *All Kinds of Families,* 14.

U.S. Federal Communications Commission. (2004, February 11). *TV channel blocking.* Washington, DC: Federal Communications Commission. Retrieved November 30, 2004, from http://www.fcc.gov/parents/channelblocking.html

Updegraff, K. A., McHale, S. M., Crouter, A. C., & Kupanoff, K. (2001). Parents' involvement in adolescents' peer relationships: A comparison of mothers' and fathers' roles. *Journal of Marriage and Family, 63,* 655–668.

Usher, C. M. (n.d.). *Boomerang kids.* Vancouver: BC Council of the Family.

V-chip, The: Where do we go from here? The reality of television ratings in the United States. (1996). Retrieved August 18, 1996, from http://www.dnai.com/~children/media/v-chip_intro.html; http://www.dnai.com/~children/media/v-chip_transcript.html

Valois, J. (1993). *Sociologie de la famille au Québec.* Anjou, QC: Centre Éducatif et Culturel.

Van Harten, P. (2004, July 22). Agency reconsiders moving foster kids. *Hamilton Spectator,* p. A3.

Vanderburgh, R. M. (1987). Modernization and aging in the Anicinabe context. In V. W. Marshall (Ed.), *Aging in Canada: Social perspectives* (2nd ed., pp. 100–110). Markham, ON: Fitzhenry & Whiteside.

Vastel, M. (1994). Quebec: The politics of survival. *Transition, 24*(4), 15, 20.

Verlinsky, Y., Rechitsky, S., Sharapova, T., Morris, R., Taranassi, M., & Kuliev, A. (2004). Preimplantation HLA testing. *Journal of the American Medical Association, 291,* 2079–2085.

Videon, T. M. (2002). The effects of parent-adolescent relationships and parental separation on adolescent well-being. *Journal of Marriage and Family, 64,* 489–503.

Vienneau, D. (1990, December 11). Marriage law will change old rules. *Toronto Star,* pp. B1, B8.

Visher, E. B., Visher, J. S., & Pasley, K. (2003). Remarriage families and stepparenting. In F. Walsh (Ed.), *Normal family processes: Growing diversity and complexity* (3rd ed., pp. 153–175). New York: Guilford.

Voydanoff, P. (1983). Unemployment: Family strategies for adaptation. In C. R. Figley & H. I. McCubbin (Eds.), *Stress and the family: Volume II. Coping with catastrophe* (pp. 90–102). New York: Brunner/Mazel.

Voydanoff, P. (2004). The effects of work demands and resources on work-to-family conflict and facilitation. *Journal of Marriage and Family, 66,* 398–412.

Wachtel, A. (1989). *Discussion paper: Child abuse.* Ottawa: Health and Welfare Canada.

Wachtel, A. (1999). *The "state of the art" in child abuse prevention, 1997.* Ottawa: Health Canada.

Waite, L. J. (2003). Why marriage matters. In M. Coleman & L. Ganong (Eds.), *Points & counterpoints: Controversial relationship and family issues in the 21st century: An anthology* (pp. 64–69). Los Angeles: Roxbury.

Waite, L. J., & Joyner, K. (2001). Emotional satisfaction and physical pleasure in sexual unions: Time horizon, sexual behavior, and sexual exclusivity. *Journal of Marriage and Family, 63,* 247–264.

Walker, C. (1977). Some variations in marital satisfaction. In R. Chester & J. Peel (Eds.), *Equalities and inequalities in family life* (pp. 127–139). London: Academic Press.

Wallerstein, J., Lewis, J., & Blakeslee, S. (2000). *The unexpected legacy of divorce: A 25 year landmark study.* New York: Hyperion.

Walsh, D. (2001). *Dr. Dave's cyberhood: Making media choices that create a healthy electronic environment for your kids.* New York: Fireside.

Walsh, F. (1998). *Strengthening family resilience.* New York: Guilford.

Walsh, F. (1999). Families in later life: Challenges and opportunities. In B. Carter & M. McGoldrick (Eds.), *The expanded family life cycle: Individual, family, and social perspectives* (3rd ed., pp. 307–326). Boston: Allyn & Bacon.

Walsh, F. (2003a). Changing families in a changing world: Reconsidering family normality. In F. Walsh (Ed.), *Normal family processes: Growing diversity and complexity* (3rd ed., pp. 3–26). New York: Guilford.

Walsh, F. (2003b). Family resilience: Strengths forged through adversity. In F. Walsh (Ed.), *Normal family processes: Growing diversity and complexity* (3rd ed., pp. 399–423). New York: Guilford.

Ward, J. A. (1988, June). *Approaches to native mental health care.* Paper presented at the Atlantic Provinces Psychiatric Association, Halifax.

Ward, M. (1978). Full house: Adoption of a large sibling group. *Child Welfare, 57,* 233–241.

Ward, M. (1979). The relationship between parents and caseworker in adoption. *Social Casework, 60,* 96–103.

Ward, M. (1995). Butterflies and bifurcations: Can chaos theory contribute to our understanding of family systems? *Journal of Marriage and the Family, 57,* 629–638.

Ward, M. (2005, June). When is a grandparent not a grandparent? *Family Focus,* F16, F17.

Ward, M., & Tremitiere, B. (1991, August). *How marriage and special-needs adoption coexist.* Paper presented at the Annual Conference of the North American Council on Adoptable Children, Atlanta.

Ward, P. (1990). *Courtship, love, and marriage in nineteenth-century English Canada.* Montreal & Kingston: McGill-Queen's University Press.

Ward, R. A., & Spitze, G. (1996a). Gender differences in parent-child coresidence experiences. *Journal of Marriage and the Family, 58,* 718–725.

Ward, R. A., & Spitze, G. (1996b). Will the children ever leave? Parent-child coresidence: History and plans. *Journal of Family Issues, 17,* 514–539.

Warren, J. A., & Johnson, P. J. (1995). The impact of workplace support on work-family role strain. *Family Relations, 44,* 163–169.

Waterfall, B. (2003). Native peoples and the social work profession: A critical analysis of colonizing problematics and the development of decolonized thought. In A. Westhues (Ed.), *Canadian social policy: Issues and perspectives* (3rd ed., pp. 50–66). Waterloo, ON: Wilfrid Laurier University Press.

Waterman, J. (1986). Family dynamics of incest with young children. In K. MacFarlane, J. Waterman, & others (Eds.), *Sexual abuse of young children: Evaluation and treatment* (pp. 204–219). New York: Guilford.

Waters, L. E. (2000). Coping with unemployment: A literature review and presentation of a new model. *International Journal of Management Review, 2,* 169–182.

Waters, L. E., & Moore, K. A. (2001). Coping with economic deprivation during unemployment. *Journal of Economic Psychology, 22,* 461–482.

Waters, L. E., & Moore, K. A. (2002). Predicting self-esteem during unemployment: The effect of gender, financial deprivation, alternate roles, and social support. *Journal of Employment Counseling, 39,* 171–189.

Waters, L. E., & Muller, J. (2003). Money or time: Comparing the effects of time structure and financial deprivation on the psychological distress of unemployed adults. *Australian Journal of Psychology, 55,* 166–175.

Weigel, D. J., & Ballard-Reisch, D. S. (1999). How couples maintain marriages: A closer look at self and spouse influences upon the use of maintenance in marriages. *Family Relations, 48,* 263–269.

Weinstein, E. (1996). I thought it was our turn: Therapeutic considerations in midlife families. In J. D. Atwood (Ed.), *Family scripts* (pp. 271–298). Washington, DC: Accelerated Development.

Weitzman, S. (2000). *"Not to people like us": Hidden abuse in upscale marriages.* New York: Basic Books.

Westermeyer, J. F. (2004). Predictors and characteristics of Erikson's life cycle model among men: A 32-year longitudinal study. *Journal of Aging and Human Development, 58,* 29–48.

Westfall, W. (1989). *Two worlds: The protestant culture of nineteenth-century Ontario.* Montreal & Kingston: McGill-Queen's University Press.

White, J. M. (1989). Marriage: A developing process. In K. Ishwaran (Ed.), *Family and marriage: Cross-cultural perspectives* (pp. 197–211). Toronto: Wall & Thompson.

White, J. M., & Klein D. M. (2002). *Family theories.* (2nd ed.). Thousand Oaks, CA: Sage.

White, L. (1994). Growing up with single parents and stepparents: Long-term effects on family solidarity. *Journal of Marriage and the Family, 56,* 935–948.

White, L., & Peterson, D. (1995). The retreat from marriage: Its effect on unmarried children's exchange with parents. *Journal of Marriage and the Family, 57,* 428–434.

Widom, C. S., & Maxfield, M. G. (2001, February). An update on the "cycle of violence." *Research in Brief.* Washington, DC: National Institute of Justice.

Wiehe, V. L., & Herring, T. (1991). *Perilous rivalry: When siblings become abusive.* Lexington, MA: Lexington Books.

Wikipedia. (2004). Generation Y. Retrieved December 1, 2004, from http://en.wikipedia.org/wiki/Generation_Y

Williams, C. (2003, November). Finances in the golden years. *Perspectives on Labour and Income* (Statistics Canada Catalogue no. 75-001-XIE), 5–13.

Williams, C. (2004, Summer). The sandwich generation. *Perspectives on Labour and Income* (Statistics Canada Catalogue no. 75-001-XIE), 5–12.

Wilson, J., & Hickman, B. W. (1999). *How to have an elegant wedding for $5,000 or less: Achieving beautiful simplicity without mortgaging your future.* Rocklin, CA: Prima.

Wingard, J., McCormack, C. S., & Neigh, S. (2003). *Progress report on homelessness in Hamilton 2003.* Hamilton, ON: Social Planning and Research Council of Hamilton.

Wiseman, J. P. (1991). *The other half: Wives of alcoholics and their social-psychological situation.* New York: Aldine de Gruyter.

Wolfe, D. A., & Jaffe, P. G. (2001, September). Emerging strategies in the prevention of family violence. *Family Focus,* F1–F3, F5.

Wolfson, L. H. (1987). *The new family law.* Toronto: Random House.

Women's Issues and Social Empowerment (W.I.S.E.). (1998). *Domestic violence information manual.* Melbourne, Australia: W.I.S.E. Retrieved February 14, 2001, from http://infoxchange.net.au/wise/DVIM/

Wood, J. T. (1996). She says/he says: Communication, caring, and conflict in heterosexual relationships. In J. T. Wood (Ed.), *Gendered relationships* (pp. 149–162). Mountainview, CA: Mayfield.

Wright, D. L., & Aquilino, W. S. (1998). Influence of emotional support exchange in marriage on caregiving wives' burden and marital satisfaction, *Family Relations, 47,* 195–204.

Wu, Z. (1994). Remarriage in Canada: A social exchange perspective. *Journal of Divorce & Remarriage, 21*(3/4), 191–224.

Wu, Z. (1995a). Premarital cohabitation and postmarital cohabiting union formation. *Journal of Family Issues, 16,* 212–232.

Wu, Z. (1995b). The stability of cohabitation relationships: The role of children. *Journal of Marriage and the Family, 57,* 231–236.

Wu, Z., & Penning, M. J. (1997). Marital instability after midlife. *Journal of Family Issues, 18,* 459–478.

Yoshikawa, H., Magnuson, K. A., Bos, J. M., & Hsueh, J. (2003). Effect of earning-supplement policies on adult economic and middle-childhood outcomes differ for the "hardest to employ." *Child Development, 74,* 1500–1521.

Youniss, J. (1980). *Parents and peers in social development.* Chicago: University of Chicago Press.

Zabin, L. S., & Hayward, S. C. (1993). *Adolescent sexual behavior and childbearing.* Newbury Park, CA: Sage.

Zelizer, V. A. (1985). *Pricing the priceless child: The changing social value of children.* New York: Basic Books.

Zhou, M. (2000). Social capital in Chinatown: The role of community-based organizations and families in the adaptation of the younger generation. In M. Zhou & J. V. Gatewood (Eds.), *Contemporary Asian America: A multidisciplinary reader* (pp. 315–335). New York: University Press.

INDEX